The Eurovision Song Contest

Lugano 1956 - Rotterdam 2021

The Complete and Independent Guide

Silverthorn Publishing
13th Year of Publication

Simon Barclay
General Editor

2021 edition
© 2021 by Simon Barclay. All rights reserved

ISBN: 9781291780901

Corrections:

As part of the revision of earlier editions, a small number of errors were discovered and this book includes the corrected figures. The main changes are:
1. The name of the artist representing Romania in 2014 was mis-spelled as Paul, instead of Paula.
2. The votes given to Slovakia and Serbia in 2010 had been transposed.
3. The votes cast by Norway and Israel in the 2010 semi-final scoreboard, were incorrectly labelled Iceland and Greece.

Contents of the 2021 Edition

Introduction to the 2021 Edition

Eurovision Winners

Section One: The Cancelled 2020 Contest
Qualification for the 2020 Contest	10
2020 Contest performers, song details:	20

Section Two: Qualification for the 2021 Contest — 23

Section Three: Contest Details & Votes — 33
Contest performers and voting tables:	1950's	34
Contest performers and voting tables:	1960's	38
Contest performers and voting tables:	1970's	48
Contest performers and voting tables:	1980's	66
Contest performers and voting tables:	1990's	86
Contest performers and voting tables:	2000's	106
Contest performers and voting tables :	2010's	142
2021 First Semi-Final performers, jury voting, televoting and combined results		202
2021 Second Semi-Final performers, jury voting, televoting and combined results		206
2021 Final performers, jury voting, televoting and combined results		210
2021 Final: Voting Order & Spokespersons		214
Round by Round voting & changes to scoreboard: Jury Voting		215
Round by Round voting & changes to scoreboard: Public Televoting & combined results		220
Country-by-Country History		224

Section Four: Statistics & Analysis — 257
	Predicting the Winners, the history of votes for the best song	258
New	12 points: comparing Juries with the Public since 2016	261
New	Zero points: comparing Juries with the Public since 2016	262
New	Jury analysis: how many favoured the winner?	263
	Marcel Bezençon Awards	264
	OGAE poll result	265
	Artist selection basis & which countries kept the same entrant from 2020	266
	Winners' Ages & Genders since 1956	267
	This year's Contestants profile - singers & backing performers	269
	Language history by country	270
	Previous voting sytem: Final results	271
New	Population weighted voting	272
	Most Successful Countries League Table	273
	Least Successful Countries League Table	274
	Most Finishes in Top 3	275
	Most Finishes in Bottom 3	275
	Best & worst at qualifying from the semi-finals	275
	Best semi-final to compete in	276
	Most consecutive semi-final failures	276
	Unluckiest semi-finals for each country	278
New	When voters change their minds: Semi-final voting compared to Final voting	279

[Continued..]

Contents of the 2021 Edition (continued)

	Page
Performance of the "Big 5"	281
Winners & losers position in the order of performance since 1975	282
Running Order analysis, where is best to perform? Previous voting system	283
Running Order analysis, where is best to perform? New voting System	284
Double Douze!	286
Are You Sure? When Juries and the Public Disagree	287
Highest number of 12's received by one country	288
Lowest number of 12's received by a winning country	288
12 Points Go To... maximum points given by Juries since 2016	289
12 Points Go To... maximum points given by the Public since 2016	290
Sharing The Love: the concentration of points awarded	291
The host country's performance since 1975	292
Nil Points!	293
Highest scores in finals	294
Largest & smallest winning margins in Finals	295
Performance of debutant countries since 1956	296
League Table of Appearances	296
Closest voting relationships	297
Each Country's Best Friends & their 10 year voting history	299
The most one-sided voting - who doesn't reciprocate?	300
And countries whose Public have never voted for another since 2016	301
Jury/Public split of points in finals since 2016	302
Most Points Received since 1975	304
East v West - the impact of geographical voting	305
Bloc voting by juries and the public in the 2018 Final	307
Complete country-by-country voting analysis since 1975 - who votes for who?	308

Introduction to the 2021 Edition

What a relief! The Eurovision Song Contest returned after being cancelled in 2020 due to the Covid-19 pandemic and it was wonderful to see it back and in front of fans.

The Netherlands were due to host the 65th Contest in 2020 following Duncan Laurence's win with "Arcade" and so it was staged this year in Rotterdam's Ahoy Arena with 3500 fans attending, still limited due to social distancing but a welcome sight nonetheless and the fans generated plenty of noise! It was the Netherlands' 5th time hosting the event, the last being in 1980. Sadly Duncan was unable to take part in the show on the night, having tested positive for Covid-19, as did a band member from Iceland's entry which prevented the group from performing live. Despite having to rely on a rehearsal video, Iceland finished an impressive 4th in the Final.

Thirty-nine countries participated, two fewer than in 2019, Bulgaria and Ukraine returned but we lost Hungary, Montenegro, Armenia and Belarus. Armenia withdrew because of continuing unrest following the 2020 war with Azerbaijan and Belarus's original song was deemed to be too political, supporting the government's stance over the recent protests in Belarus and even a second attempt breached the rules, so Belarus was disqualified. It wouldn't be Eurovision without a bizarre qualification drama.

Congratulations to rock group Måneskin and to Italy who won Eurovision for the first time since 1990 with "Zitti e buoni", although it was absent from the contest from 1998 until 2010. This was Italy's third win overall. It goes to show there's no predicting what type of song will win.

The "Big 5"'s performance was completely polarised this year. On one hand we had Italy and France finishing in the top two places but Spain, Germany and the United Kingdom finished in the bottom three. None of the bottom three received a single point from the public and nor did hosts Netherlands who finished fourth last. The United Kingdom managed to receive no points from either juries or the public, a feat which was expected to be almost impossible, but at least it was entertainingly awful!

The 2021 Edition of the Complete & Independent Guide is the 13th edition of the book and as usual it's packed with details of every Contest since 1956 along with plenty of analysis, in 332 pages. We've included a section on the cancelled 2020 contest as well, the qualification process and details of all the songs selected for that show but not used.

A few changes this year, the complete voting history now shows just the points awarded by each country and the individual scoreboards for the jury and public voting will now only be included for the current year. The book is expanding by at least 12 pages every year and with these changes we can continue to keep the price at a low level.

Over the last couple of years we have also taken the opportunity to revise our early editions and now we have available second editions of the Guides for 2008, 2009 and 2010, all in gorgeous hardcover as well as paperback. We have been able to include in these updated editions a lot of the analysis we've developed in recent years.

Simon Barclay
Editor

@silverthornpub
silverthorn-publishing@outlook.com

Eurovision Winners

Year	Host City	Winner	Artist	Song
1956	Lugano, Switzerland	Switzerland	Lys Assia	Refrain
1957	Frankfurt, Germany	Netherlands	Corry Brokken	Net Als Toen
1958	Hilversum, Netherlands	France	André Claveau	Dors Mon Amour
1959	Cannes, France	Netherlands	Teddy Scholten	Een Beetje
1960	London, United Kingdom	France	Jacqueline Boyer	Tom Pillibi
1961	Cannes, France	Luxembourg	Jean-Claude Pascal	Nous Les Amoureux
1962	Luxembourg City, Luxembourg	France	Isabelle Aubret	Un Premier Amour
1963	London, United Kingdom	Denmark	Grethe & Jørgen Ingmann	Dansevise
1964	Copenhagen, Denmark	Italy	Gigliola Cinquetti	Non Ho L'étà
1965	Naples, Italy	Luxembourg	France Gall	Poupée De Cire, Poupée De Son
1966	Luxembourg City, Luxembourg	Austria	Udo Jürgens	Merci Chérie
1967	Vienna, Austria	United Kingdom	Sandie Shaw	Puppet On A String
1968	London, United Kingdom	Spain	Massiel	La, La, La
1969	Madrid, Spain	= France	Frida Boccara	Un Jour, Un Enfant
1969	Madrid, Spain	= United Kingdom	Lulu	Boom Bang-a-bang
1969	Madrid, Spain	= Netherlands	Lenny Kuhr	De Troubadour
1969	Madrid, Spain	= Spain	Salomé	Vivo Cantando
1970	Amsterdam, Netherlands	Ireland	Dana	All Kinds Of Everything
1971	Dublin, Ireland	Monaco	Séverine	Un Banc, Un Arbre, Une Rue
1972	Edinburgh, United Kingdom	Luxembourg	Vicky Leandros	Après Toi
1973	Luxembourg City, Luxembourg	Luxembourg	Anne-Marie David	Tu Te Reconnaîtras
1974	Brighton, United Kingdom	Sweden	ABBA	Waterloo
1975	Stockholm, Sweden	Netherlands	Teach-In	Teach-In
1976	The Hague, Netherlands	United Kingdom	Brotherhood of Man	Save Your Kisses For Me
1977	London, United Kingdom	France	Marie Myriam	L'oiseau Et L'enfant
1978	Paris, France	Israel	Izhar Cohen & the Alphabeta	Abanibi
1979	Jerusalem, Israel	Israel	Milk and Honey	Hallelujah
1980	The Hague, Netherlands	Ireland	Johnny Logan	What's Another Year
1981	Dublin, Ireland	United Kingdom	Bucks Fizz	Making Your Mind Up
1982	Harrogate, United Kingdom	Germany	Nicole	Ein bißchen Frieden
1983	Munich, Germany	Luxembourg	Corinne Hermès	Si La Vie Est Cadeau
1984	Luxembourg City, Luxembourg	Sweden	Herrey's	Diggi-loo diggy-ley
1985	Gothenburg, Sweden	Norway	Bobbysocks	La Det Swinge
1986	Bergen, Norway	Belgium	Sandra Kim	J'aime La Vie
1987	Brussels, Belgium	Ireland	Johnny Logan	Hold Me Now
1988	Dublin, Ireland	Switzerland	Céline Dion	Ne Partez Pas Sans Moi
1989	Lausanne, Switzerland	Yugoslavia	Riva	Rock Me
1990	Zagreb, Yugoslavia	Italy	Toto Cutugno	Insieme: 1992
1991	Rome, Italy	Sweden	Carola	Fångad Av En Stormvind
1992	Malmö, Sweden	Ireland	Linda Martin	Why Me
1993	Millstreet, Ireland	Ireland	Niamh Kavanagh	In Your Eyes
1994	Dublin, Ireland	Ireland	P Harrington & C McGettigan	Rock 'n' Roll Kids
1995	Dublin, Ireland	Norway	Secret Garden	Nocturne
1996	Oslo, Norway	Ireland	Eimear Quinn	The Voice
1997	Dublin, Ireland	United Kingdom	Katrina and The Waves	Love shine a light
1998	Birmingham, United Kingdom	Israel	Dana International	Diva
1999	Jerusalem, Israel	Sweden	Charlotte Nilsson	Take me to your heaven
2000	Stockholm, Sweden	Denmark	Olsen Brothers	Fly on the wings of love
2001	Copenhagen, Denmark	Estonia	Tanel Padar, Dave Benton & 2XL	Everybody
2002	Tallinn, Estonia	Latvia	Marie N	I Wanna
2003	Riga, Latvia	Turkey	Sertab Erener	Everyway That I Can

Eurovision Winners

Year	Host City	Winner	Artist	Song
2004	Istanbul, Turkey	Ukraine	Ruslana	Wild Dances
2005	Kiev, Ukraine	Greece	Helena Paparizou	My Number One
2006	Athens, Greece	Finland	Lordi	Hard Rock Hallelujah
2007	Helsinki, Finland	Serbia	Marija Šerifovic	Molitva
2008	Belgrade, Serbia	Russia	Dima Bilan	Believe
2009	Moscow, Russia	Norway	Alexander Rybak	Fairytale
2010	Oslo, Norway	Germany	Lena Meyer-Landrut	Satellite
2011	Düsseldorf, Germany	Azerbaijan	Ell/Nikki	Running Scared
2012	Baku, Azerbaijan	Sweden	Loreen	Euphoria
2013	Malmö, Sweden	Denmark	Emmelie de Forest	Only Teardrops
2014	Copenhagen, Denmark	Austria	Conchita Wurst	Rise Like a Phoenix
2015	Vienna, Austria	Sweden	Måns Zelmerlöw	Heroes
2016	Stockholm, Sweden	Ukraine	Jamala	1944
2017	Kiev, Ukraine	Portugal	Salvador Sobral	Amar Pelos Dois
2018	Lisbon, Portugal	Israel	Netta	Toy
2019	Tel Aviv, Israel	Netherlands	Duncan Laurence	Arcade
2020	Cancelled			
2021	Rotterdam, Netherlands	Italy	Måneskin	Zitti e buoni

SECTION 1

The Cancelled 2020 Contest

Notes on each country's qualification competitions and details of the songs to be performed.

Eurovision 2020: Qualification for the Cancelled Contest

Albania

Representative: Arilena Ara
Born: 17 July 1998 in Shkodër, Albania (aged 21 in May 2020)
Previous appearances: none

Selection Competition: Festivali i Këngës 58   Broadcaster: RTSH
Selection Date: Artist & Song: 22 December 2019
Format: Two semi-finals each with 10 artists, Final with 12 artists
Voting basis: 100% jury vote

Top 3:

Artist	Song in Final	Points
Arilena Ara	Shaj	67
Elvana Gjata	Me tana	64
Sara Bajraktari	Ajër	50

Armenia

Representative: Athena Manoukian
Born: 22 May 1994 in Athens, Greece (age 25 in May 2020)
Previous appearances: none

Selection Competition: Depi Evratesil 2020   Broadcaster: AMPTV
Selection Date: Artist & Song: 15 February 2020
Format: Final with 12 artists
Voting basis: 50% Jury/50% Televoting

Top 3:

Artist	Song in Final	Juries	Public	Total
Athena Manoukian	Chains on You	118	50	168
ERNA	Life Faces	65	55	120
Vladimir Arzumanyan	What's Going on Mama?	58	60	118

Australia

Representative: Montaigne (real name Jessica Alyssa Cerro)
Born: 14 August 1995 in Sydney, Australia (age 24 in May 2020)
Previous appearances: none

Selection Competition: Eurovision - Australia Decides   Broadcaster: SBS
Selection Date: Artist & Song: 8 February 2020
Format: Final with 10 artists
Voting basis: 50% jury/50% public vote.

Top 3:

Artist	Song	Jury	Public	Total
Montaigne	Don't Break Me	54	53	107
Casey Donovan	Proud	40	60	100
Vanessa Amorosi	Lessons of Love	42	40	82

Austria

Representative: Vincent Bueno
Born: 10 December 1985 in Vienna, Austria (age 34 in May 2020)
Previous appearances: Backing singer at ESC2017 in Kyiv, Ukraine

Selection Competition: Internal Selection   Broadcaster: ORF
Selection Date: Artist & Song: 12 December 2019

Eurovision 2020: Qualification for the Cancelled Contest

Azerbaijan

Representative:	Samira Efendi
Born:	17 April 1991 in Baku, Azerbaijan (then USSR) (age 29 in May 2020)
Previous appearances:	none

Selection Competition:	Internal Selection	Broadcaster: İTV
Selection Date:	Artist & Song: 28 February 2020	

Belarus

Representative:	VAL
Group members:	Valeria Gribusova & Vlad Pashkevic
Previous appearances:	none

Selection Competition:	Nationalny Otbor	Broadcaster: BTRC
Selection Date:	Artist & Song: 28 February 2020	
Format:	Final with 10 artists	
Voting basis:	50% jury/50% public vote.	

Top 3:

Artist	Song	Jury	Public	Total
VAL	Da vidna	10	10	20
CHAKRAS	La-ley-la	6	12	18
Yan Yarosh	Fire	12	6	18

Belgium

Representative:	Hooverphonic
Group members:	Luka Cruysberghs, Alex Callier & Raymond Geerts
Previous appearances:	none

Selection Competition:	Internal Selection	Broadcaster: VRT
Selection Date:	Artist: 1 October 2019	Song: 17 February 2020

Bulgaria

Representative:	Victoria Georgieva
Born:	21 September 1997 in Varna, Bulgaria (age 22 in May 2020)
Previous appearances:	none

Selection Competition:	Internal Selection	Broadcaster: BNT
Selection Date:	Artist: 25 November 2019	Song: 7 March 2020

Croatia

Representative:	Damir Kedžo
Born:	24 May 1987 in Omišalj, Croatia (then Yugoslavia) (age 32 during May 2020)
Previous appearances:	none

Selection Competition:	Dora 2020	Broadcaster: HRT
Selection Date:	Artist & song: 29 February 2020	
Format:	Final with 16 artists	
Voting basis:	50% jury/50% public voting.	

Top 3:

Artist	Song	Jury	Public	Total
Damir Kedžo	Divlji vjetre	15	16	31
Mia Negovetić	When it comes to you	16	15	31
Indira Levak	You will never break my heart	14	14	28

(Result decided on public voting after the top two acts finished on equal points)

Eurovision 2020: Qualification for the Cancelled Contest

Cyprus

Representative:	Sandro Nicolas (real name Alessandro Rütten)
Born:	2 August 1996 in Heinsberg, Germany (age 23 during May 2020)
Previous appearances:	none
Selection Competition:	Internal Selection Broadcaster: CyBC
Selection Date:	Artist & Song: 29 November 2019

Czech Republic

Representative:	Benny Cristo (real name Ben da Silva Cristóvão)
Born:	8 June 1987 in Plzeň, Czech Republic (then Czechoslovakia) (age 32 during May 2020)
Previous appearances:	none
Selection Competition:	Eurovision Song CZ Broadcaster: ČT
Selection Date:	Artist & Song: 3 February 2020
Format:	Final with 7 artists
Voting basis:	50% jury/50% public voting.

Final: second round

Artist	Song	Jury	Public	Total
Benny Cristo	Kemama	10	12	22
Elis Mraz feat. Čis T	Wanna Be Like	8	10	18
Barbora Mochowa	White & Black Holes	12	2	14

Denmark

Representative:	Ben & Tan (Benjamin Rosenbohm & Tanne Balcells)
Born:	Ben: 3 June 2002 in Berlin, Germany (age 17 during May 2020)
	Tanne: 1998 in Barcelona, Spain (age 22 during May 2020)
Previous appearances:	none
Selection Competition:	Dansk Melodi Grand Prix 2020 Broadcaster: DR
Selection Date:	Artist & Song: 7 March 2020
Format:	Final with 10 artists and two voting rounds
Voting basis:	50% jury/50% public voting in first round, then 100% televoting in superfinal

Final: second round

Artist	Song	Total
Ben & Tan	Yes	61%
Sander Sanchez	Screens	20%
Emil	Ville ønske jeg havde kendt dig	19%

Estonia

Representative:	Uku Suviste
Born:	6 June 1982 in Võru, Estonia (then USSR) (age 37 during May 2020)
Previous appearances:	none
Selection Competition:	Eesti Laul 2020 Broadcaster: ERR
Selection Date:	Artist & Song: 29 February 2020
Format:	2 Semi-Finals each with 12 artists, Final with 12 artists
Voting basis:	1st round: 50% jury/50% public voting. 2nd Round: 100% public voting

Final: second round

Artist	Song	Public vote
Uku Suviste	What Love Is	68.2%
Jaagup Tuisk	Beautiful Lie	16.1%
Anett x Fredi	Write About Me	15.6%

Eurovision 2020: Qualification for the Cancelled Contest

Finland

Representative:	Aksel Kankaanranta
Born:	28 January 1998 in Turku, Finland (age 22 during May 2020)
Previous appearances:	none

Selection Competition:	Uuden Musiikin Kilpailu 2020	Broadcaster: YLE
Selection Date:	Artist & Song: 7 March 2020	
Format:	Final with six artists.	
Voting basis:	50% public vote/50% juries	

Top 3 Songs:

Artist	Song	Jury	Public	Total
Aksel Kankaanranta	Looking Back	76	94	170
Erik Vikman	Cicciolina	58	99	157
Tika	I Let My Heart Break	50	77	127

France

Representative:	Tom Leeb
Born:	21 March 1989 in Paris, France (age 31 during May 2020)
Previous appearances:	none

Selection Competition:	Internal Selection	Broadcaster: France Télévisions
Selection Date:	Artist: 14 January 2020	Song: 16 February 2020

Georgia

Representative:	Tornike Kipiani
Born:	11 December 1987 in Tbilisi, Georgia (then USSR) (age 32 during May 2020)
Previous appearances:	none

Selection Competition:	Georgian Idol	Broadcaster: GPB
Selection Date:	Artist: 31 December 2019	Song: 3 March 2020
Format:	6 elimination shows with 10 artists reducing by one after each show, leaving four artists in the Final.	
Voting basis:	100% public televote.	

Final Result:

Artist	Song	Public vote
Tornike Kipiani	Love, Hate, Love	33.82%
Barbara Samkharadze	This Is Me	31.18%
Tamar Kakalashvili	White Flag	18.38%
Mariam Gogiberidze	Writing's On The Wall	16.62%

Germany

Representative:	Ben Dolic
Born:	4 May 1997 in Ljubljana, Slovenia (age 23 during May 2020)
Previous appearances:	none

Selection Competition:	Internal selection	Broadcaster: NDR
Selection Date:	Artist & Song: 27 February 2020	

Greece

Representative:	Stefania Liberakakis
Born:	17 December 2002 in Utrecht, Netherlands (age 17 during May 2020)
Previous appearances:	none

Selection Competition:	Internal selection	Broadcaster: ERT
Selection Date:	Artist: 3 February 2020	Song: 1 March 2020

Eurovision 2020: Qualification for the Cancelled Contest

Iceland

Representative:	Daði Freyr Pétursson
Born:	30 June 1992 in Reykjavik, Iceland (age 27 during May 2020)
Previous appearances:	none
Selection Competition:	Söngvakeppnin 2020 Broadcaster: RÚV
Selection Date:	Artist & Song: 29 February 2020
Format:	2 Semi-finals, Final with 5 artists and two voting rounds
Voting basis:	50% jury/50% public vote in 1st round of Final, 100% public vote in 2nd round. Winner decided on total votes from both rounds.

Final: Second Round

Artist	Song	Round 1	Round 2	Total
Daði & Gagnamagnið	Think About Things	60324	58319	118643
Dimma	Almyrkvi	37715	42468	80183

Ireland

Representative:	Lesley Roy
Born:	17 September 1986 in Dublin, Ireland (age 33 during May 2020)
Previous appearances:	none
Selection Competition:	Internal Selection Broadcaster: RTÉ
Selection Date:	Artist & Song: 5 March 2020

Israel

Representative:	Eden Alene
Born:	7 May 2000 in Jerusalem, Israel (age 20 during May 2020)
Previous appearances:	none
Selection Competition:	HaKokhav HaBa L'Eurovizion Broadcaster: IPBC/Keshet
Selection Date:	Artist: 4 February 2020 Song: 3 March 2020
Format:	Probably the most complicated of all selection competitions. 60 artists competed in 15 audition rounds, 4 shortlisting rounds, top 20 competed head to head in "duels". 12 then competed in themed duels in 5 heats. A quarter-final followed by 2 semi-finals, then final with 2 rounds for the final 4 artists. The song was then selected in a separate competition
Voting basis:	100% jury voting in first final, 50% jury/50% public voting in second final.

Final: second round:

Artist	Song	Jury	Public	Total
Eden Alene	Halo	110	150	260
Ella-Lee Lahav	Roar	92	90	182
Orr Amrami-Brockman	Haim lhiot bah mehhoav	98	60	158

Italy

Representative:	Antonio Diodato
Born:	30 August 1981 in Aosta, Italy (age 38 during May 2020)
Previous appearances:	none
Selection Competition:	Sanremo 2020 Broadcaster: RAI
Selection Date:	Artist & Song: 8 February 2020
Format:	Final with 23 artists in first round, 3 in second round.
Voting basis:	66% press/expert juries/34% public voting

Top 3:

Artist	Song	Experts	Press	Public	Total
Diodato	Fai Rumore	36%	58%	24%	39.32
Francesco Gabbani	Viceversa	39%	24%	39%	33.94
Pinguini Tattici Nucleari	Ringo Starr	25%	18%	37%	26.80

Eurovision 2020: Qualification for the Cancelled Contest

Latvia

Representative: Samanta Tīna (real name Samanta Poļakova)
Born: 31 March 1989 in Tukums, Latvia (then USSR) (age 31 during May 2020
Previous appearances: none

Selection Competition: Supernova 2020   Broadcaster: LTV
Selection Date: Artist & Song: 8 February 2020
Format: Final with 9 artists.
Voting basis: 100% public voting by televote and internet

Top 3:

Artist	Song	Internet	Televote	Total
Samanta Tīna	Still Breathing	39%	30%	35%
Katrīna Dimanta	Heart Beats	23%	35%	28%
ANNNA	Polyester	19%	13%	16%

Lithuania

Representative: The Roop
Group members: Vaidotas Valiukevičius, Robertas Baranauskas, Mantas Banišauskas
Previous appearances: none

Selection Competition: Pabandom iš naujo! 2020 (Let's Try Again! 2020)   Broadcaster: LRT
Selection Date: Artist & Song: 15 February 2020
Format: 3 Elimination Heats, 2 semi-finals & Final with 8 artists
Voting basis: 50% jury/50% public vote

Top 3:

Artist	Song	Jury	Public	Total
The Roop	On Fire	12	12	24
Moniqué	Make Me Human	10	10	20
Monika Marija	If I Leave	8	7	15

Malta

Representative: Destiny Chukunyere
Born: 29 August 2002 in Birkirkara, Malta (age 17 during May 2020
Previous appearances: Backing singer at ESC2019 in Tel Aviv, Israel

Selection Competition: X Factor Malta 2020   Broadcaster: PBS
Selection Date: Artist & Song: 8 February 2020
Format: 2 elimination heats, a semi-final, then Final with 4 artist
Voting basis: 100% public vote in the final.

Top 2:

Artist	Final song (4 performed)	Result
Destiny Chukunyere	He Lives in You	1
Justine Shorfid	All I Want	2

Eurovision 2020: Qualification for the Cancelled Contest

Moldova

Representative:	Natalia Gordienko
Born:	11 December 1987 in Chișinău, Moldova (then USSR) (age 32 during May 2020)
Previous appearances:	Featured with Arsenium at ESC2006 in Athens, Greece
Selection Competition:	Finala națională 2020 Broadcaster: TRM
Selection Date:	Artist & Song: 29 February 2020
Format:	Final with 20 artists.
Voting basis:	50% jury/50% public vote

Top 3:

Artist	Song	Jury	Public	Total
Natalia Gordienko	Prison	12	12	24
Pasha Parfeny	My Wine	10	10	20
Maxim Zavidia	Take Control	8	7	15

Netherlands

Representative:	Jeangu Macrooy
Born:	6 November 1993 in Paramaribo, Suriname (age 26 during May 2020)
Previous appearances:	None
Selection Competition:	Internal Selection Broadcaster: AVROTROS
Selection Date:	Artist & Song: 10 January 2020

North Macedonia

Representative:	Vasil Garvanliev
Born:	2 November 1984 in Strumica, North Macedonia (then Yugoslavia) (age 35 during May 2020)
Previous appearances:	Backing singer for North Macedonia at ESC2019 in Tel Aviv, Israel
Selection Competition:	Internal Selection Broadcaster: MRT
Selection Date:	Artist & song: 15 January 2020

Norway

Representative:	Ulrikke Brandstorp
Born:	13 July 1995 in Sarpsborg, Norway (age 24 during May 2020)
Previous appearances:	none
Selection Competition:	Melodi Grand Prix 2020 Broadcaster: NRK
Selection Date:	Artist & Song: 15 February 2020
Format:	5 regional heats, Final with 5 heat winners & 5 pre-qualified artists
Voting basis:	100% public vote

Gold Duel'

Artist	Song	Public vote
Ulrikke Brandstorp	Attention	50.72%
Kristin Husøy	Pray for Me	49.28%

Eurovision 2020: Qualification for the Cancelled Contest

Poland

Representative:	Alicja Szemplińska
Born:	29 April 2002 in Ciechanów, Poland (age 18 during May 2020)
Previous appearances:	none
Selection Competition:	Szansa na Sukces - Eurowizja 2020 Broadcaster: TVP
Selection Date:	Artist & Song: 23 February 2020
Format:	3 semi-finals, Final with 3 artists
Voting basis:	50% jury/50% public vote

Top 3:

Artist	Song	Jury	Public	Total
Alicja Szemplińska	Empires	5	5	10
Albert Černý	Lucy	3	3	6
Kasia Dereń	Count on Me	1	1	2

Portugal

Representative:	Elisa Silva
Born:	11 May 1999 in Lisbon, Portugal (age 21 during May 2020)
Previous appearances:	none
Selection Competition:	Festival da Canção 2020 Broadcaster: RTP
Selection Date:	Artist & Song: 7 March 2020
Format:	2 semi-finals, Final with 8 artists
Voting basis:	50% jury/50% public vote

Top 3:

Artist	Song	Jury	Public	Total
Elisa	Medo de sentir	10	10	20
Barbara Tinoco	Passe-partout	6	12	18
Filipe Sambado	Gerbera amarela do Sul	12	4	16

Romania

Representative:	Roxen (real name Larisa Roxana Giurgiu)
Born:	5 January 2000 in Cluj-Napoca, Romania (age 20 during May 2020)
Previous appearances:	none
Selection Competition:	Selecția Naționalá 2020 Broadcaster: TVR
Selection Date:	Artist: 11 February 2020 Song: 1 March 2020
Format:	Final with 5 songs, all sung by Roxen
Voting basis:	50% jury/50% public vote

Top 3:

Artist	Song	Jury	Public	Total
Roxen	Alcohol You	5	5	10
Roxen	Storm	3	3	6
Roxen	Cherry Red	1	2	3

Russia

Representative:	Little Big
Group members:	Ilya Prusikin, Sonya Tayurskaya, Anton Lissov, Sergey Makarov
Previous appearances:	none
Selection Competition:	Internal Selection Broadcaster: Channel One
Selection Date:	Artist & Song: 7 March 2020

Eurovision 2020: Qualification for the Cancelled Contest

San Marino

Representative:	Senhit (real name Senhit Zadik Zadik)
Born:	1 October 1979 in Bologna, Italy (age 40 during May 2020)
Previous appearances:	Represented San Marino at ESC2011 in Dusseldorf, Germany
Selection Competition:	Internal Selection Broadcaster: SMRTV
Selection Date:	Artist: 6 March 2020 Song: 9 March 2020

Serbia

Representative:	Hurricane
Group members:	Sanja Vučić, Ivana Nikolić, Ksenija Knežević
Previous appearances:	none
	Sanja Vučić represented Serbia at ESC2016 in Stockholm, Sweden
	Ksenija Knežević was backing singer for Montenegro at ESC2015 in Vienna, Austria
Selection Competition:	Beovizija 2020 Broadcaster: RTS
Selection Date:	Artist & Song: 1 March 2020
Format:	Two semi-finals with 12 artists in each, final with 12 artists
Voting basis:	50% jury/50% public vote

Top 3:

Artist	Song	Jury	Public	Total
Hurricane	Hasta la vista	12	12	24
Naiva	Baš, baš	8	7	15
Igor Simić	Ples za rastanak	10	4	14

Slovenia

Representative:	Ana Soklič
Born:	10 April 1984 in Savica, Slovenia (then Yugoslavia) (age 36 during May 2020)
Previous appearances:	none
Selection Competition:	EMA 2020 Broadcaster: RTVSLO
Selection Date:	Artist & Song: 22 February 2020
Format:	12 artists in Final, then two in Superfinal
Voting basis:	100% public vote

Superfinal:

Artist	Song	Public vote
Ana Soklič	Voda	54%
Lina Kuduzović	Man Like U	46%

Spain

Representative:	Blas Cantó
Born:	26 October 1991 in Ricote, Spain (age 28 during May 2020)
Previous appearances:	none
Selection Competition:	Internal Selection Broadcaster: TVE
Selection Date:	Artist: 5 October 2019 Song: 30 January 2020

Eurovision 2020: Qualification for the Cancelled Contest

Sweden

Representative: The Mamas
Group members: Ashley Haynes, Loulou Lamotte, Dinah Yonas Manna
Previous appearances: Backing singers for Sweden at ESC2019 in Tel Aviv, Israel

Selection Competition: Melodifestivalen 2020   Broadcaster: SVT
Selection Date: Artist & Song: 7 March 2020
Format: 4 Semi-Finals, 1 Second Chance Round, Final with 12 artists.
Voting basis: 50% jury/50% public vote

Top 3:

Artist	Song	Jury	Public	Total
The Mamas	Move	65	72	137
Dotter	Bulletproof	65	71	136
Anna Bergendahl	Kingdom Come	46	61	107

Switzerland

Representative: Gjon's Tears (real name Gjon Muharremaj)
Born: 29 June 1998 in Fribourg, Switzerland (age 21 during May 2020
Previous appearances: none

Selection Competition: Internal Selection   Broadcaster: SRG SSR
Selection Date: Artist & Song: 4 March 2020

Ukraine

Representative: Go_A
Group members: Kateryna Pavlenko, Ihor Didenchuk, Taras Shevchenko, Ivan Hryhoriak
Previous appearances: none

Selection Competition: Vidbir 2020   Broadcaster: STB
Selection Date: Artist & Song: 22 February 2020
Format: 2 semi-finals with 8 artists, Final with 6 artists
Voting basis: 50% jury/50% public vote

Top 3:

Artist	Song	Jury	Public	Total
Go_A	Solovey	6	6	12
Khayat	Call for love	4	5	9
Krutь	99	5	4	9

United Kingdom

Representative: James Newman
Born: 19 October 1985 in Settle, England (age 34 during May 2020
Previous appearances: none

Selection Competition: Internal Selection   Broadcaster: BBC
Selection Date: Artist & Song: 27 February 2020

2020 Eurovision: Rotterdam, Netherlands (cancelled)

Semi-final 1: 12 May 2020

Votes would have been cast by countries participating in each semi-final plus the five automatically qualifying countries decided by draw: Germany and Italy in semi-final 1, France, UK and Spain in semi-final 2. Hosts Netherlands would have voted in semi-final 1.

Country	Artist	Song	Writer	Composer
Australia	Montaigne	Don't Break Me	Montaigne, Anthony Egizii, David Musumeci	Montaigne, Anthony Egizii, David Musumeci
Belarus	VAL	Da vidna	Mikita Naidzenau	Vladislav Pashkevich, Valeria Gribusova
Ireland	Lesley Roy	Story of My Life	Lesley Roy, Catt Gravitt, Tom Shapiro	Lesley Roy, Robert Marvin, Catt Gravitt, Tom Shapiro
Lithuania	The Roop	On Fire	Vaidotas Valiukevičius	Vaidotas Valiukevičius, Robertas Baranauskas, Mantas Banišauskas
North Macedonia	Vasil	You	Nevena Neskoska, Kalina Neskoska, Alice Schroeder	Nevena Neskoska
Russia	Little Big	Uno	Little Big	Little Big
Slovenia	Ana Soklic	Voda	Ana Soklič	Ana Soklič, Bojan Simončič, Žiga Pirnat
Sweden	The Mamas	Move	Herman Gardarfve, Melanie Wehbe, Patrik Jean	Herman Gardarfve, Melanie Wehbe, Patrik Jean
Azerbaijan	Efendi	Cleopatra	Luuk van Beers, Alan Roy Scott, Sarah Lake	Luuk van Beers, Alan Roy Scott, Sarah Lake
Belgium	Hooverphonic	Release Me	Alex Callier	Alex Callier, Luca Chiaravalli
Croatia	Damir Kedžo	Divlji vjetre	Ante Pecotić	Ante Pecotić
Cyprus	Sandro	Running	Alfie Arcuri, Sebastian Rickards, Octavian Rasinariu, Sandro	Alfie Arcuri, Sebastian Rickards, Octavian Rasinariu, Sandro, Teo DK
Israel	Eden Alene	Feker libi	Doron Medalie, Idan Raichel	Doron Medalie, Idan Raichel
Malta	Destiny	All of My Love	Bernarda Brunovic, Borislav Milanov, Sebastian Arman, Dag Lundberg, Joacim Persson	Bernarda Brunovic, Borislav Milanov, Sebastian Arman, Dag Lundberg, Joacim Persson, Cesár Sampson
Norway	Ulrikke	Attention	Kjetil Mørland, Christian Ingebrigtsen, Ulrikke Brandstorp	Kjetil Mørland, Christian Ingebrigtsen, Ulrikke Brandstorp
Romania	Roxen	Alcohol You	Ionuț Armaș, Breyan Isaac	Ionuț Armaș, Viky Red
Ukraine	Go_A	Solovey	Kateryna Pavlenko	Taras Shevchenko, Kateryna Pavlenko

2020 Eurovision: Rotterdam, Netherlands (cancelled) Semi-final 2: 14 May 2020

Votes would have been cast by countries participating in each semi-final plus the five automatically qualifying countries decided by draw: Germany and Italy in semi-final 1, France, UK and Spain in semi-final 2. Hosts Netherlands would have voted in semi-final 1.

Country	Artist	Song	Writer	Composer
Austria	Vincent Bueno	Alive	Vincent Bueno	Vincent Bueno, David "Davey" Yang, Felix van Göns, Artur Aigner
Czech Republic	Benny Cristo	Kemama	Ben Cristovao, Charles Sarpong	Osama Hussain, Rudy Ray, Filip Zangi
Estonia	Uku Suviste	What Love Is		Uku Suviste
Greece	Stefania	Supergirl	Dimitris Kontópoulos, Arcade, Sharon Vaughn	Dimitris Kontópoulos, Arcade
Iceland	Daði og Gagnamagnið	Think About Things	Daði Freyr	Daði Freyr
Moldova	Natalia Gordienko	Prison	Sharon Vaughn	Dimitris Kontopoulos, Phillip Kirkorov
Poland	Alicja	Empires	Patryk Kumor, Dominic Buczkowski-Wojtaszek, Laurell Barker, Frazer Mac	Patryk Kumor, Dominic Buczkowski-Wojtaszek, Laurell Barker, Frazer Mac
San Marino	Senhit	Freaky!	Gianluigi Fazio, Henrik Steen, Nanna Bottos	Gianluigi Fazio, Henrik Steen, Nanna Bottos
Serbia	Hurricane	Hasta la vista	Kosana Stojić, Sanja Vučić	Nemanja Antonić
Albania	Arilena Ara	Fall from the Sky	Michael Blue, Robert Stevenson, Sam Schummer	Darko Dimitrov, Lazar Cvetkoski
Armenia	Athena Manoukian	Chains on You	Athena Manoukian	Athena Manoukian, DJ Paco
Bulgaria	Victoria	Tears Getting Sober	Victoria Georgieva, Borislav Milanov, Lukas Oskar Janisch	Victoria Georgieva, Borislav Milanov, Lukas Oskar Janisch, Cornelia Wiebols
Denmark	Ben & Tan	Yes	Emil Adler Lei, Jimmy Jansson, Linnea Deb	Emil Adler Lei, Jimmy Jansson, Linnea Deb
Finland	Aksel	Looking Back	Joonas Angeria, Whitney Phillips, Connor McDonough, Riley McDonough, Toby McDonough	Joonas Angeria, Whitney Phillips, Connor McDonough, Riley McDonough, Toby McDonough
Georgia	Tornike Kipiani	Take Me as I Am	Tornike Kipiani	Tornike Kipiani
Latvia	Samanta Tina	Still Breathing	Aminata Savadogo	Samanta Tina
Portugal	Elisa	Medo de sentir	Marta Carvalho	Marta Carvalho
Switzerland	Gjon's Tears	Répondez-moi	Gjon Muharremaj, Alizé Oswald, Xavier Michel, Jeroen Swinnen	Gjon Muharremaj, Alizé Oswald, Xavier Michel, Jeroen Swinnen

2020 Eurovision: Rotterdam, Netherlands (cancelled)
FINAL: 16 May 2020

Final qualification rules: Top 10 placed countries from each semi-final. Automatic qualification: United Kingdom, France, Germany, Spain, Italy and hosts Netherlands.

Country	Artist	Song	Writer	Composer
Netherlands	Jeangu Macrooy	Grow	JAU Macrooy	JAU Macrooy, PL Perquin
France	Tom Leeb	Mon alliée (The Best in Me)	Peter Boström, Thomas G:son, John Lundvik, Tom Leeb, Amir Haddad, Lea Ivanne	Peter Boström, Thomas G:son, John Lundvik
Germany	Ben Dolic	Violent Thing	Borislav Milanov, Peter St. James, Dag Lundberg	Borislav Milanov, Peter St. James, Dag Lundberg, Jimmy Thorén, Connor Martin
Italy	Diodato	Fai rumore	Antonio Diodato	Antonio Diodato, Edwyn Roberts
Spain	Blas Cantó	Universo	Blas Cantó, Dan Hammond	Blas Cantó, Dan Hammond, Ash Hicklin, Mikolaj Trybulec, Dangelo Ortega
United Kingdom	James Newman	My Last Breath	James Newman, Adam Argyle, Ed Drewett, Iain James	James Newman, Adam Argyle, Ed Drewett, Iain James

SECTION 2

Qualification for the 2021 Contest

Notes on each country's selection process

Eurovision 2021: Qualification Process

Albania

Representative: Anxhela Peristeri
Born: 24 March 1986 in Korçë, Albania (age 35 during ESC2021)
Previous appearances: none

Artist Selection Process: Festivali i Këngës 59 Broadcaster: RTSH
Selection Date: Artist & Song: 23 December 2020
Format: Two semi-finals each with 10 artists, Final with 12 artists
Voting basis: 100% jury vote

Top 3:

Artist	Song in Final	Position
Anxhela Peristeri	Karma	1
Sardi Strugaj	Kam me t'ba me kajt	2
Festina Mejzini	Kush je ti dashuri	3

Australia

Representative: Montaigne (real name: Jessica Alyssa Cerro)
Born: 14 August 1995 in Sydney, Australia (age 25 during ESC2021)
Previous appearances: none

Artist Selection Process: Internal Selection Broadcaster: SBS
Selection Date: Artist: 2 April 2020 Song: 5 March 2021

Austria

Representative: Vincent Bueno
Born: 10 December 1985 in Vienna, Austria (age 35 in during ESC2021)
Previous appearances: Backing singer at ESC2017 in Kyiv, Ukraine

Artist Selection Process: Internal Selection Broadcaster: ORF
Selection Date: Artist: 26 March 2020 Song: 10 March 2021

Azerbaijan

Representative: Samira Efendi
Born: 17 April 1991 in Baku, Azerbaijan (then USSR) (age 30 during ESC2021
Previous appearances: none

Artist Selection Process: Internal Selection Broadcaster: İTV
Selection Date: Artist: 20 March 2020 Song: 15 March 2021

Belgium

Representative: Hooverphonic
Group members: Luka Cruysberghs, Alex Callier & Raymond Geerts
Previous appearances: none

Artist Selection Process: Internal Selection Broadcaster: VRT
Selection Date: Artist: 20 March 2020 Song: 4 March 2021

Eurovision 2021: Qualification Process

Bulgaria

Representative:	Victoria Georgieva
Born:	21 September 1997 in Varna, Bulgaria (age 23 during ESC2021
Previous appearances:	none

Artist Selection Process:	Internal Selection	Broadcaster: BNT	
Selection Date:	Artist: 21 March 2020	Song: 10 March 2021	

Croatia

Representative:	Albina (real name: Albina Grčić)
Born:	6 February 1999 in Split, Croatia (then Yugoslavia) (age 22 during ESC 2021
Previous appearances:	none

Artist Selection Process:	Dora 2021	Broadcaster: HRT
Selection Date:	Artist & song: 18 January 2021	
Format:	Final with 14 artists	
Voting basis:	50% juries/50% public voting.	

Top 3:

Artist	Song	Jury	Public	Total
Albina	Tick-Tock	78	120	198
Nina Kraljić & Alkonost Of Balkan	Rijeka	68	77	145
Mia Negovetić	She's Like A Dream	67	52	119

Cyprus

Representative:	Elena Tsagrinou
Born:	16 November 1994 in Athens, Greece (age 26 during ESC2021)
Previous appearances:	none

Artist Selection Process:	Internal Selection	Broadcaster: CyBC
Selection Date:	Artist & Song: 25 November 2020	

Czech Republic

Representative:	Benny Cristo (real name Ben da Silva Cristóvão)
Born:	8 June 1987 in Plzeň, Czech Republic (then Czechoslovakia) (age 34 during ESC2021
Previous appearances:	none

Artist Selection Process:	Internal selection	Broadcaster: ČT
Selection Date:	Artist: 13 May 2020	Song: 16 February 2021

Denmark

Representative:	Fyr & Flamme
Group members:	Jesper Groth, Laurits Emanuel
Previous appearances:	none

Artist Selection Process:	Dansk Melodi Grand Prix 2021	Broadcaster: DR
Selection Date:	Artist & Song: 6 March 2021	
Format:	Final with 8 artists and two voting rounds	
Voting basis:	100% public voting.	

Final: second round

Artist	Song	Total
Fyr & Flamme	Øve os på hinanden	37%
Jean Michel	Beautiful	34%
Chief 1 & Thomas Buttenschøn	Højt over skyerne	29%

Eurovision 2021: Qualification Process

Estonia

Representative:	Uku Suviste
Born:	6 June 1982 in Võru, Estonia (then USSR) (age 38 during May 2021)
Previous appearances:	none
Artist Selection Process:	Eesti Laul 2021 Broadcaster: ERR
Selection Date:	Artist & Song: 6 March 2021
Format:	2 Semi-Finals each with 12 artists, top 6 in each progressed to Final
Voting basis:	50% public vote/50% jury.

Final: second round

Artist	Song	Public vote
Uku Suviste	The Lucky One	46.4%
Sissi	Time	28.9%
Jüri Pootsmann	Magus melanhoolia	24.7%

Finland

Representative:	Blind Channel
Group members:	Joel Hokka, Niko Moilanen, Joonas Porko, Olli Matela, Tommi Lalli Aleksi Kaunisvesi
Previous appearances:	none
Artist Selection Process:	Uuden Musiikin Kilpailu 2021 Broadcaster: YLE
Selection Date:	Artist & Song: 7 March 2020
Format:	Final with 7 artists.
Voting basis:	75% public vote/25% juries.

Top 3 Songs:

Artist	Song	Jury	Public	Total
Blind Channel	Dark Side	72	479	551
Teflon Brothers x Pandora	I Love You	30	150	180
Ilta	Kelle mä soitan	48	101	149

France

Representative:	Barbara Pravi (real name: Barbara Piévic)
Born:	10 April 1993 in Paris, France (age 28 during ESC2021
Previous appearances:	none
Artist Selection Process:	Eurovision France, c'est vous qui décidez! Broadcaster: France Télévisions
Selection Date:	Artist & Song: 30 January 2021
Format:	Final with 12 artists in first round, then superfinal with 8 artists
Voting basis:	50% public vote/50% jury.

Top 3 Songs:

Artist	Song	Jury	Public	Total
Barbara Pravi	Voilà	104	100	204
Juliette Moraine	Pourvu qu'on m'aime	76	60	136
PONY X	Amour fou	74	50	124

Georgia

Representative:	Tornike Kipiani
Born:	11 December 1987 in Tbilisi, Georgia (then USSR) (age 33 during ESC2021
Previous appearances:	none
Artist Selection Process:	Internal selection Broadcaster: GPB
Selection Date:	Artist: 19 March 2020 Song: 15 March 2021

Eurovision 2021: Qualification Process

Germany

Representative:	Jendrik (real name: Jendrik Sigwart)
Born:	27 August 1994 in Hamburg, Germany (age 26 during ESC2021)
Previous appearances:	none

Artist Selection Process:	Internal selection	Broadcaster: NDR
Selection Date:	Artist: 6 February 2021	Song: 25 February 2021

Greece

Representative:	Stefania (real name: Stefania Liberakakis)
Born:	17 December 2002 in Utrecht, Netherlands (age 18 during ESC2021)
Previous appearances:	none

Artist Selection Process:	Internal selection	Broadcaster: ERT
Selection Date:	Artist: 18 March 2020	Song: 7 January 2021

Iceland

Representative:	Daði og Gagnamagnið (real name: Daði Freyr Pétursson)
Born:	30 June 1992 in Reykjavik, Iceland (age 28 during ESC2021)
Previous appearances:	none

Artist Selection Process:	Internal selection	Broadcaster: RÚV
Selection Date:	Artist: 23 October 2020	Song: 13 March 2021

Ireland

Representative:	Lesley Roy
Born:	17 September 1986 in Dublin, Ireland (age 34 during ESC2021)
Previous appearances:	none

Artist Selection Process:	Internal Selection	Broadcaster: RTÉ
Selection Date:	Artist: 17 December 2020	Song: 26 February 2021

Israel

Representative:	Eden Alene
Born:	7 May 2000 in Jerusalem, Israel (age 21 during ESC2021
Previous appearances:	none

Artist Selection Process:	Internal Selection	Broadcaster: IPBC/KAN
Selection Date:	Artist: 22 March 2020	Song: 25 January 2021

Italy

Representative:	Måneskin
Group members:	Damiano David, Victoria De Angelis, Thomas Raggi, Ethan Torchic
Previous appearances:	none

Artist Selection Process:	Sanremo 2021 Broadcaster: RAI
Selection Date:	Artist & Song: 6 March 2021
Format:	Final with 26 artists in first round, 3 in second round.
Voting basis:	66% press/expert juries/34% public voting

Top 3:

Artist	Song	Experts	Press	Public	Total
Måneskin	Zitti e buoni	32.97%	35.16%	53.53%	40.46%
Francesca Michielin & Fedez	Chiamami per nome	33.13%	30.13%	28.26%	30.49%
Ermal Meta	Un milione di cose da dirti	33.89%	34.71%	18.21%	28.83%

Eurovision 2021: Qualification Process

Latvia

Representative:	Samanta Tīna (real name Samanta Poļakova
Born:	31 March 1989 in Tukums, Latvia (then USSR) (age 32 during ESC2021
Previous appearances:	none
Artist Selection Process:	Internal selection Broadcaster: LTV
Selection Date:	Artist: 16 May 2020 Song: 12 March 2021

Lithuania

Representative:	The Roop
Group members:	Vaidotas Valiukevičius, Robertas Baranauskas, Mantas Banišauskas
Previous appearances:	none
Artist Selection Process:	Pabandom iš naujo! 2021 (Let's Try Again! 2021) Broadcaster: LRT
Selection Date:	Artist & Song: 15 February 2020
Format:	2 Elimination Heats, a semi-final & Final with the top 5 from the semi-final plus The Roop, who were due to perform in ESC2020.
Voting basis:	50% jury/50% public vote

Top 3:

Artist	Song	Jury	Public	Total
The Roop	Discoteque	12	12	24
Gebrasy	Where'd You Wanna Go?	10	10	20
Voldemars Petersons	Never Fall for You Again	8	7	15

Malta

Representative:	Destiny Chukunyere
Born:	29 August 2002 in Birkirkara, Malta (age 18 during ESC2021
Previous appearances:	Backing singer at ESC2019 in Tel Aviv, Israel
Artist Selection Process:	Internal Selection Broadcaster: PBS
Selection Date:	Artist: 18 May 2020 Song: 15 March 2021

Moldova

Representative:	Natalia Gordienko
Born:	11 December 1987 in Chișinău, Moldova (then USSR) (age 33 during ESC2021)
Previous appearances:	Featured with Arsenium at ESC2006 in Athens, Greece
Artist Selection Process:	Internal selection Broadcaster: TRM
Selection Date:	Artist: 26 January 2021 Song: 4 March 2021

Netherlands

Representative:	Jeangu Macrooy
Born:	6 November 1993 in Paramaribo, Suriname (age 27 during ESC2021
Previous appearances:	None
Artist Selection Process:	Internal Selection Broadcaster: AVROTROS
Selection Date:	Artist: 18 March 2020 Song: 4 March 2021

Eurovision 2021: Qualification Process

North Macedonia

Representative:	Vasil (real name: Vasil Garvanliev)
Born:	2 November 1984 in Strumica, North Macedonia (then Yugoslavia) (age 36 during ESC2021)
Previous appearances:	Backing singer for North Macedonia at ESC2019 in Tel Aviv, Israel

Artist Selection Process:	Internal Selection	Broadcaster: MRT
Selection Date:	Artist: 20 January 2021	Song: 11 March 2021

Norway

Representative:	Tix (real name: Andreas Haukeland)
Born:	12 April 1993 in Bærum, Norway (age 28 during ESC2021)
Previous appearances:	none

Artist Selection Process:	Melodi Grand Prix 2021	Broadcaster: NRK
Selection Date:	Artist & Song: 20 February 2021	
Format:	5 semi-finals, a second chance round and Final with 12 artists	
Voting basis:	100% public vote	

'Gold Duel'

Artist	Song	Public vote
Tix	Fallen Angel	57%
Keiino	Monument	43%

Poland

Representative:	Rafał (real name: Rafał Brzozowski)
Born:	8 June 1981 in Warsaw, Poland (age 39 during ESC2021)
Previous appearances:	none

Artist Selection Process:	Internal selection	Broadcaster: TVP
Selection Date:	Artist & Song: 12 March 2021	

Portugal

Representative:	The Black Mamba
Group members:	Pedro Tatanka, Miguel Casais, Marco Pombinho, Rui Pedo Vaz, Guilherme Sagueiro
Previous appearances:	none

Artist Selection Process:	Festival da Canção 2021	Broadcaster: RTP
Selection Date:	Artist & Song: 6 March 2021	
Format:	2 semi-final each with 10 artists, top 5 in each progressed to Final	
Voting basis:	50% jury/50% public vote	

Top 3:

Artist	Song	Jury	Public	Total
The Black Mamba	Love is on my side	10	10	20
Carolina Deslandes	Por um triz	12	8	20
NEEV	Dancing in the stars	5	12	3

(The Black Mamba qualified due to more public votes).

Eurovision 2021: Qualification Process

Romania

Representative:	Roxen (real name Larisa Roxana Giurgiu)
Born:	5 January 2000 in Cluj-Napoca, Romania (age 21 during ESC2021)
Previous appearances:	none

Artist Selection Process:	Internal selection	Broadcaster: TVR
Selection Date:	Artist: 31 March 2020	Song: 4 March 2021

Russia

Representative:	Manizha (real name: Manizha Khamrayeva)
Born:	8 July 1991 in Dushanbe, Tajikistan (then USSR) (age 29 during ESC2021
Previous appearances:	none

Artist Selection Process:	Evrovidenie 2021 – Natsional'nyy Otbor	Broadcaster: Channel One
Selection Date:	Artist & Song: 8 March 2021	
Format:	Final with 3 artists.	
Voting basis:	100% public voting.	

Top 3:

Artist	Song	Public
Manizha	Russian Woman	39.7%
#2Mashi	Bitter Words	35.7%
Therr Maitz	Future is Bright	24.6%

San Marino

Representative:	Senhit (real name Senhit Zadik Zadik)
Born:	1 October 1979 in Bologna, Italy (age 41 during ESC2021)
Previous appearances:	Represented San Marino at ESC2011 in Dusseldorf, Germany

Artist Selection Process:	Internal Selection	Broadcaster: SMRTV
Selection Date:	Artist: 16 May 2020	Song: 7 March 2021

Serbia

Representative:	Hurricane
Group members:	Sanja Vučić, Ivana Nikolić, Ksenija Knežević
Previous appearances:	Sanja Vučić represented Serbia at ESC2016 in Stockholm, Sweden
	Ksenija Knežević was a backing singer for Montenegro at ESC2015 in Vienna, Austria.

Artist Selection Process:	Internal selection	Broadcaster: RTS
Selection Date:	Artist: 17 December 2020	Song: 5 March 2021

Slovenia

Representative:	Ana Soklič
Born:	10 April 1984 in Savica, Slovenia (then Yugoslavia) (age 37 during ESC2021
Previous appearances:	none

Artist Selection Process:	Internal selection	Broadcaster: RTVSLO
Selection Date:	Artist: 16 May 2020	Song: 27 February 2021

Eurovision 2021: Qualification Process

Spain

Representative:	Blas Cantó
Born:	26 October 1991 in Ricote, Spain (age 29 during ESC2021)
Previous appearances:	none

Artist Selection Process:	Internal Selection	Broadcaster: TVE
Selection Date:	Artist: 18 March 2020	Song: 20 February 2021

Sweden

Representative:	Tusse (real name: Tousin Michael Chiza)
Born:	1 January 2002 in DR Congo (age 19 during ESC2021)
Previous appearances:	none

Artist Selection Process:	Melodifestivalen 2021	Broadcaster: SVT
Selection Date:	Artist & Song: 13 March 2021	
Format:	4 Semi-Finals, 1 Second Chance Round, Final with 12 artists	
Voting basis:	50% jury/50% public vote	

Top 3:

Artist	Song	Jury	Public	Total
Tusse	Voices	79	96	175
Eric Saade	Every Minute	69	49	118
The Mamas	In the Middle	50	56	106

Switzerland

Representative:	Gjon's Tears (real name Gjon Muharremaj)
Born:	29 June 1998 in Fribourg, Switzerland (age 22 during ESC2021)
Previous appearances:	none

Artist Selection Process:	Internal Selection	Broadcaster: SRG SSR
Selection Date:	Artist: 20 March 2020	Song: 10 March 2021

Ukraine

Representative:	Go_A
Group members:	Kateryna Pavlenko, Ihor Didenchuk, Taras Shevchenko, Ivan Hryhoriak
Previous appearances:	none

Artist Selection Process:	Internal selection	Broadcaster: STB
Selection Date:	Artist: 18 March 2020	Song: 4 February 2021

United Kingdom

Representative:	James Newman
Born:	19 October 1985 in Settle, England (age 35 during ESC2021)
Previous appearances:	none

Artist Selection Process:	Internal Selection	Broadcaster: BBC
Selection Date:	Artist: 19 February 2021	Song: 11 March 2021

SECTION 3

Contest Details and Voting Tables

Semi-Finals & Final results and votes awarded in each Contest

1956 Eurovision 1: Lugano, Switzerland

24 May 1956

Rank	Start	Country	Artist	Song	Writer	Composer
1	9	Switzerland	Lys Assia	Refrain	Emile Gardaz	Géo Voumard
2	10	Belgium	Mony Marc	Le Plus Beau Jour De Ma Vie	David Bée	Claude Alix
3	11	Germany	Freddy Quinn	So Geht Das Jede Nacht	Peter Mösser	Lothar Olias
4	12	France	Dany Dauberson	Il Est Là	Simone Vallauris	Simone Vallauris
5	14	Italy	Tonina Torielli	Amami Se Vuoi	Mario Panzeri	Vittorio Mascheroni
6	13	Luxembourg	Michèle Arnaud	Les Amants De Minuit	Pierre Lambry	Simone Laurencin
7	8	Netherlands	Corry Brokken	Voorgoed Voorbij	Jelle de Vries	Jelle de Vries
8	7	Italy	Franca Raimondi	Aprite Le Finestre	Pinchi	Virgilio Panzito
9	3	Belgium	Fud Leclerc	Messieurs Les Noyés De La Seine	Robert Montal	Jean Miret, Jacques Say
10	2	Switzerland	Lys Assia	Das Alte Karussell	Fernando Paggi	George Betz-Stahl
11	4	Germany	Walter Andreas Schwarz	Im Wartesaal Zum Großen Glück	Walter Andreas Schwarz	Walter Andreas Schwarz
12	5	France	Mathé Altéry	Le Temps Perdu	Rachèle Thoreau	André Lodge
13	6	Luxembourg	Michèle Arnaud	Ne Crois Pas	Jacques Lassry	Christian Guittreau
14	1	Netherlands	Jetty Paerl	De Vogels Van Holland	Annie Schmidt	Cor Lemaire

Note: Two songs were performed per country. Each country had 10 jurors who could award 1 point each to their favourite act, including those entries from their own country. The votes awarded have never been disclosed.

1957 Eurovision 2: Frankfurt, Germany

3 March 1957

Rank	Start	Country	Artist	Song	Writer	Composer	POINTS
1	6	Netherlands	Corry Brokken	Net Als Toen	Willy van Hemert	Guus Jansen	31
2	8	France	Paule Desjardins	La Belle Amour	Francis Carco	Guy Lefarge	17
3	9	Denmark	Birthe Wilke & Gustav Winckler	Skibet Skal Sejle I Nat	Paul Sörensen	Erik Fiehn	10
4	7	Germany	Margot Hielscher	Telefon, Telefon	Ralph Maria Siegel	Friedrich Meyer	8
5	2	Luxembourg	Danièle Dupré	Tant De Peine	Jacques Taber	Jean-Pierre Kemmer	8
6	4	Italy	Nunzio Gallo	Corde Della Mia Chitarra	Giuseppi Cavaliere	Mario Ruccione	7
7	1	United Kingdom	Patricia Bredin	All	Alan Stranks	Reynell Wreford	6
8	3	Belgium	Bobbejaan Schoepen	Straatdeuntje	Eric Franssen	Harry Frekin	5
9	10	Switzerland	Lys Assia	L'enfant Que J'étais	Emile Gardaz	Géo Voumard	5
10	5	Austria	Bob Martin	Wohin, Kleines Pony	Hans Werner, Kurt Svab	Kurt Svab	3

1957 Eurovision 2: Frankfurt, Germany

3 March 1957

	Austria	Belgium	Denmark	France	Germany	Italy	Monaco	Netherlands	Switzerland	United Kingdom	TOTAL
Belgium			2		2				1		5
Luxembourg	3	1				4					8
United Kingdom	1	1	1					1			6
Italy		1					1		2	2	7
Austria							2	1			3
Netherlands	6	5	3	4	1	1	1		7	1	31
Germany		1		6		1					8
France		2	2		6		1	4		2	17
Denmark						3	5			2	10
Switzerland			2		1	1		1			5

Note: each country had 10 jurors who could award 1 point each to their favourite act.

1958 Eurovision 3: Hilversum, Netherlands

12 March 1958

Rank	Start	Country	Artist	Song	Writer	Composer	POINTS
1	3	France	André Claveau	Dors Mon Amour	Hubert Giraud	Pierre Delanoë	27
2	10	Switzerland	Lys Assia	Giorgio	Fridolin Tschudi	Paul Burkhard	24
3	1	Italy	Domenico Modugno	Nel Blu Dipinto Di Blu	Franco Migliacci, Domenico Modugno	Domenico Modugno	13
4	5	Sweden	Alice Babs	Lilla Stjärna	Åke Gerhard	Åke Gerhard	10
5	9	Austria	Liane Augustin	Die Ganze Welt Braucht Liebe	Günther Léopold, Kurt Werner	Günther Léopold, Kurt Werner	8
6	7	Belgium	Fud Leclerc	Ma Petite Chatte	André Dohet	André Dohet	8
7	8	Germany	Margot Hielscher	Für Zwei Groschen Musik	Fred Rauch, Walter Brandin	Friedrich Meyer	5
8	6	Denmark	Raquel Rastenni	Jeg Rev Et Blad Ud Af Min Dagbog	Harry Jensen	Harry Jensen	3
9	2	Netherlands	Corry Brokken	Heel De Wereld	Benny Vreden	Benny Vreden	1
10	4	Luxembourg	Solange Berry	Un Grand Amour	Monique Laniece, Raymond Roche	Michel Eric	1

1959 Eurovision 4: Cannes, France

11 March 1959

Rank	Start	Country	Artist	Song	Writer	Composer	POINTS
1	5	Netherlands	Teddy Scholten	Een Beetje	Willy van Hemert	Dick Schallies	21
2	10	United Kingdom	Pearl Carr & Teddy Johnson	Sing Little Birdie	Syd Cordell	Stan Butcher	16
3	1	France	Jean Philippe	Oui, Oui, Oui, Oui	Pierre Cour	Hubert Giraud	15
4	8	Switzerland	Christa Williams	Irgendwoher	Lothar Löffler	Lothar Löffler	14
5	2	Denmark	Birthe Wilke	Uh-jeg Ville Ønske Jeg Var Dig	Carl Andersen	Otto Lington	12
6	11	Belgium	Bob Benny	Hou Toch Van Mij	Ke Riema	Hans Flower	9
7	3	Italy	Domenico Modugno	Piove	Dino Verde	Domenico Modugno	9
8	6	Germany	Alice & Ellen Kessler	Heut' Woll'n Wir Tanzen Geh'n	Astrid Voltmann	Helmut Zander	5
9	9	Austria	Ferry Graf	Der K Und K Kalypso Aus Wien	Günther Léopold	Norbert Pawlicki	4
10	7	Sweden	Brita Borg	Augustin	Åke Gerhard	Harry Sandin	4
11	4	Monaco	Jacques Pills	Mon Ami Pierrot	Raymond Bravard	Florence Veran	1

1958 Eurovision 3: Hilversum, Netherlands

12 March 1958

	Austria	Belgium	Denmark	France	Germany	Italy	Monaco	Netherlands	Sweden	Switzerland	TOTAL
Italy	1	4		1	4		1		1	1	13
Netherlands										1	1
France	7	1	9		1	6	1	1		1	27
Luxembourg										1	1
Sweden	1	1						3	2	3	10
Denmark				1			1		1		3
Belgium			1		5		1			1	8
Germany	1	1		2			1				5
Austria		1		3			1	1		2	8
Switzerland		2		3		4	4	5	6		24

1959 Eurovision 4: Cannes, France

11 March 1959

	Austria	Belgium	Denmark	France	Germany	Italy	Monaco	Netherlands	Sweden	Switzerland	United Kingdom	TOTAL
France	1	2	4		4	1	2		4	1		15
Denmark	2					1	1	1	1	1	2	12
Italy		1		3			1			3		9
Monaco	1											1
Netherlands	3	3		4	2	7	1				1	21
Germany		1		2		1						5
Sweden			1									4
Switzerland	1	1	2		1		1	3	3		5	14
Austria							1		2	1		4
United Kingdom	2	2	1	1			2	5		3		16
Belgium			2		3		1	1			2	9

Note: in both years each country had 10 jurors who could award 1 point each to their favourite act.

1960 Eurovision 5: London, United Kingdom

29 March 1960

Rank	Start	Country	Artist	Song	Writer	Composer	POINTS
1	13	France	Jacqueline Boyer	Tom Pillibi	Pierre Cour	André Popp	32
2	1	United Kingdom	Bryan Johnson	Looking High, High, High	John Watson	John Watson	25
3	8	Monaco	François Deguelt	Ce Soir-là	Pierre Dorsey	Hubert Giraud	15
4	6	Norway	Nora Brockstedt	Voi-voi	George Elgaaen	George Elgaaen	11
5	11	Germany	Wyn Hoop	Bonne Nuit, Ma Chérie!	Kurt Schwabach	Franz-Josef Breuer	11
6	5	Belgium	Fud Leclerc	Mon Amour Pour Toi	Robert Montal	Jack Say	9
7	7	Austria	Harry Winter	Du Hast Mich So Fasziniert	Robert Gilbert	Robert Stolz	6
8	12	Italy	Renato Rascel	Romantica	Dino Verde	Renato Rascel	5
9	9	Switzerland	Anita Traversi	Cielo E Terra	Mario Robbiani	Mario Robbiani	5
10	2	Sweden	Siw Malmkvist	Alla Andra Får Varann	Åke Gerhard	Ulf Kjellqvist	4
11	4	Denmark	Katy Bødtger	Det Var En Yndig Tid	Sven Buemann	Vilfred Kjær	4
12	10	Netherlands	Rudi Carrell	Wat Een Geluk	Willy van Hemert	Dick Schallies	2
13	3	Luxembourg	Camillo Felgen	So Laang We's Du Do Bast	Henri Mootz	Henri Mootz, Jean Roderes	1

1961 Eurovision 6: Cannes, France

18 March 1961

Rank	Start	Country	Artist	Song	Writer	Composer	POINTS
1	14	Luxembourg	Jean-Claude Pascal	Nous Les Amoureux	Maurice Vidalin	Jacques Datin	31
2	15	United Kingdom	The Allisons	Are You Sure?	John Alford, Bob Day	John Alford, Bob Day	24
3	10	Switzerland	Franca di Rienzo	Nous Aurons Demain	Emile Gardaz	Géo Voumard	16
4	9	France	Jean-Paul Mauric	Printemps (avril Carillonne)	Guy Favereau	Francis Baxter	13
5	16	Italy	Betty Curtis	Al Di Là	Giulio Rapetti	Carlo Donida	12
6	13	Denmark	Dario Campeotto	Angelique	Aksel Rasmussen	Aksel Rasmussen	12
7	12	Norway	Nora Brockstedt	Sommer I Palma	Egil Hagen	Jan Wølner	10
8	5	Yugoslavia	Ljiljana Petrovic	Neke Davne Zvezde	Miroslav Antic	Jože Privšek	9
9	1	Spain	Conchita Bautista	Estando Contigo	Antonio Guijarro	Augusto Algueró	8
10	6	Netherlands	Greetje Kauffeld	Wat Een Dag	Pieter Goemans	Dick Schallies	6
11	2	Monaco	Colette Deréal	Allons, Allons Les Enfants	Pierre Delanoë	Hubert Giraud	6
12	4	Finland	Laila Kinnunen	Valoa Ikkunassa	Sauvo Puhtila	Eino Hurme	6
13	8	Germany	Lale Andersen	Einmal Sehen Wir Uns Wieder	Ernst Bader	Rudolf Maluck	3
14	7	Sweden	Lill-Babs	April, April	Bo Eneby	Bobby Ericsson	2
15	3	Austria	Jimmy Makulis	Sehnsucht	Leopold Andrejewirsch	Leopold Andrejewirsch	1
16	11	Belgium	Bob Benny	September, Gouden Roos	Wim Brabants	Hans Flower	1

1960 Eurovision 5: London, United Kingdom

29 March 1960

	Austria	Belgium	Denmark	France	Germany	Italy	Luxembourg	Monaco	Netherlands	Norway	Sweden	Switzerland	United Kingdom	TOTAL
United Kingdom	3	1			1	2	5	1	5	2	1	4		25
Sweden				2		1			1					4
Luxembourg						1								1
Denmark	1			1	1		1			2	4	4	1	4
Belgium	1		2			3							1	9
Norway	1	1	2						1			4	1	11
Austria			2	3		1	1	2					2	6
Monaco			2		7		1					1	1	15
Switzerland	2	1				1								5
Netherlands						1		2						2
Germany	2	2		4			1	2	1		1			11
Italy		1					1	2	2					5
France	1	3	4		1		1	5		5	4	1	5	32

1961 Eurovision 6: Cannes, France

18 March 1961

	Austria	Belgium	Denmark	Finland	France	Germany	Italy	Luxembourg	Monaco	Netherlands	Norway	Spain	Sweden	Switzerland	United Kingdom	Yugoslavia	TOTAL
Spain					2				1	1	2		1		1		8
Monaco			1	3								1		1	1		6
Austria															1		1
Finland			1		1		2						1		2		6
Yugoslavia	3		1		2	1	2						1		1		9
Netherlands					1								4			2	6
Sweden					2												2
Germany	1		1						2				1		2		3
France						4		1	2			2	1		2	1	13
Switzerland	2		1				2	1	2	2		1	4		2		16
Belgium																	1
Norway		5														1	10
Denmark		1			1					1	8		2				12
Luxembourg	4	1	1		1		3	8	4	3		2		1		5	31
United Kingdom		1	1		2	5	1			1		3	1	7		1	24
Italy		4	4		1				1	1					1	1	12

Note: in both years each country had 10 jurors who could award 1 point each to their favourite act.

1962 Eurovision 7: Luxembourg

18 March 1962

Rank	Start	Country	Artist	Song	Writer	Composer	POINTS
1	9	France	Isabelle Aubret	Un Premier Amour	Roland Valade	Claude Henri Vic	26
2	16	Monaco	François Deguelt	Dis Rien	René Rouzaud	Henri Salvador	13
3	14	Luxembourg	Camillo Felgen	Petit Bonhomme	Maurice Vidalin	Jacques Datin	11
4	13	United Kingdom	Ronnie Carroll	Ring-a-ding Girl	Stan Butcher	Syd Cordell	10
5	12	Yugoslavia	Lola Novakovic	Ne Pali Svetlo U Sumrak	Dragutin Britvic	Jože Privšek	10
6	7	Germany	Conny Froboess	Zwei Kleine Italiener	Georg Buschor	Christian Bruhn	9
7	1	Finland	Marion Rung	Tipi-tii	Kari Tuomisaari	Kari Tuomisaari	4
8	6	Sweden	Inger Berggren	Sol Och Vår	Ulf Kjellqvist, Åke Gerhard	Ulf Kjellqvist, Åke Gerhard	4
9	15	Italy	Claudio Villa	Addio, Addio	Franco Migliacci	Domenico Modugno	3
10	11	Switzerland	Jean Philippe	Le Retour	Emile Gardaz	Géo Voumard	2
11	10	Norway	Inger Jacobsen	Kom Sol, Kom Regn	Ivar Andersen	Kjell Karlsen	2
12	5	Denmark	Ellen Winther	Vuggevise	Sejr Volmer-Sørensen	Kjeld Bonfils	2
13	8	Netherlands	De Spelbrekers	Katinka	Henry Hamhuis	Joop Stokkermans	0
14	2	Belgium	Fud Leclerc	Ton Nom	Tony Golan	Eric Channe	0
15	3	Spain	Victor Balaguer	Llámame	Miguel Portoles	Mario Selles	0
16	4	Austria	Eleonore Schwarz	Nur In Der Wiener Luft	Bruno Uher	Bruno Uher	0

1963 Eurovision 8: London, United Kingdom

23 March 1963

Rank	Start	Country	Artist	Song	Writer	Composer	POINTS
1	8	Denmark	Grethe & Jørgen Ingmann	Dansevise	Sejr Volmer-Sørensen	Otto Francker	42
2	10	Switzerland	Esther Ofarim	T'en Va Pas	Emile Gardaz	Géo Voumard	40
3	6	Italy	Emilio Pericoli	Uno Per Tutte	Alberto Testa, Giulio Rapetti	Tony Renis	37
4	1	United Kingdom	Ronnie Carroll	Say Wonderful Things	Norman Newell	Philip Green	28
5	11	France	Alain Barrière	Elle était Si Jolie	Alain Barrière	Alain Barrière	25
6	15	Monaco	Françoise Hardy	L'amour S'en Va	Françoise Hardy	Françoise Hardy	25
7	4	Austria	Carmela Corren	Vielleicht Geschieht Ein Wunder	Peter Wehle	Erwin Halletz	16
8	16	Luxembourg	Nana Mouskouri	A Force De Prier	Pierre Delanoë	Raymond Bernard	13
9	3	Germany	Heidi Brühl	Marcel	Charly Niessen	Charly Niessen	5
10	14	Belgium	Jacques Raymond	Waarom	Wim Brabants	Hans Flower	4
11	9	Yugoslavia	Vice Vukov	Brodovi	Mario Nardelli	Mario Nardelli	3
12	12	Spain	José Guardiola	Algo Prodigioso	Camillo Murillo Janero	Fernando Garcia Morcillo	2
13	5	Norway	Anita Thallaug	Solhverv	Dag Kristoffersen	Dag Kristoffersen	0
14	7	Finland	Laila Halme	Muistojeni Laulu	Börje Sundgren	Börje Sundgren	0
15	2	Netherlands	Annie Palmen	Een Speeldoos	Pieter Goemans	Pieter Goemans	0
16	13	Sweden	Monica Zetterlund	En Gång i Stockholm	Beppe Wolgers	Bobbie Ericsson	0

1962 Eurovision 7: Luxembourg

18 March 1962

	Austria	Belgium	Denmark	Finland	France	Germany	Italy	Luxembourg	Monaco	Netherlands	Norway	Spain	Sweden	Switzerland	United Kingdom	Yugoslavia	TOTAL
Finland	2										1				3		4
Belgium	2																0
Spain																	0
Austria																	0
Denmark			3										1				2
Sweden			1				1										4
Germany									2			2	3	3			9
Netherlands									1	1							0
France	2	2				3	2	1	1		3	2	3	3	1	3	26
Norway					2	2											2
Switzerland		1															2
Yugoslavia				1	3		3					1		2			10
United Kingdom	1		2	3								3		1			10
Luxembourg		3														2	11
Italy								2								1	3
Monaco	3				1	1		3		3	2						13

Note: Each country awarded from 3 points to 1 point in descending order for their 3 favourite acts.

1963 Eurovision 8: London, United Kingdom

23 March 1963

	Austria	Belgium	Denmark	Finland	France	Germany	Italy	Luxembourg	Monaco	Netherlands	Norway	Spain	Sweden	Switzerland	United Kingdom	Yugoslavia	TOTAL
United Kingdom			3	3	3				1	3	5	5	2			3	28
Netherlands									3		2						0
Germany					2				5		3	3	3	5	4		5
Austria	2	2	1	4				4		1				3	2	4	16
Norway				2				5		5			5				0
Italy		3	5						4		4	3	1	4	3		37
Finland					1			5	2	4	1	2	1		5		0
Denmark	3	5		5			2					4					42
Yugoslavia					1												3
Switzerland	5	4	4				4	3	4			2			5	5	40
France	2	1					1	1	2	4		4	1	4		2	25
Spain																	2
Sweden												1					0
Belgium	4																4
Monaco	1		2	1	5	5	3	2		2			4	1	1	1	25
Luxembourg					4	3	1							2			13

Note: Each country awarded from 5 points to 1 point in descending order for their 5 favourite acts.

1964 Eurovision 9: Copenhagen, Denmark

21 March 1964

Rank	Start	Country	Artist	Song	Writer	Composer	POINTS
1	12	Italy	Gigliola Cinquetti	Non Ho L'età	Mario Panzeri	Nicola Salerno	49
2	8	United Kingdom	Matt Monro	I Love The Little Things	Tony Hatch	Tony Hatch	17
3	10	Monaco	Romuald	Où Sont-elles Passées?	Pierre Barouh	Francis Lai	15
4	7	France	Rachel	Le Chant De Mallory	Pierre Cour	André Popp	14
5	1	Luxembourg	Hugues Aufray	Dès Que Le Printemps Revient	Jacques Plante	Hugues Aufray	14
6	6	Austria	Udo Jürgens	Warum Nur, Warum?	Udo Jürgen Bockelmann	Udo Jürgen Bockelmann	11
7	5	Finland	Lasse Mårtenson	Laiskotellen	Sauvo Puhtila	Lasse Mårtenson	9
8	3	Norway	Arne Bendiksen	Spiral	Egil Hagen	Sigurd Jansen	6
9	4	Denmark	Bjørn Tidmand	Sangen Om Dig	Morgens Dam	Aksel Rasmussen	4
10	15	Belgium	Robert Cogoi	Près De Ma Rivière	Robert Cogoi	Robert Cogoi	2
11	2	Netherlands	Anneke Grönloh	Jij Bent Mijn Leven	René de Vos	Ted Powder	2
12	16	Spain	Tim, Nelly & Tony	Caracola	Fina de Calderón	Fina de Calderón	1
13	14	Switzerland	Anita Traversi	I Miei Pensieri	Sanzio Chiesa	Giovanni Pelli	0
14	9	Germany	Nora Nova	Man Gewöhnt Sich So Schnell An Das Schöne	Niels Nobach	Rudi von der Dovenmühle	0
15	11	Portugal	António Calvário	Oração	Francisco Nicholson, Rogério Bracinha	João Nobre	0
16	13	Yugoslavia	Sabahudin Kurt	Zivot Je Sklopio Krug	Stevan Raickovic	Srcan Matijevic	0

1965 Eurovision 10: Naples, Italy

20 March 1965

Rank	Start	Country	Artist	Song	Writer	Composer	POINTS
1	15	Luxembourg	France Gall	Poupée De Cire, Poupée De Son	Serge Gainsbourg	Serge Gainsbourg	32
2	2	United Kingdom	Kathy Kirby	I Belong	Phil Peters	Peter Lee-Sterling	26
3	11	France	Guy Mardel	N'avoue Jamais	Françoise Dorin	Guy Mardel	22
4	6	Austria	Udo Jürgens	Sag Ihr, Ich Lass' Sie Grüßen	Frank Bohlen	Udo Jürgen Bockelmann	16
5	13	Italy	Bobby Solo	Se Piangi, Se Ridi	Giulio Rapetti	Roberto Satti, Gianni Marchetti	15
6	4	Ireland	Butch Moore	I'm Walking The Streets In The Rain	Teresa Conlon	Joe Harrigan, George Prendergast	11
7	14	Denmark	Birgit Brüel	For Din Skyld	Poul Henningsen	Jørgen Jersild	10
8	18	Switzerland	Yovanna	Non à Jamais Sans Toi	Jean Charles	Bob Calfati	8
9	9	Monaco	Marjorie Noël	Va Dire à L'amour	Jacques Mareuil	Raymond Bernard	7
10	10	Sweden	Ingvar Wixell	Absent Friend	Alf Henriksson	Dag Wiren	6
11	1	Netherlands	Conny Van den Bos	Het Is Genoeg	Karel Prior	Johnny Holshuyzen	5
12	17	Yugoslavia	Vice Vukov	Ceznja	Zarko Roje	Julijo Maric	2
13	7	Norway	Kirsti Sparboe	Karusell	Jolly Kramer-Johansen	Jolly Kramer-Johansen	1
14	12	Portugal	Simone de Oliviera	Sol De Inverno	Jeronimo Bragança	Carlos Nobrega e Sousa	1
15	3	Spain	Conchita Bautista	Qué Bueno, Qué Bueno	Antonio Figueroa Egea	Antonio Figueroa Egea	0
16	16	Finland	Viktor Klimenko	Aurinko Laskee Länteen	Reino Helismaa	Toivo Kärki	0
17	5	Germany	Ulla Wiesner	Paradies, Wo Bist Du?	Barbara Kist, Hans Blüm	Barbara Kist, Hans Blüm	0
18	8	Belgium	Lize Marke	Als Het Weer Lente Is	Jaak Dreesen	Jef van den Berg	0

1964 Eurovision 9: Copenhagen, Denmark

21 March 1964

	Austria	Belgium	Denmark	Finland	France	Germany	Italy	Luxembourg	Monaco	Netherlands	Norway	Portugal	Spain	Switzerland	United Kingdom	Yugoslavia	TOTAL
Luxembourg			1			5	3			3							14
Netherlands	3		5	1											1		2
Norway			3										3		3		6
Denmark											1						4
Finland					1	1		1			3	3	5			1	9
Austria	3	1		3			5		5		5			5			11
France												3					14
United Kingdom	1																17
Germany		3			5			3	3			5		1		3	0
Monaco																	15
Portugal													1	3		5	0
Italy	5	5		5		3		5	3	5		5		3	5		49
Yugoslavia							1		1								0
Switzerland																	0
Belgium																	2
Spain																	1

1965 Eurovision 10: Naples, Italy

20 March 1965

	Austria	Belgium	Denmark	Finland	France	Germany	Ireland	Italy	Luxembourg	Monaco	Netherlands	Norway	Portugal	Spain	Sweden	Switzerland	United Kingdom	Yugoslavia	TOTAL
Netherlands		6	5											5	3	5			5
United Kingdom												1						3	26
Spain																			0
Ireland									5										11
Germany					3												3		0
Austria	1																5		16
Norway																	1		1
Belgium																			0
Monaco							1												7
Sweden			3													1	5	1	6
France						3													22
Portugal						1													1
Italy		3			3	5					3	3		3	5	3			15
Denmark															5 1				10
Luxembourg	5		1	5			3		5	3	5	3		1	1	3			32
Finland																			0
Yugoslavia				1									1						2
Switzerland	3			5															8

Note: In both years each country awarded their three favourite acts either 5 points, 3 points or 1 point, apart from Belgium in 1965 which chose only two favourites and awarded 6 and 3 points.

43

1966 Eurovision 11: Luxembourg City, Luxembourg

5 March 1966

Rank	Start	Country	Artist	Song	Writer	Composer	POINTS
1	9	Austria	Udo Jürgens	Merci Chérie	Udo Jürgen Bockelmann, Thomas	Udo Jürgen Bockelmann	31
2	10	Sweden	Lill Lindfors & Svante Thuresson	Nygammal Vals Eller Hip Man	Björn Lindroth	Bengt-Arne Wallin	16
3	6	Norway	Åse Kleveland	Intet Er Nytt Under Solen	Arne Bendiksen	Arne Bendiksen	15
4	17	Ireland	Dickie Rock	Come Back To Stay	Rowland Soper	Rowland Soper	14
5	3	Belgium	Tonia	Un Peu De Poivre, Un Peu De Sel	Phil van Cauwenbergh	Paul Quintens	14
6	12	Switzerland	Madeleine Pascal	Ne Vois-tu Pas?	Roland Schweizer	Pierre Brenner	12
7	5	Yugoslavia	Berta Ambroz	Brez Besed	Elza Budav	Mojmir Sepe	9
8	11	Spain	Raphael	Yo Soy Aquél	Manuel Alejandro	Manuel Alejandro	9
9	18	United Kingdom	Kenneth McKellar	A Man Without Love	Peter Callander	Cyril Ornadel	8
10	7	Finland	Ann-Christine Nyström	Play-boy	Ossi Runne	Ossi Runne	7
11	4	Luxembourg	Michèle Torr	Ce Soir Je T'attendais	Jacques Chaumelle	Bernard Kesslair	7
12	1	Germany	Margot Eskens	Die Zeiger Der Uhr	Hans Bradtke	Walter Dobschinski	7
13	8	Portugal	Madalena Iglesias	Ele E Ela	Carlos Canelhas	Carlos Canelhas	6
14	2	Denmark	Ulla Pia	Stop, Ja Stop - Ja Stop, Mens Legen Er	Erik Kåre	Erik Kåre	4
15	16	Netherlands	Milly Scott	Fernando En Philippo	Gerrit den Braber	Kees de Bruyn	2
16	15	France	Dominique Walter	Chez Nous	Jacques Plante	Claude Carrère	1
17	13	Monaco	Tereza	Bien Plus Fort	Jean-Max Rivière	Gérard Bourgeois	0
18	14	Italy	Domenico Modugno	Dio Come Ti Amo	Domenico Modugno	Domenico Modugno	0

1967 Eurovision 12: Vienna, Austria

8 April 1967

Rank	Start	Country	Artist	Song	Writer	Composer	POINTS
1	11	United Kingdom	Sandie Shaw	Puppet On A String	Bill Martin, Phil Coulter	Bill Martin, Phil Coulter	47
2	17	Ireland	Sean Dunphy	If I Could Choose	Wesley Burrows	Michael Coffey	22
3	4	France	Noëlle Cordier	Il Doit Faire Beau Là-bas	Pierre Delanoë	Hubert Giraud	20
4	2	Luxembourg	Vicky	L'amour Est Bleu	Pierre Cour	André Popp	17
5	14	Monaco	Minouche Barelli	Boum-badaboum	Serge Gainsbourg	Serge Gainsbourg, Michel Colombier	10
6	12	Spain	Raphael	Hablemos Del Amor	Manuel Alejandro	Manuel Alejandro	9
7	10	Belgium	Louis Neefs	Ik Heb Zorgen	Phil van Cauwenbergh	Paul Quintens	8
8	15	Yugoslavia	Lado Leskovar	Vse Roze Sveta	Milan Lindic	Urban Koder	7
9	9	Germany	Inge Brück	Anouschka	Hans Blüm	Hans Blüm	7
10	7	Sweden	Östen Warnebring	Som En Dröm	Curt Peterson, Marcus Österdahl, Patrice Hellberg	Curt Peterson, Marcus Österdahl, Patrice Hellberg	7
11	16	Italy	Claudio Villa	Non Andare Più Lontano	Vito Pallavicini	Gianni Mescoli	4
12	5	Portugal	Eduardo Nascimento	O Vento Mudou	João Magalhães Pereira	Nuño Nazareth Fernandes	3
13	8	Finland	Fredi	Varjoon-suojaan	Alvi Vuorinen	Lasse Mårtenson	3
14	3	Austria	Peter Horten	Warum Es Hunderttausend Sterne Gibt	Karin Bognar	Kurt Peche	2
15	13	Norway	Kirsti Sparboe	Dukkemann	Ola Johannessen	Tor Hultin	2
16	1	Netherlands	Thérèse Steinmetz	Ring-dinge	Gerrit den Braber	Johnny Holshuysen	2
17	6	Switzerland	Géraldine	Quel Coeur Vas-tu Briser?	Gérard Gray	Daniël Faure	0

1966 Eurovision 11: Luxembourg City, Luxembourg — 5 March 1966

Voting countries (columns): Austria, Belgium, Denmark, Finland, France, Germany, Ireland, Italy, Luxembourg, Monaco, Netherlands, Norway, Portugal, Spain, Sweden, Switzerland, United Kingdom

Receiving country	TOTAL
Germany	7
Denmark	4
Belgium	14
Luxembourg	7
Yugoslavia	9
Norway	12
Finland	7
Portugal	6
Austria	31
Sweden	16
Spain	9
Switzerland	12
Monaco	0
Italy	0
France	1
Netherlands	2
Ireland	14
United Kingdom	8

1967 Eurovision 12: Vienna, Austria — 8 April 1967

Voting countries (columns): Austria, Belgium, Finland, France, Germany, Ireland, Italy, Luxembourg, Monaco, Netherlands, Norway, Portugal, Spain, Sweden, Switzerland, United Kingdom, Yugoslavia

Receiving country	TOTAL
Netherlands	2
Luxembourg	17
Austria	2
France	20
Portugal	3
Switzerland	0
Sweden	7
Finland	3
Germany	7
Belgium	8
United Kingdom	47
Spain	9
Norway	2
Monaco	10
Yugoslavia	7
Italy	4
Ireland	22

Note: In 1966, each country awarded their three favourite acts either 5 points, 3 points or 1 point. In 1967, Ten jurors from each country each awarded 1 point to their favourite act

45

1968 Eurovision 13: London, United Kingdom

6 April 1968

Rank	Start	Country	Artist	Song	Writer	Composer	POINTS
1	15	Spain	Massiel	La, La, La	Ramón Arcusa, Manuel de la Calva	Ramón Arcusa, Manuel de la Calva	29
2	12	United Kingdom	Cliff Richard	Congratulations	Bill Martin, Phil Coulter	Bill Martin, Phil Coulter	28
3	10	France	Isabelle Aubret	La Source	Guy Bonnet, Henri Dijan	Daniel Faure	20
4	14	Ireland	Pat McGeegan	Chance Of A Lifetime	John Kennedy	John Kennedy	18
5	8	Sweden	Claes-Göran Hederström	Det Börjar Verka Kärlek, Banne Mej	Peter Himmelstrand	Peter Himmelstrand	15
6	16	Germany	Wencke Myhre	Ein Hoch Der Liebe	Carl Schäuble	Horst Jankowski	11
7	17	Yugoslavia	Luci Kapurso & Hamo Hajdarhodzic	Jedan Dan	Stijepo Strazicic	Djelo Jusic, Stipica Kalogjera	8
8	7	Monaco	Line & Willy	A Chacun Sa Chanson	Roland Valade	Jean-Claude Olivier	8
9	3	Belgium	Claude Lombard	Quand Tu Reviendras	Roland Dero	Jo van Wetter	8
10	11	Italy	Sergio Endrigo	Marianne	Sergio Endrigo	Sergio Endrigo	7
11	5	Luxembourg	Chris Baldo & Sophie Garel	Nous Vivrons D'amour	Jacques Demarny	Carlos Leresche	5
12	1	Portugal	Carlos Mendes	Verão	José Alberto Diogo	Pedro Osório	5
13	6	Switzerland	Gianni Mascolo	Guardando Il Sole	Sanzio Chiesa	Aldo d'Addario	2
14	13	Norway	Odd Børre	Stress	Ola Johannessen	Tor Hultin	2
15	4	Austria	Karel Gott	Tausend Fenster	Walter Brandin	Udo Jürgen Bockelmann	2
16	9	Finland	Kristina Hautala	Kun Kello Käy	Juha Vainio	Esko Linnavalli	1
17	2	Netherlands	Ronnie Tober	Morgen	Theo Strengers	Joop Stokkermans	1

1969 Eurovision 14: Madrid, Spain

29 March 1969

Rank	Start	Country	Artist	Song	Writer	Composer	POINTS
=1	14	France	Frida Boccara	Un Jour, Un Enfant	Eddy Marnay	Emile Stern	18
=1	7	United Kingdom	Lulu	Boom Bang-a-bang	Peter Warne	Alan Moorhouse	18
=1	8	Netherlands	Lenny Kuhr	De Troubadour	Lenny Kuhr	David Hartsema	18
=1	3	Spain	Salomé	Vivo Cantando	Aniano Alcalde	Maria José de Cerato	18
5	11	Switzerland	Paola del Medico	Bonjour, Bonjour	Jack Stark	Henry Mayer	13
6	4	Monaco	Jean-Jacques	Maman, Maman	Jo Perrier	Jo Perrier	11
7	10	Belgium	Louis Neefs	Jennifer Jennings	Phil van Cauwenbergh	Paul Quintens	10
8	5	Ireland	Muriel Day & the Lindsays	The Wages Of Love	Michael Reade	Michael Reade	10
9	13	Germany	Siw Malmkvist	Primaballerina	Hans Blüm	Hans Blüm	8
10	9	Sweden	Tommy Körberg	Judy, Min Vän	Britt Lindeborg	Roger Wallis	8
11	2	Luxembourg	Romuald	Catherine	André Pascal	Paul Mauriat, André Borly	7
12	16	Finland	Jarkko & Laura	Kuin Silloin Ennen	Juha Vainio	Toivo Kärki	6
13	1	Yugoslavia	Ivan	Pozdrav Svijetu	Milan Lentic	Milan Lentic	5
14	6	Italy	Iva Zanicchi	Due Grosse Lacrime Bianche	Daiano	Piero Soffici	5
15	15	Portugal	Simone de Oliveira	Desfolhada Portuguesa	José Carlos Ary dos Santos	Nuño Nazareth Fernandes	4
16	12	Norway	Kirsti Sparboe	Oj, Oj, Oj, Så Glad, Jeg Skal Bli	Arne Bendiksen	Arne Bendiksen	1

Note: Four joint winners were declared. A tie-break system was introduced in 1970.

1968 Eurovision 13: London, United Kingdom

6 April 1968

	Austria	Belgium	Finland	France	Germany	Ireland	Italy	Luxembourg	Monaco	Netherlands	Norway	Portugal	Spain	Sweden	Switzerland	United Kingdom	Yugoslavia	TOTAL
Portugal											2		3					5
Netherlands												1				1		1
Belgium			1	1			1						1					8
Austria	1						3						2					2
Luxembourg										1						1		5
Switzerland												1					2	2
Monaco			3			1		1		2	6			1	3			8
Sweden			1			4		3		1	1				2			15
Finland																		1
France	2	6					2			3				1		2	2	20
Italy			2	4	2	1	1	1	5	2		1		3	2			7
United Kingdom		2			2			1				1		4	4			28
Norway	4	1		4	6			1	4	1		1		2				2
Ireland								1				4	1				6	18
Spain	2		3	4		1	3	1				1		2	1	5		29
Germany								1					1					11
Yugoslavia	1	1				3		1										8

1969 Eurovision 14: Madrid, Spain

29 March 1969

	Belgium	Finland	France	Germany	Ireland	Italy	Luxembourg	Monaco	Netherlands	Norway	Portugal	Spain	Sweden	Switzerland	United Kingdom	Yugoslavia	TOTAL
Yugoslavia	1			1				3	1		3	1				1	5
Luxembourg	1		2	3				3		1	2		2			1	7
Spain	3	3		1	1		2	1	2				1	3			18
Monaco	1	1				4			1		1	2	1				11
Ireland							4	1	1	1	1						10
Italy		3	6				2			3	1					2	5
United Kingdom		1		1		3			2		1	2	5	4			18
Netherlands	1					3	4	1		3	1						18
Sweden	3						2		1	2							8
Belgium					3					1		2		2	3	2	10
Switzerland	1	2		2					2						2		13
Norway														1			1
Germany	1		1							1		2	1			3	8
France				1	4	1		2	2		2	2			4		18
Portugal	1		1									2					4
Finland			1	1		1			1	1		1					6

Note: in both years, ten jurors from each country each awarded 1 point to their favourite act.

47

1970 Eurovision 15: Amsterdam, Netherlands

21 March 1970

Rank	Start	Country	Artist	Song	Writer	Composer	POINTS
1	12	Ireland	Dana	All Kinds Of Everything	Derry Lindsay, Jackie Smith	Derry Lindsay, Jackie Smith	32
2	7	United Kingdom	Mary Hopkin	Knock, Knock (who's there?)	John Carter, Geoff Stephens	John Carter, Geoff Stephens	26
3	11	Germany	Katja Ebstein	Wunder Gibt Es Immer Wieder	Günther Loose	Christian Bruhn	12
4	9	Spain	Julio Iglesias	Gwendolyne	Julio Iglesias	Julio Iglesias	8
5	6	France	Guy Bonnet	Marie Blanche	Pierre-André Dousset	Guy Bonnet	8
6	5	Switzerland	Henri Dès	Retour	Henri Dès	Henri Dès	8
7	1	Netherlands	Patricia & Hearts of Soul	Waterman	Pieter Goemans	Pieter Goemans	7
8	10	Monaco	Dominique Dussault	Marlène	Henri Dijan	Eddie Barclay, Jimmy Walter	5
9	3	Italy	Gianni Morandi	Occhi Di Ragazza	Gianfranco Baldazzi, Sergio Bardotti	Lucio Dalla	5
10	5	Belgium	Jean Vallée	Viens L'oublier	Jean Vallée	Jean Vallée	5
11	4	Yugoslavia	Eva Sršen	Pridi, Dala Ti Bom Cvet	Dušan Velkaverh	Mojmir Sepe	4
12	8	Luxembourg	David-Alexandre Winter	Je Suis Tombé Du Ciel	Eddy Marnay	Yves de Vriendt	0

Note: Only 12 countries participated due to a boycott over the voting system used in 1969.

1971 Eurovision 16: Dublin, Ireland

3 April 1971

Rank	Start	Country	Artist	Song	Writer	Composer	POINTS
1	3	Monaco	Séverine	Un Banc, Un Arbre, Une Rue	Yves Dessca	Jean-Pierre Bourtayre	128
2	6	Spain	Karina	En Un Mundo Nuevo	Tony Luz	Rafael Trabucchelli	115
3	5	Germany	Katja Ebstein	Diese Welt	Fred Jay	Dieter Zimmermann	100
4	9	United Kingdom	Clodagh Rodgers	Jack In The Box	David Myers	John Worsley	98
5	11	Italy	Massimo Ranieri	L'amore è Un Attimo	Gaetano Savio, Giancarlo Bigazzi	Federico Polito	91
6	12	Sweden	Family Four	Vita Vidder	Håkan Elmquist	Håkan Elmquist	85
7	14	Netherlands	Saskia & Serge	De Tijd	Gerrit den Braber	Joop Stokkermans	85
8	17	Finland	Markku Aro & the Koivisto Sisters	Tie Uuteen Päivään	Rauno Lehtinen	Rauno Lehtinen	84
9	15	Portugal	Tonicha	Menina Do Alto Da Serra	José Carlos Ary dos Santos	Nuño Nazareth Fernandes	83
10	7	France	Serge Lama	Un Jardin Sur La Terre	Henri Dijan, Jacques Demarny	Alice Dona	83
11	13	Ireland	Angela Farrell	One Day Love	Donald Martin, Ita Flynn	Donald Martin, Ita Flynn	79
12	4	Switzerland	Peter, Sue & Marc	Les Illusions De Nos Vingt Ans	Maurice Tézé	Peter Reber	78
13	8	Luxembourg	Monique Melsen	Pomme, Pomme, Pomme	Pierre Cour	Hubert Giraud	70
14	16	Yugoslavia	Krunoslav Slabinac	Tvoj Djecak Je Tuzan	Zvonimir Golob	Ivica Krajac	68
15	10	Belgium	Lily Castel & Jacques Raymond	Goeie Morgen, Morgen	Phil van Cauwenbergh	Paul Quintens	68
16	1	Austria	Marianne Mendt	Musik	Richard Schönherz, Manuel Rigoni	Richard Schönherz, Manuel Rigoni	66
17	18	Norway	Hanne Krogh	Lykken Er	Arne Bendiksen	Arne Bendiksen	65
18	2	Malta	Joe Grech	Marija L-maltija	Charles Misfud	Joe Grech	52

1970 Eurovision 15: Amsterdam, Netherlands — 21 March 1970

	Belgium	France	Germany	Ireland	Italy	Luxembourg	Netherlands	Spain	Sweden	Switzerland	United Kingdom	Yugoslavia	TOTAL
Netherlands		2	2	1							1	3	7
Switzerland			2				2				1		8
Italy										2		1	5
Yugoslavia											4		4
Belgium		3			1				2				5
France									4	2		2	8
United Kingdom		2	4	3	2	1	3					4	26
Luxembourg													0
Spain					3	2			3				8
Monaco	1	2			1	2		1		1			5
Germany		1				3		4	1	1			12
Ireland	9	1	2			2	5	3		6	4		32

Note: Ten jurors from each country each awarded 1 point to their favourite act.

1971 Eurovision 16: Dublin, Ireland — 3 April 1971

	Austria	Belgium	Finland	France	Germany	Ireland	Italy	Luxembourg	Malta	Monaco	Netherlands	Norway	Portugal	Spain	Sweden	Switzerland	United Kingdom	Yugoslavia	TOTAL
Austria		3	3	3	7	6	6	2	3	5	3	5	5	2	4	2	3	4	66
Malta	4	4	3	3	3	4	4	2		2	5	2	2	5	2	2	3	2	52
Monaco	4	10	7	8	10	9	4	4	5		9	10	8	2	10	10	8	10	128
Switzerland	5	3	4	6	6	5	7	2	5	4	5	4	6	2	4		6	4	78
Germany	6	7	5	8		5	6	2	5	7	5	4	7	8	6	6	7	7	100
Spain	4	4	9	10	7	9	4	4	8	10	6	8	7		6	5	5	7	115
France	3	3	3		5	6	5	2	2	8	9	5	5	5	4	8	5	5	83
Luxembourg	2	3	5	5	2	5	3		7	6	3	4	6	4	2	3		6	70
United Kingdom	4	8	6	8	5	7	3	4	8	8	5	6	7	2	5	6		3	98
Belgium	3		6	5	2	4	3	2	2	5	6	4	6	2	5	4	6	8	68
Italy	4	2	2	9	6	6		2	6	9	2	5	3	6	7	8	5	8	91
Sweden	7	6	4	5	4	3		2	4	4	9	4	3	2		9	6	6	85
Ireland	7	3	4	7	4		6	2	6	6	5	6	4	5	2	3	5	5	79
Netherlands	6	2	6	7	4	5	6	2	2	6		8	9	5	6	5	5	5	85
Portugal	4	4	5	8	5	3	2	5	3	6	5	5		10	2	2	6	6	83
Yugoslavia	6	2	3	6	7	5	4	2	2	4	4	5	4	6	2	2	3		68
Finland	4	10		4	4	6	4	2	4	4	3	6	8	3	4	4	10	6	84
Norway	3	6	3	5	2	7	2	2	3	6	2		5	2	2	4	7	4	65

Note: Two jurors from each country both awarded between 1 and 5 points per act.

1972 Eurovision 17: Edinburgh, United Kingdom
25 March 1972

Rank	Start	Country	Artist	Song	Writer	Composer	POINTS
1	17	Luxembourg	Vicky Leandros	Après Toi	Klaus Munro, Yves Dessca	Mario Panas, Klaus Munro	128
2	5	United Kingdom	The New Seekers	Beg, Steal Or Borrow	Tony Cole, Graeme Hall, Steve Wolfe	Tony Cole, Graeme Hall, Steve Wolfe	114
3	1	Germany	Mary Roos	Nur Die Liebe Läßt Uns Leben	Joachim Relin	Joachim Heider	107
4	18	Netherlands	Sandra & Andres	Als Het Om De Liefde Gaat	Hans van Hemert	Dries Holten	106
5	11	Austria	The Milestones	Falter Im Wind	Heinz Unger	Richard Schönherz, Manuel Rigoni	100
6	12	Italy	Nicola di Bari	I Giorni Dell' Arcobaleno	Dalmazio Masini	Piero Pintucci, Nicola di Bari	92
7	7	Portugal	Carlos Mendes	A Festa Da Vida	José Niza	José Calvário	90
8	8	Switzerland	Véronique Müller	C'est La Chanson De Mon Amour	Catherine Desage	Véronique Müller	88
9	13	Yugoslavia	Tereza	Muzika I Ti	Ivica Krajac	Nikica Kalogjera	87
10	4	Spain	Jaime Morey	Amanece	Ramón Arcusa	Augusto Algueró	83
11	2	France	Betty Mars	Comé-comédie	Frédéric Botton	Frédéric Botton	81
12	10	Finland	Päivi Paunu & Kim Floor	Muistathan	Juha Flinck	Juha Flinck, Nacke Johansson	78
13	14	Sweden	Family Four	Härliga Sommardag	Håkan Elmquist	Håkan Elmquist	75
14	6	Norway	Grethe Kausland & Benny Borg	Småting	Kåre Grøttum, Ivar Børsum	Kåre Grøttum, Ivar Børsum	73
15	3	Ireland	Sandie Jones	Ceol On Ghrá	Liam MacUistin	Joe Burkett	72
16	15	Monaco	Anne-Marie Godart & Peter MacLane	Comme On S'aime	Jean Drejac	Raymond Bernard	65
17	16	Belgium	Serge & Christine Ghisoland	À La Folie Ou Pas Du Tout	Daniël Nelis	Daniël Nelis, Bob Milan	55
18	9	Malta	Helen & Joseph	L-imhabba	Albert Cassola	Charles Camilleri	48

1972 Eurovision 17: Edinburgh, United Kingdom

25 March 1972

	Austria	Belgium	Finland	France	Germany	Ireland	Italy	Luxembourg	Malta	Monaco	Netherlands	Norway	Portugal	Spain	Sweden	Switzerland	United Kingdom	Yugoslavia	TOTAL
Germany	5	7	5	8		6	7	7	4	8	6	6	6	9	8	5	5	5	107
France	2	7	4		5	5	3	8	5	6	6	7	2	2	2	3	9	5	81
Ireland	4	4	3	3	4		3	6	6	5	5	6	4	4	5	3	4	3	72
Spain	5	3	4	5	7	5	3	5	4	8	5	8	6		7	3	3	2	83
United Kingdom	7	4	7	9	8	6	7	8	2	9	8	10	4	2	6	8		9	114
Norway	3	4	7	3	4	6	2	6	5	4	4		5	5	4	2	4	5	73
Portugal	4	7	2	4	3	7	9	10	5	4	5	2		7	7	6	4	4	90
Switzerland	8	4	7	5	4	6	5	7	4	6	5	7	2	5	4		4	5	88
Malta	2	2	5	2	3	4	2	2		3	4	2	2	2	3	2	6	2	48
Finland	3	8		3	4	3	3	6	3	5	8	6	4	6	4	3	5	4	78
Austria		4	4	6	6	6	6	5	5	5	9	5	5	6	10	7	3	8	100
Italy	6	6	6	5	4	3		6	6	6	5	6	7	2	8	9	3	4	92
Yugoslavia	3	8	3	4	7	5	2	8	4	9	6	4	5	8	4	2	5		87
Sweden	4	7	5	3	5	5	3	5	4	5	5	5	4	3		2	3	7	75
Monaco	3	4	5	3	4	4	3	4	5		5	6	2	3	3	2	5	4	65
Belgium	2		4	3	2	4	3	6	5	4	3	2	3	2	2	3	5	2	55
Luxembourg	8	8	6	8	9	9	9		4	7	9	8	7	2	8	6	10	10	128
Netherlands	6	2	9	6	6	8	3	7	3	5		8	5	8	6	6	9	9	106

Note: Two jurors from each country both awarded between 1 and 5 points per act.

1973 Eurovision 18: Luxembourg

7 April 1973

Rank	Start	Country	Artist	Song	Writer	Composer	POINTS
1	11	Luxembourg	Anne-Marie David	Tu Te Reconnaîtras	Vline Buggy	Claude Morgan	129
2	7	Spain	Mocedades	Eres Tú	Juan Carlos Calderón	Juan Carlos Calderón	125
3	15	United Kingdom	Cliff Richard	Power To All Our Friends	Guy Fletcher, Doug Flett	Guy Fletcher, Doug Flett	123
4	17	Israel	Ilanit	Ey-sham	Ehud Manor	Nurit Hirsh	97
5	12	Sweden	The Nova & The Dolls	You're Summer	Lars Forssell	Monica & Carl-Axel Dominique	94
6	1	Finland	Marion Rung	Tom Tom Tom	Rauno Lehtinen	Rauno Lehtinen	93
7	5	Norway	Bendik Singers	It's Just A Game	Arne Bendiksen	Arne Bendiksen	89
8	6	Monaco	Marie	Un Train Qui Part	Boris Bergman	Bernard Liamis	85
9	4	Germany	Gitte	Junger Tag	Stephan Lego	Günther-Eric Thöner	85
10	3	Portugal	Fernando Tordo	Tourada	José Carlos Ary dos Santos	Fernando Tordo	80
11	14	Ireland	Maxi	Do I Dream?	Jack Brierley, George Crosby	Jack Brierley, George Crosby	80
12	8	Switzerland	Patrick Juvet	Je Me Vais Marier, Marie	Pierre Delanoë	Patrick Juvet	79
13	10	Italy	Massimo Ranieri	Chi Sarà Con Te	Giancarlo Bigazzi	Federico Polito, Gaetano Savio	74
14	13	Netherlands	Ben Cramer	De Oude Muzikant	Pierre Kartner	Pierre Kartner	69
15	16	France	Martine Clémenceau	Sans Toi	Anne Gregory	Paul Koulak	65
16	9	Yugoslavia	Zdravko Colic	Gori Vatra	Kemal Monteno	Kemal Monteno	65
17	2	Belgium	Nicole & Hugo	Baby, Baby	Erik Marijsse	Ignace Baert	58

1973 Eurovision 18: Luxembourg

7 April 1973

	Belgium	Finland	France	Germany	Ireland	Israel	Italy	Luxembourg	Monaco	Netherlands	Norway	Portugal	Spain	Sweden	Switzerland	United Kingdom	Yugoslavia	TOTAL
Finland	9		4	6	5	5	2	6	5	5	6	5	6	7	6	9	7	93
Belgium		4	2	4	4	2	2	4	6	3	3	3	6	2	4	5	4	58
Portugal	6	4	6	5	4	5	3	4	4	5	5		8	2	8	5	6	80
Germany	5	2	7		6	4	3	7	5	5	4	6	9	6	7	5	4	85
Norway	5	8	6	6	3	9	5	7	7	3		5	6	3	7	3	6	89
Monaco	3	6	5	4	6	4	8	6		5	3	2	6	4	5	9	9	85
Spain	8	3	9	9	10	8	10	8	9	10	4	9		7	8	4	9	125
Switzerland	3	4	2	4	7	3	4	6	5	8	7	3	7	3		7	6	79
Yugoslavia	3	5	4	4	5	4	2	4	5	4	2	3	8	2	6	4		65
Italy	5	2	5	5	4	4		5	7	4	5	3	5	5	7	5	5	74
Luxembourg	6	6	10	7	8	8	9		7	9	8	8	6	8	10	10	9	129
Sweden	4	8	4	5	5	5	5	6	5	6	8	4	7		9	7	6	94
Netherlands	4	4	6	5	5	2	4	7	4		5	2	5	3	5	3	5	69
Ireland	7	3	4	4		4	5	6	6	6	6	2	7	5	5	5	5	80
United Kingdom	6	9	8	7	9	9	5	10	8	10	7	6	4	9	8		8	123
France	3	4		4	5	2	2	3	5	5	4	2	5	5	4	5	7	65
Israel	6	6	5	7	7		7	8	7	6	5	5	4	6	6	5	7	97

Note: Two jurors from each country both awarded between 1 and 5 points per act.

1974 Eurovision 19: Brighton, United Kingdom

6 April 1974

Rank	Start	Country	Artist	Song	Writer	Composer	POINTS
1	8	Sweden	ABBA	Waterloo	Stig Anderson	Benny Andersson, Björn Ulvæus	24
2	17	Italy	Gigliola Cinquetti	Sì	Mario Panzeri, Daniele Pace, Lorenzo Pilat, Corrado Conti	Mario Panzeri, Daniele Pace, Lorenzo Pilat, Corrado Conti	18
3	12	Netherlands	Mouth & MacNeal	I See A Star	Hans van Hemert	Hans van Hemert	15
4	10	Monaco	Romuald	Celui Qui Reste Et Celui Qui S'en Va	Michael Jourdan	Jean-Pierre Bourtayre	14
5	9	Luxembourg	Ireen Sheer	Bye, Bye, I Love You	Michael Kunze, Humbert Ibach	Ralph Siegel	14
6	2	United Kingdom	Olivia Newton-John	Long Live Love	Valerie Avon, Harold Spiro	Valerie Avon, Harold Spiro	14
7	6	Israel	Poogy	Natati La Khaiai	Dani Sanderson, Alon Oleartchick	Dani Sanderson	11
8	13	Ireland	Tina	Cross Your Heart	Paul Lyttle	Paul Lyttle	11
9	3	Spain	Peret	Canta Y Se Feliz	Pedro Pubill Calaf	Pedro Pubill Calaf	10
10	11	Belgium	Jacques Hustin	Fleur De Liberté	Franck F Gérald	Jacques Hustin	10
11	5	Greece	Marinella	Krassi, Thalassa Ke T'agori Mou	Pythagoras	George Katsaros	7
12	7	Yugoslavia	Korni	Generacija 42	Kornelije Kovac	Kornelije Kovac	6
13	1	Finland	Carita	Äla Mene Pois (Keep Me Warm)	Hector	Eero Koivistoinen	4
14	16	Portugal	Paulo de Carvalho	E Depois Do Adeus	José Niza	José Calvário	3
15	14	Germany	Cindy & Bert	Die Sommermelodie	Kurt Feltz	Werner Scharfenberger	3
16	4	Norway	Anne-Karine Ström & the Bendik Singers	The First Day Of Love	Philip Kruse	Frode Thingnæs	3
17	15	Switzerland	Piera Martell	Mein Ruf Nach Dir	Pepe Ederer	Pepe Ederer	3

1974 Eurovision 19: Brighton, United Kingdom

6 April 1974

	Belgium	Finland	Germany	Greece	Ireland	Israel	Italy	Luxembourg	Monaco	Netherlands	Norway	Portugal	Spain	Sweden	Switzerland	United Kingdom	Yugoslavia	TOTAL
Finland					1	2										1		4
United Kingdom	1	1	2	1	1		3	1	3		2	2			1		4	14
Spain			1						1									10
Norway	1									1		1		1				3
Greece										4		2		2		2		7
Israel					1		3			2		1	1	1				11
Yugoslavia	1	1					2	1				1	1					6
Sweden		5	2		1	2		1	1	3	2	1	1		5		1	24
Luxembourg	1		1	1	3	2	2				1	1	1	1	1		2	14
Monaco	2		2		1	1		2			2		2					14
Belgium				5				3										10
Netherlands	1	1	1	2	1	1		2	1		1	1	2	3		1	3	15
Ireland						1					2		2	2	1	1		11
Germany	1			1											1			3
Switzerland	1		1										1			1		3
Portugal															2			3
Italy	1	2			1	1		1	4			1	2			5		18

Note: 10 jurors from each country awarded 1 point each to their favourite act

55

1975 Eurovision 20: Stockholm, Sweden
22 March 1975

Rank	Start	Country	Artist	Song	Writer	Composer	POINTS
1	1	Netherlands	Teach-In	Teach-In	Will Luikinga, Eddy Ouwens	Dick Bakker	152
2	9	United Kingdom	The Shadows	Let Me Be The One	Paul Curtis	Paul Curtis	138
3	19	Italy	Wess & Dori Ghezzi	Era	Andrea lo Vecchio	Shel Shapiro	115
4	3	France	Nicole Rieu	Et Bonjour à Toi L'artiste	Pierre Delanoë, Jeff Barnel	Pierre Delanoë, Jeff Barnel	91
5	5	Luxembourg	Géraldine	Toi	Pierre Cour, Bill Martin, Phil Coulter	Bill Martin, Phil Coulter	84
6	7	Switzerland	Simone Drexel	Mikado	Simone Drexel	Simone Drexel	77
7	15	Finland	Pihasoittajat	Old Man Fiddle	Hannu Karlsson	Kim Kuusi	74
8	18	Sweden	Lars Berghagen & the Dolls	Jennie, Jennie	Lars Berghagen	Lars Berghagen	72
9	2	Ireland	The Swarbriggs	That's What Friends Are For	Jimmy Swarbrigg, Tommy Swarbrigg	Jimmy Swarbrigg, Tommy Swarbrigg	68
10	17	Spain	Sergio y Estibaliz	Tú Volverás	Juan Carlos Calderón	Juan Carlos Calderón	53
11	12	Israel	Shlomo Artzi	At Ve'ani	Ehud Manor	Shlomo Artzi	40
12	10	Malta	Renato	Singing This Song	M Idris Misfud	Sammy Galea	32
13	8	Yugoslavia	Pepel In Kri	Dan Ljubezni	Dusan Velkaverh	Tadej Hrusovar	22
14	14	Monaco	Sophie	Une Chanson C'est Une Lettre	Boris Bergman	André Popp	22
15	11	Belgium	Ann Christy	Gelukkig Zijn	Mary Boduin	Mary Boduin	17
16	16	Portugal	Duarte Mendes	Madrugada	José Luis Tinoco	José Luis Tinoco	16
17	4	Germany	Joy Fleming	Ein Lied Kann Eine Brücke Sein	Michael Holm	Rainer Pietsch	15
18	6	Norway	Ellen Nikolaysen	You Touched My Life With Summer	Svein Hundnes	Svein Hundnes	11
19	13	Turkey	Semiha Yanki	Seninle Bir Dakika	Hikmet Munir Ebcioglu	Kemal Ebcioglu	3

Note: 1975 marked the introduction of the current 12, 10, 8, 7, 6, 5, 4, 3, 2 & 1 points system.

1975 Eurovision 20: Stockholm, Sweden

22 March 1975

	Belgium	Finland	France	Germany	Ireland	Israel	Italy	Luxembourg	Malta	Monaco	Netherlands	Norway	Portugal	Spain	Sweden	Switzerland	Turkey	United Kingdom	Yugoslavia	TOTAL
Netherlands	3	10	5	8	8	12	1	10	12	10		12	7	12	12	6	4	12	8	152
Ireland	12	1	6			7	4		4		6	4	4	3	10	7		6	1	68
France	2				12		8	8	7	7	8		12	8	8	3	1	8		91
Germany									3					4						15
Luxembourg		5	3		10	6	10		5		12		8	6	4		5	3	7	84
Norway							7			2	2		2				7			11
Switzerland	8	4	10	6	2		12	2	6	5	7	1	1		7			5		77
Yugoslavia	5			2	4						3		5		5					22
United Kingdom	10	7	12	10	3	10	3	12	8	12	4	7		10	2	8			12	138
Malta	7		8			1		5			1	2			6	4	2		2	32
Belgium				7							5								3	17
Israel	1	3	1	1	1		2	1	1	3	10	5			6	2	6	1		40
Turkey																				3
Monaco		2		3		2	5	4				10	3	1	3			2	5	22
Finland			2	12	5	8		6		8				2		12	12	4		74
Portugal																				16
Spain	4	8		5	7	4	6		2	4		3				5	3		4	53
Sweden		6	7		3	3		7		6		8	6	5		1	8	7	6	72
Italy	6	12	4	4	6	5		3	10	1		6	10	7	1	10	10	10	10	115

57

1976 Eurovision 21: The Hague, Netherlands
3 April 1976

Rank	Start	Country	Artist	Song	Writer	Composer	POINTS
1	1	United Kingdom	Brotherhood of Man	Save Your Kisses For Me	Tony Hiller, Lee Sheriden, Martin Lee	Tony Hiller, Lee Sheriden, Martin Lee	164
2	17	France	Catherine Ferry	Un, Deux, Trois	Jean Paul Cara	Tony Rallo	147
3	16	Monaco	Mary Christy	Toi, La Musique Et Moi	Gilbert Sinoué	Georges Costa, André Bars	93
4	2	Switzerland	Peter, Sue & Marc	Djambo, Djambo	Peter Reber	Peter Reber	91
5	14	Austria	Waterloo & Robinson	My Little World	Gerhard Heinz	Gerhard Heinz	80
6	4	Israel	Chocolate, Menta, Mastik	Emor Shalom	Ehud Manor	Matti Caspi	77
7	13	Italy	Romina & Al Bano	We'll Live It All Again	Al Bano, Romina Power	Detto Mariano	69
8	6	Belgium	Pierre Rapsat	Judy Et Cie	Eric van Hulse	Pierre Rapsat	68
9	8	Netherlands	Sandra Reemer	The Party's Over Now	Hans van Hemert	Hans van Hemert	56
10	7	Ireland	Red Hurley	When	Brendan J Graham	Brendan J Graham	54
11	11	Finland	Fredi & The Friends	Pump-pump	Matti Siitonen	Vexi Salmi	44
12	15	Portugal	Carlos do Carmo	Uma Flor De Verde Pinho	Manuel Alégre	José Niza	24
13	10	Greece	Mariza Koch	Panaghia Mou, Panaghia Mou	Michael Fotiades	Mariza Koch	20
14	5	Luxembourg	Jürgen Marcus	Chansons Pour Ceux Qui S'aiment	Vline Buggy, Fred Jay	Jack White	17
15	3	Germany	Les Humphries Singers	Sing, Sang, Song	Kurt Hertha	Ralph Siegel	12
16	12	Spain	Braulio	Sobran Las Palabras	Braulio	Braulio	11
17	9	Yugoslavia	Ambasadori	Ne Mogu Skriti Svoju Bol	Slobodan Djurasovic	Slobodan Vujovic	10
18	18	Norway	Anne-Karine Ström	Mata Hari	Philip Kruse	Frode Thingnæs	7

1976 Eurovision 21: The Hague, Netherlands

3 April 1976

	Austria	Belgium	Finland	France	Germany	Greece	Ireland	Israel	Italy	Luxembourg	Monaco	Netherlands	Norway	Portugal	Spain	Switzerland	United Kingdom	Yugoslavia	TOTAL
United Kingdom	10	12	10	7	8	12	3	12	4	8	10	10	12	12	12	12		10	164
Switzerland	8	7	7	6	5	2	1	4		1	4	6	10	7	4		12	7	91
Germany		1		2						2	1	2		2	2	2		3	12
Israel	6	5	8		3		4		10	7		5	7	2	1	7	6	8	77
Luxembourg		6					6												17
Belgium	3		12	5		8		1	8		8	4	6	8		6	7		68
Ireland	2			3	1	7		3	12	3	6		1	6	5		10	1	54
Netherlands	4	4			4		2	8	2	4	2			4	3	4		5	56
Norway												3		1					7
Greece	7	2	4	8	6		5	6	5		7	1	4		6		2		20
Finland						1	12	2	3		3		3	10			3		44
Spain	1					10	10	10					2				1		11
Italy		3	6	10	10	6	8	7	1	5	5	7	3		8	8	4	6	69
Austria			5		7	4			7	6		8	2			3		2	80
Portugal	5	8	1	12			8	7	6	12			5	3	7	5	5		24
Monaco	12	10	2		12	5	7	5		10	12	12	8	5	10	10	8	4	93
France			3		2	3										1		12	147
Yugoslavia				4															10

59

1977 Eurovision 22: London, United Kingdom   7 May 1977

Rank	Start	Country	Artist	Song	Writer	Composer	POINTS
1	18	France	Marie Myriam	L'oiseau Et L'enfant	Joe Garcy	Jean-Paul Cara	136
2	9	United Kingdom	Lynsey de Paul & Mike Moran	Rock Bottom	Lynsey de Paul, Mike Moran	Lynsey de Paul, Mike Moran	121
3	1	Ireland	The Swarbriggs Plus Two	It's Nice To Be In Love Again	Tommy Swarbrigg, Jimmy Swarbrigg	Tommy Swarbrigg, Jimmy Swarbrigg	119
4	2	Monaco	Michèle Torr	Une Petite Française	Jean Albertini	Paul de Senneville, Olivier Toussaint	96
5	10	Greece	Pascalis, Marianna, Robert & Bessy	Mathema Solfege	Sevy Tiliakou	Georges Hatzinassios	92
6	12	Switzerland	Pepe Lienhard Band	Swiss Lady	Peter Reber	Peter Reber	71
7	17	Belgium	Dream Express	A Million In One, Two, Three	Luc Smets	Luc Smets	69
8	6	Germany	Silver Convention	Telegram	Michael Kunze	Silvester Levay	55
9	14	Spain	Micky	Enseñame A Cantar	Fernando Arbex	Fernando Arbex	52
10	16	Finland	Monica Aspelund	Lapponia	Monica Aspelund	Aarno Raninen	50
11	11	Israel	Ilanit	Ah-haa-vah Hee Shir Lish-naa-yim	Edna Peleg	Eldad Shrim	49
12	3	Netherlands	Heddy Lester	De Mallemolen	Wim Hogenkamp	Frank Affolter	35
13	15	Italy	Mia Martini	Libera	Luigi Albertelli	Salvatore Fabrizio	33
14	8	Portugal	Os Amigos	Portugal No Coração	José Carlos Ary dos Santos	Fernando Tordo	18
15	5	Norway	Anita Skorgan	Casanova	Dag Nordtømme	Svein Strugstad	18
16	7	Luxembourg	Anne Marie B	Frère Jacques	Guy Béart, Pierre Cour	Guy Béart, Pierre Cour	17
17	4	Austria	Schmetterlinge	Boom Boom Boomerang	E. Lukas Resetarits	Schuri Herrnstadt, Willi Resetarits & Herbert Zöchling-Tampier	11
18	13	Sweden	Forbes	Beatles	Sven-Olof Bagge	Claes Bure	2

1977 Eurovision 22: London, United Kingdom

7 May 1977

	Austria	Belgium	Finland	France	Germany	Greece	Ireland	Israel	Italy	Luxembourg	Monaco	Netherlands	Norway	Portugal	Spain	Sweden	Switzerland	United Kingdom	TOTAL
Ireland	5	3		10	5	10		12	8	8	8	1	12	1	4	12	8	12	119
Monaco	8	2	5	5	6	12	5	2	12	1			1	6	8	10	6	7	96
Netherlands		10	1	8		1	3	1			3		2		1		7	1	35
Austria						3				3	5								11
Norway	2	5		1					5					2		1		2	18
Germany			8			8	1	5	6	2	1	3		8	5	5		8	55
Luxembourg					1		2								7				17
Portugal				6	10			8	3	12	2	2	7		3	8	4		18
United Kingdom	12	12	4	12	4			3	2	6	12	7	4	12	12	7	1		121
Greece	4	6	6	3		6	7	4	1		10	10	5	10	6	3	10	5	92
Israel	3	1		2		4	6		4	5	7	5	10	4				4	49
Switzerland	10	8	10		2														71
Sweden	1	7	7		7	4	8	7	7	7		6					3	3	2
Spain	6		2	7	3	2	12	6				4	8	3	2		2		52
Italy				4	8	5	4	10		4		12	6	7		2	5		33
Finland		3			12	7	10	6		10	4	8	3	5	10	4		10	50
Belgium	7	4	12						10							6	12	6	69
France																			136

1978 Eurovision 23: Paris, France
22 April 1978

Rank	Start	Country	Artist	Song	Writer	Composer	POINTS
1	18	Israel	Izhar Cohen & the Alphabeta	Abanibi	Ehud Manor	Nurit Hirsh	157
2	10	Belgium	Jean Vallée	L'amour ça Fait Chanter La Vie	Jean Vallée	Jean Vallée	125
3	6	France	Joël Prévost	Il Y Aura Toujours Des Violons	Didier Barbelivien	Gérard Stern	119
4	14	Monaco	Caline & Olivier Toussaint	Les Jardins De Monaco	Didier Barbelivien, Jean Albertini	Paul de Senneville, Olivier Toussaint	107
5	1	Ireland	Colm Wilkinson	Born To Sing	Colm Wilkinson	Colm Wilkinson	86
6	13	Germany	Ireen Sheer	Feuer	John Möring	Erich Leissman, Jean Frankfurter	84
7	17	Luxembourg	Baccara	Parlez-vous Français?	Frank Dostal, Peter Zenter	Rolf Soja	73
8	15	Greece	Tania Tsanaklidou	Charlie Chaplin	Yannis Xantoulis	Sakis Tsilikis	66
9	7	Spain	José Vélez	Bailemos Un Vals	Ramón Arcusa, Manuel de la Calva	Ramón Arcusa, Manuel de la Calva	65
10	9	Switzerland	Carole Vinci	Vivre	Pierre Alain	Alain Morisod	65
11	8	United Kingdom	Co-Co	The Bad Old Days	Stephanie de Sykes, Stuart Slater	Stephanie de Sykes, Stuart Slater	61
12	3	Italy	Ricchi e Poveri	Questo Amore	Sergio Bardotti	Dario Farina, Mario Luisini	53
13	11	Netherlands	Harmony	't Is Ok	Toon Gispen, Dick Bakker	Eddy Ouwens	37
14	20	Sweden	Björn Skifs	Det Blir Alltid Värre Framåt Natten	Peter Himmelstrand	Peter Himmelstrand	26
15	19	Austria	Springtime	Mrs Caroline Robinson	Walter Markel, Gerhard Markel, Norbert Niedermayer	Walter Markel, Gerhard Markel	14
16	16	Denmark	Mabel	Boom Boom	Mabel	Mabel	13
17	5	Portugal	Gemini	Dai-li-dou	Carlos Quintas	Victor Mamêde	5
18	4	Finland	Seija Simola	Anna Rakkaudelle Tilaisuus	Reijo Karvonen, Seija Simola	Reijo Karvonen	2
19	12	Turkey	Nazar	Sevinçe	Hulki Aktunç	Daghan Baydur, Onno Tunç	2
20	2	Norway	Jahn Teigen	Mil Etter Mil	Kai Eide	Kai Eide	0

1978 Eurovision 23: Paris, France

22 April 1978

	Austria	Belgium	Denmark	Finland	France	Germany	Greece	Ireland	Israel	Italy	Luxembourg	Monaco	Netherlands	Norway	Portugal	Spain	Sweden	Switzerland	Turkey	United Kingdom	TOTAL
Ireland	6	10		3	5	5	10				10			12			8	7	10		86
Norway																					0
Italy		1	8		4	2	2	10			3	8		6	1	8		1	1	6	53
Finland			12											2		1					2
Portugal				2						4											5
France	12	8		7		10	8	6	5	10	1	5	6	3	2	5	10	6	4	8	119
Spain	7	2					6	3	6		2	4	4		6	3	3	8	7		65
United Kingdom	5	4	3	1	2	8	3		2	1	5	7	2	5	4	4	4	2	6		61
Switzerland	10	7			7	6	12	12	1	6	8	2	8	7		2	1	10		2	65
Belgium	4		5	6	12	3			7	5	7	12	5		4					12	125
Netherlands						4			12		6	1		1			1			3	37
Turkey																				1	2
Germany	1	5	1	12	1		7	1	3	3		10	7	4	7	10	7	3	8	10	84
Monaco	6	6	10	8	10	7	4	4	8	7	4		10		5	7	12	5	5		107
Greece	3		4	5	6			7	10	2					8		2	4			66
Denmark	2						1		4				1								13
Luxembourg		3	7		8	12	1	2		12		6	3	8	12	12	6		2	7	73
Israel	8	12	6	10		1	5	8		8	12	3	12		10	6	5	12	12	5	157
Austria			2		3									10	3				3		14
Sweden				4				5												4	26

1979 Eurovision 24: Jerusalem, Israel

31 March 1979

Rank	Start	Country	Artist	Song	Writer	Composer	POINTS
1	10	Israel	Milk and Honey	Hallelujah	Shimrit Orr	Kobi Oshrat	125
2	19	Spain	Betty Missiego	Su Canción	Fernando Moreno	Fernando Moreno	116
3	11	France	Anne-Marie David	Je Suis L'enfant-soleil	Eddy Marnay	Hubert Giraud	106
4	9	Germany	Dschinghis Khan	Dschinghis Khan	Bernd Meinunger	Ralph Siegel	86
5	4	Ireland	Cathal Dunne	Happy Man	Cathal Dunne	Cathal Dunne	80
6	3	Denmark	Tommy Seebach	Disco Tango	Keld Heick	Tommy Seebach	76
7	17	United Kingdom	Black Lace	Mary Ann	Peter Morris	Peter Morris	73
8	7	Greece	Elpida	Socrates	Sotia Tsotou	Doros Georghiades	69
9	1	Portugal	Manuela Bravo	Sobe, Sobe, Balão Sobe	Carlos Nobrega e Sousa	Carlos Nobrega e Sousa	64
10	8	Switzerland	Peter, Sue, Marc, Pfuri, Gorps & Kniri	Trödler Und Co	Peter Reber	Peter Reber	60
11	16	Norway	Anita Skorgan	Oliver	Philip Kruse	Anita Skorgan	57
12	14	Netherlands	Xandra	Colorado	Gerard Cox	Rob Bolland, Ferdi Bolland	51
13	13	Luxembourg	Jeane Manson	J'ai Déjà Vu ça Dans Tes Yeux	Jean Renard	Jean Renard	44
14	5	Finland	Katri-Helena	Katso Sineen Taivaan	Vexi Salmi	Matti Siitonen	38
15	2	Italy	Matia Bazar	Raggio Di Luna	Giancarlo Golzi, Salvatore Stellita	Carlo Marrale, Piero Cassano, Antoniella Ruggiero	27
16	6	Monaco	Laurent Vaguener	Notre Vie, C'est La Musique	Jean Albertini, Didier Barbelivien	P de Senneville, L Vaguener	12
17	15	Sweden	Ted Gärdestad	Satellit	Kenneth Gärdestad, Ted Gärdestad	Kenneth Gärdestad, Ted Gärdestad	8
18	12	Belgium	Micha Marah	Hey Nana	Guy Beyers	Charles Dumolin	5
19	18	Austria	Christina Simon	Heute In Jerusalem	André Heller	Peter Wolf	5

1979 Eurovision 24: Jerusalem, Israel
31 March 1979

	Austria	Belgium	Denmark	Finland	France	Germany	Greece	Ireland	Israel	Italy	Luxembourg	Monaco	Netherlands	Norway	Portugal	Spain	Sweden	Switzerland	United Kingdom	TOTAL
Portugal	7	5		2	10	4				6	3	5	3	6		6	3	4		64
Italy	3	7		8										3	8	8				27
Denmark	3		5		6	10	12	2			4	3	8		5	4	1	1	3	76
Ireland		10		6		6	10			5	7			5			8	6	4	80
Finland			4		5	5	7			7	6				1			8		38
Monaco	2	1	1		3	2		4	10	2		7			10	2	2			12
Greece	12	4	7	10	4	7		1	4		5	2	7			7		7		69
Switzerland		2	12	3	7		2	5	6	1	1	12	2	8	2	12	6		8	60
Germany	8		6	12	12		4	12			8	8	1	12	12	10	12	5	12	86
Israel	5	6		1	1		8		5	10	12	10	12	7	6	3	5	10	6	125
France			2			1		3				4	4	2	7			3	2	106
Belgium						1			7				4	4			4		10	5
Luxembourg	4	3	8	4	2	3	5	10	1	3		4			7			3		44
Netherlands				5			3	6	2	8		1								51
Sweden	1	8				8	1	8		4	2	6	6	10	3	1				8
Norway	6		10	7				7				1	5		4	5	10	2	7	57
United Kingdom										4	10		10	1					1	73
Austria	10	12	3		8	12	6		8	12	10						7	12	5	5
Spain																				116

1980 Eurovision 25: The Hague, Netherlands   19 April 1980

Rank	Start	Country	Artist	Song	Writer	Composer	POINTS
1	17	Ireland	Johnny Logan	What's Another Year	Shay Healy	Shay Healy	143
2	12	Germany	Katja Ebstein	Theater	Bernd Meinunger	Ralph Siegel	128
3	13	United Kingdom	Prima Donna	Love Enough For Two	Stephanie de Sykes, Stuart Slater	Stephanie de Sykes, Stuart Slater	106
4	9	Switzerland	Paola	Cinéma	Peter Reber, Véronique Müller	Peter Reber	104
5	15	Netherlands	Maggie MacNeal	Amsterdam	Alex Alberts	Frans Smit, Sjoukje Smit, Robert Verwey	93
6	6	Italy	Alan Sorrenti	Non So Che Darei	Alan Sorrenti	Alan Sorrenti	87
7	14	Portugal	José Cid	Um Grande, Grande Amor	José Cid	José Cid	71
8	1	Austria	Blue Danube	Du Bist Musik	Klaus-Peter Sattler	Klaus-Peter Sattler	64
9	4	Luxembourg	Sophie & Magaly	Papa Pingouin	Pierre Delanoë, Jean-Paul Cara	Ralph Siegel, Bernd Meinunger	56
10	8	Sweden	Tomas Ledin	Just Nu!	Tomas Ledin	Tomas Ledin	47
11	16	France	Profil	Hé, Hé M'sieurs Dames	Richard de Bordeaux, Richard Joffo	Sylvano Santorio	45
12	18	Spain	Trigo Limpio	Qué Date Esta Noche	José Antonio Martin	José Antonio Martin	38
13	3	Greece	Anna Vishy & the Epikouri	Autostop	Rony Sofou	Jick Nakassian	30
14	7	Denmark	Bamses Venner	Tænker Altid På Dig	Flemming Jørgensen	Bjarne Gren-Jensen	25
15	2	Turkey	Ajda Pekkan	Petr'oil	Sanar Yurdatapan	Atilla Ozdemiroglu	23
16	11	Norway	Sverre Kjellsberg & Mattis Hætta	Sámiid Ædnan	Ragnar Olsen	Sverre Kjellsberg	15
17	19	Belgium	Telex	Euro-vision	Telex	Telex	14
18	5	Morocco	Samira Bensaïd	Bitakat Hob	Malou Rouanne	Abdel Ati Amenna	7
19	10	Finland	Vesa-Matti Loiri	Huilumies	Vexi Salmi	Aarno Raninen	6

1980 Eurovision 25: The Hague, Netherlands
19 April 1980

	Austria	Belgium	Denmark	Finland	France	Germany	Greece	Ireland	Italy	Luxembourg	Morocco	Netherlands	Norway	Portugal	Spain	Sweden	Switzerland	Turkey	United Kingdom	TOTAL
Austria		1	5	5	4	4	1	10	4		3	3	6	3	4	1	4		6	64
Turkey	3								8		12									23
Greece	5		2					4	2			8	4	1				1	3	30
Luxembourg	1	8	4	3	7			8	7	1			7		3	6			8	56
Morocco																				7
Italy	2	10	3	6	2	7	2	2				1	2	12	10	10	8	6	4	87
Denmark				7		5	4				2		1		1		6	8		25
Sweden						2	10		5	10	6	10	10	6	2		5			47
Switzerland	6	2	8	12		10		12	3	5	7	2	5		2	2		2	7	104
Finland					1															6
Norway					3	6					4									15
Germany	8	7	7	2	10			5	12	3	10	12		8	12	5	7	10	10	128
United Kingdom	7	6	10	4	5	3		6		8	8	7	8	7	8	12	10	5		106
Portugal		4	6	1	6	1		7	10	4		5			5	8	2	4		71
Netherlands	12	3		10	12	8		1		12			3	4		3	3	12	2	93
France		5	1					3	1	2	1	4	3	5	6	4	1	3	5	45
Ireland	10	12	12	8	8	12			6	7		6	12	2	7	7	12		12	143
Spain	4									6	5			10				7		38
Belgium																			1	14

1981 Eurovision 26: Dublin, Ireland

4 April 1981

Rank	Start	Country	Artist	Song	Writer	Composer	POINTS
1	14	United Kingdom	Bucks Fizz	Making Your Mind Up	Andy Hill	John Danter	136
2	3	Germany	Lena Valaitis	Johnny Blue	Bernd Meinunger	Ralph Siegel	132
3	9	France	Jean Gabilou	Humanahum	Joel Gracy	Jean-Paul Cara	125
4	19	Switzerland	Peter, Sue & Marc	Io Senza Tei	Peter Reber, Nella Martinetti	Peter Reber	121
5	12	Ireland	Sheeba	Horoscopes	Joe Burkett	Jim Kelly	105
6	18	Cyprus	Island	Monika	Stavros Sideras	Doros Georghiades	69
7	5	Israel	Habibi	Halaylah	Shlomit Aharon, Yuval Dor	Shuki Levi	56
8	17	Greece	Yiannis Dimitras	Feggari Kalokerino	Yiannis Dimitras	Giorgos Niachros	55
9	11	Netherlands	Linda Williams	Het Is Een Wonder	Bart van de Laar	Cees de Wit	51
10	20	Sweden	Björn Skifs	Fångad I En Dröm	Björn Skifs, Bengt Palmers	Björn Skifs, Bengt Palmers	50
11	4	Luxembourg	Jean-Claude Pascal	C'est Peut-être Pas L'amérique	Sophie Makhno, Jean-Claude Villemino	Sophie Makhno, Jean-Claude Villemino	41
12	6	Denmark	Debbie Cameron & Tommy Seebach	Krøller Eller Ej	Keld Heick	Tommy Seebach	41
13	16	Belgium	Emly Starr	Samson	Kick Dandy, Els van den Abeele	Kick Dandy, Giuseppe Marchese	40
14	10	Spain	Bacchelli	Y Solo Tú	Amado Jaén	Amado Jaén	38
15	7	Yugoslavia	Seid-Memic Vajta	Leila	Ranko Boban	Ranko Boban	35
16	8	Finland	Riki Sorsa	Reggae OK	Olli Ojala	Jim Pembroke	27
17	1	Austria	Marty Brem	Wenn Du Da Bist	Werner Böhmler	Werner Böhmler	20
18	15	Portugal	Carlos Paião	Play-back	Carlos Paião	Carlos Paião	9
19	2	Turkey	Modern Folk Trio & Ayşegül	Dönme Dolap	Ali Kocatepe	Ali Kocatepe	9
20	13	Norway	Finn Kalvik	Aldri I Livet	Finn Kalvik	Finn Kalvik	0

1981 Eurovision 26: Dublin, Ireland

4 April 1981

	Austria	Belgium	Cyprus	Denmark	Finland	France	Germany	Greece	Ireland	Israel	Luxembourg	Netherlands	Norway	Portugal	Spain	Sweden	Switzerland	Turkey	United Kingdom	Yugoslavia	TOTAL
Austria				1		5									6	2		6			20
Turkey	5				5																9
Germany	10	10	8	8	7	8		5	6	8		3	4	12	12	12	6	12	7	3	132
Luxembourg	8	12			4	3	5		7	3	1	7	8	4	1	5	4			2	41
Israel		5			6	4	1				3	2	1	5	3	3	10	1	4		56
Denmark		3	3			1			2					2		4		4	5		41
Yugoslavia	12			2	8		12	2	5	2		5	5	1	2				1		35
Finland	3	2	7	7		2	3	8	4	7	12	6	10	10	7	6	12	10		4	27
France	7	1	2	12			6	3	3	6	10	4		3	5	10	2	5	6		125
Spain		8	12	10	3	6	4	10		4	5	10		7		7	1	3		5	38
Netherlands	4		4	6	2	7	8	1	10	10	6			6		8	8	8		10	51
Ireland	1	6	5	3			2	7		12		8	2		10		7	7	3	8	105
Norway										1											0
United Kingdom	6	7	6	4	12	10	7	12	12	5	8	1	7	8	4	1		2		12	136
Portugal				5	1	12	10	4	8		2		12							7	9
Belgium	2		10	4	12		7		1		8		6						12	6	40
Greece		4	1	5	1														2	12	55
Cyprus												8		8	10				10		69
Switzerland	2							6				12							12	12	121
Sweden							10										3		2	7	50

69

1982 Eurovision 27: Harrogate, United Kingdom

24 April 1982

Rank	Start	Country	Artist	Song	Writer	Composer	POINTS
1	18	Germany	Nicole	Ein bißchen Frieden	Bernd Meinunger	Ralph Siegel	161
2	15	Israel	Avi Toledano	Hora	Yoram Tahar-Lev	Avi Toledano	100
3	7	Switzerland	Arlette Zola	Amour on t'aime	Pierre Alain	Alain Morisod	97
4	11	Belgium	Stella	Si tu aimes ma musique	Jo May	Fred Bekky, Rony Brack, Bobott	96
5	8	Cyprus	Anna Vishy	Mono i agapi	Anna Vishy	Anna Vishy	85
6	2	Luxembourg	Svetlana	Cours après le temps	Cyril Assous	Michel Jouveaux	78
7	4	United Kingdom	Bardo	One step further	Simon Jeffries	Simon Jeffries	76
8	9	Sweden	Chips	Dag efter dag	Monica Forsberg	Lasse Holm	67
9	10	Austria	Mess	Sonntag	Rudolph Leve	Michael Scheikl	57
10	12	Spain	Lucía	Él	Ignacio Román	Francisco Cepero	52
11	17	Ireland	The Duskeys	Here Today, Gone Tomorrow	Sally Keating	Sally Keating	49
12	3	Norway	Jahn Teigen & Anita Skorgan	Adieu	Herodes Falsk	Jahn Teigen	40
13	1	Portugal	Doce	Bem-bom	António Pinho, Tózé Brito, Pedro Brito	António Pinho, Tózé Brito, Pedro Brito	32
14	14	Yugoslavia	Aska	Halo Halo	Miro Zec	Aleksandar Sanja Ilic	21
15	5	Turkey	Neço	Hani	Olcayto Ahmet Tugsuz, Fait Tugsuz	Olcayto Ahmet Tugsuz	20
16	16	Netherlands	Bill van Dijk	Jij En Ik	Liselore Gerritsen	Dick Bakker	8
17	13	Denmark	Brixx	Video-video	Jens Brixtofte	Jens Brixtofte	5
18	6	Finland	Kojo	Nuku Pommiin	Juice Leskinen	Jim Pembroke, Otto Donner	0

1982 Eurovision 27: Harrogate, United Kingdom
24 April 1982

	Austria	Belgium	Cyprus	Denmark	Finland	Germany	Ireland	Israel	Luxembourg	Netherlands	Norway	Portugal	Spain	Sweden	Switzerland	Turkey	United Kingdom	Yugoslavia	TOTAL
Portugal	2	8			2		2	1	7	4		—		6	1	5	4		32
Luxembourg		2	4	4	7	8	10	5		7	7	6	5			3	6		78
Norway	6		3	2		10	6		6		—		2	4					40
United Kingdom	12				4	1	7	2	12	1	6	4	1		5	10	—	6	76
Turkey	3				1				8	2	3				3	—			20
Finland					—														0
Switzerland	10	12	6	7	8		8	10	2	10	4	2	7	2	—	2	12	10	97
Cyprus	5	3	—		3	6		7	4	12	12	5			8		3	5	85
Sweden	8	5		8	5	2	3		3	5	8	7	4	—	4		5	2	67
Austria	—	6	7	6	6		5	4		3			8			7	10	4	57
Belgium	4	—	8	10		4	4	6	5		5	8	10	7	2	6	2	7	96
Spain		4	10			7		8	1				—	1	7	8		1	52
Denmark				—			1					3							5
Yugoslavia		1	1	3										12		4		—	21
Israel	7	7	2	1	12	12		—	10	8	1	10	6	10	10		1	3	100
Netherlands						5				—				3					8
Ireland			5	5	10	3	—	3			2	1	3	5	6	1	7	8	49
Germany	1	10	12	12		—	12	12		6	10	12	12	8	12	12	8	12	161

71

1983 Eurovision 28: Munich, Germany

23 April 1983

Rank	Start	Country	Artist	Song	Writer	Composer	POINTS
1	20	Luxembourg	Corinne Hermès	Si La Vie Est Cadeau	Alain Garcia	Jean-Pierre Millers	142
2	16	Israel	Ofra Haza	Hi	Ehud Manor	Avi Toledano	136
3	4	Sweden	Carola Häggkvist	Främling	Monica Forsberg	Lasse Holm	126
4	12	Yugoslavia	Danijel	Dzuli	Mario Mihaljevic	Danijel Popovic	125
5	14	Germany	Hoffmann & Hoffmann	Rücksicht	Volker Lechtenbrink	Michael Reinecke	94
6	3	United Kingdom	Sweet Dreams	I'm Never Giving Up	Ron Roker, Jan Pulsford, Phil Wigger	Ron Roker, Jan Pulsford, Phil Wigger	79
7	11	Netherlands	Bernadette	Sing Me A Song	Martin Duiser	Piet Souer	66
8	1	France	Guy Bonnet	Vivre	Fulbert Cant	Guy Bonnet	56
9	18	Austria	Westend	Hurricane	Heli Deinboek, Heinz Nessizius	Peter Vieweger	53
10	2	Norway	Jahn Teigen	Do Re Mi	Herodes Falsk, Jahn Teigen	Anita Skorgan, Jahn Teigen	53
11	5	Italy	Riccardo Fogli	Per Lucia	Riccardo Fogli, Vincenzo Spampinato	Maurizio Fabrizio	41
12	9	Finland	Ami Aspelund	Fantasiaa	Kaisu Liuhala	Kari Kuusamo	41
13	17	Portugal	Armando Gama	Esta Balada Que Te Dou	Armando Gama	Armando Gama	33
14	10	Greece	Christie	Mou Les	Sophia Fildissi	Antonis Plessas, Mimis Plessas	32
15	8	Switzerland	Mariella Farré	Io Cosi Non Ci Sto	Nella Martinetti	Thomas Gonzenbach, Remo Kessler	28
16	13	Cyprus	Stavros & Constantina	I Agapi Akoma Zi	Stavros Sideras	Stavros Sideras	26
17	15	Denmark	Gry Johansen	Kloden Drejer	Flemming Gernyx, Christian Jacobsen	Flemming Gernyx, Christian Jacobsen, Lars Christensen	16
18	19	Belgium	Pas de Deux	Rendez-vous	Paul Peyskens	Walter Verdin	13
=19	6	Turkey	Çetin Alp and the Short Wave	Opera	Aysel Gürel	Bugra Ugur	0
=19	7	Spain	Remedios Amaya	¿quién Maneja Mi Barca?	Isidro Muñoz	José Miguel Evóras	0

1983 Eurovision 28: Munich, Germany — 23 April 1983

	Austria	Belgium	Cyprus	Denmark	Finland	France	Germany	Greece	Israel	Italy	Luxembourg	Netherlands	Norway	Portugal	Spain	Sweden	Switzerland	Turkey	United Kingdom	Yugoslavia	TOTAL
France	3	7	4		6		4	7	1	10	3	2	3	3			10	6		3	56
Norway	10		6	8			1		4		2	8		6		3		5	5		53
United Kingdom	8	5	7	5	10	5	3	5	8	2	6	5	5	2		12	8	7	8	1	79
Sweden			1	10	1	6	12	10	6	8		3	12	4	2	2	5	4		8	126
Italy						7		2						7	3						41
Turkey																					0
Spain																					0
Switzerland	6	1				1	7			7	5		1		1				6	7	28
Finland	2		12			3		8	7		1		2				4	3			41
Greece					5										12						32
Netherlands	4	2	5	4	3	2	2	6	3	4	4		7			6	12	2	1	5	66
Yugoslavia	1	12	8	12	12		6		10	1	8	7	8		10		1	12	12		125
Cyprus		4		1			5		5				4				2				26
Germany	7	6		3	4	10		1		6	12	10	10	8	4	8	7		7	6	94
Denmark			2		7			3		3	10	12	6	10	6	7	2		2		16
Israel	12	10		7	2	8	10	4		5	7	6		5	5	5	7		10	10	136
Portugal						4			2					1		1	6	10	3	2	33
Austria		3	3	6				4				4			8	4		10	3	4	53
Belgium														12	7		3		4		13
Luxembourg	5	8	10	2	8	12	8	12	12	12		1		12	7	10	3	8		12	142

1984 Eurovision 29: Luxembourg City, Luxembourg — 5 May 1984

Rank	Start	Country	Artist	Song	Writer	Composer	POINTS
1	1	Sweden	Herrey's	Diggi-loo diggy-ley	Britt Lindeborg	Torgny Söderberg	145
2	9	Ireland	Linda Martin	Terminal 3	Sean Sherrard	Sean Sherrard	137
3	4	Spain	Bravo	Lady, lady	Amaya Saizar	Miguel Blasco Larami	106
4	10	Denmark	Hot Eyes	Det' lige det	Keld Heick	Søren Bundgård	101
5	8	Belgium	Jacques Zegers	Avanti la vie	Jacques Zegers	Henri Seroka	70
6	18	Italy	Alice & Battiato	I treni di Tozeur	Rosario Cosentino	Franco Battiato	70
7	6	United Kingdom	Belle & the Devotions	Love games	Paul Curtis, Graham Sacher	Paul Curtis, Graham Sacher	63
8	3	France	Annick Thoumazeau	Autant d'amoureux que d'étoiles	Charel Level	Vladimir Cosma	61
9	16	Finland	Kirka	Hengaillaan	Jussi Tuominen	Jukka Siikavire	46
10	2	Luxembourg	Sophie Carle	100% d'amour	Jean-Michel Bériat, Patrick Jaymes	Jean-Pierre Goussaud	39
11	19	Portugal	Maria Guinot	Silêncio e tanta gente	Maria Guinot	Maria Guinot	38
12	15	Turkey	Bes Yıl Önce, On Yıl Sonra	Halay	Ulku Aker	Selcuk Basar	37
13	14	Germany	Mary Roos	Aufrecht geh'n	Michael Kunze	Michael Reinecke	34
14	11	Netherlands	Maribelle	Ik hou van jou	Peter van Asten, Richard De Bois	Peter van Asten, Richard De Bois	34
15	7	Cyprus	Andy Paul	Anna Mari-Elena	Andy Paul	Andy Paul	31
16	17	Switzerland	Rainy Day	Welche Farbe hat der Sonnenschein	Günther Loose	Günther Loose	30
17	5	Norway	Dollie de Luxe	Lenge leve livet	Ingrid Bjørnov, Benedicte Adrian	Ingrid Bjørnov, Benedicte Adrian	29
18	12	Yugoslavia	Vlado and Isolda	Ciao amore	Milan Peric	Slobodan Bucevac	26
19	13	Austria	Anita	Einfach weg	Walter Müller	Brigitte Seuberth, Ernst Seuberth	5

1984 Eurovision 29: Luxembourg
5 May 1984

Contestant	AT	BE	CY	DK	FI	FR	DE	IE	IT	LU	NL	NO	PT	ES	SE	CH	TR	UK	YU	TOTAL
Sweden	12	7	12	12	8	6	12	12	6	6	10	10	4	4	—	10	3	7	4	145
Luxembourg	8	10	7	5				5	3	—							4		8	39
France	6	3	3					7	7		12	2	7		2	4		6		61
Spain	6	1	6	7	6	10	2	3	8	8	2	6	12	—	10	3	12	4	2	106
Norway	2	2	2	1	4		7	8	10	7		—	6		8	2				29
United Kingdom				10		1		4		1	4	8	10	3	3		1	—	1	63
Cyprus			—						4					2	4				12	31
Belgium	3	—		3	10	12	4		1	12	8	3	10	2		12	5	8		70
Ireland	10	12	10		7	3	10	—	12	5	7	4	2	10	12	1	10	12		137
Denmark	4	8	5	—	5	8	5	6	5	3	3	12	1	6	5	5	2	1	5	101
Netherlands					2	7		1		2	—			8			8	3		34
Yugoslavia			8	4		2	3												—	26
Austria	—																			5
Germany	1	6		2		4	—	2	2		5	7	5	1	6	6		2	10	34
Turkey		4	4								1		3	12	7		—	5	3	37
Finland	5	5	1	6	—	5	1					5		1	1		6	10		46
Switzerland				8	1		6		4	10		1	8			—				30
Italy	7				12		6		—	4	6			12		7	7		7	70
Portugal							8						—	5		8		10		38

75

1985 Eurovision 30: Gothenburg, Sweden

3 May 1985

Rank	Start	Country	Artist	Song	Writer	Composer	POINTS
1	13	Norway	Bobbysocks	La Det Swinge	Rolf Løvland	Rolf Løvland	123
2	10	Germany	Wind	Für Alle	Hanne Haller	Hanne Haller	105
3	16	Sweden	Kikki Danielsson	Bra Vibrationer	Ingela "Pling" Forsman	Lasse Holm	103
4	14	United Kingdom	Vikki	Love Is...	Vikki Watson, James Kaleth	Vikki Watson, James Kaleth	100
5	11	Israel	Izhar Cohen	Olé Olé	Hamutal Ben Ze'ev	Kobi Oshrat	93
6	1	Ireland	Maria Christian	Wait Until The Weekend Comes	Brendan J. Graham	Brendan J. Graham	91
7	12	Italy	Al Bano & Romina Power	Magic, Oh Magic	Christiano Minellono	Dario Farina, Michael Hoffmann	78
8	17	Austria	Gary Lux	Kinder Dieser Welt	Michael Kunze	Mick Jackson, Geoff Bastow	60
9	2	Finland	Sonja Lumme	Eläköön Elämä	Veli-Pekka Lehto	Petri Laaksonen	58
10	6	France	Roger Bens	Femme Dans Ses Rêves Aussi	Didier Pascalis	Didier Pascalis	56
11	4	Denmark	Hot Eyes	Sku' Du Spør Fra No'n	Keld Heick	Søren Bundgård	41
12	15	Switzerland	Mariella Farré & Pino Gasparini	Piano Piano	Trudi Müller-Bosshard	Anita Kerr	39
13	18	Luxembourg	Margo, Franck Olivier, Diane Solomon, Ireen Sheer, Malcolm Roberts & Chris Roberts	Children, Kinder, Enfants	Bernd Meinunger, Jean-Michel Bériat	Ralph Siegel	37
14	5	Spain	Paloma San Basilio	La Fiesta Terminó	Juan Carlos Calderón	Juan Carlos Calderón	36
15	7	Turkey	MFÖ	Di Dai Di Dai Dai (a'sik Oldum)	Mazhar Alanson, Fuat Güner, Özkan Ugur	Mazhar Alanson, Fuat Güner, Özkan Ugur	36
16	19	Greece	Takis Biniaris	Miazoume	Maro Bizani	Takis Biniaris	15
17	3	Cyprus	Lia Vishy	To Katalava Arga	Lia Vishy-Piliouri	Lia Vishy-Piliouri	15
18	9	Portugal	Adelaide	Penso Em Ti, Eu Sei	Adelaide Ferreira, Luis Fernando	Tózé Brito	9
19	8	Belgium	Linda Lepomme	Laat Me Nu Gaan	Bert Vivier	Pieter Verlinden	7

1985 Eurovision 30: Gothenburg, Sweden

3 May 1985

	Austria	Belgium	Cyprus	Denmark	Finland	France	Germany	Greece	Ireland	Israel	Italy	Luxembourg	Norway	Portugal	Spain	Sweden	Switzerland	Turkey	United Kingdom	TOTAL
Ireland	10	8	7	3	1	3	4			8	12		3	8	4	7	5	5	3	91
Finland			6					10	6	1	7				6	10	2	3	7	58
Cyprus								8	1		3					5	3			15
Denmark	5	3	3			10	6		2		2		6	1				12	4	41
Spain			1		8			6		3		1		2		6	4	1	2	36
France	3		4		5			12	7		10	3	1	3	3		12		8	56
Turkey		1			2		2											7		36
Belgium								7										2		7
Portugal																				9
Germany		10	12	10	10	8		2	4	7	5	10	8	7	10	8			1	105
Israel	7	2	5	4	6	12	7		8		6	6	10	5	8	2	7		5	93
Italy	6		10	1	4	5		2		4		12		12	12			8		78
Norway	12	12		12	7	2	12	1	12	12	6	7		6	1	12			12	123
United Kingdom	2	6		5	3	6	5	4	5	2	8	8	7	4	5	4	4	10		100
Switzerland	1	5	2	6		7	1	3				2	5			1		6		39
Sweden	4	7		8	12	7	8		10	6	4	5	12		2		8	4	6	103
Austria		4		7		1	10	5	3	10		4	2			3	1		10	60
Luxembourg	8			2		4	3			5	1		4	10	7					37
Greece			8																	15

77

1986 Eurovision 31: Bergen, Norway
3 May 1986

Rank	Start	Country	Artist	Song	Writer	Composer	POINTS
1	13	Belgium	Sandra Kim	J'aime La Vie	Rosario Marino Atria	Jean-Pierre Furnémont, Angelo	176
2	10	Switzerland	Daniela Simons	Pas Pour Moi	Nella Martinetti	Atilla Sereftug	140
3	1	Luxembourg	Sherisse Laurence	L'amour De Ma Vie	Alain Garcia, Frank Dostal	Rolf Soja	117
4	12	Ireland	Luv Bug	You Can Count On Me	Kevin Sheerin	Kevin Sheerin	96
5	17	Sweden	Lasse Holm & Monica Törnell	E' De' Det Här Du Kallar Kärlek	Lasse Holm	Lasse Holm	78
6	18	Denmark	Lise Haavik & Trax	Du Er Fuld Af Løgn	John Hatting	John Hatting	77
7	5	United Kingdom	Ryder	Runner In The Night	Maureen Darbyshire	Brian Wade	72
8	14	Germany	Ingrid Peters	Über Die Brücke Geh'n	Hans Blüm	Hans Blüm	62
9	8	Turkey	Klips ve Onlar	Halley	Ilhan Irem	Melih Kibar	53
10	9	Spain	Cadillac	Valentino	José Maria Guzmán	José Maria Guzmán	51
11	2	Yugoslavia	Doris Dragovic	Zeljo Moja	Zrinko Tutic	Zrinko Tutic	49
12	4	Norway	Ketil Stokkan	Romeo	Ketil Stokkan	Ketil Stokkan	44
13	7	Netherlands	Frizzle Sizzle	Alles Heeft Ritme	Peter Schön	Peter Schön, Rob ten Bokum	40
14	20	Portugal	Dora	Não Sejas Mau Para Mim	Guilherme Inês, Zé da Ponte, Luis Oliveira	Guilherme Inês, Zé da Ponte, Luis Oliveira	28
15	19	Finland	Kari Kuivalainen	Päivä Kahden Ihmisen	Kari Kuivalainen	Kari Kuivalainen	22
16	6	Iceland	Icy	Gleðibankinn	Magnús Eiríksson	Magnús Eiríksson	19
17	3	France	Cocktail Chic	Européennes	Georges Costa, Michel Costa	Georges Costa, Michel Costa	13
18	16	Austria	Timna Brauer	Die Zeit Ist Einsam	Peter Cornelius	Peter Janda	12
19	11	Israel	Moti Galadi & Sarai Tzuriel	Yavoh Yom	Moti Galadi	Yoram Zadok	7
20	5	Cyprus	Elpida	Tora Zo	Phivos Gavris, Petros Yiannaki	Petros Yiannaki	4

1986 Eurovision 31: Bergen, Norway
3 May 1986

	Austria	Belgium	Cyprus	Denmark	Finland	France	Germany	Iceland	Ireland	Israel	Luxembourg	Netherlands	Norway	Portugal	Spain	Sweden	Switzerland	Turkey	United Kingdom	Yugoslavia	TOTAL
Luxembourg	10	10	8	2	4	8	12	1	7	4		8	12	6		10	2		8	5	117
Yugoslavia	1	4	12					5	3	1	2	7			3	1		3	7		49
France		5	6	5		4	6	4	6			2	3			3	7				13
Norway	3		2	8	10	10	5			2	4			2	2	8	6	6			44
United Kingdom			4		3					8	1	5	6	7	6	2	4	2			72
Iceland	2	6	1	3	1	6		2	5	3	6	6			1			7		2	19
Netherlands	7	3		4	7	7		3	10	12	7	12	5	3	4		8	8	2	12	40
Turkey	4	12	5			1		8		6	12		1	10	12	12	1	10	1	4	53
Spain	12	2		12	8	3		10	8	5	3	10	2	8		7	5	5	5	6	51
Switzerland	6	7	10	10	12	12	1		12		10		8	12		6	10	12	10	8	140
Israel	8			7	2				8		8			4		5			12	1	7
Ireland							2	12	1											3	96
Belgium		1		6	6	2	4	7	2	10	5	3	7	1			12				176
Germany	5		7		5	5	7	7				4	10	5	7	4	3		3	7	62
Cyprus																					4
Austria		8					3	6		7		1			8			1			12
Sweden			3										4					4	4		78
Denmark																					77
Finland				1																	22
Portugal																					28

79

1987 Eurovision 32: Brussels, Belgium   9 May 1987

Rank	Start	Country	Artist	Song	Writer	Composer	POINTS
1	20	Ireland	Johnny Logan	Hold Me Now	Sean Sherrard	Sean Sherrard	172
2	16	Germany	Wind	Laß Die Sonne In Dein Herz	Bernd Meinunger	Ralph Siegel	141
3	7	Italy	Umberto Tozzi & Raf	Gente Di Mare	Giancarlo Bigazzi	Umberto Tozzi, Raffaele Riefoli	103
4	21	Yugoslavia	Novi Fosili	Ja Sam Za Ples	Stevo Cvikic	Rajko Dujmic	92
5	12	Netherlands	Marcha	Rechtop In De Wind	Peter Koelewijn	Peter Koelewijn	83
6	19	Denmark	Anne-Catherine Herdorf & Bandjo	En Lille Melodi	Jacob Jonia	Helga Engelbrecht	83
7	17	Cyprus	Alexia	Aspro Mavro	Maria Papapavlou	Andreas Papapavlou	80
8	2	Israel	Datner & Kushnir	Shir Habatlanim	Zohar Laskov	Zohar Laskov	73
9	1	Norway	Kate Gulbrandsen	Mitt Liv	Hanne Krogh, Rolf Løvland	Rolf Løvland	65
10	11	Greece	Bang	Stop!	Thanos Kalliris, Vassilis Dertilis	Thanos Kalliris, Vassilis Dertilis	64
11	5	Belgium	Liliane Saint-Pierre	Soldiers Of Love	Liliane Keuninckx, Gyuri Spies, Marc de Coen	Liliane Keuninckx, Gyuri Spies, Marc de Coen	56
12	6	Sweden	Lotta Engberg	Boogaloo	Christer Lundh	Mikael Wendt	50
13	14	United Kingdom	Rikki	Only The Light	Richard Peebles	Richard Peebles	47
14	15	France	Christine Minier	Les Mots D'amour N'ont Pas De Dimanche	Gérard Curci	Marc Minier	44
15	18	Finland	Vicky Rosti	Sata Salamaa	Veli-Pekka Lehto	Petri Laaksonen	32
16	4	Iceland	Halla Margarét	Hægt Og Hljótt	Valgeir Guðjónsson	Valgeir Guðjónsson	28
17	22	Switzerland	Carole Rich	Moitié Moitié	Jean-Jacques Egli	Jean-Jacques Egli	26
18	8	Portugal	Nevada	Neste Barco à Vela	Alfredo Azinheira	Alfredo Azinheira, Jorge Mendes	15
19	9	Spain	Patricia Kraus	No Estás Solo	Patricia Kraus	Rafael Martínez, Rafael Trabucchelli	10
20	3	Austria	Gary Lux	Nur Noch Gefühl	Stefanie Werger	Kenneth Westmore	8
21	13	Luxembourg	Plastic Bertrand	Amour Amour	Roger Jouret, Alec Mansion	Roger Jouret, Alec Mansion	4
22	10	Turkey	Seyyal Tanner & Lokomotif	Sarkim Sevgi üstüne	Olcayto Ahmet Tugsuz	Olcayto Ahmet Tugsuz	0

80

1987 Eurovision 32: Brussels, Belgium
9 May 1987

	Austria	Belgium	Cyprus	Denmark	Finland	France	Germany	Greece	Iceland	Ireland	Israel	Italy	Luxembourg	Netherlands	Norway	Portugal	Spain	Sweden	Switzerland	Turkey	United Kingdom	Yugoslavia	TOTAL
Norway	4	7	3	3	5	4	7			2		7		4			3	10	6				65
Israel	1	6			7	10	8		5	5		1		3	2	10		4	8		4		73
Austria								7							4								8
Iceland	3	4	5		3		10	6					5		5		4			4	8	4	28
Belgium	3		7	7		3	4		8		2	6	5				7	1	7	2			56
Sweden		1	1		4				3		12	3				7							50
Italy	6	5					12	5		12	3		4			12	12	1	7	8	1	12	103
Portugal							2	10									8						15
Spain																							10
Turkey																							0
Greece		2	12	6	2	7		3	1	6	5	8	7	5			5	6			5	5	64
Netherlands	2	3		2		12					10	10	8			2			10	7	3	8	83
Luxembourg			2	4	1					3			1	1	1	3		5	5	3	2		4
United Kingdom	5	3					5	4		10	8	5	12	10	3	5		5	2			2	47
France				12	10		3	12	12	7		4	6	2	6	4	1	7	1	6		7	44
Germany	10	10	6	10	6	6		1	6	8	8		2	8	10	1	2	2	4		10	10	141
Cyprus						5						2		6	7	8	10	3	3		6	1	80
Finland							1	8	7		6	12			8	4		8		1			32
Denmark	7				8	8	6			4	4		10	6	7	1	10	12	3	10	7	6	83
Ireland	12	12	8	5	12	1		2	10	1	7	12	3	12	8	8	6		12	12	12		172
Yugoslavia	8	8	10	8		2			2		1			7	12	6				5			92
Switzerland			4	1																		3	26

81

1988 Eurovision 33: Dublin, Ireland

30 April 1988

Rank	Start	Country	Artist	Song	Writer	Composer	POINTS
1	9	Switzerland	Céline Dion	Ne Partez Pas Sans Moi	Nella Martinetti	Atilla Sereftug	137
2	4	United Kingdom	Scott Fitzgerald	Go	Julie Forsyth	Julie Forsyth	136
3	13	Denmark	Hot Eyes	Ka' Du Se Hva' Jeg Sa'	Keld Heick	Søren Bundgård	92
4	17	Luxembourg	Lara Fabian	Croire	Alain Garcia	Jacques Cardona	90
5	15	Norway	Karoline Krüger	For Vår Jord	Erik Hillestad	Anita Skorgan	88
6	21	Yugoslavia	Srebrna Krila	Mangup	Stevo Cvikic, Rajko Dujmic	Rajko Dujmic	87
7	8	Israel	Yardena Arazi	Ben Adam	Ehud Manor	Boris Dimitshtein	85
8	10	Ireland	Jump the Gun	Take Him Home	Peter Eades	Peter Eades	79
9	7	Netherlands	Gerard Joling	Shangri-la	Peter de Wijn	Peter de Wijn	70
10	19	France	Gérard Lenorman	Chanteur De Charme	Gérard Lenorman, Claude Lemesle	Gérard Lenorman	64
11	6	Spain	La Década	La Chica Que Yo Quiero (made In Spain)	Francisco Dondiego	Enrique Piero	58
12	2	Sweden	Tommy Körberg	Stad I Ljus	Py Bäckman	Py Bäckman	52
13	18	Italy	Luca Barbarossa	Ti Scrivo	Luca Barbarossa	Luca Barbarossa	52
14	11	Germany	Maxi & Chris Garden	Lied Für Einen Freund	Bernd Meinunger	Ralph Siegel	48
15	5	Turkey	MFÖ	Sufi (hey Ya Hey)	Mazhar Alanson	Mazhar Alanson, Fuat Güner, Özkan Ugu	37
16	1	Iceland	Beathoven	Sókrates	Sverrir Stormsker	Sverrir Stormsker	20
17	14	Greece	Aphroditi Fryda	Kloun	Dimitris Sakislis	Dimitris Sakislis	10
18	20	Portugal	Dora	Voltarei	José Calvário, José Niza	José Calvário, José Niza	5
19	16	Belgium	Reynaert	Laissez Briller Le Soleil	Joseph Reynaerts, Philippe Anciaux	Joseph Reynaerts, Dany Willem	5
20	3	Finland	Boulevard	Nauravat Silmät Muistetaan	Kirsti Willberg	Pepe Willberg	3
21	12	Austria	Wilfried	Lisa Mona Lisa	Wilfried Scheutz, Klaus Kofler, Ronnie Herbholzheimer	Wilfried Scheutz, Klaus Kofler, Ronnie Herbholzheimer	0

1988 Eurovision 33: Dublin, Ireland — 30 April 1988

	Austria	Belgium	Denmark	Finland	France	Germany	Greece	Iceland	Ireland	Israel	Italy	Luxembourg	Netherlands	Norway	Portugal	Spain	Sweden	Switzerland	Turkey	United Kingdom	Yugoslavia	TOTAL
Iceland	10		4		2						1		4		8		1					20
Sweden	8	1	8					3	5		10	3	8	12						2		52
Finland										3												3
United Kingdom	2	12	10	10	6	10	6	1	7	10	12	8	1	5	3	10	5	5	12	1		136
Turkey						8	8	2		8	8	4				5	4					37
Spain	2	6				6	12	6	2	2	5	6	3	2	3			6	5	6	4	58
Netherlands		10		6	10	5	3	7	1	7	3	12	10			8		7	6	4	7	70
Israel	6	4	7	2	1	12	10	8	10		7	5	6	8	10	12	12	10	10	10	1	85
Switzerland		5			4	7			6	4		1		7	12	3	7	4	2	3	6	137
Ireland	12				12	4		10		5			3	4		1				5	2	79
Germany		7	5		7	1		5	6	1	4			10	6		3	1	3		8	48
Austria	3	3		7	5		7		8						7							0
Denmark	1	8		12		2	2	5	12			2	5	6	4		8	12		12	10	92
Greece	5			8	8	3		4		12	2	10	2	3	1	7	10	8	4	7	3	10
Norway	7	2	3	3			5		3					1	1	2	2	3	8		5	88
Belgium			12	1	3		1	12		12	6	7				4	6	2	7	8	12	5
Luxembourg	4						4															90
Italy																						52
France																						64
Portugal																						5
Yugoslavia																						87

1989 Eurovision 34: Lausanne, Switzerland
6 May 1989

Rank	Start	Country	Artist	Song	Writer	Composer	POINTS
1	22	Yugoslavia	Riva	Rock Me	Stevo Cvikic	Rajko Dujmic	137
2	7	United Kingdom	Live Report	Why Do I Always Get It Wrong	Brian Hodgson	John Beeby	130
3	12	Denmark	Birthe Kjær	Vi Maler Byen Rød	Keld Heick	Søren Bundgård	111
4	10	Sweden	Tommy Nilsson	En Dag	Tim Norell, Ola Håkansson	Tim Norell, Ola Håkansson, Alexander Bard	110
5	13	Austria	Thomas Forstner	Nur Ein Lied	Joachim Horn-Bernges	Dieter Bohlen	97
6	16	Spain	Nina	Nacida Para Amar	Juan Carlos Calderón	Juan Carlos Calderón	88
7	14	Finland	Anneli Saaristo	La Dolce Vita	Turkka Mali	Matti Puurtinen	76
8	15	France	Nathalie Pâque	J'ai Volé La Vie	Sylvain Lebel	Guy Matteoni, G G Candy	60
9	1	Italy	Anna Oxa & Fausto Leali	Avrei Voluto	Franco Ciani, Franco Berlincioni	Franco Fasano	56
10	19	Greece	Marianna	To Diko Sou Asteri	Villy Sanianou	Yiannis Kyris, Marianna Efstratiou	56
11	17	Cyprus	Fanny Polymeri & Yiannis Savvidakis	Apopse As Vrethoume	Efi Meletiou	Marios Meletiou	51
12	2	Israel	Gili ve Galit	Derech Ha'melech	Shaike Paikov	Shaike Paikov	50
13	18	Switzerland	Furbaz	Viver Senza Tei	Marie-Louise Werth	Marie-Louise Werth	47
14	21	Germany	Nino de Angelo	Flieger	Joachim Horn-Bernges	Dieter Bohlen	46
15	4	Netherlands	Justine Pelmelay	Blijf Zoals Je Bent	Cees Bergman, Geert-Jan Hessing, Aart Mol, E van Prehn, E Veerhoff	Jan Kisjes	45
16	9	Portugal	Da Vinci	Conquistador	Pedro Luis	Ricardo	39
17	8	Norway	Britt Synnøve Johansen	Venners Nærhet	Leiv N Grøtte	Inge Enoksen	30
18	3	Ireland	Kiev Connolly & the Missing Passengers	The Real Me	Kiev Connolly	Kiev Connolly	21
19	6	Belgium	Ingeborg	Door De Wind	Stef Bos	Stef Bos	13
20	11	Luxembourg	Park Café	Monsieur	Maggie Parke, Bernard Loncheval, Yves Lacomblez	Maggie Parke, Gast Waltzing	8
21	5	Turkey	Pan	Bana Bana	Timur Selçuk	Timur Selçuk	5
22	20	Iceland	Daniel August Haraldsson	Það Sem Enginn Sér	Valgeir Guðjónsson	Valgeir Guðjónsson	0

1989 Eurovision 34: Lausanne, Switzerland
6 May 1989

	Austria	Belgium	Cyprus	Denmark	Finland	France	Germany	Greece	Iceland	Ireland	Israel	Italy	Luxembourg	Netherlands	Norway	Portugal	Spain	Sweden	Switzerland	Turkey	United Kingdom	Yugoslavia	TOTAL
Italy			6		10		7	4								7	12		2			8	56
Israel		3		5	5		3		5	7		1		3				5	7		2	7	50
Ireland	3						4						2		3					7		2	21
Netherlands	4				4	7	6	1	1	3		10	1				6				3		45
Turkey																	1						5
Belgium										5				5	2							4	13
United Kingdom	8	8	2	1	6	12	12	2		4	7	6	12	7	12	12	10	10	1	1		6	130
Norway		2		6		4		6			2			2				2		5			30
Portugal	6				2		8	8	2		6		7		1		8	3	1	4			39
Sweden	12	6	8	12		2							6		8	8	5	3	3		4	12	110
Luxembourg						5											3						8
Denmark	7	4	2		12	6	5	12	10	10	1	5	3	12	10	2	2	12	8	6	10	1	111
Austria		12	10	4	1			5	8		8	12	4	6		1	7	7		3		5	97
Finland	3		3	3		10	2	5		8	10	3	8	4	5			4		10		10	76
France	5		7		3		10	10		6	5	8	10		4			1		4		3	60
Spain		7	4	8	8	8		7	12			2				6			10	2	7		88
Cyprus	2			2					7		3	4				3			4		6		51
Switzerland	1								4		4			10		10					8		47
Greece		1	12			1				2				1	6	5			12	8	5		56
Iceland			1																				0
Germany		5	1	7		3		3	3	2		7	5	8	7	5		6	6		1		46
Yugoslavia	10	10	5	10	7		1		6	12	12					4	4	8	5	12	12		137

1990 Eurovision 35: Zagreb, Yugoslavia   5 May 1990

Rank	Start	Country	Artist	Song	Writer	Composer	POINTS
1	19	Italy	Toto Cutugno	Insieme: 1992	Toto Cutugno	Toto Cutugno	149
2	14	France	Joelle Ursull	White And Black Blues	Serge Gainsbourg	Georges Ougier de Moussac	132
3	17	Ireland	Liam Reilly	Somewhere In Europe	Liam Reilly	Liam Reilly	132
4	8	Iceland	Stjörnin	Eitt Lag Enn	Aðalsteinn Ásberg Sigurðsson	Hörður G Ólafsson	124
5	1	Spain	Azúcar Moreno	Bandido	José-Luis Abel	Raúl Orellana, Jaime Stinus	96
6	7	United Kingdom	Emma	Give A Little Love Back To The World	Paul Curtis	Paul Curtis	87
7	15	Yugoslavia	Tajci	Hajde Da Ludujemo	Alka Vuica	Zrinko Tutic	81
8	11	Denmark	Lonnie Devantier	Hallo Hallo	Keld Heick	John Hatting, Torben Lendager	64
9	13	Germany	Chris Kempers & Daniel Kovac	Frei Zu Leben	Michael Kunze	Ralph Siegel	60
10	20	Austria	Simone	Keine Mauern Mehr	Mario Botazzi	Wolfgang Berry, Nana Berry	58
11	12	Switzerland	Egon Egemann	Musik Klingt In Die Welt Hinaus	Cornelia Lackner	Cornelia Lackner	51
12	3	Belgium	Philippe Lafontaine	Macédomienne	Philippe Lafontaine	Philippe Lafontaine	46
13	6	Luxembourg	Céline Carzo	Quand Je Te Rêve	Thierry Delianis	Jean-Charles France	38
14	21	Cyprus	Haris Anastasiou	Milas Poli	Haris Anastasiou	John Vickers	36
15	5	Netherlands	Maywood	Ik Wil Alles Met Je Delen	Alice May	Alice May	25
16	18	Sweden	Edin-Ådahl	Som En Vind	Mikael Wendt	Mikael Wendt	24
17	4	Turkey	Kayahan	Gözlerinin Hapsindeyim	Kayahan Acar	Kayahan Acar	21
18	10	Israel	Rita	Shara Barechovot	Tzruya Lahav	Rami Kleinstein	16
19	2	Greece	Christos Callow & Wave	Horis Skopo	Giorgos Papagiannakis	Giorgos Paleokastriris	11
20	16	Portugal	Nucha	Há Sempre Alguém	Fancisco Teotonio Pereira	Jan van Dijck, Luis Filipe	9
21	22	Finland	Beat	Fri?	Stina Engblom	Kim & Janne Engblom, Tina Krause	8
22	9	Norway	Ketil Stokkan	Brandenburger Tor	Ketil Stokkan	Ketil Stokkan	8

1990 Eurovision 35: Zagreb, Yugoslavia
5 May 1990

	Austria	Belgium	Cyprus	Denmark	Finland	France	Germany	Greece	Iceland	Ireland	Israel	Italy	Luxembourg	Netherlands	Norway	Portugal	Spain	Sweden	Switzerland	Turkey	United Kingdom	Yugoslavia	TOTAL
Spain	8	1	8		10	5	12	8	4			8		2	5	5			6	10	1	3	96
Greece	4		6							1													11
Belgium						8	8		2				4	5	1	2		7	4				46
Turkey			2			6	5						1	7	4							7	21
Netherlands	5			3			3	1			2	2				1			3	3	4		25
Luxembourg		12	5	10		12	1	4				1				3						2	38
United Kingdom	1	10	3		7	10		5			10	6	3			12	7	8	10	1		10	87
Iceland	10			1				3			8	3	8	4	10	12	4		7			4	124
Norway				12			4				4											1	8
Israel		3	4		5				7						7		6	3	2	2			16
Denmark	6		1			1		12		4	7	7	2	4	7	7	1	4	1	6		5	64
Switzerland	3		7	4	3			7	1	10	6	5	12			8	8	5					51
Germany	2		10	5	12	2		2	12	8	12	10		12	12	4	5	4	12	4		12	60
France	12	8	12	7	1		10	10	10	5					3		3	5	5	12	7		132
Yugoslavia		2		8	4				8		1	12	7	10	8	6	10	1		5	5		81
Portugal				6	8			6	3	12	5	4	6	6	6	10	2	12			2		9
Ireland	7	5		2	2	7	7		6	2	3		10	8			12	10	8	8	10	6	132
Sweden					6	4	2	10	5			12	5	1	2			2		7	6	8	24
Italy		7		7		3	6			12							10	6	8		8		149
Austria		8		5													2						58
Cyprus											5				2		12	6					36
Finland									5		3												8

1991 Eurovision 36: Rome, Italy

4 May 1991

Rank	Start	Country	Artist	Song	Writer	Composer	POINTS
1	8	Sweden	Carola	Fångad Av En Stormvind	Stephan Berg	Stephan Berg	146
2	9	France	Amina	C'est Le Dernier Qui A Parlé Qui A Raison	Amina Annabi	Wasis Diop	146
3	15	Israel	Duo Datz	Kan	Uzi Chitman	Uzi Chitman	139
4	19	Spain	Sergio Dalma	Bailar Pegados	Luis Gomez Escolar	Julio Seijas	119
5	5	Switzerland	Sandra Simó	Canzone Per Te	Renato Mascetti	Renato Mascetti	118
6	3	Malta	Paul Giordimaina & Georgina	Could It Be	Raymond Mahoney	Paul Abela	106
7	22	Italy	Peppino di Capri	Comme E' Ddoce 'o Mare	Giampiero Artegiani	Marcello Marocchi	89
8	12	Portugal	Dulce	Lusitana Paixão	Fred Micael, Zé da Ponte, J Quintela	Fred Micael, Zé da Ponte, J Quintela	62
9	21	Cyprus	Elena Patroclou	SOS	Andreas Christou	Kypros Charalambous	60
10	20	United Kingdom	Samantha Janus	A Message To Your Heart	Paul Curtis	Paul Curtis	47
11	11	Ireland	Kim Jackson	Could It Be That I'm In Love	Liam Reilly	Liam Reilly	47
12	10	Turkey	Izel Çeliköz, Rayhan Soykarçi & Can Ugurluér	Iki Dakika	Aysel Gürel	Sevket Ugurluér	44
13	4	Greece	Sofia Vossou	I Anixi	Andreas Mikroutsikos	Andreas Mikroutsikos	36
14	7	Luxembourg	Sarah Bray	Un Baiser Volé	Linda Lecomte, Mick Wersant	Patrick Hippert	29
15	2	Iceland	Stefán & Eyfi	Nina	Eyjólfur Kristjánsson	Eyjólfur Kristjánsson	26
16	18	Belgium	Clouseau	Geef Het Op	Bob Savenberg, Koen Wauters, Kris Wauters, Jan Leyers	Bob Savenberg, Koen Wauters, Kris Wauters, Jan Leyers	23
17	14	Norway	Just 4 Fun	Mrs Thompson	P G Roness, Kaare Skevik	Dag Kolsrud	14
18	17	Germany	Atlantis 2000	Dieser Traum Darf Niemals Sterben	Helmut Frey	Alfons Weindorf	10
19	13	Denmark	Anders Frandsen	Lige Der Hvor Hjertet Slår	Michael Elo	Michael Elo	8
20	16	Finland	Kaija	Hullu Yö	Jukka Välimaa	Ile Kallio	6
21	1	Yugoslavia	Baby Doll	Brazil	Dragana Saric	Zoran Vracevic	1
22	6	Austria	Thomas Forstner	Venedig Im Regen	Robby Musenbichler, Hubert Moser, Wolfgang Eltner	Robby Musenbichler, Hubert Moser, Wolfgang Eltner	0

Note: Sweden win on the higher number of '10' votes, after finishing level on total points and number of '12' votes.

1991 Eurovision 36: Rome, Italy
4 May 1991

	Austria	Belgium	Cyprus	Denmark	Finland	France	Germany	Greece	Iceland	Ireland	Israel	Italy	Luxembourg	Malta	Norway	Portugal	Spain	Sweden	Switzerland	Turkey	United Kingdom	Yugoslavia	TOTAL
Yugoslavia														1									1
Iceland	4	4	10	5	1	2																	26
Malta	2	1	8	4	5	4	5	2		12	4	7	10		6	7	6	10	6	7	7	1	106
Greece	8	12	2	12			6			1	8	10		5	1	6	5	12		2	8	4	36
Switzerland			6	8	8	7	6	7	5	2	10	2	12		3	2		8		3	3	5	118
Austria																			4				0
Luxembourg	5	2	7	7			3		4								4	1	6				29
Sweden	10	10	4	1	8	10	12	8	12	3	10	12	7		8	10	4		10	6	12	6	146
France	12	7	5	2			8		7	7	12	8			12	5	8	5	7		6	10	146
Turkey	1	5			7			4	8		7	3	8	3	2		2	7	3		5		44
Ireland					6	3	2	5			1	1	2	7	5			3	1	4	4	3	47
Portugal						5		1	8	8			1	4	7		10			1			62
Denmark									6	4													8
Norway			5	2					10			5	5	8				6	8	12		12	14
Israel		8		10			7	10	1	6			6	6	4	8	12	2	12	8	10	8	139
Finland			3	6			1	3			2		3	10		1	1		5				6
Germany	3				3	5		12		5	5	5		12	10	3	3	2	2		2	2	10
Belgium	7	6	12		4	6	4	6	2		6	6	6	6	4	8		4	12	8	1	8	23
Spain	3	6	12	6	4	1	7		2		2			10		1							119
United Kingdom	7	3	1	3		12	1		3	5	5		4	10	10	3			5				47
Cyprus	6									10	6			12	10	12	7		2	10		2	60
Italy					12	8		6	3		3			2		12		4	2	10		7	89

89

1992 Eurovision 37: Malmö, Sweden — 9 May 1992

Rank	Start	Country	Artist	Song	Writer	Composer	POINTS
1	17	Ireland	Linda Martin	Why Me	Johnny Logan	Johnny Logan	155
2	16	United Kingdom	Michael Ball	One Step Out Of Time	Tony Ryan, Paul Davies, Victor Stratton	Tony Ryan, Paul Davies, Victor Stratton	139
3	10	Malta	Mary Spiteri	Little Child	Raymond Mahoney	Georgina Abela	123
4	19	Italy	Mia Martini	Rapsodia	Giancarlo Bigazzi	Giuseppe Dati	111
5	5	Greece	Cleopatra	Olou Tou Kosmou I Elpida	Christos Lagos	Christos Lagos	94
6	3	Israel	Dafna	Ze Rak Sport	Ehud Manor	Kobi Oshrat	85
7	11	Iceland	Heart 2 Heart	Nei Eða Já	Stefán Hilmarsson	Friðrik Karlsson, Grétar Örvarsson	80
8	6	France	Kali	Monté La Riviè	Remy Bellenchombre	Kali	73
9	23	Netherlands	Humphrey Campbell	Wijs Me De Weg	Edwin Schimscheimer	Edwin Schimscheimer	67
10	15	Austria	Tony Wegas	Zusammen Geh'n	Joachim Horn-Bernges	Dieter Bohlen	63
11	9	Cyprus	Evridiki	Teriazoume	George Theophanous	George Theophanous	57
12	18	Denmark	Lotte Nilsson & Kenny Lübcke	Ält Det Som Ingen Ser	Carsten Warming	Carsten Warming	47
13	20	Yugoslavia	Extra Nena	Ljubim Te Pesmama	Gale Jankovic	Radivoje Radivojevic	44
14	1	Spain	Serafin	Todo Esto Es La Música	Luis Miguelez	Luis Miguelez, Alfredo Albuena	37
15	13	Switzerland	Daisy Auvray	Mister Music Man	Gordon Dent	Gordon Dent	32
16	22	Germany	Wind	Träume Sind Für Alle Da	Bernd Meinunger	Ralph Siegel	27
17	8	Portugal	Dinä	Amor D'água Fresca	Rosa Lobato de Faria	Nandina Veloso	26
18	21	Norway	Merethe Trøan	Visjoner	Eva Jansen	Robert Morley	23
19	4	Turkey	Aylin Vatankos	Yaz Bitti	Aylin Üçanlar	Aldogan Simsekyay	17
20	2	Belgium	Morgane	Nous On Veut Des Violons	Anne-Marie Gaspard	Claude Barzotti	11
21	14	Luxembourg	Marion Welter & Kontinent	Sou Fräi	Jang Linster, Ab van Goor	Jang Linster, Ab van Goor	10
22	7	Sweden	Christer Björkmann	I Morgon är En Annan Dag	Niklas Strömstedt	Niklas Strömstedt	9
23	12	Finland	Pave	Yamma Yamma	Hector	Pave Maijanen	4

1992 Eurovision 37: Malmö, Sweden
9 May 1992

	Austria	Belgium	Cyprus	Denmark	Finland	France	Germany	Greece	Iceland	Ireland	Israel	Italy	Luxembourg	Malta	Netherlands	Norway	Portugal	Spain	Sweden	Switzerland	Turkey	United Kingdom	Yugoslavia	TOTAL
Spain	2	1		1	3	6		4				7	3	2	1	5					1	1		37
Belgium	1					3							1					3			4			11
Israel	1		4	2		8	4		2	3			8	7	3	2	7	10	4	4	2	7	12	85
Turkey					5	7								8		8								17
Greece	4		12								7	12			4		5		3	10	8		6	94
France			3		7	1	3			5	12	6			6	10		6		12	3		7	73
Sweden				4																			4	9
Portugal					2	2	8	2		6	8	1			8	3	2						5	26
Cyprus		10			8			10	8	10	3	4	12	1	5	1	12	12	12	2			8	57
Malta	8	4	1	8			6	7				3	5		2		6	8	6	5		12	10	123
Iceland	7			5				6	8		4	5								3		4		80
Finland										1	1			10										4
Switzerland		5						8	12	12		10		4					1					32
Luxembourg																								10
Austria	12	8	8	7	6	10	12	12	4	7	2	8	7	6	7	7	3	2	5	8	10			63
United Kingdom	10	12	6	12	10		10		7			2	10	12	10	6	4	5	10	6	12	8		139
Ireland	3	7	5	10		12	5	3	6		6		6	5	12	12	1	1	7	7	5	3		155
Denmark						5	1	1	10	4	10			3			8	4	8		6			47
Italy	6		10		12		2		5				2							7				111
Yugoslavia			2		4				1	2			4						2					44
Norway		3		6	1					8	5						10					5	1	23
Germany		6		3					3							4						6		27
Netherlands	5	2	7			4	7	5		8	5							7		1	7	2		67

91

1993 Eurovision 38: Millstreet, Ireland

15 May 1993

Qualification: 7 new applicant countries took part in a preliminary heat, the top 3 qualified for the main contest.

Rank	Start	Country	Artist	Song	Writer	Composer	POINTS
1	14	Ireland	Niamh Kavanagh	In your eyes	Jimmy Walsh	Jimmy Walsh	187
2	19	United Kingdom	Sonia	Better the devil you know	Dean Collinson, Red	Dean Collinson, Red	164
3	4	Switzerland	Annie Cotton	Moi, tout simplement	Jean-Jacques Egli	Christophe Dúc	148
4	12	France	Patrick Fiori	Mama Corsica	François Valéry	François Valéry	121
5	25	Norway	Silje Vige	Alle mine tankar	Björn-Erik Vige	Björn-Erik Vige	120
6	20	Netherlands	Ruth Jacott	Vrede	Henk Westbroek	Eric van Tijn, Jochem Fluitsma	92
7	13	Sweden	Arvingarna	Eloïse	Gert Lengstrand	Lasse Holm	89
8	8	Malta	William Mangion	This time	William Mangion	William Mangion	69
9	6	Greece	Katerina Garbi	Ellada, hora tou fotos	Dimosthenis	Dimosthenis	64
10	11	Portugal	Anabela	A cidade até ser dia	Paulo Dacosta, Marco Quelhas, Pedro Abrantes	Paulo Dacosta, Marco Quelhas, Pedro Abrantes	60
11	22	Spain	Eva Santamaria	Hombres	Carlos Toro	Carlos Toro	58
12	1	Italy	Enrico Ruggeri	Sole d'Europa	Enrico Ruggeri	Enrico Ruggeri	45
13	9	Iceland	Inga	Þá veistu svarið	Friðrik Sturlúson	Jon-Kjell Seljeseth	42
14	10	Austria	Tony Wegas	Maria Magdalena	Thomas Spitzer	Christian Kolonovits, Johann Bertl	32
15	21	Croatia	Put	Don't ever cry	Dorde Novkovic	Andrej Basa	31
16	18	Bosnia & H	Fazla	Sva bol svijeta	Fahrudin Pecikoza	Dino Dervishalidovic	27
17	17	Finland	Katri-Helena	Tule luo	Jukka Saarinen	Matti Puurtinen	20
18	3	Germany	Münchener Freiheit	Viel zu weit	Stefan Zauner	Stefan Zauner	18
19	23	Cyprus	Kyriakos Zymboulakis & Demos Van	Mi stamatas	Rodoula Papalambrianou	Aristos Moschovakis	17
20	15	Luxembourg	Modern Times	Donne-moi une chance	Patrick Hippert, Jimmy Martin	Patrick Hippert, Jimmy Martin	11
21	2	Turkey	Burak Aydos, Öztürk Baybora & Serter	Esmer yarim	Burak Aydos	Burak Aydos	10
22	16	Slovenia	1X Band	Tih dezeven dan	Tomaz Kosec	Cole Moretti	9
23	5	Denmark	Tommy Seebach Band	Under stjernerne på himlen	Keld Heick	Tommy Seebach	9
24	24	Israel	Lakahat Shiru	Shiru	Yoram Tahar-Lev	Shaike Paikov	4
25	7	Belgium	Barbara	Iemand als jij	Tobana	Marc Vliegen	3

Eurosong Qualifier: Ljubliana, Slovenia

3 April 1993

Rank	Start	Country	Artist	Song	Writer	Composer	POINTS
1	6	Slovenia	1X Band	Tih dezeven dan	Tomaz Kosec	Cole Moretti	54
2	1	Bosnia & H	Fazla	Sva bol svijeta	Fahrudin Pecikoza	Dino Dervishalidovic	52
3	2	Croatia	Put	Don't ever cry	Dorde Novkovic	Andrej Basa	51
4	7	Slovakia	Elán	Amnestia na neveru	Jan Baláž	Jožef Ráž	50
5	3	Estonia	Jaanika Sillamaa	Muretut meelt ja südametuld	Leelo Tungal	Andres Valkoneni	47
6	4	Hungary	Andrea Szulák	Arva reggel	Petar Ugrin	György Jakob, Emesi Hatvani	44
7	5	Romania	Dida Dragan	Nu pleca	Adrian Ordean	Dida Dragan	38

1993 Eurovision 38: Millstreet, Ireland — 15 May 1993

	Italy	Turkey	Germany	Switzerland	Denmark	Greece	Belgium	Malta	Iceland	Austria	Portugal	France	Sweden	Ireland	Luxembourg	Slovenia	Finland	Bosnia & H	United Kingdom	Netherlands	Croatia	Spain	Cyprus	Israel	Norway
TOTAL	45	10	18	148	9	64	3	69	42	32	60	121	89	187	11	9	20	27	164	92	31	58	17	4	120
Austria				6			8	4	1		5	7	10	8				1	12	3	4	2			6
Belgium								4	12	3			10	2					12	7		5			
Bosnia & H	2				5			4				3		8		1			3	10		6		7	
Croatia	1			2				4	5			8		6					10	3		7		12	
Cyprus				6		12		1	2		3	10		7					4			5		8	
Denmark			3	10				5	4		1	12	7	6					8					2	
Finland	8			4		6		2	1		7	3							5				10		12
France	5			12	7	2		3			8							4	6				10	1	
Germany				12	2		3	4		1				8	5	6			7						10
Greece				7				5	4	1	2	3	6	8									10		12
Iceland				1		4					2	8	7	3		5		12	6						10
Ireland				4	7			2	1		6	10					3	8	12						5
Israel				4		7			3	2	8	10	5	12				6	1						
Italy				8	10	2		7						12	4		3		1	6		5			
Luxembourg	10			12	3				4		6	5	7			2		8							1
Malta	7			5		6			12	10	1	2	4								3		8		
Netherlands	2		1	8		5			7			12	3	10					4						6
Norway				3		7			2		5	6		12					8	10	4	1			
Portugal	10			1					2			12	4	6					7	5				3	8
Slovenia				8					5			4	6	12	1				10	7		2			3
Spain	2	6		3		8		4			12		10						5	7	1				
Sweden						6	1	4	7		2	8		12		3			10	5					
Switzerland	1		2					7			4	8	12									5	3	6	10
Turkey						2		5		4		7	1				3	12	8	6					10
United Kingdom				10				6	2	3	1	4	7	12								8	5		

1994 Eurovision 39: Dublin, Ireland

30 April 1994

Qualification: Bottom 6 countries from 1993 relegated, replaced with 7 new applicant countries.

Rank	Start	Country	Artist	Song	Writer	Composer	POINTS
1	3	Ireland	P Harrington & C McGettigan	Rock 'n' roll kids	Brendan J. Graham	Brendan J. Graham	226
2	24	Poland	Edyta Górniak	To nie ja!	Jacek Cygan	Stanislas Syrewicz	166
3	14	Germany	MeKaDo	Wir geben 'ne Party	Bernd Meinunger	Ralph Siegel	128
4	22	Hungary	Friderika Bayer	Kinek mondjam el vétkeimet	Szilveszter Jenei	Szilveszter Jenei	122
5	12	Malta	Moira Stafrace & Christopher Scicluna	More than love	Moira Stafrace	Christopher Scicluna	97
6	17	Norway	E Andreasson & J W Danielsen	Duett	Hans Olav Mørk	Rolf Løvland	76
7	25	France	Nina Morato	Je suis un vrai garçon	Nina Morato	Bruno Maman	74
8	8	Portugal	Sara Tavares	Chamar a música	Rosa Lobato Faria	João Carlos Mota Oliveira	73
9	23	Russia	Youddiph	Vechni stranik	Youddiph	Lev Zemlinski	70
10	6	United Kingdom	Frances Ruffelle	We will be free (Lonely symphony)	George de Angelis, Mark Dean	George de Angelis, Mark Dean	63
11	4	Cyprus	Evridiki	Ime anthropos ke ego	George Theophanous	George Theophanous	51
12	5	Iceland	Sigga	Nætur	Stefán Hilmarsson	Friðrik Karlsson	49
13	1	Sweden	Marie Bergman & Roger Pontare	Stjärnorna	Mikael Littwold	Peter Bertilsson	48
14	19	Greece	Costas Bigalis & the Sea Lovers	To trehantiri (diri diri)	Costas Bigalis	Costas Bigalis	44
15	18	Bosnia & H	Alma & Dejan	Ostani kraj mene	Edu Mulahalilovic	Adi Mulahalilovic	39
16	7	Croatia	Tony Cetinski	Nek'ti bude ljubav sva	Zeljko Krznaric	Zeljko Klasterka	27
17	20	Austria	Petra Frey	Für den Frieden der Welt	Karl Brunner, Johann Brunner	Alfons Weindorf	19
18	21	Spain	Alejandro Abad	Ella no es ella	Alejandro Abad	Alejandro Abad	17
19	15	Slovakia	Martin Durinda & Tublatanka	Nekovecná piesen	Martin Sarvas	Martin Durinda	15
20	9	Switzerland	Duilio	Sto pregando	Giuseppe Scaramella	Giuseppe Scaramella	15
21	11	Romania	Dan Bittman	Dincolo de nori	Antoniu Furtuna, Dan Bittman	Antoniu Furtuna, Dan Bittman	14
22	2	Finland	CatCat	Bye bye baby	Kari Salli, Markku 'Make' Lentonen	Kari Salli, Markku 'Make' Lentonen	11
23	13	Netherlands	Willeke Alberti	Waar is de zon	Cooth van Doesburgh	Edwin Schimscheimer	4
24	10	Estonia	Silvi Vrait	Nagu merelaine	Leelo Tungal	Ivar Must	2
25	16	Lithuania	Ovidijus Vyšniauskas	Lopšinę mylimai	Gintaras Zdebskis	Ovidijus Vyšniauskas	0

1994 Eurovision 39: Dublin, Ireland
30 April 1994

	Austria	Bosnia & H	Croatia	Cyprus	Estonia	Finland	France	Germany	Greece	Hungary	Iceland	Ireland	Lithuania	Malta	Netherlands	Norway	Poland	Portugal	Romania	Russia	Slovakia	Spain	Sweden	Switzerland	United Kingdom	TOTAL
Sweden	5				2			5		2	2		5	3	6	10						1		7		48
Finland		1							10																	11
Ireland	10	10	12	8	10	7	8	12		10	12		10	5	12	12	8	12	8	12	6	10	10	12	10	226
Cyprus						10	3		12		3		3			5	5	5		2	1	4	8	2		51
Iceland	3		6	5	5	1	4					6				2	4	3		1	3	6	8	3	6	49
United Kingdom	1	4			8			4		3	8	1		10			3	8		5	12	3	8	8		63
Croatia									5												12					27
Portugal						5	6			7		8		1	3		1			4		12	5	5	8	73
Switzerland							5							8								2				15
Estonia									2				2													2
Romania									6				7	6												14
Malta		12	7	2	7	6		3	7			10	4		1	1	7	4	10		10		4	6	1	97
Netherlands	4																									4
Germany	2	7	10	6	3	3				12	7	5	4		4	1	7	10	12	7	7	8	6		7	128
Slovakia				10			10		3					12												15
Lithuania																										0
Norway		6	3		8			2	1	5	1	3	1	7	7				4	8			4	1	4	76
Bosnia & H			4	12		2		1		1				4			2		6		8	7	6			39
Greece		5	2	7		4	2			4						4			1		5		2		3	44
Austria							2		8										5		2		1		3	19
Spain	8	3	5		4	12	7	7	4	6	10	12	6	2	10	8	12	1	2	3			12	4	2	17
Hungary	6		1	3	1		1	6			4	4	12		5	3	10	2	3		4				5	122
Russia		8		1	12	8	12	10		8	6	7	8		8	6	6	7	7	6			3	10	12	70
Poland	12		8		6			8			5	2				7		6		10						166
France	7	2		4		12																	3			74

1995 Eurovision 40: Dublin, Ireland

13 May 1995

Qualification: Bottom 6 countries from 1994 relegated, replaced with the countries relegated in 1993.

Rank	Start	Country	Artist	Song	Writer	Composer	POINTS
1	5	Norway	Secret Garden	Nocturne	Petter Skavlan	Rolf Løvland	148
2	9	Spain	Anabel Conde	Vuelve conmigo	José María Purón	José María Purón	119
3	18	Sweden	Jan Johansen	Se på mej	Ingela Pling Forsman	Håkan Almqvist, Bobby Ljunggren	100
4	12	France	Nathalie Santamaria	Il me donne rendez-vous	Didier Barbelivien	François Bernheim	94
5	19	Denmark	Aud Wilken	Fra Mols til Skagen	Lise Cabble	Mette Mathiesen, Lise Cabble	92
6	11	Croatia	Magazin & Lidija	Nostalgija	Vjekoslava Huljic	Tonci Huljic	91
7	20	Slovenia	Darja Svajger	Prisluhni mi	Primoz Peterca	Primoz Peterca, Saso Fajon	83
8	21	Israel	Liora	Amen	Hamutal Ben Ze'ev	Moshe Datz	81
9	17	Cyprus	Alexandros Panayi	Sti fotia	Alexandros Panayi	Alexandros Panayi	79
10	22	Malta	Mike Spiteri	Keep me in mind	Alfred Sant	Ray Agius	76
11	15	United Kingdom	Love City Groove	Love City Groove	Paul Hardy, Steven Rudden, Tatsiana Mais, Jay Williams	Paul Hardy, Steven Rudden, Tatsiana Mais, Jay Williams	76
12	23	Greece	Elina Constantopoulou	Pia prossefchi	Antonis Pappas	Nikos Terzis	68
13	8	Austria	Stella Jones	Die Welt dreht sich verkehrt	Mischa Krausz	Mischa Krausz	67
14	2	Ireland	Eddie Friel	Dreamin'	Richard Abbott, Barry Woods	Richard Abbott, Barry Woods	44
15	7	Iceland	Bó Halldórsson	Núna	Jón Örn Marinósson	Bó Halldórsson, Ed Welch	31
16	10	Turkey	Arzu Ece	Sev!	Zeynep Talu	Melih Kibar	21
17	6	Russia	Philipp Kirkorov	Kolybelnaya dlya vulkana	Ilya Bershadsky	Ilya Reznyk	18
18	1	Poland	Justyna	Sama	Wojciech Waglewski	Mateusz Pospieszalski, Wojciech Waglewski	15
19	4	Bosnia & H	Davor Popovic	Dvadeset i prvi vijek	Zlatan Fazlic	Zlatan Fazlic, Sinan Alimanovic	14
20	14	Belgium	Frédéric Etherlinck	La voix est libre	Pierre Theunis	Pierre Theunis	8
21	16	Portugal	Tó Cruz	Baunilha e chocolate	Rosa Lobato De Faria	António Vitorino de Almeida	5
22	13	Hungary	Czaba Szigeti	Új nèv egy règi ház fàlan	Attila Horváth	Ferenc Balázs	3
23	3	Germany	Stone & Stone	Verliebt in Dich	Cheyenne Stone	Cheyenne Stone	1

1995 Eurovision 40: Dublin, Ireland — 13 May 1995

	Austria	Belgium	Bosnia & H	Croatia	Cyprus	Denmark	France	Germany	Greece	Hungary	Iceland	Ireland	Israel	Malta	Norway	Poland	Portugal	Russia	Slovenia	Spain	Sweden	Turkey	United Kingdom	TOTAL
Poland									3	1	6				4		1							15
Ireland		5	5			1	1	1	4		3				1			5	5	3	10	5	4	44
Germany														1										1
Bosnia & H				8		3																3		14
Norway			1	6	7	2	10	4	12	6	12	10	10	6		12	12	12	7	4		12	4	148
Russia					1		2				1				10			3						18
Iceland		10				8	8		7	4		6			2		2			6	6	4		31
Austria		12	8	10		10	7	6	6	2	5	2	2	8	3	2	2		3	2	4	4	5	67
Spain		1		5									12	7		8	7		12	12		8	8	119
Turkey													1	12					8				2	21
Croatia			10			6		8	5	10	5	3	4		7	7	4			1	3	7		91
France		6		3	5				2		10	5	7		6			2		7		2	1	94
Hungary	1				2						8													3
Belgium			4				12		1	7		1					10	1						8
United Kingdom	12	7		1		7	4	3	8	12			5		5	5		4	4	5	5		3	76
Portugal																								5
Cyprus	8	8	2		4	5	3	3			2	12	6	4	8	1	8	4	4		8	1	3	79
Sweden			3	10		12		12			4	7		3	12	10	6	6	1			6	6	100
Denmark	7	3	3	5				7	10	3	7	7		2		3	5	10	6		7			92
Slovenia	3		6	2	3		6	5		8		8	3	5		4		7		1	2		10	83
Israel	6	4	7	4	8	4		10		5								8	10		12		12	81
Malta	2		12	12	6		6	2				4	8	10		6	3		2	10	1	10	7	76
Greece	5	2		7	12		5											8		8				68

1996 Eurovision 41: Oslo, Norway   **18 May 1996**

Qualification: 1995 Winner plus 22 from 29 entries based on judged preselection

Rank	Start	Country	Artist	Song	Writer	Composer	POINTS
1	17	Ireland	Eimear Quinn	The voice	Brendan Graham	Brendan Graham	162
2	12	Norway	Elisabeth Andreasson	I evighet	Torhild Nigar	Torhild Nigar	114
3	23	Sweden	One More Time	Den vilda	Nanne Grönvall	Peter Grönvall	100
4	7	Croatia	Maja Blagdan	Sveta ljubav	Zrinko Tutic	Zrinko Tutic	98
5	11	Estonia	Ivo Linna & Maarja-Liis Ilus	Kaelakee hääl	Kaari Sillamaa	Priit Pajusaar	94
6	4	Portugal	Lúcia Moniz	O meu coração não tem cor	José Fanha	Pedro Osório	92
7	15	Netherlands	Maxine & Franklin Brown	De eerste keer	Peter van Asten, Piet Souer	Peter van Asten	78
8	2	United Kingdom	Gina G	Just a little bit	Simon Tauber	Steve Rodway	77
9	5	Cyprus	Constantinos	Mono gia mas	Rodoula Papalambrianou	Andreas Giorgallis	72
10	8	Austria	George Nußbaumer	Weil's Dr Guat Got	Mischa Krausz, George Nußbaumer	Mischa Krausz, George Nußbaumer	68
11	6	Malta	Miriam Christine	In a woman's heart	Alfred Sant	Paul Abela	68
12	1	Turkey	Sebnem Paker	Beşinçi mevsim	Dr. Çuhaci	Levent Çoker	57
13	19	Iceland	Anna Mjöll	Sjúbidú	Anna Mjöll Ólafsdóttir, Ólafur Gaukur	Anna Mjöll Ólafsdóttir, Ólafur Gaukur	51
14	10	Greece	Marianna Efstratiou	Emis forame to himona anixiatika	Iro Trigoni	Costas Bigalis	36
15	20	Poland	Kasia Kowalska	Chce znac swój grzech	Kasia Kowalska	Robert Amirian	31
16	9	Switzerland	Cathy Leander	Mon coeur l'aime	Régis Mounir	Régis Mounir	22
17	16	Belgium	Lisa del Bo	Liefde is een kaartspel	Daniel Ditmar	John Terra, Sarah Brogden	22
18	22	Slovakia	Marcel Palonder	Kým nás máš	Jozef Urban	Juraj Burian	19
19	13	France	Dan Ar Braz et l'Héritage des Celtes	Diwanit bugale	Dan Ar Braz	Dan Ar Braz	18
20	3	Spain	Antonio Carbonell	¡Ay, qué deseo!	Ketama	Ketama	17
21	14	Slovenia	Regina	Dan najlepših sanj	Aleksander Kogoj	Aleksander Kogoj	16
22	21	Bosnia & H	Amila Glamocak	Za našu ljubav	Sinan Alimanovic, Aida Frijak, Adnan Bajramovic	Sinan Alimanovic, Aida Frijak, Adnan Bajramovic	13
23	18	Finland	Jasmine	Niin kaunis on taivas	Timo Niemi	Timo Niemi	9

1996 Eurovision 41: Oslo, Norway — 18 May 1996

Receiving \ Voting	AT	BE	BA	HR	CY	EE	FI	FR	GR	IS	IE	MT	NL	NO	PL	PT	SK	SI	ES	SE	CH	TR	UK	TOTAL
Turkey	3	5	5	1			5	4				10	7						8		6	—	6	**57**
United Kingdom		12		7	1	2	3	8		4		6				12		6		6	4	3	—	**77**
Spain				4	2							5				3			—					**17**
Portugal	1	6	1	10	12		3	5		4	1					—			7	4	10	5	2	**92**
Cyprus	2				—		6	2	6	10		2	6			5			10	2	5		12	**72**
Malta			12			6	6		5			—			6	10	1	10	5	5				**68**
Croatia		4	10	—	8				12	5	8	7	5	1	2	1	4	12		1	1	8	4	**98**
Austria			6					12	8			12		7	8	2	3	5				4		**68**
Switzerland		2			10					3	4	1	4				2	3	4		—		3	**22**
Greece	5		3		7				—		2				1					3			7	**36**
Estonia	8	4	8	5	3	—	12		1	12	7		1	8	10		8	8		12		2	10	**94**
Norway		8	3			5	7	7	2	8	5		3	—	4		10			10	7		8	**114**
France		7				3	2	—					10										1	**18**
Slovenia	12	1								1								—	1					**16**
Netherlands	7		2		5	4		10	10	2	10	4	—	3	7	7	5	7	6	8				**78**
Belgium				2				6					2						12				5	**22**
Ireland	6	3	12		6	1	10	3	3		—		12	10	12	8	12	1	3	7	12	12		**162**
Finland							—		7	7				2		6								**9**
Iceland	4	6					8			—	12				3							7		**51**
Poland		4			4										—		6	2				6		**31**
Bosnia & H			—	3		8	1		4	6		8	8	5	5				2					**13**
Slovakia	10	10															—	4						**19**
Sweden			4			10		3		6				6		4	7	4		—	8			**100**

99

1997 Eurovision 42: Dublin, Ireland

3 May 1997

Qualification: The 25 countries with the best average scores in the last 5 years qualified.

Rank	Start	Country	Artist	Song	Writer	Composer	POINTS
1	24	United Kingdom	Katrina and The Waves	Love shine a light	Kimberley Rew	Kimberley Rew	227
2	5	Ireland	Marc Roberts	Mysterious woman	John Farry	John Farry	157
3	2	Turkey	Sebnem Paker & Group Etnic	Dinle	Mehtap Alnitemiz	Levent Çoker	121
4	9	Italy	Jalisse	Fiumi di parole	Carmen di Domenico, Alessandra Drusian	Fabio Ricci	114
5	1	Cyprus	Chara & Andreas Konstantinou	Mana mou	Constantina Konstantinou	Constantina Konstantinou	98
6	10	Spain	Marcos Llunas	Sin rencor	Marcos Llunas	Marcos Llunas	96
7	22	France	Fanny	Sentiments songes	Jean-Paul Dreau	Jean-Paul Dreau	95
8	13	Estonia	Maarja-Liis Ilus	Keelatud maa	Kaari Sillamaa	Harmo Kallaste	82
9	18	Malta	Debbie Scerri	Let me fly	Ray Agius	Ray Agius	66
10	6	Slovenia	Tanja Ribic	Zbudi se	Zoran Predin	Sašo Lošic	60
11	12	Poland	Anna Maria Jopek	Ale jestem	Magda Czapinska	Tomasz Lewandowski	54
12	19	Hungary	VIP	Miert kell, hogy elmenj?	Krisztina Bokor Fekete, Attila Kornyei	Viktor Rakonczai, Sandor Jozsa	39
13	17	Greece	Marianna Zorba	Horepse	Manolis Manouselis	Manolis Manouselis	39
14	16	Sweden	Blond	Bara hon älskar mig	Stephan Berg	Stephan Berg	36
15	20	Russia	Alla Pugachova	Primadonna	Alla Pugachova	Alla Pugachova	33
16	21	Denmark	Kølig Kaj	Stemmen i mit liv	Thomas Laegård	Lars Pedersen	25
17	23	Croatia	ENI	Probudi me	Alida Sarar	Davor Tolja	24
18	11	Germany	Bianca Shomburg	Zeit	Bernd Meinunger	Ralph Siegel	22
19	14	Bosnia & H	Alma Cardzic	Goodbye	Milic Vukasinovic	Sinan Alimanovic, Milic Vukasinovic	22
20	25	Iceland	Paul Oscar	Minn hinsti dans	Paul Oscar	Trausti Haraldsson, Paul Oscar	18
21	4	Austria	Bettina Soriat	One step	Ina Siber, Marc Berry	Marc Berry	12
22	7	Switzerland	Barbara Berta	Dentro di me	Barbara Berta	Barbara Berta	5
23	8	Netherlands	Mrs. Einstein	Niemand heeft nog tijd	Ed Hooijmans	Ed Hooijmans	5
24	15	Portugal	Célia Lawson	Antes do adeus	Rosa Lobato de Faria	Thilo Krassmann	0
25	3	Norway	Tor Endresen	San Francisco	Tor Endresen	Tor Endresen, Arne Myksvol	0

1997 Eurovision 42: Dublin, Ireland — 3 May 1997

	Austria	Bosnia & H	Croatia	Cyprus	Denmark	Estonia	France	Germany	Greece	Hungary	Iceland	Ireland	Italy	Malta	Netherlands	Norway	Poland	Portugal	Russia	Slovenia	Spain	Sweden	Switzerland	Turkey	United Kingdom	TOTAL
Cyprus			4		7	1	4	5	12		12	3	4	7	10	2		3	1	4	10		4		5	98
Turkey	7	12				6	6	12	7	6	7	2	7	10	2			5	4		12	6	6		4	121
Norway																										0
Austria																									12	12
Ireland	10	8	6	8	10	8	10	8	3	5			10		3	3	1	10	3	1	6	10	7	6	12	157
Slovenia		7	3	2		4	7			8	3		2	4			2		10		3			10		60
Switzerland																			5							5
Netherlands																								1		5
Italy	1		10	6	4			4	5	3	1	1		12	7		8	12	7	10	8	3	10	5	3	114
Spain	3	4	5	10	2		2	2	6	10		6	3	3	6	5	4	8	8	5			8	4		96
Germany	8	1			5	3	3		1	1			5		1	10	6	2		7	2		5			22
Poland	6		1	1	8		8	7		7	2	8	1					1	8	7	4	1				54
Estonia	4						3	3		4	12		12			4	6			3	4	4	5	8	10	82
Bosnia & H																							2			22
Portugal					6																7					0
Sweden		5	7			5			8		4	5	6	6	8	8	5		2	6	7				7	36
Greece			8		3	7						7		2	5	5					1					39
Malta			2	5			1				5	4				10								12		66
Hungary	5					7	5									1	5			12				3		39
Russia								1			6					7										33
Denmark		3		3	1	12			2		10	10		8	8	7										25
France				4	12				4	2	6	12	8	1	5	12	12	6	6	2	5	7	1	2	2	95
Croatia		2		7				1	10	12						6	3	7	12	8		2	3	2		24
United Kingdom	12	10	12		12	10	12	10		12	8	12	8	8	12	6	10	7	12	8	5	12	12	7		227
Iceland	2					2								1								8			6	18

1998 Eurovision 43: Birmingham, United Kingdom

9 May 1998

Qualification: Four automatic qualifiers (UK, Germany, Spain, France), along with those countries who failed to qualify for 1997 plus FYR Macedonia, the remaining places being given to the countries with the best average scores over the last 5 years.

Rank	Start	Country	Artist	Song	Writer	Composer	POINTS
1	8	Israel	Dana International	Diva	Yoav Ginai	Tzvika Pik	176
2	16	United Kingdom	Imaani	Where are you?	Scott English, Simon Stirling, Phil Manikiza	Scott English, Simon Stirling, Phil Manikiza	166
3	10	Malta	Chiara	The one that I love	Sunny Aquilina	Jason Paul Cassar	165
4	18	Netherlands	Edsilia Rombley	Hemel en aarde	Eric van Tijn, Jochem Fluitsma	Eric van Tijn, Jochem Fluitsma	150
5	1	Croatia	Danijela	Neka mi ne svane	Petar Grašo, Remi Kasinoti	Petar Grašo, Remi Kasinoti	131
6	20	Belgium	Mélanie Cohl	Dis oui	Philippe Swan	Philippe Swan	122
7	9	Germany	Guildo Horn	Guildo hat euch lieb	Stefan Raab	Stefan Raab	86
8	22	Norway	Lars A. Fredriksen	Alltid sommer	Linda Andernach Johannesen	David Eriksen	79
9	13	Ireland	Dawn	Is always over now?	Gerry Morgan	Gerry Morgan	64
10	19	Sweden	Jill Johnson	Kärleken är	Ingela "Pling" Forsman	Bobby Ljunggren, Håkan Almqvist	53
11	17	Cyprus	Michael Hajiyanni	Genesis	Zenon Zindilis	Michael Hajiyanni	37
12	23	Estonia	Koit Toome	Mere lapsed	Peeter Pruuli	Maria and Tomi Rahula	36
13	14	Portugal	Alma Lusa	Se eu te pudesse abraçar	José Cid	José Cid	36
14	24	Turkey	Tüzmen	Unutamazsin	Canan Tunç	Erdinç Tunç	25
15	21	Finland	Edea	Aava	Tommy Mansikka-Aho	Alexi Ahoniemi	22
16	4	Spain	Mikel Herzog	¿Qué voy a hacer sin ti?	Mikel Herzog	Alberto Estébanez	21
17	7	Poland	Sixteen	To takie proste	Olga Pruszkowska	Jaroslaw Pruszkowski	19
18	12	Slovenia	Vili Resnik	Naj bogovi slišijo	Urša Vlašic	Matjaz Vlašic	17
19	25	FYR Macedonia	Vlado Janevski	Ne zori, zoro	Vlado Janevski	Grigor Koprov	16
20	2	Greece	Dionysia & Thalassa group	Mia krifi evaisthissia	Yiannis Malachias	Yiannis Valvis	12
21	6	Slovakia	Katarína Hasprová	Modlitba	Anna Wepperyová	Gabriel Dušík	8
22	15	Romania	Malina Olinescu	Eu cred	Liliana Stefan	Adrian Romcescu	6
23	11	Hungary	Charlie	A holnap már ném lesz szomorú	Attila Horváth	István Lehr	4
24	3	France	Marie-Line	Où aller	Marie-Line Marolany	Marie-Line Marolany, Jean-Philippe Dary, Micaël Sene, Moïse Crespy	3
25	5	Switzerland	Gunvor	Lass ihn	Gunvor Guggisberg	Gunvor Guggisberg, Egon Egemann	0

1998 Eurovision 43: Birmingham, United Kingdom — 9 May 1998

	Belgium	Croatia	Cyprus	Estonia	Finland	France	FYR Macedonia	Germany	Greece	Hungary	Ireland	Israel	Malta	Netherlands	Norway	Poland	Portugal	Romania	Slovakia	Slovenia	Spain	Sweden	Switzerland	Turkey	United Kingdom	TOTAL
Croatia	5		7	3	3	8	12	10	5		3	10	10	4	6	6	2		12	10	1	3	5	4	2	131
Greece			12																							12
France			1				2																			3
Spain	3		4			4						3											6			21
Switzerland																										0
Slovakia		8																								8
Poland								5		2								10								19
Israel	10		10	7	10	12	8	7	10		6		12	6	3	10	12	7	7		10	5	10	5	5	172
Germany	7			1	1				3		8			12	12	8	10	6	8		12	6	12		6	86
Malta	8		5	5	5	6	7	8	6		12	7		8	2		5	1	3	12	5		8	10	12	165
Hungary				4	4	1			2									5						3		4
Slovenia		3								6			6		4		1	8	1		6	1	2	3	8	17
Ireland	3			2		10	7	2	1	6		2	2		4	2	6	12	5	4	3	7	2			64
Portugal	1		2				4					6						4		2				6		36
Romania																										6
United Kingdom	6	12	8	8	8	3	10	1	7	10	5	12	8	7	5	7	6	12	5	1	3	7	3	12		166
Cyprus	2	4				5	3	6	12	1	10	1	1		8	5	4	4		5	4	8	7	7	3	37
Netherlands	12	10		12	6		6	4	8	12	2	8	7		10	3	7			6	7	2	4	2	10	150
Sweden			6	6		7	1		4	8	7	5	4	5	7	12	8		6	7		10		1	1	53
Belgium				10						3	4		3	10	1	3			10		8	12	4		7	122
Finland			3	4				3		5	1	5	5	3		4	3		2	8	2	2	1			22
Norway	4			2	2					4		4		2		1			10	3	8	10		1	4	79
Estonia		5			12			12						1				2	2	8	2	12	1			36
Turkey	5						5											2	4	3		4				25
FYR Macedonia	6																	3								16

1999 Eurovision 44: Jerusalem, Israel   29 May 1999

Qualification: Four automatic qualifiers (UK, Germany, Spain, France), along with those countries who failed to qualify for 1998, the remaining places being given to the countries with the best average scores over the last 5 years.

Rank	Start	Country	Artist	Song	Writer	Composer	POINTS
1	15	Sweden	Charlotte Nilsson	Take me to your heaven	Gert Lengstrand	Lars Diedricson	163
2	13	Iceland	Selma Björnsdóttir	All out of luck	Thorvaldur B. Thorvaldsson	S Björnsdóttir, T B. Thorvaldsson, S I. Baldvinsson	146
3	21	Germany	Sürpriz	Reise nach Jerusalem - Kudüs'e seyahat	Bernd Meinunger	Ralph Siegel	140
4	4	Croatia	Doris Dragovic	Marija Magdalena	Vjekoslava Huljic	Tonci Huljic	118
5	19	Israel	Eden	Yom huledeth	Moshe Datz, Gabriel Batler, Yaacov Lymay, Jacky Oved	Moshe Datz, Gabriel Batler, Yaacov Lymay, Jacky Oved	93
6	23	Estonia	Evelin Samuel and Camille	Diamond of night	Marian-Anna Kärmas & Kaari Sillamaa	Priit Pajusaar and Glen Pilvr	90
7	22	Bosnia & H	Dino and Beatrice	Putnici	Dino Dervišhalidovic	Dino Dervišhalidovic	86
8	9	Denmark	Trine Jepsen & Michael Teschl	This time (I mean it)	Ebbe Ravn	Ebbe Ravn	71
9	11	Netherlands	Marlayne	One good reason	Tjeerd Van Zanen and Alan Michael	Tjeerd Van Zanen and Alan Michael	71
10	18	Austria	Bobbie Singer	Reflection	Dave Moskin	Dave Moskin	65
11	6	Slovenia	Darja Svajger	For a thousand years	Primoz Peterca	Primoz Peterca	50
12	2	Belgium	Venessa Chinltor	Like the wind	Wim Claes, Emma Phillipa, Ilia Beyers, John Terra	Wim Claes, Emma Phillipa, Ilia Beyers, John Terra	38
13	5	United Kingdom	Precious	Say it again	Paul Varney	Paul Varney	38
14	8	Norway	Stig André Van Eijk	Living my life without you	Sem & Stig Van Eijk & Peter Brandt	Sem & Stig Van Eijk & Peter Brandt	35
15	20	Malta	Times 3	Believe 'n peace	Moira Stafrace	Chris Scicluna	32
16	7	Turkey	Tuba Önal & Grup Mystik	Dön artik	Canan Tunç	Erdinç Tunç	21
17	17	Ireland	The Mullans	When you need me	Bronagh Mullan	Bronagh Mullan	18
18	12	Poland	Mietek (Mieczyslaw) Szczesniak	Przytul mnie mocno	Wojciech Ziembicki	Seweryn Krajewski	17
19	10	France	Nayah	Je veux donner ma voix	Gilles Arcens & Luigi Rutigliano	Pascal Graczyk & René Colombies	14
20	1	Lithuania	Aiste Smilgeviciute	Strazdas	Sigitas Geda	Linas Rimša	13
21	14	Portugal	Marlain Angelidou	Tha'nai erotas	Andreas Karanikolas	George Kallis	12
22	16	Cyprus	Rui Bandeira	Como tudo começou	Tó Andrade	Jorge do Carmo	2
23	3	Spain	Lydia	No quiero escuchar	F R Fernández, A P Ramírez, A C Zamarreno, C L González	Fernando Rodriguez Fernández & Alejandro Piqueras Ramirez	1

1999 Eurovision 44: Jerusalem, Israel

29 May 1999

Country	Austria	Belgium	Bosnia & H	Croatia	Cyprus	Denmark	Estonia	France	Germany	Iceland	Ireland	Israel	Lithuania	Malta	Netherlands	Norway	Poland	Portugal	Slovenia	Spain	Sweden	Turkey	United Kingdom	TOTAL
Lithuania		5		2	5		2					3		1										13
Belgium				4			5	2			10	5			10		2		2					38
Spain				1																				1
Croatia	8		8		2		3	7	10	4	6	7	6	5	1		7	6	12	12	1	8		118
United Kingdom			1	5	4	1						4	5	8					2	4		4		38
Slovenia		2	5	12				1	12		12		10							2				50
Turkey					7	6	6	5		7					6									21
Norway	5			7	7					12	3	2	2					3	5	5			5	35
Denmark					8				4		7	6	4	4		8	1		3	3	8	2		71
France											2		7	2								5		14
Netherlands	4	12	4			7				6	1	6	8	2				2			4		8	71
Poland	2	8	6			12	10	3	2		4		3		7	10		4						17
Iceland			12		12	10	12	12	3		5	8	12	10	8	12	4	10	7	10	12	10	10	146
Cyprus																							2	2
Sweden	6	7			1	3	8	10	5	8					2	1	3	5	4	8		1	12	163
Portugal								12	7	1			12		4		10		1					12
Ireland					10	3	4		1					6								1	4	18
Austria	1	6			3	2	1		5	5					2	6	3	5	4	8	7	3	7	65
Israel	7	3	2	8			7	8	7	3	8	—			4	2	10	8	1	7	3		6	93
Malta	10	1	7	6		5		6	1	2		12		—	12	3		1					1	32
Germany	10	10	10	3		8	7	8	—		8	1	1	7	12	3	12	12	6	1	2	12		140
Bosnia & H	12		—	10		4		6							3	7	5	7	10		6	7		86
Estonia	3	4	3				—	4	6	2			1		5	5	8		8	1	10		3	90

105

2000 Eurovision 45: Stockholm, Sweden   13 May 2000

Qualification: Four automatic qualifiers (UK, Germany, Spain, France), along with those countries who failed to qualify for 1999, the remaining places being given to the countries with the best average scores over the last 5 years.

Rank	Start	Country	Artist	Song	Writer	Composer	POINTS
1	14	Denmark	Olsen Brothers	Fly on the wings of love	Jørgen Olsen	Jørgen Olsen	195
2	9	Russia	Alsou	Solo	Andrew Lane, Brandon Barnes	Andrew Lane, Brandon Barnes	155
3	21	Latvia	BrainStorm	My star	Renars Kaupers	Renars Kaupers	136
4	4	Estonia	Ines	Once in a lifetime	Jana Hallas	Pearu Paulus, Ilmar Laisaar, Alar Kotkas	98
5	15	Germany	Stefan Raab	Wadde hadde dudde da	Stefan Raab	Stefan Raab	96
6	23	Ireland	Eamonn Toal	Millennium of love	Raymond J. Smyth, Gerry Simpson	Raymond J. Smyth, Gerry Simpson	92
7	18	Sweden	Roger Pontare	When spirits are calling my name	Thomas Holmstrand, Linda Jansson, Peter Dahl	Thomas Holmstrand, Linda Jansson, Peter Dahl	88
8	7	Malta	Claudette Pace	Desire	Gerard James Borg	Philip Vella	73
9	17	Croatia	Goran Karan	Kada zaspu anđeli	Nenad Nincevic	Zdenko Runjic	70
10	22	Turkey	Pinar Ayhan & S.O.S. band	Yorgunum anla	Sühan Ayhan, Pinar Ayhan, Orkun Yazgan	Sühan Ayhan, Pinar Ayhan, Orkun Yazgan	59
11	8	Norway	Charmed	My heart goes boom	Tore Madsen	Morten Henriksen	57
12	12	Iceland	Einer Ágúst Viðisson & Telma Ágústdóttir	Tell me! (Hvert sem er)	Sigurður Örn Jónsson	Örlygur Smári	45
13	2	Netherlands	Linda Wagenmakers	No goodbyes	John O'Hare	Ellert Driessen	40
14	24	Austria	The rounder girls	All to you	Dave Moskin	Dave Moskin	34
15	19	FYC Macedonia	XXL	100\% te ljubam	Orce Zafirofski, Dragan Karanfilovski	Dragan Karanfilovski	29
16	3	United Kingdom	Nicki French	Don't play that song again	John Springate, Gary Shephard	John Springate, Gary Shephard	28
17	6	Romania	Taxi	The moon	Dan Teodorescu	Dan Teodorescu	25
18	13	Spain	Serafin Zubiri	Colgado de un sueño	José Maria Purón	José Maria Purón	18
19	20	Finland	Nina Åström	A little bit	Gerrit aan 't Goor	Luca Genta	18
20	16	Switzerland	Jane Bogaert	La vita cos'è?	Thomas Marin	Bernie Staub	14
21	11	Cyprus	Voice	Nomiza	Alexandros Panayi	Alexandros Panayi	8
22	1	Israel	Ping Pong	Sa'me'akh	Roi Arad, Guy Asif, Ronen Ben Tal	Roi Arad, Guy Asif	7
23	5	France	Sofia Mestari	On aura le ciel	Pierre Legay	Benoît Heinrich	5
24	10	Belgium	Nathalie Sorce	Envie de vivre	Silvio Pezzuto	Silvio Pezzuto	2

2000 Eurovision 45: Stockholm, Sweden — 13 May 2000

	Austria	Belgium	Croatia	Cyprus	Denmark	Estonia	Finland	France	FYR Macedonia	Germany	Iceland	Ireland	Israel	Latvia	Malta	Netherlands	Norway	Romania	Russia	Spain	Sweden	Switzerland	Turkey	United Kingdom	TOTAL
Israel	3	8	2	5				6	1	1	1	1			5					4			3		7
Netherlands		2	4	3				2					8	3	6			3			6		6	4	40
United Kingdom		1	6	6		2				5	5	7	1	10	7		4	6	3				2		28
Estonia		7	7		4		8						6			7	4			1	6		2	4	98
France				8	3	1				3			3	4		2	2	7	3		3		5		5
Romania					7	3			12	4	7	3	3	6					6	1	7			2	25
Malta	2	1	8	8	6	10	5	5	8		8	4	7			1	2	7	8	5	3	2	5	3	73
Norway	7	6	12	12					7		7	10	10		3			12			7		10	8	57
Russia									2					7	12		8				5	2			155
Belgium			3						4						1						8	1			2
Cyprus				10	12													5	2						8
Iceland		5		4					10			12	5	12	8	10	7	5	2			1		12	45
Spain					2	8	10	7	6	12	12	12	12	8		8	10	1	12			10	1	5	18
Denmark	10	12	1	4			2	10	6		6	5		8		8	3		4	10		12			195
Germany	12	6						8	3		4			2	4	6			5	12			8	6	96
Switzerland	1							1																	14
Croatia	6				10	5	6	3	10	6		6	4					8	10	2		6	8		70
Sweden		5					7		6	8	4				4	5	5		7	6		3	12	6	88
FYR Macedonia			10	2														10			2				29
Finland						7												4							18
Latvia	8	12		1	8	12	12	3		7	10	8	4		10	4	12		1	7	10	7	1	7	136
Turkey	5	3		7	1	4	4	12	5	10			2	1	2	12	1	2		1	1	5		10	59
Ireland	4	4	5		5		1	4		2	2			5	10	3	6			3	4	8	7		92
Austria							3				3	2			2					8		4	4	1	34

2001 Eurovision 46: Copenhagen, Denmark

12 May 2001

Qualification: Four automatic qualifiers (UK, Germany, Spain, France), along with those countries who failed to qualify for 2000, the remaining places being given to the countries with the best average scores over the last 5 years.

Rank	Start	Country	Artist	Song	Writer	Composer	POINTS
1	20	Estonia	Tanel Padar, Dave Benton & 2XL	Everybody	Maian-Anna Kärmas	Ivar Must	198
2	23	Denmark	Rollo & King	Never ever let you go	Stefan Nielsen	Søren Poppe	177
3	22	Greece	Antique	Die for you	Antonis Papas	Antonis Papas	147
4	14	France	Natasha Saint-Pier	Je n'ai que mon âme	Jill Kapler	Jill Kapler	142
5	7	Sweden	Friends	Listen to your heartbeat	Thomas G:son, Henrik Sethsson	Thomas G:son, Henrik Sethsson	100
6	13	Spain	David Civera	Dile que la quiero	Alejandro Abad	Alejandro Abad	76
7	17	Slovenia	Nuša Derenda	Energy	Lucienne Lonchina	Matjaz Vlašic	70
8	19	Germany	Michelle	Wer Liebe lebt	Eva Richter	Gino Trovatello, Matthias Stingl	66
9	21	Malta	Fabrizio Faniello	Another summer night	Georgina Abela	Paul Abela	48
10	10	Croatia	Vanna	Strings of my heart	Vjekoslava Huljic	Tonci Huljic	42
11	15	Turkey	Sedat Yüce	Sevgiliye son	Nurdan Güneri	Semih Güneri	41
12	6	Russia	Mumiy troll	Lady alpine blue	Ilia Lagoutenko	Ilia Lagoutenko	37
13	8	Lithuania	Skamp	You got style	Erica Quinn Jennings, Vilius Alesius, Viktoras Diawara	Viktoras Diawara, Linas Rimša	35
14	3	Bosnia & H	Nino	Hano	Nino Pršeš	Nino Pršeš	29
15	16	United Kingdom	Lindsay D.	No dream impossible	Russ Ballard, Chris Winter	Russ Ballard, Chris Winter	28
16	5	Israel	Tal Sondak	Ein davar	Shimrit Orr	Yair Klinger	25
17	11	Portugal	MTM	Só sei ser feliz assim	Marco Quelhas	Marco Quelhas	18
18	9	Latvia	Arnis Mednis	Too much	Gustavs Terzens, Arnis Mednis	Arnis Mednis	16
19	1	Netherlands	Michelle	Out on my own	André Remkes, Dirk Jan Vermeij	André Remkes, Dirk Jan Vermeij	16
20	18	Poland	Piasek	2 long	Andrzej Piaseczny	Robert Chojnacki	11
21	12	Ireland	Gary O'Shaughnessy	Without your love	Pat Sheridan	Pat Sheridan	6
22	2	Iceland	TwoTricky	Angel (Birta)	Einar Bárðarson	Einar Bárðarson, Magnus Thor Sigmundsson	3
23	4	Norway	Haldor Lægreid	On my own	Ole Henrik Antonsen, Tom-Steinar Hanssen, Ole Jørgen Olsen	Ole Henrik Antonsen, Tom-Steinar Hanssen	3

2001 Eurovision 46: Copenhagen, Denmark — 12 May 2001

Receiver	TOTAL	Bosnia & H	Croatia	Denmark	Estonia	France	Germany	Greece	Iceland	Ireland	Israel	Latvia	Lithuania	Malta	Netherlands	Norway	Poland	Portugal	Russia	Slovenia	Spain	Sweden	Turkey	United Kingdom
Netherlands	16	6									5							6	1	4				
Iceland	3			2																				
Bosnia & H	29		10	7																7		4		
Norway	3													1				3						
Israel	25	6				10		2	5														7	
Russia	37	3	4		4			5	5	8	3	8	10	2										8
Sweden	100	2		10	7	2			7	1	8	6	2	8	5	2	5	5	2	2	5		8	4
Lithuania	35								1		4	5	8	10					10			1		
Latvia	16		8		8																			
Croatia	42	7					3	7																5
Portugal	18					12												1			6			
Ireland	6																1							5
Spain	76	5	6	6	3	5	6	8	2	3	12	4	7	4	7	4	1	7	12	1	3	5	6	3
France	142	12	7	3	10	7	7	4	4	7	2	7	7	3	8	7	10	12	12	6	5	6	1	6
Turkey	41		3				2	10							3									
United Kingdom	28	10	8		5	1	4		6	4	1			4	2			2	3	3		7		
Slovenia	70			1			5			2		1		3	4	6	2	2	4		1	2		
Poland	11		1	4	1	6				6				5	1	3			8					2
Germany	66	4	2	8	2	8	10		10	10	6	12	12	12	12	10	4		6	12	10	8	3	12
Estonia	198	1		12	6		1		3	5	10	2	1		6	5	3	4	7	8	4	12	2	1
Malta	48	8	5	5	6	3	8	12	8	12	7	10	5	7	10	8	8	4	5	10	12	10	5	7
Greece	147		12		12	4	12		12				6	6		12	7	8		10	7		4	10
Denmark	177	8	12		12	4	12	6	12	12	7	10	6	6	10	12	7	8	5	10	7	10	4	10

109

2002 Eurovision 47: Tallinn, Estonia   25 May 2002

Qualification: Four automatic qualifiers (UK, Germany, Spain, France), along with the top 15 from the other participants in 2001, plus those countries which failed to qualify for the 2001 contest and Israel and Latvia by invitation.

Rank	Start	Country	Artist	Song	Writer	Composer	POINTS
1	23	Latvia	Marie N	I wanna	Marija Naumova, Marats Samauskis	Marija Naumova	176
2	20	Malta	Ira Losco	7th wonder	Gerard James Borg	Philip Vella	164
3	2	United Kingdom	Jessica Garlick	Come back	Martyn Baylay	Martyn Baylay	111
4	8	Estonia	Sahléne	Runaway	Jana Hallas	Pearu Paulus, Ilmar Laisaar, Alar Kotkas	111
5	17	France	Sandrine François	Il faut du temps	Patrick Bruel, Marie-Florence Gros	Rick Allison	104
6	1	Cyprus	One	Gimme	George Theophanous	George Theophanous	85
7	5	Spain	Rosa	Europe's living a celebration	Xasqui Ten	Toni Ten	81
8	21	Romania	Monica Anghel & Marcel Pavel	Tell me why	Mirela Fugaru	Ionel Tudor	72
9	12	Sweden	Afro-dite	Never let it go	Marcos Ubeda	Marcos Ubeda	72
10	7	Russia	Prime minister	Northern girl	Karen Kavaleryan, Evgene Fridlyand, Irina Antonyan	Kim Breitburg	55
11	6	Croatia	Vesna Pisarovic	Everything I want	Milana Vlaovic	Milana Vlaovic	44
12	10	Israel	Sarit Hadad	Light a candle	Yoav Ginai	Tzvika Pik	37
13	15	Bosnia & H	Maja Tatic	Na jastuku za dvoje	Ružica Cavic, Stevo Cvikic	Dragan Mijatovic	33
14	16	Belgium	Sergio & the Ladies	Sister	Dirk Paelinck	Mark Paelinck	33
15	22	Slovenia	Sestre	Samo ljubezen	Barbara Pešut	Robert Pešut	32
16	19	Turkey	Buket Bengisu & Saphire	Leylaklar soldu kalbinde	Sami Hodara, Figen Cakmak	Fani Hodara	29
17	4	Greece	Michalis Rakintzis	S.A.G.A.P.O.	Michalis Rakintzis	Michalis Rakintzis	27
18	3	Austria	Manuel Ortega	Say a word	Robert Pflugler	Alexander Kahr	26
19	9	FYR Macedonia	Karolina	Od nas zavisi	Vladimir Krstevski	Nikola Perevski	25
20	13	Finland	Laura	Addicted to you	Janina Frostell, Tracy Lipp	Maki Kolehmainen	24
21	18	Germany	Corinna May	I can't live without music	Bernd Meinunger	Ralph Siegel	17
22	11	Switzerland	Francine Jordi	Dans le jardin de mon âme	Francine Lehmann	Francine Lehmann	15
23	24	Lithuania	Aivaras	Happy You	Aivaras Stepukonis	Aivaras Stepukonis	12
24	14	Denmark	Malene	Tell me who you are	Michael Ronson	Michael Ronson	7

2002 Eurovision 47: Tallinn, Estonia — 25 May 2002

	Austria	Belgium	Bosnia & H	Croatia	Cyprus	Denmark	Estonia	Finland	France	FYR Macedonia	Germany	Greece	Israel	Latvia	Lithuania	Malta	Romania	Russia	Slovenia	Spain	Sweden	Switzerland	Turkey	United Kingdom	TOTAL
Cyprus	12	3		10			4	4				12		8	4	12	8	6	4	6	1			3	85
United Kingdom		6	7		1	6	6	8	1	4	8	7	5	5	8	10		1	8		2	6	2		111
Austria		5			12																	7	12		26
Greece	6	12	6	1	7				12	5	7	4	6				6	8				12		2	27
Spain			2	6	6	8	10	3			3	5	1	10	6	8	10		12		7	5			81
Croatia					5			10			4	2	2	12	7	2	2		6				8		44
Russia	3	4	10	5	3	8		1		6				3		5	12	3			12			7	55
Estonia				4				5	10								5		1			1		5	111
FYR Macedonia	5	2				1		7	3		5	1	3	3	1	3	3		7						25
Israel	4	1	12		2	10				3	2			1					7	1	10		4	1	37
Switzerland			3			3							4	4	10										15
Sweden	7			7	2	2			2				7	2	2	3		7	2	3					72
Finland						4					6	3	7	7	5		4		3	1	6			5	24
Denmark	1	10	8			5			7	8		6	10			4	1	2		8	3	10	10	4	7
Bosnia & H				3		12	7	2	6	10	10	8	8		3		7	5	10	1	8	3	3		33
Belgium	8	7	4	12	10				5	12	1		10			6		12	10	8	4	4	5	12	33
France	2		1		8			2	4	2			8						5	2		2	7	6	104
Germany	10	8	5	8		7	12	6	8	7	12	10	12		12	7		10	5	12	5	8	6	8	17
Turkey				2			2							6				4							29
Malta																									164
Romania																									72
Slovenia																									32
Latvia																									176
Lithuania																									12

2003 Eurovision 48: Riga, Latvia — 24 May 2003

Qualification: Four automatic qualifiers (UK, Germany, Spain, France), along with the top 15 from the other participants in 2002, plus those countries which failed to qualify for the 2002 contest and new entrant Ukraine.

Rank	Start	Country	Artist	Song	Writer	Composer	POINTS
1	4	Turkey	Sertab Erener	Everyway that I can	Demir Demirkan	Sertab Erener, Demir Demirkan	167
2	22	Belgium	Urban Trad	Sanomi	Yves Barbieux	Yves Barbieux	165
3	11	Russia	t.A.T.u.	Ne ver', ne boisia	Valeriy Polienko	Mars Lasar, Ivan Pogomalov	164
4	18	Norway	Jostein Hasselgård	I'm not afraid to move on	Arve Furset	Arve Furset	123
5	25	Sweden	Fame	Give me your love	Calle Kindbom, Carl Lösnitz	Calle Kindbom, Carl Lösnitz	107
6	2	Austria	Alf Poier	Weil der Mensch zählt	Alf Poier	Alf Poier	101
7	20	Poland	Ich Troje	Keine Grenzen - Zadnych granic	André Franke, J Horn-Bernges, Michal Wisniewski, Jacek Lagwa	André Franke, J Horn-Bernges, Michal Wisniewski, Jacek Lagwa	90
8	1	Iceland	Birgitta	Open your heart (Segðu mér allt)	Sveinbjörn Baldvinsson, Birgitta Haukdal	Hallgrímur Óskarsson	81
9	12	Spain	Beth	Dime	Amaya Martinez	Jesús-Maria Pérez	81
10	24	Romania	Nicola	Don't break my heart	Nicola	Mihai Alexandru	73
11	10	Germany	Lou	Let's get happy	Bernd Meinunger	Ralph Siegel	53
12	3	Ireland	Mickey Harte	We've got the world	Keith Molloy, Martin Brannigan	Keith Molloy, Martin Brannigan	53
13	14	Netherlands	Esther Hart	One more night	Alan Michael, Tjeerd van Zanen	Alan Michael, Tjeerd van Zanen	45
14	16	Ukraine	Olexandr	Hasta la vista	Mirit Shem-Ur	Tzvika Pik	30
15	8	Croatia	Claudia Beni	Više nisam tvoja	Andrej Babich	Andrej Babich	29
16	6	Bosnia & H	Mija Martina	Ne brini	Arjana Kunštek	Ines Prajo	27
17	17	Greece	Mando	Never let you go	Terry Siganos	Mando	25
18	19	France	Louisa Baileche	Monts et merveilles	Hocine Hallaf	Hocine Hallaf	19
19	13	Israel	Lior Narkis	Words for love	Yossi Gispan	Yoni Ro'en	17
20	9	Cyprus	Stelios Constantas	Feeling alive	Stelios Constantas	Stelios Constantas	15
21	23	Estonia	Ruffus	Eighties coming back	Vaiko Eplik	Vaiko Eplik	14
22	7	Portugal	Rita Guerra	Deixa-me sonhar	Paulo Martins	Paulo Martins	13
23	26	Slovenia	Karmen	Nanana	Karmen Stavec	Martin Stibernik	7
24	21	Latvia	F.L.Y.	Hello from Mars	Martin Freiman, Lauris Raynix	Martin Freiman, Lauris Raynix	5
25	5	Malta	Lynn Chircop	To dream again	Cynthia Sammut	Alfred Zammit	4
26	15	United Kingdom	Jemini	Cry baby	Martin Isherwood	Martin Isherwood	0

2003 Eurovision 48: Riga, Latvia — 24 May 2003

Contestant	Austria	Belgium	Bosnia & H	Croatia	Cyprus	Estonia	France	Germany	Greece	Iceland	Ireland	Israel	Latvia	Malta	Netherlands	Norway	Poland	Portugal	Romania	Russia	Slovenia	Spain	Sweden	Turkey	Ukraine	United Kingdom	TOTAL
Iceland	12	3		6	5	1	1	1	2		7		3	12	6	12	1				4		7	8	4		81
Austria	7	2	5	5	4	6	10	2	2	10			4	5	8	8		10			7	8	6	6		8	101
Ireland	5	1	12	4	7		6	10	7	2			1		12	6	2	7	10		2	3	8	5	1	12	53
Turkey		12	12	10	8			5		3	3	7		4		10		8			10				2	7	167
Malta																		1									4
Bosnia & H	7		8				6		1		3													12	3		27
Portugal											2											2					13
Croatia	5		6						12		6	1		2							8			3			29
Cyprus	1										4																15
Germany						2	7						2	3	2		5	4	1			4	10			4	53
Russia	8	7	3	12	10	12		8	10	8	4	10	12	1	1	2	4	12	7	7	12	6	2	3	12		164
Spain	1	10		7	6		8		5	4		12			5				5	6	1	1	4			4	81
Israel									3	6						5				5							17
Netherlands	8		2								5		5	7						10			5			1	45
United Kingdom																											0
Ukraine						3					1	4	5			1	10		2	8							30
Greece	2	6			12	10	3	5	6	12	12	3	7	6			6	5	3	1	5		12	4	7	6	25
Norway	10	5	8			10	5	7	8	7			8	10	4		3	2	6	4		5	3		8	2	123
France						4		12	4	1						4			4								19
Poland					3	8	12	6		5	10	8	10		10	3		6	8	3	3	12	3	7	10	5	90
Latvia						5					8	6		8		1				2							5
Belgium	4		10																			12				5	165
Estonia		4	1														8						1	1		3	14
Romania	6		7	1	2	7		4				6	6		6	1	7	3	12	12	6	10	5		6		73
Sweden	3		4	2	1							5				7				2		7			5	10	107
Slovenia			4	3																							7

2004 Eurovision 49: Istanbul, Turkey

Semi-final: 12 May 2004

Rank	Start	Country	Artist	Song	Writer	Composer	POINTS
1Q	20	Serbia & Mont	Željko Joksimović	Lane moje	Leontina Vukmanović	Željko Joksimović	263
2Q	11	Ukraine	Ruslana	Wild dances	Alexander Ksenofontov	Ruslana Lyzchicko	256
3Q	10	Greece	Sakis Rouvas	Shake it	Nektarios Tirakis	Nikos Terzis	238
4Q	13	Albania	Anjeza Shahini	The image of you	Agim Doçit	Edmon Zhulali	167
5Q	14	Cyprus	Lisa Andreas	Stronger every minute	Mike Konnaris	Mike Konnaris	149
6Q	22	Netherlands	Re-union	Without you	Angeline van Otterdijk	Ed van Otterdijk	146
7Q	21	Bosnia & H	Deen	In the Disco	Vesna Pisarovic	Vesna Pisarovic	133
8Q	8	Malta	Julie & Ludwig	On again...off again	Gerard James Borg	Philip Vella	74
9Q	18	Croatia	Ivan Mikulic	You are the only one	Duško Gruborovic & Marina Madrinic	Ivan Mikulic	72
10Q	15	FYR Macedonia	Tose Proeski	Life	Tose Proeski	Tose Proeski	71
11	5	Israel	David D'or	Le'ha'amin	David D'or	David D'or	57
12	17	Estonia	Neiokõsõ	Tii	Aapo Ilves	Priit Pajusaar, Glen Pilvre	57
13	19	Denmark	Tomas Thordarson	Shame on you	Ivar Lind Greiner	Ivar Lind Greiner	56
14	1	Finland	Jari Sillanpää	Takes 2 to tango	Jari Sillanpää	Mika Toivanen	51
15	7	Portugal	Sofia	Foi Magia	Paulo Neves	Paulo Neves	38
16	12	Lithuania	Linas ir Simona	What's happened to your love	Camden MS	Michalis Antonio, Linas Adomaitis	26
17	4	Latvia	Fomins & Kleins	Dziesma par laimi	Tomass Kleins	Guntars Racs	23
18	6	Andorra	Marta Roure	Jugarem a estimar-nos	Jofre Bardagí	Jofre Bardagí	12
19	2	Belarus	Aleksandra & Konstantin	My Galileo	Aleksey Solomaha	Aleksandra & Konstantin	10
20	9	Monaco	Maryon	Notre planète	Philippe Bosco	Philippe Bosco	10
21	16	Slovenia	Platin	Stay forever	Diana Lecnik	Simon Gomilsek	5
22	3	Switzerland	Piero Esteriore & the Music Stars	Celebrate	Greg Manning	Greg Manning	0

2004 Eurovision 49: Istanbul, Turkey — Semi-final: 12 May 2004

	Albania	Andorra	Austria	Belarus	Belgium	Bosnia & H	Croatia	Cyprus	Denmark	Estonia	Finland	France	FYR Macedonia	Germany	Greece	Iceland	Ireland	Israel	Latvia	Lithuania	Malta	Monaco	Netherlands	Norway	Poland	Portugal	Romania	Russia	Serbia & Mont	Slovenia	Spain	Sweden	Switzerland	Turkey	Ukraine	United Kingdom	TOTAL
Finland	7				1			6		7			2		5	3						6		3							3	8					51
Belarus				4						2						1				2															5		10
Switzerland																						2															0
Latvia				3	2			2	2	5	2				3		4	2		6	6										4			4		2	23
Israel	5	3	1											1									2						3		4						57
Andorra																															12						12
Portugal		12			4			4							3							1									6		7				38
Malta	6	5		1		4	1		4				4			2	1						3			4			3	1					2	5	74
Monaco	2	4								10					1																						10
Greece	12	8	5	8	10	5	6	12	3	4	5		7	10		6	2	12	6	8	12	4	6	5		8			10	4	7	4	3	12	10	12	238
Ukraine	3	10	4	12	8	7	8	8	6	12	8		8	6		10	10	10	10	12	10	5	7	7		12			8	8	10	6	2	8		7	256
Lithuania			2	2				7							2		3	1	8		3																26
Albania		6	7		5	6	7	1	7	1	6		12	8	8	4	5	6	5		8	3	5	8		2	6		6	5	2	7	10	6	1	6	167
Cyprus	2	6	6	6	6		2		5	6	7			4	12	8	8	4	3	4	5	12	10	4		3	1		2	3	1	3	1	5	7	10	149
FYR Macedonia	8		2			8	5		1					3	4			3			1		1				4		12	6		2	5	3	6		71
Slovenia						1	3						1																								5
Estonia	1									3	12			5		7		5	12	10	2		4	1		5			4			1	6	3	3	1	57
Croatia			8	7		10		3	3		1		6		7			8	1	3	4	7		6		1			5	7		5	6		8		72
Denmark						3					4					12					2	8	4				2					12		1			56
Serbia & Mont	4	1	12	10	7	12	12	10	10	3	10		10	12	10		6	8	4	1	4	7	12	6		10	10			12	8	12	12	7	12	8	263
Bosnia & H	10	10		5	3		10		12	8			5	7		5	7		8			8	8	12					7	10	5	10	8	10		4	133
Netherlands		7	3	5	12	2	4	5	8	8	3		3	2	4		12	7	2	5	7	8		2		6	3		1	2	5	4	4	2	4	3	146

Note: France, Poland & Russia chose not to vote in the semi-final

115

2004 Eurovision 49: Istanbul, Turkey

Final: 12 May 2004

Final qualification rules:
Top 10 countries from the 2003 Final
Top 10 countries from the 2004 Semi-Final

Automatic qualification:
United Kingdom, France, Germany, Spain

Rank	Start	Country	Artist	Song	Writer	Composer	POINTS
1	10	Ukraine	Ruslana	Wild dances	Alexander Ksenofontov	Ruslana Lyzchicko	280
2	5	Serbia & Mont	Željko Joksimović	Lane moje	Leontina Vukmanović	Željko Joksimoviæ	263
3	16	Greece	Sakis Rouvas	Shake it	Nektarios Tirakis	Nikos Terzis	252
4	22	Turkey	Athena	For Real	Gökhan & Hakan Özoğuz	Gökhan & Hakan Özoğuz	195
5	21	Cyprus	Lisa Andreas	Stronger every minute	Mike Konnaris	Mike Konnaris	170
6	24	Sweden	Lena Philipsson	It Hurts	Thomas Orup Eriksson	Thomas Orup Eriksson	170
7	9	Albania	Anjeza Shahini	The image of you	Agim Doçit	Edmon Zhulali	106
8	8	Germany	Max (Maximilian Mutzke)	Can't Wait Until Tonight	Stefan Raab	Stefan Raab	93
9	12	Bosnia & H	Deen	In the Disco	Vesna Pisarovic	Vesna Pisarovic	91
10	1	Spain	Ramón	Para Llenarme De Ti	Kike Santander	Kike Santander	87
11	14	Russia	Julia Savicheva	Believe Me	Brenda Loring	Maxim Fadeev	67
12	6	Malta	Julie & Ludwig	On again...off again	Gerard James Borg	Philip Vella	50
13	11	Croatia	Ivan Mikulic	You are the only one	Duško Gruborovic & Marina Madrinic	Ivan Mikulic	50
14	15	FYR Macedonia	Tose Proeski	Life	Tose Proeski	Tose Proeski	47
15	4	France	Jonatan Cerrada	A Chaque Pas	Jonatan Cerrada, Benjamin Robbins, Steve Balsamo	Jonatan Cerrada, Benjamin Robbins, Steve Balsamo	40
16	20	United Kingdom	James Fox	Hold On To Our Love	Gary Miller and Tim Woodcock	Gary Miller and Tim Woodcock	29
17	19	Poland	Blue Cafe	Love Song	Tatiana Okupnik	Pawel Rurak-Sokal	27
18	23	Romania	Sanda Ladosi	I Admit	Irina Gligor	George Popa	18
19	17	Iceland	Jónsi	Heaven	Magnús Þór Sigmundsson	Sveinn Rúnar Sigurðsson	16
20	7	Netherlands	Re-union	Without you	Angeline van Otterdijk	Ed van Otterdijk	11
21	2	Austria	Tie Break	Du Bist	Peter Zimmermann	Peter Zimmermann	9
22	13	Belgium	Xandee	1 Life	Dirk Paelinck	Marc Paelinck	7
23	18	Ireland	Chris Doran	If My World Stopped Turning	Brian McFadden, Jonathan Shorten	Brian McFadden, Jonathan Shorten	7
24	3	Norway	Knut Anders Sørum	High	Dan Attlerud	Thomas Thörnholm, Lars Andersson	3

2004 Eurovision 49: Istanbul, Turkey — Final: 12 May 2004

Order votes announced	Albania 2	Andorra 1	Austria 3	Belarus 6	Belgium 5	Bosnia & H 4	Croatia 18	Cyprus 9	Denmark 11	Estonia 12	Finland 14	France 15	FYR Macedonia 25	Germany 10	Greece 17	Iceland 21	Ireland 19	Israel 20	Latvia 23	Lithuania 22	Malta 26	Monaco 24	Netherlands 27	Norway 28	Poland 29	Portugal 30	Romania 31	Russia 32	Serbia & Mont 8	Slovenia 34	Spain 13	Sweden 33	Switzerland 7	Turkey 35	Ukraine 36	United Kingdom 16	TOTAL
Spain		12						7							3	1					3	3	4			12	5						6	2			87
Austria																																					9
Norway																																3					3
France	1	7			10																					2		4			4						40
Serbia & Mont	7	2	12	7	3	12	12	10	7	1	10	10	10	2	8	7	3	7	5	2	6	1	10	6	5	7	8	4		12	6	12	12	8	12	3	263
Malta	3	6	5		6	4	2		1	6		4	3		1		6	4	6	4			3	1	3	7	1	10	8	4		3		5	1	2	50
Netherlands					6					3											2	12				1											11
Germany	2	10		1		3	1		4	2	3	7	12		10	4	4	7	1	1	10	7	3	3	6	8	4		8	3	12	7	10	5		4	93
Albania		5		8		4	6	8	5		8	1	8	5	7	12	2	4	6		8	6	1	3		10	1	5	5	4	6	10	7	6	1	1	106
Ukraine	5	10	4	10	5	6	8	8		12		2	12	6		4	2	12	1	12	10	6	7	7	12	10	6	12	10	8	8	10	7	12		5	280
Croatia			3	5		10			8		1		5	1			7		12		8	4	1		8			5	5	5		8	3		7		50
Bosnia & H	10		7				10						4									4	2	10					6	10	8		5				91
Belgium		1						1													1		5														7
Russia				12		8	5	6		8	4		7	7	2			6	10	8	12		6						1	7	7	4	1	4	10		67
FYR Macedonia	6				8	5	7	12				6					5	10	7	10	1	10		2	7	6	12		12	6			4		3		47
Greece	12	8	2	6	8				3	5	6	6	7	7		6	5	10	7	12	12	10	6	2	7			7	7	6	7	4	4	10	8	12	252
Iceland							5		2	2	2											5		5				2									16
Ireland																		1														1				7	7
Poland								2		4						3			3	7	4		8	4			2	1		1	1	1			5		27
United Kingdom		4	6	1	4		4		6	7	7	5		4	4	2	8	2	4	5	7	2	8	4		3	3	6	3		3	2	1				29
Cyprus		3	8	4	2	7	4		10			12	6	8	12	10	10	2	2	3	4		12	8	4		10	8	2	1	3	6	2	1	4	10	170
Turkey	8		8	3	12		3		12	10	5	3	2	12	6	5	1	8	8	6	5	8		8	8	5			2	2	2	5	8		6	6	195
Romania								3																		4					10						18
Sweden	4	5	1	4	2	2	7	5	12	10	12	3		3		8	12	5	8	6	5			12	10	5	7	3	4	2	5		4	3	2	8	170

117

2005 Eurovision 50: Kiev, Ukraine

Semi-final: 19 May 2005

Rank	Start	Country	Artist	Song	Writer	Composer	POINTS
1Q	14	Romania	Luminita Anghel & Sistem	Let me try	Cristian Faur	Cristian Faur	235
2Q	4	Moldova	Zdob si Zdub	Boonika bate toba	Zdob si Zdub	Zdob si Zdub	207
3Q	24	Denmark	Jakob Sveistrup	Talking to you	Jacob Launbjerg & Andreas Mørck	Jacob Launbjerg & Andreas Mørck	185
4Q	20	Croatia	Boris Novkovic & Lado members	Vukovi umiru sami	Boris Novkoviæ	Franjo Valentiæ	169
5Q	15	Hungary	NOX	Forogj világ	Attila Valla	Szabolcs Harmath	167
6Q	13	Norway	Wig Wam	In my dreams	Trond "Teeny" Holter	Trond "Teeny" Holter	164
7Q	7	Israel	Shiri Maymon	Hasheket shenish'ar	Eyal Shachar & Pini Aronbayev	Pini Aronbayev	158
8Q	19	Switzerland	Vanilla Ninja	Cool vibes	David Brandes	David Brandes	114
9Q	17	FYR Macedonia	Martin Vucic	Make my day	Ognen Nedelkovski	Dragan Vucić	97
10Q	5	Latvia	Walter & Kazha	The war is not over	Martins Freimanis	Martins Freimanis	85
11	25	Poland	Ivan & Delfin	Czarna dziewczyna	Ivan Komarenko & Pawel Radziszewski	Lukasz Lazer	81
12	23	Slovenia	Omar Naber	Stop	Urša Vlašič	Omar Naber	69
13	8	Belarus	Angelica Agurbash	Love me tonight	Nektarios Tyrakis	Nikos Terzis	67
14	22	Ireland	Donna and Joseph McCaul	Love?	Karl Broderick	Karl Broderick	53
15	9	Netherlands	Glennis Grace	My impossible dream	Bruce Smith	Robert D. Fisher	53
16	10	Iceland	Selma	If I had your love	Linda Thompson	Thorvaldur Bjarni Thorvaldsson, Vignir Snær Vigfússon	52
17	3	Portugal	2B	Amar	Jose da Ponte, Alexandre Honrado, Ernesto Leite	Jose da Ponte, Alexandre Honrado, Ernesto Leite	51
18	16	Finland	Geir Rönning	Why	Steven Stewart	Mika Toivanen	50
19	21	Bulgaria	Kaffe	Lorraine	Vesselin Ivanov, Orlin Pavlov	Vesselin Ivanov	49
20	12	Estonia	Suntribe	Let's get loud	Sven Lõhmus	Sven Lõhmus	31
21	1	Austria	Global.Kryner	Y así	Christof Spörk	Christof Spörk, Edi Köhldorfer	30
22	11	Belgium	Nuno Resende	Le grand soir	Alec Mansion & Frédéric Zeitoun	Alec Mansion & Frédéric Zeitoun	29
23	18	Andorra	Marian van de Wal	La mirada interior	Rafa Tanit, Daniel Aragay & Rafa Fernández	Rafa Tanit	27
24	6	Monaco	Lise Darly	Tout de moi	Phil Bosco	Didier Fabre	22
25	2	Lithuania	Laura and the Lovers	Little by little	Billy Butt	Bobby Ljunggren	17

118

2005 Eurovision 50: Kiev, Ukraine — Semi-final: 19 May 2005

To → / From ↓	Albania	Andorra	Austria	Belarus	Belgium	Bosnia & H	Bulgaria	Croatia	Cyprus	Denmark	Estonia	Finland	France	FYR Macedonia	Germany	Greece	Hungary	Iceland	Ireland	Israel	Latvia	Lithuania	Malta	Moldova	Monaco	Netherlands	Norway	Poland	Portugal	Romania	Russia	Serbia & Mont	Slovenia	Spain	Sweden	Switzerland	Turkey	Ukraine	United Kingdom	TOTAL
Austria	5	7														1																	10			6				30
Lithuania																					8																		4	17
Portugal	3		8	10	10	6	6	4	8		5	3	12	10	12		6	8	3	10	10	10	12				1	6	8	12	12	6	7	1		12	12	12		51
Moldova				7	4	6		7	2	5	10		5				6	2	6	6		12	12	2			3		4		1	3	6	5			6	2	5	207
Latvia													10																						7					85
Monaco	10																																							22
Israel	7	12		12	3		4		3	4		1	8	1	3	6	5		7		3	2	6	5	12	10		4	6	8	8	3		4		3	6	5	6	158
Belarus					12		12		7					6		8						3	7		1			1			10						3	4		67
Netherlands	1									6			2						4	2			8	10	8		8		12	1				2		2				53
Iceland										10		6	7						1		12			3		6									7					52
Belgium																						5		1			8		12				2							29
Estonia										3							1	12	10	7	6	6	3	8		2			1				3							31
Norway	2		4	5	8	5	3	1	4	12	6	12	6	2	7	4	12	5	8	7			10	3	7	2	7	7	1	7	3	4	1	12	8	5	2	6	7	164
Romania	4		10	3	6	3	8	8	12	7	1	4	4	5	4	12	8	7	8	12	6		2	1		8	6	8	10		7	5	4		5	4	7	1	8	235
Hungary	1		7	4		3	7	8	6	1	4	5		4	2	5		7		8	5		10	12	7	1	6	12	7	10		8			3	1	8	10	1	167
Finland	3						1			8	8		7		4				1					4		3	10								10					50
FYR Macedonia	12		4			10							1		2											7				4		10	8		1					97
Andorra	6																																	10						27
Switzerland	10		1	8	2	2	3	3	5	2			6	3	6	3	3	6	2	3	7	8	1	6	2	4	2	5	2	2	2	2	5	6	4					114
Croatia		12		1	8	12	8				12	7	4	12	10	7	8	4	10		4	4		7	5		4	3	3	6	2	12	12		6	10			12	169
Bulgaria	4		12											8						1			5									1					5			49
Ireland		2							10		2						10	1							4	4	2	2	5	5		7		6	6	10				53
Slovenia	8		3		7	4		5	1			7		7	5	2	2	10	12		2	2						10	5	3	6					7	4	3	12	69
Denmark		8	6	2	5	8	6		10		7	8	5		8	10	7	10			2	7	4	6	10	12	12	10	5	3	4			8	12	7		3	10	185
Poland			5					2	1				3		5	8	4	3		1	1	1		7		5	5				5	7	12	7	2		1	8		75

2005 Eurovision 50: Kiev, Ukraine

Final: 21 May 2005

Final qualification rules:
Top 10 countries from the 2004 Final
Top 10 countries from the 2005 Semi-Final

Automatic qualification:
United Kingdom, France, Germany, Spain

Rank	Start	Country	Artist	Song	Writer	Composer	POINTS
1	19	Greece	Helena Paparizou	My number one	Christos Dantis & Natalia Germanou	Christos Dantis	230
2	3	Malta	Chiara	Angel	Chiara Siracusa	Chiara Siracusa	192
3	4	Romania	Luminita Anghel & Sistem	Let me try	Cristian Faur	Cristian Faur	158
4	11	Israel	Shiri Maymon	Hasheket shenish'ar	Eyal Shachar & Pini Aronbayev	Pini Aronbayev	154
5	23	Latvia	Walter & Kazha	The war is not over	Martins Freimanis	Martins Freimanis	153
6	7	Moldova	Zdob si Zdub	Boonika bate toba	Zdob si Zdub	Zdob si Zdub	148
7	12	Serbia & Mont	No Name	Zauvijek moja	Milan Peric	Slaven Knezovic	137
8	22	Switzerland	Vanilla Ninja	Cool vibes	David Brandes	David Brandes	128
9	5	Norway	Wig Wam	In my dreams	Trond "Teeny" Holter	Trond "Teeny" Holter	125
10	13	Denmark	Jakob Sveistrup	Talking to you	Jacob Launbjerg & Andreas Mørck	Jacob Launbjerg & Andreas Mørck	125
11	18	Croatia	Boris Novkovic & Lado members	Vukovi umiru sami	Boris Novkoviæ	Franjo Valentiæ	115
12	1	Hungary	NOX	Forogj világ	Attila Valla	Szabolcs Harmath	97
13	6	Turkey	Gülseren	Rimi rimi ley	Göksan Arman	Erdinç Tunç	92
14	21	Bosnia & H	Feminnem	Call me	Andrej Babic	Andrej Babic	79
15	20	Russia	Natalia Podolskaya	Nobody hurt no one	M.S. Applegate, J.P. Chase	Victor Drobysh	57
16	8	Albania	Ledina Celo	Tomorrow I go	Pandi Laço	Adi Hila	53
17	15	FYR Macedonia	Martin Vucic	Make my day	Ognen Nedelkovski	Dragan Vucić	52
18	9	Cyprus	Constantinos Christoforou	Ela ela	Constantinos Christoforou	Constantinos Christoforou	46
19	16	Ukraine	Greenjolly	Razom nas bahato	Greenjolly	Greenjolly	30
20	14	Sweden	Martin Stenmarck	Las Vegas	Niklas Edberger, Johan Fransson, Tim Larsson & Tobias Lundgren	Niklas Edberger, Johan Fransson, Tim Larsson & Tobias Lundgren	30
21	10	Spain	Son de sol	Brujería	Alfredo Panebianco	Alfredo Panebianco	28
22	2	United Kingdom	Javine	Touch my fire	Javine Hilton & John Themis	Javine Hilton & John Themis	18
23	24	France	Ortal	Chacun pense à soi	Saad Tabainet, Ortal	Saad Tabainet, Ortal	11
24	17	Germany	Gracia	Run & hide	John O'Flynn	David Brandes, Jane Tempest	4

2005 Eurovision 50: Kiev, Ukraine — Final: 21 May 2005

Order votes announced	Albania	Andorra	Austria	Belarus	Belgium	Bosnia & H	Bulgaria	Croatia	Cyprus	Denmark	Estonia	Finland	France	FYR Macedonia	Germany	Greece	Hungary	Iceland	Ireland	Israel	Latvia	Lithuania	Malta	Moldova	Monaco	Netherlands	Norway	Poland	Portugal	Romania	Russia	Serbia & Mont	Slovenia	Spain	Sweden	Switzerland	Turkey	Ukraine	United Kingdom	TOTAL
Hungary	23	11	1	5	8	36	12	33	24	28	9	10	39	30	32	34	16	7	13	26	38	2	18	22	4	6	20	15	3	19	35	27	14	25	29	37	21	31	17	97
United Kingdom		6		2	2	1	5	6	7		3		3	1		2		6		8	3							10	2	8	3	6		5			6	2		18
Malta	4		5	5	8			4	6	10	4	8	7		8	8	5	4	10	10	5	2		7	5	5	10			2			1	7	6	3	1			192
Romania	5	7	6	1	7	2			8	3	8		5	2			10	5	5	12		5	7	7	4	3	6	7	12		12			12	2		8	10	5	158
Norway		2		4	3	3	8		3	12	8	12			12	4	10	12	4	1	6	5	5	3	4	1		8			10	3	4	3	8		4	6	5	125
Turkey	8	7		2	10	8	3	10		8			12	4									2			12				3	10	2	3	4		6			1	92
Moldova			2	7	1	4	6		2	12	6		2	5	1	7	4	8	6	4	8	10		7	4			3	10	12	10	2	3	4		10	7	12	2	148
Albania		3				5		2					1	12	10	10							12									8					2			53
Cyprus	7						10						4			12													8	1		1							3	46
Spain		12																																		4				28
Israel	3	8	1	8	6				4	5	1	5	10	10	5	6	8	1	6		2	3	8	6	12	7	5		5	7	1			6	1	1	3	7	7	154
Serbia & Mont	6	12	3		4	10	4	12	10			2	6	12	3		2	2	2		1	4	3	1	6	4	12	1		6	4		10		4	12		3		137
Denmark	3						7	8		7	5	6		6	6		6	10	7	3	4	4	3	5	10	8	12	5	1					10	10	2	5		8	125
Sweden	10					7	7										1		1				1		3	1		12	7		2	7	5							30
FYR Macedonia				12																				8										1						52
Ukraine			10																					2	2			12												30
Germany																																								4
Croatia	2		8		12	12								8	2		7	1	2		7	6			7	2	2	2	3	5	1	10	12	8	1	8				115
Greece	12	4	4	6		6			12	2	7		8	7	12		12	2	2			1	6	4		10	4	1		10	4	12	2		4	7	12	8	12	230
Russia											7	7				1					10	7		10														4		57
Bosnia & H			10					10		4				3					1						8	6						4	8							79
Switzerland		1		10				3	4	1	12	10			4	3	3		3	2	12	8	1				3	6			7	4	8	8	7					128
Latvia		10		6	5			7	1	6	10	4			7	1	1		12	6		12	10	12	8		8	4	6		5	12	2		5	5		5	6	153
France	1	5																		5													7		3			1		11

2006 Eurovision 51: Athens, Greece — Semi-final: 18 May 2006

Rank	Start	Country	Artist	Song	Writer	Composer	POINTS
1Q	16	Finland	Lordi	Hard rock hallelujah	Mr. Lordi	Mr. Lordi	292
2Q	22	Bosnia & H	Hari Mata Hari	Lejla	Fahrudin Pecikoza & Dejan Ivanović	Željko Joksimović	267
3Q	13	Russia	Dima Bilan	Never let you go	Karen Kavaleryan, Irina Antonyan	Alexandr Lunyov	217
4Q	20	Sweden	Carola	Invincible	Thomas G:son, Carola Häggkvist	Thomas G:son, Bobby Ljunggren, Henrik Wikström	214
5Q	18	Lithuania	LT United	We are the winners	Andrius Mamontovas, Viktoras Diawara	Andrius Mamontovas, Saulius Urbonavicius	163
6Q	1	Armenia	André	Without your love	Catherine Bekian	Armen Martirosyan	150
7Q	15	Ukraine	Tina Karol	Show me your love	Tina Karol	Tina Karol	146
8Q	14	Turkey	Sibel Tüzün	Superstar	Sibel Tüzün	Sibel Tüzün	91
9Q	8	Ireland	Brian Kennedy	Every song is a cry for love	Brian Kennedy	Brian Kennedy	79
10Q	11	FYR Macedonia	Elena Risteska	Ninanajna	Rade Vrcakovski	Darko Dimitrov	76
11	12	Poland	Ich Troje	Follow my heart	Michael Wisnieski, Real McCoy, William Lennox	André Franke	70
12	7	Belgium	Kate Ryan	Je t'adore	Kate Ryan, Niklas Bergwall, Niclas Kings, Lisa Greene	Kate Ryan, Niklas Bergwall, Niclas Kings, Lisa Greene	69
13	23	Iceland	Silvia Night	Congratulations	Ágústa Eva Erlendsdóttir & Gaukur Úlfarsson	Þorvaldur Bjarni Þorvaldsson	62
14	6	Albania	Luiz Ejlli	Zjarr e ftohtë	Floran Kondi	Klodian Qafoku	58
15	9	Cyprus	Annet Artani	Why angels cry	Peter Yiannakis	Peter Yiannakis	57
16	3	Slovenia	Anžej Dežan	Mr. Nobody	Ursa Vlašić	Matjaz Vlašić	49
17	2	Bulgaria	Mariana Popova	Let me cry	Elina Gavrilova	Dani Milev	36
18	21	Estonia	Sandra	Through my window	Jana Hallas	Pearu Paulus, Ilmar Laisaar, Alar Kotkas	28
19	19	Portugal	Nonstop	Coisas de nada	José Manuel Afonso, Elvis Veiguinha	José Manuel Afonso, Elvis Veiguinha	26
20	17	Netherlands	Treble	Amambanda	Treble	Treble	22
21	10	Monaco	Séverine Ferrer	La coco-dance	J. Woodfeel, Iren Bo	J. Woodfeel, Iren Bo	14
22	5	Belarus	Polina Smolova	Mum	Andrey Kostiugov	Sergey Sukhomlin	10
23	4	Andorra	Jennifer	Sense tu	Joan Antoni Rechi	Rafael Artesero Herrero	8

2006 Eurovision 51: Athens, Greece — Semi-final: 18 May 2006

	Albania	Andorra	Armenia	Belarus	Belgium	Bosnia & H	Bulgaria	Croatia	Cyprus	Denmark	Estonia	Finland	France	FYR Macedonia	Germany	Greece	Iceland	Ireland	Israel	Latvia	Lithuania	Malta	Moldova	Monaco	Netherlands	Norway	Poland	Portugal	Romania	Russia	Serbia & Mont	Slovenia	Spain	Sweden	Switzerland	Turkey	Ukraine	United Kingdom	TOTAL
Armenia	3	6		7	12		8		12				12	12	7	10			10				2		12		3		2	12			12	3	3	10	7	3	150
Bulgaria	8	2	3	7					8				4	6		3												1					5			1			36
Slovenia	7	5	2	2	3	7		6				1		3					4			5	3	3							7						2		49
Andorra		12																														8							8
Belarus			1			5		7						12		7		5												6							1		10
Albania		8	7						1	3	3	3	3		3		4				2	7		6	7		4	2		2		1	2	2	10	3		2	58
Belgium	7		3	4						5	6	4					2	5	5	4	4	6	1	7	3	6	2	4		1	1	5	2	5	2				69
Ireland	1			12	3						2											4		10			1		4		1	3		1	1		3	8	79
Cyprus	4	7					2	8					8		2	12																			1			7	57
Monaco				1																		4		10			1												14
FYR Macedonia	12	3	8	10		10							2		6	2	3	7	2	3	8	1	4		2	2			1		10	8	4		6				76
Poland			3	8	4	3							10		5	5	6	4	12	12	12	8	12	2	1	4		7	7		6	4		7	8		10	1	70
Russia			4	12	2	12								2	8		5	3	3	6	6	3	10		10	1	8	10	10	5	5	2	3	12		4	10		217
Turkey	6				8												1	10	8	8	10	10	5				6	8	8		8	10	10				12		91
Ukraine			10	8	10	4						8	5	4	12	4	8	3	7	10	1	3	6	4	6	8	6	10	5	10	5	2	3	7		7		12	146
Finland	10	2	4	8	4	12								1	1	1	12	10	1	5	12	10	7		5	5	12	10	8	8	8	10	10	12	8	6	12	12	292
Netherlands	2	5		6	7	2			3																											5	6	10	22
Lithuania					5	6			4			8	7		12		8					12	7	8	4	10	10	5	3	4	3	6			5	2	5		163
Portugal	12		7																	10				5							4	7	7	4	7				26
Sweden	5	8		5	5	6			5			10			10		7	1	1	7		2	7	5	8	12	7	12	6	3	4	7	7		7	12	4	6	214
Estonia			5	3								5																						8					28
Bosnia & H	10	1	3		6							12		10			7	6		1	3	2	8	12	4	12	5	6	12	7	12	12	1	10	12	12	8	4	267
Iceland						1						7	1					2		1	7			1		7		3			2		6	6				5	62

2006 Eurovision 51: Athens, Greece

Final: 20 May 2006

Final qualification rules:
Top 10 countries from the 2005 Final
Top 10 countries from the 2006 Semi-Final

Automatic qualification:
United Kingdom, France, Germany, Spain

Rank	Start	Country	Artist	Song	Writer	Composer	POINTS
1	17	Finland	Lordi	Hard rock hallelujah	Mr. Lordi	Mr. Lordi	292
2	10	Russia	Dima Bilan	Never let you go	Karen Kavaleryan, Irina Antonyan	Alexandr Lunyov	248
3	13	Bosnia & H	Hari Mata Hari	Lejla	Fahrudin Pecikoza & Dejan Ivanović	Željko Joksimović	229
4	12	Romania	Mihai Traistariu	Tornero	Cristian Hriscu, Mihaela Deac	Eduard Cîrcotă	172
5	22	Sweden	Carola	Invincible	Thomas G:son, Carola Häggkvist	Thomas G:son, Bobby Ljunggren, Henrik Wikström	170
6	14	Lithuania	LT United	We are the winners	Andrius Mamontovas, Viktoras Diawara	Andrius Mamontovas, Saulius Urbonavicius	162
7	18	Ukraine	Tina Karol	Show me your love	Tina Karol	Tina Karol	145
8	24	Armenia	André	Without your love	Catherine Bekian	Armen Martirosyan	129
9	16	Greece	Anna Vissi	Everything	Anna Vissi	Nikos Karvelas	128
10	21	Ireland	Brian Kennedy	Every song is a cry for love	Brian Kennedy	Brian Kennedy	93
11	23	Turkey	Sibel Tüzün	Superstar	Sibel Tüzün	Sibel Tüzün	91
12	20	Croatia	Severina	Moja štikla	Severina Vučković	Boris Novković, Franjo Valentić	56
13	11	FYR Macedonia	Elena Risteska	Ninanajna	Rade Vrcakovski	Darko Dimitrov	56
14	8	Germany	Texas Lightning	No, no, never	Jane Comerford	Jane Comerford	36
15	5	Norway	Christine Guldbrandsen	Alvedansen	Kjetil Fluge, Christine Guldbrandsen	Kjetil Fluge, Atle Halstensen, Christine Guldbrandsen	36
16	1	Switzerland	Six4One	If we all give a little	Bernd Meinunger	Ralph Siegel	30
17	4	Latvia	Cosmos	I hear your heart	Molly-Ann Leikin, Guntars Račs	Reinis Sējāns, Andris Sējāns	30
18	9	Denmark	Sidsel Ben Semmane	Twist of love	Niels Drevsholt	Niels Drevsholt	26
19	15	United Kingdom	Daz Sampson	Teenage life	Daz Sampson, John Matthews	Daz Sampson, John Matthews	25
20	2	Moldova	Arsenium & Natalia Gordienko	Loca	Arsenium	Arsenium	22
21	6	Spain	Las Ketchup	Bloody Mary	Manuel Ruiz Gómez (Queco)	Manuel Ruiz Gómez (Queco)	18
22	19	France	Virginie Pouchin	Il était temps	Corneille	Corneille	5
23	3	Israel	Eddie Butler	Ze hazman	Osnat Tsabag, Orly Burg	Eddie Butler	4
24	7	Malta	Fabrizio Faniello	I do	Aldo Spiteri, Fabrizio Faniello	Aldo Spiteri, Fabrizio Faniello	1

2006 Eurovision 51: Athens, Greece — Final: 20 May 2006

Order votes announced	Albania 37	Andorra 26	Armenia 24	Belarus 34	Belgium 28	Bosnia & H 13	Bulgaria 38	Croatia 20	Cyprus 31	Denmark 9	Estonia 30	Finland 17	France 19	FYR Macedonia 11	Germany 8	Greece 16	Iceland 35	Ireland 21	Israel 3	Latvia 4	Lithuania 14	Malta 7	Moldova 2	Monaco 36	Netherlands 32	Norway 5	Poland 33	Portugal 27	Romania 12	Russia 10	Serbia & Mont 29	Slovenia 25	Spain 6	Sweden 22	Switzerland 1	Turkey 23	Ukraine 18	United Kingdom 15	TOTAL
Switzerland						4			3							1						12		6				1		3			2						30
Moldova													4															3	12							1			22
Israel																																							4
Latvia			1	1						1	3	5				2	4	4		6	8		3	8						1				2			4	2	30
Norway	6																8							1	3					7							3	3	36
Spain	1	12														2																							18
Malta																																							1
Germany	5				1					3								3		3		5			3	1						4	5		7			5	36
Denmark																									6						8	6		8					26
Russia	4	6	12	2	3	6	10	7	8	2	10	12	2	8	6	8	5	5	12		12	5	10	12	2	4	10		8	4	5	4	7	6	4	5	12	1	248
FYR Macedonia	3			3		8	6	8		6	4		7		5	7	2	6	10	2	1		4		8	4	3	7		6	8	6	7	10	1	6		6	56
Romania	2	3	4	4	2	2	2	5	10				2	2	7	6	3	2	10		12	10	5			8	4	10			4	5	12	6	12	3	1		172
Bosnia & H	12		5	4	6		7	12	2	8	4	10	6	12	1	4	10	6	2	2	4	1	4	12	6	5	8	2	7	6	12	12	1	10	12	12	10	10	229
Lithuania		7		6	4		1	6	4	7	8	8		3			3	2	3	10		3		7	5	2	8	4		5	3	3	4	3			5	10	162
United Kingdom		2						1	1	4	2				8			8		1					2		1												25
Greece	8	1	8	2	10	1	12		12	3		1	5	7	8		1	3	7	8	3	8	1		5		12	6	10	8	6			4	5	4		7	128
Finland		10		7	8	7	5	10	5	12	12		8	6	10	12	12	5	5	5	10	7	6	7	7	12		4	4		7	8	10	12	8	7	7	12	292
Ukraine		5	10	10	5	5	3	4	6	10	7	2	3	5	1	5	6	1	6	5	7	2	8		1	10	6	12	3	10	2	2	3	1		8			145
France			2																					3															5
Croatia						12								10	2									4							10	10							56
Ireland		4	3					2		5	6	4	1		4		1		5	4	6	4	4	10	4	7	2	5	2		7	1		5	6		2	8	93
Sweden	10	8	6	5	5	3	5	3	6	10	7	7	3	5	12		7	7		7	5	6	2	5		10	7	8	5	2	1	7	6		2	7	6	4	170
Turkey	7				7	10	4		7					4	3	3			1		2		7		12				6	12					10		7	3	91
Armenia				8	12		8									10			8						10		5		1				8			10	8		129

Notes: Serbia-Montenegro withdrew due to a dispute over the representing act, Croatia were awarded an automatic place in the Final

2007 Eurovision 52: Helsinki, Finland
Semi-final: 10 May 2007

Rank	Start	Country	Artist	Song	Writer	Composer	POINTS
1Q	15	Serbia	Marija Šerifovic	Molitva	Saša Milošević Mare	Vladimir Graić	298
2Q	22	Hungary	Magdi Rúzsa	Unsubstantial Blues	Imre Mózsik	Magdi Rúzsa	224
3Q	26	Turkey	Kenan Dogulu	Shake it up shekerim	Kenan Dogulu	Kenan Dogulu	197
4Q	4	Belarus	Dmitry Koldun	Work your magic	Karen Kavaleryan	Philip Kirkorov	176
5Q	28	Latvia	Bonaparti.lv	Questa Notte	Kjell Jennstig, Torbjörn Wassenius, Francesca Russo	Kjell Jennstig	168
6Q	1	Bulgaria	Elitsa Todorova, Stoyan Yankulov	Water	Elitsa Todorova	Elitsa Todorova, Stoyan Yankoulov	146
7Q	25	Slovenia	Alenka Gotar	Cvet z juga	Andrej Babiæ	Andrej Babiæ	140
8Q	6	Georgia	Sopho	My Story	Bibi Kvachadze	Beqa Jafaridze	123
9Q	18	FYR Macedonia	Karolina	Mojot Svet	Grigor Koprov, O Nedelkovski, V Dojcinovski	Grigor Koprov, O Nedelkovski, V Dojcinovski	97
10Q	9	Moldova	Natalia Barbu	Fight	Buga	Brasoveanu	91
11	17	Portugal	Sabrina	Dança comigo (vem ser feliz)	Emanuel, Tó Maria Vinhas	Emanuel	88
12	21	Andorra	Anonymous	Salvem el món	Anonymous	Anonymous	80
13	5	Iceland	Eirikur Hauksson	Valentine lost	Peter Fenner	Sveinn Rúnar Sigurðsson	77
14	14	Poland	The Jet Set	Time to party	Kamil Varen, David Junior Serame	Mateusz Krezan	75
15	3	Cyprus	Evridiki	Comme ci, comme ça	Poseidonas Giannopoulos	Dimitris Korgialas	65
16	13	Croatia	Dragonfly feat. Dado Topic	Vjerujem u ljubav	Dado Topic	Dado Topic	54
17	11	Albania	Aida & Frederik Ndoci	Hear my plea	Pandi Laço	Adrian Hila	49
18	19	Norway	Guri Schanke	Ven a bailar conmigo	Thomas G:son	Thomas G:son	48
19	12	Denmark	DQ	Drama Queen	Peter Andersen, Claus Christensen	Peter Andersen, Simon Munk	45
20	8	Switzerland	DJ BoBo	Vampires are alive	DJ BoBo	DJ BoBo	40
21	10	Netherlands	Edsilia Rombley	On top of the world	Tjeerd Oosterhuis, Martin Gijzemijter	Tjeerd Oosterhuis	38
22	23	Estonia	Gerli Padar	Partners in crime	Hendrik Sal-Saller	Berit Vaher	33
23	7	Montenegro	Stevan Faddy	Ajde kroci	Milan Periæ	Slaven Knezoviæ	33
24	2	Israel	Teapacks	Push the button	Kobi Oz	Kobi Oz	17
25	20	Malta	Olivia Lewis	Vertigo	Gerald James Borg	Philip Vella	15
26	24	Belgium	The KMG's	Love power	Paul Curtiz, Sexyfire	Paul Curtiz	14
27	27	Austria	Eric Papilaya	Get a life - Get alive	Austin Howard	Gerg Usek	4
28	16	Czech Rep	Kabát	Malá dáma	Kabát	Kabát	1

2007 Eurovision 52: Helsinki, Finland — Semi-final: 10 May 2007

	Albania	Andorra	Armenia	Austria	Belarus	Belgium	Bosnia & H	Bulgaria	Croatia	Cyprus	Czech Republic	Denmark	Estonia	Finland	France	FYR Macedonia	Georgia	Germany	Greece	Hungary	Iceland	Ireland	Israel	Latvia	Lithuania	Malta	Moldova	Montenegro	Netherlands	Norway	Poland	Portugal	Romania	Russia	Serbia	Slovenia	Spain	Sweden	Switzerland	Turkey	Ukraine	United Kingdom	TOTAL
Bulgaria	1		1	6		2	3		6	12	10			2	8	7	3	4	10	8			6			3	5	5				5	1		5	3	10			12	2	6	146
Israel	8		4			5		7			2		3		6			3	12		1				4									1									17
Cyprus	4		12		3		2	6		10	5	1	7	12	5	4	4		7	2	4	6	4	10	10	7	12	4		3	4	1	3	12	4			3			12	10	65
Belarus			8		8	1	5	3	5	7		10	6	4	4	3	1	3	6	10	4		8	6	5	10	8	4	5	3	3	1		10	4		3	12		5	10		176
Iceland	7												10												8					12			12			5							77
Georgia		6					5					3	2			3			6				8			10									8	2	3				10		123
Montenegro		5	7		4	10			1			4						8	2	5		2	3												8						6		33
Switzerland					5														3				1	4				6		1						2							40
Moldova		2		7	4		10		3							10	7	1	8		8	5	5			8		7	1			12			3		6		1		6		91
Albania	10				5	10	7	12	8	1	6			1				2		1	2	10		1	3	6	6	6	1										7			1	38
Denmark		3	3	5									4	5		6		5			10	8	3	2	1	1		7	10	4		2			3	8		4	7			7	49
Croatia	6															2	6		8					3					4			2			6				5			3	45
Poland	3	2		7	4	7			2		7	7										5	5					7							3							5	54
Serbia	2	10		4	5		10		7	4	8	12	4	8	3	12	8	10	5	12	2	10	7	2	1	1	1	1	10	8	5	4	6	8		12	5	10	12	12	8	5	298
Czech Republic																																											1
Portugal	12		6							1					10	1		7	4					3			7	10	4		10				1	1	8						88
FYR Macedonia			3	5					8			6									7						1	2			2	2	2		10	10						7	97
Norway														1																								6	5				48
Malta	6																										4																15
Andorra					4				2			7	5	5	1	5		6			6	4	2	8	2	5	3		8	2	6	6		4		4		2	8			2	80
Hungary		8	6	8	1	12	6	4	7	5	7	12	8	10	12		10	2			12	7		12	7		1	10		10	8	10	10	3		6	1	8	6		4		224
Estonia			3				4				4			6			2					3			6			2	2		2	2							4				33
Belgium							10				1						12																										14
Slovenia	8			2		6	6	5	10		3	8	12	7	1	5	5		1	7	3	1		5		5	3	8	8	2	6	7	4	4		4	12	2		3		2	140
Turkey	12		10	10	6	12	8	5		5	1	5	12	7	12		2	12		6		12	10			12	10	3	12	10	1	8	8	7		6	1	7	10		1	4	197
Austria		1															12													6	12	8					2	7	3			12	4
Latvia				1	2	8			4		3	3	12	3			5						10				2		7	7			5	2		7		1	2		3	8	168

127

2007 Eurovision 52: Helsinki, Finland

Final: 12 May 2007

Final qualification rules:
Top 10 countries from the 2006 Final
Top 10 countries from the 2007 Semi-Final

Automatic qualification:
United Kingdom, France, Germany, Spain, Finland

Rank	Start	Country	Artist	Song	Writer	Composer	POINTS
1	17	Serbia	Marija Šerifovic	Molitva	Saša Milošević Mare	Vladimir Graić	268
2	18	Ukraine	Verka Serduchka	Dancing Lasha Tumbai	Andrei Danilko	Andrei Danilko	235
3	15	Russia	Serebro	Song # 1	Daniil Babichev	Maxim Fadeev	207
4	22	Turkey	Kenan Dogulu	Shake it up shekerim	Kenan Dogulu	Kenan Dogulu	163
5	21	Bulgaria	Elitsa Todorova, Stoyan Yankulov	Water	Elitsa Todorova	Elitsa Todorova, Stoyan Yankoulov	157
6	3	Belarus	Dmitry Koldun	Work your magic	Karen Kavaleryan	Philip Kirkorov	145
7	10	Greece	Sarbel	Yassou Maria	Mack	Alex Papakonstantinou, Marcus Englöf	139
8	23	Armenia	Hayko	Anytime you need	Karen Kavaleryan	Hayko	138
9	8	Hungary	Magdi Rúzsa	Unsubstantial Blues	Imre Mózsik	Magdi Rúzsa	128
10	24	Moldova	Natalia Barbu	Fight	Buga	Brasoveanu	109
11	1	Bosnia & H	Marija Sestic	Rijeka bez imena	Aleksandra Milutinovic, Goran Kovacic	Aleksandra Milutinovic, Goran Kovacic	106
12	11	Georgia	Sopho	My Story	Bibi Kvachadze	Beqa Jafaridze	97
13	20	Romania	Todomondo	Liubi, liubi, I love you	Mister M, Vlad Crepu, Ghedi Kamara	Mister M	84
14	6	FYR Macedonia	Karolina	Mojot Svet	Grigor Koprov, O Nedelkovski, V Dojcinovski	Grigor Koprov, O Nedelkovski, V Dojcinovski	73
15	7	Slovenia	Alenka Gotar	Cvet z juga	Andrej Babiæ	Andrej Babiæ	66
16	14	Latvia	Bonaparti.lv	Questa Notte	Kjell Jennstig, Torbjörn Wassenius, Francesca Russo	Kjell Jennstig	54
17	5	Finland	Hanna Pakarinen	Leave me alone	Martti Vuorinen, Hanna Pakarinen	Martti Vuorinen, Miikka Huttunen	53
18	12	Sweden	The Ark	The worrying kind	The Ark	The Ark	51
19	16	Germany	Roger Cicero	Frauen regieren die Welt	Frank Ramond, Matthias Hass	Frank Ramond, Matthias Hass	49
20	2	Spain	NASH	I love you mi vida	Tony Sanchez-Ohlsson, Rebeca Pous del Toro	Thomas G:son, Andreas Rickstrand	43
21	9	Lithuania	4Fun	Love or leave	Julija Ritčik	Julija Ritčik	28
22	13	France	Les Fatals Picards	L'amour à la Française	I Callot, L Honel, P Léger, J-M Sauvagnargues, Y Giraud	I Callot, L Honel, P Léger, J-M Sauvagnargues, Y Giraud	19
23	19	United Kingdom	Scooch	Flying the flag (for you)	Andrew Hill, Morten Schjolin, Russ Spencer, Paul Tarry	Andrew Hill, Morten Schjolin, Russ Spencer, Paul Tarry	19
24	4	Ireland	Dervish	They can't stop the spring	John Waters, Tommy Moran	John Waters, Tommy Moran	5

2007 Eurovision 52: Helsinki, Finland — Final: 12 May 2007

Order votes announced	Albania	Andorra	Armenia	Austria	Belarus	Belgium	Bosnia & H	Bulgaria	Croatia	Cyprus	Czech Republic	Denmark	Estonia	Finland	France	FYR Macedonia	Georgia	Germany	Greece	Hungary	Iceland	Ireland	Israel	Latvia	Lithuania	Malta	Moldova	Montenegro	Netherlands	Norway	Poland	Portugal	Romania	Russia	Serbia	Slovenia	Spain	Sweden	Switzerland	Turkey	Ukraine	United Kingdom	TOTAL
	16	4	3	5	2	14	13	32	19	18	26	7	30	11	6	41	9	22	8	42	37	28	21	36	23	29	39	1	27	24	31	15	17	35	10	20	38	33	25	12	34	40	
Bosnia & H	8			8					10		4	7			1	4		3		4				8				7	7	6			1		8	8		6	8	10			106
Spain	12					3	7	1		6	2		7		6	7	8		1	4	4		2		7	2	10	4			7	8	1	12	2				5	10			43
Belarus	2	10					4																12			10	10	3				1									12		145
Ireland	5					1																																	1				5
Finland		7			1						5	4	6				1	1	5		12				5					4						10	3	12	6				53
FYR Macedonia	3						8	10	8																			10							10	10					4		73
Slovenia				4	4		7		7		5					6			1	4	8	5		4		5		8		4	4	3	8	3	5		3						66
Hungary		6		2		5			4	12		8		4			5	7	5					5	1	1			4	8	2	2		3	12	5		8	3		4	2	128
Lithuania		1		2			3	1					2	10										10																		3	28
Greece	7		8	3	3	8		12		12			5		3	3		10		7	8	1	1	6	12		6		5		5		10		4		2		4	4		10	139
Georgia			5		6	6	1	6		2				7						2	5		6			5	4		2			3		7				4	4	5	8		97
Sweden		2		2				3				12	2	8				10			10	12		10						12	5	2				2							51
France	4	8	2						1													10	1					6															19
Latvia					3	4	2	5	3	7	6	5	2	3	2	5	7	6	8	6	1	6	6	7	10	4	8	6	3	3	3	4	2	5	7	6	4	5				4	54
Russia	3	5	12	7		7	12	6		3	8	6	12	3	8	12	6	8	4	12	2	4	8	3	6	6	5	12	8	5	8	5	6		3	12	5	1	7	8	10	6	207
Germany	1		7			1	5	3	12	4	8	3	1	1	4	2	10		7	3	7	8	10	12	8	8	7	2	1	10	8	5	4	5	6	12	1	10	12	5		1	49
Serbia	6	12	4	12			5		5		12		8	12	12	2	2	12	4	12	6	4	10	12	8			12	12	2	12	12	4	8		4	7	3	2		8	3	268
Ukraine			6	4	10							10		6	10		10	2	7	3		8		1	8	12	7	2	12	1	2	12	4	8	3	2	7	3	2	3		8	235
United Kingdom																					3	7				12			10														19
Romania	10			3		4		2			5		1		7	4	2	4	2	8		3	7	7		7	12		6	3		7	5	1	6	7	12	5		2	2		84
Bulgaria			4	6	1		6		6	10			10		5	1	6	12	12	10			1	2	6	3	3	5		5	5	6	5	4	6	7	10	1		6	3	5	157
Turkey			10		12		10	7		8	10		2		12	10	10	2	6	1	3					1	1	1	12	1	10	10	7	2	1	1	8	7	10		1	12	163
Armenia		4		5	5	10		8		2				2		1	12	2	10				5			2	2		10			10		10		1	6		12	12	5	138
Moldova	4	3		8			4	4		2				2		3	3		10	5			4		2					1			12	6	1			2	7	7	7		109

129

2008 Eurovision 53: Belgrade, Serbia
Semi-final 1: 20 May 2008

Votes are cast by countries participating in each semi-final plus two of the four automatically qualifying countries decided by draw: Germany & Spain in semi-final 1, United Kingdom & France in semi-final 2. The hosts, Serbia, were drawn to vote in semi-final 2. The top 9 countries ranked by televoting in each semi-final qualify for the final. The back-up jury also chose an additional act that finished outside the top 9 in each semi-final.

Rank	Start	Country	Artist	Song	Writer	Composer	POINTS
1Q	19	Greece	Kalomira	Secret Combination	Poseidon Yannopoulos	Konstantinos Pantzis	156
2Q	14	Armenia	Sirusho	Qele, Qele	Sirusho	H A Der-Hovagimian	139
3Q	18	Russia	Dima Bilan	Believe	Dima Bilan & Jim Beanz	Dima Bilan & Jim Beanz	135
4Q	9	Norway	Maria	Hold On Be Strong	Mira Craig	Mira Craig	106
5Q	2	Israel	Boaz	The Fire In Your Eyes	Dana International & Shai Kerem	Dana International	104
6Q	7	Azerbaijan	Elnur & Samir	Day After Day	Zahra Badalbeyli	Govher Hasanzadeh	96
7Q	17	Romania	Nico & Vlad	Pe-o Margine De Lume	Andreea Andrei & Adina Șuteu	Andrei Tudor	94
8Q	16	Finland	Teräsbetoni	Missä Miehet Ratsastaa	J Ahola	J Ahola	79
9Q	13	Bosnia & Herzegovina	Laka	Pokušaj	Elvir Lakovic Laka	Elvir Lakovic Laka	72
10J	10	Poland	Isis Gee	For Life	Isis Gee	Isis Gee	42
12	4	Moldova	Geta Burlacu	A Century Of Love	Viorica Demici	Oleg Baraliuc	36
11	8	Slovenia	Rebeka Dremelj	Vrag Naj Vzame	Amon	Josip Miani-Pipi	36
13	15	Netherlands	Hind	Your Heart Belongs To Me	Hind Laroussi Tahiri & Tjeerd van Zanen	Hind Laroussi Tahiri, Tjeerd van Zanen & Bas van den Heuvel	27
14	1	Montenegro	Stefan Filipović	Zauvijek Volim Te	Ognen Nedelkovski	Grigor Koprov	23
15	11	Ireland	Dustin the Turkey	Irelande Douze Pointe	Darren Smith, Simon Fine & Dustin The Turkey	Darren Smith, Simon Fine & Dustin The Turkey	22
16	12	Andorra	Gisela	Casanova	Jordi Cubino	Jordi Cubino	22
17	6	Belgium	Ishtar	O Julissi	Michel Vangheluwe	Michel Vangheluwe	16
18	3	Estonia	Kreisiraadio	Leto Svet	Priit Pajusaar, Glen Pilvre, Peeter Oja, Hannes Võrno & Tarmo Leinatamm	Priit Pajusaar, Glen Pilvre, Peeter Oja, Hannes Võrno & Tarmo Leinatamm	8
19	5	San Marino	Miodio	Complice	Nicola Della Valle	Francesco Sancisi	5

2008 Eurovision 53: Belgrade, Serbia

Semi-final 1: 20 May 2008

	Andorra	Armenia	Azerbaijan	Belgium	Bosnia & H	Estonia	Finland	Germany	Greece	Ireland	Israel	Moldova	Montenegro	Netherlands	Norway	Poland	Romania	Russia	San Marino	Slovenia	Spain	TOTAL
Montenegro	7	7		7	12														1	10		23
Israel		7	10		5		10	4	5				5	6	10	4	6	8	2	4	4	104
Estonia	1	6	5				7					1					10	5	5			8
Moldova	2								4													36
San Marino									3													5
Belgium						6								10								16
Azerbaijan	8	2		5	3	4	5	8	7	5	5	10	3	4		10	7	10				96
Slovenia		4	1		10			1	2		2	2	10	5		2	1	2				36
Norway	10	8	7	1	4	8	12	5		8	6	3	4	1	2	7	4	7	7	2	2	106
Poland		1	3				2		1	12					1		2	3	10		3	42
Ireland				4	2	7		7			3		1	1							1	22
Andorra						3				1	4				12					1	12	22
Bosnia & H			4	12		1	8	10	12	3	10	6	12	7	3	12	5		8	12	10	72
Armenia	3			8		2	4		6	2	1	5	6	12	7		3		3	5		139
Netherlands		3	2	2		12		2		6		8	2		6	5		4	4	3	6	27
Finland	12			2	1		1	3	8	7	8	12		3	5	3		1	6	6	8	79
Romania	6	5	6	6		10	6	6	10	4	12	7	8	2	8	8				3	5	94
Russia	4	12	8	3	7		3	12		10	7	4	7	8	4	6	8	6	12	7	8	135
Greece	5	10	12	10	8	5											12				7	156

131

2008 Eurovision 53: Belgrade, Serbia

Semi-final 2: 22 May 2008

Votes are cast by countries participating in each semi-final plus two of the four automatically qualifying countries decided by draw: Germany & Spain in semi-final 1, United Kingdom & France in semi-final 2. The hosts, Serbia, were drawn to vote in semi-final 2. The top 9 countries ranked by televoting in each semi-final qualify for the final. The back-up jury also chose an additional act that finished outside the top 9 in each semi-final.

Rank	Start	Country	Artist	Song	Writer	Composer	POINTS
1Q	4	Ukraine	Ani Lorak	Shady Lady	Karen Kavaleryan	Philip Kirkorov	152
2Q	19	Portugal	Vânia Fernandes	Senhora Do Mar (Negras Águas)	Carlos Coelho	Andrej Babić	120
3Q	13	Denmark	Simon Mathew	All Night Long	Jacob Launbjerg, Svend Gudiksen & Nis Bøgvad	Jacob Launbjerg, Svend Gudiksen & Nis Bøgvad	112
4Q	11	Croatia	Kraljevi Ulice & 75 Cents	Romanca	Miran Hadži Veljković	Miran Hadži Veljković	112
5Q	14	Georgia	Diana Gurtskaya	Peace Will Come	Karen Kavaleryan	Kim Breitburg	107
6Q	10	Latvia	Pirates Of The Sea	Wolves Of The Sea	Jonas Liberg, Johan Sahlen, Claes Andreasson, Torbjorn Wassenius	Jonas Liberg, Johan Sahlen, Claes Andreasson, Torbjorn Wassenius	86
7Q	3	Turkey	Mor ve Ötesi	Deli	Mor ve Ötesi	Mor ve Ötesi	85
8Q	1	Iceland	Euroband	This Is My Life	Paul Oscar & Peter Fenner	Örlygur Smári	68
9Q	6	Albania	Olta Boka	Zemrën E Lamë Peng	Pandi Laço	Adrian Hila	67
10	18	FYR Macedonia	Tamara, Vrčak & Adrijan	Let Me Love You	Rade Vrchakovski-Vrcak	Rade Vrchakovski-Vrcak	64
11	12	Bulgaria	Deep Zone & Balthazar	DJ, Take Me Away	Dian Savov	Dian Savov	56
12J	2	Sweden	Charlotte Perrelli	Hero	Fredrik Kempe	Fredrik Kempe & Bobby Ljunggren	54
13	7	Switzerland	Paolo Meneguzzi	Era Stupendo	Pablo Meneguzzo & Vincenzo Incenzo	Pablo Meneguzzo	47
14	16	Malta	Morena	Vodka	Gerard James Borg	Philip Vella	38
15	17	Cyprus	Evdokia Kadi	Femme Fatale	Vangelis Evagelou	Nicos Evagelou	36
16	5	Lithuania	Jeronimas Milius	Nomads In The Night	Jeronimas Milius	Vytautas Diškevičius	30
17	9	Belarus	Ruslan Alehno	Hasta La Vista	Eleonora Melnik	Taras Demchuk	27
18	8	Czech Republic	Tereza Kerndlová	Have Some Fun	Gordon Pogoda	Gordon Pogoda & Stano Simor	9
19	15	Hungary	Csézy	Candlelight	Imre Mózsik	Viktor Rakonczai	6

2008 Eurovision 53: Belgrade, Serbia — Semi-final 2: 22 May 2008

Receiver \ Voter	Albania	Belarus	Bulgaria	Croatia	Cyprus	Czech Republic	Denmark	France	FYR Macedonia	Georgia	Hungary	Iceland	Latvia	Lithuania	Malta	Portugal	Serbia	Sweden	Switzerland	Turkey	Ukraine	United Kingdom	TOTAL
Iceland	5				1		10	8			7		2	2	5	5		10	4	3	1	4	68
Sweden	1				4		12	1			1			3	7	3	3		3	2		6	54
Turkey	12	3	7				8	10	8	5	4	8		7	8	12	8	6	7		5	10	85
Ukraine		12	12	7	10	12	7	3	6	12	8	6	6			2		3	1	12			152
Lithuania									10	10		1	12		12			7	10		3		30
Albania		5		10		1		5	12						1					8	3		67
Switzerland	10				7		5	7	1					6		2				1			47
Czech Republic				2	2				5														9
Belarus							6		4	4		7	5	6	6	10	2	8			10	5	27
Latvia		6	1	6		5		2	10	6	10	4		12		6	10	4	6	5	2		86
Croatia	3	7	6		6	3	3	6	7	8	3	5	7	5	2	1	5			6	7		112
Bulgaria		2		1	8	2		4	3	3	12	5	1	1	4	8		12	5		6		56
Denmark	4	4		3	5	10			2		2	12	8	8	10	7	7	1			4	1	112
Georgia		10			12	8	1				2	2	10	10		4	4			10	12		107
Hungary							4			1		3	4		3		1						6
Malta	8		3	4		6	2			2	5						12	2	2	4		2	38
Cyprus	2		8														6	5	8	7		12	36
FYR Macedonia	7		10	12	4	4					6		3	4	3				12				64
Portugal	6	8	5	8	3	7		12		7		10									8	7	120

2008 Eurovision 53: Belgrade, Serbia

Final: 24 May 2008

Final qualification rules:
Top 9 countries from each semi-final decided by televoting, plus one from each semi-final decided by a back-up jury.

Automatic qualification:
United Kingdom, France, Germany, Spain, Serbia

Rank	Start	Country	Artist	Song	Writer	Composer	POINTS
1	24	Russia	Dima Bilan	Believe	Dima Bilan & Jim Beanz	Dima Bilan & Jim Beanz	272
2	18	Ukraine	Ani Lorak	Shady Lady	Karen Kavaleryan	Philip Kirkorov	230
3	21	Greece	Kalomira	Secret Combination	Poseidon Yannopoulos	Konstantinos Pantzis	218
4	5	Armenia	Sirusho	Qele, Qele	Sirusho	H A Der-Hovagimian	199
5	25	Norway	Maria	Hold On Be Strong	Mira Craig	Mira Craig	182
6	23	Serbia	Jelena Tomašević & Bora Dugic	Oro	Dejan Ivanović	Željko Joksimović	160
7	12	Turkey	Mor ve Ötesi	Deli	Mor ve Ötesi	Mor ve Ötesi	138
8	20	Azerbaijan	Elnur & Samir	Day After Day	Zahra Badalbeyli	Govher Hasanzadeh	132
9	7	Israel	Boaz	The Fire In Your Eyes	Dana International & Shai Kerem	Dana International	124
10	6	Bosnia & H	Laka	Pokušaj	Elvir Lakovic Laka	Elvir Lakovic Laka	110
11	17	Georgia	Diana Gurtskaya	Peace Will Come	Karen Kavaleryan	Kim Breitburg	83
12	14	Latvia	Pirates Of The Sea	Wolves Of The Sea	Jonas Liberg, Johan Sahlen, Claes Andreasson, Torbjorn Wassenius	Jonas Liberg, Johan Sahlen, Claes Andreasson, Torbjorn Wassenius	83
13	13	Portugal	Vânia Fernandes	Senhora Do Mar (Negras Águas)	Carlos Coelho	Andrej Babić	69
14	11	Iceland	Euroband	This Is My Life	Paul Oscar & Peter Fenner	Örlygur Smári	64
15	16	Denmark	Simon Mathew	All Night Long	Jacob Launbjerg, Svend Gudiksen & Nis Bøgvad	Jacob Launbjerg, Svend Gudiksen & Nis Bøgvad	60
16	22	Spain	Rodolfo Chikilicuatre	Baila El Chiki Chiki	Rodolfo Chikilicuatre	Rodolfo Chikilicuatre	55
17	3	Albania	Olta Boka	Zemërn E Lamë Peng	Pandi Laço	Adrian Hila	55
18	15	Sweden	Charlotte Perrelli	Hero	Fredrik Kempe	Fredrik Kempe & Bobby Ljunggren	47
19	19	France	Sébastien Tellier	Divine	Sebastien Tellier, Amandine de La Richardière	Sebastien Tellier	47
20	1	Romania	Nico & Vlad	Pe-o Margine De Lume	Andreea Andrei & Adina Şuteu	Andrei Tudor	45
21	9	Croatia	Kraljevi Ulice & 75 Cents	Romanca	Miran Hadži Veljković	Miran Hadži Veljković	44
22	8	Finland	Teräsbetoni	Missä Miehet Ratsastaa	J Ahola	J Ahola	35
23	4	Germany	No Angels	Disappear	Remee, Hanne Sorvaag & Thomas Troelsen	Remee, Hanne Sorvaag & Thomas Troelsen	14
24	10	Poland	Isis Gee	For Life	Isis Gee	Isis Gee	14
25	2	United Kingdom	Andy Abraham	Even If	Andy Abraham, Andy Watkins & Paul Wilson	Andy Abraham, Andy Watkins & Paul Wilson	14

2008 Eurovision 53: Belgrade, Serbia — Final: 24 May 2008

Order votes announced	Albania (7)	Andorra (22)	Armenia (25)	Azerbaijan (33)	Belarus (38)	Belgium (8)	Bosnia & H (6)	Bulgaria (11)	Croatia (36)	Cyprus (14)	Czech Republic (26)	Denmark (43)	Estonia (5)	Finland (35)	France (17)	FYR Macedonia (2)	Georgia (42)	Germany (4)	Greece (34)	Hungary (21)	Iceland (16)	Ireland (31)	Israel (13)	Latvia (10)	Lithuania (39)	Malta (30)	Moldova (15)	Montenegro (41)	Netherlands (28)	Norway (20)	Poland (23)	Portugal (19)	Romania (18)	Russia (40)	San Marino (9)	Serbia (12)	Slovenia (24)	Spain (27)	Sweden (37)	Switzerland (32)	Turkey (29)	Ukraine (3)	United Kingdom (1)	TOTAL
Romania																											12								1			12				3		45
United Kingdom																																			6								1	14
Albania				1			1	12	8	3						12			10									7				4			3		4			8	1			55
Germany								12																																2				14
Armenia	2				7	12	6	8		10					12	1	12	6	12		1		8				2	1	12		12		4	12	8	5	5	10	2	8	10	7		199
Bosnia & H			3		4			2	12	2		2		6	2	5	3	5							3			10	7	3	5				10	12	10		10	7	6			110
Israel	4		6	7		5	5		2	2			10	8	6		1	3	1	3	7			1			6	5	3	4	2	3	1	1	10	7	3		7	1	6	5		124
Finland																		2				2		5													8			3		1		35
Croatia			2			10																						2								3								44
Poland																					10																						4	14
Iceland												12		7	10	2				5													8	2										64
Turkey	10			12	3		8	5	3			6		4	8	7	6		1		7		4	2		6	6	2	10	8	5	7	8		4			4		6			4	138
Portugal		10			8	10			4									4								7			5						5	1			3	10		3	6	69
Latvia		2			2					1		8								1	3	12			10	12				7	1			2	2									83
Sweden	3				1		7	3		7	2	2	3			8				2	12	1	1	7	1	5	3		10	12	7													47
Denmark										6	4		5	2		3			4		5	6	2	8	2	10	8	5			1	5												60
Georgia			10	6	8		3	10		12	8	7	4	5					6	1	8	4	10	10	5	4	4				7	1		7				4					3	83
Ukraine	8	6	5	10	10	6			5	5		8	6	3	10	7	7	4	3	6			3	3	6	5	8		10		1	12	3	8	12				5		4		5	230
France	3		4											2		10	4	12						4	8	10		4	5		1		2										2	47
Azerbaijan		7			2	8	7		3	4	10		1		3	8		1	3	12		4	2		7	2		4	2		7	12	2	10		6	1		4		12	8		132
Greece	12	8	8	6	8			7		12	5	6		1	5	3	7	12		8			5	8	12		1	6	8		7	3	12	3	12	8	6	3	1	5	7	10	5	218
Spain	1	12	1		2	4			10	4				1		10	4	8	8	7			7	3		1	10	12	1	6		10	7			10		4	3	4	3	2	2	55
Serbia	5		3	2	1		12	4	5	8	6		10	1	7	6	8	7	5	10	2	5	12	12	12	8	10	12	8	6	4	6	7	4			12	5	6	12	5		12	160
Russia	6	5	12	8	12	3	4	6	6			10	8	10	7	10	8		7	7	2	7	7	6	4	3	5		1	5	6	2	10	5		10	7	5	6	12	5	2	12	272
Norway	7	1	7	5	5	2	2	1	1		7		12	8	1		5		2	4	10						5	8	4		8	6	5		7	4		6	12		2	6	7	182

135

2009 Eurovision 54: Moscow, Russia

Semi-final 1: 12 May 2009

Votes are cast by countries participating in each semi-final plus two of the four automatically qualifying countries decided by draw: Germany & United Kingdom in semi-final 1, Spain & France in semi-final 2. The hosts, Russia, were drawn to vote in semi-final 2. The top 9 countries ranked by televoting in each semi-final qualify for the final. The back-up jury also chose an additional act that finished outside the top 9 in each semi-final.

Rank	Start	Country	Artist	Song	Writer	Composer	POINTS
1Q	12	Iceland	Yohanna	Is It True?	Óskar Páll Sveinsson, Chris Neil, Tinatin Japaridze	Óskar Páll Sveinsson, Chris Neil, Tinatin Japaridze	174
2Q	9	Turkey	Hadise	Düm Tek Tek	Sinan Akçıl, Hadise Açıkgöz, Stefaan Fernande	Sinan Akçıl	172
3Q	18	Bosnia & H	Regina	Bistra Voda	Aleksandar Čović	Aleksandar Čović	125
4Q	5	Sweden	Malena Ernman	La Voix	Fredrik Kempe and Malena Ernman	Fredrik Kempe	105
5Q	6	Armenia	Inga & Anush	Jan Jan	Vardan Zadoyan & Avet Barseghyan	Mane Hakobyan	99
6Q	17	Malta	Chiara	What If We	Gregory Bilsen	Marc Paelinck	86
7Q	10	Israel	Noa & Mira Awad	There Must Be Another Way	Noa, Mira Awad, Gil Dor	Noa, Mira Awad, Gil Dor	75
8Q	16	Portugal	Flor-de-lis	Todas As Ruas Do Amor	Pedro Marques	Pedro Marques, Paulo Pereira	70
9Q	14	Romania	Elena	The Balkan Girls	Laurențiu Duță, Alexandru Pelin	Laurențiu Duță, Ovidiu Bistriceanu, Daris Mangal	67
10	13	FYR Macedonia	Next Time	Neshto Shto Ke Ostane	Elvir Mekic	Jovan Jovanov & Damjan Lazarov	45
11	1	Montenegro	Andrea Demirovic	Just Get Out of My Life	Bernd Meinunger & Jose Juan Santana Rodriguez	Ralph Siegel	44
12J	15	Finland	Waldo's People	Lose Control	Waldo, A. Lehtonen, Karima, A. Kratz Gutå A. Lehtonen, Karima		42
13	4	Belarus	Petr Elfimov	Eyes That Never Lie	Valery Prokhozhy	Petr Elfimov	25
14	8	Switzerland	Lovebugs	The Highest Heights	Adrian Sieber, Thomas Rechberger, Florian Senn, Lovebugs	Adrian Sieber, Thomas Rechberger, Florian Senn, Lovebugs	15
15	7	Andorra	Susanne Georgi	La Teva Decisió (Get A Life)	Rune Braager, Lene Dissing, Marcus Winther-John, Pernille Georgi, Susanne Georgi	Rune Braager, Lene Dissing, Marcus Winther-John, Pernille Georgi, Susanne Georgi	8
16	11	Bulgaria	Krassimir Avramov	Illusion	Krassimir Avramov, William Tabanau, Casie Tabanau	Krassimir Avramov, William Tabanau	7
17	3	Belgium	Copycat	Copycat	Jacques Duvall	Benjamin Schoos	1
18	2	Czech Republic	Gipsy.cz	Aven Romale	Radoslav Gipsy Bang	Radoslav Gipsy Bang	0

2009 Eurovision 54: Moscow, Russia

Semi-final 1: 12 May 2009

	Andorra	Armenia	Belarus	Belgium	Bosnia & H	Bulgaria	Czech Republic	Finland	FYR Macedonia	Germany	Iceland	Israel	Malta	Montenegro	Portugal	Romania	Sweden	Switzerland	Turkey	United Kingdom	TOTAL
Montenegro	1	5	3		10				8	2		1	6		1			2	5		44
Czech Republic																					0
Belgium		1																			1
Belarus		4		4	4	1	1	4			1	4	1				1				25
Sweden	7	8	7	4			6	10	3	4	10	7	8	2	8	4		4	4	7	105
Armenia	8		10	10	1	8	12	1	2	10	2	10	3	4	4	8	5	1	10	5	99
Andorra																					8
Switzerland	2		2		2			5							2		2				15
Turkey	5	10	6	12	12	12	5	7	12	12	7	6	10	8	5	12	7	12		12	172
Israel	8	7	4	3		4	4	6	1	5	6		4	5		3	6	5	3	1	75
Bulgaria									5										2		7
Iceland	10	12	12	7	7	6	10	12	4	6		12	12	7	12	10	12	7	8	8	174
FYR Macedonia					8	10	3				4			10	10	2		6	6	6	45
Romania	4	2	1	2	6	5		2	7	1	12	8	2	6	3		10		7	2	67
Finland	3			1	3	2	2			7	8	2	5	3		1	3			4	42
Portugal	12	3		6	5	3	7	3		3	5	5		1	6	7	4	10		6	70
Malta	6		8	8		7	8	8		8	3	3		12	7	6	8	3		10	86
Bosnia & H			5	5					10	8			7			5	8	8	12	3	125

137

2009 Eurovision 54: Moscow, Russia
Semi-final 2: 14 May 2009

Votes are cast by countries participating in each semi-final plus two of the four automatically qualifying countries decided by draw: Germany & United Kingdom in semi-final 1, Spain & France in semi-final 2. The hosts, Russia, were drawn to vote in semi-final 2. The top 9 countries ranked by televoting in each semi-final qualify for the final. The back-up jury also chose an additional act that finished outside the top 9 in each semi-final.

Rank	Start	Country	Artist	Song	Writer	Composer	POINTS
1Q	6	Norway	Alexander Rybak	Fairytale	Alexander Rybak	Alexander Rybak	201
2Q	12	Azerbaijan	AySel & Arash	Always	Arash Labaf, Robert Uhlmann, Elin Wrethov, Anderz Wrethov	A Labaf, R Uhlmann, J Bejerholm, M Englof, A Papaconstantinou	180
3Q	18	Estonia	Urban Symphony	Rändajad	Sven Lõhmus	Sven Lõhmus	115
4Q	13	Greece	Sakis Rouvas	This Is Our Night	Graig Porteils & Cameron Giles-Webb	Dimitris Kontopoulos	110
5Q	15	Moldova	Nelly Ciobanu	Hora Din Moldova	Nelly Ciobanu	Veaceslav Daniliuc .	106
6Q	17	Ukraine	Svetlana Loboda	Be my Valentine! (Anti-crisis Girl)	Yevgeny Matyushenko	Svetlana Loboda	80
7Q	16	Albania	Kejsi Tola	Carry Me In Your Dreams	Agim Doçi	Edmond Zhulali	73
8Q	9	Denmark	Brinck	Believe Again	Lars Halvor Jensen, Martin Michael Larsson, Ronan Keating	Lars Halvor Jensen, Martin Michael Larsson, Ronan Keating	69
9Q	14	Lithuania	Sasha Son	Love	Dmitrij Šavrov (Sasha Son)	Dmitrij Šavrov (Sasha Son)	66
10	4	Serbia	Marko Kon & Milaan	Cipela	Marko Kon, Aleksandar Kobac	Marko Kon, Aleksandar Kobac, Milan Nikolic	60
11	2	Ireland	Sinéad Mulvey & Black Daisy	Et Cetera	Niall Mooney, Jonas Gladnikoff, Daniele Moretti & Christina Schilling	Niall Mooney, Jonas Gladnikoff, Daniele Moretti & Christina Schilling	52
12	5	Poland	Lidia Kopania	I Don't Wanna Leave	Alex Geringas, Bernd Klimpel, Rike Boomgaarden, Dee Adam	Alex Geringas, Bernd Klimpel, Rike Boomgaarden, Dee Adam	43
13J	1	Croatia	Igor Cukrov featuring Andrea	Lijepa Tena	Vjekoslava Huljić	Tonči Huljić	33
14	7	Cyprus	Christina Metaxa	Firefly	Nikolas Metaxas	Nikolas Metaxas	32
15	11	Hungary	Zoli Ádok	Dance With Me	Kasai	Szabó Zé	16
16	10	Slovenia	Quartissimo featuring Martina	Love Symphony	Andrej Babić	Andrej Babić	14
17	19	Netherlands	The Toppers	Shine	Gordon Heuckeroth	Gordon Heuckeroth	11
18	8	Slovakia	Kamil Mikulčík & Nela Pocisková	Leť Tmou	Anna Žigová, Petronela Kolevská	Rastislav Dubovský	8
19	3	Latvia	Intars Busulis	Probka	Janis Elsbergs, Sergej Timofejev	Karlis Lacis	7

2009 Eurovision 54: Moscow, Russia
Semi-final 2: 14 May 2009

	Albania	Azerbaijan	Croatia	Cyprus	Denmark	Estonia	France	Greece	Hungary	Ireland	Latvia	Lithuania	Moldova	Netherlands	Norway	Poland	Russia	Serbia	Slovakia	Slovenia	Spain	Ukraine	TOTAL
Croatia	1			2					1				3				3	12		10		1	33
Ireland	7	1	1		10	4	1				5	7	2	3	4	3		3		2			52
Latvia												6											7
Serbia	6		12	4		1			2						2				3	12	5		60
Poland	8		8	8	3		12	5				3		6	3					8	5	6	43
Norway		12			12	12	4	1	10	10	10	3	1	2		10	10	8	10		12	10	201
Cyprus	4	2			7	6	3	8	3	8	1	12	10	12		1	1	2	1				32
Slovakia				3				12		2		1								5	4	2	8
Denmark	5		2					2		1		5		7									69
Slovenia	2		7			8				7	3							5					14
Hungary	3				8														2				16
Azerbaijan		8	6	10	8	10	10	7	12	6	8	10	12	8	6	12	12	6	12	6		12	180
Greece	12	4	3	12	2	5	6		6	12	4	4	6	10	1	2	4	10	5	4	7	4	110
Lithuania		6	5	1	5	7	2		5	5	7		4	4	7	4	5			3	6	5	66
Moldova		7	10	7		2	7	6	4		2			1	10	5	8	7	7	7	1	8	106
Albania		5			6	3	5	10	8	3	6	2	5	5	5	6	2	1	4		8	3	73
Ukraine		10		6				3	7	4		8	8			7	7		6		10		80
Estonia		3	4	5	4		8	4			12		7		8	8	6	4	8	1	2	7	115
Netherlands	10				1													4	8			7	11

139

2009 Eurovision 54: Moscow, Russia

Final: 16 May 2009

Final qualification rules: Top 9 countries from each semi-final decided by televoting, plus one from each semi-final decided by a back-up jury.
Automatic qualification: United Kingdom, France, Germany, Spain, Russia

Final points scoring system: televoting by all countries participating in semi-finals/final equals 50% of points awarded, 50% also determined by a jury from each country.

Rank	Start	Country	Artist	Song	Writer	Composer	POINTS
1	20	Norway	Alexander Rybak	Fairytale	Alexander Rybak	Alexander Rybak	387
2	7	Iceland	Yohanna	Is It True?	Óskar Páll Sveinsson, Chris Neil, Tinatin Japaridze	Óskar Páll Sveinsson, Chris Neil, Tinatin Japaridze	218
3	11	Azerbaijan	AySel & Arash	Always	Arash Labaf, Robert Uhlmann, Elin Wrethov, Anderz Wrethov	A Labaf, R Uhlmann, J Bejerholm, M Englof, A Papaconstantinou	207
4	18	Turkey	Hadise	Düm Tek Tek	Sinan Akçıl, Hadise Açıkgöz, Stefaan Fernande	Sinan Akçıl	177
5	23	United Kingdom	Jade Ewen	It's My Time	Andrew Lloyd Webber & Diane Warren	Andrew Lloyd Webber & Diane Warren	173
6	15	Estonia	Urban Symphony	Rändajad	Sven Lõhmus	Sven Lõhmus	129
7	8	Greece	Sakis Rouvas	This Is Our Night	Graig Porteils & Cameron Giles-Webb	Dimitris Kontopoulos	120
8	3	France	Patricia Kaas	Et S'il Fallait Le Faire	Anse Lazio	Fred Blondin	107
9	12	Bosnia & H	Regina	Bistra Voda	Aleksandar Čović	Aleksandar Čović	106
10	9	Armenia	Inga & Anush	Jan Jan	Vardan Zadoyan, Avet Barseghyan	Mane Hakobyan	92
11	10	Russia	Anastasia Prikhodko	Mamo	Konstantin Meladzé, Diana Golde	Konstantin Meladzé	91
12	21	Ukraine	Svetlana Loboda	Be my Valentine! (Anti-crisis Girl)	Yevgeny Matyushenko	Svetlana Loboda	76
13	16	Denmark	Brinck	Believe Again	Lars Halvor Jensen, Martin Michael Larsson, Ronan Keating	Lars Halvor Jensen, Martin Michael Larsson, Ronan Keating	74
14	13	Moldova	Nelly Ciobanu	Hora Din Moldova	Nelly Ciobanu	Veaceslav Daniliuc	69
15	6	Portugal	Flor-de-lis	Todas As Ruas Do Amor	Pedro Marques	Pedro Marques, Paulo Pereira	57
16	2	Israel	Noa & Mira Awad	There Must Be Another Way	Noa, Mira Awad, Gil Dor	Noa, Mira Awad, Gil Dor	53
17	19	Albania	Kejsi Tola	Carry Me In Your Dreams	Agim Doçi	Edmond Zhulali	48
18	5	Croatia	Igor Cukrov featuring Andrea	Lijepa Tena	Vjekoslava Huljić	Tonči Huljić	45
19	22	Romania	Elena	The Balkan Girls	Laurențiu Duță, Alexandru Pelin	Laurențiu Duță, Ovidiu Bistriceanu, Daris Mangal	40
20	17	Germany	Alex Swings Oscar Sings!	Miss Kiss Kiss Bang	Alex Christensen, Steffen Haefeliger	Alex Christensen, Steffen Haefeliger	35
21	4	Sweden	Malena Ernman	La Voix	Fredrik Kempe & Malena Ernman	Fredrik Kempe	33
22	14	Malta	Chiara	What If We	Gregory Bilsen	Marc Paelinck	31
23	1	Lithuania	Sasha Son	Love	Dmitrij Šavrov (Sasha Son)	Dmitrij Šavrov (Sasha Son)	23
24	25	Spain	Soraya	La Noche Es Para Mí (The Night Is For Me)	Felipe Pedroso	Jason Gill, Dimitri Stassos, Irini Michas	23
25	24	Finland	Waldo's People	Lose Control	Waldo, A. Lehtonen, Karima, A. Kratz Gută	A. Lehtonen, Karima	22

2009 Eurovision 54: Moscow, Russia — Final: 16 May 2009

Order votes announced	Albania	Andorra	Armenia	Azerbaijan	Belarus	Belgium	Bosnia & H	Bulgaria	Croatia	Cyprus	Czech Republic	Denmark	Estonia	Finland	France	FYR Macedonia	Germany	Greece	Hungary	Iceland	Ireland	Israel	Latvia	Lithuania	Malta	Moldova	Montenegro	Netherlands	Norway	Poland	Portugal	Romania	Russia	Serbia	Slovakia	Slovenia	Spain	Sweden	Switzerland	Turkey	Ukraine	United Kingdom	TOTAL
Lithuania	26	14	39	41	3	2	23	17	32	28	6	36	31	15	9	20	5	22	40	8	35	10	12	18	4	37	13	30	42	29	33	34	11	27	21	38	1	7	16	25	24	19	23
Israel		7		1			8	1				1	2		10						7		7										10		5						1	4	53
France	2	3	6		7	8	6				4		5	4			3	6		6	3	5	5	6			4	6	1				10	3	5	7	3		1		3	1	107
Sweden	1	2		5		1						2	6	7	2	4		2		3					4	2	1		4										7		3		33
Croatia							12					4	3			4				1							8							5		6							45
Portugal	6					6	1						8		7					7						2											8						57
Iceland	6	8	5		2			5	2	5	7	10		10		2	5	4	7		12		8	8	12	3	5	7	12	1	8	10	3		6	5	1	10	5	2		8	218
Greece	12		10	2		5		12	7	12	2	8	7			1	6		4			10	8	7	7		2	1		2	4	8	4	6	8	4	1	2	5	6	2	5	120
Armenia					1	7		6		4	12			1	7			2		1			6	5		6	8	5	3	3		7	5		3		4	3	2		2		92
Russia			12		8					1	8						5	4					4				2										4			4	8		91
Azerbaijan	4		1		10	3	3	8	10	8	10	8	8	1		3		8	10	5			10	10	1	10	6	10	10			4	7	4	4	1	4	8		12	10	3	207
Bosnia & H	5		2	2	6			4	12		10		7	2		10	2						4	2			12	4				12		12	8	10		5	4	8			106
Moldova			7			4			3	2				6					10	2		1								3			1										69
Malta		1															4				5		1	1		7			3	5	12	3		7			5						31
Estonia				4	4				6		7			3	5	3	1	5	6	10	6		10	10	6	7		2	8	8		1	8		12	1					4	6	129
Denmark	5									6				12					3	4	4		3	2	5	5		8	6	7	1	2		1		8				4	5		74
Germany	3					2	2				1	7			5	5		3				3					3	2			3											7	35
Turkey	10		4	12	3	12	7	10		10	1	6	1	8	12	12	10	7	5			12	12	12	6	8	10	12		12	3	6	12	10			2	6	12			12	177
Albania											5		12		8	7	8	7	2					4	2	4	3	8	6	10	6	5	2	2	1	2	12	1	6	3			48
Norway	7	10	8		12	10		2	8	4	3	12	12		8	8	12	10	12	12	8	12	12	12	10	12	10	12		12		5	12	10	10	12	12	12	12	3	12	10	387
Ukraine		8	3	10	6			1		2			1				8		8	8		2	2	4	2	4		3	2	10	6		2	2	1	3	6	1	6	5		2	76
Romania				3		4			5	7	6		4			5					2	4		3	10	12				4	2			2	7	3	7				12		40
United Kingdom	8	4	7		3		4	7	4		3	3			4	6	8	12	1		10		2	3	10	1	10	3	5	4	10		6	8		3	10			5	6		173
Finland																				8					3													4					22
Spain		12																1													7								3				23

141

2010 Eurovision 55: Oslo, Norway

Semi-final 1: 25 May 2010

Votes are cast by countries participating in each semi-final plus the four automatically qualifying countries decided by draw: Germany, France & Spain in semi-final 1, United Kingdom in semi-final 2. The hosts, Norway, were drawn to vote in semi-final 2. Points awarded are the combined totals of the televoting and jury votes. The top 10 countries in each semi-final qualify for the final.

Rank	Start	Country	Artist	Song	Writer	Composer	POINTS
1Q	10	Belgium	Tom Dice	Me And My Guitar	Tom Dice, Jeroen Swinnen & Ashley Hicklin	Tom Dice, Jeroen Swinnen & Ashley Hicklin	167
2Q	13	Greece	Giorgos Alkaios & Friends	OPA	Giannis Antoniou & Friends	Giorgos Alkaios	133
3Q	17	Iceland	Hera Björk	Je Ne Sais Quoi	Örlygur Smári & Hera Björk	Örlygur Smári & Hera Björk	123
4Q	14	Portugal	Filipa Azevedo	Há Dias Assim	Augusto Madureira	Augusto Madureira	89
5Q	7	Serbia	Milan Stanković	Ovo Je Balkan	Goran Bregović, Marina Tucaković & Ljiljana Jorgovanović	Goran Bregović	79
6Q	12	Albania	Juliana Pasha	It's All About You	Pirro Çako	Ardit Gjebrea	76
7Q	2	Russia	Peter Nalitch & Friends	Lost And Forgotten	Peter Nalitch	Peter Nalitch	74
8Q	8	Bosnia & H	Vukašin Brajić	Thunder And Lightning	Dino Šaran	Dino Šaran	59
9Q	16	Belarus	3+2	Butterflies	Malka Chaplin	Maxim Fadeev	59
10Q	1	Moldova	Sunstroke Project & Olia Tira	Run Away	Alina Galetskaya	Anton Ragoza & Sergey Stepanov	52
11	5	Finland	Kuunkuiskaajat	Työki Ellää	Timo Kiiskinen	Timo Kiiskinen	49
12	11	Malta	Thea Garrett	My Dream	Sunny Aquilina	Jason Cassar	45
13	9	Poland	Marcin Mroziński	Legenda	Marcin Mroziński	Marcin Nierubiec	44
14	3	Estonia	Malcolm Lincoln	Siren	Robin Juhkental	Robin Juhkental	39
15	15	FYR Macedonia	Gjoko Taneski	Jas Ja Imam Silata	Kristijan Gabroski	Kristijan Gabroski	37
16	4	Slovakia	Kristina Pelakova	Horehronie	Kamil Peteraj	Martin Kavulic	24
17	6	Latvia	Aisha	What For?	Guntars Racs	Janis Lusens	11

2010 Eurovision 55: Oslo, Norway

Semi-final 1: 25 May 2010

	Albania	Belarus	Belgium	Bosnia & H	Estonia	Finland	France	FYR Macedonia	Germany	Greece	Iceland	Latvia	Malta	Moldova	Poland	Portugal	Russia	Serbia	Slovakia	Spain	TOTAL
Moldova	3	10	2	2			3	7		4			7			8	5	1		5	52
Russia	7	12	5	1	12	3			1	3		10	1	12	8	1		4			74
Estonia	1	1		5		12				1	2	12			5	4		6			39
Slovakia			1		10	2					5		2		1	5					24
Finland		7	7		6				3		6	6					3		2	2	49
Latvia						5					3										11
Serbia	3		3	12	1		12	10	4	7	3	3	3	3	6	2	4		6	6	79
Bosnia & Herzegovina	7	4					6	8		5		4		1			2	12	5		59
Poland	6	3	6				7		7					2			6			3	44
Belgium	4	8		4	8	10	10	4	12	10	12	8	12	6	12	12	10	7	10	8	167
Malta	2	2		6	3	1		6	2	2	4	1	6		4	3			12	1	45
Albania			8	7	2	4	2	12	5	12	10		8		7			2		4	76
Greece	10		10	8	5	8	4	3	8		8		4	7	2	10	7	10	8	10	133
Portugal	5		4	3		6	8	2	10		7	7		5				5	4	12	89
FYR Macedonia	12			10							1			4		7	1	8	1		37
Belarus		3			4		1	5	6	6		5	5	8	3	6	12		3		59
Iceland	8	6	12		7	7	5	1		8		2	10	10	10		8	3	7	7	123

2010 Eurovision 55: Oslo, Norway

Semi-final 2: 27 May 2010

Votes are cast by countries participating in each semi-final plus the four automatically qualifying countries decided by draw: Germany, France & Spain in semi-final 1, United Kingdom in semi-final 2. The hosts, Norway, were drawn to vote in semi-final 2. Points awarded are the combined totals of the televoting and jury votes. The top 10 countries in each semi-final qualify for the final.

Rank	Start	Country	Artist	Song	Writer	Composer	POINTS
1Q	17	Turkey	maNga	We Could Be The Same	Evren Özdemir, maNga, Fiona Movery Akıncı	maNga	118
2Q	7	Azerbaijan	Safura	Drip Drop	Sandra Bjurman	Anders Bagge, Stefan Örn	113
3Q	16	Georgia	Sofia Nizharadze	Shine	Hanne Sorvaag, Harry Sommerdahl & Christian Leuzzi	Hanne Sorvaag, Harry Sommerdahl & Christian Leuzzi	106
4Q	10	Romania	Paula Seling & Ovi	Playing With Fire	Ovidiu Cernăuţeanu	Ovidiu Cernăuţeanu	104
5Q	4	Denmark	Chanée & N'evergreen	In A Moment Like This	Thomas G:son, Henrik Sethsson & Erik Bernholm	Thomas G:son, Henrik Sethsson & Erik Bernholm	101
6Q	2	Armenia	Eva Rivas	Apricot Stone	Karen Kavaleryan	Armen Martirosyan	83
7Q	8	Ukraine	Alyosha	Sweet People	Olena Kucher	Olena Kucher, Borys Kukoba & Vadim Lisitsa	77
8Q	3	Israel	Harel Skaat	Milim	Noam Horev	Tomer Adaddi	71
9Q	12	Ireland	Niamh Kavanagh	It's For You	Niall Mooney, Mårten Eriksson, Jonas Gladnikoff & Lina Eriksson	Niall Mooney, Mårten Eriksson, Jonas Gladnikoff & Lina Eriksson	67
10Q	14	Cyprus	Jon Lilygreen & The Islanders	Life Looks Better In Spring	Nasos Lambrianides	Nasos Lambrianides, Melis Konstantinou	67
11	6	Sweden	Anna Bergendahl	This Is My Life	Kristian Lagerström	Bobby Ljunggren	62
12	1	Lithuania	InCulto	East European Funk	InCulto	InCulto	44
13	15	Croatia	Feminnem	Lako Je Sve	Neda Parmać, Pamela Ramljak	Branimir Mihaljević	33
14	9	Netherlands	Sieneke	Ik Ben Verliefd (Sha-la-lie)	Pierre Kartner	Pierre Kartner	29
15	13	Bulgaria	Miro	Angel Si Ti	Miroslav Kostadinov	Miroslav Kostadinov	19
16	11	Slovenia	Ansambel Žlindra & Kalamari	Narodnozabavni Rock	Leon Oblak	Marino Legovič	6
17	5	Switzerland	Michael von der Heide	Il Pleut de L'Or	Michael von der Heide, Heike Kospach, André Grüter	Michael von der Heide, Pele Loriano	2

2010 Eurovision 55: Oslo, Norway

Semi-final 2: 27 May 2010

	Armenia	Azerbaijan	Bulgaria	Croatia	Cyprus	Denmark	Georgia	Ireland	Israel	Lithuania	Netherlands	Norway	Romania	Slovenia	Sweden	Switzerland	Turkey	Ukraine	United Kingdom	TOTAL
Lithuania	2			1	2	1	8	12				5			4			2	7	44
Armenia		7	8		12		10		12	1	10		10		5	3	4	8		83
Israel	8	6	1		4		5				12	7	3	5	8			6	5	71
Denmark	5		2	4	3		3	4	7	5	4	8	12	10	12	5	6	5		101
Switzerland							2													2
Sweden	3	2		2	1	12		5	5	3	6	12	1	8		10	2		3	62
Azerbaijan			7	10	10	5	12	10	2	2	1	2	8	1	3	6	12	12		113
Ukraine	10	8	6	6	6	3	7	2	2	10	2	4	5	6	1	2	3		2	77
Netherlands	4	5	4		8	4	1	3	4	6		3		4	7	4	5			29
Romania				5		8	4	6	8		3	10					8	3	12	104
Slovenia				3																6
Ireland	1	4				6			3	7	8	6	4	2		12	1	1	10	67
Bulgaria				12	5	7		1	10	4			6	12			7	4	6	19
Cyprus	6	3	5			2		7	6		5			7	6	7			4	67
Croatia	7	1	3							12			2	3	2	1		7	1	33
Georgia	12	10	10	7	7			8		8	7	1	7		10	8	10	10	8	106
Turkey		12	12	8		10	6													118

2010 Eurovision 55: Oslo, Norway

Final: 29 May 2010

Final qualification rules: Top 10 placed countries from each semi-final. Automatic qualification: United Kingdom, France, Germany, Spain, Norway.
Points awarded are the combined totals of the televoting and jury votes from each of the 39 participating countries.

Rank	Start	Country	Artist	Song	Writer	Composer	POINTS
1	22	Germany	Lena Meyer-Landrut	Satellite	Julie Frost & John Gordon	Julie Frost & John Gordon	246
2	14	Turkey	maNga	We Could Be The Same	Evren Özdemir, maNga, Fiona Movery Akıncı	maNga	170
3	19	Romania	Paula Seling & Ovi	Playing With Fire	Ovidiu Cernăuțeanu	Ovidiu Cernăuțeanu	162
4	25	Denmark	Chanée & N'evergreen	In A Moment Like This	Thomas G:son, Henrik Sethsson & Erik Bernholm	Thomas G:son, Henrik Sethsson & Erik Bernholm	149
5	1	Azerbaijan	Safura	Drip Drop	Sandra Bjurman	Anders Bagge, Stefan Örn	145
6	7	Belgium	Tom Dice	Me And My Guitar	Tom Dice, Jeroen Swinnen & Ashley Hicklin	Tom Dice, Jeroen Swinnen & Ashley Hicklin	143
7	21	Armenia	Eva Rivas	Apricot Stone	Karen Kavaleryan	Armen Martirosyan	141
8	11	Greece	Giorgos Alkaios & Friends	OPA	Giannis Antoniou & Friends	Giorgos Alkaios	140
9	13	Georgia	Sofia Nizharadze	Shine	Hanne Sorvaag, Harry Sommerdahl & Christian Leuzzi	Hanne Sorvaag, Harry Sommerdahl & Christian Leuzzi	136
10	17	Ukraine	Alyosha	Sweet People	Olena Kucher	Olena Kucher, Borys Kukoba & Vadim Lisitsa	108
11	20	Russia	Peter Nalitch & Friends	Lost And Forgotten	Peter Nalitch	Peter Nalitch	90
12	18	France	Jessy Matador	Allez Olla Olé	H Ducamin & J Ballue	H Ducamin & J Ballue	82
13	8	Serbia	Milan Stanković	Ovo Je Balkan	Goran Bregović, Marina Tucaković & Ljiljana Jorgovanović	Goran Bregović	72
14	24	Israel	Harel Skaat	Milim	Noam Horev	Tomer Adaddi	71
15	2	Spain	Daniel Diges	Algo Pequeñito (Something Tiny)	Jesús Cañadilla, Luis Miguel de la Varga, Alberto Jodar, Daniel Diges	Jesús Cañadilla, Luis Miguel de la Varga, Alberto Jodar, Daniel Diges	68
16	15	Albania	Juliana Pasha	It's All About You	Pirro Çako	Ardit Gjebrea	62
17	6	Bosnia & H	Vukašin Brajić	Thunder And Lightning	Dino Šaran	Dino Šaran	51
18	23	Portugal	Filipa Azevedo	Há Dias Assim	Augusto Madureira	Augusto Madureira	43
19	16	Iceland	Hera Björk	Je Ne Sais Quoi	Örlygur Smári & Hera Björk	Örlygur Smári & Hera Björk	41
20	3	Norway	Didrik Solli-Tangen	My Heart Is Yours	Hanne Sørvaag & Fredrik Kempe	Hanne Sørvaag & Fredrik Kempe	35
21	5	Cyprus	Jon Lilygreen & The Islanders	Life Looks Better In Spring	Nasos Lambrianides	Nasos Lambrianides, Melis Konstantinou	27
22	4	Moldova	Sunstroke Project & Olia Tira	Run Away	Alina Galetskaya	Anton Ragoza & Sergey Stepanov	27
23	10	Ireland	Niamh Kavanagh	It's For You	Jonas Gladnikoff & Lina Eriksson	Niall Mooney, Mårten Eriksson, Jonas Gladnikoff & Lina Eriksson	25
24	9	Belarus	3+2	Butterflies	Malka Chaplin	Maxim Fadeev	18
25	12	United Kingdom	Josh Dubovie	That Sounds Good To Me	Pete Waterman, Mike Stock, Steve Crosby	Pete Waterman, Mike Stock, Steve Crosby	10

2010 Eurovision 55: Oslo, Norway — Final: 29 May 2010

Voting announcement order	Albania	Armenia	Azerbaijan	Belarus	Belgium	Bosnia & H	Bulgaria	Croatia	Cyprus	Denmark	Estonia	Finland	France	FYR Macedonia	Georgia	Germany	Greece	Iceland	Ireland	Israel	Latvia	Lithuania	Malta	Moldova	Netherlands	Norway	Poland	Portugal	Romania	Russia	Serbia	Slovakia	Slovenia	Spain	Sweden	Switzerland	Turkey	Ukraine	United Kingdom	TOTAL
Azerbaijan	5	39	15	29	31	9	22	7	27	18	12	10	19	35	37	3	16	17	2	34	24	28	25	36	33	26	8	14	1	13	4	21	11	20	38	30	6	23	32	145
Spain	7			6	5	7	12		10	2				3	8		1	4	3	7	2		12	7		7	8			8			5			2	12	12		68
Norway	2		6	4	1		2			5	7	4		2	2					1	5	8	3	4				12	2	4		3						4		35
Moldova								4						6	6													3	10											27
Cyprus	6						4	4		1			5		1		12	10	2			1						6				2			4		8			27
Bosnia & Herzegovina								10					7														10				12		4		3			1		51
Belgium	3					12		8	1	10	3	6	10	7		12	6	10	10		4	7	10	3	6	3	10	5	4	5	5	10		1	2	7	5			143
Serbia							1			7	4					5	5	8	4						1					2			8	1	7	10	8			72
Belarus				2	8		5		6	8	1	1			12					6				3			1													18
Ireland	12				12			1	12		2	7	4			2								2	3	1								5					7	25
Greece	1		2		4	6	5	8	5	6			2	5	3	8		8	5	5	4	12	7	5	8		4	8	7	10	10	5		1	6	1	5	7	12	140
United Kingdom	8					4	6				8	8	12	10	5	10	5	2	1		7	4				1			8							3		8		10
Georgia		12	8	7		10	10		8		6			12		1				8	3	2	6	8	8	2	4			3	7		1	1	6	1	5	7	12	136
Turkey		12	12	3	10	5			4	12		12			5	4	10	2	4		7	4	2	12	7	2	2		8	12	4		2	3	5	3		8	10	170
Albania					3		8	6	5	4	4	5	8	12	5	3	3	7		8	3	2	6	10		6		2	1			6				8	7		1	62
Iceland				2	8						1		1		7					10	1	5	2																1	41
Ukraine	8		10			3		3	6	3			2	1		3	8	6	6	2	12	6	5	6	7	4	3	7	5	3		1	3	2	6		1	5	5	108
France	6					2			3	7	4	5		8	7		4	5		3	7			8	5	10	6			6			7	10	5	3			2	82
Romania	5	1	7	1				8	8	7	1		6	4			7	3	6	8	3	2	5	12	12	10	6	10			7		3	12	10	4		2	8	162
Russia		10	3	12						8				8	10	6	6	1		10	8	5	2	10		4	5	2			4	6	7	6			4	10		90
Armenia				5	7		8		7	3	10	10	6		10	7	7		6	12	1	10	5	6	12	10	7	1	6	3	1	4			10		6	6	5	141
Germany	10		1		10	8	3	6	4	12	12	12	3	8	4	6	2	12		12	12	3	4	6	4	12	5		6	12	8	12	10	8	1	4	2	2	4	246
Portugal		4							2			10	8			6					6		1		10				3	6	2		6	12	6	12	4	10		43
Israel	4	5	5	8	2	1		6		5	5	2	1	2	4			1						1	10	5	12	4	12	1		8	6			5			3	71
Denmark	2		4					2						2				12	12	4	10	3	8	2	2	8						7	12	4	8				6	149

147

2011 Eurovision 56: Düsseldorf, Germany — Semi-final 1: 10 May 2011

Votes are cast by countries participating in each semi-final plus the five automatically qualifying countries decided by draw: United Kingdom and Spain in semi-final 1, France, Germany and Italy in semi-final 2. Points awarded are based on the combined votes of the viewers and jury from each country voting in this semi-final. The top 10 countries in each semi-final qualify for the final.

Rank	Start	Country	Artist	Song	Writer	Composer	POINTS
1Q	19	Greece	Loucas Yiorkas feat Stereo Mike	Watch My Dance	Eleana Vrachali	Giannis Christodoulopoulos	133
2Q	18	Azerbaijan	Ell/Nikki	Running Scared	Stefan Örn, Sandra Bjurman	Stefan Örn, Sandra Bjurman, Iain Farquharson	122
3Q	10	Finland	Paradise Oskar	Da Da Dam	Axel Ehnström	Axel Ehnström	103
4Q	14	Iceland	Sjonni's Friends	Coming Home	Thorunn Clausen & Sjonni Brink	Sjonni Brink	100
5Q	17	Lithuania	Evelina Sašenko	C'est Ma Vie	Andrius Kairys	Paulius Zdanavičius	81
6Q	9	Georgia	Eldrine	One More Day	DJ Rock, Mikheil Chelidze	Beso Tsikhelashvili	74
7Q	15	Hungary	Kati Wolf	What About My Dreams?	Péter Geszti, Johnny K Palmer	Viktor Rakonczai, Gergő Rácz	72
8Q	6	Serbia	Nina	Čaroban	Kristina Kovač	Kristina Kovač	67
9Q	7	Russia	Alexej Vorobjov	Get You	Alexej Vorobjov, Nadir Khayat, AJ Junior, Bilal Hajji, Eric Sanicola	Alexej Vorobjov, Nadir Khayat, AJ Junior, Bilal Hajji, Eric Sanicola	64
10Q	8	Switzerland	Anna Rossinelli	In Love For A While	David Klein	David Klein	55
11	11	Malta	Glen Vella	One Life	Fleur Balzan	Paul Giordimaina	54
12	4	Armenia	Emmy	Boom Boom	Sosi Khanikyan	Hayk Harutyunyan, Hayk Hovhannisyan	54
13	5	Turkey	Yüksek Sadakat	Live It Up	Ergün Arsal	Kutlu Özmakinaci	47
14	3	Albania	Aurela Gaçe	Feel The Passion	Sokol Marsi	Shpetim Saraci	47
15	13	Croatia	Daria	Celebrate	Boris Djurdjevic & Marina Mudrinić	Boris Djurdjevic	41
16	12	San Marino	Senit	Stand By	Radiosa Romani	Radiosa Romani	34
17	2	Norway	Stella Mwangi	Haba Haba	Stella Mwangi	Big City/Beyond51	30
18	16	Portugal	Homens Da Luta	Luta É Alegria	Nuno Duarte	Vasco Duarte	22
19	1	Poland	Magdalena Tul	Jestem	Magdalena Tul	Magdalena Tul	18

2011 Eurovision 56: Düsseldorf, Germany
Semi-final 1: 10 May 2011

	Albania	Armenia	Azerbaijan	Croatia	Finland	Georgia	Greece	Hungary	Iceland	Lithuania	Malta	Norway	Poland	Portugal	Russia	San Marino	Serbia	Spain	Switzerland	Turkey	United Kingdom	TOTAL
Poland	1	1	1			4		4		2		3							2		5	18
Norway					8		12		10		4		1	2					6	8		30
Albania	12		2	7		8	8				7		2	4	8	8		3	5	7	1	47
Armenia			12			3			4		2											54
Turkey	12			12	7	3				3	3	7		1	2	7		2	5			47
Serbia	2	12	5	5	3	5	3	3	5	5		4	6	3	4	10		6	12	3		67
Russia	3	3	8	2	6		10	8	3	6		6	3	5		3	6				2	64
Switzerland		8	3		1	6		1	6	12	8	12	5	8	5	1	2	6		10		55
Georgia		6	3	3			10	6	12	7		2	10		12	2	4	4	10	1	6	74
Finland	6	7	7	4		6		2		1	6						3			2		103
Malta	8	5	6	1		1	2		1		12					12	5			5	6	54
San Marino	7		4							8		10	4	10	1	4	12	12	8		7	34
Croatia		2			10		6	12	7		1	5		6	3		8	10		6	10	41
Iceland	4			6	12		5					8	12	7	7		10	8	4		3	100
Hungary						2	1		2		10	1	8	6	10	5		5	3	12	12	72
Portugal	5	4		10	2	10	4	5	2	10			12	7	10	5	1	1	1	4	4	22
Lithuania	10	10	10	8	5	12	7	7	8	4	5	1	8	12	6	6	7	7	7	4	8	81
Azerbaijan					4	7		10					7		6							122
Greece																						133

2011 Eurovision 56: Düsseldorf, Germany

Semi-final 2: 12 May 2011

Votes are cast by countries participating in each semi-final plus the five automatically qualifying countries decided by draw: United Kingdom and Spain in semi-final 1, France, Germany and Italy in semi-final 2. Points awarded are based on the combined votes of the viewers and jury from each country voting in this semi-final. The top 10 countries in each semi-final qualify for the final.

Rank	Start	Country	Artist	Song	Writer	Composer	POINTS
1Q	8	Sweden	Eric Saade	Popular	Fredrik Kempe	Fredrik Kempe	155
2Q	18	Denmark	A Friend in London	New Tomorrow	Lise Cabble, Jakob Schack Glaesner	Lise Cabble, Jakob Schack Glaesner	135
3Q	13	Slovenia	Maja Keuc	No One	Urša Vlašič	Matjaž Vlašič	112
4Q	14	Romania	Hotel FM	Change	Alexandra Ivan, Gabriel Băruța	Gabriel Băruța	111
5Q	1	Bosnia & H	Dino Merlin	Love in Rewind	Dino Merlin	Dino Merlin	109
6Q	6	Ukraine	Mika Newton	Angel	Maryna Skomorohova	Ruslan Kvinta	81
7Q	2	Austria	Nadine Beiler	The Secret is Love	Nadine Beiler	Thomas Rabitsch	69
8Q	19	Ireland	Jedward	Lipstick	Daniel Priddy, Lars Halvor Jensen, Martin Michael Larsson	Daniel Priddy, Lars Halvor Jensen, Martin Michael Larsson	68
9Q	15	Estonia	Getter Jaani	Rockefeller Street	Sven Lõhmus	Sven Lõhmus	60
10Q	7	Moldova	Zdob și Zdub	So Lucky	Andy Schuman, Marc Elsner	Mihai Gincu, Marc Elsner	54
11	4	Belgium	Witloof Bay	With Love Baby	Benoît Giaux, RoxorLoops	Benoît Giaux, RoxorLoops	53
12	10	Bulgaria	Poli Genova	Na Inat	Sebastian Arman, David Bronner, Borislav Milanov, Poli Genova	Sebastian Arman, David Bronner, Borislav Milanov, Poli Genova	48
13	5	Slovakia	TWiiNS	I'm Still Alive	Bryan Todd, Sandra Nordstrom, Branislav Jancich	Bryan Todd, Sandra Nordstrom, Branislav Jancich	48
14	16	Belarus	Anastasiya Vinnikova	I Love Belarus	Eugene Oleinik, Svetlana Geraskova	Eugene Oleinik	45
15	12	Israel	Dana International	Ding Dong	Dana International	Dana International	38
16	11	FYR Macedonia	Vlatko Ilievski	Rusinka	Marko Marinkovikj-Slatkaristika, Jovan Jovanov	Grigor Koprov, Vladimir Dojchinovski	36
17	17	Latvia	Musiqq	Angel in Disguise	Marats Ogleznevs	Marats Ogleznevs	25
18	9	Cyprus	Christos Mylordos	San Aggelos S'Agapisa	Mihalis Antoniou	Andreas Anastasiou	16
19	3	The Netherlands	3JS	Never Alone	Jaap Kwakman, Jan Dulles, Jaap de Witte	Jaap Kwakman, Jan Dulles, Jaap de Witte	13

2011 Eurovision 56: Düsseldorf, Germany

Semi-final 2: 12 May 2011

	Austria	Belarus	Belgium	Bosnia & H	Bulgaria	Cyprus	Denmark	Estonia	France	FYR Macedonia	Germany	Ireland	Israel	Italy	Latvia	Moldova	Netherlands	Romania	Slovakia	Slovenia	Sweden	Ukraine	TOTAL
Bosnia & Herzegovina	12	5	4			4	7	2	10	12	7	2	1	4	2		10		12	12	8	4	109
Austria		6		7	10		5		1		12		1	5			3		5	7	4	1	69
Netherlands			8		5																		13
Belgium	1	3		8	6	2		1	6			5	2	2	3	6	6	8		2			53
Slovakia	3		3	6	3	5	1	7		3		4	8	6	1	7		3	10	3	3	12	48
Ukraine		12		4	2		12	12	12	6	5	8	4	7	7	8		2	4	6			81
Moldova		10					4		3	5	1	1	12	3		3	12	12	7	5	3		54
Sweden	10	8	12	5		12			12	2	2			8		5	2	7				5	155
Cyprus																1						6	16
Bulgaria	2		1			10	4		3	1	4	1	3	10				4		4	1		48
FYR Macedonia		7		10										1						8		7	36
Israel		6	2			1		5	7	7	3	6	6		4	5	5	4			5		38
Slovenia	8			12	8	7	8	6	5	10	6	3	7	12	5		8	10	8		7		112
Romania	6		10		1	8	6	6	8	4		10	5		8	12	4		6			8	111
Estonia	5	1	6		4		3		4						6						6	10	60
Belarus				2		3	2	4		8		7	10			10		1	1				45
Latvia	4	2	7	1	12			10	2		10	12			12	2	7	5	3	10	2	3	25
Denmark	7	4		3	7	6		3			8						1	6	2	1	12	2	135
Ireland			5	3			10								10						10		68

2011 Eurovision 56: Düsseldorf, Germany

Final: 14 May 2011

Final qualification rules: Top 10 placed countries from each semi-final. Automatic qualification: United Kingdom, France, Germany, Spain, Italy. Points awarded are based on the combined votes of the viewers and jury from each of the 43 participating countries.

Rank	Start	Country	Artist	Song	Writer	Composer	POINTS
1	19	Azerbaijan	Ell/Nikki	Running Scared	Stefan Örn, Sandra Bjurman	Stefan Örn, Sandra Bjurman, Iain Farquharson	221
2	12	Italy	Raphael Gualazzi	Madness of Love	Raphael Gualazzi	Raphael Gualazzi	189
3	7	Sweden	Eric Saade	Popular	Fredrik Kempe	Fredrik Kempe	185
4	23	Ukraine	Mika Newton	Angel	Maryna Skomorohova	Ruslan Kvinta	159
5	3	Denmark	A Friend in London	New Tomorrow	Lise Cabble, Jakob Schack Glæsner	Lise Cabble, Jakob Schack Glæsner	134
6	2	Bosnia & H	Dino Merlin	Love in Rewind	Dino Merlin	Dino Merlin	125
7	9	Greece	Loucas Yiorkas feat Stereo Mike	Watch My Dance	Eleana Vrachali	Giannis Christodoulopoulos	120
8	6	Ireland	Jedward	Lipstick	Daniel Priddy, Lars Halvor Jensen, Martin Michael Larsson	Daniel Priddy, Lars Halvor Jensen, Martin Michael Larsson	119
9	25	Georgia	Eldrine	One More Day	DJ Rock, Mikheil Chelidze	Beso Tsikhelashvili	110
10	16	Germany	Lena Meyer-Landrut	Taken by a Stranger	Gus Seyffert, Nicole Morier, Monica Birkenes	Gus Seyffert, Nicole Morier, Monica Birkenes	107
11	14	United Kingdom	Blue	I Can	Ciaron Bell, Ben Collier, Ian Hope, Duncan James, Liam Keenan, Lee Ryan, StarSign	Ciaron Bell, Ben Collier, Ian Hope, Duncan James, Liam Keenan, Lee Ryan, StarSign	100
12	15	Moldova	Zdob și Zdub	So Lucky	Andy Schuman, Marc Elsner	Mihai Gincu, Marc Elsner	97
13	20	Slovenia	Maja Keuc	No One	Urša Vlašič	Matjaž Vlašič	96
14	24	Serbia	Nina	Čaroban	Kristina Kovač	Kristina Kovač	85
15	11	France	Amaury Vassili	Sognu	Jean-Pierre Marcellesi, Julie Miller	Daniel Moyne, Quentin Bachelet	82
16	10	Russia	Alexej Vorobjov	Get You	Alexej Vorobjov, Nadir Khayat, AJ Junior, Bilal Hajji, Eric Sanicola	Alexej Vorobjov, Nadir Khayat, AJ Junior, Bilal Hajji, Eric Sanicola	77
17	17	Romania	Hotel FM	Change	Alexandra Ivan, Gabriel Băruța	Gabriel Băruța	77
18	18	Austria	Nadine Beiler	The Secret is Love	Nadine Beiler	Thomas Rabitsch	64
19	4	Lithuania	Evelina Sašenko	C'est Ma Vie	Andrius Kairys	Paulius Zdanavičius	63
20	21	Iceland	Sjonni's Friends	Coming Home	Thorunn Clausen & Sjonni Brink	Sjonni Brink	61
21	1	Finland	Paradise Oskar	Da Da Dam	Axel Ehnström	Axel Ehnström	57
22	5	Hungary	Kati Wolf	What About My Dreams?	Péter Geszti, Johnny K Palmer	Viktor Rakonczai, Gergő Rácz	53
23	22	Spain	Lucía Pérez	Que Me Quiten Lo Bailao	Rafael Artesero	Rafael Artesero	50
24	8	Estonia	Getter Jaani	Rockefeller Street	Sven Lõhmus	Sven Lõhmus	44
25	13	Switzerland	Anna Rossinelli	In Love For A While	David Klein	David Klein	19

2011 Eurovision 56: Düsseldorf, Germany
Final: 14 May 2011

Order votes announced	Albania	Armenia	Austria	Azerbaijan	Belarus	Belgium	Bosnia & H	Bulgaria	Croatia	Cyprus	Denmark	Estonia	Finland	France	FYR Macedonia	Georgia	Germany	Greece	Hungary	Iceland	Ireland	Israel	Italy	Latvia	Lithuania	Malta	Moldova	Netherlands	Norway	Poland	Portugal	Romania	Russia	San Marino	Serbia	Slovakia	Slovenia	Spain	Sweden	Switzerland	Turkey	Ukraine	United Kingdom	TOTAL
	31	9	15	20	29	42	36	2	28	5	14	40	7	26	10	25	19	24	34	11	37	39	4	43	35	32	41	3	8	16	33	30	1	18	27	12	21	38	17	23	22	6	13	
Finland											5	7		5	12		2	3		10	3				1				12	5									7	5		6		57
Bosnia & Herzegovina	7		12	2		7		2	7				12	7	12		7	3			12	10	4	6	1	5		8	4	3		1	2	4	12	6	12		8	12	10		5	125
Denmark					1	4		7	2	3		10				12	6		10	12	12		4	7		5		12	7	12	6	1		4	7	6	8	1	8	12	10	4	6	134
Lithuania													12	2						5	10								3	1		7	2		8			6	10					63
Hungary			2	2	8		7	3			12		10		6			6		4	4	12		10		8	3	5				1				8		7	5			4		53
Ireland			4				2			10	10	12	6	10		1	8		10	7	7	5			7	6	6	10	10			7		6	1	10	8	6	12			1	12	119
Sweden	4			3	4	7	5		4	8	2	12	7		6			6	8	4	4	12		4		8	3	5	2		2	3	1	8	2		4	5			4	2	3	185
Estonia					5	2										12					7	5	2		4	6	6	10			10			3										44
Greece	10	7		8		8		10		12	8	5			3	6	10	1	8	7	4	8	2		7	8	3	5				8	8	8	3	5	3		6	8	6	3		120
Russia	4	8		4	5		4	4		2	4		4		4	4	5	1	3		7			4	6	6	6	10			2		3	3	4				4	7	5	7	8	77
France	2	5		1	3	12			6	7	1		3		1	2	3	12		1		8		1		1	5	5		4	2			12	2					4	1		7	82
Italy	12	6	6		3	6	6			1			4		5	7		10	4	3	5			12	10	10	2	10	5	10	10	6		12	5	4		10		4			7	189
Switzerland	6	2		5	2					4	3				5		4	2		2	6	1	10	5	3	7	4	7	1	4	3		4	2			1				6		10	19
United Kingdom			5	7	7		3		1		8			4		5			1		8		8	8	4			4	5		5	12	7			5	7		6	8		7		100
Moldova		5				1		10			4			3				4			1		6	2	2		12				3			12	3		3	3	3	7		3		97
Germany			10		8		3	4	1	12	1	8	5		2	8			1	6	1	6	6	2	8	2	10	7		8		10	12	1	10		5	8	4	7		5	8	107
Romania			1	6		10	7			6		2		6	10		12		2			3	6	3		3	2	4	6				5							1	12	7		77
Austria	3					3		5	3				1		4			5				4	12		4		12	1											3	1			2	64
Azerbaijan	8		8		6	3	8		10	8	8						12		7	8				2	8	12	10	6		8	8	10	12	10		3			3	1	12	10		221
Slovenia			3				12		12		4	2			10				6		2	3		3		3		2			1	4	5	1		7			5	2	2			96
Iceland						6	1				7		8		4				12				5			2		1	8		4				1	1			1				4	61
Spain	5										6		8	12	8				5												12	5	10	5									1	50
Ukraine	3	12		12	10			8	5	5					7	10	7					7	7	8	5	4	4	3	6	2	7	2	10		6	2	6	2	2					159
Serbia	1	1	7		8		10	1	8				2		8				5						12		8			6	12	5	6			12	10		1					85
Georgia	10			10	12							3										2				7		3		7				7				4			8	12		110

153

2012 Eurovision 57: Baku, Azerbaijan

Semi-final 1: 22 May 2012

Votes are cast by countries participating in each semi-final plus the five automatically qualifying countries decided by draw: Italy and Spain in semi-final 1, France, Germany and the United Kingdom in semi-final 2. Hosts Azerbaijan voted in semi-final 1. Points awarded are based on the combined votes of the viewers and jury from each of the countries voting in this semi-final. The top 10 countries in each semi-final qualify for the final.

Rank	Start	Country	Artist	Song	Writer	Composer	POINTS
1Q	14	Russia	Buranovskiye Babushki	Party for Everybody	Olga Tuktareva, Mary S Applegate	Viktor Drobysh, Timofei Leontiev	152
2Q	5	Albania	Rona Nishliu	Suus	Rona Nishliu	Florent Boshnjaku	146
3Q	6	Romania	Mandinga	Zaleilah	Elena Ionescu, Dihigo Omar Secada, Costi Ionita	Costi Ionita	120
4Q	3	Greece	Eleftheria Eleftheriou	Aphrodisiac	Dimitri Stassos, Mikaela Stenström, Dajana Lööf	Dimitri Stassos, Mikaela Stenström, Dajana Lööf	116
5Q	17	Moldova	Pasha Parfeny	Lăutar	Pasha Parfeny	Pasha Parfeny, Alex Brashovean	100
6Q	18	Ireland	Jedward	Waterline	Nick Jarl & Sharon Vaughn	Nick Jarl & Sharon Vaughn	92
7Q	12	Cyprus	Ivi Adamou	La La Love	Alex Papaconstantinou, Bjorn Djupström, Alexandra Zakka & Viktor Svensson	Alex Papaconstantinou, Bjorn Djupström, Alexandra Zakka & Viktor Svensson	91
8Q	2	Iceland	Greta Salóme & Jónsi	Never Forget	Gréta Salóme	Gréta Salóme	75
9Q	13	Denmark	Soluna Samay	Should've Known Better	Chief 1, Remee & Isam B	Chief 1 & Remee	63
10Q	15	Hungary	Compact Disco	Sound of Our Hearts	Behnam Lotfi, Gábor Pál, Attila Sándor, Csaba Walkó	Behnam Lotfi, Gábor Pál, Attila Sándor, Csaba Walkó	52
11	7	Switzerland	Sinplus	Unbreakable	Gabriel Broggini, Ivan Broggini	Gabriel Broggini, Ivan Broggini	45
12	9	Finland	Pernilla	När Jag Blundar	Jonas Karlsson	Jonas Karlsson	41
13	10	Israel	Izabo	Time	Ran Shem-Tov & Shiri Hadar	Ran Shem-Tov & Shiri Hadar	33
14	11	San Marino	Valentina Monetta	The Social Network Song (Oh Oh - Uh - Oh Oh)	Timothy Touchton & José Santana Rodriguez	Ralph Siegel	31
15	1	Montenegro	Rambo Amadeus	Euro Neuro	Rambo Amadeus	Rambo Amadeus	20
16	4	Latvia	Anmary	Beautiful Song	Rolands Ūdris	Ivars Makstnieks	17
17	8	Belgium	Iris	Would You?	Nina Sampermans, Jean Bosco Safari, Walter Mannaerts	Nina Sampermans, Jean Bosco Safari, Walter Mannaerts	16
18	16	Austria	Trackshittaz	Woki Mit Deim Popo	Lukas Plöchl, Manuel Hoffelner	Lukas Plöchl	8

2012 Eurovision 57: Baku, Azerbaijan
Semi-final 1: 22 May 2012

	Albania	Austria	Azerbaijan	Belgium	Cyprus	Denmark	Finland	Greece	Hungary	Iceland	Ireland	Israel	Italy	Latvia	Moldova	Montenegro	Romania	Russia	San Marino	Spain	Switzerland	TOTAL
Montenegro	12																		8			20
Iceland		2		5	8	10	10	5	4			4	1	5	2	5		1	3	6	4	75
Greece	8	1	10	8	12	4				5	10	3	5		10	10	12	5	7	3	3	116
Latvia			3								4				4	2		4				17
Albania		12	12	10	10	7	5	10	10	3	1	5	12	4	1	12	4	2	10	4	12	146
Romania	5	5	7	4	6	1		8	3	4	12	8	10		12	7		8	6	12	2	120
Switzerland	3	3			2				8	2		1			8				1			45
Belgium	2						2	4			6		8	7			2			1		16
Finland	1			1						7	3	2					1					41
Israel		7	5		1	8	3							6		4		6			1	33
San Marino	10		1	3		3		2	12			10	3	1		6	5			2		31
Cyprus	6							12	5	12	5		7		7		7	7				91
Denmark		10	8	12	4		1	1		8	7	12	6	3	3	8	3	3	4	8		63
Russia		4	2	6	7	12	8	7	1	6	8		2	8			6		2		10	152
Hungary	7	6		2	5	5	12							12	6		8			7	8	52
Austria			6				4		7	1					5						6	8
Moldova	4	8	4		3	6	6	6	2		2	6	4	2		3	10	12	5	10	5	100
Ireland				7		2	7	3	6	10		7		10		1		10	12	5	7	92

155

2012 Eurovision 57: Baku, Azerbaijan

Semi-final 2: 24 May 2012

Votes are cast by countries participating in each semi-final plus the five automatically qualifying countries decided by draw: Italy and Spain in semi-final 1, France, Germany and the United Kingdom in semi-final 2. Hosts Azerbaijan voted in semi-final 1. Points awarded are based on the combined votes of the viewers and jury from each of the countries voting in this semi-final. The top 10 countries in each semi-final qualify for the final.

Rank	Start	Country	Artist	Song	Writer	Composer	POINTS
1Q	11	Sweden	Loreen	Euphoria	Thomas G:son & Peter Boström	Thomas G:son & Peter Boström	181
2Q	1	Serbia	Željko Joksimović	Nije Ljubav Stvar	Marina Tucaković & Miloš Roganović	Željko Joksimović	159
3Q	18	Lithuania	Donny Montell	Love Is Blind	Brandon Stone & Jodie Rose	Brandon Stone	107
4Q	14	Estonia	Ott Lepland	Kuula	Aapo Ilves	Ott Lepland	100
5Q	13	Turkey	Can Bonomo	Love Me Back	Can Bonomo	Can Bonomo	80
6Q	17	Bosnia & H	MayaSar	Korake Ti Znam	Maja Sarihodžić	Maja Sarihodžić	77
7Q	4	Malta	Kurt Calleja	This Is The Night	Johan Jämtberg, Mikael Gunnerås & Kurt Calleja	Johan Jämtberg, Mikael Gunnerås & Kurt Calleja	70
8Q	7	Ukraine	Gaitana	Be My Guest	Gaitana	Gaitana and KIWI Project	64
9Q	2	FYR Macedonia	Kaliopi	Crno I Belo	Kaliopi	Romeo Grill	53
10Q	16	Norway	Tooji	Stay	Tooji, Figge Boström & Peter Boström	Tooji, Figge Boström & Peter Boström	45
11	8	Bulgaria	Sofi Marinova	Love Unlimited	Donka Vasileva	Krum Geopriev & Iasen Kozev	45
12	10	Croatia	Nina Badrić	Nebo	Nina Badrić	Nina Badrić	42
13	6	Portugal	Filipa Sousa	Vida Minha	Carlos Coelho	Andrej Babic	39
14	12	Georgia	Anri Jokhadze	I'm A Joker	Bibi Kvachadze	Rusudan Chkhaidze	36
15	3	Netherlands	Joan Franka	You And Me	Joan Franka	Joan Franka, Jessica Hoogenboom	35
16	5	Belarus	Litesound	We Are The Heroes	Dmitry Kariakin, Vladimir Kariakin	Dmitry Kariakin, Vladimir Kariakin	35
17	9	Slovenia	Eva Boto	Verjamem	Igor Pirković	Vladimir Graić, Hari Mata Hari	31
18	15	Slovakia	Max Jason Mai	Don't Close Your Eyes	Max Jason Mai	Max Jason Mai	22

2012 Eurovision 57: Baku, Azerbaijan
Semi-Final 2: 26 May 2012

	Belarus	Bosnia & H	Bulgaria	Croatia	Estonia	France	FYR Macedonia	Georgia	Germany	Lithuania	Malta	Netherlands	Norway	Portugal	Serbia	Slovakia	Slovenia	Sweden	Turkey	Ukraine	United Kingdom	TOTAL
Serbia	8	10	12	10	1	12	12	10	10	2	5	10	10	8		8	12	8		8	3	159
FYR Macedonia	2	8	7	7				1			1				8		6		8	5		53
Netherlands					7				8	3			3			2	2	1	7		4	35
Malta	5		6	5	3		2	4		6		2			3		4	4	6	6	12	70
Belarus				2		8	1	8		7	4	1				5			1	12		35
Portugal		4		3		2	3	6	3	1		6	5		4	1	3	6				39
Ukraine	12	2	5	1	5	3	6			5	6		2	2	2				10		2	64
Bulgaria		3					4		2		2		6	6	10							45
Slovenia		5		8			7		4						12	12		7				31
Croatia	1	12				6	8	12	1	10	8	12	12	10	7	3	8			1	8	42
Sweden	7	7	10		12	7		3	12	12	12	7	1	1		10	10		5	7		181
Georgia	6				4	10	10		6		7	8	8	12			1	7	3	10		36
Turkey		6	8		2	1			7	8		3		4	1	3		12		2	6	80
Estonia	4		3							4	3			3		10		3		3	7	100
Slovakia					6	4		2	5			5	4	4	5	4	5	10	4			22
Norway	3	1	2		8	5	5	5			10	5		3	5	6	5	5	12			45
Bosnia & Herzegovina			1	12								4	4	5	6	7	7	2	2	4	1	77
Lithuania	10		4	4	10						10		7	7							10	104

157

2012 Eurovision 57: Baku, Azerbaijan

Final: 26 May 2012

Final qualification rules: Top 10 placed countries from each semi-final. Automatic qualification: United Kingdom, France, Germany, Spain, Italy & hosts Azerbaijan. Points awarded are based on the combined votes of the viewers and jury from each of the 42 participating countries.

Rank	Start	Country	Artist	Song	Writer	Composer	POINTS
1	17	Sweden	Loreen	Euphoria	Thomas G:son & Peter Boström	Thomas G:son & Peter Boström	372
2	6	Russia	Buranovskiye Babushki	Party For Everybody	Olga Tuktareva, Mary S Applegate	Viktor Drobysh, Timofei Leontiev	259
3	24	Serbia	Željko Joksimović	Nije Ljubav Stvar	Marina Tucaković & Miloš Roganović	Željko Joksimović	214
4	13	Azerbaijan	Sabina Babayeva	When The Music Dies	Anders Bagge, Sandra Bjurman, Stefan Örn, Johan Kronlund	Anders Bagge, Johan Kronlund, Sandra Bjurman, Stefan Örn	150
5	3	Albania	Rona Nishliu	Suus	Rona Nishliu	Florent Boshnjaku	146
6	11	Estonia	Ott Lepland	Kuula	Aapo Ilves	Ott Lepland	120
7	18	Turkey	Can Bonomo	Love Me Back	Can Bonomo	Can Bonomo	112
8	20	Germany	Roman Lob	Standing Still	Wayne Hector, Jamie Cullum, Steve Robson	Wayne Hector, Jamie Cullum, Steve Robson	110
9	10	Italy	Nina Zilli	L'Amore È Femmina (Out Of Love)	Nina Zilli, Christian Rabb, Kristoffer Sjökvist, Frida Molander & Charlie Mason	Christian Rabb, Kristoffer Sjökvist, Frida Molander & Charlie Mason	101
10	19	Spain	Pastora Soler	Quédate Conmigo (Stay With Me)	Antonio Sánchez	Antonio Sánchez, Thomas G:son & Erik Bernholm	97
11	26	Moldova	Pasha Parfeny	Lăutar	Pasha Parfeny	Pasha Parfeny, Alex Brashovean	81
12	14	Romania	Mandinga	Zaleilah	Elena Ionescu, Dihigo Omar Secada, Costi Ionita	Costi Ionita	71
13	22	FYR Macedonia	Kaliopi	Crno I Belo	Kaliopi	Romeo Grill	71
14	4	Lithuania	Donny Martell	Love Is Blind	Brandon Stone & Jodie Rose	Brandon Stone	70
15	25	Ukraine	Gaitana	Be My Guest	Gaitana	Gaitana and KIWI Project	65
16	8	Cyprus	Ivi Adamou	La La Love	A Papaconstantinou, B Djupström, A Zakka & V Svensson	A Papaconstantinou, B Djupström, A Zakka & V Svensson	65
17	16	Greece	Eleftheria Eleftheriou	Aphrodisiac	Dimitri Stassos, Mikaela Stenström, Dajana Lööf	Dimitri Stassos, Mikaela Stenström, Dajana Lööf	64
18	5	Bosnia & H	MayaSar	Korake Ti Znam	Maja Sarihodžić	Maja Sarihodžić	55
19	23	Ireland	Jedward	Waterline	Nick Jarl & Sharon Vaughn	Nick Jarl & Sharon Vaughn	46
20	7	Iceland	Greta Salóme & Jónsi	Never Forget	Gréta Salómé	Gréta Salómé	46
21	21	Malta	Kurt Calleja	This Is The Night	Johan Jämtberg, Mikael Gunnerås & Kurt Calleja	Johan Jämtberg, Mikael Gunnerås & Kurt Calleja	41
22	9	France	Anggun	Echo (You And I)	William Rousseau & Anggun	Jean Pierre Pilot & William Rousseau	21
23	15	Denmark	Soluna Samay	Should've Known Better	Chief 1, Remee & Isam B	Chief 1 & Remee	21
24	2	Hungary	Compact Disco	Sound Of Our Hearts	Behnam Lotfi, Gábor Pál, Attila Sándor, Csaba Walkó	Behnam Lotfi, Gábor Pál, Attila Sándor, Csaba Walkó	19
25	1	United Kingdom	Engelbert Humperdinck	Love Will Set You Free	Martin Terefe & Sacha Skarbek	Martin Terefe & Sacha Skarbek	12
26	12	Norway	Tooji	Stay	Tooji, Figge Boström & Peter Boström	Tooji, Figge Boström & Peter Boström	7

2012 Eurovision 57: Baku, Azerbaijan — Final: 26 May 2012

Order votes announced	Albania	Austria	Azerbaijan	Belarus	Belgium	Bosnia & H	Bulgaria	Croatia	Cyprus	Denmark	Estonia	Finland	France	FYR Macedonia	Georgia	Germany	Greece	Hungary	Iceland	Ireland	Israel	Italy	Latvia	Lithuania	Malta	Moldova	Montenegro	Netherlands	Norway	Portugal	Romania	Russia	San Marino	Serbia	Slovakia	Slovenia	Spain	Sweden	Switzerland	Turkey	Ukraine	United Kingdom	TOTAL
	1	4	8	6	7	15	17	21	20	31	30	34	11	23	35	38	14	40	26	42	41	36	32	29	9	16	2	24	28	25	3	39	10	37	22	19	33	27	18	13	5	12	
United Kingdom					1																																					12	12
Hungary																				4						1					7		12	2	8					1	5		19
Albania		8	10	12	10	6	4	5	4	5		6	3	12	3	6	10	8				12	1		1		1	1		8	1		12	1	8	3		1	12	1			146
Lithuania			4	8			5				3			7	12					7			4		4		10	1	6			5								5		7	70
Bosnia & Herzegovina		7						10										8									1	1						5		7			1	10			55
Russia	3	5	10		8	3	6	6	5	8	8	8	4	4	5	7	4	7	7	6	7	10	10	6	3	6	4	4	8	8	4		10	7	3	8	8	7	1	7	10	3	259
Iceland			12			1			1	6	6	7			3	3		6		8	3	5					6	4	5					4		4	4						46
Cyprus	6		2														12		8		4		3		10	5	1				2	2					5						65
France	2					2													6	2					12	2	6			2								2					21
Italy	7			4				2	2	3	7		1		4	2	3	5	10	8	4		8	4	10	5	4	7	4	7		6	7		5	5	1				4	4	101
Estonia								8				10	10	5	10	4			10	8				8	12	10	1	7	7			10		10	10		6				1		120
Norway																			1				3					3				1			6								7
Azerbaijan	4			4	3	7	10	3	8	1			2	2	2		5	5		1	8	7		4	12	5	5			4	8	10	4	3	6			7	7	12	4	2	150
Romania		6		7				12	3		5	5			10		7			5	6			8	12	2			2	3		1		10			10		3	4	12	12	71
Denmark											2				1				5		2	2																			5		21
Greece	12		5		2	1	1						8	6	8	5									6	4				3		3		4					3		5		64
Sweden	5	12	7	6	12	8	8		10	12	12	12	12	8	7	12	6	12	12	12	12		12	10	12	7		12	12	3	10	12	3	10	12	10	12		7	12	6	12	372
Turkey	10	3	12		7	4	7		3	2		3	5			8		3	2	5	1			1	1				1	12	3		5		4			6	3			1	112
Spain		6			6	5	3		6		4	6	6		7		8	1	2		10		7		8		6	6	3		6		1					4	8			8	97
Germany	2	4		3				4		10	10	1	7		2		1	10	2	10			3	7	2	4	3	2		10							3		4		6	6	110
Malta			8	3		12								1		5					5	1	7					5					2									5	41
FYR Macedonia	8			2		10	2	8		4		4						4	4	3				7		3	8					8	6	12	1	6							71
Ireland		1		1	4	1	8	3				2			6	10						1												1	7							10	46
Serbia	1	10	3	4	5	10	12	12	7	4			8	10			8	4	4	3	5	5	5	5	5	3	12	5	10	5	5	4	6		7	12		5	6		7	2	214
Ukraine				10								4		3	6		1	2				3	6	2	7	8		10	1	1	12	8				1	2	10	2			5	65
Moldova		1		5				1	7		1						2	2			5						3			6		7					7		2	8			81

2013 Eurovision 58: Malmö, Sweden

Semi-final 1: 14 May 2013

Votes are cast by countries participating in each semi-final plus the five automatically qualifying countries decided by draw: Italy and United Kingdom in semi-final 1, France, Germany and Spain in semi-final 2. Hosts Sweden voted in semi-final 1. Points awarded are based on the combined votes of the viewers and jury from each of the countries voting in this semi-final. The top 10 countries in each semi-final qualify for the

Rank	Start	Country	Artist	Song	Writer	Composer	POINTS
1Q	5	Denmark	Emmelie de Forest	Only Teardrops	Lise Cabble, Julia Fabrin Jakobsen, Thomas Stengaard	Lise Cabble, Julia Fabrin Jakobsen, Thomas Stengaard	167
2Q	6	Russia	Dina Garipova	What If	Gabriel Alares, Joakim Björnberg, Leonid Gutkin	Gabriel Alares, Joakim Björnberg, Leonid Gutkin	156
3Q	7	Ukraine	Zlata Ognevich	Gravity	Karen Kavaleryan	Mikhail Nekrasov	140
4Q	12	Moldova	Aliona Moon	O Mie	Yuliana Scutaru	Pasha Parfeny	95
5Q	15	Belgium	Roberto Bellarosa	Love Kills	Iain James, Jukka Immonen	Iain James, Jukka Immonen	75
6Q	8	Netherlands	Anouk	Birds	Anouk Teeuwe	Tore Johansson, Martin Gjerstad	75
7Q	11	Belarus	Alyona Lanskaya	Solayoh	Martin King	Marc Paelinck	64
8Q	13	Ireland	Ryan Dolan	Only Love Survives	Wez Devine, Ryan Dolan	Wez Devine, Ryan Dolan	54
9Q	10	Lithuania	Andrius Pojavis	Something	Andrius Pojavis	Andrius Pojavis	53
10Q	2	Estonia	Birgit Õigemeel	Et Uus Saaks Alguse	Mihkel Mattisen & Silvia Soro	Mihkel Mattisen	52
11	16	Serbia	Moje 3	Ljubav Je Svuda	Marina Tucaković	Saša Milošević Mare	46
12	9	Montenegro	Who See	Igranka	Dejan Dedovic, Mario Djordjevic, Djordje Miljenovic	Djordje Miljenovic	41
13	4	Croatia	Klapa s mora	Mižerja	Goran Topolovac	Goran Topolovac	38
14	1	Austria	Natália Kelly	Shine	Andreas Grass, Nikola Paryla, Alexander Kahr	Andreas Grass, Nikola Paryla, Alexander Kahr	27
15	14	Cyprus	Despina Olympiou	An Me Thimasai	Zenon Zintillis	Andreas Giorgallis	11
16	3	Slovenia	Hannah	Straight Into Love	Hannah Mancini, Marko Primuzak	Hannah Mancini, Gregor Zemljic, Erik Margan, Matija Rodic	8

2013 Eurovision 58: Malmö, Sweden

Semi-final 1: 14 May 2013

	Austria	Belarus	Belgium	Croatia	Cyprus	Denmark	Estonia	Ireland	Italy	Lithuania	Moldova	Montenegro	Netherlands	Russia	Serbia	Slovenia	Sweden	Ukraine	United Kingdom	TOTAL
Austria			3	4	2	4	1	4	2		3				2	1			1	27
Estonia	3	5	1			1		8	5	4	5		4	5			6	1	4	52
Slovenia				5								3								8
Croatia	5				1															38
Denmark	12	8	10	12	8		12	12	6	1	7	5	3	4	10	2	12	6	12	167
Russia	10	10	7	8	10	12	10	10	4	6	8	8	12		8	8	10	4	10	156
Ukraine	2	12	8	7	12	8	6	2	12	10	12	7	7		6	10	1	7	2	140
Netherlands	8		12			10	7	5	1	12		12	8	7	5	12	8		8	75
Montenegro		2	6	6	3	5	4	6	10	7	6			1	12	3	2	8	7	41
Lithuania		7			6	2	3	3	7		2	6	2	2	4			5		53
Belarus	7		5	1	5	6	5		8	8	10	4	6	12	7	4	5	12		64
Moldova	1	6	4	2	7	3	2	6		3		1	5	6		7	3	10	6	95
Ireland	4	4	2			7	8			5	4	10	10	8			7	3	3	54
Cyprus																				11
Belgium	6	3		3		7		7				1				6	7		5	75
Serbia		1		10	4				3	2		10	1			5	4	2		46

2013 Eurovision 58: Malmö, Sweden

Semi-final 2: 16 May 2013

Votes are cast by countries participating in each semi-final plus the five automatically qualifying countries decided by draw: Italy and United Kingdom in semi-final 1, France, Germany and Spain in semi-final 2. Hosts Sweden voted in semi-final 1. Points awarded are based on the combined votes of the viewers and jury from each of the countries voting in this semi-final. The top 10 countries in each semi-final qualify for the

Rank	Start	Country	Artist	Song	Writer	Composer	POINTS
1Q	4	Azerbaijan	Farid Mammadov	Hold Me	John Ballard & Ralph Charlie Al Fahel	Dimitrios Kontopoulos	139
2Q	9	Greece	Koza Mostra feat. Agathon Iakovidis	Alcohol is Free	Stathis Pachidis, Ilias Kozas	Ilias Kozas	121
3Q	13	Norway	Margaret Berger	I Feed You My Love	Karin Park, Robin Lynch, Niklas Olovson	Karin Park, Robin Lynch, Niklas Olovson	120
4Q	6	Malta	Gianluca	Tomorrow	Boris Cezek & Dean Muscat	Boris Cezek & Dean Muscat	118
5Q	17	Romania	Cezar	It's My Life	Cristian Faur	Cristian Faur	83
6Q	8	Iceland	Eythor Ingi	Ég Á Líf	Örlygur Smári & Pétur Örn Gudmundsson	Örlygur Smári & Pétur Örn Gudmundsson	72
7Q	11	Armenia	Dorians	Lonely Planet	Vardan Zadoyan	Tony Iommi	69
8Q	12	Hungary	ByeAlex	Kedvesem (Zoohacker Remix)	Alex Márta	Alex Márta, Zoltán Palásti Kovács	66
9Q	5	Finland	Krista Siegfrids	Marry Me	Krista Siegfrids, Erik Nyholm, Kristoffer Karlsson, Jessica Lundström	Krista Siegfrids, Erik Nyholm, Kristoffer Karlsson, Jessica Lundström	64
10Q	15	Georgia	Nodi Tatishvili & Sophie Gelovani	Waterfall	Thomas G:son	Thomas G:son & Erik Bernholm	63
11	2	San Marino	Valentina Monetta	Crisalide (Vola)	Mauro Balestri	Ralph Siegel	47
12	7	Bulgaria	Elitsa Todorova feat. Stoyan Yankulov	Samo Shampioni (Only Champions)	Elitsa Todorova, Christian Talev	Elitsa Todorova, Christian Talev	45
13	16	Switzerland	Takasa	You And Me	Georg Schlunegger, Roman Camenzind, Fred Herrmann	Georg Schlunegger, Roman Camenzind, Fred Herrmann	41
14	10	Israel	Moran Mazor	Rak Bishvilo	Gal Sarig	Han Harari	40
15	14	Albania	Adrian Lulgjuraj & Bledar Sejko	Identitet	Eda Sejko	Bledar Sejko	31
16	3	FYR Macedonia	Esma & Lozano	Pred Da Se Razdeni	Magdalena Cvetkovska	Darko Dimitrov, Lazar Cvetkovski, Simeon Atanasov	28
17	1	Latvia	PeR	Here We Go	Ralfs Eilands	Ralfs Eilands, Arturas Burke	13

2013 Eurovision 58: Malmö, Sweden — Semi-final 2: 16 May 2013

	Albania	Armenia	Azerbaijan	Bulgaria	Finland	France	FYR Macedonia	Georgia	Germany	Greece	Hungary	Iceland	Israel	Latvia	Malta	Norway	Romania	San Marino	Spain	Switzerland	TOTAL
Latvia							2	7				3								1	13
San Marino		4	1				5	1		1	2		4	3	6		4		10		47
FYR Macedonia	12			5	1	5									5						28
Azerbaijan	8			12	3		2	12		12	12	8	12		12	5	12		2	4	139
Finland	1		3			8	5		3		5	7	1	7	1	8	3		8	3	64
Malta	6	7	12		5	7	8	6	5	5	8	6	2	8		12	7			2	118
Bulgaria	4	10	4			2	12	4		2	1			6		1	1		6	7	45
Iceland		1		10	12	1	3		12									10	7		72
Greece	10	8	7	4	7			2	8		10	2	6	10	7	10	10	12	5	10	121
Israel	3	6	6	8	2	4		5	4		3	1		5		7	2		3	6	40
Armenia	7			6		12	6	10	6	7			8	1	8		5				69
Hungary				7	8	3		3	10			12	3	2		4	6	4		12	66
Norway		5	5		10		7	8	2	4	7	4	5	12	3		8	5	12	8	120
Albania			2	3			10			8		5				2		6		5	31
Georgia		12	10	1	6		4			6	4		7	4	4			1	4		63
Switzerland	2	2		2	4	10			1	3	6	10			2	3					41
Romania	5	3	8			6	1		7	10			10		10	6			1		83

163

2013 Eurovision 58: Malmö, Sweden

Final: 18 May 2013

Final qualification rules: Top 10 placed countries from each semi-final. Automatic qualification: United Kingdom, France, Germany, Spain, Italy & hosts Sweden.
Points awarded are based on the combined votes of the viewers and jury from each of the 39 participating countries.

Rank	Start	Country	Artist	Song	Writer	Composer	POINTS
1	18	Denmark	Emmelie de Forest	Only Teardrops	Lise Cabble, Julia Fabrin Jakobsen, Thomas Stengaard	Lise Cabble, Julia Fabrin Jakobsen, Thomas Stengaard	281
2	20	Azerbaijan	Farid Mammadov	Hold Me	John Ballard & Ralph Charlie Al Fahel	Dimitrios Kontopoulos	234
3	22	Ukraine	Zlata Ognevich	Gravity	Karen Kavaleryan	Mikhail Nekrasov	214
4	24	Norway	Margaret Berger	I Feed You My Love	Karin Park, Robin Lynch, Niklas Olovson	Karin Park, Robin Lynch, Niklas Olovson	191
5	10	Russia	Dina Garipova	What If	Gabriel Alares, Joakim Björnberg, Leonid Gutkin	Gabriel Alares, Joakim Björnberg, Leonid Gutkin	174
6	21	Greece	Koza Mostra feat. Agathon Iakovidis	Alcohol Is Free	Stathis Pachidis, Ilias Kozas	Ilias Kozas	152
7	23	Italy	Marco Mengoni	L'Essenziale	Roberto Casalino	Francesco De Benedittis, Roberto Casalino, Marco Mengoni	126
8	9	Malta	Gianluca	Tomorrow	Boris Cezek & Dean Muscat	Boris Cezek & Dean Muscat	120
9	13	Netherlands	Anouk	Birds	Anouk Teeuwe	Tore Johansson, Martin Gjerstad	114
10	17	Hungary	ByeAlex	Kedvesem (Zoohacker Remix)	Alex Márta	Alex Márta, Zoltán Palásti Kovács	84
11	3	Moldova	Aliona Moon	O Mie	Yuliana Scutaru	Pasha Parfeny	71
12	6	Belgium	Roberto Bellarosa	Love Kills	Iain James, Jukka Immonen	Iain James, Jukka Immonen	71
13	14	Romania	Cezar	It's My Life	Cristian Faur	Cristian Faur	65
14	16	Sweden	Robin Stjernberg	You	Robin Stjernberg, Joy Deb, Linnea Deb, Joakim Harestad Haukaas	Robin Stjernberg, Joy Deb, Linnea Deb, Joakim Harestad Haukaas	62
15	25	Georgia	Nodi Tatishvili & Sophie Gelovani	Waterfall	Thomas G:son	Thomas G:son & Erik Bernholm	50
16	8	Belarus	Alyona Lanskaya	Solayoh	Martin King	Marc Paelinck	48
17	19	Iceland	Eyþór Ingi	Ég Á Líf	Örlygur Smári & Pétur Örn Gudmundsson	Örlygur Smári & Pétur Örn Gudmundsson	47
18	12	Armenia	Dorians	Lonely Planet	Vardan Zadoyan	Tony Iommi	41
19	15	United Kingdom	Bonnie Tyler	Believe in Me	Desmond Child, Lauren Christy, Christopher Braide	Desmond Child, Lauren Christy, Christopher Braide	23
20	7	Estonia	Birgit Õigemeel	Et Uus Saaks Alguse	Mihkel Mattisen & Silvia Soro	Mihkel Mattisen	19
21	11	Germany	Cascada	Glorious	Yann Peifer, Manuel Reuter, Andres Ballinas, Tony Cornelissen	Yann Peifer, Manuel Reuter, Andres Ballinas, Tony Cornelissen	18
22	2	Lithuania	Andrius Pojavis	Something	Andrius Pojavis	Andrius Pojavis	17
23	1	France	Amandine Bourgeois	L'enfer Et Moi	Boris Bergman	David Salkin	14
24	4	Finland	Krista Siegfrids	Marry Me	Krista Siegfrids, Erik Nyholm, Kristoffer Karlsson, Jessica Lundström	Krista Siegfrids, Erik Nyholm, Kristoffer Karlsson, Jessica Lundström	13
25	5	Spain	ESDM	Contigo Hasta El Final (With You Until The End)	Raquel del Rosario, David Feito, Juan Suárez	Raquel del Rosario, David Feito, Juan Suárez	8
26	26	Ireland	Ryan Dolan	Only Love Survives	Wez Devine, Ryan Dolan	Wez Devine, Ryan Dolan	5

2013 Eurovision 58: Malmö, Sweden — Final: 18 May 2013

Order votes announced	Albania 3	Armenia 15	Austria 5	Azerbaijan 13	Belarus 19	Belgium 22	Bulgaria 21	Croatia 37	Cyprus 36	Denmark 31	Estonia 25	Finland 17	France 28	FYR Macedonia 35	Georgia 34	Germany 26	Greece 29	Hungary 10	Iceland 27	Ireland 30	Israel 7	Italy 16	Latvia 20	Lithuania 39	Malta 24	Moldova 12	Montenegro 32	Netherlands 4	Norway 14	Romania 11	Russia 23	San Marino 1	Serbia 8	Slovenia 33	Spain 18	Sweden 2	Switzerland 38	Ukraine 9	United Kingdom 6	TOTAL
France	2														1				2													8						1		14
Lithuania			3	3	5									1						1										12										17
Moldova		2	2	1	4	3				2			4	7	1					3	1	6					5			12	6		6		2		4	1	8	71
Finland							3					6	3			1					4											3								13
Spain	6																					2																		8
Belgium		3							1	5	2	3	5					4		4		6	2				5			12	8		6	2		7			3	71
Estonia												6											10	3																19
Belarus	5			7							5			5	5	5	1	8	5	3	3		5	1	2	4	3	8	10		8	5	3							48
Malta	6		2	8	7	12	8		3	4	5	8	2	3	3	5	3		8		1	10	5		1	7	7	8	10	5			8	10	1		1	12	7	120
Russia	7				8	4	5	6	5	7	12	2	6	6	6	2			6		4		12	7	2	7	7	4	6	3					6	5	2	4	10	174
Germany	3	6			2																					1									3		1			18
Armenia					2		8			10			7		10			3					4			1			12		2	1								41
Netherlands	4		8			12		2			7	8	12	2		5		5	8	6	3		6	4	2	1	3		8		3			7		8	4	6		114
Romania	5		4	6						1	6	5				2	10		6	7					7	10			6							4	5			65
United Kingdom													1							7	5		4		5		1			3						1				23
Sweden						1		1		8	1	4				3		3	4	5		3		5		5		3	12			6	1	1	4					62
Hungary	8			4	2		6	4			4	10	7		12	12	2		8					2			10	7	2		2		2	6		3	10			84
Denmark	1	4	5	5		10	2	10	7		8	7	12	12	7	10	7	10	12	12	8	12	6	5	6	6	10	10	7	6	4	6	12	12	8	8	3	5	12	281
Iceland		5			1					1	6	5			8	8		6						2				4					4				5		2	47
Azerbaijan	7	12			10	5	12	7	8	6			8		12	4	12	12	12	12	8	12	3	12	12	8	12	2	7	10	12	2	5	12	8	3	6	10		234
Greece	10	8	7	4	6	2	7	5	12	3	6	1		4		6		1	1		2	7	1	10	4	2	8	1	2	7	10	12		3	7		8		8	152
Ukraine		12		12	12	8	10	12	10		10		10	10	8		8	7	3	8	10	5	7	10	10	12	8	5	5	4	10	2	10		10	6			5	214
Italy	12	1				6		8	6	12	3		10	8	2	7	6		7	8	2		7	6	10		6	5	1	1	1	4	4	8	12		6	10	8	126
Norway	2	3	10	2	3	7	1	3	4		12				4		4	2	3			8	8	8	3	3	4	6	5	8	7	7	7	5	5	12	7	3	5	191
Georgia		10															5									2	3		1		5					2		7		50
Ireland									2																														1	5

165

2014 Eurovision 59: Copenhagen, Denmark
Semi-final 1: 6 May 2014

Votes are cast by countries participating in each semi-final plus the five automatically qualifying countries decided by draw: Spain and France in semi-final 1, Italy, Germany and the UK in semi-final 2. Hosts Denmark voted in semi-final 1. Points awarded are based on the combined votes of the viewers and jury from each of the countries voting in this semi-final. The top 10 countries in each semi-final qualify for the final.

Rank	Start	Country	Artist	Song	Writer	Composer	POINTS
1Q	14	Netherlands	The Common Linnets	Calm After the Storm	Ilse DeLange, JB Meijers, Rob Crosby, Matthew Crosby, Jake Etheridge	Ilse DeLange, JB Meijers, Rob Crosby, Matthew Crosby, Jake Etheridge	150
2Q	4	Sweden	Sanna Nielsen	Undo	Fredrik Kempe, David Kreuger, Hamed "K-One" Pirouzpanah	Fredrik Kempe, David Kreuger, Hamed "K-One" Pirouzpanah	131
3Q	16	Hungary	András Kállay-Saunders	Running	András Kállay-Saunders	András Kállay-Saunders & Krisztián Szakos	127
4Q	1	Armenia	Aram MP3	Not Alone	Garik Papoyan	Aram MP3	121
5Q	9	Ukraine	Mariya Yaremchuk	Tick-Tock	Mariya Yaremchuk & Sandra Bjurman	Mariya Yaremchuk	118
6Q	7	Russia	Tolmachevy Sisters	Shine	John Ballard, Ralph Charlie, Gerard James Borg	Philipp Kirkorov & Dimitris Kontopoulos	63
7Q	15	Montenegro	Sergej Ćetković	Moj Svijet	Sergej Ćetković & Emina Sandal	Sergej Ćetković	63
8Q	5	Iceland	Pollapönk	No Prejudice	Heidar Orn Kristjansson, Haraldur Freyr Gislason, John Grant	Heidar Orn Kristjansson	61
9Q	8	Azerbaijan	Dilara Kazimova	Start a Fire	Stefan Örn, Johan Kronlund, Alessandra Günthardt	Stefan Örn, Johan Kronlund, Alessandra Günthardt	57
10Q	12	San Marino	Valentina Monetta	Maybe (Forse)	Mauro Balestri	Ralph Siegel	40
11	13	Portugal	Suzy	Quero Ser Tua	Emanuel	Emanuel	39
12	3	Estonia	Tanja	Amazing	Tanja	Timo Vendt, Tanja	36
13	2	Latvia	Aarzemnieki	Cake to Bake	Guntis Veilands	Guntis Veilands	33
14	10	Belgium	Axel Hirsoux	Mother	Rafael Artesero & Ashley Hicklin	Rafael Artesero & Ashley Hicklin	28
15	6	Albania	Hersi	One Night's Anger	Jorgo Papingji	Gentian Lako	22
16	11	Moldova	Cristina Scarlat	Wild Soul	Lidia Scarlat	Ivan Akulov	13

2014 Eurovision 59: Copenhagen, Denmark

Semi-final 1: 10 May 2014

	Albania	Armenia	Azerbaijan	Belgium	Denmark	Estonia	France	Hungary	Iceland	Latvia	Moldova	Montenegro	Netherlands	Portugal	Russia	San Marino	Spain	Sweden	Ukraine	TOTAL
Armenia	5			3	5	5	12	8	3	6		10	12	4	12	10	6	8	12	121
Latvia		5	7	5	1	6		2	6					3		2		1		33
Estonia			5						5	10							2	5		36
Sweden	6	4		8	10	7	4	10	10	8	10	5	8	8	6	3	12		10	131
Iceland				4	8	2	6	6		5			7	1		7	3	7	3	61
Albania				2	2	1	8					12	1			5				22
Russia	7	7	10	1	4	4		5	2	4	12	4	4	5		6		2	6	63
Azerbaijan	3	12		7	7		2	1	1	2	6	7	5	2	10	4	5		5	57
Ukraine		6	12			10		3	7	7	8	8		7	7	1		6		118
Belgium	4		4				1				7	2	3		4				2	28
Moldova			6						4	1		6			1		1			13
San Marino	8	2	6	6	3	3	5	7			1	3	2		3		1	4	4	40
Portugal	1	3	1						12	12	3	1				12	8			39
Netherlands	2	10	3	10	12	12	10	12			2		2	12	2		7	12	7	150
Montenegro	12	8	2		6		7	4			5		6	6	5		4	3	1	63
Hungary	10	1	8	12		8	3		8	3	4		10	10	8	8	10	10	8	127

2014 Eurovision 59: Copenhagen, Denmark

Semi-final 2: 8 May 2014

Votes are cast by countries participating in each semi-final plus the five automatically qualifying countries decided by draw: Spain and France in semi-final 1, Italy, Germany and the UK in semi-final 2. Hosts Denmark voted in semi-final 1. Points awarded are based on the combined votes of the viewers and jury from each of the countries voting in this semi-final. The top 10 countries in each semi-final qualify for the final.

Rank	Start	Country	Artist	Song	Writer	Composer	POINTS
1Q	6	Austria	Conchita Wurst	Rise Like a Phoenix	Charly Mason, Joey Patulka, Ali Zuckowski, Julian Maas	Charly Mason, Joey Patulka, Ali Zuckowski, Julian Maas	169
2Q	15	Romania	Paula Seling & Ovi	Miracle	Ovi, Philip Halloun, Frida Amundsen, Beyond51	Ovi, Philip Halloun, Frida Amundsen, Beyond51	125
3Q	8	Finland	Softengine	Something Better	Henri Oskár, Topi Latukka	Topi Latukka	97
4Q	12	Switzerland	Sebalter	Hunter of Stars	Sebastiano Paù-Lessi	Sebastiano Paù-Lessi	92
5Q	10	Belarus	Teo	Cheesecake	Dmitry Novik	Yury Vashchuk (Teo)	87
6Q	3	Norway	Carl Espen	Silent Storm	Josefin Winther	Josefin Winther	77
7Q	13	Greece	Freaky Fortune feat. RiskyKidd	Rise Up	Freaky Fortune & RiskyKidd	Freaky Fortune	74
8Q	5	Poland	Donatan & Cleo	My Słowianie - We Are Slavic	Cleo	Donatan	70
9Q	1	Malta	Firelight	Coming Home	Richard Edwards Micallef	Richard Edwards Micallef	63
10Q	14	Slovenia	Tinkara Kovač	Round and Round	Tinkara Kovač, Hannah Mancini, Tina Piš	Raay	52
11	7	Lithuania	Vilija Matačiūnaitė	Attention	Vilija Matačiūnaitė	Vilija Matačiūnaitė & Viktoras Vaupšas	36
12	9	Ireland	Can-Linn (feat. Kasey Smith)	Heartbeat	Jonas Gladnikoff, Rasmus Palmgren, Patrizia Helander	Hazel Kaneswaran, Jonas Gladnikoff, Rasmus Palmgren, Patrizia Helander	35
13	11	FYR Macedonia	Tijana	To The Sky	Elena Risteska Ivanovska, Darko Dimitrov	Darko Dimitrov, Lazar Cvetkoski	33
14	2	Israel	Mei Finegold	Same Heart	Rami Talmid	Rami Talmid	19
15	4	Georgia	The Shin and Mariko	Three Minutes to Earth	Eugen Eliu	Zaza Miminoshvili	15

2014 Eurovision 59: Copenhagen, Denmark

Semi-final 2: 10 May 2014

	Austria	Belarus	Finland	FYR Macedonia	Georgia	Germany	Greece	Ireland	Israel	Italy	Lithuania	Malta	Norway	Poland	Romania	Slovenia	Switzerland	United Kingdom	TOTAL
Austria		7	12	6	10	4	12	12	10	12	10	10	8	10	12	10	12	12	169
Belarus	10		7	2	12		8	1	7		12	6	1	7	8	6	10		87
F.Y.R. Macedonia		1	1		2				2	2		3				12			33
Finland	8			10	1	5	4	10	3	8	5		12	8	5	2	8	8	97
Georgia		5	4			1	1				6	2		1					15
Greece	3	12			3	6		4	6	6		8	6	5	7	3	4	1	74
Ireland	4			7			2		1			4	3		2	1	1	5	35
Israel		2	3	5		2	6								1				19
Lithuania		6			7			5		1			5	2				10	36
Malta	1	4	5	12	8	3	7	3		5	1		2	4	3	4	5	7	63
Norway	5		10	4	5	7	3	8	4		8	7		6	4	5	2		77
Poland	2	10		3		12	10	2	12	10	4	1	7			7	3	4	70
Romania	12	8	6	8	6	8		7	8	4	2	12	10				7	6	125
Slovenia	7		2		4		5	6	5	7	3		4	3	6		6	2	52
Switzerland	6	3	8	1		10				3	7	5		12	10	8		3	92

2014 Eurovision 59: Copenhagen, Denmark
Final: 10 May 2014

Final qualification rules: Top 10 placed countries from each semi-final. Automatic qualification: United Kingdom, France, Germany, Spain, Italy & hosts Denmark. Points awarded are based on the combined votes of the viewers and jury from each of the 37 participating countries.

Rank	Start	Country	Artist	Song	Writer	Composer	POINTS
1	11	Austria	Conchita Wurst	Rise Like a Phoenix	Charly Mason, Joey Patulka, Ali Zuckowski, Julian Maas	Charly Mason, Joey Patulka, Ali Zuckowski, Julian Maas	290
2	24	The Netherlands	The Common Linnets	Calm After the Storm	Ilse DeLange, JB Meijers, Rob Crosby, Matthew Crosby, Jake Etheridge	Ilse DeLange, JB Meijers, Rob Crosby, Matthew Crosby, Jake Etheridge	238
3	13	Sweden	Sanna Nielsen	Undo	Fredrik Kempe, David Kreuger, Hamed "K-One" Pirouzpanah	Fredrik Kempe, David Kreuger, Hamed "K-One" Pirouzpanah	218
4	7	Armenia	Aram MP3	Not Alone	Garik Papoyan	Aram MP3	174
5	21	Hungary	András Kállay-Saunders	Running	András Kállay-Saunders	András Kállay-Saunders, Krisztián Szakos	143
6	1	Ukraine	Mariya Yaremchuk	Tick-Tock	Mariya Yaremchuk & Sandra Bjurman	Mariya Yaremchuk	113
7	15	Russia	Tolmachevy Sisters	Shine	John Ballard, Ralph Charlie, Gerard James Borg	Philipp Kirkorov & Dimitris Kontopoulos	89
8	5	Norway	Carl Espen	Silent Storm	Josefin Winther	Josefin Winther	88
9	23	Denmark	Basim	Cliché Love Song	Lasse Lindorff, Daniel Fält,	Lasse Lindorff, Daniel Fält,	74
10	19	Spain	Ruth Lorenzo	Dancing in the Rain	Basim Moujahid, Kim Novak-Zorde Ruth Lorenzo, Julian Emery, James Lawrence Irvin	Basim Moujahid, Kim Novak-Zorde Ruth Lorenzo, Julian Emery, James Lawrence Irvin	74
11	18	Finland	Softengine	Something Better	Henri Oskár, Topi Latukka	Topi Latukka	72
12	6	Romania	Paula Seling & Ovi	Miracle	Ovi, Philip Halloun, Frida Amundsen, Beyond51	Ovi, Philip Halloun, Frida Amundsen, Beyond51	72
13	20	Switzerland	Sebalter	Hunter of Stars	Sebastiano Paù-Lessi	Sebastiano Paù-Lessi	64
14	9	Poland	Donatan & Cleo	My Słowianie - We Are Slavic	Cleo	Donatan	62
15	4	Iceland	Pollapönk	No Prejudice	Heidar Orn Kristjansson, Haraldur Freyr Gislason, John Grant	Heidar Orn Kristjansson	58
16	2	Belarus	Teo	Cheesecake	Dmitry Novik	Yury Vashchuk (Teo)	43
17	26	United Kingdom	Molly	Children of the Universe	Molly Smitten-Downes, Anders Hansson	Molly Smitten-Downes, Anders Hansson	40
18	12	Germany	Elaiza	Is it Right?	Elżbieta Steinmetz, Adam Kesselhaut	Elżbieta Steinmetz, Frank Kretschmer	39
19	8	Montenegro	Sergej Ćetković	Moj Svijet	Sergej Ćetković & Emina Sandal	Sergej Ćetković	37
20	10	Greece	Freaky Fortune feat. RiskyKidd	Rise Up	Freaky Fortune & RiskyKidd	Freaky Fortune	35
21	16	Italy	Emma	La Mia Città	Emma Marrone	Emma Marrone	33
22	3	Azerbaijan	Dilara Kazimova	Start a Fire	Stefan Örn, Johan Kronlund, Alessandra Günthardt	Stefan Örn, Johan Kronlund, Alessandra Günthardt	33
23	22	Malta	Firelight	Coming Home	Richard Edwards Micallef	Richard Edwards Micallef	32
24	25	San Marino	Valentina Monetta	Maybe (Forse)	Mauro Balestri	Ralph Siegel	14
25	17	Slovenia	Tinkara Kovač	Round and Round	Tinkara Kovač, Hannah Mancini, Tina Piš	Raay	9
26	14	France	Twin Twin	Moustache	Lorent Ardouvin, François Ardouvin	Pierre Beyres, Kim N'Guyen	2

2014 Eurovision 59: Copenhagen, Denmark — Final: 10 May 2014

Order votes announced	Albania 4	Armenia 15	Austria 30	Azerbaijan 1	Belarus 19	Belgium 32	Denmark 6	Estonia 24	FYR Macedonia 17	France 12	Finland 28	Georgia 36	Germany 20	Greece 2	Hungary 25	Iceland 16	Ireland 27	Israel 21	Italy 33	Latvia 14	Lithuania 29	Malta 11	Moldova 26	Montenegro 7	Netherlands 10	Norway 23	Poland 3	Portugal 22	Romania 8	Russia 9	San Marino 5	Slovenia 37	Spain 31	Sweden 18	Switzerland 35	Ukraine 34	United Kingdom 13	TOTAL
Ukraine			5	10	8	4	1	8		2		6			2			5	10	7	5		10	7			5			7			6					113
Belarus		8		7										5				1			3		5	1						12	12					6		43
Azerbaijan					3							7												1						10	12				5	1		33
Iceland			2				5	3	4		7		2		5		7		7	5	8	2			6	6		3		1	8		1	4		6	4	58
Norway			1	6	4		6		8	7	2		5	3		1	2	8				8	12	1	10		7	1	1			5		3	5	1		88
Romania		8	8		1	5	2	5	12	4	12	12	6	7	7	2	7	6	5	10		6	3	10	7	4	1	4		8	6		4	5				72
Armenia			12		10				4		5	4	10	3	7	3	2	2	8		8	8	2			2	1		7	8		7		2		10		174
Montenegro	6								12					1	3							6									6	1						37
Poland									5		5		10		10	3			8			1	2	4		2				4		1		2	2	7		62
Greece	2	7		2	7		4		3			4					12	2						2						5								35
Austria	5			4	6		8	4		12	10	10	7	12	10	10	12	12	3	6	7	10	7	2	12	10	8	12	8	5	10	12	12	12	12	8	12	290
Germany	4	6		1	1		12			10	4	5		2	8	7	4	10				7	6		8	8		8	2	2					7	5	7	39
Sweden	7						10	12		4	12	2	12	10	12	12		10	12	8		5	8	3	8	8	8	8	12	2	10		10		6	12	7	218
France				8						1					4							12					4	2						1				2
Russia			6	5											1			3		2			8	6				2							2			89
Italy	10											8		10		5				6		12		8	2													33
Slovenia																							1	8														9
Finland	12		4					1	6	5		1	4	4	6		6	4		3	4			5	2	7	3		5		3			6	4		6	72
Spain		2					4		2	3	6		1	6	1	5	5	7	2	4	2	3			3	5	2	7	6						8	2	5	74
Switzerland		5		8	5		3	7					3			6	1			1	2				4		10	6	10	6				7			1	64
Hungary	8		7					10	10		6		8	4		6	3		1		4	3		12	5		3	5			7	4	2	8	1	3	10	143
Malta	1				5						3				4									4								3					3	32
Denmark		1							7	6						8	10				1			1	1	1	6	10	4	6	1		6	8	3			74
Netherlands		4	10		2			12	2	8	8		12	8	12	12			4	12	12			12		12	12	5	3	3	2		7	10	10	2	3	238
San Marino	3	3		3											4							4	1					10			5							14
United Kingdom											3						8									3							5					40

2015 Eurovision 60: Vienna, Austria

Semi-final 1: 19 May 2015

Votes are cast by countries participating in each semi-final plus the five automatically qualifying countries decided by draw: France and Spain in semi-final 1, Italy, Germany and the UK in semi-final 2. Hosts Austria voted in semi-final 1. Special guests Australia voted in both semi-finals. Points awarded are based on the combined votes of the viewers and jury from each of the countries voting in this semi-final. The top 10 countries in each semi-final qualify for the final.

Rank	Start	Country	Artist	Song	Writer	Composer	POINTS
1Q	12	Russia	Polina Gagarina	A Million Voices	Gabriel Alares, Joakim Björnberg, Katrina Noorbergen, Leonid Gutkin, Vladimir Matetsky	Gabriel Alares, Joakim Björnberg, Katrina Noorbergen, Leonid Gutkin, Vladimir Matetsky	182
2Q	3	Belgium	Loïc Nottet	Rhythm Inside	Beverly Jo Scott	Loïc Nottet	149
3Q	7	Estonia	Elina Born & Stig Rästa	Goodbye to Yesterday	Stig Rästa	Stig Rästa	105
4Q	16	Georgia	Nina Sublatti	Warrior	Nina Sublatti	Nina Sublatti, Thomas G:son	98
5Q	15	Romania	Voltaj	De la capat (All over Again)	Calin Gavril Goia, Gabriel Constantin, Adrian Cristescu, Paduraru Silviu-Marian, Stevens, Andrei-Madalin Leonte	Calin Gavril Goia, Gabriel Constantin, Adrian Cristescu, Paduraru Silviu-Marian, Alstani Victor-Razvan	89
6Q	6	Greece	Maria Elena Kyriakou	One Last Breath	Vangelis Konstantinidis, Evelina Tziora	Efthivoulos Theocharous, Maria-Elena Kyriakou	81
7Q	2	Armenia	Genealogy	Face the Shadow	Inna Mkrtchyan	Armen Martirosyan	77
8Q	10	Hungary	Boggie	Wars for Nothing	Sára Hélène Bori	Áron Sebestyén / Boglárka Csemer	67
9Q	9	Serbia	Bojana Stamenov	Beauty Never Lies	Charlie Mason	Vladimir Graić	63
10Q	14	Albania	Elhaida Dani	I'm Alive	Sokol Marsi	Arber Elshani, Kristijan Lekaj	62
11	1	Moldova	Eduard Romanyuta	I Want Your Love	Erik Lewander, Hayley Aitken, Tom Andrews	Erik Lewander, Hayley Aitken, Tom Andrews	41
12	11	Belarus	Uzari & Maimuna	Time	Gerylana/Maimuna	Uzari	39
13	13	Denmark	Anti Social Media	The Way You Are	Remee, Chief 1	Remee, Chief 1	33
14	4	Netherlands	Trijntje Oosterhuis	Walk Along	Anouk Teeuwe	Tobias Karlsson	33
15	8	FYR Macedonia	Daniel Kajmakoski	Autumn Leaves	Joacim Persson	Joacim Persson	28
16	5	Finland	Pertti Kurikan Nimipäivät	Aina mun pitää	Pertti Kurikan Nimipäivät	Pertti Kurikan Nimipäivät	13

2015 Eurovision 60: Vienna, Austria

Semi-final 1: 19 May 2015

	Albania	Armenia	Australia	Austria	Belarus	Belgium	Denmark	Estonia	Finland	France	FYR Macedonia	Georgia	Greece	Hungary	Moldova	Netherlands	Romania	Russia	Serbia	Spain	TOTAL
Moldova	2	6			5							10					8		5		41
Armenia	5				7			10		5	7	8	7		4	5	1	12		4	77
Belgium	6	1	8	6	6		12	5	12	12	6	5	6	10	5	12	7	8	7	10	149
Netherlands	1				1	6	2	4	3	2	1	2					3			3	33
Finland					1		2	4						2					4		13
Greece	12	8	6	4	3	3		1	2	3	4	4		3	3	6	6	5	6	2	81
Estonia		4	5	10	8	5	8		8	4	2	3	4	8	2	8	2	10	2	12	105
FYR Macedonia	10		3					2							1				12		28
Serbia		5	12	7	4	4	1		4	1	12		2	4		7		4			63
Hungary	3	7	2	5			4	12	7	6						4	10	2	8		67
Belarus		7					3					12	3		8			6			39
Russia	7	10	10	12	12	8	10	8	10	10	8	7	12	12	7	10	12		10	7	182
Denmark		2	4	1		1		7	1	7	10	1	1	7		3	5			1	33
Albania	8	3	1	3		10						6	10	1	6			3		6	62
Romania	8	3	6	8	2	7	6	3	6	8			5	5	12	2		1	3	8	89
Georgia	4	12	7	2	10	2	5	6	5		3		8	6	10	1	4	7	1	5	98

173

2015 Eurovision 60: Vienna, Austria — Semi-final 2: 21 May 2015

Votes are cast by countries participating in each semi-final plus the five automatically qualifying countries decided by draw: France and Spain in semi-final 1, Italy, Germany and the UK in semi-final 2. Hosts Austria voted in semi-final 1. Special guests Australia voted in both semi-finals. Points awarded are based on the combined votes of the viewers and jury from each of the countries voting in this semi-final. The top 10 countries in each semi-final qualify for the final.

Rank	Start	Country	Artist	Song	Writer	Composer	POINTS
1Q	13	Sweden	Måns Zelmerlöw	Heroes	Linnea Deb, Joy Deb, Anton Hård af Segerstad	Linnea Deb, Joy Deb, Anton Hård af Segerstad	217
2Q	10	Latvia	Aminata	Love Injected	Aminata Savadogo	Aminata Savadogo	155
3Q	9	Israel	Nadav Guedj	Golden Boy	Doron Medalie	Doron Medalie	151
4Q	6	Norway	Mørland & Debrah Scarlett	A Monster Like Me	Kjetil Mørland	Kjetil Mørland	123
5Q	16	Slovenia	Maraaya	Here for You	Charlie Mason, Raay	Raay, Marjetka Vovk	92
6Q	15	Cyprus	John Karayiannis	One Thing I Should Have Done	Mike Connaris	Mike Connaris	87
7Q	1	Lithuania	Monika Linkyte & Vaidas Baumila	This Time	Monika Liubinaitė	Vytautas Bikus	67
8Q	17	Poland	Monika Kuszynska	In the Name of Love	Monika Kuszyńska	Kuba Raczyński	57
9Q	4	Montenegro	Knez	Adio	Marina Tucaković & Dejan Ivanović	Željko Joksimović	57
10Q	11	Azerbaijan	Elnur Hüseynov	Hour of the Wolf	Sandra Bjurman, Nicolas Rebscher, Nicklas Lif, Lina Hansson	Nicolas Rebscher, Nicklas Lif, Lina Hansson	53
11	5	Malta	Amber	Warrior	Matt Muxu Mercieca	Elton Zarb	43
12	2	Ireland	Molly Sterling	Playing with Numbers	Greg French & Molly Sterling	Greg French & Molly Sterling	35
13	8	Czech Republic	Marta Jandová & Václav Noid Bárta	Hope Never Dies	Tereza Šoralová	Václav Noid Bárta	33
14	7	Portugal	Leonor Andrade	Há um mar que nos separa	Miguel Gameiro	Miguel Gameiro	19
15	12	Iceland	Maria Ólafs	Unbroken	Ásgeir Orri Ásgeirsson, Sæþór Kristjánsson, Maria Ólafsdóttir, Pálmi Ragnar Ásgeirsson	Ásgeir Orri Ásgeirsson, Sæþór Kristjánsson, Pálmi Ragnar Ásgeirsson	14
16	3	San Marino	Michele Perniola & Anita Simoncini	Chain of Lights	John O'Flynn	Ralph Siegel	11
17	14	Switzerland	Mélanie René	Time to Shine	Mélanie René	Mélanie René	4

2015 Eurovision 60: Vienna, Austria — Semi-final 2: 21 May 2015

	Australia	Azerbaijan	Cyprus	Czech Republic	Germany	Iceland	Ireland	Israel	Italy	Latvia	Lithuania	Malta	Montenegro	Norway	Poland	Portugal	San Marino	Slovenia	Sweden	Switzerland	United Kingdom	TOTAL
Lithuania	4	7	7	1		4	7	4		10		4					3			3	3	67
Ireland		2	1	5	2					4	2		2				5	1	3		8	35
San Marino			2										5									11
Montenegro	3	10		6					6	2				3		5		10	7	1	5	57
Malta	8		6	4		10	3	7	4	7	8		10		6	8	7	6	12	10	5	43
Norway		3		7	7		4	10	1			5	6			8	8	6	12	6	2	123
Portugal					1	10	1	1	2	1	8	1	4		8	1	4	4	1		1	19
Czech Republic					4			8					1					3				33
Israel	7	8	10	2	8	8	8		12	3	4	10	3	8	10	10	6	5	10	7	12	151
Latvia	10	6	8	8	10	7	12	2	8		12	7	7	7	7	7	6	8	8	8	10	155
Azerbaijan	2		5	10		2		3			6	8		2	3	3	10		4			53
Iceland		5					2				1		7		2				2			14
Sweden	12	4	12	12	12	12	10	12	10	12	10	12	8	12	12	12	12	12		12	7	217
Switzerland		1				1								1	1							4
Cyprus	6	12		3	5	5	6	5	7	6	3	2	12	6	4	6	2	7	6	5	6	87
Slovenia	5		3		6	6		6	3	8	7	3		4	5	4	1		5	4		92
Poland	1		4		3	3	5		5	5	5	6		5		2		2		2	4	57

2015 Eurovision 60: Vienna, Austria

Final: 23 May 2015

Final qualification rules: Top 10 placed countries from each semi-final. Automatic qualification: United Kingdom, France, Germany, Spain, Italy, hosts Austria and special guests Australia.
Points awarded are based on the combined votes of the viewers and jury from each of the 40 participating countries.

Rank	Start	Country	Artist	Song	Writer	Composer	POINTS
1	10	Sweden	Måns Zelmerlöw	Heroes	Linnea Deb, Joy Deb, Anton Hård af Segerstad	Linnea Deb, Joy Deb, Anton Hård af Segerstad	365
2	25	Russia	Polina Gagarina	A Million Voices	Gabriel Alares, Joakim Björnberg, Katrina Noorbergen, Leonid Gutkin, Vladimir Matetsky	Gabriel Alares, Joakim Björnberg, Katrina Noorbergen, Leonid Gutkin, Vladimir Matetsky	303
3	27	Italy	Il Volo	Grande amore	Ciro Esposito / Francesco Boccia	Ciro Esposito / Francesco Boccia	292
4	13	Belgium	Loïc Nottet	Rhythm Inside	Beverly Jo Scott	Loïc Nottet	217
5	12	Australia	Guy Sebastian	Tonight Again	Guy Sebastian, David Ryan Harris, Louis Schoorl	Guy Sebastian, David Ryan Harris, Louis Schoorl	196
6	19	Latvia	Aminata	Love Injected	Aminata Savadogo	Aminata Savadogo	186
7	4	Estonia	Elina Born & Stig Rästa	Goodbye to Yesterday	Stig Rästa	Stig Rästa	106
8	9	Norway	Mørland & Debrah Scarlett	A Monster Like Me	Kjetil Mørland	Kjetil Mørland	102
9	3	Israel	Nadav Guedj	Golden Boy	Doron Medalie	Doron Medalie	97
10	8	Serbia	Bojana Stamenov	Beauty Never Lies	Charlie Mason	Vladimir Graić	53
11	23	Georgia	Nina Sublatti	Warrior	Nina Sublatti	Nina Sublatti, Thomas G:son	51
12	24	Azerbaijan	Elnur Hüseynov	Hour of the Wolf	Sandra Bjurman, Nicolas Rebscher, Nicklas Lif, Lina Hansson	Nicolas Rebscher, Nicklas Lif, Lina Hansson	49
13	16	Montenegro	Knez	Adio	Marina Tucaković & Dejan Ivanović	Željko Joksimović	44
14	1	Slovenia	Maraaya	Here for You	Charlie Mason, Raay	Raay, Marjetka Vovk	39
15	20	Romania	Voltaj	De la capăt (All over Again)	C G Goia, G Constantin, A Cristescu, P Silviu-Marian, A Victor-Razvan, M-A Stevens, A-M Leonte	Calin Gavril Goia, Gabriel Constantin, Adrian Cristescu, Paduraru Silviu-Marian, Alstani Victor-Razvan	35
16	6	Armenia	Genealogy	Face the Shadow	Inna Mkrtchyan	Armen Martirosyan	34
17	26	Albania	Elhaida Dani	I'm Alive	Sokol Marsi	Arber Elshani, Kristijan Lekaj (Zzap'n'Chriss)	34
18	7	Lithuania	Monika Linkyte & Vaidas Baumila	This Time	Monika Liubinaitė	Vytautas Bikus	30
19	15	Greece	Maria Elena Kyriakou	One Last Breath	Vangelis Konstantinidis, Evelina Tziora	Efthivoulos Theocharous, Maria-Elena Kyriakou	23
20	22	Hungary	Boggie	Wars for Nothing	Sára Héléne Bori	Áron Sebestyén / Boglárka Csemer	19
21	21	Spain	Edurne	Amanecer	Tony Sánchez-Ohlsson, Peter Boström & Thomas G:son	Tony Sánchez-Ohlsson, Peter Boström & Thomas G:son	15
22	11	Cyprus	John Karayiannis	One Thing I Should Have Done	Mike Connaris	Mike Connaris	11
23	18	Poland	Monika Kuszyńska	In the Name of Love	Monika Kuszyńska	Kuba Raczyński	10
24	5	United Kingdom	Electro Velvet	Still in Love with You	David Mindel & Adrian Bax White	David Mindel & Adrian Bax White	5
25	2	France	Lisa Angell	N'oubliez pas	Laure Izon / M. Albert	Michel Illouz / M. Albert	4
26	14	Austria	The Makemakes	I Am Yours	Jimmy Harry and The Makemakes	Jimmy Harry and The Makemakes	0
27	17	Germany	Ann Sophie	Black Smoke	Michael Harwood, Ella McMahon, Tonino Speciale	Michael Harwood, Ella McMahon, Tonino Speciale	0

2015 Eurovision 60: Vienna, Austria — Final: 23 May 2015

Order votes announced	Albania	Armenia	Australia	Austria	Azerbaijan	Belarus	Belgium	Cyprus	Czech Republic	Denmark	Estonia	Finland	France	FYR Macedonia	Georgia	Germany	Greece	Hungary	Iceland	Ireland	Israel	Italy	Latvia	Lithuania	Malta	Moldova	Montenegro	Netherlands	Norway	Poland	Portugal	Romania	Russia	San Marino	Serbia	Slovenia	Spain	Sweden	Switzerland	United Kingdom	TOTAL
Slovenia	7	16	20	23	9	6	14	36	21	12	39	3	15	24	40	19	4	26	35	17	31	34	10	28	2	8	1	29	37	30	38	5	32	33	11	25	22	18	13	27	39
France					3																						4							1							4
Israel	5		2	2		2		6				1		8	1	5			2		6	8	3	4	5		3	5	4	4	7	1		2	6		1	4	3	5	97
Estonia	4		3	6	4	7	2	2	2	6		3		2	2	2		7	5			2	1	8	3	8	1	4	3	2	7	1	7	2	2		3	3			106
United Kingdom																				1					1						1										5
Armenia			5	3		4	3		2				3	3	12	5	1		10				7				4	5					6							4	34
Lithuania			4	4					3	1	2				3	2			1	7								4						1					5	1	30
Serbia	2							8						10							2	3	7				12							6		6			5		53
Norway	7		12	7	6	10	12		10	3	4	4	8	5	7	4	4	4	10	4		5	2	5	2			3		3	6			6		4		7	5		102
Sweden	7		6	5		8				12	10	12	2			10		10	12	10	10	12	12	10	10	8	5	10	12	12	8	8	8	7	8	12	8		10	12	365
Cyprus																	10											1			5			1		1					11
Australia	3	1		12		6	4	4	5	4	5	5	3		4	7	5	8	8	5	7	6	2	3	6	4		3		3	6	6	4	6	3	4	4	12	8	10	196
Belgium	1	4	6	5		8		7	6	8	7	7	12	1		8	7	12	4	2	4	7	12	7		6	5	10	7	5	5	7	10	5	4	12	3	10	2	3	217
Austria																																									0
Greece	10	5																																8							23
Montenegro	6	8		2										4																				12	12	10		2			44
Germany																																									0
Poland			5													1				3		1																			10
Latvia	2		4	1		5	7	3	5	4	6	6	7		4	6	3	5	3	12		4		12	4	2		2	8	10	2	5	2	8	1	7	4	5	4	2	186
Romania					1		5	1	2					12	10			1			5					12					4						5				35
Spain													5								1					1	2			3	3		1			1			1		15
Hungary							1			1	8		1			1										5						4		4							19
Georgia	10		6	5	10	3			4		1						2	3			5			6		3	2						5								51
Azerbaijan									12					12	10		2						10	2		10	8						3	4				2			49
Russia	8	12							8	10	12	8	10	6	5	12	8	6	3	8	8	10	8		7	10	7	6	2	6	10	3			10	5	10	6	7	6	303
Albania							6					2		12			6								12	7	10														34
Italy	12	6	8	10	8	1	8	12	7	5	3	2	6	7	8	3	12	2	6	6	12		8	1	12	7	6	7	5	7	12	12	12	10	7	8	12	8	6	8	292

177

2016 Eurovision 61: Stockholm, Sweden
Semi-final 1: 10 May 2016

Votes are cast by countries participating in each semi-final plus the five automatically qualifying countries decided by draw: France and Spain in semi-final 1, Italy, Germany and the UK in semi-final 2. Hosts Sweden voted in semi-final 1. This semi-final marked the first time the new voting system was used, with each voting country now awarding two sets of points, one from their professional jury and one from their public vote. The top 10 countries in each semi-final qualify for the final.

Rank	Start	Country	Artist	Song	Writer	Composer	POINTS
1Q	9	Russia	Sergey Lazarev	You Are The Only One	John Ballard, Ralph Charlie	Dimitris Kontopoulos, Philip Kirkorov	342
2Q	7	Armenia	Iveta Mukuchyan	LoveWave	Iveta Mukuchyan, Stephanie Crutchfield	Lilith Navasardyan, Levon Navasardyan	243
3Q	18	Malta	Ira Losco	Walk On Water	Lisa Desmond, Tim Larsson, Tobias Lundgren, Molly Pettersson-Hammar & Ira Losco	Lisa Desmond, Tim Larsson, Tobias Lundgren, Molly Pettersson-Hammar & Ira Losco	209
4Q	4	Hungary	Freddie	Pioneer	Borbála Csarnai	Szabó Zé	197
5Q	6	Netherlands	Douwe Bob	Slow Down	Douwe Bob Posthuma, Jeroen Overman, Jan-Peter Hoekstra	Douwe Bob Posthuma, Jeroen Overman, Jan-Peter Hoekstra, Matthijs van Duijvenbode	197
6Q	14	Azerbaijan	Samra	Miracle	Amir Aly, Jakke Erixson, Henrik Wikström	Amir Aly, Jakke Erixson, Henrik Wikström	185
7Q	12	Austria	ZOË	Loin d'ici	Christof Straub & Zoë Straub	Christof Straub & Zoë Straub	170
8Q	11	Cyprus	Minus One	Alter Ego	Thomas G:son, Minus One	Thomas G:son, Minus One	164
9Q	10	Czech Republic	Gabriela Gunčíková	I Stand	Aidan O'Connor, Sara Biglert	Christian Schneider, Sara Biglert	161
10Q	5	Croatia	Nina Kraljić	Lighthouse	Andreas Grass & Nikola Paryla	Andreas Grass & Nikola Paryla	133
11	17	Bosnia & H	Dalal & Deen feat. Ana Rucner and Jala	Ljubav Je	Almir Ajanović, Jasmin Fazlić	Almir Ajanović	104
12	8	San Marino	Serhat	I Didn't Know	Nektarios Tyrakis	Olcayto Ahmet Tuğsuz	68
13	15	Montenegro	Highway	The Real Thing	Srdjan Sekulovic Skansi	Skansi, Luka Vojvodić, Maro Market	60
14	16	Iceland	Greta Salóme	Hear Them Calling	Greta Salóme Stefánsdóttir	Greta Salóme Stefánsdóttir	51
15	1	Finland	Sandhja	Sing It Away	Sandhja Kuivalainen, Petri Matara, Milos Rosas, Markus Savijoki	Heikki Korhonen, Markus Savijoki, Milos Rosas, Petri Matara, Sandhja Kuivalainen	51
16	2	Greece	Argo	Utopian Land	Vladimiros Sofianides	Vladimiros Sofianides	44
17	3	Moldova	Lidia Isac	Falling Stars	Gabriel Alares, Sebastian Lestapier, Ellen Berg, Leonid Gutkin	Gabriel Alares, Sebastian Lestapier, Ellen Berg, Leonid Gutkin	33
18	13	Estonia	Jüri Pootsmann	Play	Stig Rästa, Vallo Kikas, Fred Krieger	Stig Rästa, Vallo Kikas, Fred Krieger	24

2016 Eurovision 61: Stockholm, Sweden

Combined Jury & Public Votes

Semi-final 1: 10 May 2016

	Armenia	Austria	Azerbaijan	Bosnia & H	Croatia	Cyprus	Czech Republic	Estonia	Finland	France	Greece	Hungary	Iceland	Malta	Moldova	Montenegro	Netherlands	Russia	San Marino	Spain	Sweden	TOTAL
Finland	8	2					7	7				5	2	5			2			3	10	51
Greece	10		6			15										3		10				44
Moldova	6		5			2					3			4				11				33
Hungary	6	8	15	5	16	12	18	10	4	2	14		8	8	9	7	9	10	7	15	4	197
Croatia	5	13	4	17		8	8	3	7	12	4	3	7		7	15	17	5	1	2	4	133
Netherlands	8	16		1	7	4	13	20	18	7	3	12	22	7	4	2	17		18	10	16	197
Armenia		9	13	10	8	17	12	3	8	12	18	7	8	16	18	15	17	24	8	22	8	243
San Marino		5		10				4	3	15	6	5	1	11	4	2	4					68
Russia	19	15	24	15	16	22	8	13	14	10	22	20	22	22	22	18	9		15	16	20	342
Czech Republic	7	11	5	16	16	5		6	10	4	3	11	8	5	11	5	6	6	6	13	7	161
Cyprus	8	2	1	2	12		5	16	7	9	20	9	6	14	7	5	13	8	13	4	3	164
Austria	5		6	6	7	5	10	10	13	22	7	8	12	2	7		16	10	3	12	9	170
Estonia		1	3						13					2	3			2				24
Azerbaijan		4		16	3	12	13	7	2	7	5	19	10	10	12	12	7	17	16	5	8	185
Montenegro	10		7	11	6	1		7			6			7				3	10			60
Iceland		6			1		4		9	6		1		3		18			8	6	5	51
Bosnia & H	2	12	15		16	13	9	10	8	10	5	16	10		1	18	7		6		12	104
Malta	22	12	12	7	8		9								11	14	9	10	5	8	10	209

179

2016 Eurovision 61: Stockholm, Sweden

Semi-final 2: 12 May 2016

Votes are cast by countries participating in each semi-final plus the five automatically qualifying countries decided by draw: France and Spain in semi-final 1, Italy, Germany and the UK in semi-final 2. Hosts Sweden voted in semi-final 1. Each voting country now awards two sets of points, one from their professional jury and one from their public vote. The top 10 countries in each semi-final qualify for the final.

Rank	Start	Country	Artist	Song	Writer	Composer	POINTS
1Q	10	Australia	Dami Im	Sound of Silence	DNA (David Musumeci & Anthony Egizii)	DNA (David Musumeci & Anthony Egizii)	330
2Q	14	Ukraine	Jamala	1944	Jamala	Jamala	287
3Q	18	Belgium	Laura Tesoro	What's The Pressure?	Sanne Putseys, Birsen Uçar	Sanne Putseys, Louis Favre, Yannick Werther	274
4Q	9	Lithuania	Donny Montell	I've Been Waiting For This Night	Jonas Thander, Beatrice Robertsson	Jonas Thander, Beatrice Robertsson	222
5Q	12	Bulgaria	Poli Genova	If Love Was A Crime	Borislav Milanov, Sebastian Arman, Joacim Bo Persson	Borislav Milanov, Sebastian Arman, Joacim Bo Persson	220
6Q	2	Poland	Michał Szpak	Color Of Your Life	Kamil Varen	Andy Palmer	151
7Q	4	Israel	Hovi Star	Made of Stars	Doron Medalie	Doron Medalie	147
8Q	1	Latvia	Justs	Heartbeat	Aminata Savadogo	Aminata Savadogo	132
9Q	16	Georgia	Nika Kocharov & Young Georgian Lolitaz	Midnight Gold	Kote Kalandadze	Kote Kalandadze, Thomas G:Son	123
10Q	6	Serbia	Sanja Vučić ZAA	Goodbye (Shelter)	Ivana Peters	Ivana Peters	105
11	8	FYR Macedonia	Kaliopi	Dona	Kaliopi	Romeo Grill	88
12	5	Belarus	IVAN	Help You Fly	Alexander Ivanov, Timofei Leontiev, Mary Susane Applegate	Victor Drobysh	84
13	15	Norway	Agnete	Icebreaker	Agnete Johnsen, Gabriel Alares, Ian Curnow	Agnete Johnsen, Gabriel Alares, Ian Curnow	63
14	11	Slovenia	ManuElla	Blue And Red	Leon Oblak	Manuella Brechko, Marjan Hvala	57
15	7	Ireland	Nicky Byrne	Sunlight	Nicky Byrne, Wayne Hector, Ronan Hardiman	Nicky Byrne, Wayne Hector, Ronan Hardiman	46
16	17	Albania	Eneda Tarifa	Fairytale	Olsa Toqi	Olsa Toqi	45
17	13	Denmark	Lighthouse X	Soldiers Of Love	Søren Bregendal, Johannes Nymark, Martin Skriver, Sebastian Owens, Daniel Durr, Katrine Klith Andersen	Søren Bregendal, Johannes Nymark, Martin Skriver, Sebastian Owens, Daniel Durr, Katrine Klith Andersen	34
18	3	Switzerland	Rykka	The Last Of Our Kind	Christina Rieder, Mike James, Jeff Dawson, Warne Livesey	Christina Rieder, Mike James, Jeff Dawson, Warne Livesey	28

2016 Eurovision 61: Stockholm, Sweden
Combined Jury & Public Votes
Semi-final 2: 12 May 2016

	Albania	Australia	Belarus	Belgium	Bulgaria	Denmark	FYR Macedonia	Georgia	Germany	Ireland	Israel	Italy	Latvia	Lithuania	Norway	Poland	Serbia	Slovenia	Switzerland	Ukraine	United Kingdom	TOTAL
Latvia	1	5	5	3		5	9	13	8	11	7			19	5	11		10	6	9	5	132
Poland	2		6	12	6	6	1	10	12	10	6	13	4	10	14		2	7	7	13	10	151
Switzerland	3	1	2	1		2		7	1	5	1							7				28
Israel	4	16		11	7	5	6	7	14	9		8	2	6	6	8	7	4	10	9	6	147
Belarus		6			10	1		6	2	3	3	1	8	6		12	5	2	1	15	3	84
Serbia	8	5	5	2	13		22	2	1			11	5		5	1		12	15	3		105
Ireland		7		4		8					3	2	1	1	5	2			2	2	9	46
FYR Macedonia	24	6			8						10	2					24	10	4			88
Lithuania	4	15	20	11	6	17	5	12	7	15	9	5	22		20	6	5	1	8	14	20	222
Australia	16		15	22	19	20	8	12	17	14	24	15	16	17	20	20	11	11	18	19	16	330
Slovenia	7	4		7	1		10			8		6	3	1			10					57
Bulgaria	14	18	12	13		10	16	5	11	15	13	7	10	5	16	9	10	11	7	5	13	220
Denmark	5	1	3	5				4		3	4		2		5	1			1			34
Ukraine	10	3	19	11	16	6	16	24	14	4	17	22	22	18	10	24	16	16	10		9	287
Norway	10	5	9	4	1	16	2	1		1	5	7	11	6	1		3	2	2	1	1	63
Georgia			4	8	7		1		15	18	14	8		18		14	5	1		12	13	123
Albania				2	2		12	13									8	3	10			45
Belgium	8	24	16		20	20	8	13	14	18	14	9	10	9	14	8	10	19	15	14	11	274

2016 Eurovision 61: Stockholm, Sweden

FINAL: 14 May 2016

Final qualification rules: Top 10 placed countries from each semi-final. Automatic qualification: United Kingdom, France, Germany, Spain, Italy and hosts Sweden. Each of the 42 participating countries now awards two sets of points, one from their professional jury and one from their public vote.

Rank	Start	Country	Artist	Song	Writer	Composer	POINTS
1	21	Ukraine	Jamala	1944	Jamala	Jamala	534
2	13	Australia	Dami Im	Sound of Silence	DNA (David Musumeci & Anthony Egizii)	DNA (David Musumeci & Anthony Egizii)	511
3	18	Russia	Sergey Lazarev	You Are The Only One	John Ballard, Ralph Charlie	Dimitris Kontopoulos, Philip Kirkorov	491
4	8	Bulgaria	Poli Genova	If Love Was A Crime	Borislav Milanov, Sebastian Arman, Joacim Bo Persson	Borislav Milanov, Sebastian Arman, Joacim Bo Persson	307
5	9	Sweden	Frans	If I Were Sorry	Frans Jeppsson Wall, Fredrik Andersson, Michael Saxell, Oscar Fogelström	Frans Jeppsson Wall, Fredrik Andersson, Michael Saxell, Oscar Fogelström	261
6	11	France	Amir	J'ai cherché	Nazim Khaled, Amir Haddad	Nazim Khaled, Amir Haddad, Johan Errami	257
7	26	Armenia	Iveta Mukuchyan	LoveWave	Iveta Mukuchyan, Stephanie Crutchfield	Lilith Navasardyan, Levon Navasardyan	249
8	12	Poland	Michał Szpak	Color Of Your Life	Kamil Varen	Andy Palmer	229
9	16	Lithuania	Donny Montell	I've Been Waiting For This Night	Jonas Thander, Beatrice Robertsson	Jonas Thander, Beatrice Robertsson	200
10	1	Belgium	Laura Tesoro	What's The Pressure?	Sanne Putseys, Birsen Uçar	Sanne Putseys, Louis Favre, Yannick Werther	181
11	3	Netherlands	Douwe Bob	Slow Down	Douwe Bob Posthuma, Jeroen Overman, Jan-Peter Hoekstra	Douwe Bob Posthuma, Jeroen Overman, Jan-Peter Hoekstra, Matthijs van Duijvenbode	153
12	22	Malta	Ira Losco	Walk On Water	Lisa Desmond, Tim Larsson, Tobias Lundgren, Molly Pettersson-Hammar & Ira Losco	Lisa Desmond, Tim Larsson, Tobias Lundgren, Molly Pettersson-Hammar & Ira Losco	153
13	24	Austria	ZOË	Loin d'ici	Christof Straub & Zoe Straub	Christof Straub & Zoe Straub	151
14	7	Israel	Hovi Star	Made of Stars	Doron Medalie	Doron Medalie	135
15	20	Latvia	Justs	Heartbeat	Aminata Savadogo	Aminata Savadogo	132
16	6	Italy	Francesca Michielin	No Degree Of Separation	Francesca Michielin, Federica Abbate, Norma Jean Martine	Fabio Gargiulo, Federica Abbate, Cheope	124
17	4	Azerbaijan	Samra	Miracle	Amir Aly, Jakke Erixson, Henrik Wikström	Amir Aly, Jakke Erixson, Henrik Wikström	117
18	15	Serbia	Sanja Vučić ZAA	Goodbye (Shelter)	Ivana Peters	Ivana Peters	115
19	5	Hungary	Freddie	Pioneer	Borbála Csarnai	Szabó Zé	108
20	23	Georgia	Nika Kocharov & Young Georgian Lolitaz	Midnight Gold	Kote Kalandadze	Kote Kalandadze, Thomas G:Son	104
21	14	Cyprus	Minus One	Alter Ego	Thomas G:son, Minus One	Thomas G:son, Minus One	96
22	19	Spain	Barei	Say Yay!	Barei, Ruben Villanueva & Victor Pua	Barei, Ruben Villanueva & Victor Pua	77
23	17	Croatia	Nina Kraljić	Lighthouse	Andreas Grass & Nikola Paryla	Andreas Grass & Nikola Paryla	73
24	25	United Kingdom	Joe And Jake	You're Not Alone	Matt Schwartz, Justin Benson, Siva Kaneswaran	Matt Schwartz, Justin Benson, Siva Kaneswaran	62
25	2	Czech Republic	Gabriela Gunčíková	I Stand	Aidan O'Connor, Sara Biglert	Christian Schneider, Sara Biglert	41
26	10	Germany	Jamie-Lee	Ghost	Anna Leyne	Anna Leyne, Thomas Burchia, Conrad Hensel	11

2016 Eurovision 61: Stockholm, Sweden — Combined Jury & Public Votes — FINAL: 14 May 2016

To → / From ↓	Belgium	Czech Republic	Netherlands	Azerbaijan	Hungary	Italy	Israel	Bulgaria	Sweden	Germany	France	Poland	Australia	Cyprus	Serbia	Lithuania	Croatia	Russia	Spain	Latvia	Ukraine	Malta	Georgia	Austria	United Kingdom	Armenia	TOTAL
Albania	2				18	3		12	3		24	5	24			4		14	6		6	2			5	2	181
Armenia		1						7	2			1	5	12				14	3		10	13	18				41
Australia	3	4	3			10		18	15	2					4	8	1	5	7		10	6		4	8		153
Austria	5	4	6					5	15		13	12	15			1	6	11			10	10		3		2	117
Azerbaijan					11	3		16		2	8	5	9		4	5		24	1	5	20	11		1			108
Belarus	4		10	10	3			5	10		4	12	7		1	10		17	5	5	17	5		7		10	124
Belgium		1	14			10	2	11	1		16		16		12	6	14	6			5		7	8		7	135
Bosnia & H		6		9	1						11		13	20	5			11		15	19	2		5		2	307
Bulgaria	10		2	1		2	2		3		6		13	5	1			18	4		10	7	3	4		20	261
Croatia			10			8	3	2	7	1	10	4	17	14				14			10	7		6		4	11
Cyprus						2	8	3	5		12	2	1	13	3		1	22			7	6				16	257
Czech Republic	2		7	6	13		5	7	14	5		8	10		3		8	10		1	12	6	4	4		8	229
Denmark	16		14			2	6	16	2	5	20		11		4		1		15	15	2		1	3			511
Estonia			6							22	3	1	14	7	1	10		12		15	15	2	6			3	96
Finland		3	10		2	7		4	22		5		15	1	6		8	2	5		12	5	10				115
France	4		7		12	3	15	7			7	6					4	7	4		10	4	16	14	7		200
FYR Macedonia	8	2	1		1	5	20				2	11	19	11	8		3	18			7						73
Georgia	10		7	2			3	3	6	1	4	4	9		10	2		8	13	22			12				491
Germany	5		7		4	12		4	18		10	11			1			12	2	13		8	7	2			77
Greece		1	1	5			7				10	3	12	20			11	22	8	4	5	1	18				132
Hungary	2	8	7	1		4	11			1	8	15	5		3		5	10		8	12	10	6	1			534
Iceland	6	5	18	1				18		7	10	18		4	7		3	15		4					10		153
Ireland	12	2	8		6	4	15	7		3	10	6			12	1		8	8	5	4			1			104
Israel	7		2			14				20	4	15		1	3			10	4		20	3		8			151
Italy		4			8	7	2	12	10	6	7		2	8	12			22	5			6	1				62
Latvia	3	3		2	2	15		5	11		18		19				22	4	4		6	2	4	1			249
Lithuania	5			2	6	2	7		4	9	17		8	19	18	14	1			4	4						
Malta		3	6	5	15	1	18		8		15	5		14	2	4		13	7								
Moldova		8					2	6		6	15	2		7	1	19	8	1	22	3		4	12	10			
Montenegro	3	7	10	4	2	7			6	1	4	18	2	6	18		8	12			14	10	10				
Netherlands	16	1	6	7	1	12		9	10	17			3	10				14	10								
Norway	7	6	12	3	13	7	1	11	18	14	2	6	7	3	8												
Poland	4	6	7	6	10	1	11	17	1	2	8	5	11	24	8	4				2							
Russia	16	1	2	10	5	6	11	4	10	8	5	4	8	24													
San Marino	4	3	10	3	4	7	5	5	8	4	17	6	5	24	3	6	1	8	2								
Serbia	5	5	10	7	12	1	12	3	8	4	13	19	10	2	5												
Slovenia	8	1	3	1	2	12	5	4	9	17	8	10	7	19	6	4											
Spain	3	2	10	8	1	12	1	17	5	12	12	7	6	2	18												
Sweden	3	7	10	4	11	10	24	8	10	14	2	7	5	4													
Switzerland	10	5	9	8	1	8	3	5	13	12	7	6	2	3	10	14		7									
Ukraine	10	17	2	6	3	5	8	9	15	12	13	9															
United Kingdom	3	13	6	10	14	9	2	15	12																		

2017 Eurovision 62: Kiev, Ukraine

Semi-final 1: 9 May 2017

Votes are cast by countries participating in each semi-final plus the five automatically qualifying countries decided by draw: Italy, Spain and United Kingdom in semi-final 1, France and Germany in semi-final 2. Hosts Ukraine also voted in semi-final 2. Each voting country awards two sets of points, one from their professional jury and one from their public vote. The top 10 countries in each semi-final qualify for the final.

Rank	Start	Country	Artist	Song	Writer	Composer	POINTS
1Q	9	Portugal	Salvador Sobral	Amar Pelos Dois	Luísa Sobral	Luísa Sobral	370
2Q	12	Moldova	Sunstroke Project	Hey Mamma	Alina Galetcaia	Anton Ragoza, Serghei Ialovitki, Seghei Stepanov, Mihail Cebotarenco	291
3Q	1	Sweden	Robin Bengtsson	I Can't Go On	David Kreuger, Hamed "K-One" Pirouzpanah, Robin Stjernberg	David Kreuger, Hamed "K-One" Pirouzpanah, Robin Stjernberg	227
4Q	5	Belgium	Blanche	City Lights	Pierre Dumoulin, Ellie Delvaux	Pierre Dumoulin, Emmanuel Delcourt	165
5Q	15	Cyprus	Hovig	Gravity	Thomas G:son	Thomas G:son	164
6Q	3	Australia	Isaiah	Don't Come Easy	DNA (David Musumeci & Anthony Egizii), Michael Angelo	DNA (David Musumeci & Anthony Egizii), Michael Angelo	160
7Q	16	Armenia	Artsvik	Fly With Me	Avet Barseghyan, David Tserunyan	Lilith Navasaryan, Levon Navasardyan	152
8Q	8	Azerbaijan	Dihaj	Skeletons	Sandra Bjurman	Isa Melikov	150
9Q	11	Poland	Kasia Moś	Flashlight	Kasia Moś, Rickard Bonde Truumeel, Pete Barringer	Kasia Moś, Rickard Bonde Truumeel, Pete Barringer	119
10Q	10	Greece	Demy	This Is Love	Romy Papadea, John Ballard	Dimitris Kontopoulos	115
11	2	Georgia	Tamara Gachechiladze	Keep The Faith	Tamara Gachechiladze	Anri Jokhadze	99
12	7	Finland	Norma John	Blackbird	Lasse Piirainen, Leena Tirronen	Lasse Piirainen, Leena Tirronen	92
13	14	Czech Republic	Martina Bárta	My Turn	DWB, Kyler Niko	DWB, Kyler Niko	83
14	4	Albania	Lindita	World	Lindita, Big Basta	Klodian Qafoku	76
15	13	Iceland	Svala	Paper	Svala Bjorgvinsdottir, Lily Elise	Svala Bjorgvinsdottir, Einar Egilsson, Lester Mendez, Lily Elise	60
16	6	Montenegro	Slavko Kalezić	Space	Adis Eminić, Iva Boršić, Momcilo Zekovic Zeko	Momčilo Zeković Zeko	56
17	17	Slovenia	Omar Naber	On My Way	Omar Naber	Omar Naber	36
18	18	Latvia	Triana Park	Line	Agnese Rakovska	Agnese Rakovska, Kristaps Ērglis, Kristians Rakovskis	21

2017 Eurovision 62: Kiev, Ukraine — Combined Jury & Public Votes — Semi-final 1: 9 May 2017

	Albania	Armenia	Australia	Azerbaijan	Belgium	Cyprus	Czech Republic	Finland	Georgia	Greece	Iceland	Italy	Latvia	Moldova	Montenegro	Poland	Portugal	Slovenia	Spain	Sweden	United Kingdom	TOTAL
Sweden	14	9	16	6	17	13	12	19	12	5	18	11	9	9	9	9	15	12	9		3	227
Georgia	1	14		18	3	1		3	6	10	7	4		7		10	9	5	8	6	1	99
Australia	6	4		9	11	9	12	8	6		16	1	10	6	4	8	6	15	8	14	7	160
Albania				13						15		15	15	10	22			1				76
Belgium	11	6	4	7		7	9	10	5	5	9	11			2	15	8	10	10	13	8	165
Montenegro		1	7	13		6	2	3		7	2	5		8				6	1	1		56
Finland	5		9		3	14	4			1	6		5	3	13	5	14	8	5	15	3	92
Azerbaijan	7		4		5	16	16		22	8	6	12	3	16	11			10	5	17	20	150
Portugal	18	14	16	20	19	24	14	22	20	15	24	14	24	18	16	24		20	24	17	5	370
Greece	14	15	4		6	5		2	2		1	4	6	7		4	7		6	6	18	115
Poland	4	4	12	4	12	7	16	2	3	2	5	8		4			1	4	3	15	18	119
Moldova	19	18	22	15	11		16	14	9	10	8	19	14		15	10	22	10	17	6	20	291
Iceland	4	3	2	2	2			10	3				12	2		1			8	9	2	60
Czech Republic		4	4	4	6	1			1		5		7	2	2	3	14	10	10	4	8	83
Cyprus	3	24	6		12		9	13	12	18	8	6	6	7	5	7	3	4		12	9	164
Armenia	10		10		7	13	5	8	17	20		6	5	14	8	12	4	1	4	3	5	152
Slovenia					2		1	3	4						9	8	4		4	1		36
Latvia				5				1			1			5					2		7	21

2017 Eurovision 62: Kiev, Ukraine

Semi-final 2: 11 May 2017

Votes are cast by countries participating in each semi-final plus the five automatically qualifying countries decided by draw: Italy, Spain and United Kingdom in semi-final 1, France and Germany in semi-final 2. Hosts Ukraine also voted in semi-final 2. Each voting country awards two sets of points, one from their professional jury and one from their public vote. The top 10 countries in each semi-final qualify for the final.

Rank	Start	Country	Artist	Song	Writer	Composer	POINTS
1Q	15	Bulgaria	Kristian Kostov	Beautiful Mess	Borislav Milanov, Sebastian Arman, Joacim Persson, Alexander Blay, Alex	Borislav Milanov, Sebastian Arman, Joacim Persson, Alexander Blay, Alex	403
2Q	7	Hungary	Joci Pápai	Origo	József Pápai	József Pápai	231
3Q	18	Israel	IMRI	I Feel Alive	Dolev Ram, Penn Hazut	Dolev Ram, Penn Hazut	207
4Q	6	Netherlands	OG3NE	Lights And Shadows	Rick Vol	Rick Vol, Rory de Kievit	200
5Q	12	Norway	JOWST	Grab The Moment	Jonas McDonnell	Joakim With Steen	189
6Q	5	Romania	Ilinca ft. Alex Florea	Yodel It!	Alexa Niculae	Mihai Alexandru	174
7Q	2	Austria	Nathan Trent	Running On Air	Nathan Trent, Bernhard Penzias	Nathan Trent, Bernhard Penzias	147
8Q	11	Croatia	Jacques Houdek	My Friend	Jacques Houdek, Ines Prajo, Arjana Kunštek, Fabrizio Laucella	Jacques Houdek, Siniša Reljić, Tony Malm	141
9Q	14	Belarus	Naviband	Story Of My Life	Artem Lukyanenka	Artem Lukyanenka	110
10Q	8	Denmark	Anja	Where I Am	Anja Nissen, Michael D'Arcy, Angel Tupai	Anja Nissen, Michael D'Arcy, Angel Tupai	101
11	1	Serbia	Tijana Bogićević	In Too Deep	Borislav Milanov, Joacim Persson, Lisa Desmond, Johan Alkenae	Borislav Milanov, Joacim Persson, Lisa Desmond, Johan Alkenae	98
12	13	Switzerland	Timebelle	Apollo	Elias Näslin, Alessandra Günthardt, Nicolas Günthardt	Elias Näslin, Alessandra Günthardt, Nicolas Günthardt	97
13	9	Ireland	Brendan Murray	Dying To Try	Jörgen Elofsson, James Newman	Jörgen Elofsson, James Newman	86
14	17	Estonia	Koit Toome & Laura	Verona	Sven Lõhmus	Sven Lõhmus	85
15	3	FYR Macedonia	Jana Burčeska	Dance Alone	Joacim Persson, Alex Omar, Bobi-Leon Milanov, Florence A.	Joacim Persson, Alex Omar, Bobi-Leon Milanov, Florence A.	69
16	4	Malta	Claudia Faniello	Breathlessly	Gerard James Borg	Philip Vella, Sean Vella	55
17	16	Lithuania	Fusedmarc	Rain Of Revolution	Denis Zujev, Michail Levin	Denis Zujev, Viktoria Ivanovskaja, Michail Levin	42
18	10	San Marino	Valentina Monetta & Jimmie Wilson	Spirit Of The Night	Jutta Staudenmayer, Steven Barnacle	Ralph Siegel	1

2017 Eurovision 62: Kiev, Ukraine

Combined Jury & Public Votes — Semi-final 2: 11 May 2017

	Austria	Belarus	Bulgaria	Croatia	Denmark	Estonia	France	FYR Macedonia	Germany	Hungary	Ireland	Israel	Lithuania	Malta	Netherlands	Norway	Romania	San Marino	Serbia	Switzerland	Ukraine	TOTAL
Serbia	6	4	2	12	8	1	6	12	7	4	2			2	6	6		2		18		98
Austria		6	12	9	10	5	4	3	10	11	10	11	4	1	14	4	9	8	7	9		147
FYR Macedonia			12	6			8			2		5	1	8		3		4	15	3	3	69
Malta	6	5	7	1		4	6	8	3		5	2	6		3		1	1	2			55
Romania	7	5	7	7	8	12	12	13	7	7	12	13	6	11	9	8		8	6	7	9	174
Netherlands	12	8	9	14	17	8	5	8	13	16	8	4	5	9		11	12	15	8	12	6	200
Hungary	15	10	8	22	7	10	7	11	10		6	19	7	6	10	8	12	13	24	13	13	231
Denmark		2	4	8		8	2	7	1	6	1	4	6	5	11	14	10	5	4	3		101
Ireland	13	3	1		7	14	1	1	4	5		1	12	5	2	2	9	2		2	2	86
San Marino									1													1
Croatia	11	7	12			5	2	8	11	10	7		2	8	6	2	12	10	10	10	8	141
Norway	5	16	8	4	22	13	3		14	12	9	10	19		12		4	10	4	10	14	189
Switzerland	6	2	7	1	5	3	4	6	2	1	8	3	8	5	4	5	16	5	4		2	97
Belarus	8		5	10		6	13			5	1	13	11	7	3		1		2	1	24	110
Bulgaria	20	24		14	18	22	15	22	22	24	22	18	20	24	24	24	16	20	18	18	18	403
Lithuania		8				1		4			12					10		6			1	42
Estonia	2	9	2		3		6	6	3	4	3	13	12	5		5	3		12	1	8	85
Israel	5	7	20	8	11	4	22	7	8	9	10		3	20	12	14	11	7		9	8	207

187

2017 Eurovision 62: Kiev, Ukraine

FINAL: 13 May 2017

Final qualification rules: Top 10 placed countries from each semi-final. Automatic qualification: United Kingdom, France, Germany, Spain, Italy and hosts Ukraine. Each of the 42 participating countries awards two sets of points, one from their professional jury and one from their public vote.

Rank	Start	Country	Artist	Song	Writer	Composer	POINTS
1	11	Portugal	Salvador Sobral	Amar Pelos Dois	Luísa Sobral	Luísa Sobral	758
2	25	Bulgaria	Kristian Kostov	Beautiful Mess	Borislav Milanov, Sebastian Arman, Joacim Persson, Alexander Blay, Alex	Borislav Milanov, Sebastian Arman, Joacim Persson, Alexander Blay, Alex	615
3	7	Moldova	Sunstroke Project	Hey, Mamma!	Alina Galetcaia	Anton Ragoza, Serghei Ialovitki, Seghei Stepanov, Mihail Cebotarenco	374
4	23	Belgium	Blanche	City Lights	Pierre Dumoulin, Ellie Delvaux	Pierre Dumoulin, Emmanuel Delcourt	363
5	24	Sweden	Robin Bengtsson	I Can't Go On	David Kreuger, Hamed "K-One" Pirouzpanah, Robin Stjernberg	David Kreuger, Hamed "K-One" Pirouzpanah, Robin Stjernberg	344
6	9	Italy	Francesco Gabbani	Occidentali's Karma	Francesco Gabbani, Fabio Ilacqua, Luca Chiaravalli	Francesco Gabbani, Filippo Gabbani, Luca Chiaravalli	334
7	20	Romania	Ilinca ft. Alex Florea	Yodel It!	Alexa Niculae	Mihai Alexandru	282
8	8	Hungary	Joci Pápai	Origo	József Pápai	József Pápai	200
9	14	Australia	Isaiah	Don't Come Easy	DNA (David Musumeci & Anthony Egizii), Michael Angelo	DNA (David Musumeci & Anthony Egizii), Michael Angelo	173
10	17	Norway	JOWST	Grab The Moment	Jonas McDonnell	Joakim With Steen	158
11	6	Netherlands	OG3NE	Lights And Shadows	Rick Vol	Rick Vol, Rory de Kievit	150
12	26	France	Alma	Requiem	Nazim Khaled, Alexandra Maquet	Nazim Khaled	135
13	13	Croatia	Jacques Houdek	My Friend	Jacques Houdek, Ines Prajo, Arjana Kunštek, Fabrizio Laucella	Jacques Houdek, Siniša Reljić, Tony Malm	128
14	12	Azerbaijan	Dihaj	Skeletons	Sandra Bjurman	Isa Melikov	120
15	18	United Kingdom	Lucie Jones	Never Give Up On You	Emmelie de Forest, Daniel Salcedo, Lawrie Martin	Emmelie de Forest, Daniel Salcedo, Lawrie Martin	111
16	4	Austria	Nathan Trent	Running On Air	Nathan Trent, Bernhard Penzias	Nathan Trent, Bernhard Penzias	93
17	3	Belarus	Naviband	Story Of My Life	Artem Lukyanenka	Artem Lukyanenka	83
18	5	Armenia	Artsvik	Fly With Me	Avet Barseghyan, David Tserunyan	Lilith Navasaryan, Levon Navasardyan	79
19	15	Greece	Demy	This Is Love	Romy Papadea, John Ballard	Dimitris Kontopoulos	77
20	10	Denmark	Anja	Where I Am	Anja Nissen, Michael D'Arcy, Angel Tupai	Anja Nissen, Michael D'Arcy, Angel Tupai	77
21	19	Cyprus	Hovig	Gravity	Thomas G:son	Thomas G:son	68
22	2	Poland	Kasia Mos	Flashlight	Kasia Moś, Rickard Bonde Truumeel, Pete Barringer	Kasia Moś, Rickard Bonde Truumeel, Pete Barringer	64
23	1	Israel	IMRI	I Feel Alive	Dolev Ram, Penn Hazut	Dolev Ram, Penn Hazut	39
24	22	Ukraine	O Torvald	Time	Kamenchuk Yevhen	Zhenia Galych, Denys Miziuk	36
25	21	Germany	Levina	Perfect Life	Lindy Robbins, Dave Bassett, Lindsey Ray	Lindy Robbins, Dave Bassett, Lindsey Ray	6
26	16	Spain	Manel Navarro	Do It For Your Lover	Manel Navarro, Antonio Rayo	Manel Navarro, Antonio Rayo	5

2017 Eurovision 62: Kiev, Ukraine
Combined Jury & Public Votes
FINAL: 13 May 2017

	United Kingdom	Ukraine	Switzerland	Sweden	Spain	Slovenia	Serbia	San Marino	Romania	Portugal	Poland	Norway	Netherlands	Montenegro	Moldova	Malta	Lithuania	Latvia	Italy	Israel	Ireland	Iceland	Hungary	Greece	Germany	Georgia	FYR Macedonia	France	Finland	Estonia	Denmark	Czech Republic	Cyprus	Croatia	Bulgaria	Belgium	Belarus	Azerbaijan	Austria	Australia	Armenia	Albania	TOTAL
Israel												5				7											1	9							8		1	5			1		39
Poland	10					4	1	1	2			3	1				1		3		7	3		3	2		1	1				1		5	7		2	6	2				64
Belarus	1	20														2	5	8					2			6				2		3		1	2	4	2	12	7				83
Austria	3						4		1	10	4			1	4		3	6	1					3		5						4			12	3				3			93
Armenia				4	3	3	5	4			2		3	4	2	1	2		4	3	7		2		2	13		1		4	7	2	1		4					1		7	79
Netherlands	4	3	7	3	1	1		7	12	3	8	4		3	6	3		9			4	6	8	10	8	1	8	6	8	4	6	8	6	9	4	10			10				150
Moldova	16	16	8	16	13	3	14	8	20	18	6	8	5	7		1	8	2	20	8	8	6	10	13	7		3	7	4	4	11	8	6	4	10	7	5	20	3	22	14		374
Hungary	12	12	12	4		5	22	4	10	2	5	4	6		1	5	2	3	4	1	2	12	4		4		8	2	15	9	3	8	18		6	1	8	7	10				200
Italy	2		8	7	18	12	14	13	6	4		9	2	18	4	24	13		10	10	1	3	5	11	4	7	8	15	4	5	10	10	18	7		5		6	12			24	334
Denmark	2			5					5			8	8										5				7		5	5		6		3			3			13			77
Portugal	20	20	24	22	24	20	20	19	13	12	22	22	24	8	13	18	24	22	10	24	15	24	19	13	22	20	17	24	20	18	15	20	15	17	7	17	11	16	20	14	22	14	758
Azerbaijan		6	8			4	5	6	6		1	1	3	5	15				12		1		4	10	11	22	10						1		5	4			10			2	120
Croatia	5	7		2	8	12	3	3	4	5	5	3	4	17	4	9		5	6		3		5		5		8	7	5	7					1	2		1	4			7	128
Australia	10	2	4	10		7			1		7	1					1			7		10	7					3	3		10		4			5						4	173
Greece					2							3		12				5					2	24			4	10					24									4	77
Spain										5																4																	5
Norway		1	5	6		10		10		2	3		7			5			3	5	2	2	6	5	10	9	2	8			13	7		2		11	3		3	5		8	158
United Kingdom					1		5	6	5		5	1	5			7	16	4			4	7	3	3	4		3	3	2	14		5	1			2			1	15	4	8	111
Cyprus				2						1		10		1		4		5				5	2	24				10	5						3	5							68
Romania	7	4	4	3	7	2	4	6		7	7		8	10	24	11	4	8	10	7	20	5		7	6	6	4	10	3	6	4	10	4	6	11	6		5	10		2	7	282
Germany		3			2																3																						6
Ukraine											2									4						4						7											36
Belgium	8	6	13	6	8	11	3	13	5	18	22	20	12	7	2	5	14	22	9	14	17	12	8	5	10	9		8	10	14	8	4	5	18			11	4	10		5	5	363
Sweden	12	7	11		10	7	3	2	9	8	7	11	10	8	11	7	9	4	10	6	6	16	4	3	4	13	6	8	18	6	24	7	11	6	2		24	3	5	12	9	2	344
Bulgaria	19	2	14	14	16	15	16	14	18	8	14	20	18	8	18	18	14	15	10	13	6	10	22	12	13	13	24	9	13	19	14	14	17	18	12	14	24	14	17	13	7	20	615
France	7	11	3	3	3		2	14	4	10				5	5	4			7	10			1	4		3	11		1	1			5	3		12	4	5		13	11	6	135

2018 Eurovision 63: Lisbon, Portugal

Semi-final 1: 8 May 2018

Votes are cast by countries participating in each semi-final plus the five automatically qualifying countries decided by draw: Spain and United Kingdom in semi-final 1, France, Italy and Germany in semi-final 2. Hosts Portugal voted in semi-final 1. Each voting country awards two sets of points, one from their professional jury and one from their public vote. The top 10 countries in each semi-final qualify for the final.

Rank	Start	Country	Artist	Song	Writer	Composer	POINTS
1Q	7	Israel	Netta	Toy	Doron Medalie & Stav Beger	Doron Medalie & Stav Beger	283
2Q	19	Cyprus	Eleni Foureira	Fuego	Alex Papaconstantinou, Geraldo Sandell, Anderz Wrethov, Didrick, Viktor Svensson	Alex Papaconstantinou, Geraldo Sandell, Anderz Wrethov, Didrick, Viktor Svensson	262
3Q	5	Czech Republic	Mikolas Josef	Lie To Me	Mikolas Josef	Mikolas Josef	232
4Q	13	Austria	Cesár Sampson	Nobody But You	Sebastian Arman, Cesár Sampson, Joacim Persson, Johan Alkenäs, Borislav Milanov	Sebastian Arman, Cesár Sampson, Joacim Persson, Johan Alkenäs, Borislav Milanov	231
5Q	9	Estonia	Elina Nechayeva	La Forza	Elina Nechayeva, Ksenia Kuchukova	Mihkel Mattisen, Timo Vendt	201
6Q	18	Ireland	Ryan O'Shaughnessy	Together	Ryan O'Shaughnessy, Mark Caplice, Laura Elizabeth Hughes	Ryan O'Shaughnessy, Mark Caplice, Laura Elizabeth Hughes	179
7Q	10	Bulgaria	Equinox	Bones	Borislav Milanov, Joacim Persson, Brandon Treyshun Campbell, Dag Lundberg	Borislav Milanov, Joacim Persson, Brandon Treyshun Campbell, Dag Lundberg	177
8Q	3	Albania	Eugent Bushpepa	Mall	Eugent Bushpepa	Eugent Bushpepa	162
9Q	6	Lithuania	Ieva Zasimauskaitė	When We're Old	Vytautas Bikus	Vytautas Bikus	119
10Q	15	Finland	Saara Aalto	Monsters	Saara Aalto, Joy Deb, Linnea Deb, Ki Fitzgerald	Saara Aalto, Joy Deb, Linnea Deb, Ki Fitzgerald	108
11	1	Azerbaijan	Aisel	X My Heart	Sandra Bjurman	Dimitris Kontopoulos	94
12	4	Belgium	Sennek	A Matter Of Time	Laura Groeseneken, Alex Callier, Maxime Tribeche	Laura Groeseneken, Alex Callier, Maxime Tribeche	91
13	17	Switzerland	ZiBBZ	Stones	Laurell Barker, Corinne Gfeller	Laurell Barker, Corinne Gfeller, Stefan Gfeller	86
14	14	Greece	Yianna Terzi	Oniro Mou	Yianna Terzi, Aris Kalimeris, Michalis Papathanasiou, Dimitris Stamatiou	Yianna Terzi, Aris Kalimeris, Michalis Papathanasiou, Dimitris Stamatiou	81
15	16	Armenia	Sevak Khanagyan	Qami	Anna Danielyan, Victoria Maloyan	Sevak Khanagyan	79
16	8	Belarus	Alekseev	Forever	Yevgeny Matyushenko	Kirill Pavlov	65
17	12	Croatia	Franka	Crazy	Franka Batelic	Branimir Mihaljevic	63
18	11	FYR Macedonia	Eye Cue	Lost And Found	Bojan Trajkovski	Bojan Trajkovski, Darko Dimitrov	24
19	2	Iceland	Ari Ólafsson	Our Choice	Thorunn Clausen	Thorunn Clausen	15

2018 Eurovision 63: Lisbon, Portugal — Semi-final 1: 8 May 2018

Combined Jury & Public Votes

	Albania	Armenia	Austria	Azerbaijan	Belarus	Belgium	Bulgaria	Croatia	Cyprus	Czech Republic	Estonia	Finland	FYR Macedonia	Greece	Iceland	Ireland	Israel	Lithuania	Portugal	Spain	Switzerland	United Kingdom	TOTAL
Azerbaijan	12		4					5	10	10	3		12	15	1		15		7				94
Iceland					7	1				4			2								1		15
Albania		5	7	7	12	4	6	8	7	8	1	7	22	18	12	1	4	1	5	9	10	8	162
Belgium	4	9	7	2	2		12	1		10	7	5			2	2	2	16	10				91
Czech Republic	2	14	18	8	18	18	10	20	8		7	7	14	8	17	8	15	12	4	11	11	2	232
Lithuania	1		2	1	6	4	10	8	3		20	4			3	12	2		18	3	7	12	119
Israel	14	16	18	14	16	10	12	12	20	3	1	22	8	6	18	15		8	4	19	13	13	283
Belarus	7	11		24			2		5		6	3		1				6					65
Estonia	6	13	6	4	3	5	4	6	11	5		12	4	18	12	18	7	16	20	8	13	10	201
Bulgaria	11	2	9	6	10	2		6	16	9	7	10	20	13		9	3	5	7	11	3	18	177
FYR Macedonia	8			6			5	1						3			1						24
Croatia		1	2	5	8		4		4		2		16	5			6		1		4	5	63
Austria	3	10		5	5	22	16	7	4	7	20	16			14	15	20	20	11	8	18	10	231
Greece	13	10		10		1	10	6	20	1			4		1	1		5	4		2	3	81
Finland	8				3	2	2		2	1	17		2		14	11	13		4	7	7	10	108
Armenia			10		16	12	8		4	10		3		5			5		4			2	79
Switzerland	3	3	9	3		8		7		6	2	5	1	1	5	5	9	6	3	6		4	86
Ireland			17	6	3			15	2	12	11	10	1	4	12		4	16	8	14	16	11	179
Cyprus	24	22	7	15	7		15	14		7	12	12	10	19	5	19	10	5	10	20	11	8	262

2018 Eurovision 63: Lisbon, Portugal
Semi-final 2: 10 May 2018

Votes are cast by countries participating in each semi-final plus the five automatically qualifying countries decided by draw: Spain and United Kingdom in semi-final 1, France, Italy and Germany in semi-final 2. Hosts Portugal voted in semi-final 1. Each voting country awards two sets of points, one from their professional jury and one from their public vote. The top 10 countries in each semi-final qualify for the final.

Rank	Start	Country	Artist	Song	Writer	Composer	POINTS
1Q	1	Norway	Alexander Rybak	That's How You Write A Song	Alexander Rybak	Alexander Rybak	266
2Q	15	Sweden	Benjamin Ingrosso	Dance You Off	MAG, Louis Schoorl, K Nita, Benjamin Ingrosso	MAG, Louis Schoorl, K Nita, Benjamin Ingrosso	254
3Q	7	Moldova	DoReDos	My Lucky Day	John Ballard	Philipp Kirkorov	235
4Q	9	Australia	Jessica Mauboy	We Got Love	Anthony Egizii, David Musumeci, Jessica Mauboy	Anthony Egizii, David Musumeci	212
5Q	5	Denmark	Rasmussen	Higher Ground	Niclas Arn, Karl Eurén	Niclas Arn, Karl Eurén	204
6Q	18	Ukraine	Melovin	Under The Ladder	Mike Ryals	Melovin	179
7Q	8	Netherlands	Waylon	Outlaw In 'Em	Waylon, Ilya Toshinskiy, Jim Beaver	Waylon, Ilya Toshinskiy, Jim Beaver	174
8Q	17	Slovenia	Lea Sirk	Hvala, ne!	Lea Sirk	Lea Sirk, Tomy DeClerque	132
9Q	3	Serbia	Sanja Ilić & Balkanika	Nova Deca	Danica Krstajić	Aleksandar Sanja Ilić, Tatjana Karajanov Ilić	117
10Q	13	Hungary	AWS	Viszlát Nyár	Örs Siklósi	Bence Brucker, Dániel Kökényes, Áron Veress, Soma Schiszler	111
11	2	Romania	The Humans	Goodbye	Cristina Caramarcu	Alexandru Matei, Alin Neagoe	107
12	14	Latvia	Laura Rizzotto	Funny Girl	Laura Rizzotto	Laura Rizzotto	106
13	12	Malta	Christabelle	Taboo	Muxu, Christabelle	Thomas G:son, Johnny Sanchez	101
14	11	Poland	Gromee feat. Lukas Meijer	Light Me Up	Andrzej Gromala, Lukas Meijer, Mahan Moin, Christian Rabb	Andrzej Gromala, Lukas Meijer, Mahan Moin, Christian Rabb	81
15	6	Russia	Julia Samoylova	I Won't Break	Netta Nimrodi, Leonid Gutkin, Arie Burshtein	Netta Nimrodi, Leonid Gutkin, Arie Burshtein	65
16	16	Montenegro	Vanja Radovanović	Inje	Vladimir Radovanovic	Vladimir Radovanovic	40
17	4	San Marino	Jessika feat. Jenifer Brening	Who We Are	Mathias Strasser, Christof Straub, Zoe Straub, Jenifer Brening, Stefan Moessle	Mathias Strasser, Christof Straub, Zoe Straub, Jenifer Brening, Stefan Moessle	28
18	10	Georgia	Ethno-Jazz Band Iriao	For You	Irina Sanikidze	David Malazonia; Mikheil Mdinaradze	24

2018 Eurovision 63: Lisbon, Portugal — Combined Jury & Public Votes — Semi-final 2: 10 May 2018

	Australia	Denmark	France	Georgia	Germany	Hungary	Italy	Latvia	Malta	Moldova	Montenegro	Netherlands	Norway	Poland	Romania	Russia	San Marino	Serbia	Slovenia	Sweden	Ukraine	TOTAL
Norway	14	18	6	10	9	15	13	9	18	10	11	20		11	8	18	14	14	17	22	9	266
Romania			9	14		12	12	3	2	24	8	2	2	3		4		1	6	3	2	107
Serbia		1	10		7	8	5		1	10	24	1	1		10	13	6		16	4		117
San Marino	2						5		15						5	1						28
Denmark	18		5	3	10	17	17	7	16	5	4	12	12	8	8	7	12	9	8	12	14	204
Russia			3	6			2	12	3	15	8		4		1		1	7			3	65
Moldova	20	8	12	15	9	10	14	14	8		9	10	5	2	24	24	16	5	11	7	12	235
Netherlands	2	12	8	11	10	12	3	9	5	8	6		15	11	11		6	10	11	12	12	174
Australia		20	18		15	13	7	14	17	15	3	8	18	11	7	4	4	9	6	17	6	212
Georgia						1		7								3					13	24
Poland		4	11		14	11	3		1			10	7			2	2				7	81
Malta	10	9	6	4	6		8	7		2	7	1	6	1	10		8	4	8	9		101
Hungary	7			6	8		6	3		1	1	8	2	16	13	9	8	12	8	4	2	111
Latvia	5		10	15	10	2				3		7	7	11	1		5	3		1	11	106
Sweden	20	9	8	14	12	4	6	16	17	2	8	18	22	17	2	13	17	13	14		11	254
Montenegro		20							5						7			17	8		3	40
Slovenia	6	7	7	1	5	5	7	4		6	10	11	8	11	4	2	6	10		11	11	132
Ukraine	12	8	3	17	1	6	8	11	8	15	17	8	7	14	5	16	11	2	3	7		179

2018 Eurovision 63: Lisbon, Portugal

FINAL: 12 May 2018

Final qualification rules: Top 10 placed countries from each semi-final. Automatic qualification: United Kingdom, France, Germany, Spain, Italy and hosts Portugal. Each of the 43 participating countries awards two sets of points, one from their professional jury and one from their public vote.

Rank	Start	Country	Artist	Song	Writer	Composer	POINTS
1	22	Israel	Netta	Toy	Doron Medalie & Stav Beger	Doron Medalie & Stav Beger	529
2	25	Cyprus	Eleni Foureira	Fuego	Alex Papaconstantinou, Geraldo Sandell, Anderz Wrethov, Didrick, Viktor Svensson	Alex Papaconstantinou, Geraldo Sandell, Anderz Wrethov, Didrick, Viktor Svensson	436
3	5	Austria	Cesár Sampson	Nobody But You	Sebastian Arman, Cesár Sampson, Joacim Persson, Johan Alkenäs, Borislav Milanov	Sebastian Arman, Cesár Sampson, Joacim Persson, Johan Alkenäs, Borislav Milanov	342
4	11	Germany	Michael Schulte	You Let Me Walk Alone	Michael Schulte, Thomas Stengaard, Katharina Müller, Nisse Ingwersen	Michael Schulte, Thomas Stengaard, Katharina Müller, Nisse Ingwersen	340
5	26	Italy	Ermal Meta e Fabrizio Moro	Non Mi Avete Fatto Niente	Ermal Meta, Fabrizio Moro, Andrea Febo	Ermal Meta, Fabrizio Moro, Andrea Febo	308
6	14	Czech Republic	Mikolas Josef	Lie To Me	Mikolas Josef	Mikolas Josef	281
7	20	Sweden	Benjamin Ingrosso	Dance You Off	MAG, Louis Schoorl, K Nita, Benjamin Ingrosso	MAG, Louis Schoorl, K Nita, Benjamin Ingrosso	274
8	6	Estonia	Elina Nechayeva	La Forza	Elina Nechayeva, Ksenia Kuchukova	Mihkel Mattisen, Timo Vendt	245
9	15	Denmark	Rasmussen	Higher Ground	Niclas Arn, Karl Eurén	Niclas Arn, Karl Eurén	226
10	19	Moldova	DoReDos	My Lucky Day	John Ballard	Philipp Kirkorov	209
11	12	Albania	Eugent Bushpepa	Mall	Eugent Bushpepa	Eugent Bushpepa	184
12	4	Lithuania	Ieva Zasimauskaitė	When We're Old	Vytautas Bikus	Vytautas Bikus	181
13	13	France	Madame Monsieur	Mercy	Emilie Satt, Jean-Karl Lucas	Emilie Satt, Jean-Karl Lucas	173
14	18	Bulgaria	Equinox	Bones	Borislav Milanov, Joacim Persson, Brandon Treyshun Campbell, Dag Lundberg	Borislav Milanov, Joacim Persson, Brandon Treyshun Campbell, Dag Lundberg	166
15	7	Norway	Alexander Rybak	That's How You Write A Song	Alexander Rybak	Alexander Rybak	144
16	24	Ireland	Ryan O'Shaughnessy	Together	Ryan O'Shaughnessy, Mark Caplice, Laura Elizabeth Hughes	Ryan O'Shaughnessy, Mark Caplice, Laura Elizabeth Hughes	136
17	1	Ukraine	Melovin	Under The Ladder	Mike Ryals	Melovin	130
18	23	Netherlands	Waylon	Outlaw In 'Em	Waylon, Ilya Toshinskiy, Jim Beaver	Waylon, Ilya Toshinskiy, Jim Beaver	121
19	10	Serbia	Sanja Ilić & Balkanika	Nova Deca	Danica Krstajić	Aleksandar S Ilić, Tatjana K Ilić	113
20	16	Australia	Jessica Mauboy	We Got Love	Anthony Egizii, David Musumeci, Jessica Mauboy	Anthony Egizii, David Musumeci	99
21	21	Hungary	AWS	Viszlát Nyár	Örs Siklósi	Bence Brucker, Dániel Kökényes, Áron Veress, Soma Schiszler	93
22	3	Slovenia	Lea Sirk	Hvala, ne!	Lea Sirk	Lea Sirk, Tomy DeClerque	64
23	2	Spain	Amaia y Alfred	Tu Canción	Raul Gomez Garcia, Sylvia Ruth Santoro	Raul Gomez Garcia, Sylvia Ruth Santoro	61
24	9	United Kingdom	SuRie	Storm	Nicole Blair, Gil Lewis, Sean Hargreaves	Nicole Blair, Gil Lewis, Sean Hargreaves	48
25	17	Finland	Saara Aalto	Monsters	Saara Aalto, Joy Deb, Linnea Deb, Ki Fitzgerald	Saara Aalto, Joy Deb, Linnea Deb, Ki Fitzgerald	46
26	8	Portugal	Cláudia Pascoal	O Jardim	Isaura	Isaura	39

2018 Eurovision 63: Lisbon, Portugal — Combined Jury & Public Votes — FINAL: 12 May 2018

To / From	Albania	Armenia	Australia	Austria	Azerbaijan	Belarus	Belgium	Bulgaria	Croatia	Cyprus	Czech Republic	Denmark	Estonia	Finland	France	FYR Macedonia	Georgia	Germany	Greece	Hungary	Iceland	Ireland	Israel	Italy	Latvia	Lithuania	Malta	Moldova	Montenegro	Netherlands	Norway	Poland	Portugal	Romania	Russia	San Marino	Serbia	Slovenia	Spain	Sweden	Switzerland	Ukraine	United Kingdom	TOTAL
Ukraine	4				14	12		1		2	12				4	4	8						7	8	3			15	7		2	12	4		8	5					1		1	130
Spain		7		5			1			7		6			5			6				1								1			14	10							1	5	1	61
Slovenia					8				7					2	2	4				5			4		1			3	6				3	1		6	8							64
Lithuania			3			4		10	12	6	7	6	22				9	8							16	15	5			1	15	1	3	6	3	6	8			7	8	2	12	181
Austria	2	7	5		6	5		16		2	5	18	18	10	7	12	9	15	7		11	12	13	7	7	15	1	13		13	16	12		12			4	12	8	12	8	7	12	342
Estonia	4	2	8	2		10		2		5	5	7		10	7		9	2	3	7	17	5	8	10	18	12		7	5	4		6	8	3	9	5	3	5	3		10	4	6	245
Norway	7	1		3	7	18			5	5		8	6	12		12				7	7	7		12	2	7	4		7	2		4			5		9	5	3	10		4	5	144
Portugal													3		8				3		4						1			2						1					13			39
United Kingdom	3											3			3			1	2			6		6	2				2							3								48
Serbia	3			8					12						1	18			2							7		2	24							3					12			113
Germany	14	5	12	16	5		7		3	3	3	24	6	1	8	3	7		2	1	14	10	8	13	3	7	4	8		24	18	11	8	8	4	14	10	4	13		12		3	340
Albania		12		9	12	7			5	6		2		9		18	4			10	10	2	8	12		10	1		20			7	10			1		5			18	7	7	184
France	12	9					11		6	4		6		5			4	8	5	7	9	4	6		10	15	8	6		6	8	3	5	2	2			2	10	5	7			173
Czech Republic	1	14	4	15	6	11	8	11	9	13		2	5	5	3	9	3	7	7	8	11	7	12	13	4	8	8	11		6	4	4	2	3	2	10	5	11	14	3		14	5	281
Denmark			10		5	10	5		2		5		8	13	2		12	3		24	12	2	6	12	5	10	2			8	10	6		2	7	6	4			12	2	11	2	226
Australia		2			3	2					2	12			10	5		7	5	7			7		6		9	7			6	4	5	2	5	2			2	8		2	1	99
Finland			4														3			3	3		6					11	4											9			4	46
Bulgaria		11	7	6	11	6	7		8	12	5	1	7	7	6	7	6		5		15	10	1		7		9	11		6	13	2	7	5		2	2		5	6	2		14	166
Moldova	2		12				2		8	10	6		10	10	1	1	3		11	2		1	10		12				8	8			6	19	24	9	6	12			2	6	4	209
Sweden	4	12	12	8	2	1	8		12	12	8	11	5	8		7	12	12	8	1		2	10	12	12	2	7	7	2		13	6	5		11	8	12		2		5	6	2	274
Hungary				3	8	2		5		4	2		3	8	10		5		6				3	10			2		3		7	10						3			1	1		93
Israel	6	18	18	19	13	8	16	14	16	10	22	3		19	24	18	15	11	10	16	15	13		9	8	7	14	22	1	4	7	10	2	8	18	24	9	1	22	17	6	22	17	529
Netherlands	3			1			22			4		5		2	6		5	5		8		3			5	3		1	3		9	8		8			7	3		1		8	2	121
Ireland	7		12	8		4	4	1		14	14	4		2	1			15		3	4		6			4	9	1		4	1	1	3	1		4	7	7	5			8		136
Cyprus	20	19	7	1	14	15	11	15	10		8	6	12	7	3	18	10	9	24	7		17	5	8	1	7	22	13	6	11	7	8	5	12	11	7	10	14	20	16	6	4	13	436
Italy	24	3		10	5	4	6	6	15	2	2		7	10	10	6	5	12		6			5		6		22	8	12	7		5	14	6	7	12	14	10	10		8	5	8	308

195

2019 Eurovision 64: Tel Aviv, Israel
Semi-final 1: 14 May 2019

Votes are cast by countries participating in each semi-final plus the five automatically qualifying countries decided by draw: France and Spain in semi-final 1, Italy, UK and Germany in semi-final 2. Hosts Israel voted in semi-final 1. Each voting country awards two sets of points, one from their professional jury and one from the public vote. The top 10 countries in each semi-final qualify for the final.

Rank	Start	Country	Artist	Song	Writer	Composer	POINTS
1Q	12	Australia	Kate Miller-Heidke	Zero Gravity	Kate Miller-Heidke, Keir Nuttall	Kate Miller-Heidke, Keir Nuttall, Julian Hamilton	261
2Q	6	Czech Republic	Lake Malawi	Friend of a Friend	Jan Steinsdoerfer, Maciej Mikolaj	Jan Steinsdoerfer, Maciej Mikolaj	242
3Q	13	Iceland	Hatari	Hatrið mun sigra	Hatari	Hatari	221
4Q	14	Estonia	Victor Crone	Storm	Stig Rästa, Victor Crone, Fred Krieger	Stig Rästa, Vallo Kikas, Victor Crone, Sebastian Lestapier	198
5Q	16	Greece	Katerine Duska	Better Love	Katerine Duska, David Sneddon	Katerine Duska, Leon of Athens, David Sneddon, Phil Cook	185
6Q	5	Slovenia	Zala Kralj & Gašper Šantl	Sebi	Zala Kralj & Gašper Šantl	Zala Kralj & Gašper Šantl	167
7Q	9	Serbia	Nevena Božović	Kruna	Nevena Božović	Nevena Božović, Darko Dimitrov	156
8Q	17	San Marino	Serhat	Say Na Na Na	Serhat, Mary Susan Applegate	Serhat	150
9Q	1	Cyprus	Tamta	Replay	Alex Papaconstantinou, Teddy Sky, Viktor Svensson, Albin Nedler, Kristoffer Fogelmark	Alex Papaconstantinou, Teddy Sky, Viktor Svensson, Albin Nedler, Kristoffer Fogelmark	149
10Q	8	Belarus	ZENA	Like It	Yuliya Kireyeva	Yuliya Kireyeva, Victor Drobysh	122
11	4	Poland	Tulia	Fire of Love (Pali się)	Allan Rich, Jude Friedman, Sonia Krasny	Nadia Dalin	120
12	7	Hungary	Joci Pápai	Az én apám	Ferenc Molnár	Joci Pápai, Ferenc Molnár	97
13	10	Belgium	Eliot	Wake Up	Pierre Dumoulin, Eliot Vassamillet	Pierre Dumoulin, Eliot Vassamillet	70
14	11	Georgia	Oto Nemsadze	Keep on Going	Diana Giorgadze	Roma Giorgadze	62
15	15	Portugal	Conan Osiris	Telemóveis	Conan Osiris	Conan Osiris	51
16	2	Montenegro	D mol	Heaven	Adis Eminić	Dejan Božović	46
17	3	Finland	Darude feat. Sebastian Rejman	Look Away	Sebastian Rejman & Ville Virtanen	Sebastian Rejman & Ville Virtanen	23

2019 Eurovision 64: Tel Aviv, Israel — Combined Jury & Public Votes — Semi-final 1: 14 May 2019

	Australia	Belarus	Belgium	Cyprus	Czech Republic	Estonia	Finland	France	Georgia	Greece	Hungary	Iceland	Israel	Montenegro	Poland	Portugal	San Marino	Serbia	Slovenia	Spain	TOTAL
Cyprus	3	4	4		11	8		6	15	24	3	1	12	12	4	2	18	8	7	7	149
Montenegro				4						5							10	20	7		46
Finland	2					12				4		2			1					2	23
Poland	13	11	5		14	9	16	8			14	8		9		3	5	3	4		120
Slovenia	4	8	3	5	17	7	12	2	12	6	10	10	7		16	15	7	17		7	167
Czech Republic	22	10	14	3		20	13	8	13	9	14	22	12		12	16	7	11	17	13	242
Hungary	7	2	2			8	3	10	1			3	7	6	9	7		18	8		97
Belarus	2		4	6	11	11		4	10	9	12	9	5	5	2	6	1	8	10	7	122
Serbia	3	4	5	11	10	6	4	9	9	12	9	6	1	19	14	7	7		17	3	156
Belgium				13	3	4	2	5	2			5	3		4	12	2		6	9	70
Georgia	5	11		17	1			6		10	2		7	2			1				62
Australia		18	22	4	10	6	20	14	4	18	10	22	20	12	22	12	12	12	4	19	261
Iceland	22	13	17	9	6	8	16	22	6	9	11		3	10	17	8	14	6	14	10	221
Estonia	7	18	19	7	8		16	2	16	3	14	14	20	2	7	17	8	4	9	7	198
Portugal	4	2	9	3	2		3	12	2						2					12	51
Greece	15	5	10	24	5	4	7	8	14		5	8	12	13		5	24	4	10	12	185
San Marino	7	10	2	10	12	13	4		12	4	12	6	7	20	6	9		5	3	8	150

2019 Eurovision 64: Tel Aviv, Israel — Semi-final 2: 16 May 2019

Votes are cast by countries participating in each semi-final plus the five automatically qualifying countries decided by draw: France and Spain in semi-final 1, Italy, UK and Germany in semi-final 2. Hosts Israel voted in semi-final 1. Each voting country awards two sets of points, one from their professional jury and one from their public vote. The top 10 countries in each semi-final qualify for the final.

Rank	Start	Country	Artist	Song	Writer	Composer	POINTS
1Q	16	Netherlands	Duncan Laurence	Arcade	Duncan Laurence, Joel Sjöö, Wouter Hardy	Duncan Laurence, Joel Sjöö, Wouter Hardy	280
2Q	17	North Macedonia	Tamara Todevska	Proud	Kosta Petrov, Sanja Popovska	Robert Bilbilov, Lazar Cvetkoski, Darko Dimitrov	239
3Q	8	Sweden	John Lundvik	Too Late for Love	John Lundvik, Anderz Wrehov, Andreas Stone Johansson	John Lundvik, Anderz Wrehov, Andreas Stone Johansson	238
4Q	4	Switzerland	Luca Hänni	She Got Me	Laurell Barker, Mac Frazer, Luca Hänni, Jon Hällgren, Lukas Hällgren	Laurell Barker, Mac Frazer, Luca Hänni, Jon Hällgren, Lukas Hällgren	232
5Q	18	Azerbaijan	Chingiz	Truth	Borislav Milanov, Trey Campbell, Bo J, Hostess	Borislav Milanov, Trey Campbell, Bo J, Pablo Dinero, Hostess and Chingiz	224
6Q	13	Russia	Sergey Lazarev	Scream	Sharon Vaughn, Dimitris Kontopoulos	Philip Kirkorov, Dimitris Kontopoulos	217
7Q	15	Norway	KEiiNO	Spirit in the Sky	Alexander Olsson, Tom Hugo, Fred Buljo, Alexandra Rotan	Tom Hugo, Henrik Tala, Fred Buljo, Rüdiger Schramm	210
8Q	11	Malta	Michela	Chameleon	Joacim Perrson, Paula Winger, Borislav Milanov, Johan Alkenäs	Joacim Perrson, Paula Winger, Borislav Milanov, Johan Alkenäs	157
9Q	14	Albania	Jonida Maliqi	Ktheju tokës	Eriona Rushiti	Eriona Rushiti	96
10Q	7	Denmark	Leonora	Love Is Forever	Lise Cabble, Melanie Wehbe, Emil Lei	Lise Cabble, Melanie Wehbe, Emil Lei	94
11	12	Lithuania	Jurij Veklenko	Run with the Lions	Eric Lumiere, Ash Hicklin, Pele Loriano	Eric Lumiere, Ash Hicklin, Pele Loriano	93
12	3	Moldova	Anna Odobescu	Stay	Georgios Kalpakidis, Thomas Reil, Jeppe Reil, Maria Broberg	Georgios Kalpakidis, Thomas Reil, Jeppe Reil, Maria Broberg	85
13	6	Romania	Ester Peony	On a Sunday	Ioana Victoria Badea	Ester Alexandra Crețu, Alexandru Șerbu	71
14	10	Croatia	Roko	The Dream	Jacques Houdek, Charlie Mason, Andrea Čubrić	Jacques Houdek	64
15	5	Latvia	Carousel	That Night	Sabīne Žuga	Mārcis Vasiļevskis, Sabīne Žuga	50
16	1	Armenia	Srbuk	Walking Out	Garik Papoyan	Lost Capital, tokionine	49
17	9	Austria	PÆNDA	Limits	PÆNDA	PÆNDA	21
18	2	Ireland	Sarah McTernan	22	Janieck van de Polder, Marcia Sondeijker, Roel Rats	Janieck van de Polder, Marcia Sondeijker, Roel Rats	16

2019 Eurovision 64: Tel Aviv, Israel — Combined Jury & Public Votes — Semi-final 2: 18 May 2019

	Albania	Armenia	Austria	Azerbaijan	Croatia	Denmark	Germany	Ireland	Italy	Latvia	Lithuania	Malta	Moldova	Netherlands	North Macedonia	Norway	Romania	Russia	Sweden	Switzerland	United Kingdom	TOTAL
Armenia	3		1					2		2		6	6	7	8			16				49
Ireland		8			1				8				5								3	16
Moldova	11	14	19	3	2	2	20	16	5	3	9	5	6	6	7	2	24	10	6	5	4	85
Switzerland		3		12	18	10	4	1	6		19	12	1	16	3	15	10	6	16		6	232
Latvia	1	2		5		6		5	5			1	24	1		1		12		7		50
Romania		2	6	8			4	1	12	12	3	2	1	7		13		3	12	4	6	71
Denmark	11	16	13	3	1	22	5	5	12	16	15	17		22	5	22	5	2		18	14	94
Sweden	1					2	12	17		1	6						1		8			238
Austria	5	2	13	1		5	3	1	1	1		1		5	10		7	3	1	5	8	21
Croatia	6	17	2	12	8	5	8	8	10	6	4		10	11	11	7	7	8	4	4	9	64
Malta	5		3	3		4	1	12		16		6	5	2		12		1	7	4	12	157
Lithuania	10	19	4	24	6	6	7	7	7	15	14	13	18	10	17	7	14		10	4	5	93
Russia			3	11	11		2		15				2		24	2	5	7	2	12		217
Albania	12	6	13	5	10	20	12	17	8	8	9	12	7	12	3		5	8	17	16	10	96
Norway	14	14	16	12	15	15	18	16	7	15	18	22	7		14	15	14	8	15	18	7	210
Netherlands	20	14	13	17	24	11	18	10	8	5	4	8	6	10		8	14	16	6	15	12	280
North Macedonia	17		13		12	8	7	8	10	16	15	11	14	8	13	12	17	16	9	4	14	239
Azerbaijan																						224

2019 Eurovision 64: Tel Aviv, Israel
FINAL: 18 May 2019

Final qualification rules: Top 10 placed countries from each semi-final. Automatic qualification: United Kingdom, France, Germany, Spain, Italy and hosts Israel. Each of the 43 participating countries awards two sets of points, one from their professional jury and one from their public vote.

Rank	Start	Country	Artist	Song	Writer	Composer	POINTS
1	12	Netherlands	Duncan Laurence	Arcade	Duncan Laurence, Joel Sjöö, Wouter Hardy	Duncan Laurence, Joel Sjöö, Wouter Hardy	498
2	22	Italy	Mahmood	Soldi	Dardust, Mahmood	Dardust, Mahmood, Charlie Charles	472
3	5	Russia	Sergey Lazarev	Scream	Sharon Vaughn, Dimitris Kontopoulos	Philip Kirkorov, Dimitris Kontopoulos	370
4	24	Switzerland	Luca Hänni	She Got Me	Laurell Barker, Mac Frazer, Luca Hänni, Jon Hällgren, Lukas Hällgren	Laurell Barker, Mac Frazer, Luca Hänni, Jon Hällgren, Lukas Hällgren	364
5	9	Sweden	John Lundvik	Too Late for Love	John Lundvik, Anderz Wrehov, Andreas Stone Johansson	John Lundvik, Anderz Wrehov, Andreas Stone Johansson	334
6	15	Norway	KEiiNO	Spirit in the Sky	Alexander Olsson, Tom Hugo, Fred Buljo, Alexandra Rotan	Tom Hugo, Henrik Tala, Fred Buljo, Rüdiger Schramm	331
7	8	North Macedonia	Tamara Todevska	Proud	Kosta Petrov, Sanja Popovska	Robert Bilbilov, Lazar Cvetkoski, Darko Dimitrov	305
8	20	Azerbaijan	Chingiz	Truth	Borislav Milanov, Trey Campbell, Bo J, Hostess	Borislav Milanov, Trey Campbell, Bo J, Pablo Dinero, Hostess and Chingiz	302
9	25	Australia	Kate Miller-Heidke	Zero Gravity	Kate Miller-Heidke, Keir Nuttall	Kate Miller-Heidke, Keir Nuttall, Julian Hamilton	284
10	17	Iceland	Hatari	Hatrið mun sigra	Hatari	Hatari	232
11	3	Czech Republic	Lake Malawi	Friend of a Friend	Jan Steinsdoerfer, Maciej Trybulec, Albert Černý	Jan Steinsdoerfer, Maciej Trybulec, Albert Černý	157
12	6	Denmark	Leonora	Love Is Forever	Lise Cabble, Melanie Wehbe, Emil Lei	Lise Cabble, Melanie Wehbe, Emil Lei	120
13	11	Cyprus	Tamta	Replay	Alex Papaconstantinou, Teddy Sky, Viktor Svensson, Albin Nedler, Kristoffer Fogelmark	Alex Papaconstantinou, Teddy Sky, Viktor Svensson, Albin Nedler, Kristoffer Fogelmark	109
14	1	Malta	Michela	Chameleon	Joacim Perrson, Paula Winger, Borislav Milanov, Johan Alkenäs	Joacim Perrson, Paula Winger, Borislav Milanov, Johan Alkenäs	107
15	10	Slovenia	Zala Kralj & Gašper Šantl	Sebi	Zala Kralj & Gašper Šantl	Zala Kralj & Gašper Šantl	105
16	21	France	Bilal Hassani	Roi	Emilie Satt, Jean-Karl Lucas	Emilie Satt, Jean-Karl Lucas	105
17	2	Albania	Jonida Maliqi	Ktheju tokës	Eriona Rushiti	Eriona Rushiti	90
18	23	Serbia	Nevena Božović	Kruna	Nevena Božović	Nevena Božović, Darko Dimitrov	89
19	7	San Marino	Serhat	Say Na Na Na	Serhat, Mary Susan Applegate	Serhat	77
20	18	Estonia	Victor Crone	Storm	Stig Rästa, Victor Crone, Fred Krieger	Stig Rästa, Vallo Kikas, Victor Crone,	76
21	13	Greece	Katerine Duska	Better Love	Katerine Duska, David Sneddon	Katerine Duska, Leon of Athens, David Sneddon, Phil Cook	74
22	26	Spain	Miki	La Venda	Adrià Salas	Adrià Salas	54
23	14	Israel	Kobi Marimi	Home	Inbar Wizman, Ohad Shragai	Inbar Wizman, Ohad Shragai	35
24	19	Belarus	ZENA	Like It	Yuliya Kireyeva	Yuliya Kireyeva, Victor Drobysh	31
25	4	Germany	S!sters	Sister	Laurell Barker, Tom Oehler, Marine Kaltenbacher, Thomas Stengaard	Laurell Barker, Tom Oehler, Marine Kaltenbacher, Thomas Stengaard	24
26	16	United Kingdom	Michael Rice	Bigger Than Us	Laurell Barker, Anna-Klara Folin, John Lundvik, Jonas Thander	Laurell Barker, Anna-Klara Folin, John Lundvik, Jonas Thander	11

2019 Eurovision 64: Tel Aviv, Israel — Combined Jury & Public Votes — FINAL: 18 May 2019

	Albania	Armenia	Australia	Austria	Azerbaijan	Belarus	Belgium	Croatia	Cyprus	Czech Republic	Denmark	Estonia	Finland	France	Georgia	Germany	Greece	Hungary	Iceland	Ireland	Israel	Italy	Latvia	Lithuania	Malta	Moldova	Montenegro	Netherlands	North Macedonia	Norway	Poland	Portugal	Romania	Russia	San Marino	Serbia	Slovenia	Spain	Sweden	Switzerland	United Kingdom	TOTAL
Malta	10		5					3	3	3			1			3					4	8	1			1	6	8	11		4			6			1		2			107
Albania	4		12	3		12			2							5													20				2	3	7					10		90
Czech Republic		3	7	3				1																7			15	4		12	1	10	2			4	12	6	1		1	157
Germany							5	7							12		8						3	5		10	1					8								6		24
Russia	13	17	4	5	24	13	1	2	20	12	3	8	4	3	8	8		7	4	8	12	8	16	13	14	17	20	5	6	1	3	10	13		22	8		4	3	3	4	370
Denmark							1				8	18	4	5	7	5	18	6	1		1	16	7			4	3	12		9	5	1		5		2	7	4	7	1	9	120
San Marino	10							2							10					2					1	8	8		8			1				1						77
North Macedonia	18	10	7	12	11	10		17	7	7	10	15	7	7	2	7	1	10	8	5		10	8	11	8	12	13	4		10	8	5	7	4	1	24	14		2	14	12	305
Sweden	6	14	20	6	2	2	2	5		12	22	7	19	10	8	3		4	20	14	6	2	10	4	11	2	8	20	8	20		2	1			8	7	18		12	15	334
Slovenia		2	4		5			10		10			7		4			3	1				2				4			1	14	3		6		10		1				105
Cyprus	7				3	8	2					15		7		24			8	5	6			6		5		1	2	1				8	12	3		5	7		1	109
Netherlands	7	16	12	15	7	16	18	10	11	10	14	15	13	17	13	15	6	9	12	16	14	5	17	19	17	9	1		14	15	10	20	17	5	9	3	11	16	18	16	10	498
Greece	6				6	3	3		24					12										4	4	7	5		2			3		10	18							74
Israel									5	3					4					3									1	2			3		1							35
Norway	5	5	12	9	1	8	7	5	1	10	17	10	10	8		17		10	12	18	10	10	8	8	7	1		12	5		9	10	4	10	3	4	6	7	16	15	12	331
United Kingdom	2														1			2		3					1					2										1		11
Iceland	3	18	6			7	13	3		10	4	5	12	6	3	2	2	12		6	18	7	7	12		1	2	7	2	10	15	3	5	9	8	5	7	3	8	8	8	232
Estonia								1		2	10		8						3			5	15	4	24					2						6	1					76
Belarus	1				6							1						8															15						10		31
Azerbaijan	11	3	3		11		18		6		9	6	2	6		8		7	4	7	10	8	10	15	10	16	3	4	5	8	4	8	16	24	8	3	10	8	8		10	302
France	3	4	13	5		11		3	7	12	4	3			5		4	1	1		6	5	7	2	24	5	7		15		6	2	1			1	3	4		5	2	105
Italy	13	15	5	17	11	10	20	24	16	10			8	18	1	18		11	9	5	18			12			7	16	15	10	7	13	8	1	20	17	16	16	12	17	18	472
Serbia			1	6				12				4			3				2								24		10	4	7	3	3		7		10			7		89
Switzerland	14	15		22	8	8	12	14	8	5	12	14	16	4	3	16	7	8	12	17	10	3	1	2	8	4		16		12	5	6	14	2		11	9	13	11		12	364
Australia	3	1		3	2	2	8		2	8	2	2	2			15	5	1	20	14	11	12	6	3	3	10	4	4	10	4	18	11	14	4	7	7	2	15	11	4	18	284
Spain					2		6		4		1		7				4				5							3				12		1		2				5	2	54

201

2021 Eurovision 65: Rotterdam, Netherlands

Semi-final 1: 18 May 2021

Votes are cast by countries participating in each semi-final plus the five automatically qualifying countries decided by draw: Germany and Italy in semi-final 1, France, Spain and the United Kingdom in semi-final 2. Hosts Netherlands voted in semi-final 1. Each voting country awards two sets of points, one from their professional jury and one from their public vote. The top 10 countries in each semi-final qualify for the final.

Rank	Start	Country	Artist	Song	Writer	Composer	POINTS
1Q	16	Malta	Destiny	Je me casse	Malin Christin, Amanuel Dermont, Nicklas Eklund, Pete Barringer	Malin Christin, Amanuel Dermont, Nicklas Eklund, Pete Barringer	325
2Q	15	Ukraine	Go_A	Shum	Kateryna Pavlenko	Taras Shevchenko, Kateryna Pavlenko	267
3Q	3	Russia	Manizha	Russian Woman	Manizha Sanghin	Ori Avni, Ori Kaplan	225
4Q	1	Lithuania	The Roop	Discoteque	Vaidotas Valiukevičius, Mantas Banišauskas, Kalle Lindroth	Vasil Garvanliev, Davor Jordanovski, Borche Kuzmanovski	203
5Q	12	Israel	Eden Alene	Set Me Free	Amit Mordechay, Ido Netzer, Noam Zlatin, Ron Carmi	Amit Mordechay, Ido Netzer, Noam Zlatin, Ron Carmi	192
6Q	8	Cyprus	Elena Tsagrinou	El Diablo	Thomas Stengaard, Jimmy Thörnfeldt, Laurell Barker, Oxa	Thomas Stengaard, Jimmy Thörnfeldt, Laurell Barker, Oxa	170
7Q	4	Sweden	Tusse	Voices	Joy Deb, Linnea Deb, Jimmy Thörnfeldt, Anderz Wrethov	Joy Deb, Linnea Deb, Jimmy Thörnfeldt, Anderz Wrethov	142
8Q	14	Azerbaijan	Efendi	Mata Hari	Amy van der Wel, Luuk van Beers, Josh Earl, Tony Cornelissen	Amy van der Wel, Luuk van Beers, Josh Earl, Tony Cornelissen	138
9Q	11	Belgium	Hooverphonic	The Wrong Place	Alex Callier, Charlotte Foret	Alex Callier, Charlotte Foret	117
10Q	9	Norway	Tix	Fallen Angel	Andreas Haukeland, Emelie Hollow, Mathias Haukeland	Andreas Haukeland	115
11	10	Croatia	Albina	Tick-Tock	Tihana Buklijaš Bakić, Max Cinnamon	Branimir Mihaljević	110
12	13	Romania	Roxen	Amnesia	Adelina Stîngă, Viky Red	Adelina Stîngă, Viky Red	85
13	2	Slovenia	Ana Soklič	Amen	Charlie Mason, Ana Soklič, Žiga Pirnat	Ana Soklič, Žiga Pirnat, Bojan Simončič	44
14	5	Australia	Montaigne	Technicolour	Jess Cerro, Dave Hammer	Jess Cerro, Dave Hammer	28
15	6	North Macedonia	Vasil	Here I Stand	Vasil Garvanliev	Vasil Garvanliev, Davor Jordanovski, Borche Kuzmanovski	23
16	7	Ireland	Lesley Roy	Maps	Lesley Roy, Philip Strand, Emelie Eriksson, Lukas Hällgren	Lesley Roy, Philip Strand, Emelie Eriksson, Lukas Hällgren	20

2021 Eurovision 65: Rotterdam, Netherlands — Jury Votes — Semi-final 1: 18 May 2021

	Australia	Azerbaijan	Belgium	Croatia	Cyprus	Germany	Ireland	Israel	Italy	Lithuania	Malta	Netherlands	North Macedonia	Norway	Romania	Russia	Slovenia	Sweden	Ukraine	TOTAL
Lithuania	2		2	6	3	4	5	12	7		4	3			8	2		7	1	66
Slovenia		4			6	7		3			5		3	4	7				4	36
Russia	7	12	12	8	8	7	8	6	5	3	1	12	7	3	5		10	6		117
Sweden	6	6	6	1	7	12	1	5	4	8	10	5	1	10	4	7			3	91
Australia				2		1									2	1	4		12	26
North Macedonia	3	3	3		2		2		1		2			1	6			1		12
Ireland	3	3	3		2	5	4	10	1	4			4	1	3	8	12	1	2	16
Cyprus	10			10			4	2	3	2	8		4	5	3	8	12	4		92
Norway	1		7				3	1	6	1		4	2			3	3	8		38
Croatia		5	1	4	5	2	10	7	2	10	3		8		1		7		8	57
Belgium		2		4	4				10			10		8		6	5	2	10	70
Israel	8	1	4	7	1	3			12	7		8	12	2		10	2	10	6	99
Romania		7	5	3	10	6				5	12	1		6		4	8	3	7	58
Azerbaijan	5						7	4			6	2	6	7		5	1	5		47
Ukraine	4	8	10	5		8	6	8	8	12	7	6	5	7	10	12	6	12		103
Malta	12	10	8	12	12	10	12			6		7	10	12	12	12			5	174

2021 Eurovision 65: Rotterdam, Netherlands — Public Votes — Semi-final 1: 18 May 2021

	Australia	Azerbaijan	Belgium	Croatia	Cyprus	Germany	Ireland	Israel	Italy	Lithuania	Malta	Netherlands	North Macedonia	Norway	Romania	Russia	Slovenia	Sweden	Ukraine	TOTAL
Lithuania	8	3	8	3	12	12	12	5	8		7	8	4	12	6	7		10	12	137
Slovenia				5									3							8
Russia	7	8	2	10	7	6	1	12	7	8	2	5	8	4	5		7	3	6	108
Sweden		1	7		3		4	2		5	10	2		10		2	2		3	51
Australia																1			1	2
North Macedonia	2			1											2		8			11
Ireland																				4
Cyprus	6	4	3	6		1	6	6	2	1	12	1	6	3	4	5	1	4	4	78
Norway	3	10	6	2	1	4	2	4	1	4	6	3	12	1	3	6	6	12	2	77
Croatia	5	2			2	7	7	3		6			2		1		12	2		53
Belgium						3		1	4	10	5	7	2	2	1	3	4	5	5	47
Israel	4	12	4	4	10	5	5		3	2		6	1	5	10	4		6	7	93
Romania		5	1		5		3	7	10		3		7							27
Azerbaijan	1		5	8	4	2		8	5	3	8	4	7	6	7	10	3	1	10	91
Ukraine	12	7	10	12	6	10	8	8	12	12	4	10	5	7	12	12	10	7		164
Malta	10	6	12	7	8	8	10	10	6	7		12	10	8	8	8	5	8	8	151

2021 Eurovision 65: Rotterdam, Netherlands
Combined Jury & Public Votes
Semi-final 1: 18 May 2021

	Australia	Azerbaijan	Belgium	Croatia	Cyprus	Germany	Ireland	Israel	Italy	Lithuania	Malta	Netherlands	North Macedonia	Norway	Romania	Russia	Slovenia	Sweden	Ukraine	TOTAL
Lithuania	10	3	10	9	15	16	17	17	15		11	11	4	12	14	9		17	13	**203**
Slovenia		4		5	6			3			5		6	4	7				4	**44**
Russia	14	20	14	18	15	13	9	18	12	8	3	17	15	7	10		17	9	6	**225**
Sweden	6	7	13	1	10	12	5	7	4	8	20	7	1	20	4	9	2		6	**142**
Australia				2		1				8					2	2			13	**28**
North Macedonia				1			2								8		12			**23**
Ireland	5	3	3						1	1	3	1		1				1		**20**
Cyprus	16	4	3	16		6	10	16	5	8	20		10	8	7	13	13	8	6	**170**
Norway	4	10	13	2	1	4	5	6	7	8	6	7	2		3	6	9	20	2	**115**
Croatia	5	7	1		7	9	17	4	2	1	3		20	1	1	3	19	2	8	**110**
Belgium		2		4	4	3		8	14	20		17	2	2	1	9	9	7	15	**117**
Israel	12	13	8	11	11	8	5		15	9	5	14	13	13	10	14	2	16	13	**192**
Romania			6	3	15	6	3			5	15	1		2					7	**85**
Azerbaijan	6		5	8	4	2	7	7	5	3	14	6	13	12	7	14	11	4	10	**138**
Ukraine	16	15	20	17	6	18	14	12	12	24		16	10	14	22	17	11	12		**267**
Malta	22	16	20	19	20	18	22	18	14	13		19	20	20	20	20	11	20	13	**325**

2021 Eurovision 65: Rotterdam, Netherlands
Semi-final 2: 20 May 2021

Votes are cast by countries participating in each semi-final plus the five automatically qualifying countries decided by draw: Germany and Italy in semi-final 1, France, Spain and the United Kingdom in semi-final 2. Hosts Netherlands voted in semi-final 1. Each voting country awards two sets of points, one from their professional jury and one from their public vote. The top 10 countries in each semi-final qualify for the final.

Rank	Start	Country	Artist	Song	Writer	Composer	POINTS
1Q	16	Switzerland	Gjon's Tears	Tout l'Univers	Wouter Hardy, Nina Sampermans, Gjon Muharremaj	Wouter Hardy, Nina Sampermans, Gjon Muharremaj, Xavier Michel	291
2Q	8	Iceland	Daði og Gagnamagnið	10 Years	Daði Freyr Pétursson	Daði Freyr Pétursson	288
3Q	13	Bulgaria	Victoria	Growing Up is Getting Old	Victoria Georgieva, Maya Nalani, Oliver Björkvall, Helena Larsson	Victoria Georgieva, Maya Nalani, Oliver Björkvall, Helena Larsson	250
4Q	12	Portugal	The Black Mamba	Love is on my Side	Tatanka	Tatanka	239
5Q	14	Finland	Blind Channel	Dark Side	Aleksi Kaunisvesi, Joonas Porko, Joel Hokka, Niko Moilanen, Olli Matela	Aleksi Kaunisvesi, Joonas Porko, Joel Hokka, Niko Moilanen, Olli Matela	234
6Q	4	Greece	Stefania	Last Dance	Dimitris Kontopoulos, Arcade, Sharon Vaughn	Dimitris Kontopoulos, Arcade	184
7Q	7	Moldova	Natalia Gordienko	Sugar	Mikhail Gutseriev, Sharon Vaughn	Dimitris Kontopoulos, Phillipp Kirkorov	179
8Q	9	Serbia	Hurricane	Loco Loco	Sanja Vučić	Nemanja Antonić, Darko Dimitrov	124
9Q	1	San Marino	Senhit	Adrenalina	Thomas Stengaard, Joy Deb, Linnea Deb, Jimmy Thörnfeldt, Kenny Silverdique, Suzi Pancenkov, Malou Linn Eloise Ruotsalainen, Chanel Tukia, Senhit Zadik, Dillard Tramar	Thomas Stengaard, Joy Deb, Linnea Deb, Jimmy Thörnfeldt, Kenny Silverdique, Suzi Pancenkov, Malou Linn Eloise Ruotsalainen, Chanel Tukia, Senhit Zadik, Dillard Tramar	118
10Q	11	Albania	Anxhela Peristeri	Karma	Olti Curri	Kledi Bahiti	112
11	17	Denmark	Fyr & Flamme	Øve os på hinanden	Laurits Emanuel	Laurits Emanuel	89
12	5	Austria	Vincent Bueno	Amen	Tobias Carshey, Ashley Hicklin, Jonas Thander	Tobias Carshey, Ashley Hicklin, Jonas Thander	66
13	2	Estonia	Uku Suviste	The Lucky One	Uku Suviste, Sharon Vaughn	Uku Suviste	58
14	6	Poland	Rafał	The Ride	Joakim Övrenius, Thomas Karlsson, Clara Rubensson, Johan Mauritzson	Joakim Övrenius, Thomas Karlsson, Clara Rubensson, Johan Mauritzson	35
15	3	Czech Republic	Benny Cristo	Omaga	Benny Cristo	Filip Vlček	23
16	10	Georgia	Tornike Kipiani	You	Tornike Kipiani	Tornike Kipiani	16
17	15	Latvia	Samanta Tīna	The Moon is Rising	Samanta Tīna, Aminata Savadogo, Oskars Uhaņs	Samanta Tīna, Aminata Savadogo, Oskars Uhaņs	14

2021 Eurovision 65: Rotterdam, Netherlands — Semi-final 2: 20 May 2021

Jury Votes

	Albania	Austria	Bulgaria	Czech Republic	Denmark	Estonia	Finland	France	Georgia	Greece	Iceland	Latvia	Moldova	Poland	Portugal	San Marino	Serbia	Spain	Switzerland	United Kingdom	TOTAL
San Marino	8	1	2	2	5	1	2	8	1	10	3	2	10	10			2	3	2	4	76
Estonia			7						3	1		3	3	4	1		1	1	3	2	29
Czech Republic			5					2	6	4			1		5						23
Greece	10		10	5	2	3	6	12			7		8	12	3	10	8	7	1		104
Austria	7		6		3	4	5		5		4	1			2		3	6	7		53
Poland	3		3		1					2						12					18
Moldova		2	12	1				1						7	2	8			6		56
Iceland	4	10		10	8	8	8	6	7			12		3	10	1	12	8	8	12	140
Serbia	5	6		4		5	3	5		3					4	4		4			56
Georgia			1																		1
Albania		3	4	1	10	2	4		10		5	5	5	6	8	7					74
Portugal	1	7	8	12	4	6	7	10	8		8	8	2	1		2	7		5		128
Bulgaria	2	8		7	6	10	12	4	4	5	10	6	12	5	12	5	10	10			149
Finland	6	5		6	7	7		7			6	7	4	2	6	3	6		12		84
Latvia													4								4
Switzerland	12	12		8	12	12	10	3	12		12	10	7	8		6	5	12		8	156
Denmark		4		3			1				1										9

2021 Eurovision 65: Rotterdam, Netherlands — Public Votes — Semi-final 2: 20 May 2021

	Albania	Austria	Bulgaria	Czech Republic	Denmark	Estonia	Finland	France	Georgia	Greece	Iceland	Latvia	Moldova	Poland	Portugal	San Marino	Serbia	Spain	Switzerland	United Kingdom	TOTAL
San Marino	7				2	4	1		12	2	3			2			3	4		2	42
Estonia			1	1	6		7					10	3						1		29
Czech Republic																					0
Greece	10		8	2	3		2		10		5	1	12		10	5	8	1	2	1	80
Austria	3				4						2								4		13
Poland		1						1			1		7							7	17
Moldova		6		12	12		5	12		12	6	12		7	12	12	12	3			123
Iceland		10	6	10	7		12	6	7	5		7	6	10	7	8	7	8	7	12	148
Serbia	4	12	10	5				7	1	4			1	1	2	7		2	12		68
Georgia			2		1	3					3	3		3	3						15
Albania		2	4			5	3	3	2	10	8	5	2	5	1	2	1		8		38
Portugal	6	7	5	4	8	5	6	10		3	4		4	5		3	4	12	10	6	111
Bulgaria	8	4		6	5	2	4	5	8	6		2	5	4	5	4	6	10	3	10	101
Finland	5	5	12	8	10	10		2	6	8	10	8	8	12	6	10	10	6	6	8	150
Latvia						1			5							1				4	10
Switzerland	12	8	7	7	3	6	10	8	3	7	7	6	10	8	8	6	5	7		3	135
Denmark	2	3	3	3		8	8	4	4	1	12	4		6	4	1	2	5	5	5	80

208

2021 Eurovision 65: Rotterdam, Netherlands
Combined Jury & Public Votes
Semi-final 2: 20 May 2021

	Albania	Austria	Bulgaria	Czech Republic	Denmark	Estonia	Finland	France	Georgia	Greece	Iceland	Latvia	Moldova	Poland	Portugal	San Marino	Serbia	Spain	Switzerland	United Kingdom	TOTAL
San Marino	15	1	2	2	7	5	3	8	13	12	6	2	10	12			5	7	2	6	118
Estonia			8	1	6		7		3	1		13	6	4	1		1	1	4	2	58
Czech Republic			5					2	6	4			1		5						23
Greece	20		18	7	5	3	8	12	10		12	1	20	12	13	15	16	8	3	1	184
Austria	10		6		7	4	5		5		6	1			2		3	6	11		66
Poland		1	3		1			1		2	1		7			12				7	35
Moldova	3	8	12	12		12	5	13		24	6	16		14	12	20	16	3		3	179
Iceland	5	20	6	20	20	15	20	12	14	12		19	12	13	17	9	19	16	15	24	288
Serbia	9	18	10	9		5	3	12	3	7	2		1	1	6	11		6	16	5	124
Georgia			3		1	3						3		3	3						16
Albania		5	8	1	10	2	7	3	2	16	5	5	7	6	9	9	1	2	13	1	112
Portugal	7	14	13	16	12	11	13	20	10	8	16	13	6	6		5	11	22	20	16	239
Bulgaria	10	12		13	11	12	16	9	16	14	14	8	17	9	17	9	16	15	15	17	250
Finland	11	10	12	14	17	17		9	10	8	16	15	8	14	12	13	16	6	12	14	234
Latvia						1			5				4							4	14
Switzerland	24	20	7	15	19	18	20	11	15	7	19	16	17	16	15	12	10	19		11	291
Denmark	2	7	3	6		8	9	4	4	1	13	4		6	4	1	2	5	5	5	89

209

2021 Eurovision 65: Rotterdam, Netherlands

FINAL: 22 May 2021

Final qualification rules: Top 10 placed countries from each semi-final. Automatic qualification: United Kingdom, France, Germany, Spain, Italy and hosts Israel. Each of the 39 participating countries awards two sets of points, one from their professional jury and one from their public vote.

Rank	Start	Country	Artist	Song	Writer	Composer	POINTS
1	24	Italy	Måneskin	Zitti e buoni	Måneskin	Måneskin	524
2	20	France	Barbara Pravi	Voilà	Barbara Pravi, Igit, Lili Poe	Barbara Pravi, Igit	499
3	11	Switzerland	Gjon's Tears	Tout l'Univers	Wouter Hardy, Nina Sampermans, Gjon Muharremaj	Wouter Hardy, Nina Sampermans, Gjon Muharremaj, Xavier Michel	432
4	12	Iceland	Daði og Gagnamagnið	10 Years	Daði Freyr Pétursson	Daði Freyr Pétursson	378
5	19	Ukraine	Go_A	Shum	Kateryna Pavlenko	Taras Shevchenko, Kateryna Pavlenko	364
6	16	Finland	Blind Channel	Dark Side	Aleksi Kaunisvesi, Joonas Porko, Joel Hokka, Niko Moilanen, Olli Matela	Aleksi Kaunisvesi, Joonas Porko, Joel Hokka, Niko Moilanen, Olli Matela	301
7	6	Malta	Destiny	Je me casse	Malin Christin, Amanuel Dermont, Nicklas Eklund, Pete Barringer	Malin Christin, Amanuel Dermont, Nicklas Eklund, Pete Barringer	255
8	18	Lithuania	The Roop	Discoteque	Vaidotas Valiukevičius, Mantas Banišauskas, Kalle Lindroth	Vasil Garvanliev, Davor Jordanovski, Borche Kuzmanovski	220
9	5	Russia	Manizha	Russian Woman	Manizha Sanghin	Ori Avni, Ori Kaplan	204
10	10	Greece	Stefania	Last Dance	Dimitris Kontopoulos, Arcade, Sharon Vaughn	Dimitris Kontopoulos, Arcade	170
11	17	Bulgaria	Victoria	Growing Up is Getting Old	Victoria Georgieva, Maya Nalani, Oliver Björkvall, Helena Larsson	Victoria Georgieva, Maya Nalani, Oliver Björkvall, Helena Larsson	170
12	7	Portugal	The Black Mamba	Love is on my Side	Tatanka	Tatanka	153
13	14	Moldova	Natalia Gordienko	Sugar	Mikhail Gutseriev, Sharon Vaughn	Dimitris Kontopoulos, Phillipp Kirkorov	115
14	25	Sweden	Tusse	Voices	Joy Deb, Linnea Deb, Jimmy Thörnfeldt, Anderz Wrethov	Joy Deb, Linnea Deb, Jimmy Thörnfeldt, Anderz Wrethov	109
15	8	Serbia	Hurricane	Loco Loco	Sanja Vučić	Nemanja Antonić, Darko Dimitrov	102
16	1	Cyprus	Elena Tsagrinou	El Diablo	Thomas Stengaard, Jimmy Thörnfeldt, Laurell Barker, Oxa	Thomas Stengaard, Jimmy Thörnfeldt, Laurell Barker, Oxa	94
17	3	Israel	Eden Alene	Set Me Free	Amit Mordechay, Ido Netzer, Noam Zlatin, Ron Carmi	Amit Mordechay, Ido Netzer, Noam Zlatin, Ron Carmi	93
18	22	Norway	Tix	Fallen Angel	Andreas Haukeland, Emelie Hollow, Mathias Haukeland	Andreas Haukeland	75
19	4	Belgium	Hooverphonic	The Wrong Place	Alex Callier, Charlotte Foret	Alex Callier, Charlotte Foret	74
20	21	Azerbaijan	Efendi	Mata Hari	Amy van der Wel, Luuk van Beers, Josh Earl, Tony Cornelissen	Amy van der Wel, Luuk van Beers, Josh Earl, Tony Cornelissen	65
21	2	Albania	Anxhela Peristeri	Karma	Olti Curri	Kledi Bahiti	57
22	26	San Marino	Senhit	Adrenalina	Thomas Stengaard, Joy Deb, Linnea Deb, Jimmy Thörnfeldt, Kenny Silverdique, Suzi Pancenkov, Malou Linn Eloise Ruotsalainen, Chanel Tukia, Senhit Zadik Zadik, Dillard Tramar	Thomas Stengaard, Joy Deb, Linnea Deb, Jimmy Thörnfeldt, Kenny Silverdique, Suzi Pancenkov, Malou Linn Eloise Ruotsalainen, Chanel Tukia, Senhit Zadik Zadik, Dillard Tramar	50
23	23	Netherlands	Jeangu Macrooy	Birth of a New Age	Jeangu Macrooy	Jeangu Macrooy, Pieter Perquin	11
24	13	Spain	Blas Cantó	Voy a quedarme	Blas Cantó, Leroy Sánchez, Daniel Ortega, Dan Hammond	Blas Cantó, Leroy Sánchez, Daniel Ortega, Dan Hammond	6
25	15	Germany	Jendrik	I Don't Feel Hate	Jendrik Sigwart, Christoph Oswald	Jendrik Sigwart, Christoph Oswald	3
26	9	United Kingdom	James Newman	Embers	James Newman, Conor Blake, Danny Shah, Tom Hollings, Samuel Brennan	James Newman, Conor Blake, Danny Shah, Tom Hollings, Samuel Brennan	0

2021 Eurovision 65: Rotterdam, Netherlands — Jury Votes — FINAL: 22 May 2021

Voting country	Albania	Australia	Austria	Azerbaijan	Belgium	Bulgaria	Croatia	Cyprus	Czech Republic	Denmark	Estonia	Finland	France	Georgia	Germany	Greece	Iceland	Ireland	Israel	Italy	Latvia	Lithuania	Malta	Moldova	Netherlands	North Macedonia	Norway	Poland	Portugal	Romania	Russia	San Marino	Serbia	Slovenia	Spain	Sweden	Switzerland	Ukraine	United Kingdom	TOTAL
Order votes announced	4	24	11	8	22	20	30	21	31	34	6	25	36	32	23	15	28	17	1	13	16	33	5	18	39	7	9	2	26	29	35	3	19	14	10	37	38	27	12	
Cyprus	7	4											2			12							4	1	1	2					2	2			6					50
Albania			5				5			7								3	3				12		1															22
Israel				3		3		4	3	1			5							4		1			4	8		6	5		5		2	1	3	4	3	7	6	73
Belgium		1					4	6	2		1	4	6			3	3		6	5	1	7	12	10	6	1	8	3	5				2	6		1	3	6	1	71
Russia		12	4	12	5	5	3	10	7	4	1	1	10	1	2	2	2	10	7	7	2			7	8	5	8	1		12	4	7		6	8	3	6	6		104
Malta	8		7	7	1	6	1	1	12	4	5	1	8	8	8	6	1	10	5	6	1	3		2	7		12	10	4			7	5	5	8	12	6	5		208
Portugal				2									8				10						6			12		8		10					5		7	2		126
Serbia	1		7				7			3				5									1									5								20
United Kingdom														2						2																				0
Greece	6	3			8	4		12	6	8	3	2	2	4			5		8	10	4	6	6	3	5	6		2	7		7	8	3	3	1					91
Switzerland	12	10	5	1	1		8	2	5	12	12	12	7	10	8		12	5	1		12	8	10	5	10		7	7	7		7	4	1	7	10	5		8	8	267
Iceland		12		6	3		10		8	10	8	3	3	6				8	10	12	10	4	4	3	10	4	2	10	8	7	1		7	10	7	7	5	4	10	198
Spain						4										10			4																1				2	6
Moldova				8	12						7								10				6		3					6	12	5								53
Germany			2																							1				1										3
Finland	3		1		8			3	1	8	7	2		4			5		1	10	5		2			7		2		8	7	1	10	4			1		4	83
Bulgaria			5	1	6			5	4	6	6	12		3			8	1	1	12	5	8		3		6			12	2	6	3	6		10		10			140
Lithuania	2						2				2	3		3	1			4	10		6			5		4			2	5		6				7	4			55
Ukraine		5		6	10				10	4	4			7			3	6	4	1	7	12	5		3				6	4		5		2		8				97
France	10	7	8	4		7	6	7				7			12		6	12	8	3	3	5	3	4	12	7			6		10	12	12	2	12	6	12	10	12	248
Azerbaijan	2													5				2	2	2			6	6	2					1		1					2	3		32
Norway		3	3		2					3				2																	8					2		1		15
Netherlands																													1											11
Italy	4	6	6		2	10		8	6	2	3	6	1	12	6		7				8		8			10	5	5	3	3	10	10	8	12		10	8	10	12	206
Sweden				5	4		12			5		5	4		4			2							2	3	10						4							46
San Marino	5													2	7			7					1					12											3	37

2021 Eurovision 65: Rotterdam, Netherlands

Public Votes — **FINAL: 22 May 2021**

To → / From ↓	Cyprus	Albania	Israel	Belgium	Russia	Malta	Portugal	Serbia	United Kingdom	Greece	Switzerland	Iceland	Spain	Moldova	Germany	Finland	Bulgaria	Lithuania	Ukraine	France	Azerbaijan	Norway	Netherlands	Italy	Sweden	San Marino	TOTAL
Albania	2									8	12			7		3	5		4	6		1		10	1		44
Australia										5	5	10			1	3		6	10	4		1		7			35
Austria		1	12		6	2		12		4	4					4		3	7	6		1		8		3	20
Azerbaijan											5					5	7		8	2		7		10	1		3
Belgium					7					2				1		6			10	12	4			8	3		100
Bulgaria					3			5			3					8		6	6	10	2			12	1		47
Croatia					3			12		12	5	4				6		3	8	7				10			27
Cyprus			2		1					8						4	7	5	6	8				10	2		82
Czech Republic					5	1				3		7		12		4		1	10	2				6			0
Denmark						2					6	12				7		4	1	3		8		5	10		79
Estonia					6						2	3				12		10	5	7		4		8	1		165
Finland				1			8				6	12		2				5	10	6		4		8	3		180
France				5	4			3		2	6	4		7		1		10	12			8		10	2		0
Georgia												1		2		8		10	6	5		3		12	7		62
Germany					4	5		3		2	4	6				8			4	10	5	1		7		3	0
Greece					1	3						10		2		6	12	5	4	8	2			7			218
Iceland							2					6				12			8	7		1		10			30
Ireland					10	4		2			3	10				5		12	8	7	2			6	1		165
Israel					7					3	6	1				4		3	12	8	2			10			267
Italy					10			4			8	6		2		5		12	12	1						3	251
Latvia											4	5				8		12	6	3		2		7	1		33
Lithuania				2	4						6	3				7			12	8		5		10	1		60
Malta	2							4				5				6		1	7	3		10		12	8		0
Moldova					12					7	4	8				5		2	10	6	1			8	3		318
Netherlands							1	6		10	7					4	2	3	5	12		3		2			63
North Macedonia	6				1			12			7			6		2			4	5	3			8			13
Norway						3					2	10				6	12		5	4				7	8		
Poland					2	1				2	7	8				6		4	12	5	3			10			
Portugal											6	3		8		5		3	10	12		7		7	4		
Romania		1				2					5	1		12	3	6		3	7	8	4			10			
Russia											5					8	2	2	7	6	4			10	12	3	
San Marino	8					1		6		7	3			6		4	2		5	10				12			
Serbia	2					6				3	1	5				7			8	10	4			12			
Slovenia						1		12		8	5	3				4			7	6		2		10			
Spain					3	1					7	5				2	8	4	7	6	12			10			
Sweden					2						5	10				12		4	7	4	6	8		3			
Switzerland		7				8		12				5				4		1	2	6	6			10	3		
Ukraine				1	4											8		10		4	5	3		12	2		
United Kingdom						6					1	10				7	8	12	4	5	2			3			

San Marino cannot use televoting as they share Italy's telephone system so, in accordance with the Rules, "a substitute result is calculated by the audience result of a pre-selected group of countries."

(source: eurovision.tv)

2021 Eurovision 65: Rotterdam, Netherlands — **Combined Jury & Public Votes** — **FINAL: 22 May 2021**

	Albania	Australia	Austria	Azerbaijan	Belgium	Bulgaria	Croatia	Cyprus	Czech Republic	Denmark	Estonia	Finland	France	Georgia	Germany	Greece	Iceland	Ireland	Israel	Italy	Latvia	Lithuania	Malta	Moldova	Netherlands	North Macedonia	Norway	Poland	Portugal	Romania	Russia	San Marino	Serbia	Slovenia	Spain	Sweden	Switzerland	Ukraine	United Kingdom	TOTAL
Cyprus	9	4											2		7	7			3				6	1		8					14	8	2		6					94
Albania							1			7						24				10			12			10						2	2	1	3	4	7	7	6	57
Israel				12		3	5	2		1			10	4	7			3	6	4		1			1	8	8	6		1	5		2	1	3	1		7	1	93
Belgium				3			7	4	3	1	6	5	6		7	3	2		6	5		9			4	8	8	3	5	1	3			6		3	3	7		74
Russia		1						9	7		1	1	10	4	8	3	4	3	17	7	11	4		22	6	2		3	4			1	6	5	11	14	3	4	6	204
Malta	8	20		18			7	11		6	5			1		9	2	14	10	6	2	3	7	7	8	5	15	4	14			1			6	3	6	5		255
Portugal			6	7		6	3	1	12				16	1	8		12	2				6	4	2	6			8	4	10		7		12		14	15	2		153
Serbia	1	2	12	2		5	19	1			5		3		3					4		3				24							5			1	12			102
United Kingdom																																								0
Greece	14			10		12		24		15	19	2	12	12			4					7	6	15	10	2	1		2	18	7	15	6	11	1					170
Switzerland	24	15	15	4	16	3	13	2	8	18	6	19	13	10	12	8	18	8	18	14	16	14	10	7	12	13	9	14	13	14	6	7	2	12	17	10		15	9	432
Iceland	20	22			8		14		15	22	11	20	7	7	9			18	1	17	15	7	5	5	18	4	12	18	11		1		12	13	12	17	10	10	20	378
Spain					4																																		2	6
Moldova	7			9		12			12		5	2	2	2		10			2		2				10				8	18	15	11								115
Germany			2																											1										3
Finland	6	3	5	5	14	9	6	7	5	15	6		1	4	8	6	17	5	4	18	12	7	9	5	4	2	6	8	5	14	8	5	17	8	2	12	5	8	11	301
Bulgaria	5	2	5	1	6		12	12	4	6	6	10			13	8	8	1	1		5	2	6	12	3	3	6	4	12	2	6	5	6		12		10		13	170
Lithuania		6	3		7		2	5	1	4	12	8	7	13	13	8	4	16	13		18		6	2		4	12	12	3	3	2	6		7	6	7	5	10	12	220
Ukraine	4	15	7	14	20		8	6	10	1	9	10	12	13	9	6	11	14	16		13	24	6	10	8	4	8	5	12	12	7	5	8	7	6	12	2		4	364
France	16	11	14	6	12	17	13	15	12	3	17	13		5	22	2	13	19	16	4	6	13	6	10	24	12	8	5	18	4	6	22	8	7	24	12	18	15	17	499
Azerbaijan	2					4	2			11	4	4		8	1		1	2	4		2			7	2	3	1			4	12		4				2	6		65
Norway		1	1	7	1														7			5	10					3				22		2		10		1	2	75
Netherlands		3	3		2								2													2			1											11
Italy	14	13	14	10	10	22	22	18	12	5	11	14	10	20	13	14	12	6	13	3	15	20	12	8	2	18	12	15	10	13	20	22	20	22	10	13	18	24	3	524
Sweden	1			5	7	1					1	8	3		4	7	10	1			1	1	16	3		3	18	1	4				4				3	2		109
San Marino	5			3						5			4						3				1					12											3	50

Eurovision 2021 - Jury Voting Order & National Spokespersons

Order	Country	Spokesperson
4	Albania	Andri Xhahu
24	Australia	Joel Creasey
11	Austria	Philipp Hansa
8	Azerbaijan	Ell & Nikki
22	Belgium	Danira Boukhriss
20	Bulgaria	Joanna Dragneva
30	Croatia	Ivan Dorian Molnar
21	Cyprus	Loukas Hamatsos
31	Czech Republic	Taťána Kuchařová
34	Denmark	Tina Müller
6	Estonia	Sissi Nyila Benita
25	Finland	Katri Norrlin
36	France	Carla Lazarri
32	Georgia	Oto Nemsadze
23	Germany	Barbara Schöneberger
15	Greece	Manolis Gkinis
28	Iceland	Hannes Óli Ágústsson
17	Ireland	Ryan O'Shaughnessy
1	Israel	Lucy Ayoub
13	Italy	Carolina Di Domenico
16	Latvia	Aminata Savadogo
33	Lithuania	Andrius Mamontovas
5	Malta	Stephanie Spiteri
18	Moldova	Sergey Stepanov
39	Netherlands	Romy Monteiro
7	North Macedonia	Vane Markoski
9	Norway	Silje Skjemstad Cruz
2	Poland	Ida Nowakowska
26	Portugal	Maria Elisa Silva
29	Romania	Cătălina Ponor
35	Russia	Polina Gagarina
3	San Marino	Monica Fabbri
19	Serbia	Dragana Kosjerina
14	Slovenia	Lorella Flego
10	Spain	Nieves Álvarez
37	Sweden	Carola Häggkvist
38	Switzerland	Angélique Beldner
40	Switzerland	Sinplus
27	Ukraine	Tayanna Reshetnyak
12	United Kingdom	Amanda Holden

Eurovision 2021: Final - Round by Round Leaderboard (Jury points)

Voting round:

1 Israel

Posn	Country	Pts	Lead
1st	Switzerland	12	2
2nd	Lithuania	10	2
3rd	France	8	1
4th	Russia	7	1
5th	Belgium	6	1
6th	Malta	5	1
7th	Ukraine	4	1
8th	Cyprus	3	1
9th	Azerbaijan	2	1
10th	Bulgaria	1	1
11th	Albania	0	0
12th	Israel	0	0
13th	Portugal	0	0
14th	Serbia	0	0
15th	United Kingdom	0	0
16th	Greece	0	0
17th	Iceland	0	0
18th	Spain	0	0
19th	Moldova	0	0
20th	Germany	0	0
21st	Finland	0	0
22nd	Norway	0	0
23rd	Netherlands	0	0
24th	Italy	0	0
25th	Sweden	0	0
26th	San Marino	0	0

2 Poland

Posn	Country	Pts	Lead
1st	Switzerland	19	7
2nd	San Marino	12	2
3rd	Iceland	10	0
4th	Lithuania	10	1
5th	Belgium	9	0
6th	Malta	9	1
7th	Russia	8	0
8th	Portugal	8	0
9th	France	8	2
10th	Cyprus	6	1
11th	Italy	5	1
12th	Ukraine	4	1
13th	Israel	3	1
14th	Finland	2	0
15th	Azerbaijan	2	1
16th	Bulgaria	1	1
17th	Albania	0	0
18th	Serbia	0	0
19th	United Kingdom	0	0
20th	Greece	0	0
21st	Spain	0	0
22nd	Moldova	0	0
23rd	Germany	0	0
24th	Norway	0	0
25th	Netherlands	0	0
26th	Sweden	0	0

3 San Marino

Posn	Country	Pts	Lead
1st	Switzerland	23	3
2nd	France	20	4
3rd	Malta	16	0
4th	Lithuania	16	1
5th	Italy	15	3
6th	San Marino	12	2
7th	Iceland	10	1
8th	Belgium	9	1
9th	Russia	8	0
10th	Portugal	8	0
11th	Greece	8	3
12th	Israel	6	2
13th	Moldova	5	1
14th	Bulgaria	4	1
15th	Ukraine	4	1
16th	Cyprus	3	1
17th	Finland	3	1
18th	Albania	2	2
19th	Azerbaijan	2	2
20th	Serbia	0	0
21st	United Kingdom	0	0
22nd	Spain	0	0
23rd	Germany	0	0
24th	Norway	0	0
25th	Netherlands	0	0
26th	Sweden	0	0

4 Albania

Posn	Country	Pts	Lead
1st	Switzerland	35	5
2nd	France	30	6
3rd	Malta	24	5
4th	Italy	19	2
5th	San Marino	17	1
6th	Lithuania	16	2
7th	Greece	14	4
8th	Cyprus	10	0
9th	Iceland	10	1
10th	Belgium	9	1
11th	Russia	8	0
12th	Portugal	8	2
13th	Finland	6	0
14th	Israel	6	1
15th	Moldova	5	1
16th	Bulgaria	4	0
17th	Azerbaijan	4	0
18th	Ukraine	4	2
19th	Albania	2	1
20th	Serbia	1	1
21st	United Kingdom	0	0
22nd	Spain	0	0
23rd	Germany	0	0
24th	Norway	0	0
25th	Netherlands	0	0
26th	Sweden	0	0

5 Malta

Posn	Country	Pts	Lead
1st	Switzerland	45	12
2nd	France	33	9
3rd	Malta	24	4
4th	Greece	20	1
5th	Italy	19	1
6th	San Marino	18	2
7th	Lithuania	16	1
8th	Portugal	15	1
9th	Cyprus	14	0
10th	Albania	14	4
11th	Iceland	10	1
12th	Belgium	9	0
13th	Ukraine	9	1
14th	Finland	8	0
15th	Russia	8	0
16th	Sweden	8	2
17th	Israel	6	1
18th	Moldova	5	1
19th	Bulgaria	4	0
20th	Azerbaijan	4	3
21st	Serbia	1	1
22nd	United Kingdom	0	0
23rd	Spain	0	0
24th	Germany	0	0
25th	Norway	0	0
26th	Netherlands	0	0

Voting round:

6 Estonia

Posn	Country	Pts	Lead
1st	Switzerland	57	14
2nd	France	43	18
3rd	Malta	25	3
4th	Italy	22	2
5th	Portugal	20	0
6th	Greece	20	2
7th	Lithuania	18	0
8th	Iceland	18	0
9th	San Marino	18	3
10th	Finland	15	1
11th	Cyprus	14	0
12th	Albania	14	1
13th	Ukraine	13	3
14th	Bulgaria	10	1
15th	Belgium	9	1
16th	Russia	8	0
17th	Sweden	8	2
18th	Israel	6	1
19th	Moldova	5	1
20th	Azerbaijan	4	3
21st	Serbia	1	1
22nd	United Kingdom	0	0
23rd	Spain	0	0
24th	Germany	0	0
25th	Norway	0	0
26th	Netherlands	0	0

7 North Macedonia

Posn	Country	Pts	Lead
1st	Switzerland	63	13
2nd	France	50	18
3rd	Italy	32	2
4th	Malta	30	8
5th	Iceland	22	2
6th	Portugal	20	0
7th	Greece	20	2
8th	San Marino	18	0
9th	Lithuania	18	2
10th	Cyprus	16	1
11th	Finland	15	1
12th	Albania	14	1
13th	Israel	14	1
14th	Ukraine	13	0
15th	Serbia	13	2
16th	Sweden	11	1
17th	Bulgaria	10	2
18th	Russia	9	0
19th	Belgium	9	4
20th	Moldova	5	1
21st	Azerbaijan	4	4
22nd	United Kingdom	0	0
23rd	Spain	0	0
24th	Germany	0	0
25th	Norway	0	0
26th	Netherlands	0	0

8 Azerbaijan

Posn	Country	Pts	Lead
1st	Switzerland	63	9
2nd	France	54	17
3rd	Malta	37	5
4th	Italy	32	2
5th	Greece	30	8
6th	Portugal	22	0
7th	Iceland	22	1
8th	Russia	21	2
9th	Ukraine	19	1
10th	San Marino	18	0
11th	Lithuania	18	2
12th	Cyprus	16	0
13th	Sweden	16	1
14th	Finland	15	1
15th	Albania	14	0
16th	Israel	14	1
17th	Serbia	13	0
18th	Moldova	13	1
19th	Belgium	12	1
20th	Bulgaria	11	7
21st	Azerbaijan	4	4
22nd	United Kingdom	0	0
23rd	Spain	0	0
24th	Germany	0	0
25th	Norway	0	0
26th	Netherlands	0	0

9 Norway

Posn	Country	Pts	Lead
1st	Switzerland	70	12
2nd	France	58	9
3rd	Malta	49	12
4th	Italy	37	6
5th	Greece	31	5
6th	Sweden	26	2
7th	Iceland	24	2
8th	Israel	22	0
9th	Ukraine	22	0
10th	Portugal	22	1
11th	Russia	21	3
12th	San Marino	18	0
13th	Lithuania	18	1
14th	Bulgaria	17	1
15th	Cyprus	16	1
16th	Finland	15	1
17th	Albania	14	1
18th	Serbia	13	0
19th	Moldova	13	1
20th	Belgium	12	8
21st	Azerbaijan	4	4
22nd	United Kingdom	0	0
23rd	Spain	0	0
24th	Germany	0	0
25th	Norway	0	0
26th	Netherlands	0	0

10 Spain

Posn	Country	Pts	Lead
1st	Switzerland	80	10
2nd	France	70	13
3rd	Malta	57	20
4th	Italy	37	5
5th	Greece	32	1
6th	Iceland	31	4
7th	Portugal	27	1
8th	Sweden	26	1
9th	Israel	25	3
10th	Cyprus	22	0
11th	Ukraine	22	1
12th	Bulgaria	21	0
13th	Russia	21	1
14th	Lithuania	20	2
15th	San Marino	18	3
16th	Finland	15	1
17th	Albania	14	1
18th	Serbia	13	0
19th	Moldova	13	1
20th	Belgium	12	8
21st	Azerbaijan	4	4
22nd	United Kingdom	0	0
23rd	Spain	0	0
24th	Germany	0	0
25th	Norway	0	0
26th	Netherlands	0	0

Eurovision 2021: Final - Round by Round Leaderboard (Jury points)

Voting round:

11 Austria

Posn	Country	Pts	Lead
1st	Switzerland	90	12
2nd	France	78	17
3rd	Malta	61	18
4th	Italy	43	0
5th	Iceland	43	9
6th	Portugal	34	2
7th	Greece	32	6
8th	Bulgaria	26	0
9th	Sweden	26	1
10th	Israel	25	3
11th	Cyprus	22	0
12th	Ukraine	22	1
13th	Russia	21	1
14th	Lithuania	20	2
15th	San Marino	18	2
16th	Finland	16	2
17th	Albania	14	1
18th	Serbia	13	0
19th	Moldova	13	1
20th	Belgium	12	8
21st	Azerbaijan	4	1
22nd	Netherlands	3	1
23rd	Germany	2	2
24th	United Kingdom	0	0
25th	Spain	0	0
26th	Norway	0	0

12 United Kingdom

Posn	Country	Pts	Lead
1st	Switzerland	98	8
2nd	France	90	29
3rd	Malta	61	8
4th	Iceland	53	10
5th	Italy	43	2
6th	Portugal	41	9
7th	Greece	32	1
8th	Bulgaria	31	0
9th	Israel	31	5
10th	Sweden	26	4
11th	Cyprus	22	0
12th	Ukraine	22	1
13th	Russia	21	0
14th	San Marino	21	1
15th	Finland	20	0
16th	Lithuania	20	6
17th	Albania	14	1
18th	Belgium	13	0
19th	Serbia	13	0
20th	Moldova	13	9
21st	Azerbaijan	4	1
22nd	Netherlands	3	1
23rd	Spain	2	0
24th	Germany	2	2
25th	United Kingdom	0	0
26th	Norway	0	0

13 Italy

Posn	Country	Pts	Lead
1st	Switzerland	98	5
2nd	France	93	25
3rd	Malta	68	7
4th	Iceland	61	14
5th	Portugal	47	4
6th	Italy	43	8
7th	Israel	35	3
8th	Greece	32	0
9th	Lithuania	32	1
10th	Bulgaria	31	1
11th	Finland	30	4
12th	Sweden	26	3
13th	Ukraine	23	1
14th	Cyprus	22	1
15th	Russia	21	0
16th	San Marino	21	3
17th	Belgium	18	4
18th	Albania	14	1
19th	Serbia	13	0
20th	Moldova	13	9
21st	Azerbaijan	4	1
22nd	Netherlands	3	1
23rd	Spain	2	0
24th	Germany	2	0
25th	Norway	2	2
26th	United Kingdom	0	0

14 Slovenia

Posn	Country	Pts	Lead
1st	Switzerland	105	10
2nd	France	95	22
3rd	Malta	73	2
4th	Iceland	71	16
5th	Italy	55	8
6th	Portugal	47	11
7th	Israel	36	1
8th	Greece	35	1
9th	Finland	34	2
10th	Lithuania	32	1
11th	Bulgaria	31	2
12th	Russia	29	3
13th	Sweden	26	2
14th	Belgium	24	1
15th	Ukraine	23	1
16th	Cyprus	22	1
17th	San Marino	21	7
18th	Albania	14	1
19th	Serbia	13	0
20th	Moldova	13	9
21st	Azerbaijan	4	1
22nd	Netherlands	3	1
23rd	Spain	2	0
24th	Germany	2	0
25th	Norway	2	2
26th	United Kingdom	0	0

15 Greece

Posn	Country	Pts	Lead
1st	Switzerland	105	5
2nd	France	100	21
3rd	Malta	79	8
4th	Iceland	71	12
5th	Italy	59	12
6th	Portugal	47	8
7th	Bulgaria	39	3
8th	Israel	36	1
9th	Greece	35	1
10th	Finland	34	0
11th	Cyprus	34	2
12th	Lithuania	32	1
13th	Russia	31	3
14th	San Marino	28	1
15th	Belgium	27	1
16th	Sweden	26	2
17th	Ukraine	24	1
18th	Moldova	23	9
19th	Albania	14	1
20th	Serbia	13	9
21st	Azerbaijan	4	1
22nd	Netherlands	3	1
23rd	Spain	2	0
24th	Germany	2	0
25th	Norway	2	2
26th	United Kingdom	0	0

Voting round:

16 Latvia

Posn	Country	Pts	Lead
1st	Switzerland	117	14
2nd	France	103	22
3rd	Malta	81	0
4th	Iceland	81	14
5th	Italy	67	20
6th	Portugal	47	3
7th	Bulgaria	44	6
8th	Finland	38	0
9th	Lithuania	38	2
10th	Israel	36	1
11th	Greece	35	1
12th	Cyprus	34	2
13th	Russia	32	1
14th	Ukraine	31	3
15th	San Marino	28	1
16th	Belgium	27	1
17th	Sweden	26	3
18th	Moldova	23	9
19th	Albania	14	1
20th	Serbia	13	9
21st	Azerbaijan	4	1
22nd	Netherlands	3	1
23rd	Spain	2	0
24th	Germany	2	0
25th	Norway	2	2
26th	United Kingdom	0	0

17 Ireland

Posn	Country	Pts	Lead
1st	Switzerland	122	7
2nd	France	115	24
3rd	Malta	91	2
4th	Iceland	89	22
5th	Italy	67	20
6th	Portugal	47	2
7th	Bulgaria	45	3
8th	Lithuania	42	4
9th	Finland	38	1
10th	Ukraine	37	1
11th	Israel	36	1
12th	Greece	35	1
13th	Cyprus	34	2
14th	Russia	32	2
15th	Belgium	30	2
16th	San Marino	28	2
17th	Sweden	26	3
18th	Moldova	23	9
19th	Albania	14	1
20th	Serbia	13	4
21st	Norway	9	3
22nd	Azerbaijan	6	3
23rd	Netherlands	3	1
24th	Spain	2	0
25th	Germany	2	2
26th	United Kingdom	0	0

18 Moldova

Posn	Country	Pts	Lead
1st	Switzerland	125	6
2nd	France	119	21
3rd	Malta	98	4
4th	Iceland	94	27
5th	Italy	67	10
6th	Bulgaria	57	8
7th	Portugal	49	6
8th	Greece	43	1
9th	Russia	42	0
10th	Lithuania	42	4
11th	Finland	38	1
12th	Ukraine	37	1
13th	Israel	36	1
14th	Cyprus	35	5
15th	Belgium	30	2
16th	San Marino	28	2
17th	Sweden	26	3
18th	Moldova	23	9
19th	Albania	14	1
20th	Serbia	13	1
21st	Azerbaijan	12	3
22nd	Norway	9	6
23rd	Netherlands	3	1
24th	Spain	2	0
25th	Germany	2	2
26th	United Kingdom	0	0

19 Serbia

Posn	Country	Pts	Lead
1st	France	131	5
2nd	Switzerland	126	25
3rd	Iceland	101	3
4th	Malta	98	23
5th	Italy	75	12
6th	Bulgaria	63	9
7th	Portugal	54	6
8th	Finland	48	2
9th	Greece	46	4
10th	Russia	42	0
11th	Lithuania	42	4
12th	Israel	38	1
13th	Ukraine	37	2
14th	Cyprus	35	5
15th	Belgium	30	0
16th	Sweden	30	2
17th	San Marino	28	5
18th	Moldova	23	9
19th	Albania	14	1
20th	Serbia	13	1
21st	Azerbaijan	12	3
22nd	Norway	9	6
23rd	Netherlands	3	1
24th	Spain	2	0
25th	Germany	2	2
26th	United Kingdom	0	0

20 Bulgaria

Posn	Country	Pts	Lead
1st	France	138	12
2nd	Switzerland	126	23
3rd	Malta	103	2
4th	Iceland	101	16
5th	Italy	85	22
6th	Bulgaria	63	3
7th	Portugal	60	6
8th	Greece	54	5
9th	Finland	49	7
10th	Russia	42	0
11th	Lithuania	42	1
12th	Israel	41	4
13th	Ukraine	37	2
14th	Cyprus	35	0
15th	Moldova	35	5
16th	Belgium	30	0
17th	Sweden	30	2
18th	San Marino	28	14
19th	Albania	14	1
20th	Serbia	13	1
21st	Azerbaijan	12	3
22nd	Norway	9	3
23rd	Spain	6	1
24th	Netherlands	5	3
25th	Germany	2	2
26th	United Kingdom	0	0

Eurovision 2021: Final - Round by Round Leaderboard (Jury points)

Voting round:

21 Cyprus

Posn	Country	Pts	Lead
1st	France	145	17
2nd	Switzerland	128	15
3rd	Malta	113	12
4th	Iceland	101	8
5th	Italy	93	25
6th	Bulgaria	68	2
7th	Greece	66	5
8th	Portugal	61	9
9th	Finland	52	4
10th	Russia	48	6
11th	Lithuania	42	1
12th	Israel	41	4
13th	Ukraine	37	2
14th	Cyprus	35	0
15th	Moldova	35	1
16th	Belgium	34	4
17th	Sweden	30	2
18th	San Marino	28	14
19th	Albania	14	1
20th	Serbia	13	1
21st	Azerbaijan	12	3
22nd	Norway	9	3
23rd	Spain	6	1
24th	Netherlands	5	3
25th	Germany	2	2
26th	United Kingdom	0	0

22 Belgium

Posn	Country	Pts	Lead
1st	France	145	5
2nd	Switzerland	140	22
3rd	Malta	118	14
4th	Iceland	104	9
5th	Italy	95	21
6th	Bulgaria	74	8
7th	Greece	66	4
8th	Portugal	62	2
9th	Finland	60	5
10th	Russia	55	8
11th	Ukraine	47	5
12th	Lithuania	42	1
13th	Israel	41	6
14th	Cyprus	35	0
15th	Moldova	35	1
16th	Belgium	34	0
17th	Sweden	34	6
18th	San Marino	28	14
19th	Albania	14	1
20th	Serbia	13	1
21st	Azerbaijan	12	3
22nd	Norway	9	3
23rd	Spain	6	1
24th	Netherlands	5	3
25th	Germany	2	2
26th	United Kingdom	0	0

23 Germany

Posn	Country	Pts	Lead
1st	France	157	7
2nd	Switzerland	150	24
3rd	Malta	126	19
4th	Iceland	107	6
5th	Italy	101	27
6th	Bulgaria	74	8
7th	Greece	66	4
8th	Portugal	62	2
9th	Finland	60	3
10th	Russia	57	5
11th	Ukraine	52	9
12th	Lithuania	43	1
13th	Israel	42	1
14th	Cyprus	41	3
15th	Sweden	38	3
16th	Moldova	35	1
17th	Belgium	34	6
18th	San Marino	28	14
19th	Albania	14	1
20th	Serbia	13	1
21st	Azerbaijan	12	3
22nd	Norway	9	3
23rd	Spain	6	1
24th	Netherlands	5	3
25th	Germany	2	2
26th	United Kingdom	0	0

24 Australia

Posn	Country	Pts	Lead
1st	France	164	4
2nd	Switzerland	160	22
3rd	Malta	138	23
4th	Iceland	115	8
5th	Italy	107	31
6th	Bulgaria	76	10
7th	Greece	66	4
8th	Portugal	62	2
9th	Finland	60	2
10th	Russia	58	1
11th	Ukraine	57	11
12th	Cyprus	46	3
13th	Lithuania	43	2
14th	Israel	41	3
15th	Sweden	38	3
16th	Moldova	35	1
17th	Belgium	34	6
18th	San Marino	28	14
19th	Albania	14	1
20th	Serbia	13	1
21st	Azerbaijan	12	3
22nd	Norway	9	1
23rd	Netherlands	8	2
24th	Spain	6	4
25th	Germany	2	2
26th	United Kingdom	0	0

25 Finland

Posn	Country	Pts	Lead
1st	Switzerland	172	1
2nd	France	171	32
3rd	Malta	139	16
4th	Iceland	123	10
5th	Italy	113	27
6th	Bulgaria	86	18
7th	Greece	68	6
8th	Russia	62	0
9th	Portugal	62	2
10th	Finland	60	3
11th	Ukraine	57	11
12th	Cyprus	46	0
13th	Lithuania	46	3
14th	Sweden	43	2
15th	Israel	41	6
16th	Moldova	35	1
17th	Belgium	34	6
18th	San Marino	28	14
19th	Albania	14	1
20th	Serbia	13	1
21st	Azerbaijan	12	3
22nd	Norway	9	1
23rd	Netherlands	8	2
24th	Spain	6	4
25th	Germany	2	2
26th	United Kingdom	0	0

Voting round:

26 Portugal

Posn	Country	Pts	Lead
1st	Switzerland	179	2
2nd	France	177	34
3rd	Malta	143	12
4th	Iceland	131	15
5th	Italy	116	18
6th	Bulgaria	98	26
7th	Russia	72	4
8th	Greece	68	6
9th	Portugal	62	2
10th	Finland	60	1
11th	Ukraine	59	13
12th	Cyprus	46	0
13th	Lithuania	46	3
14th	Sweden	43	2
15th	Israel	41	2
16th	Belgium	39	4
17th	Moldova	35	7
18th	San Marino	28	14
19th	Albania	14	1
20th	Serbia	13	1
21st	Azerbaijan	12	3
22nd	Norway	9	0
23rd	Netherlands	9	3
24th	Spain	6	4
25th	Germany	2	2
26th	United Kingdom	0	0

27 Ukraine

Posn	Country	Pts	Lead
1st	France	187	0
2nd	Switzerland	187	39
3rd	Malta	148	13
4th	Iceland	135	7
5th	Italy	128	30
6th	Bulgaria	98	26
7th	Russia	72	4
8th	Greece	68	4
9th	Portugal	64	4
10th	Finland	60	1
11th	Ukraine	59	11
12th	Israel	48	2
13th	Cyprus	46	0
14th	Lithuania	46	1
15th	Belgium	45	2
16th	Sweden	43	8
17th	Moldova	35	7
18th	San Marino	28	13
19th	Azerbaijan	15	1
20th	Albania	14	1
21st	Serbia	13	3
22nd	Norway	10	1
23rd	Netherlands	9	3
24th	Spain	6	4
25th	Germany	2	2
26th	United Kingdom	0	0

28 Iceland

Posn	Country	Pts	Lead
1st	Switzerland	199	6
2nd	France	193	44
3rd	Malta	149	14
4th	Italy	135	0
5th	Iceland	135	29
6th	Bulgaria	106	32
7th	Russia	74	0
8th	Portugal	74	2
9th	Greece	72	7
10th	Finland	65	3
11th	Ukraine	62	14
12th	Israel	48	2
13th	Cyprus	46	0
14th	Lithuania	46	1
15th	Belgium	45	2
16th	Sweden	43	8
17th	Moldova	35	7
18th	San Marino	28	13
19th	Azerbaijan	15	1
20th	Albania	14	1
21st	Serbia	13	3
22nd	Norway	10	1
23rd	Netherlands	9	3
24th	Spain	6	4
25th	Germany	2	2
26th	United Kingdom	0	0

29 Romania

Posn	Country	Pts	Lead
1st	Switzerland	206	9
2nd	France	197	36
3rd	Malta	161	23
4th	Italy	138	3
5th	Iceland	135	27
6th	Bulgaria	108	24
7th	Portugal	84	10
8th	Russia	74	1
9th	Finland	73	1
10th	Greece	72	5
11th	Ukraine	67	19
12th	Israel	48	2
13th	Cyprus	46	0
14th	Lithuania	46	1
15th	Belgium	45	2
16th	Sweden	43	2
17th	Moldova	41	13
18th	San Marino	28	13
19th	Azerbaijan	15	1
20th	Albania	14	1
21st	Serbia	13	3
22nd	Norway	10	1
23rd	Netherlands	9	3
24th	Spain	6	3
25th	Germany	3	3
26th	United Kingdom	0	0

30 Croatia

Posn	Country	Pts	Lead
1st	Switzerland	214	11
2nd	France	203	39
3rd	Malta	164	14
4th	Italy	150	5
5th	Iceland	145	37
6th	Bulgaria	108	23
7th	Portugal	85	7
8th	Russia	78	5
9th	Finland	73	1
10th	Greece	72	5
11th	Ukraine	67	14
12th	Israel	53	5
13th	Lithuania	48	2
14th	Cyprus	46	1
15th	Belgium	45	2
16th	Sweden	43	2
17th	Moldova	41	13
18th	San Marino	28	8
19th	Serbia	20	5
20th	Azerbaijan	15	1
21st	Albania	14	4
22nd	Norway	10	1
23rd	Netherlands	9	3
24th	Spain	6	3
25th	Germany	3	3
26th	United Kingdom	0	0

Eurovision 2021: Final - Round by Round Leaderboard (Jury points)

Voting round:

31 Czech Republic

Posn	Country	Pts	Lead
1st	Switzerland	219	6
2nd	France	213	42
3rd	Malta	171	15
4th	Italy	156	3
5th	Iceland	153	41
6th	Bulgaria	112	15
7th	Portugal	97	17
8th	Russia	80	6
9th	Finland	74	2
10th	Greece	72	5
11th	Ukraine	67	14
12th	Israel	53	5
13th	Belgium	48	0
14th	Lithuania	48	2
15th	Cyprus	46	3
16th	Sweden	43	2
17th	Moldova	41	13
18th	San Marino	28	8
19th	Serbia	20	5
20th	Azerbaijan	15	1
21st	Albania	14	4
22nd	Norway	10	1
23rd	Netherlands	9	3
24th	Spain	6	3
25th	Germany	3	3
26th	United Kingdom	0	0

32 Georgia

Posn	Country	Pts	Lead
1st	Switzerland	229	16
2nd	France	213	41
3rd	Malta	172	4
4th	Italy	168	9
5th	Iceland	159	43
6th	Bulgaria	116	11
7th	Portugal	105	25
8th	Russia	80	6
9th	Finland	74	0
10th	Ukraine	74	2
11th	Greece	72	19
12th	Israel	53	2
13th	Lithuania	51	3
14th	Belgium	48	2
15th	Cyprus	46	3
16th	Sweden	43	2
17th	Moldova	41	13
18th	San Marino	28	8
19th	Azerbaijan	20	0
20th	Serbia	20	6
21st	Albania	14	3
22nd	Netherlands	11	1
23rd	Norway	10	4
24th	Spain	6	3
25th	Germany	3	3
26th	United Kingdom	0	0

33 Lithuania

Posn	Country	Pts	Lead
1st	Switzerland	237	19
2nd	France	218	40
3rd	Italy	178	3
4th	Malta	175	12
5th	Iceland	163	45
6th	Bulgaria	118	7
7th	Portugal	111	25
8th	Ukraine	86	6
9th	Russia	80	6
10th	Finland	74	2
11th	Greece	72	17
12th	Belgium	55	1
13th	Israel	54	3
14th	Lithuania	51	5
15th	Cyprus	46	3
16th	Sweden	43	2
17th	Moldova	41	13
18th	San Marino	28	8
19th	Azerbaijan	20	0
20th	Serbia	20	6
21st	Albania	14	3
22nd	Netherlands	11	1
23rd	Norway	10	4
24th	Spain	6	3
25th	Germany	3	3
26th	United Kingdom	0	0

34 Denmark

Posn	Country	Pts	Lead
1st	Switzerland	249	31
2nd	France	218	39
3rd	Malta	179	1
4th	Italy	178	5
5th	Iceland	173	49
6th	Bulgaria	124	13
7th	Portugal	111	25
8th	Ukraine	86	6
9th	Finland	82	2
10th	Russia	80	8
11th	Greece	72	17
12th	Israel	55	0
13th	Belgium	55	4
14th	Lithuania	51	5
15th	Cyprus	46	1
16th	Sweden	45	4
17th	Moldova	41	8
18th	San Marino	33	12
19th	Albania	21	1
20th	Azerbaijan	20	0
21st	Serbia	20	7
22nd	Norway	13	2
23rd	Netherlands	11	5
24th	Spain	6	3
25th	Germany	3	3
26th	United Kingdom	0	0

35 Russia

Posn	Country	Pts	Lead
1st	Switzerland	250	32
2nd	France	218	30
3rd	Italy	188	5
4th	Malta	183	10
5th	Iceland	173	43
6th	Bulgaria	130	19
7th	Portugal	111	25
8th	Ukraine	86	4
9th	Finland	82	2
10th	Russia	80	1
11th	Greece	79	19
12th	Israel	60	2
13th	Belgium	58	5
14th	Moldova	53	2
15th	Lithuania	51	3
16th	Cyprus	48	3
17th	Sweden	45	12
18th	San Marino	33	5
19th	Azerbaijan	28	7
20th	Albania	21	1
21st	Serbia	20	7
22nd	Norway	13	2
23rd	Netherlands	11	5
24th	Spain	6	3
25th	Germany	3	3
26th	United Kingdom	0	0

Voting round:

36 France

Posn	Country	Pts	Lead
1st	Switzerland	257	39
2nd	France	218	30
3rd	Italy	188	5
4th	Malta	183	7
5th	Iceland	176	46
6th	Bulgaria	130	11
7th	Portugal	119	28
8th	Greece	91	1
9th	Russia	90	4
10th	Ukraine	86	4
11th	Finland	82	17
12th	Israel	65	1
13th	Belgium	64	11
14th	Moldova	53	2
15th	Lithuania	51	1
16th	Cyprus	50	4
17th	Sweden	46	9
18th	San Marino	37	9
19th	Azerbaijan	28	7
20th	Albania	21	1
21st	Serbia	20	7
22nd	Norway	13	2
23rd	Netherlands	11	5
24th	Spain	6	3
25th	Germany	3	3
26th	United Kingdom	0	0

37 Sweden

Posn	Country	Pts	Lead
1st	Switzerland	262	38
2nd	France	224	26
3rd	Italy	198	3
4th	Malta	195	12
5th	Iceland	183	53
6th	Bulgaria	130	11
7th	Portugal	119	25
8th	Ukraine	94	1
9th	Russia	93	2
10th	Greece	91	9
11th	Finland	82	13
12th	Israel	69	4
13th	Belgium	65	12
14th	Moldova	53	2
15th	Lithuania	51	1
16th	Cyprus	50	4
17th	Sweden	46	9
18th	San Marino	37	9
19th	Azerbaijan	28	7
20th	Albania	21	1
21st	Serbia	20	5
22nd	Norway	15	4
23rd	Netherlands	11	5
24th	Spain	6	3
25th	Germany	3	3
26th	United Kingdom	0	0

38 Switzerland

Posn	Country	Pts	Lead
1st	Switzerland	262	26
2nd	France	236	30
3rd	Italy	206	5
4th	Malta	201	13
5th	Iceland	188	48
6th	Bulgaria	140	14
7th	Portugal	126	30
8th	Russia	96	2
9th	Ukraine	94	3
10th	Greece	91	8
11th	Finland	83	14
12th	Israel	69	4
13th	Belgium	65	10
14th	Lithuania	55	2
15th	Moldova	53	3
16th	Cyprus	50	4
17th	Sweden	46	9
18th	San Marino	37	7
19th	Azerbaijan	30	9
20th	Albania	21	1
21st	Serbia	20	5
22nd	Norway	15	4
23rd	Netherlands	11	5
24th	Spain	6	3
25th	Germany	3	3
26th	United Kingdom	0	0

39 Netherlands

Posn	Country	Pts	Lead
1st	Switzerland	267	19
2nd	France	248	40
3rd	Malta	208	2
4th	Italy	206	8
5th	Iceland	198	58
6th	Bulgaria	140	14
7th	Portugal	126	22
8th	Russia	104	7
9th	Ukraine	97	6
10th	Greece	91	8
11th	Finland	83	10
12th	Israel	73	2
13th	Belgium	71	16
14th	Lithuania	55	2
15th	Moldova	53	3
16th	Cyprus	50	4
17th	Sweden	46	9
18th	San Marino	37	5
19th	Azerbaijan	32	10
20th	Albania	22	2
21st	Serbia	20	5
22nd	Norway	15	4
23rd	Netherlands	11	5
24th	Spain	6	3
25th	Germany	3	3
26th	United Kingdom	0	0

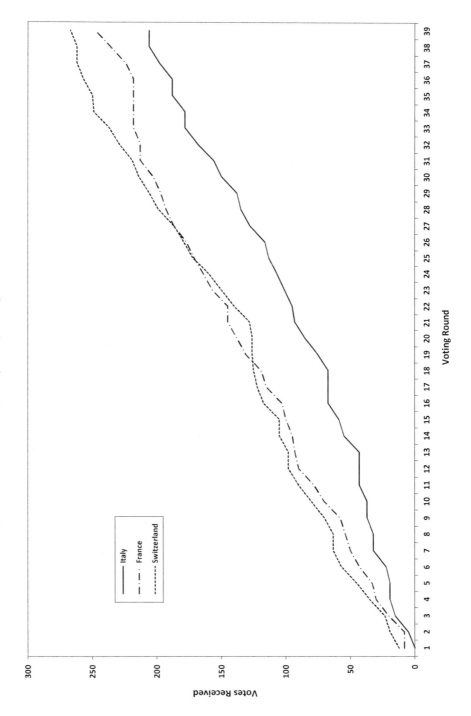

Eurovision 2021: Final - Round by Round Leaderboard (Combined Public Voting & Total points)

Public televoting points, announced in ascending order of jury votes as broadcast:

	United Kingdom 0 pts			Germany 0 pts			Spain 0 pts			Netherlands 0 pts			Norway 60 pts		
Posn	Country	Pts	Lead	Country	Pts	Lead	Country	Pts	Lead	Country	Pts	Lead	Country	Pts	Lead
1st	Switzerland	267	19	Switzerland	267	19	Switzerland	267	19	Switzerland	267	19	Switzerland	267	19
2nd	France	248	40	France	248	40	France	248	40	France	248	40	France	248	40
3rd	Malta	208	2	Malta	208	2	Malta	208	2	Malta	208	2	Malta	208	2
4th	Italy	206	8	Italy	206	8	Italy	206	8	Italy	206	8	Italy	206	8
5th	Iceland	198	58	Iceland	198	58	Iceland	198	58	Iceland	198	58	Iceland	198	58
6th	Bulgaria	140	14	Bulgaria	140	14	Bulgaria	140	14	Bulgaria	140	14	Bulgaria	140	14
7th	Portugal	126	22	Portugal	126	22	Portugal	126	22	Portugal	126	22	Portugal	126	22
8th	Russia	104	7	Russia	104	7	Russia	104	7	Russia	104	7	Russia	104	7
9th	Ukraine	97	6	Ukraine	97	6	Ukraine	97	6	Ukraine	97	6	Ukraine	97	6
10th	Greece	91	8	Greece	91	8	Greece	91	8	Greece	91	8	Greece	91	8
11th	Finland	83	10	Finland	83	10	Finland	83	10	Finland	83	10	Finland	83	8
12th	Israel	73	2	Israel	73	2	Israel	73	2	Israel	73	2	Norway	75	2
13th	Belgium	71	16	Belgium	71	16	Belgium	71	16	Belgium	71	16	Israel	73	2
14th	Lithuania	55	2	Lithuania	55	2	Lithuania	55	2	Lithuania	55	2	Belgium	71	16
15th	Moldova	53	3	Moldova	53	3	Moldova	53	3	Moldova	53	3	Lithuania	55	2
16th	Cyprus	50	4	Cyprus	50	4	Cyprus	50	4	Cyprus	50	4	Moldova	53	3
17th	Sweden	46	9	Sweden	46	9	Sweden	46	9	Sweden	46	9	Cyprus	50	4
18th	San Marino	37	5	San Marino	37	5	San Marino	37	5	San Marino	37	5	Sweden	46	9
19th	Azerbaijan	32	10	Azerbaijan	32	10	Azerbaijan	32	10	Azerbaijan	32	10	San Marino	37	5
20th	Albania	22	2	Albania	22	2	Albania	22	2	Albania	22	2	Azerbaijan	32	10
21st	Serbia	20	5	Serbia	20	5	Serbia	20	5	Serbia	20	5	Albania	22	2
22nd	Norway	15	4	Norway	15	4	Norway	15	4	Norway	15	4	Serbia	20	9
23rd	Netherlands	11	5	Netherlands	11	5	Netherlands	11	5	Netherlands	11	5	Netherlands	11	5
24th	Spain	6	3	Spain	6	3	Spain	6	3	Spain	6	3	Spain	6	3
25th	Germany	3	3	Germany	3	3	Germany	3	3	Germany	3	3	Germany	3	3
26th	United Kingdom	0	0	United Kingdom	0	0	United Kingdom	0	0	United Kingdom	0	0	United Kingdom	0	0

Public televoting points, announced in ascending order of jury votes as broadcast:

	Serbia 82 pts			Albania 35 pts			Azerbaijan 33 pts			San Marino 13 pts			Sweden 63 pts		
Posn	Country	Pts	Lead	Country	Pts	Lead	Country	Pts	Lead	Country	Pts	Lead	Country	Pts	Lead
1st	Switzerland	267	19	Switzerland	267	19	Switzerland	267	19	Switzerland	267	19	Switzerland	267	19
2nd	France	248	40	France	248	40	France	248	40	France	248	40	France	248	40
3rd	Malta	208	2	Malta	208	2	Malta	208	2	Malta	208	2	Malta	208	2
4th	Italy	206	8	Italy	206	8	Italy	206	8	Italy	206	8	Italy	206	8
5th	Iceland	198	58	Iceland	198	58	Iceland	198	58	Iceland	198	58	Iceland	198	58
6th	Bulgaria	140	14	Bulgaria	140	14	Bulgaria	140	14	Bulgaria	140	14	Bulgaria	140	14
7th	Portugal	126	22	Portugal	126	22	Portugal	126	22	Portugal	126	22	Portugal	126	17
8th	Russia	104	2	Russia	104	2	Russia	104	2	Russia	104	2	Sweden	109	5
9th	Serbia	102	5	Serbia	102	5	Serbia	102	5	Serbia	102	5	Russia	104	2
10th	Ukraine	97	6	Ukraine	97	6	Ukraine	97	6	Ukraine	97	6	Serbia	102	5
11th	Greece	91	8	Greece	91	8	Greece	91	8	Greece	91	8	Ukraine	97	6
12th	Finland	83	8	Finland	83	8	Finland	83	8	Finland	83	8	Greece	91	8
13th	Norway	75	2	Norway	75	2	Norway	75	2	Norway	75	2	Finland	83	8
14th	Israel	73	2	Israel	73	2	Israel	73	2	Israel	73	2	Norway	75	2
15th	Belgium	71	16	Belgium	71	14	Belgium	71	6	Belgium	71	6	Israel	73	2
16th	Lithuania	55	2	Albania	57	2	Azerbaijan	65	8	Azerbaijan	65	8	Belgium	71	6
17th	Moldova	53	3	Lithuania	55	3	Albania	57	2	Albania	57	2	Azerbaijan	65	8
18th	Cyprus	50	4	Moldova	53	3	Lithuania	55	2	Lithuania	55	2	Albania	57	2
19th	Sweden	46	9	Cyprus	50	4	Moldova	53	3	Moldova	53	3	Lithuania	55	2
20th	San Marino	37	5	Sweden	46	9	Cyprus	50	4	San Marino	50	0	Moldova	53	3
21st	Azerbaijan	32	10	San Marino	37	5	Sweden	46	9	Cyprus	50	4	San Marino	50	0
22nd	Albania	22	11	Azerbaijan	32	21	San Marino	37	26	Sweden	46	35	Cyprus	50	39
23rd	Netherlands	11	5	Netherlands	11	5	Netherlands	11	5	Netherlands	11	5	Netherlands	11	5
24th	Spain	6	3	Spain	6	3	Spain	6	3	Spain	6	3	Spain	6	3
25th	Germany	3	3	Germany	3	3	Germany	3	3	Germany	3	3	Germany	3	3
26th	United Kingdom	0	0	United Kingdom	0	0	United Kingdom	0	0	United Kingdom	0	0	United Kingdom	0	0

Eurovision 2021: Final - Round by Round Leaderboard (Combined Public Voting & Total points)

Public televoting points, announced in ascending order of jury votes as broadcast:

Cyprus 44 pts

Posn	Country	Pts	Lead
1st	Switzerland	267	19
2nd	France	248	40
3rd	Malta	208	2
4th	Italy	206	8
5th	Iceland	198	58
6th	Bulgaria	140	14
7th	Portugal	126	17
8th	Sweden	109	5
9th	Russia	104	2
10th	Serbia	102	5
11th	Ukraine	97	3
12th	Cyprus	94	3
13th	Greece	91	8
14th	Finland	83	8
15th	Norway	75	2
16th	Israel	73	2
17th	Belgium	71	6
18th	Azerbaijan	65	8
19th	Albania	57	2
20th	Lithuania	55	2
21st	Moldova	53	3
22nd	San Marino	50	39
23rd	Netherlands	11	5
24th	Spain	6	3
25th	Germany	3	3
26th	United Kingdom	0	0

Moldova 62 pts

Posn	Country	Pts	Lead
1st	Switzerland	267	19
2nd	France	248	40
3rd	Malta	208	2
4th	Italy	206	8
5th	Iceland	198	58
6th	Bulgaria	140	14
7th	Portugal	126	11
8th	Moldova	115	6
9th	Sweden	109	5
10th	Russia	104	2
11th	Serbia	102	5
12th	Ukraine	97	3
13th	Cyprus	94	3
14th	Greece	91	8
15th	Finland	83	8
16th	Norway	75	2
17th	Israel	73	2
18th	Belgium	71	6
19th	Azerbaijan	65	8
20th	Albania	57	2
21st	Lithuania	55	5
22nd	San Marino	50	39
23rd	Netherlands	11	5
24th	Spain	6	3
25th	Germany	3	3
26th	United Kingdom	0	0

Lithuania 165 pts

Posn	Country	Pts	Lead
1st	Switzerland	267	19
2nd	France	248	28
3rd	Lithuania	220	12
4th	Malta	208	2
5th	Italy	206	8
6th	Iceland	198	58
7th	Bulgaria	140	14
8th	Portugal	126	11
9th	Moldova	115	6
10th	Sweden	109	5
11th	Russia	104	2
12th	Serbia	102	5
13th	Ukraine	97	3
14th	Cyprus	94	3
15th	Greece	91	8
16th	Finland	83	8
17th	Norway	75	2
18th	Israel	73	2
19th	Belgium	71	6
20th	Azerbaijan	65	8
21st	Albania	57	7
22nd	San Marino	50	39
23rd	Netherlands	11	5
24th	Spain	6	3
25th	Germany	3	3
26th	United Kingdom	0	0

Belgium 3 pts

Posn	Country	Pts	Lead
1st	Switzerland	267	19
2nd	France	248	28
3rd	Lithuania	220	12
4th	Malta	208	2
5th	Italy	206	8
6th	Iceland	198	58
7th	Bulgaria	140	14
8th	Portugal	126	11
9th	Moldova	115	6
10th	Sweden	109	5
11th	Russia	104	2
12th	Serbia	102	5
13th	Ukraine	97	3
14th	Cyprus	94	3
15th	Greece	91	8
16th	Finland	83	8
17th	Norway	75	1
18th	Israel	74	1
19th	Belgium	74	9
20th	Azerbaijan	65	8
21st	Albania	57	7
22nd	San Marino	50	39
23rd	Netherlands	11	5
24th	Spain	6	3
25th	Germany	3	3
26th	United Kingdom	0	0

Israel 20 pts

Posn	Country	Pts	Lead
1st	Switzerland	267	19
2nd	France	248	28
3rd	Lithuania	220	12
4th	Malta	208	2
5th	Italy	206	8
6th	Iceland	198	58
7th	Bulgaria	140	14
8th	Portugal	126	11
9th	Moldova	115	6
10th	Sweden	109	5
11th	Russia	104	2
12th	Serbia	102	5
13th	Ukraine	97	3
14th	Cyprus	94	1
15th	Israel	93	2
16th	Greece	91	8
17th	Finland	83	8
18th	Norway	75	1
19th	Belgium	74	9
20th	Azerbaijan	65	8
21st	Albania	57	7
22nd	San Marino	50	39
23rd	Netherlands	11	5
24th	Spain	6	3
25th	Germany	3	3
26th	United Kingdom	0	0

Public televoting points, announced in ascending order of jury votes as broadcast:

Finland 218 pts

Posn	Country	Pts	Lead
1st	Finland	301	34
2nd	Switzerland	267	19
3rd	France	248	28
4th	Lithuania	220	12
5th	Malta	208	2
6th	Italy	206	8
7th	Iceland	198	58
8th	Bulgaria	140	14
9th	Portugal	126	11
10th	Moldova	115	6
11th	Sweden	109	5
12th	Russia	104	2
13th	Serbia	102	5
14th	Ukraine	97	3
15th	Cyprus	94	1
16th	Israel	93	2
17th	Greece	91	16
18th	Norway	75	1
19th	Belgium	74	9
20th	Azerbaijan	65	8
21st	Albania	57	7
22nd	San Marino	50	39
23rd	Netherlands	11	5
24th	Spain	6	3
25th	Germany	3	3
26th	United Kingdom	0	0

Greece 79 pts

Posn	Country	Pts	Lead
1st	Finland	301	34
2nd	Switzerland	267	19
3rd	France	248	28
4th	Lithuania	220	12
5th	Malta	208	2
6th	Italy	206	8
7th	Iceland	198	28
8th	Greece	170	30
9th	Bulgaria	140	14
10th	Portugal	126	11
11th	Moldova	115	6
12th	Sweden	109	5
13th	Russia	104	2
14th	Serbia	102	5
15th	Ukraine	97	3
16th	Cyprus	94	1
17th	Israel	93	18
18th	Norway	75	1
19th	Belgium	74	9
20th	Azerbaijan	65	8
21st	Albania	57	7
22nd	San Marino	50	39
23rd	Netherlands	11	5
24th	Spain	6	3
25th	Germany	3	3
26th	United Kingdom	0	0

Ukraine 267 pts

Posn	Country	Pts	Lead
1st	Ukraine	364	63
2nd	Finland	301	34
3rd	Switzerland	267	19
4th	France	248	28
5th	Lithuania	220	12
6th	Malta	208	2
7th	Italy	206	8
8th	Iceland	198	28
9th	Greece	170	30
10th	Bulgaria	140	14
11th	Portugal	126	11
12th	Moldova	115	6
13th	Sweden	109	5
14th	Russia	104	2
15th	Serbia	102	8
16th	Cyprus	94	1
17th	Israel	93	18
18th	Norway	75	1
19th	Belgium	74	9
20th	Azerbaijan	65	8
21st	Albania	57	7
22nd	San Marino	50	39
23rd	Netherlands	11	5
24th	Spain	6	3
25th	Germany	3	3
26th	United Kingdom	0	0

Russia 100 pts

Posn	Country	Pts	Lead
1st	Ukraine	364	63
2nd	Finland	301	34
3rd	Switzerland	267	19
4th	France	248	28
5th	Lithuania	220	12
6th	Malta	208	2
7th	Italy	206	2
8th	Russia	204	6
9th	Iceland	198	28
10th	Greece	170	30
11th	Bulgaria	140	14
12th	Portugal	126	11
13th	Moldova	115	6
14th	Sweden	109	7
15th	Serbia	102	8
16th	Cyprus	94	1
17th	Israel	93	18
18th	Norway	75	1
19th	Belgium	74	9
20th	Azerbaijan	65	8
21st	Albania	57	7
22nd	San Marino	50	39
23rd	Netherlands	11	5
24th	Spain	6	3
25th	Germany	3	3
26th	United Kingdom	0	0

Portugal 27 pts

Posn	Country	Pts	Lead
1st	Ukraine	364	63
2nd	Finland	301	34
3rd	Switzerland	267	19
4th	France	248	28
5th	Lithuania	220	12
6th	Malta	208	2
7th	Italy	206	2
8th	Russia	204	6
9th	Iceland	198	28
10th	Greece	170	17
11th	Portugal	153	13
12th	Bulgaria	140	25
13th	Moldova	115	6
14th	Sweden	109	7
15th	Serbia	102	8
16th	Cyprus	94	1
17th	Israel	93	18
18th	Norway	75	1
19th	Belgium	74	9
20th	Azerbaijan	65	8
21st	Albania	57	7
22nd	San Marino	50	39
23rd	Netherlands	11	5
24th	Spain	6	3
25th	Germany	3	3
26th	United Kingdom	0	0

Eurovision 2021: Final - Round by Round Leaderboard (Combined Public Voting & Total points)

Public televoting points, announced in ascending order of jury votes as broadcast:

	Bulgaria 30 pts			**Iceland 180 pts**			**Italy 318 pts**			**Malta 47 pts**			**France 251 pts**		
Posn	Country	Pts	Lead	Country	Pts	Lead	Country	Pts	Lead	Country	Pts	Lead	Country	Pts	Lead
1st	Ukraine	364	63	Iceland	378	14	Italy	524	146	Italy	524	146	Italy	524	25
2nd	Finland	301	34	Ukraine	364	63	Iceland	378	14	Iceland	378	14	France	499	121
3rd	Switzerland	267	19	Finland	301	34	Ukraine	364	63	Ukraine	364	63	Iceland	378	14
4th	France	248	28	Switzerland	267	19	Finland	301	34	Finland	301	34	Ukraine	364	63
5th	Lithuania	220	12	France	248	28	Switzerland	267	19	Switzerland	267	12	Finland	301	34
6th	Malta	208	2	Lithuania	220	12	France	248	28	Malta	255	7	Switzerland	267	12
7th	Italy	206	2	Malta	208	2	Lithuania	220	12	France	248	28	Malta	255	35
8th	Russia	204	6	Italy	206	2	Malta	208	4	Lithuania	220	16	Lithuania	220	16
9th	Iceland	198	28	Russia	204	34	Russia	204	34	Russia	204	34	Russia	204	34
10th	Greece	170	0	Greece	170	0	Greece	170	0	Greece	170	0	Greece	170	0
11th	Bulgaria	170	17	Bulgaria	170	17	Bulgaria	170	17	Bulgaria	170	17	Bulgaria	170	17
12th	Portugal	153	38	Portugal	153	38	Portugal	153	38	Portugal	153	38	Portugal	153	38
13th	Moldova	115	6	Moldova	115	6	Moldova	115	6	Moldova	115	6	Moldova	115	6
14th	Sweden	109	7	Sweden	109	7	Sweden	109	7	Sweden	109	7	Sweden	109	7
15th	Serbia	102	8	Serbia	102	8	Serbia	102	8	Serbia	102	8	Serbia	102	8
16th	Cyprus	94	1	Cyprus	94	1	Cyprus	94	1	Cyprus	94	1	Cyprus	94	1
17th	Israel	93	18	Israel	93	18	Israel	93	18	Israel	93	18	Israel	93	18
18th	Norway	75	1	Norway	75	1	Norway	75	1	Norway	75	1	Norway	75	1
19th	Belgium	74	9	Belgium	74	9	Belgium	74	9	Belgium	74	9	Belgium	74	9
20th	Azerbaijan	65	8	Azerbaijan	65	8	Azerbaijan	65	8	Azerbaijan	65	8	Azerbaijan	65	8
21st	Albania	57	7	Albania	57	7	Albania	57	7	Albania	57	7	Albania	57	7
22nd	San Marino	50	39	San Marino	50	39	San Marino	50	39	San Marino	50	39	San Marino	50	39
23rd	Netherlands	11	5	Netherlands	11	5	Netherlands	11	5	Netherlands	11	5	Netherlands	11	5
24th	Spain	6	3	Spain	6	3	Spain	6	3	Spain	6	3	Spain	6	3
25th	Germany	3	3	Germany	3	3	Germany	3	3	Germany	3	3	Germany	3	3
26th	United Kingdom	0	0	United Kingdom	0	0	United Kingdom	0	0	United Kingdom	0	0	United Kingdom	0	0

Public televoting points, announced in ascending order of jury votes as broadcast:

	Switzerland 165 pts		
Posn	Country	Pts	Lead
1st	Italy	524	25
2nd	France	499	67
3rd	Switzerland	432	54
4th	Iceland	378	14
5th	Ukraine	364	63
6th	Finland	301	46
7th	Malta	255	35
8th	Lithuania	220	16
9th	Russia	204	34
10th	Greece	170	0
11th	Bulgaria	170	17
12th	Portugal	153	38
13th	Moldova	115	6
14th	Sweden	109	7
15th	Serbia	102	8
16th	Cyprus	94	1
17th	Israel	93	18
18th	Norway	75	1
19th	Belgium	74	9
20th	Azerbaijan	65	8
21st	Albania	57	7
22nd	San Marino	50	39
23rd	Netherlands	11	5
24th	Spain	6	3
25th	Germany	3	3
26th	United Kingdom	0	0

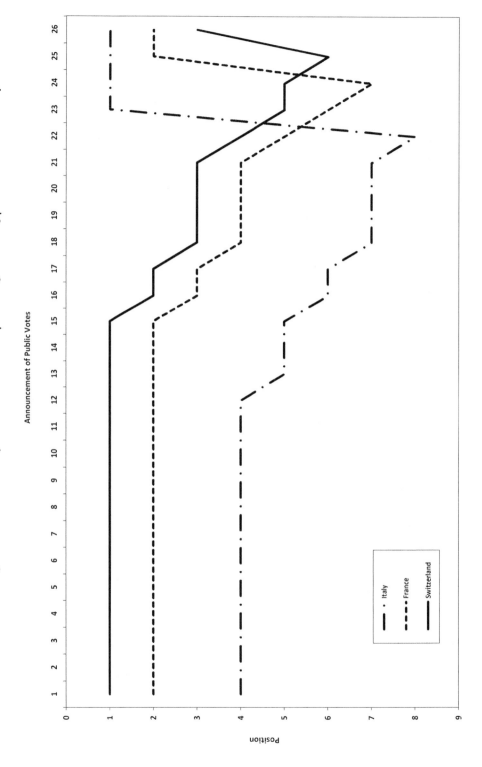

Eurovision 2021: Country-by-country history, points scored and final positions for each act.

Albania

			Semi-Final		Final	
Year	Artist	Song	Points	Position	Points	Position
2004	Anjeza Shahini	The Image Of You	167	4	106	7
2005	Ledina Celo	Tomorrow I Go	-	-	53	16
2006	Luiz Ejlli	Zjarr E Ftohtë	58	15	-	-
2007	Aida & Frederik Ndoci	Hear My Plea	49	17	-	-
2008	Olta Boka	Zemrën E Lamë Peng	67	9	55	17
2009	Kejsi Tola	Carry Me In Your Dreams	73	7	48	17
2010	Juliana Pasha	It's All About You	76	6	62	16
2011	Aurela Gaçe	Feel The Passion	47	14	-	-
2012	Rona Nishliu	Suus	146	2	146	5
2013	Adrian Lulgjuraj & Bledar Sejko	Identitet	31	15	-	-
2014	Hersi	One Night's Anger	22	15	-	-
2015	Elhaida Dani	I'm Alive	62	10	34	17
2016	Eneda Tarifa	Fairytale	45	16	-	-
2017	Lindita	World	76	14	-	-
2018	Eugent Bushpepa	Mall	162	8	184	11
2019	Jonida Maliqi	Ktheju tokës	96	9	90	17
2021	Anxhela Peristeri	Karma	112	10	57	21

Andorra

			Semi-Final		Final	
Year	Artist	Song	Points	Position	Points	Position
2004	Marta Roure	Jugarem A Estimar-nos	12	18	-	-
2005	Marian van de Wal	La Mirada Interior	27	23	-	-
2006	Jennifer	Sense Tu	8	23	-	-
2007	Anonymous	Salvem El Món	80	12	-	-
2008	Gisela	Casanova	22	16	-	-
2009	Susanne Georgi	La Teva Decisió (Get A Life)	8	15	-	-

Armenia

			Semi-Final		Final	
Year	Artist	Song	Points	Position	Points	Position
2006	André	Without Your Love	150	7	129	8
2007	Hayko	Anytime You Need	-	-	138	8
2008	Sirusho	Qele, Qele	139	2	199	4
2009	Inga & Anush	Jan Jan	99	5	92	10
2010	Eva Rivas	Apricot Stone	76	6	141	7
2011	Emmy	Boom Boom	54	12	-	-
2012	-		-	-	-	-
2013	Dorians	Lonely Planet	69	7	41	18
2014	Aram MP3	Not Alone	121	4	174	4
2015	Genealogy	Face the Shadow	77	7	34	16
2016	Iveta Mukuchyan	LoveWave	243	2	249	7
2017	Artsvik	Fly With Me	152	7	79	18
2018	Sevak Khanagyan	Qami	79	15	-	-
2019	Srbuk	Walking Out	49	16	-	-

Australia

			Semi-Final		Final	
Year	Artist	Song	Points	Position	Points	Position
2015	Guy Sebastian	Tonight Again	-	-	196	5
2016	Dami Im	Sound of Silence	330	1	511	2
2017	Isaiah	Don't Come Easy	160	6	173	9
2018	Jessica Mauboy	We Got Love	212	4	99	20
2019	Kate Miller-Heidke	Zero Gravity	261	1	284	9
2021	Montaigne	Technicolour	28	14	-	-

Austria

Year	Artist	Song	Semi-Final Points	Semi-Final Position	Final Points	Final Position
1957	Bob Martin	Wohin, Kleines Pony			3	10
1958	Liane Augustin	Die Ganze Welt Braucht Liebe			8	5
1959	Ferry Graf	Der K. Und K. Kalypso Aus Wien			4	9
1960	Harry Winter	Du Hast Mich So Fasziniert			6	7
1961	Jimmy Makulis	Sehnsucht			1	15
1962	Eleonore Schwarz	Nur In Der Wiener Luft			0	13
1963	Carmela Corren	Vielleicht Geschieht Ein Wunder			16	7
1964	Udo Jürgens	Warum Nur, Warum?			11	6
1965	Udo Jürgens	Sag Ihr, Ich Lass' Sie Grüßen			16	4
1966	Udo Jürgens	Merci Chérie			31	1
1967	Peter Horten	Warum Es Hunderttausend Sterne Gibt			2	14
1968	Karel Gott	Tausend Fenster			2	13
1969	-				-	-
1970	-				-	-
1971	Marianne Mendt	Musik			66	6
1972	The Milestones	Falter Im Wind			100	5
1973	-	-			-	-
1974	-	-			-	-
1975	-	-			-	-
1976	Waterloo and Robinson	My Little World			80	5
1977	Schmetterlinge	Boom Boom Boomerang			11	17
1978	Springtime	Mrs. Caroline Robinson			14	15
1979	Christina Simon	Heute In Jerusalem			5	18
1980	Blue Danube	Du Bist Musik			64	8
1981	Marty Brem	Wenn Du Da Bist			20	17
1982	Mess	Sonntag			57	9
1983	Westend	Hurricane			53	9
1984	Anita	Einfach Weg			5	19
1985	Gary Lux	Kinder Dieser Welt			60	8
1986	Timna Brauer	Die Zeit Ist Einsam			12	18
1987	Gary Lux	Nur Noch Gefühl			8	20
1988	Wilfried	Lisa Mona Lisa			0	21
1989	Thomas Forstner	Nur Ein Lied			97	5
1990	Simone	Keine Mauern Mehr			58	10
1991	Thomas Forstner	Venedig Im Regen			0	22
1992	Tony Wegas	Zusammen Geh'n			63	9
1993	Tony Wegas	Maria Magdalena			32	14
1994	Petra Frey	Für Den Frieden Der Welt			19	17
1995	Stella Jones	Die Welt Dreht Sich Verkehrt			67	13
1996	George Nußbaumer	Weil's Dr Guat Got			68	10
1997	Bettina Soriat	One Step			12	21
1998	-				-	-
1999	Bobbie Singer	Reflection			65	9
2000	The Rounder Girls	All To You			34	14
2001	-	-			-	-
2002	Manuel Ortega	Say A Word			26	18
2003	Alf Poier	Weil Der Mensch Zählt			101	6
2004	Tie Break	Du Bist	-	-	9	21
2005	Global.Kryner	Y Así	30	21	-	-
2006	-	-	-	-	-	-
2007	Eric Papilaya	Get A Life - Get Alive	4	27	-	-
2008	-	-	-	-	-	-
2009	-	-	-	-	-	-
2010	-	-	-	-	-	-
2011	Nadine Beiler	The Secret is Love	69	7	64	18
2012	Trackshittaz	Woki Mit Deim Popo	8	18	-	-
2013	Natália Kelly	Shine	27	14	-	-
2014	Conchita Wurst	Rise Like a Phoenix	169	1	290	1
2015	The Makemakes	I Am Yours	-	-	0	26
2016	ZOË	Loin d'ici	170	7	151	13
2017	Nathan Trent	Running On Air	147	7	93	16
2018	Cesár Sampson	Nobody But You	231	4	342	3
2019	PÆNDA	Limits	21	17	-	-
2021	Vincent Bueno	Amen	66	12	-	-

Azerbaijan

Year	Artist	Song	Semi-Final Points	Semi-Final Position	Final Points	Final Position
2008	Elnur & Samir	Day After Day	96	6	132	8
2009	AySel & Arash	Always	180	2	207	3
2010	Safura	Drip Drop	113	2	145	5
2011	Ell/Nikki	Running Scared	122	2	221	1
2012	Sabina Babayeva	When The Music Dies	-	-	150	4
2013	Farid Mammadov	Hold Me	139	1	234	2
2014	Dilara Kazimova	Start a Fire	57	9	33	22
2015	Elnur Hüseynov	Hour of the Wolf	53	10	49	12
2016	Samra	Miracle	185	6	117	17
2017	Dihaj	Skeletons	150	8	120	14
2018	Aisel	X My Heart	94	11	-	-
2019	Chingiz	Truth	224	5	302	8
2021	Efendi	Mata Hari	138	8	65	20

Belarus

Year	Artist	Song	Semi-Final Points	Semi-Final Position	Final Points	Final Position
2004	Aleksandra & Konstantin	My Galileo	10	19	-	-
2005	Angelica Agurbash	Love Me Tonight	67	13	-	-
2006	Polina Smolova	Mum	10	22	-	-
2007	Dmitry Koldun	Work Your Magic	176	4	143	6
2008	Ruslan Alenho	Hasta La Vista	27	17	-	-
2009	Petr Elfimov	Eyes That Never Lie	25	13	-	-
2010	3+2	Butterflies	59	9	18	24
2011	Anastasiya Vinnikova	I Love Belarus	45	14	-	-
2012	Litesound	We Are The Heroes	35	16	-	-
2013	Alyona Lanskaya	Solayoh	64	7	48	16
2014	Teo	Cheesecake	87	5	43	16
2015	Uzari & Maimuna	Time	39	12	-	-
2016	IVAN	Help You Fly	84	12	-	-
2017	Naviband	Story Of My Life	110	9	83	17
2018	Alekseev	Forever	65	16	-	-
2019	ZENA	Like It	122	10	31	24

Belgium

Year	Artist	Song	Semi-Final Points	Semi-Final Position	Final Points	Final Position
1956	(1) Mony Marc	Le Plus Beau Jour De Ma Vie			-	2
1956	(2) Fud Leclerc	Messieurs Les Noyés De La Seine			-	2
1957	Bobbejaan Schoepen	Straatdeuntje			5	8
1958	Fud Leclerc	Ma Petite Chatte			8	5
1959	Bob Benny	Hou Toch Van Mij			9	6
1960	Fud Leclerc	Mon Amour Pour Toi			9	6
1961	Bob Benny	September, Gouden Roos			1	15
1962	Fud Leclerc	Ton Nom			0	13
1963	Jacques Raymond	Waarom			4	10
1964	Robert Cogoi	Près De Ma Rivière			2	10
1965	Lize Marke	Als Het Weer Lente Is			0	15
1966	Tonia	Un Peu De Poivre, Un Peu De Sel			14	4
1967	Louis Neefs	Ik Heb Zorgen			8	7
1968	Claude Lombard	Quand Tu Reviendras			8	7
1969	Louis Neefs	Jennifer Jennings			10	7
1970	Jean Vallée	Viens L'oublier			5	8
1971	Lily Castel and Jacques Raymond	Goeie Morgen, Morgen			68	14
1972	Serge and Christine Ghisoland	À La Folie Ou Pas Du Tout			55	17
1973	Nicole and Hugo	Baby, Baby			58	17
1974	Jacques Hustin	Fleur De Liberté			10	9
1975	Ann Christy	Gelukkig Zijn			17	15
1976	Pierre Rapsat	Judy Et Cie.			68	8
1977	Dream Express	A Million In One, Two, Three			69	7
1978	Jean Vallée	L'amour ça Fait Chanter La Vie			125	2
1979	Micha Marah	Hey Nana			5	18

Belgium (continued)

Year	Artist	Song	Semi-Final Points	Semi-Final Position	Final Points	Final Position
1980	Telex	Euro-vision			14	17
1981	Emly Starr	Samson			40	13
1982	Stella	Si Tu Aimes Ma Musique			96	4
1983	Pas de Deux	Rendez-vous			13	18
1984	Jacques Zegers	Avanti La Vie			70	5
1985	Linda Lepomme	Laat Me Nu Gaan			7	19
1986	Sandra Kim	J'aime La Vie			176	1
1987	Liliane Saint-Pierre	Soldiers Of Love			56	11
1988	Reynaert	Laissez Briller Le Soleil			5	18
1989	Ingeborg	Door De Wind			13	19
1990	Philippe Lafontaine	Macédomienne			46	12
1991	Clouseau	Geef Het Op			23	16
1992	Morgane	Nous On Veut Des Violons			11	20
1993	Barbara	Iemand Als Jij			3	25
1994	-				-	-
1995	Frédéric Etherlinck	La Voix Est Libre			8	20
1996	Lisa del Bo	Liefde Is Een Kaartspel			22	16
1997	-				-	-
1998	Mélanie Cohl	Dis Oui			122	6
1999	Venessa Chinitor	Like The Wind			38	12
2000	Nathalie Sorce	Envie De Vivre			2	24
2001	-				-	-
2002	Sergio & the Ladies	Sister			33	13
2003	Urban Trad	Sanomi			165	2
2004	Xandee	1 Life	-	-	7	22
2005	Nuno Resende	Le Grand Soir	29	22	-	-
2006	Kate Ryan	Je T'adore	69	12	-	-
2007	The KMG's	Love Power	14	26	-	-
2008	Ishtar	O Julissi	16	17	-	-
2009	Copycat	Copycat	1	17	-	-
2010	Tom Dice	Me and My Guitar	167	1	143	6
2011	Witloof Bay	With Love Baby	53	11	-	-
2012	Iris	Would You?	16	17	-	-
2013	Roberto Bellarosa	Love Kills	75	5	71	12
2014	Axel Hirsoux	Mother	28	14	-	-
2015	Loïc Nottet	Rhythm Inside	149	2	217	4
2016	Laura Tesoro	What's The Pressure?	274	3	181	10
2017	Blanche	City Lights	165	4	363	4
2018	Sennek	A Matter Of Time	91	12	-	-
2019	Eliot	Wake Up	70	13	-	-
2021	Hooverphonic	The Wrong Place	117	9	74	19

Bosnia & Herzegovina

Year	Artist	Song	Semi-Final Points	Semi-Final Position	Final Points	Final Position
1993	Fazla	Sva Bol Svijeta			27	16
1994	Alma & Dejan	Ostani Kraj Mene			39	15
1995	Davor Popovic	Dvadeset I Prvi Vijek			14	19
1996	Amila Glamocak	Za Našu Ljubav			13	22
1997	Alma Cardzic	Goodbye			22	18
1998	-				-	-
1999	Dino & Beatrice	Putnici			86	7
2000	-				-	-
2001	Nino	Hano			29	14
2002	Maja	Na Jastuku Za Dvoje			33	13
2003	Mija Martina	Ne Brini			27	16
2004	Deen	In The Disco	133	7	91	9
2005	Feminnem	Call Me	-	-	79	14
2006	Hari Mata Hari	Lejla	267	2	229	3
2007	Marija Sestic	Rijeka Bez Imena	-	-	106	11
2008	Laka	Pokušaj	72	9	110	10
2009	Regina	Bistra Voda	125	3	106	9
2010	Vukašin Brajić	Thunder And Lightning	58	8	51	17

Bosnia & Herzegovina (continued)

			Semi-Final		Final	
Year	Artist	Song	Points	Position	Points	Position
2011	Dino Merlin	Love in Rewind	109	5	125	6
2012	MayaSar	Korake Ti Znam	77	6	55	18
2013	-	-	-	-	-	-
2014	-	-	-	-	-	-
2015	-	-	-	-	-	-
2016	Dalal & Deen feat. Ana Rucner and Jala	Ljubav Je	104	11	-	-

Bulgaria

			Semi-Final		Final	
Year	Artist	Song	Points	Position	Points	Position
2005	Kaffe	Lorraine	49	19	-	-
2006	Mariana Popova	Let Me Cry	36	17	-	-
2007	Elitsa Todorova & Stoyan Yankulov	Water	146	6	157	5
2008	Deep Zone & Balthazar	DJ, Take Me Away	56	11	-	-
2009	Krassimir Avramov	Illusion	7	16	-	-
2010	Miro	Angel Si Ti	19	15	-	-
2011	Poli Genova	Na Inat	48	12	-	-
2012	Sofi Marinova	Love Unlimited	45	11	-	-
2013	Elitsa Todorova feat. Stoyan Yankulov	Samo Shampioni (Only Champions)	45	12	-	-
2014	-	-	-	-	-	-
2015	-	-	-	-	-	-
2016	Poli Genova	If Love Was A Crime	220	5	307	4
2017	Kristian Kostov	Beautiful Mess	403	1	615	2
2018	Equinox	Bones	177	7	166	14
2019	-	-	-	-	-	-
2021	Victoria	Growing Up is Getting Old	250	3	170	11

Croatia

			Semi-Final		Final	
Year	Artist	Song	Points	Position	Points	Position
1993	Put	Don't Ever Cry			31	15
1994	Tony Cetinski	Nek'ti Bude Ljubav Sva			27	16
1995	Magazin & Lidija	Nostalgija			91	6
1996	Maja Blagdan	Sveta Ljubav			98	4
1997	ENI	Probudi Me			24	17
1998	Danijela	Neka Mi Ne Svane			131	5
1999	Doris Dragovic	Marija Magdalena			118	4
2000	Goran Karan	Kada Zaspu Andeli			70	9
2001	Vanna	Strings Of My Heart			42	10
2002	Vesna Pisarovic	Everything I Want			44	11
2003	Claudia Beni	Više Nisam Tvoja			29	15
2004	Ivan Mikulic	You Are The Only One	72	9	50	12
2005	Boris Novkovic feat. Lado members	Vukovi Umiru Sami	169	4	115	11
2006	Severina	Moja štikla	-	-	56	12
2007	Dragonfly feat. Dado Topic	Vjerujem U Ljubav	54	16	-	-
2008	Kraljevi Ulice & 75 Cents	Romanca	112	4	44	21
2009	Igor Cukrov featuring Andrea	Lijepa Tena	33	13	45	18
2010	Feminnem	Lako Je Sve	33	13	-	-
2011	Daria	Celebrate	41	15	-	-
2012	Nina Badrić	Nebo	42	12	-	-
2013	Klapa s mora	Mižerja	38	13	-	-
2014	-	-	-	-	-	-
2015	-	-	-	-	-	-
2016	Nina Kraljić	Lighthouse	133	10	73	23
2017	Jacques Houdek	My Friend	141	8	128	13
2018	Franka	Crazy	63	17	-	-
2019	Roko	The Dream	64	17	-	-
2021	Albina	Tick-Tock	110	11	-	-

Cyprus

Year	Artist	Song	Semi-Final Points	Semi-Final Position	Final Points	Final Position
1981	Island	Monika			69	6
1982	Anna Vishy	Mono I Agapi			85	5
1983	Stavros & Constantina	I Agapi Akoma Zi			26	16
1984	Andy Paul	Anna Mari-elena			31	15
1985	Lia Vishy	To Katalava Arga			15	16
1986	Elpida	Tora Zo			4	20
1987	Alexia	Aspro Mavro			80	7
1988	-				-	-
1989	Fanny Polymeri & Yiannis Savvidakis	Apopse As Vrethoume			51	11
1990	Haris Anastasiou	Milas Poli			36	14
1991	Elena Patroclou	SOS			60	9
1992	Evridiki	Teriazoume			57	10
1993	Kyriakos Zymboulakis & Demos Van Beke	Mi Stamatas			17	19
1994	Evridiki	Ime Anthropos Ke Ego			51	11
1995	Alexandros Panayi	Sti Fotia			79	9
1996	Constantinos	Mono Gia Mas			72	9
1997	Chara & Andreas Konstantinou	Mana Mou			98	5
1998	Michael Hajiyanni	Genesis			37	11
1999	Marlain Angelidou	Tha'nai Erotas			2	22
2000	Voice	Nomiza			8	21
2001	-				-	-
2002	One	Gimme			85	6
2003	Stelios Constantas	Feeling Alive			15	20
2004	Lisa Andreas	Stronger Every Minute	149	5	170	5
2005	Constantinos Christoforou	Ela Ela	-	-	46	18
2006	Annet Artani	Why Angels Cry	57	13	-	-
2007	Evridiki	Comme Ci, Comme ça	65	15	-	-
2008	Evdokia Kadi	Femme Fatale	36	15	-	-
2009	Christina Metaxa	Firefly	32	14	-	-
2010	Jon Lilygreen & The Islanders	Life Looks Better In Spring	67	10	27	21
2011	Christos Mylordos	San Aggelos S'Agapisa	16	18	-	-
2012	Ivi Adamou	La La Love	91	7	65	16
2013	Despina Olympiou	An Me Thimasai	11	15	-	-
2014	-		-	-	-	-
2015	John Karayiannis	One Thing I Should Have Done	87	6	11	22
2016	Minus One	Alter Ego	164	8	96	20
2017	Hovig	Gravity	164	5	68	21
2018	Eleni Foureira	Fuego	262	2	436	2
2019	Tamta	Replay	149	9	109	13
2021	Elena Tsagrinou	El Diablo	170	6	94	16

Czech Republic

Year	Artist	Song	Semi-Final Points	Semi-Final Position	Final Points	Final Position
2007	Kabát	Malá Dáma	1	28	-	-
2008	Tereza Kerndlová	Have Some Fun	9	18	-	-
2009	Gipsy.cz	Aven Romale	0	18	-	-
2010	-	-	-	-	-	-
2011	-	-	-	-	-	-
2012	-	-	-	-	-	-
2013	-	-	-	-	-	-
2014	-	-	-	-	-	-
2015	Marta Jandová & Václav Noid Bárta	Hope Never Dies	33	13	-	-
2016	Gabriela Gunčíková	I Stand	161	9	41	25
2017	Martina Bárta	My Turn	83	13	-	-
2018	Mikolas Josef	Lie To Me	232	3	281	6
2019	Lake Malawi	Friend of a Friend	242	2	157	11
2021	Benny Cristo	Omaga	23	15	-	-

Denmark

Year	Artist	Song	Semi-Final Points	Semi-Final Position	Final Points	Final Position
1957	Birthe Wilke & Gustav Winckler	Skibet Skal Sejle I Nat			10	3
1958	Raquel Rastenni	Jeg Rev Et Blad Ud Af Min Dagbog			3	8
1959	Birthe Wilke	Uh-jeg Ville Ønske Jeg Var Dig			12	5
1960	Katy Bødtger	Det Var En Yndig Tid			4	10
1961	Dario Campeotto	Angelique			12	5
1962	Ellen Winther	Vuggevise			2	10
1963	Grethe & Jørgen Ingmann	Dansevise			42	1
1964	Bjørn Tidmand	Sangen Om Dig			4	9
1965	Birgit Brüel	For Din Skyld			10	7
1966	Ulla Pia	Stop, Ja Stop - Ja Stop, Mens Legen Er Go			4	14
1967	-	-			-	-
1968	-	-			-	-
1969	-	-			-	-
1970	-	-			-	-
1971	-	-			-	-
1972	-	-			-	-
1973	-	-			-	-
1974	-	-			-	-
1975	-	-			-	-
1976	-	-			-	-
1977	-	-			-	-
1978	Mabel	Boom Boom			13	16
1979	Tommy Seebach	Disco Tango			76	6
1980	Bamses Venner	Tænker Altid På Dig			25	14
1981	Debbie Cameron & Tommy Seebach	Krøller Eller Ej			41	11
1982	Brixx	Video-video			5	17
1983	Gry Johansen	Kloden Drejer			16	17
1984	Hot Eyes	Det' Lige Det			101	4
1985	Hot Eyes	Sku' Du Spør Fra No'n			41	11
1986	Lise Haavik & Trax	Du Er Fuld Af Løgn			77	6
1987	Anne-Catherine Herdorf & Bandjo	En Lille Melodi			83	5
1988	Hot Eyes	Ka' Du Se Hva' Jeg Sa'			92	3
1989	Birthe Kjær	Vi Maler Byen Rød			111	3
1990	Lonnie Devantier	Hallo Hallo			64	8
1991	Anders Frandsen	Lige Der Hvor Hjertet Slår			8	19
1992	Lotte Nilsson & Kenny Lübcke	Ålt Det Som Ingen Ser			47	11
1993	Tommy Seebach Band	Under Stjernerne På Himlen			9	22
1994	-	-			-	-
1995	Aud Wilken	Fra Mols Til Skagen			92	5
1996	-	-			-	-
1997	Kølig Kaj	Stemmen I Mit Liv			25	16
1998	-	-			-	-
1999	Trine Jepsen & Michael Teschl	This Time (I Mean It)			71	8
2000	Olsen brothers	Fly On The Wings Of Love			195	1
2001	Rollo & King	Never Ever Let You Go			177	2
2002	Malene	Tell Me Who You Are			7	24
2003	-	-			-	-
2004	Tomas Thordarson	Shame On You	56	13	-	-
2005	Jakob Sveistrup	Talking To You	185	3	125	9
2006	Sidsel Ben Semmane	Twist Of Love	-	-	26	18
2007	DQ	Drama Queen	45	19	-	-
2008	Simon Mathew	All Night Long	112	3	60	15
2009	Brinck	Believe Again	69	8	74	13
2010	Chanée & N'evergreen	In A Moment Like This	101	5	149	4
2011	A Friend in London	New Tomorrow	135	2	134	5
2012	Soluna Samay	Should've Known Better	65	9	21	23
2013	Emmelie de Forest	Only Teardrops	167	1	281	1
2014	Basim	Cliché Love Song	-	-	74	9
2015	Anti Social Media	The Way You Are	33	13	-	-
2016	Lighthouse X	Soldiers Of Love	34	17	-	-
2017	Anja	Where I Am	101	10	77	20
2018	Rasmussen	Higher Ground	204	5	226	9
2019	Leonora	Love Is Forever	94	10	120	12
2021	Fyr & Flamme	Øve os på hinanden	89	11	-	-

Estonia

			Semi-Final		Final	
Year	Artist	Song	Points	Position	Points	Position
1994	Silvi Vrait	Nagu Merelaine			2	24
1995	-				-	-
1996	Ivo Linna & Maarja-Liis Ilus	Kaelakee Hääl			94	5
1997	Maarja-Liis Ilus	Keelatud Maa			82	8
1998	Koit Toome	Mere Lapsed			36	12
1999	Evelin Samuel & Camille	Diamond Of Night			90	6
2000	Ines	Once In A Lifetime			98	4
2001	Tanel Padar, Dave Benton & 2XL	Everybody			198	1
2002	Sahléne	Runaway			111	3
2003	Ruffus	Eighties Coming Back			14	21
2004	Neiokõsõ	Tii	57	11	-	-
2005	Suntribe	Let's Get Loud	31	20	-	-
2006	Sandra	Through My Window	28	18	-	-
2007	Gerli Padar	Partners In Crime	33	22	-	-
2008	Kreisiraadio	Leto Svet	8	18	-	-
2009	Urban Symphony	Rändajad	115	3	129	6
2010	Malcolm Lincoln	Siren	39	14	-	-
2011	Getter Jaani	Rockefeller Street	60	9	44	24
2012	Ott Lepland	Kuula	100	4	120	6
2013	Birgit Õigemeel	Et Uus Saaks Alguse	52	10	19	20
2014	Tanja	Amazing	36	12	-	-
2015	Elina Born & Stig Rästa	Goodbye to Yesterday	105	3	106	7
2016	Jüri Pootsmann	Play	24	18	-	-
2017	Koit Toome & Laura	Verona	85	14	-	-
2018	Elina Nechayeva	La Forza	201	5	245	8
2019	Victor Crone	Storm	198	4	76	20
2021	Uku Suviste	The Lucky One	58	13	-	-

Finland

			Semi-Final		Final	
Year	Artist	Song	Points	Position	Points	Position
1961	Laila Kinnunen	Valoa Ikkunassa			6	10
1962	Marion Rung	Tipi-tii			4	7
1963	Laila Halme	Muistojeni Laulu			0	13
1964	Lasse Mårtenson	Laiskotellen			9	7
1965	Viktor Klimenko	Aurinko Laskee Länteen			0	15
1966	Ann-Christine Nyström	Play-boy			7	10
1967	Fredi	Varjoon-suojaan			3	12
1968	Kristina Hautala	Kun Kello Käy			1	16
1969	Jarkko & Laura	Kuin Silloin Ennen			6	12
1970	-				-	-
1971	Markku Aro & Koivisto Sisters	Tie Uuteen Päivään			84	8
1972	Päivi Paunu & Kim Floor	Muistathan			78	12
1973	Marion Rung	Tom Tom Tom			93	6
1974	Carita	Äla Mene Pois (Keep Me Warm)			4	13
1975	Pihasoittajat	Old Man Fiddle			74	7
1976	Fredi & The Friends	Pump-pump			44	11
1977	Monica Aspelund	Lapponia			50	10
1978	Seija Simola	Anna Rakkaudelle Tilaisuus			2	18
1979	Katri-Helena	Katso Sineen Taivaan			38	14
1980	Vesa-Matti Loiri	Huilumies			6	19
1981	Riki Sorsa	Reggae OK			27	16
1982	Kojo	Nuku Pommiin			0	18
1983	Ami Aspelund	Fantasiaa			41	11
1984	Kirka	Hengaillaan			46	9
1985	Sonja Lumme	Eläköön Elämä			58	9
1986	Kari Kuivalainen	Päivä Kahden Ihmisen			22	15
1987	Vicky Rosti	Sata Salamaa			32	15
1988	Boulevard	Nauravat Silmät Muistetaar			3	20
1989	Anneli Saaristo	La Dolce Vita			76	7
1990	Beat	Fri?			8	21
1991	Kaija	Hullu Yö			6	20
1992	Pave	Yamma Yamma			4	23

Finland (continued)

Year	Artist	Song	Semi-Final Points	Semi-Final Position	Final Points	Final Position
1993	Katri-Helena	Tule Luo			20	17
1994	CatCat	Bye Bye Baby			11	22
1995	-	-			-	-
1996	Jasmine	Niin Kaunis On Taivas			9	23
1997	-	-			-	-
1998	Edea	Aava			22	15
1999	-	-			-	-
2000	Nina Åström	A Little Bit			18	18
2001	-	-			-	-
2002	Laura	Addicted To You			24	20
2003	-	-			-	-
2004	Jari Sillanpää	Takes 2 To Tango	51	14	-	-
2005	Geir Rönning	Why?	50	18	-	-
2006	Lordi	Hard Rock Hallelujah	292	1	292	1
2007	Hanna Pakarinen	Leave Me Alone	-	-	53	17
2008	Teräsbetoni	Missä Miehet Ratsastaa	79	8	35	22
2009	Waldo's People	Lose Control	42	12	22	25
2010	Kuunkuiskaajat	Työlki Ellää	49	11	-	-
2011	Paradise Oskar	Da Da Dam	103	3	57	21
2012	Pernilla	När Jag Blundar	41	12	-	-
2013	Krista Siegfrids	Marry Me	64	9	13	24
2014	Softengine	Something Better	97	3	72	11
2015	Pertti Kurikan Nimipäivät	Aina mun pitää	13	16	-	-
2016	Sandhja	Sing It Away	51	15	-	-
2017	Norma John	Blackbird	92	12	-	-
2018	Saara Aalto	Monsters	108	10	46	25
2019	Darude feat. Sebastian Rejman	Look Away	23	17	-	-
2021	Blind Channel	Dark Side	234	5	301	6

France

Year	Artist	Song	Semi-Final Points	Semi-Final Position	Final Points	Final Position
1956	(1) Mathé Altéry	Le Temps Perdu			-	2
1956	(2) Dany Dauberson	Il Est Là			-	2
1957	Paule Desjardins	La Belle Amour			17	2
1958	André Claveau	Dors Mon Amour			27	1
1959	Jean Philippe	Oui, Oui, Oui, Oui			15	3
1960	Jacqueline Boyer	Tom Pillibi			32	1
1961	Jean-Paul Mauric	Printemps (avril Carillonne)			13	4
1962	Isabelle Aubret	Un Premier Amour			26	1
1963	Alain Barrière	Elle était Si Jolie			25	5
1964	Rachel	Le Chant De Mallory			14	4
1965	Guy Mardel	N'avoue Jamais			22	3
1966	Dominique Walter	Chez Nous			1	16
1967	Noëlle Cordier	Il Doit Faire Beau Là-bas			20	3
1968	Isabelle Aubret	La Source			20	3
1969	Frida Boccara	Un Jour, Un Enfant			18	1
1970	Guy Bonnet	Marie Blanche			8	4
1971	Serge Lama	Un Jardin Sur La Terre			83	9
1972	Betty Mars	Comé-comédie			81	11
1973	Martine Clémenceau	Sans Toi			65	15
1974	-	-			-	-
1975	Nicole Rieu	Et Bonjour à Toi L'artiste			91	4
1976	Catherine Ferry	Un, Deux, Trois			147	2
1977	Marie Myriam	L'oiseau Et L'enfant			136	1
1978	Joël Prévost	Il Y Aura Toujours Des Violons			119	3
1979	Anne-Marie David	Je Suis L'enfant-soleil			106	3
1980	Profil	Hé, Hé M'sieurs Dames			45	11
1981	Jean Gabilou	Humanahum			125	3
1982	-	-			-	-
1983	Guy Bonnet	Vivre			56	8
1984	Annick Thoumazeau	Autant D'amoureux Que D'étoiles			61	8
1985	Roger Bens	Femme Dans Ses Rêves Aussi			56	10

France (continued)

Year	Artist	Song	Semi-Final Points	Semi-Final Position	Final Points	Final Position
1986	Cocktail Chic	Européennes			13	17
1987	Christine Minier	Les Mots D'amour N'ont Pas De Dimanche			44	14
1988	Gérard Lenorman	Chanteur De Charme			64	10
1989	Nathalie Pâque	J'ai Volé La Vie			60	8
1990	Joelle Ursull	White And Black Blues			132	2
1991	Amina	C'est Le Dernier Qui A Parlé Qui A Raison			146	1
1992	Kali	Monté La Riviè			73	8
1993	Patrick Fiori	Mama Corsica			121	5
1994	Nina Morato	Je Suis Un Vrai Garçon			74	7
1995	Nathalie Santamaria	Il Me Donne Rendez-vous			94	4
1996	Dan Ar Braz & l'Héritage des Celtes	Diwanit Bugale			18	19
1997	Fanny	Sentiments Songes			95	7
1998	Marie-Line	Où Aller			3	24
1999	Nayah	Je Veux Donner Ma Voix			14	17
2000	Sofia Mestari	On Aura Le Ciel			5	23
2001	Natasha Saint-Pier	Je N'ai Que Mon âme			142	4
2002	Sandrine François	Il Faut Du Temps			104	5
2003	Louisa Baileche	Monts Et Merveilles			19	18
2004	Jonatan Cerrada	A Chaque Pas	-	-	40	15
2005	Ortal	Chacun Pense à Soi	-	-	11	23
2006	Virginie Pouchin	Il était Temps	-	-	5	22
2007	Les Fatals Picards	L'amour à La Française	-	-	19	22
2008	Sébastien Tellier	Divine	-	-	47	19
2009	Patricia Kaas	Et S'il Fallait Le Faire	-	-	107	8
2010	Jessy Matador	Allez Olla Olé	-	-	82	12
2011	Amaury Vassili	Sognu	-	-	82	15
2012	Anggun	Echo (You And I)	-	-	21	22
2013	Amandine Bourgeois	L'enfer Et Moi	-	-	14	23
2014	Twin Twin	Moustache	-	-	2	26
2015	Lisa Angell	N'oubliez pas	-	-	4	25
2016	Amir	J'ai cherché	-	-	257	6
2017	Alma	Requiem	-	-	135	12
2018	Madame Monsieur	Mercy	-	-	173	13
2019	Bilal Hassani	Roi	-	-	105	16
2021	Barbara Pravi	Voilà	-	-	499	2

Georgia

Year	Artist	Song	Semi-Final Points	Semi-Final Position	Final Points	Final Position
2007	Sopho	My Story	123	8	97	12
2008	Diana Gurtskaya	Peace Will Come	107	5	83	11
2009	-	-	-	-	-	-
2010	Sofia Nizharadze	Shine	106	3	136	9
2011	Eldrine	One More Day	74	6	110	9
2012	Anri Jokhadze	I'm A Joker	36	14	-	-
2013	Nodi Tatishvili & Sophie Gelovani	Waterfall	63	10	50	15
2014	The Shin and Mariko	Three Minutes to Earth	15	15	-	-
2015	Nina Sublatti	Warrior	98	4	51	11
2016	Nika Kocharov & Young Georgian Lolitaz	Midnight Gold	123	9	104	20
2017	Tamara Gachechiladze	Keep The Faith	99	11	-	-
2018	Ethno-Jazz Band Iriao	For You	24	18	-	-
2019	Oto Nemsadze	Keep On Going	62	14	-	-
2021	Tornike Kipiani	You	16	16	-	-

Germany

Year	Artist	Song	Semi-Final Points	Semi-Final Position	Final Points	Final Position
1956	(1) Walter Andreas Schwarz	Im Wartesaal Zum Großen Glück			-	2
1956	(2) Freddy Quinn	So Geht Das Jede Nacht			-	2
1957	Margot Hielscher	Telefon, Telefon			8	4
1958	Margot Hielscher	Für Zwei Groschen Musik			5	7
1959	Alice & Ellen Kessler	Heut' Woll'n Wir Tanzen Geh'n			5	8
1960	Wyn Hoop	Bonne Nuit, Ma Chérie!			11	4
1961	Lale Andersen	Einmal Sehen Wir Uns Wieder			3	13
1962	Conny Froboess	Zwei Kleine Italiener			9	6
1963	Heidi Brühl	Marcel			5	9
1964	Nora Nova	Man Gewöhnt Sich So Schnell An Das Schöne			0	13
1965	Ulla Wiesner	Paradies, Wo Bist Du?			0	15
1966	Margot Eskens	Die Zeiger Der Uhr			7	10
1967	Inge Brück	Anouschka			7	8
1968	Wencke Myhre	Ein Hoch Der Liebe			11	6
1969	Siw Malmkvist	Primaballerina			8	9
1970	Katja Ebstein	Wunder Gibt Es Immer Wieder			12	3
1971	Katja Ebstein	Diese Welt			100	3
1972	Mary Roos	Nur Die Liebe Läßt Uns Leben			107	3
1973	Gitte	Junger Tag			85	8
1974	Cindy & Bert	Die Sommermelodie			3	14
1975	Joy Fleming	Ein Lied Kann Eine Brücke Sein			15	17
1976	Les Humphries Singers	Sing, Sang, Song			12	15
1977	Silver Convention	Telegram			55	8
1978	Ireen Sheer	Feuer			84	6
1979	Dschinghis Khan	Dschinghis Khan			86	4
1980	Katja Ebstein	Theater			128	2
1981	Lena Valaitis	Johnny Blue			132	2
1982	Nicole	Ein Bißchen Frieden			161	1
1983	Hoffmann & Hoffmann	Rücksicht			94	5
1984	Mary Roos	Aufrecht Geh'n			34	13
1985	Wind	Für Alle			105	2
1986	Ingrid Peters	Über Die Brücke Geh'n			62	8
1987	Wind	Laß Die Sonne In Dein Herz			141	2
1988	Maxi & Chris Garden	Lied Für Einen Freund			48	14
1989	Nino de Angelo	Flieger			46	14
1990	Chris Kempers & Daniel Kovac	Frei Zu Leben			60	9
1991	Atlantis 2000	Dieser Traum Darf Niemals Sterben			10	18
1992	Wind	Träume Sind Für Alle Da			27	16
1993	Münchener Freiheit	Viel Zu Weit			18	18
1994	MeKaDo	Wir Geben 'ne Party			128	3
1995	Stone & Stone	Verliebt In Dich			1	23
1996	-	-			-	-
1997	Bianca Shomburg	Zeit			22	18
1998	Guildo Horn	Guildo Hat Euch Lieb			86	7
1999	Sürpriz	Reise Nach Jerusalem - Kudüs'e Seyahat			140	3
2000	Stefan Raab	Wadde Hadde Dudde Da			96	5
2001	Michelle	Wer Liebe Lebt			66	8
2002	Corinna May	I Can't Live Without Music			17	21
2003	Lou	Let's Get Happy			53	11
2004	Max (Maximilian Mutzke)	Can't Wait Until Tonight	-	-	93	8
2005	Gracia	Run & Hide	-	-	4	24
2006	Texas Lightning	No, No, Never	-	-	36	14
2007	Roger Cicero	Frauen Regieren Die Welt	-	-	49	19
2008	No Angels	Disappear	-	-	14	23
2009	Alex Swings Oscar Sings!	Miss Kiss Kiss Bang	-	-	35	20
2010	Lena Meyer-Landrut	Satellite	-	-	246	1
2011	Lena Meyer-Landrut	Taken by a Stranger	-	-	107	10
2012	Roman Lob	Standing Still	-	-	110	8
2013	Cascada	Glorious	-	-	18	21
2014	Elaiza	Is it Right?	-	-	39	18
2015	Ann Sophie	Black Smoke	-	-	0	27
2016	Jamie-Lee	Ghost	-	-	11	26
2017	Levina	Perfect Life	-	-	6	25
2018	Michael Schulte	You Let Me Walk Alone	-	-	340	4

Germany (continued)

Year	Artist	Song	Semi-Final Points	Semi-Final Position	Final Points	Final Position
2019	S!sters	Sister	-	-	24	25
2021	Jendrik	I Don't Feel Hate	-	-	3	25

Greece

Year	Artist	Song	Semi-Final Points	Semi-Final Position	Final Points	Final Position
1974	Marinella	Krassi, Thalassa Ke T'agori Mou			7	11
1975	-	-			-	-
1976	Mariza Koch	Panaghia Mou, Panaghia Mou			20	13
1977	Pascalis, Marianna, Robert & Bessy	Mathema Solfege			92	5
1978	Tania Tsanaklidou	Charlie Chaplin			66	8
1979	Elpida	Socrates			69	8
1980	Anna Vishy & the Epikouri	Autostop			30	13
1981	Yiannis Dimitras	Feggari Kalokerino			55	8
1982	-				-	-
1983	Christie	Mou Les			32	14
1984	-	-			-	-
1985	Takis Biniaris	Miazoume			15	16
1986	-	-			-	-
1987	Bang	Stop!			64	10
1988	Aphroditi Fryda	Kloun			10	17
1989	Marianna	To Diko Sou Asteri			56	9
1990	Christos Callow & Wave	Horis Skopo			11	9
1991	Sofia Vossou	I Anixi			36	13
1992	Cleopatra	Olou Tou Kosmou I Elpida			94	5
1993	Katerina Garbi	Ellada, Hora Tou Fotos			64	9
1994	Costas Bigalis & the Sea Lovers	To Trehantiri (Diri Diri)			44	14
1995	Elina Constantopoulou	Pia Prossefchi			63	12
1996	Marianna Efstratiou	Emis Forame To Himona Anixiatika			36	14
1997	Marianna Zorba	Horepse			39	12
1998	Dionysia & Thalassa Group	Mia Krifi Evaisthissia			12	20
1999	-	-			-	-
2000	-	-			-	-
2001	Antique	Die For You			147	3
2002	Michalis Rakintzis	SAGAPO			27	17
2003	Mando	Never Let You Go			25	17
2004	Sakis Rouvas	Shake It	238	3	252	3
2005	Helena Paparizou	My Number One	-	-	230	1
2006	Anna Vissi	Everything	-	-	128	9
2007	Sarbel	Yassou Maria	-	-	139	7
2008	Kalomira	Secret Combination	156	1	218	3
2009	Sakis Rouvas	This Is Our Night	110	4	120	7
2010	Giorgos Alkaios & Friends	OPA	133	2	140	8
2011	Loucas Yiorkas feat Stereo Mike	Watch My Dance	133	1	120	7
2012	Eleftheria Eleftheriou	Aphrodisiac	116	4	64	17
2013	Koza Mostra feat. Agathon Iakovidis	Alcohol is Free	121	2	152	6
2014	Freaky Fortune feat. RiskyKidd	Rise Up	74	7	35	20
2015	Maria Elena Kyriakou	One Last Breath	81	6	23	19
2016	Argo	Utopian Land	44	16	-	-
2017	Demy	This Is Love	115	10	77	19
2018	Yianna Terzi	Oniro Mou	81	14	-	-
2019	Katerine Duska	Better Love	185	5	74	21
2021	Stefania	Last Dance	184	6	170	10

Hungary

Year	Artist	Song	Semi-Final Points	Semi-Final Position	Final Points	Final Position
1994	Friderika Bayer	Kinek Mondjam El Vétkeimet			122	4
1995	Czaba Szigeti	Új Nèv Egy Règi Hàz Fàlan			3	22
1996	-	-			-	-
1997	VIP	Miert Kell, Hogy Elmenj?			39	12
1998	Charlie	A Holnap Már Ném Lesz Szomorú			4	23
1999	-	-			-	-
2000	-	-			-	-
2001	-	-			-	-
2002	-	-			-	-
2003	-	-			-	-
2004	-	-			-	-
2005	NOX	Forogj Világ			97	12
2006	-	-			-	-
2007	Magdi Rúzsa	Unsubstantial Blues			128	9
2008	Csézy	Candlelight	6	19	-	-
2009	Zoli Ádok	Dance With Me	16	15	-	-
2010	-	-	-	-	-	-
2011	Kati Wolf	What About My Dreams?	72	7	53	22
2012	Compact Disco	Sound of Our Hearts	52	10	19	24
2013	ByeAlex	Kedvesem (Zoohacker Remix)	66	8	84	10
2014	András Kállay-Saunders	Running	127	3	143	5
2015	Boggie	Wars for Nothing	67	8	19	20
2016	Freddie	Pioneer	197	4	108	19
2017	Joci Pápai	Origo	231	2	200	8
2018	AWS	Viszlát Nyár	111	10	93	21
2019	Joci Pápai	Az én apám	97	12	-	-

Iceland

Year	Artist	Song	Semi-Final Points	Semi-Final Position	Final Points	Final Position
1986	Icy	Gleðibankinn			19	16
1987	Halla Margarét	Hægt Og Hljótt			28	16
1988	Beathoven	Sókrates			20	16
1989	Daníel Águst Haraldsson	Það Sem Enginn Sér			0	22
1990	Stjórnin	Eitt Lag Enn			124	4
1991	Stefán & Eyfi	Nina			26	15
1992	Heart 2 Heart	Nei Eða Já			80	7
1993	Inga	Þá Veistu Svarið			42	13
1994	Sigga	Nætur			49	12
1995	Bó Halldórsson	Núna			31	15
1996	Anna Mjöll	Sjúbídú			51	13
1997	Paul Oscar	Minn Hinsti Dans			18	20
1998	-	-			-	-
1999	Selma Björnsdóttir	All Out Of Luck			146	2
2000	Einer Águst Víðisson & Telma Águstdóttir	Tell Me!			45	12
2001	TwoTricky	Angel			3	22
2002	-	-			-	-
2003	Birgitta	Open Your Heart			81	8
2004	Jónsi	Heaven	-	-	16	19
2005	Selma	If I Had Your Love	52	16	-	-
2006	Silvia Night	Congratulations	62	13	-	-
2007	Eiríkur Hauksson	Valentine Lost	77	13	-	-
2008	Euroband	This Is My Life	68	8	64	14
2009	Yohanna	Is It True?	174	1	218	2
2010	Hera Björk	Je Ne Sais Quoi	123	3	41	19
2011	Sjonni's Friends	Coming Home	100	4	61	20
2012	Greta Salóme & Jónsi	Never Forget	75	8	46	20
2013	Eythor Ingi	Ég Á Líf	72	6	47	17
2014	Pollapönk	No Prejudice	61	8	58	15
2015	María Ólafs	Unbroken	14	15	-	-
2016	Greta Salóme	Hear Them Calling	51	14	-	-
2017	Svala	Paper	60	15	-	-
2018	Ari Ólafsson	Our Choice	15	19	-	-

Iceland (continued)

Year	Artist	Song	Semi-Final Points	Semi-Final Position	Final Points	Final Position
2019	Hatari	Hatrið mun sigra	221	3	232	10
2021	Daði og Gagnamagnið	10 Years	288	2	378	4

Ireland

Year	Artist	Song	Semi-Final Points	Semi-Final Position	Final Points	Final Position
1965	Butch Moore	I'm Walking The Streets In The Rain			11	6
1966	Dickie Rock	Come Back To Stay			14	4
1967	Sean Dunphy	If I Could Choose			22	2
1968	Pat McGeegan	Chance Of A Lifetime			18	4
1969	Muriel Day & the Lindsays	The Wages Of Love			10	7
1970	Dana	All Kinds Of Everything			32	1
1971	Angela Farrell	One Day Love			79	11
1972	Sandie Jones	Ceol On Ghrá			72	15
1973	Maxi	Do I Dream?			80	10
1974	Tina	Cross Your Heart			11	7
1975	The Swarbriggs	That's What Friends Are For			68	9
1976	Red Hurley	When			54	10
1977	The Swarbriggs Plus Two	It's Nice To Be In Love Again			119	3
1978	Colm Wilkinson	Born To Sing			86	5
1979	Cathal Dunne	Happy Man			80	5
1980	Johnny Logan	What's Another Year			143	1
1981	Sheeba	Horoscopes			105	5
1982	The Duskeys	Here Today, Gone Tomorrow			49	11
1983	-				-	-
1984	Linda Martin	Terminal 3			137	2
1985	Maria Christian	Wait Until The Weekend Comes			91	6
1986	Luv Bug	You Can Count On Me			96	4
1987	Johnny Logan	Hold Me Now			172	1
1988	Jump the Gun	Take Him Home			79	8
1989	Kiev Connolly & the Missing Passengers	The Real Me			21	18
1990	Liam Reilly	Somewhere In Europe			132	2
1991	Kim Jackson	Could It Be That I'm In Love			47	10
1992	Linda Martin	Why Me			155	1
1993	Niamh Kavanagh	In Your Eyes			187	1
1994	Paul Harrington & Charlie McGettigar	Rock 'n' Roll Kids			226	1
1995	Eddie Friel	Dreamin'			44	14
1996	Eimear Quinn	The Voice			162	1
1997	Marc Roberts	Mysterious Woman			157	2
1998	Dawn	Is Always Over Now?			64	9
1999	The Mullans	When You Need Me			18	18
2000	Eamonn Toal	Millennium Of Love			92	6
2001	Gary O'Shaughnessy	Without Your Love			6	21
2002	-				-	-
2003	Mickey Harte	We've Got The World			53	11
2004	Chris Doran	If My World Stopped Turning	-	-	7	22
2005	Donna & Joseph McCaul	Love?	53	14	-	-
2006	Brian Kennedy	Every Song Is A Cry For Love	79	10	93	10
2007	Dervish	They Can't Stop The Spring	-	-	5	24
2008	Dustin the Turkey	Irelande Douze Pointe	22	15	-	-
2009	Sinéad Mulvey & Black Daisy	Et Cetera	52	11	-	-
2010	Niamh Kavanagh	It's For You	67	9	25	23
2011	Jedward	Lipstick	68	8	119	8
2012	Jedward	Waterline	92	6	46	19
2013	Ryan Dolan	Only Love Survives	54	8	5	26
2014	Can-Linn (feat. Kasey Smith)	Heartbeat	35	12	-	-
2015	Molly Sterling	Playing with Numbers	35	12	-	-
2016	Nicky Byrne	Sunlight	46	15	-	-
2017	Brendan Murray	Dying To Try	86	13	-	-
2018	Ryan O'Shaughnessy	Together	179	6	136	16
2019	Sarah McTernan	22	16	18	-	-
2021	Lesley Roy	Maps	20	16	-	-

Israel

Year	Artist	Song	Semi-Final Points	Semi-Final Position	Final Points	Final Position
1973	Ilanit	Ey-sham			97	4
1974	Poogy	Natati La Khaiai			11	7
1975	Shlomo Artzi	At Ve'ani			40	11
1976	Chocolate, Menta, Mastik	Emor Shalom			77	6
1977	Ilanit	Ah-haa-vah Hee Shir Lish-naa-yim			49	11
1978	Izhar Cohen & the Alphabeta	Abanibi			157	1
1979	Milk & Honey	Hallelujah			125	1
1980	-	-			-	-
1981	Habibi	Halaylah			56	7
1982	Avi Toledano	Hora			100	2
1983	Ofra Haza	Hi			136	2
1984	-	-			-	-
1985	Izhar Cohen	Olé Olé			93	5
1986	Moti Galadi & Sarai Tzuriel	Yavoh Yom			7	19
1987	Datner & Kushnir	Shir Habatlanim			73	8
1988	Yardena Arazi	Ben Adam			85	7
1989	Gili ve Galit	Derech Ha'melech			50	12
1990	Rita	Shara Barechovot			16	18
1991	Duo Datz	Kan			139	3
1992	Dafna	Ze Rak Sport			85	6
1993	Lakahat Shiru	Shiru			4	24
1994	-	-			-	-
1995	Liora	Amen			81	8
1996	-	-			-	-
1997	-	-			-	-
1998	Dana International	Diva			172	1
1999	Eden	Yom Huledeth			93	5
2000	Ping Pong	Sa'me'akh			7	22
2001	Tal Sondak	Ein Davar			25	16
2002	Sarit Hadad	Light A Candle			37	12
2003	Lior Narkis	Words For Love			17	19
2004	David D'or	Le'ha'amin	57	11	-	-
2005	Shiri Maymon	Hasheket Shenish'ar	158	7	154	4
2006	Eddie Butler	Ze Hazman	-	-	4	23
2007	Teapacks	Push The Button	17	24	-	-
2008	Boaz	The Fire In Your Eyes	104	5	124	9
2009	Noa & Mira Awad	There Must Be Another Way	75	7	53	16
2010	Harel Skaat	Milim	71	8	71	14
2011	Dana International	Ding Dong	38	15	-	-
2012	Izabo	Time	33	13	-	-
2013	Moran Mazor	Rak Bishvilo	40	14	-	-
2014	Mei Finegold	Same Heart	19	14	-	-
2015	Nadav Guedj	Golden Boy	151	3	97	9
2016	Hovi Star	Made of Stars	147	7	135	14
2017	IMRI	I Feel Alive	207	3	39	23
2018	Netta	Toy	283	1	529	1
2019	Kobi Marimi	Home	-	-	35	23
2021	Eden Alene	Set Me Free	192	5	93	17

Italy

Year	Artist	Song	Semi-Final Points	Semi-Final Position	Final Points	Final Position
1956	(1) Tonina Torielli	Amami Se Vuoi			-	2
1956	(2) Franca Raimondi	Aprite Le Finestre			-	2
1957	Nunzio Gallo	Corde Della Mia Chitarra			7	6
1958	Domenico Modugno	Nel Blu Dipinto Di Blu			13	3
1959	Domenico Modugno	Piove			9	6
1960	Renato Rascel	Romantica			5	8
1961	Betty Curtis	Al Di Là			12	5
1962	Claudio Villa	Addio, Addio			3	9
1963	Emilio Pericoli	Uno Per Tutte			37	3
1964	Gigliola Cinquetti	Non Ho L'étà			49	1
1965	Bobby Solo	Se Piangi, Se Ridi			15	5

Italy (continued)

Year	Artist	Song	Semi-Final Points	Semi-Final Position	Final Points	Final Position
1966	Domenico Modugno	Dio Come Ti Amo			0	17
1967	Claudio Villa	Non Andare Più Lontano			4	11
1968	Sergio Endrigo	Marianne			7	10
1969	Iva Zanicchi	Due Grosse Lacrime Bianche			5	13
1970	Gianni Morandi	Occhi Di Ragazza			5	8
1971	Massimo Ranieri	L'amore è Un Attimo			91	5
1972	Nicola di Bari	I Giorni Dell' Arcobaleno			92	6
1973	Massimo Ranieri	Chi Sarà Con Te			74	13
1974	Gigliola Cinquetti	Si			18	2
1975	Wess & Dori Ghezzi	Era			115	3
1976	Romina & Al Bano	We'll Live It All Agair			69	7
1977	Mia Martini	Liberà			33	13
1978	Ricchi e Poveri	Questo Amore			53	12
1979	Matia Bazar	Raggio Di Luna			27	15
1980	Alan Sorrenti	Non So Che Darei			87	6
1981	-	-			-	-
1982	-	-			-	-
1983	Riccardo Fogli	Per Lucia			41	11
1984	Alice & Battiatc	I Treni Di Tozeur			70	5
1985	Al Bano & Romina Power	Magic, Oh Magic			78	7
1986	-	-			-	-
1987	Umberto Tozzi & Raf	Gente Di Mare			103	3
1988	Luca Barbarossa	Ti Scrivo			52	12
1989	Anna Oxa & Fausto Leali	Avrei Voluto			56	9
1990	Toto Cutugno	Insieme: 1992			149	1
1991	Peppino di Capri	Comme E' Ddoce 'o Mare			89	7
1992	Mia Martini	Rapsodia			111	4
1993	Enrico Ruggeri	Sole D'europa			45	12
1994	-	-			-	-
1995	-	-			-	-
1996	-	-			-	-
1997	Jalisse	Fiumi Di Parole			114	4
1998	-	-			-	-
1999	-	-			-	-
2000	-	-			-	-
2001	-	-			-	-
2002	-	-			-	-
2003	-	-			-	-
2004	-	-	-	-	-	-
2005	-	-	-	-	-	-
2006	-	-	-	-	-	-
2007	-	-	-	-	-	-
2008	-	-	-	-	-	-
2009	-	-	-	-	-	-
2010	-	-	-	-	-	-
2011	Raphael Gualazzi	Madness of Love	-	-	189	2
2012	Nina Zilli	L'Amore È Femmina (Out Of Love)	-	-	101	9
2013	Marco Mengoni	L'Essenziale	-	-	126	7
2014	Emma	La Mia Città	-	-	33	21
2015	Il Volo	Grande amore	-	-	292	3
2016	Francesca Michielin	No Degree Of Separation	-	-	124	16
2017	Francesco Gabbani	Occidentali's Karma	-	-	334	6
2018	Ermal Meta e Fabrizio Moro	Non Mi Avete Fatto Niente	-	-	308	5
2019	Mahmood	Soldi	-	-	472	2
2021	Måneskin	Zitti e buoni	-	-	524	1

Latvia

			Semi-Final		Final	
Year	Artist	Song	Points	Position	Points	Position
2001	Arnis Mednis	Too Much			16	18
2002	Marie N	I Wanna			176	1
2003	FLY	Hello from Mars			5	24
2004	Fomins & Kleins	Dziesma Par Laimi	23	17	-	-
2005	Walter & Kazha	The War Is Not Over	85	10	153	5
2006	Cosmos	I Hear Your Heart	-	-	30	16
2007	Bonaparti.lv	Questa Notte	168	5	54	16
2008	Pirates Of The Sea	Wolves Of The Sea	86	6	83	12
2009	Intars Busulis	Probka	7	19	-	-
2010	Aisha	What For?	11	17	-	-
2011	Musiqq	Angel in Disguise	25	17	-	-
2012	Anmary	Beautiful Song	17	16	-	-
2013	PeR	Here We Go	13	17	-	-
2014	Aarzemnieki	Cake to Bake	33	13	-	-
2015	Aminata	Love Injected	155	2	186	6
2016	Justs	Heartbeat	132	8	132	15
2017	Triana Park	Line	21	18	-	-
2018	Laura Rizzotto	Funny Girl	106	12	-	-
2019	Carousel	That Night	50	15	-	-
2021	Samanta Tīna	The Moon is Rising	14	17	-	-

Lithuania

			Semi-Final		Final	
Year	Artist	Song	Points	Position	Points	Position
1994	Ovidijus Vyšniauskas	Lopšine mylimai			0	25
1995	-	-			-	-
1996	-	-			-	-
1997	-	-			-	-
1998	-	-			-	-
1999	Aiste Smilgeviciute	Strazdas			13	20
2000	-				-	-
2001	Skamp	You Got Style			35	13
2002	Aivaras	Happy You			12	23
2003	-	-			-	-
2004	Linas ir Simona	What's Happened To Your Love?	26	16	-	-
2005	Laura & the Lovers	Little By Little	17	25	-	-
2006	LT United	We Are The Winners	163	5	162	6
2007	4Fun	Love Or Leave	-	-	28	21
2008	Jeronimas Milius	Nomads In The Night	30	16	-	-
2009	Sasha Son	Love	66	9	23	23
2010	InCulto	East European Funk	44	12	-	-
2011	Evelina Sašenko	C'est Ma Vie	81	5	63	19
2012	Donny Montell	Love is Blind	107	3	70	14
2013	Andrius Pojavis	Something	53	9	17	22
2014	Vilija Matačiūnaitė	Attention	36	11	-	-
2015	Monika Linkyte & Vaidas Baumila	This Time	67	7	30	18
2016	Donny Montell	I've Been Waiting For This Night	222	4	200	9
2017	Fusedmarc	Rain Of Revolution	42	17	-	-
2018	Ieva Zasimauskaitė	When We're Old	119	9	181	12
2019	Jurij Veklenko	Run With The Lions	93	11	-	-
2021	The Roop	Discoteque	203	4	220	8

Luxembourg

			Semi-Final		Final	
Year	Artist	Song	Points	Position	Points	Position
1956	(1) Michèle Arnaud	Les Amants De Minuit			-	2
1956	(2) Michèle Arnaud	Ne Crois Pas			-	2
1957	Danièle Dupré	Tant De Peine			8	4
1958	Solange Berry	Un Grand Amour			1	9
1959	-	-			-	-
1960	Camillo Felgen	So Laang We's Du Do Bast			1	13
1961	Jean-Claude Pascal	Nous Les Amoureux			31	1

Luxembourg (continued)

			Semi-Final		Final	
Year	Artist	Song	Points	Position	Points	Position
1962	Camillo Felgen	Petit Bonhomme			11	3
1963	Nana Mouskouri	A Force De Prier			13	8
1964	Hugues Aufray	Dès Que Le Printemps Revient			14	4
1965	France Gall	Poupée De Cire, Poupée De Son			32	1
1966	Michèle Torr	Ce Soir Je T'attendais			7	10
1967	Vicky	L'amour Est Bleu			17	4
1968	Chris Baldo & Sophie Garel	Nous Vivrons D'amour			5	11
1969	Romuald	Cathérine			7	11
1970	David-Alexandre Winter	Je Suis Tombé Du Ciel			0	12
1971	Monique Melsen	Pomme, Pomme, Pomme			70	13
1972	Vicky Leandros	Après Toi			128	1
1973	Anne-Marie David	Tu Te Reconnaîtras			129	1
1974	Ireen Sheer	Bye, Bye, I Love You			14	4
1975	Géraldine	Toi			84	5
1976	Jürgen Marcus	Chansons Pour Ceux Qui S'aiment			17	4
1977	Anne Marie B	Frère Jacques			17	16
1978	Baccara	Parlez-vous Français?			73	7
1979	Jeane Manson	J'ai Déjà Vu ça Dans Tes Yeux			44	13
1980	Sophie & Magaly	Papa Pingouin			56	9
1981	Jean-Claude Pascal	C'est Peut-être Pas L'Amérique			41	11
1982	Svetlana	Cours Après le Temps			78	6
1983	Corinne Hermès	Si La Vie Est Cadeau			142	1
1984	Sophie Carle	100% D'amour			39	10
1985	Margo, Franck Olivier, Diane Solomon, Ireen	Children, Kinder, Enfants			37	13
1986	Sherisse Laurence	L'amour De Ma Vie			117	3
1987	Plastic Bertrand	Amour Amour			4	21
1988	Lara Fabian	Croire			90	4
1989	Park Café	Monsieur			8	20
1990	Céline Carzo	Quand Je Te Rêve			38	13
1991	Sarah Bray	Un Baiser Volé			29	14
1992	Marion Welter & Kontinent	Sou Fräi			10	21
1993	Modern Times	Donne-moi Une Chance			11	20

Malta

			Semi-Final		Final	
Year	Artist	Song	Points	Position	Points	Position
1971	Joe Grech	Marija L-maltija			52	18
1972	Helen & Joseph	L-imhabba			48	18
1973	-	-			-	-
1974	-	-			-	-
1975	Renato	Singing This Song			32	12
1976	-	-			-	-
1977	-	-			-	-
1978	-	-			-	-
1979	-	-			-	-
1980	-	-			-	-
1981	-	-			-	-
1982	-	-			-	-
1983	-	-			-	-
1984	-	-			-	-
1985	-	-			-	-
1986	-	-			-	-
1987	-	-			-	-
1988	-	-			-	-
1989	-	-			-	-
1990	-	-			-	-
1991	Paul Giordimaina & Georgina	Could It Be			106	6
1992	Mary Spiteri	Little Child			123	3
1993	William Mangion	This Time			69	8
1994	Moira Stafrace & Christopher Scicluna	More Than Love			97	5
1995	Mike Spiteri	Keep Me In Mind			76	10
1996	Miriam Christine	In A Woman's Heart			68	10
1997	Debbie Scerri	Let Me Fly			66	9

Malta (continued)

Year	Artist	Song	Semi-Final Points	Semi-Final Position	Final Points	Final Position
1998	Chiara	The One That I Love			165	3
1999	Times 3	Believe 'n Peace			32	15
2000	Claudette Pace	Desire			73	8
2001	Fabrizio Faniello	Another Summer Night			48	9
2002	Ira Losco	7th Wonder			164	2
2003	Lynn Chirchop	To Dream Again			4	25
2004	Julie & Ludwig	On Again... Off Again	74	8	50	12
2005	Chiara	Angel	-	-	192	2
2006	Fabrizio Faniello	I Do	-	-	1	24
2007	Olivia Lewis	Vertigo	15	25	-	-
2008	Morena	Vodka	38	14	-	-
2009	Chiara	What If We	86	6	31	22
2010	Thea Garrett	My Dream	45	12	-	-
2011	Glen Vella	One Life	54	11	-	-
2012	Kurt Calleja	This Is The Night	70	7	41	21
2013	Gianluca	Tomorrow	118	4	120	8
2014	Firelight	Coming Home	63	9	32	23
2015	Amber	Warrior	43	11	-	-
2016	Ira Losco	Walk On Water	209	3	153	12
2017	Claudia Faniello	Breathlessly	55	16	-	-
2018	Christabelle	Taboo	101	13	-	-
2019	Michela	Chameleon	157	8	107	14
2021	Destiny	Je me casse	325	1	255	7

Moldova

Year	Artist	Song	Semi-Final Points	Semi-Final Position	Final Points	Final Position
2005	Zdob si Zdub	Boonika Bate Toba	207	2	148	6
2006	Arsenium & Natalia Gordienko	Loca	-	-	22	20
2007	Natalia Barbu	Fight	91	10	109	10
2008	Geta Burlacu	A Century Of Love	36	12	-	-
2009	Nelly Ciobanu	Hora Din Moldova	106	5	69	14
2010	Sunstroke Project & Olia Tira	Run Away	52	10	27	22
2011	Zdob și Zdub	So Lucky	54	10	97	12
2012	Pasha Parfeny	Lăutar	100	5	81	11
2013	Aliona Moon	O Mie	95	4	71	11
2014	Cristina Scarlat	Wild Soul	13	16	-	-
2015	Eduard Romanyuta	I Want Your Love	41	11	-	-
2016	Lidia Isac	Falling Stars	33	17	-	-
2017	Sunstroke Project	Hey Mamma	291	2	374	3
2018	DoReDos	My Lucky Day	235	3	209	10
2019	Anna Odobescu	Stay	85	12	-	-
2021	Natalia Gordienko	Sugar	179	7	115	13

Monaco

Year	Artist	Song	Semi-Final Points	Semi-Final Position	Final Points	Final Position
1959	Jacques Pills	Mon Ami Pierrot			1	11
1960	François Deguelt	Ce Soir-là			15	3
1961	Colette Deréal	Allons, Allons Les Enfants			6	10
1962	François Deguelt	Dis Rien			13	2
1963	Françoise Hardy	L'amour S'en Va			25	5
1964	Romuald	Où Sont-elles Passées?			15	3
1965	Marjorie Noël	Va Dire à L'amour			7	9
1966	Tereza	Bien Plus Fort			0	17
1967	Minouche Barelli	Boum-badaboum			10	5
1968	Line & Willy	A Chacun Sa Chanson			8	7
1969	Jean-Jacques	Maman, Maman			11	6
1970	Dominique Dussault	Marlène			5	8
1971	Séverine	Un Banc, Un Arbre, Une Rue			128	1
1972	Anne-Marie Godart & Peter MacLane	Comme On S'aime			65	16
1973	Marie	Un Train Qui Part			85	8

Monaco (continued)

Year	Artist	Song	Semi-Final Points	Semi-Final Position	Final Points	Final Position
1974	Romuald	Celui Qui Reste Et Celui Qui S'en Va			14	4
1975	Sophie	Une Chanson C'est Une Lettre			22	13
1976	Mary Christy	Toi, La Musique Et Moi			93	3
1977	Michèle Torr	Une Petite Française			96	4
1978	Caline & Olivier Toussaint	Les Jardins De Monaco			107	4
1979	Laurent Vaguener	Notre Vie, C'est La Musique			12	16
1980	-	-			-	-
1981	-	-			-	-
1982	-	-			-	-
1983	-	-			-	-
1984	-	-			-	-
1985	-	-			-	-
1986	-	-			-	-
1987	-	-			-	-
1988	-	-			-	-
1989	-	-			-	-
1990	-	-			-	-
1991	-	-			-	-
1992	-	-			-	-
1993	-	-			-	-
1994	-	-			-	-
1995	-	-			-	-
1996	-	-			-	-
1997	-	-			-	-
1998	-	-			-	-
1999	-	-			-	-
2000	-	-			-	-
2001	-	-			-	-
2002	-	-			-	-
2003	-	-			-	-
2004	Maryon	Notre Planète	10	19	-	-
2005	Lise Darly	Tout De Moi	22	24	-	-
2006	Séverine Ferrer	La Coco-dance	14	21	-	-

Montenegro

Year	Artist	Song	Semi-Final Points	Semi-Final Position	Final Points	Final Position
2007	Stevan Faddy	Ajde Kroci	33	22	-	-
2008	Stefan Filipović	Zauvijek Volim Te	23	14	-	-
2009	Andrea Demirovic	Just Get Out of My Life	44	11	-	-
2010	-	-	-	-	-	-
2011	-	-	-	-	-	-
2012	Rambo Amadeus	Euro Neuro	20	15	-	-
2013	Who See	Igranka	41	12	-	-
2014	Sergej Ćetković	Moj Svijet	63	7	37	19
2015	Knez	Adio	57	9	44	13
2016	Highway	The Real Thing	60	13	-	-
2017	Slavko Kalezić	Space	56	16	-	-
2018	Vanja Radovanović	Inje	40	16	-	-
2019	D mol	Heaven	46	16	-	-

Morocco

Year	Artist	Song	Semi-Final Points	Semi-Final Position	Final Points	Final Position
1980	Samira Bensaïd	Bitakat Hob			7	18

Netherlands

Year	Artist	Song	Semi-Final Points	Semi-Final Position	Final Points	Final Position
1956	(1) Corry Brokken	Voorgoed Voorbij			-	2
1956	(2) Jetty Paerl	De Vogels Van Holland			-	2
1957	Corry Brokken	Net Als Toen			31	1
1958	Corry Brokken	Heel De Wereld			1	9
1959	Teddy Scholten	Een Beetje			21	1
1960	Rudi Carrell	Wat Een Geluk			2	12
1961	Greetje Kauffeld	Wat Een Dag			6	10
1962	De Spelbrekers	Katinka			0	13
1963	Annie Palmen	Een Speeldoos			0	13
1964	Anneke Grönloh	Jij Bent Mijn Leven			2	10
1965	Conny Van den Bos	Het Is Genoeg			5	11
1966	Milly Scott	Fernando En Philippo			2	15
1967	Thérèse Steinmetz	Ring-dinge			2	14
1968	Ronnie Tober	Morgen			1	16
1969	Lenny Kuhr	De Troubadour			18	1
1970	Patricia & Hearts of Soul	Waterman			7	7
1971	Saskia & Serge	De Tijd			85	6
1972	Sandra & Andres	Als Het Om De Liefde Gaat			106	4
1973	Ben Cramer	De Oude Muzikant			69	14
1974	Mouth & MacNeal	I See A Star			15	3
1975	Teach-In	Ding-A-Dong			152	1
1976	Sandra Reemer	The Party's Over Now			56	9
1977	Heddy Lester	De Mallemolen			35	12
1978	Harmony	't Is Ok			37	13
1979	Xandra	Colorado			51	12
1980	Maggie MacNeal	Amsterdam			93	5
1981	Linda Williams	Het Is Een Wonder			51	9
1982	Bill van Dijk	Jij En Ik			8	16
1983	Bernadette	Sing Me A Song			66	7
1984	Maribelle	Ik Hou Van Jou			34	13
1985	-				-	-
1986	Frizzle Sizzle	Alles Heeft Ritme			40	13
1987	Marcha	Rechtop In De Wind			83	5
1988	Gerard Joling	Shangri-la			70	9
1989	Justine Pelmelay	Blijf Zoals Je Bent			45	15
1990	Maywood	Ik Wil Alles Met Je Delen			25	15
1991	-				-	-
1992	Humphrey Campbell	Wijs Me De Weg			67	13
1993	Ruth Jacott	Vrede			92	6
1994	Willeke Alberti	Waar Is De Zon			4	23
1995	-				-	-
1996	Maxine & Franklin Brown	De Eerste Keer			78	7
1997	Mrs Einstein	Niemand Heeft Nog Tijd			5	22
1998	Edsilia Rombley	Hemel En Aarde			150	4
1999	Marlayne	One Good Reason			71	9
2000	Linda Wagenmakers	No Goodbyes			40	13
2001	Michelle	Out On My Own			16	18
2002	-	-			-	-
2003	Esther Hart	One More Night			45	13
2004	Re-union	Without You	146	6	11	20
2005	Glennis Grace	My Impossible Dream	53	14	-	-
2006	Treble	Amambanda	22	19	-	-
2007	Edsilia Rombley	On Top Of The World	38	21	-	-
2008	Hind	Your Heart Belongs To Me	27	13	-	-
2009	The Toppers	Shine	11	17	-	-
2010	Sieneke	Ik Ben Verliefd (Sha-la-lie)	29	14	-	-
2011	3JS	Never Alone	13	19	-	-
2012	Joan Franka	You And Me	35	15	-	-
2013	Anouk	Birds	75	6	114	9
2014	The Common Linnets	Calm After the Storm	150	1	238	2
2015	Trijntje Oosterhuis	Walk Along	33	14	-	-
2016	Douwe Bob	Slow Down	197	5	153	11
2017	OG3NE	Lights And Shadows	200	4	150	11
2018	Waylon	Outlaw In 'Em	174	7	121	18

Netherlands (continued)

			Semi-Final		Final	
Year	Artist	Song	Points	Position	Points	Position
2019	Duncan Laurence	Arcade	280	1	498	1
2021	Jeangu Macrooy	Birth of a New Age	-	-	11	23

North Macedonia

			Semi-Final		Final	
Year	Artist	Song	Points	Position	Points	Position
1998	Vlado Janevski	Ne Zori, Zoro			16	19
1999	-	-			-	-
2000	XXL	100% Te Ljubam			29	15
2001	-	-			-	-
2002	Karolina	Od Nas Zavisi			25	19
2003	-	-			-	-
2004	Tose Proeski	Life	71	10	47	14
2005	Martin Vucic	Make My Day	97	9	52	17
2006	Elena Risteska	Ninanajna	76	8	56	12
2007	Karolina	Mojot Svet	97	9	73	14
2008	Tamara, Vrčak & Adrijan	Let Me Love You	64	10	-	-
2009	Next Time	Neshto Shto Ke Ostane	45	10	-	-
2010	Gjoko Taneski	Jas Ja Imam Silata	37	15	-	-
2011	Vlatko Ilievski	Rusinka	36	16	-	-
2012	Kaliopi	Crno I Belo	53	9	71	13
2013	Esma & Lozano	Pred Da Se Razdeni	28	16	-	-
2014	Tijana	To The Sky	33	13	-	-
2015	Daniel Kajmakoski	Autumn Leaves	28	15	-	-
2016	Kaliopi	Dona	88	11	-	-
2017	Jana Burčeska	Dance Alone	69	15	-	-
2018	Eye Cue	Lost And Found	24	18	-	-
2019	Tamara Todevska	Proud	239	2	305	7
2021	Vasil	Here I Stand	23	15	-	-

Norway

			Semi-Final		Final	
Year	Artist	Song	Points	Position	Points	Position
1960	Nora Brockstedt	Voi-voi			11	4
1961	Nora Brockstedt	Sommer I Palma			10	7
1962	Inger Jacobsen	Kom Sol, Kom Regn			2	10
1963	Anita Thallaug	Solhverv			0	13
1964	Arne Bendiksen	Spiral			6	8
1965	Kirsti Sparboe	Karusell			1	13
1966	Åse Kleveland	Intet Er Nytt Under Solen			15	3
1967	Kirsti Sparboe	Dukkemann			2	14
1968	Odd Børre	Stress			2	13
1969	Kirsti Sparboe	Oj, Oj, Oj, Så Glad, Jeg Skal Bli			1	16
1970	-	-			-	-
1971	Hanne Krogh	Lykken Er...			65	17
1972	Grethe Kausland & Benny Borg	Småting			73	14
1973	Bendik Singers	It's Just A Game			89	7
1974	Anne-Karine Ström & the Bendik Singers	The First Day Of Love			3	14
1975	Ellen Nikolaysen	You Touched My Life With Summer			11	18
1976	Anne-Karine Ström	Mata Hari			7	17
1977	Anita Skorgan	Casanova			18	14
1978	Jahn Teigen	Mil Etter Mil			0	20
1979	Anita Skorgan	Oliver			57	11
1980	Sverre Kjellsberg & Mattis Hætta	Sámiid Ædnan			15	16
1981	Finn Kalvik	Aldri I Livet			0	20
1982	Jahn Teigen & Anita Skorgan	Adieu			40	12
1983	Jahn Teigen	Do Re Mi			53	9
1984	Dollie de Luxe	Lenge Leve Livet			29	17
1985	Bobbysocks	La Det Swinge			123	1
1986	Ketil Stokkan	Romeo			44	12
1987	Kate Gulbrandsen	Mitt Liv			65	9
1988	Karoline Krüger	For Vår Jord			88	5

Norway (continued)

Year	Artist	Song	Semi-Final Points	Semi-Final Position	Final Points	Final Position
1989	Britt Synnøve Johansen	Venners Nærhet			30	17
1990	Ketil Stokkan	Brandenburger Tor			8	21
1991	Just 4 Fun	Mrs Thompson			14	17
1992	Merethe Trøan	Visjoner			23	18
1993	Silje Vige	Alle Mine Tankar			120	4
1994	Elisabeth Andreasson & Jan Werner Danielsen	Duett			76	6
1995	Secret Garden	Nocturne			148	1
1996	Elisabeth Andreasson	I Evighet			114	2
1997	Tor Endresen	San Francisco			0	24
1998	Lars Fredriksen	Alltid Sommer			79	8
1999	Stig André Van Eijk	Living My Life Without You			35	13
2000	Charmed	My Heart Goes Boom			57	11
2001	Haldor Lægreid	On My Own			3	22
2002	-	-	-	-	-	-
2003	Jostein Hasselgård	I'm Not Afraid To Move On			123	4
2004	Knut Anders Sørum	High	-	-	3	24
2005	Wig Wam	In My Dreams	164	6	125	9
2006	Christine Guldbrandsen	Alvedansen	-	-	36	14
2007	Guri Schanke	Ven A Bailar Conmigo	48	18	-	-
2008	Maria	Hold On Be Strong	106	4	182	5
2009	Alexander Rybak	Fairytale	201	1	387	1
2010	Didrik Solli-Tangen	My Heart Is Yours	-	-	35	20
2011	Stella Mwangi	Haba Haba	30	17	-	-
2012	Tooji	Stay	45	10	7	26
2013	Margaret Berger	I Feed You My Love	120	3	191	4
2014	Carl Espen	Silent Storm	77	6	88	8
2015	Mørland & Debrah Scarlett	A Monster Like Me	123	4	102	8
2016	Agnete	Icebreaker	63	13	-	-
2017	JOWST	Grab The Moment	189	5	158	10
2018	Alexander Rybak	That's How You Write A Song	266	1	144	15
2019	KEiiNO	Spirit In The Sky	210	7	331	6
2021	Tix	Fallen Angel	115	10	75	18

Poland

Year	Artist	Song	Semi-Final Points	Semi-Final Position	Final Points	Final Position
1994	Edyta Górniak	To Nie Ja!			166	2
1995	Justyna	Sama			15	18
1996	Kasia Kowalska	Chce Znac Swój Grzech			31	15
1997	Anna Maria Jopek	Ale Jestem			54	11
1998	Sixteen	To Takie Proste			19	17
1999	Mietek (Mieczyslaw) Szczesniak	Przytul Mnie Mocno			17	19
2000	-	-			-	-
2001	Piasek	2 Long			11	20
2002	-	-			-	-
2003	Ich Troje	Keine Grenzen - Zadnych Granic			90	7
2004	Blue Cafe	Love Song	-	-	27	17
2005	Ivan & Delfin	Czarna Dziewczyna	81	11	-	-
2006	Ich Troje	Follow My Heart	70	11	-	-
2007	The Jet Set	Time To Party	75	14	-	-
2008	Isis Gee	For Life	42	10	14	24
2009	Lidia Kopania	I Don't Wanna Leave	43	12	-	-
2010	Marcin Mroziński	Legenda	44	13	-	-
2011	Magdalena Tul	Jestem	18	19	-	-
2012	-	-	-	-	-	-
2013	-	-	-	-	-	-
2014	Donatan & Cleo	My Słowianie - We Are Slavic	70	8	62	14
2015	Monika Kuszynska	In the Name of Love	57	8	10	23
2016	Michał Szpak	Color Of Your Life	151	6	229	8
2017	Kasia Moś	Flashlight	119	9	64	22
2018	Gromee feat. Lukas Meijer	Light Me Up	81	14	-	-
2019	Tulia	Fire of Love (Pali się)	120	11	-	-
2021	Rafał Brzozowski	The Ride	35	14	-	-

Portugal

Year	Artist	Song	Semi-Final Points	Semi-Final Position	Final Points	Final Position
1964	António Calvário	Oração			0	13
1965	Simone de Oliviera	Sol De Inverno			1	13
1966	Madalena Iglesias	Ele E Ela			6	13
1967	Eduardo Nascimento	O Vento Mudou			3	12
1968	Carlos Mendes	Verão			5	11
1969	Simone de Oliviera	Desfolhada Portuguesa			4	15
1970	-				-	-
1971	Tonicha	Menina Do Alto Da Serra			83	9
1972	Carlos Mendes	A Festa Da Vida			90	7
1973	Fernando Tordo	Tourada			80	10
1974	Paulo de Carvalho	E Depois Do Adeus			3	14
1975	Duarte Mendes	Madrugada			16	16
1976	Carlos do Carmo	Uma Flor De Verde Pinho			24	12
1977	Os Amigos	Portugal No Coração			18	14
1978	Gemini	Dai-li-dou			5	17
1979	Manuela Bravo	Sobe, Sobe, Balão Sobe			64	9
1980	José Cid	Um Grande, Grande Amor			71	7
1981	Carlos Paião	Play-back			9	18
1982	Doce	Bem-bom			32	13
1983	Armando Gama	Esta Balada Que Te Dou			33	13
1984	Maria Guinot	Silêncio E Tanta Gente			38	11
1985	Adelaïde	Penso Em Ti, Eu Sei			9	18
1986	Dora	Não Sejas Mau Para Mim			28	14
1987	Nevada	Neste Barco à Vela			15	18
1988	Dora	Voltarei			5	18
1989	Da Vinci	Conquistador			39	16
1990	Nucha	Há Sempre Alguém			9	20
1991	Dulce	Lusitana Paixão			62	8
1992	Diná	Amor D'água Fresca			26	17
1993	Anabela	A Cidade Até Ser Dia			60	10
1994	Sara Tavares	Chamar A Música			73	8
1995	Tó Cruz	Baunilha E Chocolate			5	21
1996	Lúcia Moniz	O Meu Coração Não Tem Cor			92	6
1997	Célia Lawson	Antes Do Adeus			0	24
1998	Alma Lusa	Se Eu Te Pudesse Abraçar			36	12
1999	Rui Bandeira	Como Tudo Começou			12	21
2000	-				-	-
2001	MTM	Só Sei Ser Feliz Assim			18	17
2002	-				-	-
2003	Rita Guerra	Deixa-me Sonhar			13	22
2004	Sofia	Foi Magia	38	15	-	-
2005	2B	Amar	51	17	-	-
2006	Nonstop	Coisas De Nada	26	19	-	-
2007	Sabrina	Dança Comigo (vem Ser Feliz)	88	11	-	-
2008	Vânia Fernandes	Senhora Do Mar (Negras Águas)	120	2	69	13
2009	Flor-de-lis	Todas As Ruas Do Amor	70	8	57	15
2010	Filipa Azevedo	Há Dias Assim	89	4	43	18
2011	Homens Da Luta	Luta É Alegria	22	18	-	-
2012	Filipa Sousa	Vida Minha	39	13	-	-
2013	-		-	-	-	-
2014	Suzy	Quero Ser Tua	39	11	-	-
2015	Leonor Andrade	Há um mar que nos separa	19	14	-	-
2016	-		-	-	-	-
2017	Salvador Sobral	Amar Pelos Dois	370	1	758	1
2018	Cláudia Pascoal	O Jardim	-	-	39	26
2019	Conan Osiris	Telemóveis	51	15	-	-
2021	The Black Mamba	Love is on My Side	239	4	153	12

Romania

Year	Artist	Song	Semi-Final Points	Semi-Final Position	Final Points	Final Position
1994	Dan Bittman	Dincolo De Nori			14	21
1995	-	-			-	-
1996	-	-			-	-
1997	-	-			-	-
1998	Malina Olinescu	Eu Cred			6	22
1999	-	-			-	-
2000	Taxi	The Moon			25	17
2001	-	-			-	-
2002	Monica Anghel & Marcel Pavel	Tell Me Why			72	8
2003	Nicola	Don't Break My Heart			73	10
2004	Sanda Ladosi	I Admit	-	-	18	18
2005	Luminita Anghel & Sistem	Let Me Try	235	1	158	3
2006	Mihai Traistariu	Tornero	-	-	172	4
2007	Todomondo	Liubi, Liubi, I Love You	-	-	84	13
2008	Nico & Vlad	Pe-o Margine De Lume	94	7	45	20
2009	Elena	The Balkan Girls	67	9	40	19
2010	Paula Seling & Ovi	Playing With Fire	104	4	162	3
2011	Hotel FM	Change	111	4	77	17
2012	Mandinga	Zaleilah	120	3	71	12
2013	Cezar	It's My Life	83	5	65	13
2014	Paula Seling & Ovi	Miracle	125	2	72	12
2015	Voltaj	De la capat (All over Again)	89	5	35	15
2016	-	-	-	-	-	-
2017	Ilinca ft. Alex Florea	Yodel It!	174	6	282	7
2018	The Humans	Goodbye	107	11	-	-
2019	Ester Peony	On A Sunday	71	13	-	-
2021	Roxen	Amnesia	85	12	-	-

Russia

Year	Artist	Song	Semi-Final Points	Semi-Final Position	Final Points	Final Position
1994	Youddiph	Vechni Stranik			70	9
1995	Philipp Kirkorov	Kolybelnaya Dlya Vulkana			18	17
1996	-	-			-	-
1997	Alla Pugachova	Primadonna			33	15
1998	-	-			-	-
1999	-	-			-	-
2000	Alsou	Solo			155	2
2001	Mumiy Troll	Lady Alpine Blue			37	12
2002	Prime Minister	Northern Girl			55	10
2003	t.A.T.u.	Ne Ver', Ne Boisia			164	3
2004	Julia Savicheva	Believe Me	-	-	67	11
2005	Natalia Podolskaya	Nobody Hurt No One	-	-	57	15
2006	Dima Bilan	Never Let You Go	217	3	248	2
2007	Serebro	Song # 1	-	-	207	3
2008	Dima Bilan	Believe	135	3	272	1
2009	Anastasia Prikhodko	Mamo	-	-	91	11
2010	Peter Nalitch & Friends	Lost And Forgotten	74	7	90	11
2011	Alexej Vorobjov	Get You	64	9	77	16
2012	Buranovskiye Babushki	Party for Everybody	152	1	259	2
2013	Dina Garipova	What If	156	2	174	5
2014	Tolmachevy Sisters	Shine	63	6	89	7
2015	Polina Gagarina	A Million Voices	182	1	303	2
2016	Sergey Lazarev	You Are The Only One	342	1	491	3
2017	-	-	-	-	-	-
2018	Julia Samoylova	I Won't Break	65	15	-	-
2019	Sergey Lazarev	Scream	217	6	370	3
2021	Manizha	Russian Woman	225	3	204	9

San Marino

Year	Artist	Song	Semi-Final Points	Semi-Final Position	Final Points	Final Position
2008	Miodio	Complice	5	19	-	-
2009	-	-	-	-	-	-
2010	-	-	-	-	-	-
2011	Senit	Stand By	34	16	-	-
2012	Valentina Monetta	The Social Network Song (Oh Oh - Uh - Oh Oh)	31	14	-	-
2013	Valentina Monetta	Crisalide (Vola)	47	11	-	-
2014	Valentina Monetta	Maybe (Forse)	40	10	14	24
2015	Michele Perniola & Anita Simoncini	Chain of Lights	11	16	-	-
2016	Serhat	I Didn't Know	68	12	-	-
2017	Valentina Monetta & Jimmie Wilsor	Spirit Of The Night	1	18	-	-
2018	Jessika feat. Jenifer Brening	Who We Are	28	17	-	-
2019	Serhat	Say Na Na Na	150	8	77	19
2021	Senhit	Adrenalina	118	9	50	22

Serbia

Year	Artist	Song	Semi-Final Points	Semi-Final Position	Final Points	Final Position
2007	Marija Šerifović	Molitva	298	1	268	1
2008	Jelena Tomašević feat Bora Dugic	Oro	-	-	160	6
2009	Marko Kon & Milaan	Cipela	60	10	-	-
2010	Milan Stanković	Ovo Je Balkan	79	5	72	13
2011	Nina	Čaroban	67	8	85	14
2012	Željko Joksimović	Nije Ljubav Stvar	159	2	214	3
2013	Moje 3	Ljubav Je Svuda	46	11	-	-
2014	-	-	-	-	-	-
2015	Bojana Stamenov	Beauty Never Lies	63	9	53	10
2016	Sanja Vučić ZAA	Goodbye (Shelter)	105	10	115	18
2017	Tijana Bogićević	In Too Deep	98	11	-	-
2018	Sanja Ilić & Balkanika	Nova Deca	117	9	113	19
2019	Nevena Božović	Kruna	156	7	89	18
2021	Hurricane	Loco Loco	124	8	102	15

Serbia & Montenegro

Year	Artist	Song	Semi-Final Points	Semi-Final Position	Final Points	Final Position
2004	Željko Joksimović	Lane Moje	263	1	263	2
2005	No Name	Zauvijek Moja	-	-	137	7
2006	-	-	-	-	-	-

Slovakia

Year	Artist	Song	Semi-Final Points	Semi-Final Position	Final Points	Final Position
1994	Martin Durinda & Tublatanka	Nekovecná Piesen			15	19
1995	-	-			-	-
1996	Marcel Palonder	Kým Nás Máš			19	18
1997	-	-			-	-
1998	Katarína Hasprová	Modlitba			8	21
1999	-	-			-	-
2000	-	-			-	-
2001	-	-			-	-
2002	-	-			-	-
2003	-	-			-	-
2004	-	-	-	-	-	-
2005	-	-	-	-	-	-
2006	-	-	-	-	-	-
2007	-	-	-	-	-	-
2008	-	-	-	-	-	-
2009	Kamil Mikulčík & Nela Pociskova	Leť Tmou	8	18	-	-
2010	Kristina Pelakova	Horehronie	24	16	-	-
2011	TWiiNS	I'm Still Alive	48	13	-	-
2012	Max Jason Mai	Don't Close Your Eyes	22	18	-	-

Slovenia

Year	Artist	Song	Semi-Final Points	Semi-Final Position	Final Points	Final Position
1993	1X Band	Tih Dezeven Dan			9	22
1994	-	-			-	-
1995	Darja Svajger	Prisluhni Mi			83	7
1996	Regina	Dan Najlepših Sanj			16	21
1997	Tanja Ribic	Zbudi Se			60	10
1998	Vili Resnik	Naj Bogovi Slišijo			17	18
1999	Darja Svajger	For A Thousand Years			50	11
2000	-	-			-	-
2001	Nuša Derenda	Energy			70	7
2002	Sestre	Samo Ljubezen			32	15
2003	Karmen	Nanana			7	23
2004	Platin	Stay Forever	5	21	-	-
2005	Omar Naber	Stop	69	12	-	-
2006	Anžej Dežan	Mr Nobody	49	16	-	-
2007	Alenka Gotar	Cvet Z Juga	140	7	66	15
2008	Rebeka Dremelj	Vrag Naj Vzame	36	11	-	-
2009	Quartissimo featuring Martina	Love Symphony	14	16	-	-
2010	Ansambel Žlindra & Kalamari	Narodnozabavni Rock	6	16	-	-
2011	Maja Keuc	No One	112	3	96	13
2012	Eva Boto	Verjamem	31	17	-	-
2013	Hannah	Straight Into Love	8	16	-	-
2014	Tinkara Kovač	Round and Round	52	10	9	17
2015	Maraaya	Here for You	92	5	39	14
2016	ManuElla	Blue And Red	57	14	-	-
2017	Omar Naber	On My Way	36	17	-	-
2018	Lea Sirk	Hvala, ne!	132	8	64	22
2019	Zala Kralj & Gašper Šantl	Sebi	167	6	105	15
2021	Ana Soklič	Amen	44	13	-	-

Spain

Year	Artist	Song	Semi-Final Points	Semi-Final Position	Final Points	Final Position
1961	Conchita Bautista	Estando Contigo			8	9
1962	Victor Balaguer	Llámame			0	13
1963	José Guardiola	Algo Prodigioso			2	12
1964	Tim, Nelly & Tony	Caracola			1	12
1965	Conchita Bautista	Qué Bueno, Qué Bueno			0	15
1966	Raphael	Yo Soy Aquél			9	7
1967	Raphael	Hablemos Del Amor			9	6
1968	Massiel	La, La, La...			29	1
1969	Salomé	Vivo Cantando			18	1
1970	Julio Iglesias	Gwendolyne			8	4
1971	Karina	En Un Mundo Nuevo			115	2
1972	Jaime Morey	Amanece			83	10
1973	Mocedades	Eres Tú			125	2
1974	Peret	Canta Y Se Feliz			10	9
1975	Sergio & Estíbaliz	Tú Volverás			53	10
1976	Braulio	Sobran Las Palabras			11	16
1977	Micky	Enséñame A Cantar			52	9
1978	José Vélez	Bailemos Un Vals			65	9
1979	Betty Missiego	Su Canción			116	2
1980	Trigo Limpio	Qué Date Esta Noche			38	12
1981	Bacchelli	Y Solo Tú			38	14
1982	Lucía	Él			52	10
1983	Remedios Amaya	¿Quién Maneja Mi Barca?			0	9
1984	Bravo	Lady, Lady			106	3
1985	Paloma San Basilic	La Fiesta Terminó			36	14
1986	Cadillac	Valentino			51	10
1987	Patricia Kraus	No Estás Solo			10	19
1988	La Década	La Chica Que Yo Quiero (Made In Spain)			58	11
1989	Nina	Nacida Para Amar			88	6
1990	Azúcar Moreno	Bandido			96	5
1991	Sergio Dalma	Bailar Pegados			119	4

Spain (continued)

Year	Artist	Song	Semi-Final Points	Semi-Final Position	Final Points	Final Position
1992	Serafin	Todo Esto Es La Música			37	14
1993	Eva Santamaria	Hombres			58	11
1994	Alejandro Abad	Ella No Es Ella			17	18
1995	Anabel Conde	Vuelve Conmigo			119	2
1996	Antonio Carbonell	¡Ay, Qué Deseo!			17	20
1997	Marcos Llunas	Sin Rencor			96	6
1998	Mikel Herzog	¿Qué Voy A Hacer Sin Ti?			21	16
1999	Lydia	No Quiero Escuchar			1	23
2000	Serafín Zubiri	Colgado De Un Sueño			18	18
2001	David Civera	Dile Que La Quiero			76	6
2002	Rosa	Europe's Living A Celebration			81	7
2003	Beth	Dime			81	8
2004	Ramón	Para Llenarme De Ti	-	-	87	10
2005	Son de sol	Brujería	-	-	28	21
2006	Las Ketchup	Bloody Mary	-	-	18	21
2007	NASH	I Love You Mi Vida	-	-	43	20
2008	Rodolfo Chikilicuatre	Baila El Chiki Chiki	-	-	55	16
2009	Soraya	La Noche Es Para Mí	-	-	23	24
2010	Daniel Diges	Algo Pequeñito (Something Tiny)	-	-	68	15
2011	Lucía Pérez	Que Me Quiten Lo Bailao	-	-	50	23
2012	Pastora Soler	Quédate Conmigo (Stay With Me)	-	-	97	10
2013	ESDM	Contigo Hasta El Final (With You Until The End)	-	-	8	25
2014	Ruth Lorenzo	Dancing in the Rain	-	-	74	10
2015	Edurne	Amanecer	-	-	15	21
2016	Barei	Say Yay!	-	-	77	22
2017	Manel Navarro	Do It For Your Lover	-	-	5	26
2018	Amaia y Alfred	Tu Canción	-	-	61	23
2019	Miki	La Venda	-	-	54	22
2021	Blas Cantó	Voy a quedarme	-	-	6	24

Sweden

Year	Artist	Song	Semi-Final Points	Semi-Final Position	Final Points	Final Position
1958	Alice Babs	Lilla Stjärna			10	4
1959	Brita Borg	Augustin			4	9
1960	Siw Malmkvist	Alla Andra Får Varann			4	10
1961	Lill-Babs	April, April			2	14
1962	Inger Berggren	Sol Och Vår			4	7
1963	Monica Zetterlund	En Gång I Stockholm			0	13
1964	-				-	-
1965	Ingvar Wixell	Absent Friend			6	10
1966	Lill Lindfors & Svante Thuresson	Nygammal Vals Eller Hip Man Svinaherde			16	2
1967	Östen Warnebring	Som En Dröm			7	8
1968	Claes-Göran Hederström	Det Börjar Verka Kärlek, Banne Mej			15	5
1969	Tommy Körberg	Judy, Min Vän			8	9
1970	-	-			-	-
1971	Family Four	Vita Vidder			85	6
1972	Family Four	Härliga Sommardag			75	13
1973	The Nova & The Dolls	You're Summer			94	5
1974	ABBA	Waterloo			24	1
1975	Lars Berghagen & The Dolls	Jennie, Jennie			72	8
1976	-	-			-	-
1977	Forbes	Beatles			2	18
1978	Björn Skifs	Det Blir Alltid Värre Framåt Natter			26	14
1979	Ted Gärdestad	Satellit			3	17
1980	Tomas Ledin	Just Nu!			47	10
1981	Björn Skifs	Fångad I En Dröm			50	10
1982	Chips	Dag Efter Dag			67	8
1983	Carola Häggkvist	Främling			126	3
1984	Herrey's	Diggi-loo Diggy-ley			145	1
1985	Kikki Danielsson	Bra Vibrationer			103	3
1986	Lasse Holm and Monica Törnell	E' De' Det Här Du Kallar Kärlek			78	5
1987	Lotta Engberg	Boogaloo			50	12

Sweden (continued)

Year	Artist	Song	Semi-Final Points	Semi-Final Position	Final Points	Final Position
1988	Tommy Körberg	Stad I Ljus			52	12
1989	Tommy Nilsson	En Dag			110	4
1990	Edin-Ådahl	Som En Vind			24	16
1991	Carola	Fångad Av En Stormvind			146	1
1992	Christer Björkmann	I Morgon är En Annan Dag			9	22
1993	Arvingarna	Eloïse			89	7
1994	Marie Bergman & Roger Pontare	Stjärnorna			48	13
1995	Jan Johansen	Se På Mej			100	3
1996	One More Time	Den Vilda			100	3
1997	Blond	Bara Hon älskar Mig			36	14
1998	Jill Johnson	Kärleken är			53	10
1999	Charlotte Nilsson	Take Me To Your Heaven			163	1
2000	Roger Pontare	When Spirits Are Calling My Name			88	7
2001	Friends	Listen To Your Heartbeat			100	5
2002	Afro-dite	Never Let It Go			72	8
2003	Fame	Give Me Your Love			107	5
2004	Lena Philipsson	It Hurts	-	-	170	5
2005	Martin Stenmarck	Las Vegas	-	-	30	19
2006	Carola	Invincible	214	4	170	5
2007	The Ark	The Worrying Kind	-	-	51	18
2008	Charlotte Perrelli	Hero	54	12	47	18
2009	Malena Ernman	La Voix	105	4	33	21
2010	Anna Bergendahl	This Is My Life	62	11	-	-
2011	Eric Saade	Popular	155	1	185	3
2012	Loreen	Euphoria	181	1	372	1
2013	Robin Stjernberg	You	-	-	62	14
2014	Sanna Nielsen	Undo	131	2	218	3
2015	Måns Zelmerlöw	Heroes	217	1	365	1
2016	Frans	If I Were Sorry	-	-	261	5
2017	Robin Bengtsson	I Can't Go On	227	3	344	5
2018	Benjamin Ingrosso	Dance You Off	254	2	274	7
2019	John Lundvik	Too Late For Love	238	3	334	5
2021	Tusse	Voices	142	7	109	14

Switzerland

Year	Artist	Song	Semi-Final Points	Semi-Final Position	Final Points	Final Position
1956	(1) Lys Assia	Refrain			-	1
1956	(2) Lys Assia	Das Alte Karussell			-	2
1957	Lys Assia	L'enfant Que J'étais			5	8
1958	Lys Assia	Giorgio			24	2
1959	Christa Williams	Irgendwoher			14	4
1960	Anita Traversi	Cielo E Terra			5	8
1961	Franca di Rienzo	Nous Aurons Demain			16	13
1962	Jean Philippe	Le Retour			2	10
1963	Esther Ofarim	T'en Va Pas			40	2
1964	Anita Traversi	I Miei Pensieri			0	13
1965	Yovanna	Non à Jamais Sans Toi			8	8
1966	Madeleine Pascal	Ne Vois-tu Pas?			12	6
1967	Géraldine	Quel Coeur Vas-tu Briser?			0	17
1968	Gianni Mascolo	Guardando Il Sole			2	13
1969	Paola del Medico	Bonjour, Bonjour			13	5
1970	Henri Dès	Retour			8	4
1971	Peter, Sue & Marc	Les Illusions De Nos Vingt Ans			78	12
1972	Véronique Müller	C'est La Chanson De Mon Amour			88	8
1973	Patrick Juvet	Je Me Vais Marier, Marie			79	12
1974	Piera Martell	Mein Ruf Nach Dir			3	14
1975	Simone Drexel	Mikado			77	6
1976	Peter, Sue & Marc	Djambo, Djambo			91	4
1977	Pepe Lienhard Band	Swiss Lady			71	6
1978	Carole Vinci	Vivre			65	9
1979	Peter, Sue & Marc & Pfuri, Gorps & Kniri	Trödler Und Co			60	10
1980	Paola	Cinéma			104	4

Switzerland (continued)

Year	Artist	Song	Semi-Final Points	Semi-Final Position	Final Points	Final Position
1981	Peter, Sue & Marc	Io Senza Tei			121	4
1982	Arlette Zola	Amour On T'aime			97	3
1983	Mariella Farré	Io Così Non Ci Sto			28	15
1984	Rainy Day	Welche Farbe Hat Der Sonnenschein			30	16
1985	Mariella Farré & Pino Gasparini	Piano Piano			39	12
1986	Daniela Simons	Pas Pour Moi			140	2
1987	Carole Rich	Moitié Moitié			26	17
1988	Céline Dion	Ne Partez Pas Sans Moi			137	1
1989	Furbaz	Viver Senza Tei			47	13
1990	Egon Egemann	Musik Klingt In Die Welt Hinaus			51	11
1991	Sandra Simò	Canzone Per Te			118	5
1992	Daisy Auvray	Mister Music Man			32	15
1993	Annie Cotton	Moi, Tout Simplement			148	3
1994	Duilio	Sto Pregando			15	19
1995	-	-			-	-
1996	Cathy Leander	Mon Coeur L'aime			22	16
1997	Barbara Berta	Dentro Di Me			5	22
1998	Gunvor	Lass Ihn			0	25
1999	-	-			-	-
2000	Jane Bogaert	La Vita Cos'è?			14	20
2001	-	-			-	-
2002	Francine Jordi	Dans Le Jardin De Mon Âme			15	22
2003	-	-			-	-
2004	Piero Esteriore & the MusicStars	Celebrate	0	22	-	-
2005	Vanilla Ninja	Cool Vibes	114	8	128	8
2006	Six4One	If We All Give A Little	-	-	30	16
2007	DJ BoBo	Vampires Are Alive	40	20	-	-
2008	Paolo Meneguzzi	Era Stupendo	47	13	-	-
2009	Lovebugs	The Highest Heights	15	14	-	-
2010	Michael von der Heide	Il Pleut de L'Or	2	17	-	-
2011	Anna Rossinelli	In Love For A While	55	10	19	25
2012	Sinplus	Unbreakable	45	11	-	-
2013	Takasa	You And Me	41	13	-	-
2014	Sebalter	Hunter of Stars	92	4	64	13
2015	Mélanie René	Time to Shine	4	17	-	-
2016	Rykka	The Last Of Our Kind	28	18	-	-
2017	Timebelle	Apollo	97	12	-	-
2018	ZiBBZ	Stones	86	13	-	-
2019	Luca Hänni	She Got Me	232	4	364	4
2021	Gjon's Tears	Tout l'Univers	291	1	432	3

Turkey

Year	Artist	Song	Semi-Final Points	Semi-Final Position	Final Points	Final Position
1975	Semiha Yanki	Seninle Bir Dakika			3	19
1976	-	-			-	-
1977	-	-			-	-
1978	Nazar	Sevinçe			2	18
1979	-	-			-	-
1980	Ajda Pekkan	Petr'oil			23	15
1981	Modern Folk Trio & Aysegül	Dönme Dolap			9	18
1982	Neço	Hani			20	15
1983	Çetin Alp & the Short Wave	Opera			0	19
1984	Bes Yil Önce, On Yil Sonra	Halay			37	12
1985	MFÖ	Di Dai Di Dai Dai (A'sik Oldum			36	14
1986	Klips ve Onlar	Halley			53	9
1987	Seyyal Tanner & Lokomotif	Sarkim Sevgi üstüne			0	22
1988	MFÖ	Sufi (Hey Ya Hey)			37	15
1989	Pan	Bana Bana			5	21
1990	Kayahan	Gözlerinin Hapsindeyim			21	17
1991	Izel Çeliköz, Rayhan Soykarçi & Can Ugurluér	Iki Dakika			44	12
1992	Aylin Vatankos	Yaz Bitti			17	19
1993	Burak Aydos, Öztürk Baybora & Serter	Esmer Yarim			10	21

Turkey (continued)

Year	Artist	Song	Semi-Final Points	Semi-Final Position	Final Points	Final Position
1994	-	-			-	-
1995	Arzu Ece	Sev!			21	16
1996	Sebnem Paker	Besinçi Mevsim			57	12
1997	Sebnem Paker & Group Etnic	Dinle			121	3
1998	Tüzmen	Unutamazsin			25	14
1999	Tuba Önal & Grup Mystik	Dön Artik			21	16
2000	Pinar Ayhan & SOS Band	Yorgunum Anla			59	10
2001	Sedat Yüce	Sevgiliye Son			41	11
2002	Buket Bengisu & Saphire	Leylaklar Soldu Kalbinde			29	16
2003	Sertab Erener	Everyway That I Can			167	1
2004	Athena	For Real	-	-	195	4
2005	Gülseren	Rimi Rimi Ley	-	-	92	13
2006	Sibel Tüzün	Superstar	91	9	91	11
2007	Kenan Dogulu	Shake It Up Shekerim	197	3	163	4
2008	Mor ve Ötesi	Deli	85	7	138	7
2009	Hadise	Düm Tek Tek	172	2	177	4
2010	maNga	We Could Be The Same	118	1	170	2
2011	Yüksek Sadakat	Live It Up	47	13	-	-
2012	Can Bonomo	Love Me Back	80	5	112	7

Ukraine

Year	Artist	Song	Semi-Final Points	Semi-Final Position	Final Points	Final Position
2003	Olexandr	Hasta La Vista			30	14
2004	Ruslana	Wild Dances	256	2	280	1
2005	Greenjolly	Razom Nas Bahato	-	-	30	19
2006	Tina Karol	Show Me Your Love	146	6	145	7
2007	Verka Serduchka	Dancing Lasha Tumbai	-	-	235	2
2008	Ani Lorak	Shady Lady	152	1	230	2
2009	Svetlana Loboda	Be my Valentine! (Anti-crisis Girl)	80	6	76	12
2010	Alyosha	Sweet People	77	7	108	10
2011	Mika Newton	Angel	81	6	159	4
2012	Gaitana	Be My Guest	64	8	65	15
2013	Zlata Ognevich	Gravity	140	3	214	3
2014	Mariya Yaremchuk	Tick-Tock	118	5	113	6
2015	-	-	-	-	-	-
2016	Jamala	1944	287	2	534	1
2017	O Torvald	Time	-	-	36	24
2018	Melovin	Under The Ladder	179	6	130	17
2019	-	-	-	-	-	-
2021	Go_A	Shum	267	2	364	5

United Kingdom

Year	Artist	Song	Semi-Final Points	Semi-Final Position	Final Points	Final Position
1957	Patricia Bredin	All			6	7
1958	-	-			-	-
1959	Pearl Carr & Teddy Johnson	Sing Little Birdie			16	2
1960	Bryan Johnson	Looking High, High, High			25	2
1961	The Allisons	Are You Sure?			24	2
1962	Ronnie Carroll	Ring-a-ding Girl			10	4
1963	Ronnie Carroll	Say Wonderful Things			28	4
1964	Matt Monro	I Love The Little Things			17	2
1965	Kathy Kirby	I Belong			26	2
1966	Kenneth McKellar	A Man Without Love			8	9
1967	Sandie Shaw	Puppet On A String			47	1
1968	Cliff Richard	Congratulations			28	2
1969	Lulu	Boom Bang-a-bang			18	1
1970	Mary Hopkin	Knock, Knock (Who's There?)			26	2
1971	Clodagh Rodgers	Jack In The Box			98	4
1972	The New Seekers	Beg, Steal Or Borrow			114	2
1973	Cliff Richard	Power To All Our Friends			123	3

United Kingdom (continued)

Year	Artist	Song	Semi-Final Points	Semi-Final Position	Final Points	Final Position
1974	Olivia Newton-John	Long Live Love			14	4
1975	The Shadows	Let Me Be The One			138	2
1976	Brotherhood of Man	Save Your Kisses For Me			164	1
1977	Lynsey de Paul & Mike Moran	Rock Bottom			121	2
1978	Co-Co	The Bad Old Days			61	11
1979	Black Lace	Mary Ann			73	7
1980	Prima Donna	Love Enough For Two			106	3
1981	Bucks Fizz	Making Your Mind Up			136	1
1982	Bardo	One Step Further			76	7
1983	Sweet Dreams	I'm Never Giving Up			79	6
1984	Belle & The Devotions	Love Games			63	7
1985	Vikki	Love Is...			100	4
1986	Ryder	Runner In The Night			72	7
1987	Rikki	Only The Light			47	13
1988	Scott Fitzgerald	Go			136	2
1989	Live Report	Why Do I Always Get It Wrong			130	2
1990	Emma	Give A Little Love Back To The World			87	6
1991	Samantha Janus	A Message To Your Heart			47	10
1992	Michael Ball	One Step Out Of Time			139	2
1993	Sonia	Better The Devil You Know			164	2
1994	Frances Ruffelle	We Will Be Free (Lonely Symphony)			63	10
1995	Love City Groove	Love City Groove			76	10
1996	Gina G	Just A Little Bit			77	8
1997	Katrina & The Waves	Love Shine A Light			227	1
1998	Imaani	Where Are You?			166	2
1999	Precious	Say It Again			38	14
2000	Nicki French	Don't Play That Song Again			28	16
2001	Lindsay D	No Dream Impossible			28	15
2002	Jessica Garlick	Come Back			111	3
2003	Jemini	Cry Baby			0	26
2004	James Fox	Hold On To Our Love	-	-	29	16
2005	Javine	Touch My Fire	-	-	18	22
2006	Daz Sampson	Teenage Life	-	-	25	19
2007	Scooch	Flying The Flag (For You)	-	-	19	22
2008	Andy Abraham	Even If	-	-	14	25
2009	Jade Ewen	It's My Time	-	-	173	5
2010	Josh Dubovie	That Sounds Good To Me	-	-	10	25
2011	Blue	I Can	-	-	100	11
2012	Engelbert Humperdinck	Love Will Set You Free	-	-	12	25
2013	Bonnie Tyler	Believe in Me	-	-	23	19
2014	Molly	Children of the Universe	-	-	40	17
2015	Electro Velvet	Still in Love with You	-	-	5	24
2016	Joe And Jake	You're Not Alone	-	-	62	24
2017	Lucie Jones	Never Give Up On You	-	-	111	15
2018	SuRie	Storm	-	-	48	24
2019	Michael Rice	Bigger Than Us	-	-	11	26
2021	James Newman	Embers	-	-	0	26

Yugoslavia

Year	Artist	Song	Semi-Final Points	Semi-Final Position	Final Points	Final Position
1961	Ljiljana Petrovic	Neke Davne Zvezde			9	8
1962	Lola Novakovic	Ne Pali Svetlo U Sumrak			10	4
1963	Vice Vukov	Brodovi			3	11
1964	Sabahudin Kurt	Zivot Je Sklopio Krug			0	13
1965	Vice Vukov	Ceznja			2	12
1966	Berta Ambroz	Brez Besed			9	7
1967	Lado Leskovar	Vse Roze Sveta			7	8
1968	Luci Kapurso & Hamo Hajdarhodzic	Jedan Dan			8	7
1969	Ivan	Pozdrav Svijetu			5	13
1970	Eva Sršen	Pridi, Dala Ti Bom Cvet			4	11
1971	Krunoslav Slabinac	Tvoj Djecak Je Tuzan			68	14
1972	Tereza	Muzika I Ti			87	9

Yugoslavia (continued)

			Semi-Final		Final	
Year	Artist	Song	Points	Position	Points	Position
1973	Zdravko Colic	Gori Vatra			65	15
1974	Korni	Generacija 42			6	12
1975	Pepel In Kri	Dan Ljubezni			22	13
1976	Ambasadori	Ne Mogu Skriti Svoju Bol			10	18
1977	-	-			-	-
1978	-	-			-	-
1979	-	-			-	-
1980	-	-			-	-
1981	Seid-Memic Vajta	Leila			35	15
1982	Aska	Halo Halo			21	14
1983	Danijel	Dzuli			125	4
1984	Vlado & Isolda	Ciao Amore			26	18
1985	-	-			-	-
1986	Doris Dragovic	Zeljo Moja			49	11
1987	Novi Fosili	Ja Sam Za Ples			92	4
1988	Srebrna Krila	Mangup			87	6
1989	Riva	Rock Me			137	1
1990	Tajci	Hajde Da Ludujemo			81	7
1991	Baby Doll	Brazil			1	21
1992	Extra Nena	Ljubim Te Pesmama			44	12

SECTION 4

Statistics and Records

Facts & Figures and Full Analysis of the Results

Eurovision Winners - Which countries are best at predicting the winner?

1. Under the 1975-2015 scoring system

Contest & Winner

	Netherlands 1975	United Kingdom 1976	France 1977	Israel 1978	Israel 1979	Ireland 1980	United Kingdom 1981	Germany 1982	Luxembourg 1983	Sweden 1984	Norway 1985	Belgium 1986	Ireland 1987	Switzerland 1988	Yugoslavia 1989	Italy 1990	Sweden 1991	Ireland 1992	Ireland 1993	Ireland 1994	Norway 1995	Ireland 1996	United Kingdom 1997
Albania	-	-	-	-	-	-	-	-	-	-	-	-	-	-	-	-	-	-	-	-	-	-	-
Andorra	-	-	-	-	-	-	-	-	-	-	-	-	-	-	-	-	-	-	-	-	-	-	-
Armenia	-	-	-	-	-	-	-	-	-	-	-	-	-	-	-	-	-	-	-	-	-	-	-
Australia	-	-	-	-	-	-	-	-	-	-	-	-	-	-	-	-	-	-	-	-	-	-	-
Austria	-	10	7	8	8	10	4	1	5	12	12	6	12	0	10	7	10	10	8	10	0	7	12
Azerbaijan	-	-	-	-	-	-	-	-	-	-	-	-	-	-	-	-	-	-	-	-	-	-	-
Belarus	-	-	-	-	-	-	-	-	-	-	-	-	-	-	-	-	-	-	-	-	-	-	-
Belgium	3	12	4	12	2	12	8	10	8	7	12	W	12	4	10	8	10	7	2	-	5	3	-
Bosnia-H	-	-	-	-	-	-	-	-	-	-	-	-	-	-	-	-	-	-	8	10	1	12	10
Bulgaria	-	-	-	-	-	-	-	-	-	-	-	-	-	-	-	-	-	-	-	-	-	-	-
Croatia	-	-	-	-	-	-	-	-	-	-	-	-	-	-	-	-	-	-	6	12	0	0	12
Cyprus	-	-	-	-	-	-	4	12	10	12	0	10	8	-	5	12	6	5	7	8	7	6	7
Czech Republic	-	-	-	-	-	-	-	-	-	-	-	-	-	-	-	-	-	-	-	-	-	-	-
Denmark	-	-	-	6	6	12	10	12	2	12	12	10	5	0	10	6	12	10	6	-	2	-	12
Estonia	-	-	-	-	-	-	-	-	-	-	-	-	-	-	-	-	-	-	-	10	-	12	10
Finland	10	10	12	10	12	8	3	10	8	8	4	12	12	5	7	8	8	10	3	7	-	10	-
France	5	7	W	8	1	8	7	-	12	6	2	12	1	1	3	4	0	0	10	8	10	6	12
Georgia	-	-	-	-	-	-	-	-	-	-	-	-	-	-	-	-	-	-	-	-	-	-	-
Germany	8	8	12	12	0	12	4	W	8	12	12	1	6	12	1	6	12	10	5	12	4	-	10
Greece	-	12	7	5	4	12	6	-	12	-	1	-	0	10	0	10	0	12	6	0	12	10	10
Hungary	-	-	-	-	-	-	-	-	-	-	-	-	-	-	-	-	-	-	-	10	6	-	12
Iceland	-	-	-	-	-	-	-	-	-	-	10	0	7	6	3	12	7	3	12	12	0	8
Ireland	8	3	10	8	12	W	10	12	-	12	12	12	W	10	12	12	3	W	W	W	10	W	12
Israel	12	12	10	W	W	-	12	12	12	-	12	5	4	4	12	1	10	0	5	-	10	-	-
Italy	1	4	10	8	0	1	-	-	12	6	6	-	12	7	0	W	0	2	12	-	-	-	8
Latvia	-	-	-	-	-	-	-	-	-	-	-	-	-	-	-	-	-	-	-	-	-	-	-
Lithuania	-	-	-	-	-	-	-	-	-	-	-	-	-	-	-	-	-	-	-	10	-	-	-
Luxembourg	10	8	10	12	8	7	5	0	W	6	7	10	10	1	5	10	7	10	7	-	-	-	-
Malta	12	-	-	-	-	-	-	-	-	-	-	-	-	-	-	-	0	12	12	5	6	4	1
Moldova	-	-	-	-	-	-	-	-	-	-	-	-	-	-	-	-	-	-	-	-	-	-	-
Monaco	10	10	4	3	8	-	-	-	-	-	-	-	-	-	-	-	-	-	-	-	-	-	-
Montenegro	-	-	-	-	-	-	-	-	-	-	-	-	-	-	-	-	-	-	-	-	-	-	-
Morocco	-	-	-	-	0	-	-	-	-	-	-	-	-	-	-	-	-	-	-	-	-	-	-
Netherlands	W	10	8	12	1	6	12	6	1	10	-	10	12	10	8	8	-	10	10	12	-	12	12
Nth Macedonia	-	-	-	-	-	-	-	-	-	-	-	-	-	-	-	-	-	-	-	-	-	-	-
Norway	12	12	3	8	12	12	3	10	0	10	0	8	8	8	7	0	8	7	12	12	W	10	6
Poland	-	-	-	-	-	-	-	-	-	-	-	-	-	-	-	-	-	-	-	8	12	12	10
Portugal	7	12	5	10	12	5	6	12	12	4	0	12	8	12	4	10	10	4	6	12	12	8	7
Romania	-	-	-	-	-	-	-	-	-	-	-	-	-	-	-	-	-	-	-	8	-	-	-
Russia	-	-	-	-	-	-	-	-	-	-	-	-	-	-	-	-	-	-	-	12	12	-	12
San Marino	-	-	-	-	-	-	-	-	-	-	-	-	-	-	-	-	-	-	-	-	-	-	-
Serbia**	8	10	-	-	-	-	10	12	12	4	-	10	6	6	W	6	6	2	-	-	-	-	-
Slovakia	-	-	-	-	-	-	-	-	-	-	-	-	-	-	-	-	-	-	-	6	-	7	-
Slovenia	-	-	-	-	-	-	-	-	-	-	-	-	-	-	-	-	-	-	12	-	7	12	8
Spain	12	12	10	6	12	7	8	12	7	4	1	10	10	8	0	12	4	1	10	10	4	0	5
Sweden	12	-	6	0	10	7	8	8	10	W	12	6	12	12	8	10	W	10	12	10	0	7	12
Switzerland	6	12	12	12	5	12	8	12	3	10	6	10	12	W	5	8	10	6	12	12	-	12	12
Turkey	4	-	-	12	-	0	8	12	8	3	0	12	10	12	8	6	12	1	-	12	12	7
Ukraine	-	-	-	-	-	-	-	-	-	-	-	-	-	-	-	-	-	-	-	-	-	-	-
United Kingdom	12	W	6	5	12	12	W	8	0	7	12	10	12	10	12	0	12	8	12	10	4	0	W

*W denotes the winner, which is excluded from the average calcuations. **Serbia includes Serbia-Montenegro & Yugoslavia

Contest & Winner

	Israel 1998	Sweden 1999	Denmark 2000	Estonia 2001	Latvia 2002	Turkey 2003	Ukraine 2004	Greece 2005	Finland 2006	Serbia 2007	Russia 2008	Norway 2009	Germany 2010	Azerbaijan 2011	Sweden 2012	Denmark 2013	Austria 2014	Sweden 2015	Average points given to winner*	% of times 12 points given to winner	% of times 0 points given to winner	
	-	-	-	-	-	-	5	12	0	1	6	7	10	8	5	1	5	7	5.6	8%	8%	Albania
	-	-	-	-	-	-	10	4	10	0	5	10	-	-	-	-	-	-	6.5	0%	17%	Andorra
	-	-	-	-	-	-	-	-	0	7	12	8	0	0	-	4	0	7	4.2	11%	44%	Armenia
	-	-	-	-	-	-	-	-	-	-	-	-	-	-	-	-	-	12	12.0	100%	0%	Australia
	-	6	10	-	10	12	4	4	-	12	-	-	-	8	12	5	W	7	7.8	21%	6%	Austria
	-	-	-	-	-	-	-	-	-	-	8	8	1	W	7	5	1	6	5.1	0%	0%	Azerbaijan
	-	-	-	-	-	-	10	0	7	7	12	12	0	6	6	1	0	10	5.9	17%	25%	Belarus
	10	7	10	-	8	12	5	12	8	7	3	10	10	3	12	10	12	12	8.2	27%	0%	Belgium
	-	12	-	4	5	12	6	6	7	12	4	10	8	8	8	-	-	-	7.9	22%	0%	Bosnia-H
	-	-	-	-	-	-	-	12	5	6	6	2	3	0	8	2	-	-	4.9	11%	11%	Bulgaria
	0	0	0	2	2	10	8	5	10	12	6	8	6	10	7	10	-	-	6.0	14%	24%	Croatia
	10	6	4	-	4	8	8	12	5	3	8	10	4	8	10	7	-	10	7.2	12%	3%	Cyprus
	-	-	-	-	-	-	-	-	-	8	7	3	-	-	-	-	-	-	7.0	0%	0%	Czech Republic
	-	10	W	8	7	-	5	2	12	6	0	12	12	0	12	W	8	12	7.8	34%	9%	Denmark
	7	12	8	W	12	0	12	0	12	0	12	12	12	8	12	8	4	10	8.7	45%	15%	Estonia
	10	-	10	-	6	-	8	3	W	12	10	8	12	5	12	7	12	12	8.7	26%	0%	Finland
	12	3	7	8	8	10	2	8	8	8	1	8	3	6	12	12	10	8	6.6	15%	5%	France
	-	-	-	-	-	-	-	-	-	6	8	-	0	8	7	10	7	-	6.8	0%	13%	Georgia
	7	2	12	10	12	10	6	12	10	8	7	12	W	0	12	10	7	10	8.3	34%	5%	Germany
	10	-	-	12	10	7	7	W	12	4	7	10	2	5	6	7	12	4	7.2	24%	12%	Greece
	0	-	-	-	-	-	-	12	-	12	10	12	-	7	12	10	10	10	9.5	38%	8%	Hungary
	-	10	12	10	-	3	12	12	2	7	0	12	3	8	12	12	10	12	7.8	36%	11%	Iceland
	6	5	12	10	-	0	7	2	10	4	5	8	8	0	12	12	12	10	8.5	36%	6%	Ireland
	W	8	12	6	12	7	12	7	7	3	12	12	0	4	12	8	12	10	8.4	42%	6%	Israel
	-	-	-	-	-	-	-	-	-	-	-	-	-	0	0	12	12	12	6.0	29%	24%	Italy
	-	-	12	12	W	0	12	0	8	3	12	12	12	2	12	6	6	12	8.6	57%	14%	Latvia
	-	3	-	12	12	-	12	1	10	0	12	12	10	8	10	2	10	10	8.4	31%	6%	Lithuania
	-	-	-	-	-	-	-	-	-	-	-	-	-	-	-	-	-	-	7.4	6%	6%	Luxembourg
	12	12	8	12	7	4	8	6	7	8	8	8	4	12	6	6	10	10	7.7	27%	4%	Malta
	-	-	-	-	-	-	-	4	6	5	10	8	0	10	7	6	7	8	6.5	0%	9%	Moldova
	-	-	-	-	-	-	6	0	0	-	-	-	-	-	-	-	-	-	5.1	0%	25%	Monaco
	-	-	-	-	-	-	-	-	-	12	8	10	-	-	7	10	2	5	7.7	14%	0%	Montenegro
	-	-	-	-	-	-	-	-	-	-	-	-	-	-	-	-	-	-	0.0	0%	100%	Morocco
	6	8	10	12	-	12	7	10	7	8	1	12	4	6	12	10	12	10	8.8	31%	0%	Netherlands
	8	-	0	-	7	-	8	7	6	12	6	8	8	0	6	12	3	5	6.4	13%	13%	Nth Macedonia
	3	12	10	10	-	10	7	4	12	10	5	W	12	0	12	7	10	12	8.0	29%	11%	Norway
	10	6	-	12	-	2	12	1	12	8	6	12	7	8	-	-	0	12	8.3	39%	6%	Poland
	12	10	-	0	-	8	10	3	6	5	6	5	1	8	3	-	12	8	9.3	32%	6%	Portugal
	7	-	1	-	0	10	6	10	4	6	10	5	3	10	10	6	8	8	6.6	0%	6%	Romania
	-	-	12	6	10	0	12	4	8	5	W	12	6	12	12	4	5	8	8.4	44%	6%	Russia
	-	-	-	-	-	-	-	-	-	-	0	-	-	10	3	0	0	7	3.3	0%	50%	San Marino
	-	-	-	-	-	-	10	12	7	W	10	10	8	0	10	12	-	8	9.4	21%	5%	Serbia**
	0	-	-	-	-	-	-	-	-	-	-	10	12	7	12	-	-	-	7.7	29%	14%	Slovakia
	7	7	-	12	5	10	8	2	8	12	7	12	10	0	10	12	12	12	8.8	38%	5%	Slovenia
	12	6	10	8	12	3	8	8	10	1	5	12	12	0	12	8	12	8	7.6	27%	7%	Spain
	5	0	12	8	5	8	10	12	12	10	0	12	12	3	W	10	12	W	8.4	33%	11%	Sweden
	10	-	10	-	8	-	0	7	8	12	0	8	12	1	7	3	12	12	8.5	39%	6%	Switzerland
	5	6	1	12	6	W	12	12	7	0	5	3	10	12	6	-	-	-	7.5	33%	9%	Turkey
	-	-	-	-	-	2	W	0	7	6	12	12	5	10	6	5	8	-	7.3	20%	10%	Ukraine
	5	12	12	12	8	7	5	12	12	0	0	10	4	0	12	12	12	12	8.2	45%	16%	United Kingdom

Eurovision Winners - Which countries are best at predicting the winner?

2. Under the current scoring system, showing separate jury and public voting for each year's winner

	\<\< Jury voting \>\>								\<\< Public voting \>\>							
	Ukraine 2016	Portugal 2017	Israel 2018	Netherlands 2019	Italy 2021	Average points given to winner*	% of times 12 points given to winner	% of times 0 points given to winner	Ukraine 2016	Portugal 2017	Israel 2018	Netherlands 2019	Italy 2021	Average points given to winner*	% of times 12 points given to winner	% of times 0 points given to winner
Albania	0	6	5	0	4	3.0	0%	40%	6	8	1	7	10	6.4	0%	0%
Andorra	-	-	-	-	-	-	-	-	-	-	-	-	-	-	-	-
Armenia	0	12	8	6	-	6.5	25%	25%	10	10	10	10	-	10.0	0%	0%
Australia	2	7	6	6	6	5.4	0%	0%	8	7	12	6	7	8.0	20%	0%
Austria	0	8	12	8	6	6.8	20%	20%	10	12	7	7	8	8.8	20%	0%
Azerbaijan	10	8	1	0	0	3.8	0%	40%	10	8	12	7	10	9.4	20%	0%
Belarus	7	10	0	6	-	5.8	0%	25%	10	7	8	10	-	8.8	0%	0%
Belgium	3	8	6	6	2	5.0	0%	0%	2	12	10	12	8	8.8	40%	0%
Bosnia-H	12	-	-	-	-	12.0	100%	0%	7	-	-	-	-	7.0	0%	0%
Bulgaria	0	0	4	-	10	3.5	0%	50%	10	7	10	-	12	9.8	25%	0%
Croatia	0	7	10	6	12	7.0	20%	20%	10	10	6	4	10	8.0	0%	0%
Cyprus	0	8	0	5	8	4.2	0%	40%	7	7	10	6	10	8.0	0%	0%
Czech Republic	0	12	12	6	6	7.2	40%	20%	12	8	10	4	6	8.0	20%	0%
Denmark	12	10	3	7	0	6.4	20%	20%	3	5	0	7	5	4.0	0%	20%
Estonia	7	8	0	7	3	5.0	0%	20%	8	10	0	8	8	6.8	0%	20%
Finland	0	8	12	8	6	6.8	20%	20%	12	12	7	5	8	8.8	40%	0%
France	0	12	12	12	0	7.2	60%	40%	10	12	12	5	10	9.8	40%	0%
Georgia	12	12	3	8	12	9.4	60%	0%	10	8	12	5	8	8.6	20%	0%
Germany	7	10	1	8	6	6.4	0%	0%	6	12	10	7	7	8.4	20%	0%
Greece	2	5	4	0	4	3.0	0%	20%	6	8	6	6	10	7.2	0%	0%
Hungary	0	12	6	1	-	4.8	25%	25%	12	7	10	8	-	9.3	25%	0%
Iceland	0	12	8	7	7	6.8	20%	20%	0	12	7	5	5	5.8	20%	20%
Ireland	0	5	7	8	0	4.0	0%	40%	4	10	6	8	6	6.8	0%	0%
Israel	12	12	W	12	0	9.0	75%	25%	8	12	W	2	7	7.3	25%	0%
Italy	10	5	2	0	W	4.3	0%	25%	12	5	7	5	W	7.3	25%	0%
Latvia	12	12	0	12	8	8.8	60%	20%	10	10	8	5	7	8.0	0%	0%
Lithuania	8	12	6	12	10	9.6	40%	0%	10	12	1	7	10	8.0	20%	0%
Luxembourg	-	-	-	-	-	-	-	-	-	-	-	-	-	-	-	-
Malta	0	10	6	7	0	4.6	0%	40%	4	8	8	10	12	8.4	20%	0%
Moldova	12	7	10	3	0	6.4	20%	20%	10	6	12	6	8	8.4	20%	0%
Monaco	-	-	-	-	-	-	-	-	-	-	-	-	-	-	-	-
Montenegro	0	0	0	0	-	0.0	0%	0%	8	8	1	1	-	4.5	0%	0%
Morocco	-	-	-	-	-	-	-	-	-	-	-	-	-	-	-	-
Netherlands	3	12	5	W	0	5.0	25%	25%	7	12	10	W	2	7.8	25%	0%
Nth Macedonia	12	10	1	7	10	8.0	20%	0%	6	7	3	7	8	6.2	0%	0%
Norway	4	10	0	7	5	5.2	0%	20%	4	12	7	8	7	7.6	20%	0%
Poland	12	12	0	0	5	5.8	40%	40%	12	10	10	10	10	10.4	20%	0%
Portugal	-	W	1	12	3	5.3	33%	0%	-	W	1	8	7	5.3	0%	0%
Romania	-	6	0	5	3	3.5	0%	25%	-	7	8	12	10	9.3	25%	0%
Russia	0	-	8	0	10	4.5	0%	50%	10	-	10	5	10	8.8	0%	0%
San Marino	12	12	12	3	10	9.8	60%	0%	12	7	12	6	12	9.8	60%	0%
Serbia	12	12	2	0	8	6.8	40%	20%	7	8	7	3	12	7.4	20%	0%
Slovakia	-	-	-	-	-	-	-	-	-	-	-	-	-	-	-	-
Slovenia	12	12	1	6	12	8.6	60%	0%	7	8	0	5	10	6.0	0%	20%
Spain	0	12	10	8	0	6.0	20%	40%	7	12	12	8	10	9.8	40%	0%
Sweden	0	12	7	12	10	8.2	40%	20%	7	10	10	6	3	7.2	0%	0%
Switzerland	6	12	1	10	8	7.4	20%	0%	4	12	5	6	10	7.4	20%	0%
Turkey	-	-	-	-	-	-	-	-	-	-	-	-	-	-	-	-
Ukraine	W	10	10	-	12	10.7	33%	0%	W	10	12	-	12	11.3	67%	0%
United Kingdom	10	12	10	6	0	7.6	20%	20%	5	8	7	4	3	5.4	0%	0%

*W denotes the winner, which is excluded from the average calcuations.

Eurovision Winners - Are juries better than the public at predicting the winner?

(since the introduction of the current points system in 2016)

12 Points given to Winners by JURIES	Times	12 Points given to Winners by the PUBLIC	Times
Albania	0	Albania	0
Armenia	1	Armenia	0
Australia	0	Australia	1
Austria	1	Austria	1
Azerbaijan	0	Azerbaijan	1
Belarus	0	Belarus	0
Belgium	0	Belgium	2
Bosnia-H	1	Bosnia-H	0
Bulgaria	0	Bulgaria	1
Croatia	1	Croatia	0
Cyprus	0	Cyprus	0
Czech Republic	2	Czech Republic	1
Denmark	1	Denmark	0
Estonia	0	Estonia	0
Finland	1	Finland	2
France	3	France	2
Georgia	3	Georgia	1
Germany	0	Germany	1
Greece	0	Greece	0
Hungary	1	Hungary	1
Iceland	1	Iceland	1
Ireland	0	Ireland	0
Israel	3	Israel	1
Italy	0	Italy	1
Latvia	3	Latvia	0
Lithuania	2	Lithuania	1
Malta	0	Malta	1
Moldova	1	Moldova	1
Montenegro	0	Montenegro	0
Netherlands	1	Netherlands	1
Nth Macedonia	1	Nth Macedonia	0
Norway	0	Norway	1
Poland	2	Poland	1
Portugal	1	Portugal	0
Romania	0	Romania	1
Russia	0	Russia	0
San Marino	3	San Marino	3
Serbia	2	Serbia	1
Slovenia	3	Slovenia	0
Spain	1	Spain	2
Sweden	2	Sweden	0
Switzerland	1	Switzerland	1
Ukraine	1	Ukraine	2
United Kingdom	1	United Kingdom	0
Total by Juries:	**44**	**Total by Public:**	**33**

Eurovision Winners - Giving the winners zero points: are juries worse then the public?

(since the introduction of the current points system in 2016)

Zero Points given to Winners by JURIES	Times	Zero Points given to Winners by the PUBLIC	Times
Albania	2	Albania	0
Armenia	1	Armenia	0
Australia	0	Australia	0
Austria	1	Austria	0
Azerbaijan	2	Azerbaijan	0
Belarus	1	Belarus	0
Belgium	0	Belgium	0
Bosnia-H	0	Bosnia-H	0
Bulgaria	2	Bulgaria	0
Croatia	1	Croatia	0
Cyprus	2	Cyprus	0
Czech Republic	1	Czech Republic	0
Denmark	1	Denmark	1
Estonia	1	Estonia	1
Finland	1	Finland	0
France	2	France	0
Georgia	0	Georgia	0
Germany	0	Germany	0
Greece	1	Greece	0
Hungary	1	Hungary	0
Iceland	1	Iceland	1
Ireland	2	Ireland	0
Israel	1	Israel	0
Italy	1	Italy	0
Latvia	1	Latvia	0
Lithuania	0	Lithuania	0
Malta	2	Malta	0
Moldova	1	Moldova	0
Montenegro	4	Montenegro	0
Netherlands	1	Netherlands	0
Nth Macedonia	0	Nth Macedonia	0
Norway	1	Norway	0
Poland	2	Poland	0
Portugal	0	Portugal	0
Romania	1	Romania	0
Russia	2	Russia	0
San Marino	0	San Marino	0
Serbia	1	Serbia	0
Slovenia	0	Slovenia	1
Spain	2	Spain	0
Sweden	1	Sweden	0
Switzerland	0	Switzerland	0
Ukraine	0	Ukraine	0
United Kingdom	1	United Kingdom	0
Total by Juries:	**45**	**Total by Public:**	**4**

Eurovision 2021: How Many Jurors Placed the Overall Winner First?

Each country's jury votes were calculated based on 5 individual's scores. So how many of these 5 jurors thought the Italy was the best song? The ranking of Italy by each juror is given below, along with the overall ranking and points given by each jury as a group.

Jury	Juror 1	Juror 2	Juror 3	Juror 4	Juror 5	Ranked winner first?	Jury ranking	Points given
Albania	16th	4th	21st	7th	3rd	0	7th	4
Australia	7th	24th	4th	3rd	4th	0	5th	6
Austria	11th	7th	3rd	2nd	1st	1	5th	6
Azerbaijan	14th	19th	6th	14th	6th	0	14th	0
Belgium	17th	15th	16th	6th	7th	0	9th	2
Bulgaria	5th	4th	1st	7th	3rd	1	2nd	10
Croatia	1st	2nd	3rd	2nd	4th	1	1st	12
Cyprus	4th	4th	5th	4th	5th	0	3rd	8
Czech Republic	1st	14th	7th	3rd	7th	1	5th	6
Denmark	23rd	14th	23rd	22nd	10th	0	24th	0
Estonia	15th	5th	13th	21st	4th	0	8th	3
Finland	3rd	4th	10th	4th	4th	0	5th	6
France	23rd	10th	3rd	8th	22nd	0	11th	0
Georgia	1st	1st	3rd	3rd	1st	3	1st	12
Germany	16th	3rd	7th	13th	1st	1	5th	6
Greece	15th	1st	13th	15th	12th	1	7th	4
Iceland	17th	5th	2nd	5th	2nd	0	4th	7
Ireland	24th	4th	15th	24th	21st	0	17th	0
Israel	17th	18th	8th	11th	19th	0	15th	0
Italy	-	-	-	-	-	-	-	-
Latvia	2nd	4th	11th	2nd	12th	0	3rd	8
Lithuania	1st	2nd	4th	6th	4th	1	2nd	10
Malta	18th	9th	13th	4th	8th	0	11th	0
Moldova	18th	24th	9th	25th	18th	0	21st	0
Netherlands	12th	13th	17th	12th	12th	0	13th	0
North Macedonia	7th	1st	3rd	1st	6th	2	2nd	10
Norway	7th	20th	12th	6th	3rd	0	6th	5
Poland	17th	22nd	7th	2nd	5th	0	6th	5
Portugal	12th	3rd	16th	1st	11th	1	8th	3
Romania	4th	12th	3rd	18th	18th	0	8th	3
Russia	1st	5th	2nd	7th	5th	1	2nd	10
San Marino	2nd	1st	5th	1st	4th	2	2nd	10
Serbia	7th	3rd	6th	9th	1st	1	3rd	8
Slovenia	3rd	7th	2nd	2nd	1st	1	1st	12
Spain	17th	12th	21st	14th	11th	0	13th	0
Sweden	5th	1st	3rd	20th	6th	1	2nd	10
Switzerland	14th	1st	14th	2nd	2nd	1	3rd	8
Ukraine	1st	2nd	4th	1st	1st	3	1st	12
United Kingdom	14th	24th	14th	15th	9th	0	17th	0

Number of jurors ranking the winner as their favourite:						23	12%	
Number of jurors placing the winner in the bottom 5:						10	5%	
Number of juries in which no-one ranked the winner first:						21	55%	

Eurovision 2021: Marcel Bezençon Awards

Press Award (given to the best act as judged by the accredited press and media)

Year	Country	Song	Artist	Position
2002	France	Il faut du temps	Sandrine François	5th
2003	Turkey	Everyway That I Can	Sertab Erener	1st
2004	Serbia & Montenegro	Lane moje	Željko Joksimovic	2nd
2005	Malta	Angel	Chiara	2nd
2006	Finland	Hard Rock Hallelujah	Lordi	1st
2007	Ukraine	Dancing Lasha Tumbai	Verka Serduchka	2nd
2008	Portugal	Senhora do mar (Negras águas)	Vânia Fernandes	13th
2009	Norway	Fairytale	Alexander Rybak	1st
2010	Israel	Milim	Harel Skaat	14th
2011	Finland	Da Da Dam	Paradise Oskar	21st
2012	Azerbaijan	When the Music Dies	Sabina Babayeva	4th
2013	Georgia	Waterfall	Nodi and Sophie	15th
2014	Austria	Rise Like a Phoenix	Conchita Wurst	1st
2015	Italy	Grande amore	Il Volo	3rd
2016	Russia	You Are the Only One	Sergey Lazarev	3rd
2017	Italy	Occidentali's Karma	Francesco Gabbani	6th
2018	France	Mercy	Madame Monsieur	13th
2019	Netherlands	Arcade	Duncan Laurence	1st
2021	France	Voilà	Barbara Pravi	2nd

Artistic Award (given to the best artist as judged by the commentators)

Year	Country	Song	Artist	Position
2002*	Sweden	Never Let It Go	Afro-dite	8th
2003*	Netherlands	One More Night	Esther Hart	13th
2004*	Ukraine	Wild Dances	Ruslana	1st
2005*	Greece	My Number One	Helena Paparizou	1st
2006*	Sweden	Invincible	Carola	5th
2007*	Serbia	Molitva	Marija Šerifovic	1st
2008*	Ukraine	Shady Lady	Ani Lorak	2nd
2009*	France	Et s'il fallait le faire	Patricia Kaas	8th
2010	Israel	Milim	Harel Skaat	14th
2011	Ireland	Lipstick	Jedward	8th
2012	Sweden	Euphoria	Loreen	1st
2013	Azerbaijan	Hold Me	Farid Mammadov	2nd
2014	Netherlands	Calm After the Storm	The Common Linnets	2nd
2015	Sweden	Heroes	Måns Zelmerlöw	1st
2016	Ukraine	1944	Jamala	1st
2017	Portugal	Amar pelos dois	Salvador Sobral	1st
2018	Cyprus	Fuego	Eleni Foureira	2nd
2019	Australia	Zero Gravity	Kate Miller-Heidke	9th
2021	France	Voilà	Barbara Pravi	2nd

* Awarded by previous winners until 2010

Composer Award (given to the best song as judged by a jury of participating composers)

Year	Country	Song	Artist	Position
2004	Cyprus	Lisa Andreas	Stronger Every Minute	5th
2005	Serbia & Montenegro	No Name	Zauvijek moja	7th
2006	Bosnia & Herzegovina	Hari Mata Hari	Lejla	3rd
2007	Hungary	Magdi Rúzsa	Unsubstantial Blues	9th
2008	Romania	Nico & Vlad	Pe-o margine de lume	20th
2009	Bosnia & Herzegovina	Regina	Bistra voda	9th
2010	Israel	Harel Skaat	Milim	14th
2011	France	Amaury Vassili	Sognu	15th
2012	Sweden	Loreen	Euphoria	1st
2013	Sweden	Robin Stjernberg	You	14th
2014	Netherlands	The Common Linnets	Calm After the Storm	2nd
2015	Norway	Mørland & Debrah Scarlett	A Monster Like Me	8th
2016	Australia	Dami Im	Sound of Silence	2nd
2017	Portugal	Amar pelos dois	Salvador Sobral	1st
2018	Bulgaria	Equinox	Bones	14th
2019	Italy	Soldi	Mahmood	2nd
2021	Switzerland	Tout l'Univers	Gjon's Tears	3rd

Eurovision 2021: OGAE Poll Results

How do the votes by members of OGAE compare to the final result? (Top ten countries shown)

2013

Position	OGAE Poll	Contest Position
1	Denmark	1
2	San Marino	SF
3	Norway	4
4	Germany	21
5	Italy	7
6	Netherlands	9
7	Ukraine	3
8	United Kingdom	19
9	Sweden	14
10	Russia	5

2014

Position	OGAE Poll	Contest Position
1	Sweden	3
2	Hungary	5
3	Israel	SF
4	Austria	1
5	United Kingdom	17
6	Armenia	4
7	Norway	8
8	Spain	10
9	Greece	20
10	Montenegro	19

2015

Position	OGAE Poll	Contest Position
1	Italy	3
2	Sweden	1
3	Estonia	7
4	Norway	8
5	Slovenia	14
6	Australia	5
7	Israel	9
8	Spain	21
9	Azerbaijan	12
10	Belgium	4

2016

Position	OGAE Poll	Contest Position
1	France	6
2	Russia	3
3	Australia	2
4	Bulgaria	4
5	Italy	16
6	Spain	22
7	Austria	13
8	Latvia	15
9	Ukraine	1
10	Hungary	19

2017

Position	OGAE Poll	Contest Position
1	Italy	6
2	Belgium	4
3	Sweden	5
4	France	12
5	Estonia	SF
6	Portugal	1
7	Bulgaria	2
8	FYR Macedonia	SF
9	Israel	23
10	Finland	SF

2018

Position	OGAE Poll	Contest Position
1	Israel	1
2	France	13
3	Finland	25
4	Australia	20
5	Czech Republic	6
6	Bulgaria	14
7	Belgium	SF
8	Greece	SF
9	Cyprus	2
10	Denmark	9

2019

Position	OGAE Poll	Contest Position
1	Italy	2
2	Switzerland	4
3	Netherlands	1
4	Norway	6
5	Cyprus	13
6	Sweden	5
7	Azerbaijan	8
8	Iceland	10
9	Russia	3
10	Greece	21

2021

Position	OGAE Poll	Contest Position
1	Malta	7
2	Switzerland	3
3	France	2
4	Lithuania	8
5	Cyprus	16
6	San Marino	22
7	Sweden	14
8	Italy	1
9	Ukraine	5
10	Azerbaijan	20

Source: OGAEinternational.com. OGAE is an international Eurovision fan organisation.

Eurovision 2021: Which Countries Selected their artists from ESC2020?
Internal Selection or National Competition?

Which method of choosing a representative is most popular? And which is most successful? (Artists only)

An unusual year in 2021, as most countries used internal selection to bring back the artists who would have represented their countries in the cancelled 2020 show.

Spare a thought for those artists who did not get to perform despite being selected last year, especially those who were internally "deselected".

Most impressively, both Uku Suviste for Estonia and The Roop for Lithuania qualified through their national competitions for the second year running.

Country	2021	Same Act as 2020?	2021 Position
Albania	Competition	No	21
Australia	Internal	Yes	SF
Austria	Internal	Yes	SF
Azerbaijan	Internal	Yes	20
Belgium	Internal	Yes	19
Bulgaria	Internal	Yes	11
Croatia	Competition	No	SF
Cyprus	Internal	Yes	16
Czech Republic	Internal	Yes	SF
Denmark	Competition	No	SF
Estonia	Competition	Yes	SF
Finland	Competition	No	6
France	Competition	No	2
Georgia	Internal	Yes	SF
Germany	Internal	No	25
Greece	Internal	Yes	10
Iceland	Internal	Yes	4
Ireland	Internal	Yes	SF
Israel	Internal	Yes	17
Italy	Competition	No	1
Latvia	Internal	Yes	SF
Lithuania	Competition	Yes	8
Malta	Internal	Yes	7
Moldova	Internal	Yes	13
Netherlands	Internal	Yes	23
North Macedonia	Internal	Yes	SF
Norway	Competition	No	18
Poland	Internal	No	SF
Portugal	Competition	No	12
Romania	Internal	Yes	SF
Russia	Competition	No	9
San Marino	Internal	Yes	22
Serbia	Internal	Yes	15
Slovenia	Internal	Yes	SF
Spain	Internal	Yes	24
Sweden	Competition	No	14
Switzerland	Internal	Yes	3
Ukraine	Internal	Yes	5
United Kingdom	Internal	Yes	26

% Internal Selection	69%	(2019: 34%)
% National Competition	31%	(2019: 66%)
% Countries bringing back their 2020 Act		69%

Previous Years' Top 3 (in final)

Year	Winner	2nd	3rd
2019	internal	competition	internal
2018	competition	internal	internal
2017	competition	internal	competition
2016	competition	internal	internal
2015	competition	internal	competition
2014	internal	internal	competition
2013	competition	competition	competition
2012	competition	competition	internal
2011	competition	competition	competition
2010	competition	internal	competition
2009	competition	competition	internal
2008	competition	internal	competition
2007	competition	competition	internal
2006	competition	internal	internal

Previous Years' Bottom 3 (in final)

Year	Last	2nd Last	3rd Last
2019	competition	competition	competition
2018	competition	internal	competition
2017	competition	competition	competition
2016	competition	internal	competition
2015	competition	competition	internal
2014	competition	competition	internal
2013	competition	internal	competition
2012	competition	internal	competition
2011	competition	competition	competition
2010	competition	internal	competition
2009	competition	competition	competition
2008	competition	competition	competition
2007	internal	competition	competition
2006	competition	competition	competition

Eurovision Winners - Average age and gender (solo performers & duos only)

Year	Winner	Performer	Date of Contest	Date of Birth	Age
1956	Switzerland	Lys Assia	24 May 1956	03 March 1924	32
1957	Netherlands	Corry Brokken	03 March 1957	03 December 1932	24
1958	France	André Claveau	12 March 1958	17 December 1911	46
1959	Netherlands	Teddy Scholten	11 March 1959	11 May 1926	32
1960	France	Jacqueline Boyer	29 March 1960	23 April 1941	18
1961	Luxembourg	Jean-Claude Pascal	18 March 1961	24 October 1927	33
1962	France	Isabelle Aubret	18 March 1962	28 July 1938	23
1963	Denmark	Grethe and Jørgen Ingmann - Grethe	23 March 1963	17 June 1938	24
		Grethe and Jørgen Ingmann - Jørgen	23 March 1963	26 April 1925	37
1964	Italy	Gigliola Cinquetti	21 March 1964	20 December 1947	16
1965	Luxembourg	France Gall	20 March 1965	09 October 1947	17
1966	Austria	Udo Jürgens	05 March 1966	30 September 1934	31
1967	United Kingdom	Sandie Shaw	08 April 1967	26 February 1947	20
1968	Spain	Massiel	06 April 1968	02 August 1947	20
1969	Spain	Salomé	29 March 1969	21 June 1943	25
	United Kingdom	Lulu	29 March 1969	03 November 1948	20
	Netherlands	Lenny Kuhr	29 March 1969	22 February 1950	19
	France	Frida Boccara	29 March 1969	29 October 1940	28
1970	Ireland	Dana	21 March 1970	30 August 1951	18
1971	Monaco	Séverine	03 April 1971	10 October 1948	22
1972	Luxembourg	Vicky Leandros	25 March 1972	23 August 1949	22
1973	Luxembourg	Anne-Marie David	07 April 1973	23 May 1952	20
1974	Sweden	ABBA	06 April 1974	-	-
1975	Netherlands	Teach-In	22 March 1975	-	-
1976	United Kingdom	Brotherhood of Man	03 April 1976	-	-
1977	France	Marie Myriam	07 May 1977	08 May 1957	19
1978	Israel	Izhar Cohen and the Alphabeta	22 April 1978	13 May 1951	26
1979	Israel	Gali Atari and Milk and Honey	31 March 1979	29 December 1953	25
1980	Ireland	Johnny Logan	19 April 1980	13 May 1954	25
1981	United Kingdom	Bucks Fizz	04 April 1981	-	-
1982	Germany	Nicole	24 April 1982	25 October 1964	17
1983	Luxembourg	Corinne Hermès	23 April 1983	16 November 1961	21
1984	Sweden	Herreys	05 May 1984	-	-
1985	Norway	Bobbysocks! - Hanne Krogh	04 May 1985	24 January 1956	29
		Bobbysocks! - Elisabeth Andreassen	04 May 1985	28 March 1958	27
1986	Belgium	Sandra Kim	03 May 1986	15 October 1972	13
1987	Ireland	Johnny Logan	09 May 1987	13 May 1954	32
1988	Switzerland	Celine Dion	30 April 1988	30 March 1968	20
1989	Yugoslavia	Riva	06 May 1989	-	-
1990	Italy	Toto Cutugno	05 May 1990	07 July 1943	46
1991	Sweden	Carola	04 May 1991	08 September 1966	24
1992	Ireland	Linda Martin	09 May 1992	17 April 1947	45
1993	Ireland	Niamh Kavanagh	15 May 1993	13 February 1968	25
1994	Ireland	Paul Harrington & Charlie McGettigan - Paul	30 April 1994	08 May 1960	33
		Paul Harrington & Charlie McGettigan - Charlie	30 April 1994	07 December 1950	43
1995	Norway	Secret Garden - Fionnuala Sherry	13 May 1995	20 September 1962	32
		Secret Garden - Rolf Løvland	13 May 1995	19 April 1955	40

Eurovision Winners - Average age and gender (solo performers & duos only)

Year	Winner	Performer	Date of Contest	Date of Birth	Age
1996	Ireland	Eimear Quinn	18 May 1996	01 January 1973	23
1997	United Kingdom	Katrina and the Waves	03 May 1997	-	-
1998	Israel	Dana International	09 May 1998	02 February 1969	29
1999	Sweden	Charlotte Nilsson	29 May 1999	07 October 1974	24
2000	Denmark	Olsen Brothers - Jørgen	13 May 2000	15 March 1950	50
		Olsen Brothers - Niels	13 May 2000	13 April 1954	46
2001	Estonia	Tanel Padar, Dave Benton and 2XL - Tanel	12 May 2001	27 October 1980	20
		Tanel Padar, Dave Benton and 2XL - Dave	12 May 2001	31 January 1951	50
2002	Latvia	Marie N	25 May 2002	23 June 1973	28
2003	Turkey	Sertab Erener	24 May 2003	04 December 1964	38
2004	Ukraine	Ruslana	15 May 2004	24 May 1973	30
2005	Greece	Helena Paparizou	21 May 2005	31 January 1982	23
2006	Finland	Lordi	20 May 2006	-	-
2007	Serbia	Marija Šerifović	12 May 2007	14 November 1984	22
2008	Russia	Dima Bilan	24 May 2008	24 December 1981	26
2009	Norway	Alexander Rybak	16 May 2009	13 May 1986	23
2010	Germany	Lena Meyer-Landrut	29 May 2010	23 May 1991	19
2011	Azerbaijan	Ell/Nikki - Eldar Gasimov	14 May 2011	04 June 1989	21
		Ell/Nikki - Nigar Jamal	14 May 2011	07 September 1980	30
2012	Sweden	Loreen	26 May 2012	16 October 1983	28
2013	Denmark	Emmelie de Forest	18 May 2013	28 February 1993	20
2014	Austria	Conchita Wurst (performs as female)	10 May 2014	06 November 1988	25
2015	Sweden	Måns Zelmerlöw	23 May 2015	13 June 1986	28
2016	Ukraine	Jamala	14 May 2016	27 August 1983	32
2017	Portugal	Salvador Sobral	13 May 2017	28 December 1989	27
2018	Israel	Netta	12 May 2018	22 January 1993	25
2019	Netherlands	Duncan Laurence	18 May 2019	11 April 1994	25
2021	Italy	Måneskin	22 May 2021	-	-

66 performers	Average: 27
50 solo acts	Average (solo acts): 25
21 male performers	Average (men): 33
45 female performers	Average (women): 24

Eurovision 2021: What type of act?

What artist did each country choose to send to this year's Contest? Do previous years influence their choice?

Country	Represented by	Accompanied by*
Albania	solo female	none
Australia	solo female	female backing singers/dancers
Austria	solo male	none
Azerbaijan	solo female	female backing singers/dancers
Belgium	mixed group	none
Bulgaria	solo female	none
Croatia	solo female	male dancers
Cyprus	solo female	female dancers
Czech Republic	solo male	mixed dancers
Denmark	male duo	mixed backing singers
Estonia	solo male	none
Finland	male group	none
France	solo female	none
Georgia	solo male	none
Germany	solo male	female backing singers/dancers
Greece	solo female	male dancers
Iceland	mixed group	none
Ireland	solo female	none
Israel	solo female	male dancers
Italy	mixed group	none
Latvia	solo female	female dancers
Lithuania	mixed group	none
Malta	solo female	female backing singers/dancers
Moldova	solo female	male dancers
Netherlands	solo male	mixed backing singers/dancers
North Macedonia	solo male	none
Norway	solo male	male dancers
Poland	solo male	male dancers
Portugal	male group	none
Romania	solo female	mixed dancers
Russia	solo female	mixed backing singers
San Marino	solo female	mixed dancers
Serbia	female group	none
Slovenia	solo female	none
Spain	solo male	none
Sweden	solo male	mixed dancers
Switzerland	solo male	none
Ukraine	mixed group	none
United Kingdom	solo male	male musicians/dancers
	solo female	17 (44%)
	solo male	13 (33%)
	others	9

* only includes clearly visible backing singers

Eurovision 2021: Language selection over 9 year period (predominant language only)

Country	2012	2013	2014	2015	2016	2017	2018	2019	2021
Albania	Albanian	Albanian	English	English	English	English	Albanian	Albanian	Albanian
Armenia		English	English	English	English	English	Armenian	English	
Australia				English	English	English	English	English	English
Austria	German	English	English	English	French	English	English	English	English
Azerbaijan	English	English	English	English	English	English	English	English	English
Belarus	English	English	English	English	English	Belarusian	English	English	
Belgium	English	English	English	English	English	English	English	English	English
Bosnia & H	Bosnian				Bosnian				
Bulgaria	Bulgarian	Bulgarian			English	English	English		English
Croatia	Croatian	Croatian			English	English	English	English	English
Cyprus	English	Greek		English	English	English	English	English	English
Czech Republic			English	English	English	English	English	English	English
Denmark	English	English	English	English	English	English	English	English	Danish
Estonia	Estonian	Estonian	English	English	English	English	Italian	English	English
Finland	Swedish	English	English	Finnish	English	English	English	English	English
France	French	French	French	French	French	French	French	French	French
Georgia	English	English	English	English	English	English	Georgian	Georgian	English
Germany	English	English	English	English	English	English	English	English	English
Greece	English	Greek	English	English	English	English	Greek	English	English
Hungary	English	Hungarian	English	English	English	Hungarian	Hungarian	Hungarian	
Iceland	English	Icelandic	English	English	English	English	English	Icelandic	English
Ireland	English	English	English	English	English	English	English	English	English
Israel	English	Hebrew	English	English	English	English	English	English	English
Italy	English	Italian	Italian	Italian	Italian	Italian	Italian	Italian	Italian
Latvia	English	English	English	English	English	English	English	English	English
Lithuania	English	English	English	English	English	English	English	English	English
Malta	English	English	English	English	English	English	English	English	English
Moldova	English	Romanian	English	English	English	English	English	English	English
Montenegro	English	Montenegrin	Montenegrin	Montenegrin	English	English	Montenegrin	English	
Netherlands	English	English	English	English	English	English	English	English	English
Nth Macedonia	Macedonian	Macedonian	English	English	Macedonian	English	English	English	English
Norway	English	English	English	English	English	English	English	English	English
Poland			Polish	English	English	English	English	Polish	English
Portugal	Portuguese		Portuguese	Portuguese		Portuguese	Portuguese	Portuguese	English
Romania	Spanish	English	English	Romanian		English	English	English	English
Russia	Udmurt	English	English	English	English		English	English	Russian
San Marino	English	Italian	English	English	English	English	English	English	English
Serbia	Serbian	Serbian		English	English	English	Serbian	Serbian	Serbian
Slovakia	English								
Slovenia	Slovene	English	English	English	English	English	Slovene	Slovene	English
Spain	Spanish	Spanish	English	Spanish	English	Spanish	Spanish	Spanish	Spanish
Sweden	English	English	English	English	English	English	English	English	English
Switzerland	English	English	English	English	English	English		English	French
Turkey	English								
Ukraine	English	English	English		English	English	English		Ukrainian
United Kingdom	English	English	English	English	English	English	English	English	English
Number of songs:	42	39	37	40	42	42	43	41	39
Sung in English:	27	22	32	33	37	36	29	30	30
Percentage:	64%	56%	86%	83%	88%	86%	67%	73%	77%

denotes winner

2021 Eurovision 65: Rotterdam, Netherlands
FINAL Scoreboard Under Previous Voting System
FINAL: 22 May 2021

To ↓ / From →	Albania	Australia	Austria	Azerbaijan	Belgium	Bulgaria	Croatia	Cyprus	Czech Republic	Denmark	Estonia	Finland	France	Georgia	Germany	Greece	Iceland	Ireland	Israel	Italy	Latvia	Lithuania	Malta	Moldova	Netherlands	North Macedonia	Norway	Poland	Portugal	Romania	Russia	San Marino	Serbia	Slovenia	Spain	Sweden	Switzerland	Ukraine	United Kingdom	TOTAL
Cyprus	6	3										3	2	1	1	7				6				10	5	5			1		8	6			1					42
Albania										5		2				12							8	7		6	2										4	4	3	33
Israel			8				2	1					4	5	4	4		1	3	2					4	4		3	1							1				32
Belgium						5		1			3		1		1		6								2									1						21
Russia			12	12	1	2	4	5	2	4	2	5			2		1	6	10	5	4			12		1	10	1						1	6		10		2	92
Malta	10	3					2				7								5	4									4					5	3	10	3	1	4	117
Portugal		4	4		2	3	1					4			3		6			3		3	4		3		2	4	5			4	2		3		8			74
Serbia			6				10						12	5												12				8		5		8			7			45
United Kingdom																																								0
Greece	7			6		7		12	4				7	7	4								10	10							4	8	4	6						89
Switzerland	12	7	10		10		6		3	10	8	10	10	6			12	5	12	8	10	8	6	4	8	8	5	8	10	4	2	5		7	10	3		8	5	239
Iceland	12	12			5		8		12	12	5	12	2	2	6		10		12		7	4		10	1	1	7	12	6					7	7	12	6	6	12	213
Spain																																			1					0
Moldova	4		5			8			10				3																3	12	10	7								69
Germany															10		3		2	12	2																			0
Finland	3	2	2	1	8	6	3	4	8	8	10			10		4	2	2	2	12	5	5	5	1			1	5	2	10	6	1	8	3		5	2	5	6	151
Bulgaria	2	1			4			7		3	2			8	5	5	3				2		3	8				7	7		1	3	3		8		5	8	8	70
Lithuania		4						2			7	5						8	6	10	12		1				8			1		2			2	2	1	1	7	111
Ukraine		8	5	10	12	4	5	3	5	4	4	6	8	8	5		5	7	8	7	6	3	7	7	6	2	8	4	7	6	5	2	6	2	4	6	10		7	198
France	10	5	7	2	7	3	10	8	7	10	7		12	1	12		8	12	7		3	7	2	6	12	7	3	2	12	5	3	10	12	4	12	7	10	10	1	265
Azerbaijan														4					1					3				1			7		1					2		20
Norway			4							6		1						4				1	2							2						4				29
Netherlands	1																						7																	1
Italy	8	6	8	7	6	12	12	10	8	2	6	8	6	12	8	10	7	3	4		8	10	10	5	10	10	6	10	4	7	12	12	10	12	5	8	12	12	6	296
Sweden					3					7	3			3	3		4						12			12														41
San Marino	1										1																	6												14

(The basis for calculating points has changed several times in recent years. This table uses the jury/televote 50/50 variant).

271

Eurovision 2021: Population Weighted Voting

Just for fun, how would the leaderboard look if the total votes available were weighted based on each country's population sizes? We've applied the weightings only to the Public voting in the real Contest. Just assume the whole population of Europe votes!

					Weighted basis	
Populations	Population (m)	% of total pop	Votes to award		Points	Position
Albania	2.877	0.37%	8.48	Italy	302	1
Australia	25.499	3.32%	75.12	Ukraine	278	2
Austria	9.006	1.17%	26.53	Finland	236	3
Azerbaijan	10.139	1.32%	29.87	France	233	4
Belgium	11.589	1.51%	34.14	Iceland	200	5
Bulgaria	6.948	0.90%	20.47	Lithuania	200	5
Croatia	4.105	0.53%	12.09	Switzerland	164	7
Cyprus	1.207	0.16%	3.56	Cyprus	97	8
Czech Republic	10.708	1.39%	31.55	Russia	78	9
Denmark	5.792	0.75%	17.06	Moldova	77	10
Estonia	1.326	0.17%	3.91	Serbia	56	11
Finland	5.540	0.72%	16.32	Malta	50	12
France	65.273	8.50%	192.30	Bulgaria	48	13
Georgia	3.989	0.52%	11.75	Azerbaijan	47	14
Germany	83.783	10.91%	246.83	Albania	39	15
Greece	10.423	1.36%	30.71	Portugal	38	16
Iceland	0.341	0.04%	1.00	Norway	32	17
Ireland	4.937	0.64%	14.54	Sweden	26	18
Israel	8.655	1.13%	25.50	Israel	24	19
Italy	60.461	7.87%	178.12	Greece	23	20
Latvia	1.886	0.25%	5.56	San Marino	12	21
Lithuania	2.722	0.35%	8.02	Belgium	2	22
Malta	0.441	0.06%	1.30	Netherlands	0	23
Moldova	4.033	0.53%	11.88	Spain	0	23
Netherlands	17.134	2.23%	50.48	Germany	0	23
North Macedonia	2.083	0.27%	6.14	United Kingdom	0	23
Norway	5.421	0.71%	15.97			
Poland	37.846	4.93%	111.50			
Portugal	10.196	1.33%	30.04			
Romania	19.237	2.51%	56.67			
Russia	145.934	19.01%	429.93			
San Marino	0.339	0.04%	1.00			
Serbia	8.737	1.14%	25.74			
Slovenia	2.078	0.27%	6.12			
Spain	46.754	6.09%	137.74			
Sweden	10.099	1.32%	29.75			
Switzerland	8.654	1.13%	25.50			
Ukraine	43.733	5.70%	128.84			
United Kingdom	67.886	8.84%	199.99			
TOTAL	767.811	100.00%	2262.00			

Total votes available: 58 x 39 countries = 2262

(source: OECD)

The Most Successful Countries in Eurovision history....

Rank 2021	Rank 2019	Change	Country	Winners	2nd	3rd	4th	5th
1	1	0	Ireland	7	3	2	3	3
2	2	0	Sweden	6	1	6	2	9
3	3	0	United Kingdom	5	15	3	4	1
4	4	0	France	5	5	7	6	3
5	5	0	Netherlands	5	1	1	2	2
6	6	0	Luxembourg	5	0	2	2	4
7	7	0	Israel	4	2	1	2	2
8	12	+4	Italy	3	3	5	2	4
9	8	-1	Denmark	3	1	3	2	3
10	9	-1	Norway	3	1	1	4	3
11	10	-1	Germany	2	4	5	3	3
12	11	-1	Spain	2	4	1	2	1
13	13	0	Switzerland	2	3	4	5	2
14	14	0	Ukraine	2	2	1	1	1
15	15	0	Austria	2	0	1	1	4
16	16	0	Russia	1	4	4	0	1
17	17	0	Belgium	1	2	0	3	2
18	18	0	Monaco	1	1	3	3	1
19	19	0	Turkey	1	1	1	3	0
20	20	0	Azerbaijan	1	1	1	1	1
21	21	0	Greece	1	0	3	0	2
22	22	0	Latvia	1	0	1	0	1
23	23	0	Serbia	1	0	1	0	0
24	24	0	Estonia	1	0	0	2	1
24	24	0	Yugoslavia	1	0	0	2	1
26	26	0	Finland	1	0	0	0	0
26	26	0	Portugal	1	0	0	0	0
28	28	0	Malta	0	2	2	0	1
29	29	0	Iceland	0	2	0	2	0
30	30	0	Bulgaria	0	1	0	1	1
31	31	0	Cyprus	0	1	0	0	3
32	32	0	Australia	0	1	0	0	1
33	33	0	Poland	0	1	0	0	0
33	33	0	Serbia & Montenegro	0	1	0	0	0
35	35	0	Romania	0	0	2	1	0
36	36	0	Bosnia & Herzegovina	0	0	1	0	0
36	36	0	Moldova	0	0	1	0	0
38	38	0	Croatia	0	0	0	2	1
39	39	0	Armenia	0	0	0	2	0
40	40	0	Hungary	0	0	0	1	1
41	41	0	Albania	0	0	0	0	1
42	42	0	Andorra	0	0	0	0	0
42	42	0	Belarus	0	0	0	0	0
42	42	0	Czech Republic	0	0	0	0	0
42	42	0	North Macedonia	0	0	0	0	0
42	42	0	Georgia	0	0	0	0	0
42	42	0	Lithuania	0	0	0	0	0
42	42	0	Montenegro	0	0	0	0	0
42	42	0	Morocco	0	0	0	0	0
42	42	0	San Marino	0	0	0	0	0
42	42	0	Slovakia	0	0	0	0	0
42	42	0	Slovenia	0	0	0	0	0

...And The Least Successful Countries in Eurovision history
(although they at least made it to the Final...)

Rank 2021	Rank 2019	Change	Country	Last	2nd last	3rd Last	4th Last	5th Last
1	1	0	Norway	9	3	2	4	1
2	2	0	Austria	6	3	5	3	1
3	3	0	Belgium	6	2	7	4	2
4	4	0	Finland	5	4	5	2	7
5	6	+1	United Kingdom	5	2	3	2	0
6	5	-1	Germany	4	3	4	4	1
7	7	0	Switzerland	4	1	1	3	3
8	8	0	Spain	3	3	3	6	5
9	9	0	Turkey	3	3	0	1	4
10	10	0	Luxembourg	3	1	3	0	1
11	11	0	Malta	3	1	0	2	0
12	12	0	Sweden	2	2	2	1	2
13	13	0	Ireland	2	1	2	1	1
14	14	0	Yugoslavia	1	5	0	1	2
15	15	0	Portugal	1	4	4	4	4
16	16	0	Netherlands	1	4	3	4	2
17	17	0	France	1	3	5	2	3
18	18	0	Denmark	1	1	3	3	3
19	19	0	Cyprus	1	1	1	2	2
20	20	0	Lithuania	1	1	1	2	1
21	21	0	Monaco	1	1	1	1	1
22	22	0	Iceland	1	1	0	0	1
23	23	0	Italy	1	0	1	1	4
24	24	0	Israel	0	3	1	2	1
25	25	0	Estonia	0	2	0	0	0
26	26	0	Hungary	0	1	2	1	0
27	27	0	Slovenia	0	1	1	2	1
28	28	0	Belarus	0	1	1	0	0
29	29	0	Poland	0	1	0	1	2
30	30	0	Bosnia & Herzegovina	0	1	0	0	1
31	31	0	Morocco	0	1	0	0	0
31	31	0	Czech Republic	0	1	0	0	0
32	33	+1	San Marino	0	0	1	0	1
33	33	0	Latvia	0	0	1	0	0
33	33	0	Ukraine	0	0	1	0	0
36	36	0	Greece	0	0	0	2	1
37	37	0	Moldova	0	0	0	1	2
38	38	0	Romania	0	0	0	1	1
38	38	0	Croatia	0	0	0	1	1
40	40	0	Slovakia	0	0	0	0	1
40	40	0	Azerbaijan	0	0	0	0	1
42	42	0	Albania	0	0	0	0	0
42	42	0	Andorra	0	0	0	0	0
42	42	0	Armenia	0	0	0	0	0
42	42	0	Bulgaria	0	0	0	0	0
42	42	0	North Macedonia	0	0	0	0	0
42	42	0	Georgia	0	0	0	0	0
42	42	0	Montenegro	0	0	0	0	0
42	42	0	Russia	0	0	0	0	0
42	42	0	Serbia	0	0	0	0	0
42	42	0	Serbia & Montenegro	0	0	0	0	0

The Most Finishes in the Top 3...

Country	Top 3	Winners	2nd	3rd
United Kingdom	23	5	15	3
France	17	5	5	7
Sweden	13	6	1	6
Ireland	12	7	3	2
Italy	11	3	3	5
Germany	11	2	4	5
Switzerland	9	2	3	4
Russia	9	1	4	4
Netherlands	7	5	1	1
Luxembourg	7	5	0	2
Israel	7	4	2	1
Denmark	7	3	1	3
Spain	7	2	4	1

... And the Most Finishes in the Bottom 3

Country	Bottom 3	Last	2nd last	3rd Last
Belgium	15	6	2	7
Norway	14	9	3	2
Austria	14	6	3	5
Finland	14	5	4	5
Germany	12	4	4	4
United Kingdom	10	5	2	3
Spain	9	3	3	3
Portugal	9	1	4	4
France	9	1	3	5
Netherlands	8	1	4	3
Luxembourg	7	3	1	3
Switzerland	6	4	1	1
Turkey	6	3	3	0
Sweden	6	2	2	2

Failing to Qualify for the Final

Who has been eliminated at the semi-final stage the most times?

Country	Failures	Appearances	Failure rate
Monaco	3	3	100%
Slovakia	4	4	100%
Andorra	6	6	100%
Montenegro	9	11	82%
San Marino	8	10	80%
Czech Republic	6	8	75%
Switzerland	11	15	73%
Belarus	10	14	71%
Slovenia	11	16	69%
North Macedonia	11	16	69%
Latvia	11	16	69%
Portugal	9	13	69%
Poland	9	13	69%
Belgium	10	15	67%
Bulgaria	8	12	67%
Netherlands	9	14	64%
Estonia	10	16	63%
Croatia	8	13	62%
Ireland	9	15	60%
Finland	8	16	50%
Malta	7	14	50%
Albania	7	15	47%
Iceland	7	15	47%
Cyprus	6	13	46%
Lithuania	7	16	44%
Israel	6	14	43%
Austria	6	15	40%
Georgia	5	13	38%
Moldova	5	14	36%
Denmark	5	14	36%
Hungary	3	10	30%
Serbia	3	11	27%
Armenia	3	11	27%
Norway	3	12	25%
Romania	3	13	23%
Australia	1	5	20%
Greece	2	12	17%
Turkey	1	7	14%
Bosnia & H	1	8	13%
Russia	1	11	9%
Sweden	1	12	8%
Azerbaijan	1	12	8%

..And the Most Successful Semi-Finalists

Country	Failures	Appearances	Success Rate
Ukraine	0	12	100%

The Best Semi-Final to Compete In

(Analysis of Semi-Finalists since the introduction of the two Semi-Finals in 2008)

Year	Winner	Second	Third	Last place
2008	Semi-final 1	Semi-final 2	Semi-final 1	n/a (United Kingdom)
2009	Semi-final 2	Semi-final 1	Semi-final 2	Semi-final 1
2010	n/a (Germany)	Semi-final 2	Semi-final 2	n/a (United Kingdom)
2011	Semi-final 1	n/a (Italy)	Semi-final 2	Semi-final 1
2012	Semi-final 2	Semi-final 1	Semi-final 2	Semi-final 2
2013	Semi-final 1	Semi-final 2	Semi-final 1	Semi-final 1
2014	Semi-final 2	Semi-final 1	Semi-final 1	n/a (France)
2015	Semi-final 2	Semi-final 1	n/a (Italy)	n/a (Germany)
2016	Semi-final 2	Semi-final 2	Semi-final 1	n/a (Germany)
2017	Semi-final 1	Semi-final 2	Semi-final 1	n/a (Spain)
2018	Semi-final 1	Semi-final 1	Semi-final 1	n/a (Portugal)
2019	Semi-final 2	n/a (Italy)	Semi-final 2	n/a (United Kingdom)
2021	n/a (Italy)	n/a (France)	Semi-final 2	n/a (United Kingdom)

Average points received in the Final by SF Qualifiers   **Average position in Final by SF Qualifiers**

Year	Semi-final 1	Semi-final 2	Semi-final 1	Semi-final 2
2008	133	87	10	13
2009	83	118	14	11
2010	69	113	15	10
2011	87	110	15	11
2012	82	113	15	12
2013	101	100	13	12
2014	111	76	10	14
2015	87	93	12	12
2016	163	245	15	10
2017	242	183	12	13
2018	254	134	10	14
2019	279	124	14	8
2021	190	202	13	11

Winner's position in the Semi-finals   **Performance by SF Winners in Final**

Year	Winner	Position in SF	Semi-final winners	Finished in Final
2008	Russia	3rd	Greece & Ukraine	3rd & 2nd
2009	Norway	1st	Iceland & Norway	2nd & 1st
2010	Germany	n/a	Belgium & Turkey	6th & 2nd
2011	Azerbaijan	2nd	Greece & Sweden	7th & 3rd
2012	Sweden	1st	Russia & Sweden	2nd & 1st
2013	Denmark	1st	Denmark & Azerbaijan	1st & 2nd
2014	Austria	1st	Netherlands & Austria	2nd & 1st
2015	Sweden	1st	Russia & Sweden	2nd & 1st
2016	Ukraine	2nd	Russia & Australia	3rd & 2nd
2017	Portugal	1st	Portugal & Bulgaria	1st & 2nd
2018	Israel	1st	Israel & Norway	1st & 15th
2019	Netherlands	1st	Australia & Netherlands	9th & 1st
2021	Italy	n/a	Malta & Switzerland	7th & 3rd

Most semi-final consecutive failures

Country	Number of Years	Last Final appearance*
Andorra	6	Never qualified
Georgia	4	2016
Latvia	4	2016
Montenegro	4	2015
Slovakia	4	Never qualified
Romania	3	2017
Poland	3	2017
Croatia	3	2017
Monaco	3	Never qualified
Armenia	2	2017
Austria	2	2018
Ireland	2	2018
Australia	1	2019
Czech Republic	1	2019
Denmark	1	2019
Estonia	1	2019
Hungary	1	2018
Nth Macedonia	1	2019
Slovenia	1	2019

This year saw the qualification for the Final by these countries for the first time for at least 3 years:

Country	Last Final appearance*
Belgium	2017

* Includes only the years when semi-finals were held.

Eurovision 2021: Jinxed Semi-finalists

Do countries despair when they've been drawn in their 'unlucky' semi-final?

Country	2008	2009	2010	2011	2012	2013	2014	2015	2016	2017	2018	2019	2021	SF1	SF2	SF1	SF2	Difference
Finland	1	1	1	1	1	2	2	1	1	1	1	1	2	10	3	40%	100%	60%
Czech Republic	2	1	-	-	-	-	-	2	1	1	1	1	2	5	3	60%	0%	60%
Lithuania	2	2	2	1	2	1	2	2	2	2	1	2	1	4	9	100%	44%	56%
Turkey	2	1	2	1	2	-	-	-	-	-	-	-	-	2	3	50%	100%	50%
Russia	1	AQ	1	1	1	1	1	1	1	-	2	2	1	9	2	100%	50%	50%
Cyprus	2	2	2	2	1	1	-	2	1	1	1	1	1	7	5	86%	40%	46%
Montenegro	1	1	-	-	1	1	1	2	1	1	2	1	-	8	2	13%	50%	38%
Ireland	1	2	2	2	1	1	2	2	2	2	1	2	1	5	8	60%	25%	35%
Australia	-	-	-	-	-	-	-	-	2	1	2	1	1	3	2	67%	100%	33%
Latvia	2	2	1	2	1	2	1	2	2	1	2	2	2	4	9	0%	33%	33%
Moldova	1	2	1	2	1	1	1	1	1	1	2	2	2	8	5	50%	80%	30%
Slovenia	1	2	2	2	2	1	2	2	2	1	2	1	1	5	8	20%	50%	30%
Croatia	2	2	2	1	2	1	-	-	1	2	1	2	1	5	6	20%	50%	30%
Bosnia-H	1	1	1	2	2	-	-	-	1	-	-	-	-	4	2	75%	100%	25%
Nth Macedonia	2	1	1	2	2	2	2	1	2	2	1	2	1	5	8	0%	25%	25%
Hungary	2	2	-	1	1	2	1	1	1	2	2	1	-	6	5	83%	60%	23%
Israel	1	1	2	2	1	2	2	2	2	2	1	AQ	1	5	7	80%	57%	23%
Norway	1	2	AQ	1	2	2	2	2	2	2	2	2	1	3	9	67%	89%	22%
Greece	1	2	1	1	1	2	2	1	1	1	1	1	2	9	4	78%	100%	22%
Netherlands	1	2	2	2	2	1	1	1	1	2	2	2	AQ	5	7	60%	43%	17%
Belarus	2	1	1	2	2	1	2	1	2	2	1	1	-	6	6	50%	33%	17%
Azerbaijan	1	2	2	1	AQ	2	1	2	1	1	1	2	1	7	5	86%	100%	14%
Sweden	2	1	2	2	2	AQ	1	2	AQ	1	2	2	1	4	7	100%	86%	14%
Serbia	AQ	2	1	1	2	1	-	1	2	2	2	1	2	5	6	80%	67%	13%
San Marino	1	-	-	1	1	2	1	2	1	2	2	1	2	6	5	33%	20%	13%
Bulgaria	2	1	2	2	2	2	-	-	2	2	1	-	2	2	8	50%	38%	13%
Denmark	2	2	2	2	1	1	AQ	1	2	2	2	2	2	3	9	67%	78%	11%
Austria	-	-	-	2	1	1	2	AQ	1	2	1	2	2	4	5	50%	60%	10%
Estonia	1	2	1	2	2	1	1	1	1	2	1	1	2	8	5	50%	60%	10%
Poland	1	2	1	1	-	-	2	2	2	1	2	1	2	5	6	40%	50%	10%
Malta	2	1	1	1	2	2	2	2	1	2	2	2	1	5	8	60%	50%	10%
Albania	2	2	1	1	1	2	1	1	2	1	1	2	2	7	6	57%	67%	10%
Romania	1	1	2	2	1	2	2	1	-	2	2	2	1	5	7	80%	71%	9%
Armenia	1	1	2	1	-	2	1	1	1	1	1	2	-	8	3	75%	67%	8%
Iceland	2	1	1	1	1	2	1	2	1	1	1	1	2	9	4	67%	75%	8%
Switzerland	2	1	2	1	1	2	2	2	2	2	1	2	2	4	9	25%	33%	8%
Belgium	1	1	1	2	1	1	1	1	2	1	1	1	1	11	2	45%	50%	5%
Portugal	2	1	1	1	2	-	1	2	-	1	AQ	1	2	6	4	50%	50%	0%
Georgia	2	-	2	1	2	2	2	1	2	1	2	1	2	4	8	50%	50%	0%
Slovakia	-	2	1	2	2	-	-	-	-	-	-	-	-	1	3	0%	0%	0%
Ukraine	2	2	2	2	2	1	1	-	2	AQ	2	-	1	3	7	100%	100%	0%
Andorra	1	1	-	-	-	-	-	-	-	-	-	-	-	2	0	0%	-	-

Appearances in: SF1, SF2. Qualification %: SF1, SF2.

Qualification shown in **bold**.

Eurovision 2021 - Which countries' voters changed their minds during the final?

Given a bigger choice of acts to vote on in the final, how did semi-final voters react? (Public & Jury voting)

Semi-final 1

	Points received	Australia	Azerbaijan	Belgium	Croatia	Cyprus	Germany	Ireland	Israel	Italy	Lithuania	Malta	Netherlands	North Macedonia	Norway	Romania	Russia	Slovenia	Sweden	Ukraine	TOTAL
Malta	Semi final	22	16	20	19	20	18	22	18	14	13		19	20	20	20	20	11	20	13	325
	Final	20	7	7	3	11	8	14	10	7	3	11	8	5	15	14	4	5	14	5	160
	% change	-9%	-56%	-65%	-84%	-45%	-56%	-36%	-44%	-50%	-77%		-58%	-75%	-25%	-30%	-80%	-55%	-30%	-62%	-51%
Ukraine	Semi final	16	15	20	17	6	18	14	12	12	24	11	16	10	14	22	17	11	12		267
	Final	15	14	20	8	6	9	14	16	13	24	6	8	4	8	12	7	7	12		203
	% change	-6%	-7%	0%	-53%	0%	-50%	0%	33%	8%	0%	-45%	-50%	-60%	-43%	-45%	-59%	-36%	0%		-24%
Russia	Semi final	14	20	14	18	15	13	9	18	12	8	3	17	15	7	10		17	9	6	225
	Final	1	18	7	7	9	7		17	7	4		8	2				9	3	4	103
	% change	-93%	-10%	-50%	-61%	-40%	-46%	-100%	-6%	-42%	-50%	-100%	-53%	-87%	-100%	-100%		-47%	-67%	-33%	-54%
Lithuania	Semi final	10	3	10	9	15	16	17	17	15		11	11	4	12	14	9	11	17	13	203
	Final	6		7	2	5	13	16	13	17		6	3		12	3	2	7	7	10	122
	% change	-40%	-100%	-30%	-78%	-67%	-19%	-6%	-24%	13%		-45%	-73%	-100%	0%	-79%	-78%	-36%	-59%	-23%	-40%
Israel	Semi final	12	13	8	11	11	8	5		15	9	5	14	13	13	10	14	2	16	13	192
	Final		12		5	2				4	1		4	8	8	1	5	1	4	7	62
	% change	-100%	-8%	-100%	-55%	-82%	-100%	-100%		-73%	-89%	-100%	-71%	-38%	-38%	-90%	-64%	-50%	-75%	-46%	-68%
Cyprus	Semi final	16	4	3	16			10	16	5	8	20	1	10	8	7	13	13	8	6	170
	Final	4					6		3			6		8			14				42
	% change	-75%	-100%	-100%	-100%		17%	-100%	-81%	-100%	-100%	-70%	-100%	-20%	-100%	-100%	8%	-100%	-100%	-100%	-75%
Sweden	Semi final	6	7	13	1	10	12	5	7	4	8	20	7	1	20	4	9	2		6	142
	Final		5	7			4	1			1	16		3	18					2	57
	% change	-100%	-29%	-46%	-100%	-100%	-67%	-80%	-100%	-100%	-88%	-20%	-100%	200%	-10%	-100%	-100%	-100%		-67%	-60%
Azerbaijan	Semi final	6		5	8	4	2	7	7	5	3	14	6	13	12	7	14	11	4	10	138
	Final				2			2	4				2	3	1	4	12			6	36
	% change	-100%		-100%	-75%	-100%	-100%	-71%	-43%	-100%	-100%	-100%	-67%	-77%	-92%	-43%	-14%	-100%	-100%	-40%	-74%
Belgium	Semi final		2		4	4	3		8	14	20		17	2	2	1	9	9	7	15	117
	Final		3			4		3	6	5	9		6				3	6	1	7	53
	% change		50%		-100%	0%	-100%	n/a	-25%	-64%	-55%		-65%	-100%	-100%	-100%	-67%	-33%	-86%	-53%	-55%
Norway	Semi final	4	10	13	2	1	4	5	6	7	8	6	7	2		3	6	9	20	2	115
	Final	1	7	1			1	7		2	5	10						2	10	1	47
	% change	-75%	-30%	-92%	-100%	-100%	-75%	40%	-100%	-71%	-38%	67%	-100%	-100%		-100%	-100%	-78%	-50%	-50%	-59%

Eurovision 2021 - Which countries' voters changed their minds during the final?

Given a bigger choice of acts to vote on in the final, how did semi-final voters react? (Public & Jury voting)

Semi-final 2

	Points received	Albania	Austria	Bulgaria	Czech Republic	Denmark	Estonia	Finland	France	Georgia	Greece	Iceland	Latvia	Moldova	Poland	Portugal	San Marino	Serbia	Spain	Switzerland	United Kingdom	TOTAL
Switzerland	Semi final	24	20	7	15	19	18	20	11	15	7	19	16	17	16	15	12	10	19		11	280
	Final	24	15	3	8	18	14	19	13	10	4	18	16	7	14	13	7	2	17		9	222
	% change	0%	-25%	-57%	-47%	-5%	-22%	-5%	18%	-33%	-43%	-5%	0%	-59%	-13%	-13%	-42%	-80%	-11%		-18%	-21%
Iceland	Semi final	5	20	6	20	20	15	20	12	14	12		19	12	13	17	9	19	16	15	24	264
	Final		22		15	22	11	20	7	7			15	5	18	11		12	12	10	20	187
	% change	-100%	10%	-100%	-25%	10%	-27%	0%	-42%	-50%	-100%		-21%	-58%	38%	-35%	-100%	-37%	-25%	-33%	-17%	-29%
Bulgaria	Semi final	10	12		13	11	12	16	9	16	14	14	8	17	9	17	9	16	15	15	17	233
	Final	5	5		4	6	6	10		4	8	8	5	12		11	5	6	12	10	13	118
	% change	-50%	-58%		-69%	-45%	-50%	-38%	-100%	-75%	-43%	-43%	-38%	-29%	-100%	-29%	-44%	-63%	-20%	-33%	-24%	-49%
Portugal	Semi final	7	14	13	16	12	11	13	20	10	8	16	13	6	6		5	11	22	20	16	223
	Final		7	6	12		5		16	8		12		2	8			5	6	15	7	102
	% change	-100%	-50%	-54%	-25%	-100%	-55%	-100%	-20%	-20%	-100%	-25%	-100%	-67%	33%		-100%	-55%	-73%	-25%	-56%	-54%
Finland	Semi final	11	10	12	14	17	17		9	10	8	16	15	8	14	12	13	16	6	12	14	220
	Final	6	5	9	5	15	19		1		6	17	12	5	8	5		17	2	5	11	142
	% change	-45%	-50%	-25%	-64%	-12%	12%		-89%	-100%	-25%	6%	-20%	-38%	-43%	-58%	-62%	6%	-67%	-58%	-21%	-35%
Greece	Semi final	20		18	7	5	3	8	12	10		12	1	20	12	13	15	16	8	3	1	183
	Final	14		10	8			2	12	12		4		15		2	15	6	1			101
	% change	-30%	0%	-44%	14%	-100%	-100%	-75%	0%	20%		-67%	-100%	-25%	-100%	-85%	0%	-63%	-88%	-100%	-100%	-45%
Moldova	Semi final	3	8	12	12	7	12	5	13		24	6	16		14	12	20	16	3		3	176
	Final	7		12	12	5		2	7	2	10					8	11					71
	% change	133%	-100%	0%	0%	-29%	-100%	-60%	-46%	n/a	-58%	-100%	-100%		-100%	-33%	-45%	-100%	-100%	0%	-100%	-60%
Serbia	Semi final	9	18	10	9		5	3	12	3	7	2		1	1	6	11		6	16	5	119
	Final	1	12	5					3											12		33
	% change	-89%	-33%	-50%	-100%	0%	-100%	-100%	-75%	-100%	-100%	-100%	0%	-100%	-100%	-100%	-100%		-100%	-25%	-100%	-72%
San Marino	Semi final	15	1	2	2	7	5	3	8	13	12	6	2	10	12	12		5	7	2	6	112
	Final	5				5			4	7	7				12	8					3	40
	% change	-67%	-100%	-100%	-100%	-29%	-100%	n/a	-50%	-46%	-42%	-100%	-100%	-100%	0%	-33%		-100%	-100%	-100%	-50%	-64%
Albania	Semi final		5	8	1	10	2	7	3	2	16	5	5	7	6	9	9	1	2	13	1	111
	Final					7					7						2			7		23
	% change		-100%	-100%	-100%	-30%	-100%	-100%	-100%	-100%	-56%	-100%	-100%	-100%	-100%	-100%	-78%	-100%	-100%	-46%	-100%	-79%

Performance of the "Big 5"

Since automatic qualification to the final was introduced in 2004.

Contest	Countries in Final		France		Germany		Spain		United Kingdom		Italy	
Final	Voting	Max pts	Points	% of max	Points	% of max	Points	% of max	Points	% of max	Points	% of max
2004	36	420	40	10%	93	22%	87	21%	29	7%	-	0%
2005	39	456	11	2%	4	1%	28	6%	18	4%	-	0%
2006	38	444	5	1%	36	8%	18	4%	25	6%	-	0%
2007	42	492	19	4%	49	10%	43	9%	19	4%	-	0%
2008	43	504	47	9%	14	3%	55	11%	14	3%	-	0%
2009	42	492	107	22%	35	7%	23	5%	173	35%	-	0%
2010	38	444	82	18%	246	55%	68	15%	10	2%	-	0%
2011	43	504	82	16%	107	21%	50	10%	100	20%	189	38%
2012	42	492	21	4%	110	22%	97	20%	12	2%	101	21%
2013	39	456	14	3%	18	4%	8	2%	23	5%	126	28%
2014	37	432	2	0%	39	9%	74	17%	40	9%	33	8%
2015	40	468	4	1%	0	0%	15	3%	5	1%	292	62%
2016	42	984	257	26%	11	1%	77	8%	62	6%	124	13%
2017	42	984	135	14%	6	1%	5	1%	111	11%	334	34%
2018	42	984	173	18%	340	35%	61	6%	48	5%	308	31%
2019	41	960	105	11%	24	3%	54	6%	11	1%	472	49%
2021	39	912	499	55%	3	0%	6	1%	0	0%	524	57%

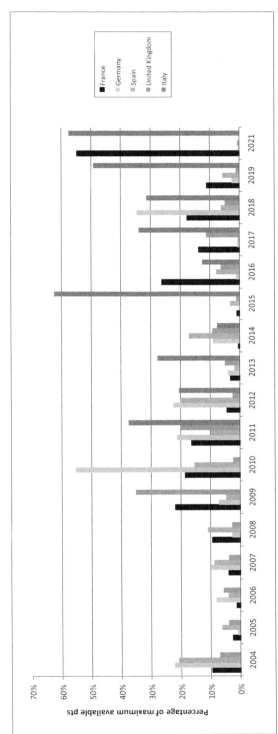

Eurovision Winners & Losers by Order of Performance

By Contest Year

Contest	Finalists	Position in Running Order			
		Winner	Second	Third	Last
1975	19	1	9	19	13
1976	18	1	17	16	18
1977	18	18	9	1	13
1978	20	18	10	6	2
1979	19	10	19	11	18
1980	19	17	12	13	10
1981	20	14	3	9	13
1982	18	18	15	7	6
1983	20	20	16	4	6 & 7
1984	19	1	9	4	13
1985	19	13	10	16	8
1986	20	13	10	1	5
1987	22	20	16	7	10
1988	21	9	4	13	12
1989	22	22	7	12	20
1990	22	19	14	17	9
1991	22	8	9	15	6
1992	23	17	16	10	12
1993	25	14	19	4	7
1994	25	3	24	14	16
1995	23	5	9	18	3
1996	23	17	12	23	18
1997	25	24	5	2	3
1998	25	8	16	10	5
1999	23	15	13	21	3
2000	24	14	9	21	10
2001	23	20	23	22	4
2002	24	23	20	2	14
2003	26	4	22	11	15
2004	24	10	5	16	3
2005	24	19	3	4	17
2006	24	17	10	13	7
2007	24	17	18	15	4
2008	25	24	18	21	2
2009	25	20	7	11	24
2010	25	22	14	19	12
2011	25	19	12	7	13
2012	26	17	6	24	12
2013	26	18	20	22	26
2014	26	11	24	13	14
2015	27	10	25	27	17
2016	26	21	13	18	10
2017	26	11	25	7	16
2018	26	22	25	5	8
2019	26	12	22	5	16
2021	26	24	20	11	9

By Position in Running Order

Running Order	Number of times:	
	Winner	Last
1	3	0
2	0	2
3	1	4
4	1	2
5	1	2
6	0	3
7	0	3
8	2	2
9	1	2
10	3	4
11	2	0
12	1	4
13	2	5
14	3	2
15	1	1
16	0	3
17	6	2
18	4	3
19	3	0
20	4	1
21	1	0
22	3	0
23	1	0
24	3	1
25	0	0
26	0	1
27	0	0

(Since the introduction of the modern points scoring system in 1975)

The Best & Worst Positions in the Order of Performance: 1975-2015

(Finals only. From the introduction of the modern points system in 1975 until the change to two sets of votes in 2016.)

Running Order	0 pts	1 pt	2 pts	3 pts	4 pts	5 pts	6 pts	7 pts	8 pts	10 pts	12 pts	Any	Points	Rank	Av Pts	Rank
1	617	60	42	54	58	48	45	43	46	48	46	490	2749	10	2.483	16
2	765	45	32	32	36	43	37	37	37	20	23	342	1817	24	1.641	26
3	680	55	46	49	44	36	38	44	40	38	37	427	2330	15	2.105	20
4	681	41	44	51	51	43	51	41	34	40	30	426	2326	16	2.101	21
5	689	48	48	41	44	44	43	40	40	29	41	418	2303	19	2.080	24
6	699	39	50	51	36	41	47	32	47	35	30	408	2233	21	2.017	25
7	635	46	61	51	50	45	51	48	35	52	33	472	2584	13	2.334	18
8	656	41	59	46	47	58	38	48	40	41	33	451	2465	14	2.227	19
9	622	48	57	53	44	44	35	48	56	49	51	485	2813	8	2.541	14
10	581	35	49	35	57	63	45	55	61	57	69	526	3322	3	3.001	6
11	613	50	48	50	48	65	53	53	43	39	45	494	2776	9	2.508	15
12	606	53	51	47	48	39	55	46	51	65	46	501	2945	4	2.660	11
13	641	46	39	36	54	43	39	50	47	59	53	466	2849	6	2.574	13
14	626	53	42	50	58	42	52	47	39	58	40	481	2742	11	2.477	17
15	693	52	39	46	31	51	37	44	39	35	40	414	2319	17	2.095	22
16	691	45	44	41	40	47	46	47	41	32	34	417	2312	18	2.087	23
17	571	44	44	38	46	50	63	63	54	55	79	536	3429	1	3.098	3
18	537	46	53	71	51	53	68	61	59	51	57	570	3335	2	3.013	5
19	559	50	49	45	53	41	55	42	61	48	50	494	2892	5	2.746	9
20	516	34	48	43	38	34	29	47	41	60	68	442	2828	7	2.952	7
21	466	49	37	40	46	42	51	43	38	30	36	412	2280	20	2.597	12
22	428	42	39	48	37	46	30	34	46	52	55	429	2608	12	3.043	4
23	400	39	28	32	47	34	41	34	36	44	33	368	2157	22	2.809	8
24	292	25	29	30	27	30	27	27	42	42	47	326	2102	23	3.401	2
25	250	14	22	21	12	19	22	23	23	25	20	201	1231	25	2.729	10
26	149	5	5	4	4	4	3	4	3	1	2	35	167	27	0.908	27
27	1	2	2	2	0	2	6	6	8	2	9	39	292	26	7.300	1
First 3	2062	160	120	135	138	127	120	124	123	106	106	1259	6896		2.076	
Top Half	311	528	562	537	544	539	513	522	516	489	465	5213	29457		5.333	
Bottom Half	369	579	546	571	564	569	594	585	591	618	642	5857	34749		5.581	
Last 3	1651	142	140	156	144	167	160	166	184	190	211	1660	10327		3.119	
Last	565	40	51	43	49	47	44	56	60	58	72	520	3282		3.025	

Notes:

The change to the way points were awarded in the 2016 Contest, meaning that the number of points was effectively been doubled, made comparisons with previous years almost meaningless. A simple inclusion of the total points awarded from 2016 onwards would distort the statistics calculated under the old system. We have therefore presented two sets of figures, one for the "old" scoring system from 1975 to 2015 and one for 2016 onwards under the new scoring system.

The average points awarded figure has been recalculated to take account of the times no votes were given.

Countries performing second in the running order have received no votes from individual countries 765 times, making it by far the worst place to perform. In fact, performing in the first 3 is pretty much fatal for your chances, compared to performing in the last 3.

On average the act performing first has received the 16th highest average votes and the act performing last has received the 5th highest average votes.

Performing in the second half of the contest remains a big advantage, with three of the top five acts this year performing in the last five places in the running order.

The Best & Worst Positions in the Order of Performance: 2016 onwards

(Finals only. Since the change to the points system in 2016.)

Running Order	0 pts	1 pt	2 pts	3 pts	4 pts	5 pts	6 pts	7 pts	8 pts	9 pts	10 pts	11 pts	12 pts	13 pts	14 pts	15 pts	16 pts
1	99	8	4	5	10	8	3	5	8	1	5	1	5	0	2	1	2
2	115	11	10	6	4	3	4	6	1	0	4	0	0	1	1	1	0
3	86	11	6	12	11	6	7	10	7	0	3	0	5	0	2	0	0
4	96	13	7	9	4	6	7	7	4	2	4	0	4	0	0	1	2
5	56	9	10	12	9	8	4	7	10	1	7	2	7	8	1	3	3
6	70	8	7	11	13	9	5	11	8	5	6	0	8	1	0	1	2
7	66	8	7	10	6	9	8	13	14	3	8	1	3	2	2	0	2
8	56	9	11	6	12	9	7	13	7	1	8	2	9	4	3	2	1
9	54	11	14	7	6	5	10	10	4	1	6	4	7	2	4	6	1
10	118	4	6	8	6	5	2	4	4	0	4	0	3	1	1	0	0
11	40	9	3	10	7	5	7	7	10	1	6	3	3	7	5	3	4
12	53	8	5	2	8	14	7	10	2	5	16	3	8	2	3	5	5
13	72	6	4	6	6	9	10	3	3	8	4	5	5	3	2	8	1
14	80	6	4	7	12	11	6	11	7	3	7	5	3	1	3	1	0
15	79	3	10	3	6	9	5	7	6	2	13	3	9	1	1	1	1
16	114	7	11	4	3	3	3	6	5	1	4	1	2	0	1	1	1
17	85	7	10	12	4	7	8	10	6	2	4	2	5	2	1	1	1
18	63	10	7	5	7	10	11	6	11	1	9	3	5	1	7	3	0
19	108	9	7	3	5	4	10	4	5	1	3	3	1	0	0	1	0
20	36	5	11	10	11	9	13	13	18	1	12	7	10	3	0	2	2
21	81	6	10	11	6	6	4	4	5	0	11	0	4	2	0	3	0
22	56	6	4	4	8	7	6	9	6	3	9	4	2	6	2	5	7
23	80	6	4	8	6	13	6	6	11	3	6	1	4	3	4	0	0
24	35	10	7	11	18	7	11	13	10	5	5	7	8	3	8	2	4
25	39	3	9	8	7	3	4	8	11	2	9	6	4	6	12	6	5
26	64	7	11	6	12	12	9	10	4	1	11	3	7	0	3	1	1
First 3	300	30	20	23	25	17	14	21	16	1	12	1	10	1	5	2	2
Top Half	1238	138	112	122	121	110	104	133	96	36	95	28	83	36	36	40	26
Bottom Half	1133	108	132	110	126	123	121	123	123	30	119	52	92	44	51	25	27
Last 3	185	28	29	33	41	26	25	37	36	8	31	17	25	0	0	0	0
Last	93	8	11	9	13	14	9	12	10	1	11	3	8	0	0	0	0

Notes:

Performing second consistently remains the worst place in the running order to perform, both for total points and average points.

Eleventh is the best over the last 5 years, this year that position was taken by 3rd placed Switzerland.

The bottom half of the draw remains the best, this year 4 of the top 6 countries performed in the bottom half of the running order.

The country performing last has achieved 30% more points than the country performing first, over the last 5 years.

The Best & Worst Positions in the Order of Performance: 2016 onwards

(Finals only. Since the change to the points system in 2016.)

Running Order	17 pts	18 pts	19 pts	20 pts	22 pts	24 pts	Any	Total Points	Rank	Av Pts	Rank
1	0	0	0	0	0	1	70	457	20	2.70	20
2	0	0	0	1	0	0	55	256	26	1.51	26
3	0	1	0	1	0	0	85	457	20	2.67	21
4	1	0	0	0	1	0	76	415	22	2.41	22
5	3	4	0	2	1	1	117	899	8	5.20	7
6	0	2	1	0	0	0	104	639	17	3.67	16
7	0	2	0	3	1	0	109	730	15	4.17	12
8	1	3	0	1	1	2	120	851	10	4.84	10
9	0	6	1	4	3	2	123	977	7	5.52	5
10	0	1	0	0	0	1	60	306	25	1.72	24
11	4	5	3	10	6	10	139	1464	1	8.18	1
12	5	3	1	2	1	0	127	1031	4	5.73	4
13	5	3	1	1	0	3	109	886	9	4.90	9
14	0	0	0	1	0	0	102	585	18	3.21	18
15	3	2	1	1	0	2	104	749	12	4.09	13
16	0	1	0	0	0	0	70	315	24	1.71	25
17	0	1	0	0	0	0	100	509	19	2.75	19
18	1	2	2	0	2	2	123	844	11	4.54	11
19	0	0	2	0	0	2	79	385	23	2.06	23
20	1	0	1	1	0	2	152	990	6	5.27	6
21	1	3	3	2	4	2	108	738	14	3.90	14
22	6	6	2	2	4	4	134	1190	3	6.26	3
23	1	2	0	0	3	1	111	677	16	3.54	17
24	1	1	0	0	1	1	157	995	5	5.18	8
25	4	9	3	5	2	3	154	1397	2	7.24	2
26	0	2	0	1	1	2	130	746	13	3.85	15
First 3	0	1	0	2	0	1	210	1170		2.294	
Top Half	22	37	9	29	17	24	1454	11392		4.232	
Bottom Half	24	38	16	18	24	25	1551	12505		4.659	
Last 3	0	0	0	0	0	0	336	1786		3.428	
Last	0	0	0	0	0	0	109	603		2.985	

Double Douze! Countries receiving the maximum 24 points in a Final since 2016

Country	Contest	Performer	24 points	Out of	%	Position
Portugal	2017	Salvador Sobral	7	41	17%	1
France	2021	Barbara Pravi	2	38	5%	2
Italy	2019	Mahmood	2	40	5%	2
Bulgaria	2017	Kristian Kostov	2	41	5%	2
Italy	2017	Francesco Gabbani	2	41	5%	6
Ukraine	2016	Jamala	2	41	5%	1
Australia	2016	Dami Im	2	41	5%	2
Russia	2016	Sergey Lazarev	2	41	5%	3
Israel	2018	Netta	2	42	5%	1
Germany	2018	Michael Schulte	2	42	5%	4
Ukraine	2021	Go_A	1	38	3%	5
Italy	2021	Måneskin	1	38	3%	1
Greece	2021	Stefania	1	38	3%	10
Switzerland	2021	Gjon's Tears	1	38	3%	3
Serbia	2021	Hurricane	1	38	3%	14
Cyprus	2021	Elena Tsagrinou	1	38	3%	16
Russia	2019	Sergey Lazarev	1	40	3%	3
North Macedonia	2019	Tamara Todevska	1	40	3%	7
Cyprus	2019	Tamta	1	40	3%	13
Greece	2019	Katerine Duska	1	40	3%	21
Azerbaijan	2019	Chingiz	1	40	3%	8
Serbia	2019	Nevena Božovic	1	40	3%	18
Sweden	2017	Robin Bengtsson	1	41	2%	5
Romania	2017	Ilinca ft. Alex Florea	1	41	2%	7
Hungary	2017	Joci Pápai	1	41	2%	8
Greece	2017	Demy	1	41	2%	19
Cyprus	2017	Hovig	1	41	2%	21
Armenia	2016	Iveta Mukuchyan	1	41	2%	7
Belgium	2016	Laura Tesoro	1	41	2%	10
Cyprus	2018	Eleni Foureira	1	42	2%	2
Denmark	2018	Rasmussen	1	42	2%	9
Italy	2018	Ermal Meta & Fabrizio Moro	1	42	2%	5
Moldova	2018	DoReDoS	1	42	2%	10
Serbia	2018	Sanja Ilić & Balkanika	1	42	2%	19

Quadruple Douze! When juries & public both gave maximum points in semi-finals & finals in 2021

Voting country	Points given to	Jury (SF)	Public (SF)	Jury (F)	Public (F)
Lithuania	Ukraine	12	12	12	12
Albania	Switzerland	12	12	12	12

Are You Sure? Countries whose juries gave the complete opposite to their voting public in 2021

Voting country	Points given to	By jury	By public	SF/Final
Germany	Sweden	12	0	Semi-final 1
Bulgaria	Moldova	12	0	Semi-final 2
France	Greece	12	0	Semi-final 2
Poland	Greece	12	0	Semi-final 2
San Marino	Poland	12	0	Semi-final 2
Malta	Albania	12	0	Final
Czech Republic	Portugal	12	0	Final
France	Greece	12	0	Final
Bulgaria	Moldova	12	0	Final
Moldova	Bulgaria	12	0	Final
Poland	San Marino	12	0	Final
Portugal	Bulgaria	12	0	Final
Norway	Lithuania	0	12	Semi-final 1
Italy	Ukraine	0	12	Semi-final 1
Czech Republic	Moldova	0	12	Semi-final 2
Estonia	Moldova	0	12	Semi-final 2
Portugal	Moldova	0	12	Semi-final 2
Bulgaria	Finland	0	12	Semi-final 2
Azerbaijan	Israel	0	12	Final
Austria	Serbia	0	12	Final
Belgium	France	0	12	Final
Czech Republic	Moldova	0	12	Final
France	Ukraine	0	12	Final
Georgia	Greece	0	12	Final
Malta	Italy	0	12	Final
Norway	Lithuania	0	12	Final
Poland	Ukraine	0	12	Final
Slovenia	Serbia	0	12	Final
Sweden	Finland	0	12	Final
Switzerland	Serbia	0	12	Final
United Kingdom	Lithuania	0	12	Final

This year the jury and public voting differences produced some interesting patterns. The jury members of Bulgaria and Moldova gave each other maximum points, yet their voting public gave each nothing. The San Marino jury gave Poland 12 points in the semi-final and then two days later, the Poland jury gave San Marino 12 points.

It also highlights diaspora voting, as the public of Austria and Switzerland both gave 12 points to Serbia again, yet received nothing in return, again. And the United Kingdom public yet again gave maximum points to Lithuania, as they did in the 2019 semi-final, and the final and semi-final of the 2016 and 2018 Contests. Either all the Lithuanians in the UK call in to vote for Lithuania or not many people actually vote in the UK.

Highest number of 12 points scored by one entry

1. Under the old scoring system from 1975 to 2015, including semi-finals.

Country	Contest	Performer	12 points	Out of	%	Position
Portugal	2017 Final (Jury)	Salvadore Sobral	18	41	44%	1
Sweden	2012 Final	Loreen	18	41	44%	1
Norway	2009 Final	Alexander Rybak	16	41	39%	1
Sweden	2015 Semi	Måns Zelmerlöw	14	20	70%	1
Austria	2014 Final	Conchita Wurst	13	36	36%	1
Sweden	2015 Final	Måns Zelmerlöw	12	39	31%	1
United Kingdom	1997	Katrina and The Waves	10	24	42%	1
Azerbaijan	2013 Final	Farid Mammadov	10	38	26%	2
Greece	2005 Final	Helena Paparizou	10	38	26%	1
Germany	1982	Nicole	9	17	53%	1
Estonia	2001	Tanel Padar, Dave Benton & 2XL	9	22	41%	1
Serbia & Montenegro	2004 Semi	Željko Joksimović	9	35	26%	1
Bosnia & Herzegovina	2006 Semi	Hari Mata Hari	9	37	24%	2
Germany	2010 Final	Lena Meyer-Landrut	9	38	24%	1
Italy	2015 Final	Il Volo	9	39	23%	3
Serbia	2007 Semi	Marija Šerifovic	9	41	22%	1
Serbia	2007 Final	Marija Šerifovic	9	41	22%	1

2. Under the current scoring system from 2016 onwards, including semi-finals, with separate jury and public scores.

Country	Contest	Performer	12 points	Out of	%	Position
Portugal	2017 Final (Jury)	Salvadore Sobral	18	41	44%	1
Portugal	2017 Final (Public)	Salvadore Sobral	12	41	29%	1
Russia	2019 Final (Public)	Sergey Lazarev	11	40	28%	3
Ukraine	2016 Final (Jury)	Jamala	11	41	27%	2
Sweden	2019 Final (Public)	John Lundvik	10	40	25%	5
Russia	2016 Final (Public)	Sergey Lazarev	10	41	24%	1
Portugal	2017 Semi (Public)	Salvadore Sobral	9	20	45%	1
Australia	2016 Semi (Jury)	Dami Im	9	20	45%	1
Sweden	2018 Semi (Jury)	Benjamin Ingrosso	9	20	45%	1
Australia	2016 Final (Jury)	Dami Im	9	41	22%	1
Austria	2018 Final (Jury)	Cesár Sampson	9	42	21%	3
Malta	2021 Semi (Jury)	Destiny	8	18	44%	1
Moldova	2021 Semi (Public)	Natalia Gordienko	8	19	42%	4
Norway	2019 Final (Public)	KEiiNO	8	40	20%	6
Israel	2018 Final (Public)	Netta	8	42	19%	1
Sweden	2018 Final (Jury)	Benjamin Ingrosso	8	42	19%	7
Switzerland	2021 Final (Jury)	Gjon's Tears	8	38	21%	1
France	2021 Final (Jury)	Barbara Pravi	8	38	21%	2

Final winners with the lowest number of 12 points

Country	Contest	Performer	12 points	Out of	%
Netherlands	2019 (Public)	Duncan Laurence	2	40	5%
United Kingdom	1981	Bucks Fizz	2	19	11%
Azerbaijan	2011	Ell/Nikki	3	42	7%
Israel	1998	Dana International	3	24	13%
Ireland	1992	Linda Martin	3	22	14%
Italy	1990	Toto Cutugno	3	21	14%
Switzerland	1988	Céline Dion	3	20	15%
France	1977	Marie Myriam	3	17	18%
Italy	2021 (Jury)	Måneskin	4	38	11%
Turkey	2003	Sertab Erener	4	25	16%
Yugoslavia	1989	Riva	4	21	19%
Sweden	1991	Carola	4	21	19%

Maximum Points: Recent Final History (Jury Voting)

Who has received the maximum points from each country in Finals since the voting system changed?

Voting country	Stockholm 2016	Kiev 2017	Lisbon 2018	Tel Aviv 2019	Rotterdam 2021
Albania	Australia	Italy	Italy	North Macedonia	Switzerland
Andorra	-	-	-	-	-
Armenia	France	Portugal	Sweden	Sweden	-
Australia	Belgium	United Kingdom	Sweden	Sweden	Malta
Austria	Australia	Netherlands	Israel	North Macedonia	Iceland
Azerbaijan	Russia	Belarus	Albania	Russia	Russia
Belarus	Russia	Bulgaria	Cyprus	Malta	-
Belgium	Australia	Sweden	Austria	Italy	Switzerland
Bosnia & H	Ukraine	-	-	-	-
Bulgaria	Armenia	Austria	Austria	-	Moldova
Croatia	Australia	Hungary	Lithuania	Italy	Italy
Cyprus	Russia	Greece	Sweden	Greece	Greece
Czech Rep	Sweden	Portugal	Israel	Sweden	Portugal
Denmark	Ukraine	Sweden	Denmark	Sweden	Switzerland
Estonia	Sweden	Bulgaria	Austria	Sweden	Switzerland
Finland	Sweden	Sweden	Israel	Sweden	Switzerland
France	Italy	Portugal	Israel	Netherlands	Greece
Georgia	Ukraine	Portugal	Sweden	Czech Rep	Italy
Germany	Israel	Norway	Sweden	Italy	France
Greece	Russia	Cyprus	Cyprus	Cyprus	Cyprus
Hungary	Australia	Portugal	Denmark	Czech Rep	-
Iceland	Netherlands	Portugal	Austria	Sweden	Switzerland
Ireland	Belgium	Belgium	Cyprus	Sweden	France
Israel	Ukraine	Portugal	Austria	Netherlands	Switzerland
Italy	Spain	Azerbaijan	Norway	Denmark	Lithuania
Latvia	Ukraine	Portugal	Sweden	Netherlands	Switzerland
Lithuania	Australia	Portugal	Austria	Netherlands	Ukraine
Malta	United Kingdom	Italy	Cyprus	Italy	Albania
Moldova	Ukraine	Romania	Estonia	North Macedonia	Bulgaria
Montenegro	Malta	Greece	Serbia	Serbia	-
Netherlands	Australia	Portugal	Denmark	Sweden	France
North Macedonia	Ukraine	Bulgaria	Estonia	Italy	Serbia
Norway	Italy	Bulgaria	Denmark	Czech Rep	Malta
Poland	Ukraine	Portugal	Austria	Australia	San Marino
Portugal	-	Azerbaijan	Estonia	Netherlands	Bulgaria
Romania	-	Netherlands	Austria	Australia	Malta
Russia	Armenia	-	Moldova	Azerbaijan	Moldova
San Marino	Ukraine	Portugal	Israel	Italy	France
Serbia	Ukraine	Portugal	Sweden	North Macedonia	France
Slovakia	-	-	-	-	-
Slovenia	Ukraine	Portugal	Sweden	Czech Rep	Italy
Spain	Armenia	Portugal	Cyprus	Sweden	France
Sweden	Australia	Portugal	Cyprus	Netherlands	Malta
Switzerland	Australia	Portugal	Denmark	North Macedonia	France
Turkey	-	-	-	-	-
Ukraine	Lithuania	Belarus	France	-	Italy
United Kingdom	Georgia	Portugal	Austria	North Macedonia	France

Maximum Points: Recent Final History (Public Voting)

Who has received the maximum points from each country in Finals since the voting system changed?

Voting country	Stockholm 2016	Kiev 2017	Lisbon 2018	Tel Aviv 2019	Rotterdam 2021
Albania	Australia	Italy	Italy	Russia	Switzerland
Andorra	-	-	-	-	-
Armenia	Russia	Cyprus	Cyprus	Russia	-
Australia	Belgium	Moldova	Israel	Norway	Iceland
Austria	Poland	Portugal	Czech Rep	Switzerland	Serbia
Azerbaijan	Russia	Bulgaria	Israel	Russia	Israel
Belarus	Russia	Bulgaria	Ukraine	Russia	-
Belgium	Poland	Portugal	Netherlands	Netherlands	France
Bosnia & H	Serbia	-	-	-	-
Bulgaria	Russia	France	Cyprus	Italy	Italy
Croatia	Serbia	Hungary	Serbia		Serbia
Cyprus	Bulgaria	Greece	Bulgaria	Greece	Greece
Czech Rep	Ukraine	Bulgaria	Ukraine	Russia	Moldova
Denmark	Sweden	Sweden	Germany	Norway	Iceland
Estonia	Russia	Belgium	Lithuania	Russia	Finland
Finland	Ukraine	Portugal	Estonia	Iceland	Iceland
France	Armenia	Portugal	Israel	Israel	Ukraine
Georgia	Armenia	Azerbaijan	Israel	Cyprus	Greece
Germany	Russia	Portugal	Italy	Norway	Lithuania
Greece	Cyprus	Cyprus	Cyprus	Cyprus	Cyprus
Hungary	Ukraine	Bulgaria	Denmark	Iceland	-
Iceland	Sweden	Portugal	Denmark	Norway	Finland
Ireland	Lithuania	Romania	Lithuania	Norway	Lithuania
Israel	France	Portugal	Czech Rep	Russia	Ukraine
Italy	Ukraine	Moldova	Albania	Albania	Ukraine
Latvia	Russia	Belgium	Lithuania	Russia	Lithuania
Lithuania	Latvia	Portugal	Estonia	Russia	Ukraine
Malta	Australia	Italy	Italy	Italy	Italy
Moldova	Russia	Romania	Israel	Russia	Russia
Montenegro	Serbia	Croatia	Serbia	Serbia	-
Netherlands	Belgium	Portugal	Germany	Norway	France
North Macedonia	Serbia	Bulgaria	Albania	Albania	Serbia
Norway	Lithuania	Portugal	Lithuania	Sweden	Lithuania
Poland	Ukraine	Belgium	Ukraine	Iceland	Ukraine
Portugal	-	Moldova	Spain	Spain	France
Romania	-	Moldova	Moldova	Netherlands	Moldova
Russia	Armenia	-	Moldova	Azerbaijan	Cyprus
San Marino	Ukraine	Bulgaria	Israel	Russia	Italy
Serbia	Russia	Hungary	Hungary	North Macedonia	Italy
Slovakia	-	-	-	-	-
Slovenia	Serbia	Croatia	Serbia	North Macedonia	Serbia
Spain	Bulgaria	Portugal	Israel	Italy	France
Sweden	Australia	Belgium	Denmark	Norway	Finland
Switzerland	Serbia	Portugal	Serbia	Italy	Serbia
Turkey	-	-	-	-	-
Ukraine	Russia	Moldova	Israel	-	Italy
United Kingdom	Lithuania	Bulgaria	Lithuania	Norway	Lithuania

Eurovision 2021 - Sharing the Love

Which countries spread their votes in the Final around the most?

Voting country	Countries receiving votes	Average points to top 3 Jury	Average points to top 3 Public	Average points to top 3 Combined	Average points to rest Jury	Average points to rest Public	Average points to rest Combined
Albania	14	8.67	9.33	18.00	1.39	1.3	2.70
Australia	14	7.67	5.33	13.00	1.52	1.8	3.35
Austria	14	8.00	6.33	14.33	1.48	1.7	3.17
Azerbaijan	16	1.33	5.33	6.67	2.35	1.8	4.17
Belgium	13	4.67	8.00	12.67	1.91	1.5	3.39
Bulgaria	16	5.67	8.33	14.00	1.78	1.4	3.22
Croatia	14	8.67	7.33	16.00	1.39	1.6	2.96
Cyprus	13	5.67	6.00	11.67	1.78	1.7	3.52
Czech Republic	14	7.00	3.67	10.67	1.61	2.0	3.65
Denmark	14	4.00	4.67	8.67	2.00	1.9	3.91
Estonia	13	8.33	5.67	14.00	1.43	1.8	3.22
Finland	13	8.33	7.00	15.33	1.43	1.6	3.04
France	15	2.33	5.33	11.50	2.22	1.8	4.04
Georgia	15	7.33	4.33	11.67	1.57	2.0	3.52
Germany	13	9.33	6.33	15.67	1.30	1.7	3.00
Greece	14	3.00	7.33	10.33	2.13	1.6	3.70
Iceland	13	8.33	6.00	14.33	1.43	1.7	3.17
Ireland	14	5.67	5.33	11.00	1.78	1.8	3.61
Israel	13	6.67	7.00	13.67	1.65	1.6	3.26
Italy	15	1.00	0.33	4.00	2.39	2.5	4.87
Latvia	12	7.67	4.67	12.33	1.52	1.9	3.43
Lithuania	14	7.67	8.00	15.67	1.52	1.5	3.00
Malta	15	4.33	5.00	9.33	1.96	1.9	3.83
Moldova	15	2.33	6.00	8.33	2.22	1.7	3.96
Netherlands	15	5.67	7.00	12.67	1.78	1.6	3.39
North Macedonia	14	7.67	6.67	14.33	1.52	1.7	3.17
Norway	13	5.33	4.33	9.67	1.83	2.0	3.78
Poland	15	4.00	7.33	11.33	2.00	1.6	3.57
Portugal	14	5.33	8.33	13.67	1.83	1.4	3.26
Romania	13	4.67	7.67	12.33	1.91	1.5	3.43
Russia	15	3.67	7.00	10.67	2.04	1.6	3.65
San Marino	13	8.67	8.33	17.00	1.39	1.4	2.83
Serbia	14	7.00	7.67	14.67	1.61	1.5	3.13
Slovenia	13	7.00	7.00	14.00	1.61	1.6	3.22
Spain	13	7.33	9.67	17.00	1.57	1.3	2.83
Sweden	13	7.00	4.67	11.67	1.61	1.9	3.52
Switzerland	14	6.67	5.33	18.00	1.65	1.8	3.48
Ukraine	14	10.00	8.00	18.00	1.22	1.5	2.70
United Kingdom	15	6.67	3.00	9.67	1.65	2.1	3.78

Notes:

The combined public and juries of Azerbaijan this year gave some points to 16 different countries, whereas Latvia focussed their points on just 12 countries.

Italy's public gave an average of 1 point to each of the other top 3 countries, and its jury gave almost nothing, compared to the 2.39 points given by its jury to each of the other countries.

In this table, "top 3" refers to the final overall standings, so Italy, France & Switzerland in 2021.

Eurovision Hosts Performance

Since the introduction of the modern points system in 1975. Two sets of points were awarded from 2016 onwards.

Year	Host Country	Points	% of max	Finished	Out of	Countries voting
1975	Sweden	72	33%	8	19	19
1976	Netherlands	56	27%	9	18	18
1977	United Kingdom	121	59%	2	18	18
1978	France	119	52%	3	20	20
1979	Israel	125	58%	1	19	19
1980	Netherlands	93	43%	5	19	19
1981	Ireland	105	46%	5	20	20
1982	United Kingdom	76	37%	7	18	18
1983	Germany	94	41%	5	20	20
1984	Luxembourg	39	18%	10	19	19
1985	Sweden	103	48%	3	19	19
1986	Norway	44	19%	12	20	20
1987	Belgium	56	22%	11	22	22
1988	Ireland	79	33%	8	21	21
1989	Switzerland	47	19%	13	22	22
1990	Yugoslavia	81	32%	7	22	22
1991	Italy	89	35%	7	22	22
1992	Sweden	9	3%	22	23	23
1993	Ireland	187	65%	1	25	25
1994	Ireland	226	78%	1	25	25
1995	Ireland	44	17%	14	23	23
1996	Norway	114	43%	2	23	23
1997	Ireland	157	55%	2	25	25
1998	United Kingdom	166	58%	2	25	25
1999	Israel	93	35%	5	23	23
2000	Sweden	88	32%	7	24	24
2001	Denmark	177	67%	2	23	23
2002	Estonia	111	40%	4	24	24
2003	Latvia	5	2%	24	26	26
2004	Turkey	195	46%	4	24	36
2005	Ukraine	30	7%	19	24	39
2006	Greece	128	29%	9	24	38
2007	Finland	53	11%	17	24	42
2008	Serbia	160	32%	6	25	43
2009	Russia	91	18%	11	25	42
2010	Norway	35	8%	20	25	39
2011	Germany	107	21%	10	25	43
2012	Azerbaijan	150	30%	4	26	42
2013	Sweden	62	14%	14	26	39
2014	Denmark	74	17%	9	26	37
2015	Austria	0	0%	26	27	40
2016	Sweden	261	27%	5	26	42
2017	Ukraine	36	4%	24	26	42
2018	Portugal	39	4%	26	26	43
2019	Israel	35	4%	23	26	41
2021	Netherlands	11	1%	23	26	39

(% of max is based on the number of countries voting, less one. It also reflects the maximum possible points that each country can award, 12 from 1975 to 2015 and 24 from 2016 onwards.)

Nil Points! Countries finishing with No Points

1. Under the old scoring system from 1975 to 2015

Year	Country	Performer	Song
1962	Belgium	Fud Leclerc	Ton nom
1962	Spain	Victor Balaguer	Llámame
1962	Austria	Eleonore Schwarz	Nur in der Wiener Luft
1962	Netherlands	De Spelbrekers	Katinka
1963	Netherlands	Annie Palmen	Een speeldoos
1963	Norway	Anita Thallaug	Solhverv
1963	Finland	Laila Halme	Muistojeni laulu
1963	Sweden	Monica Zetterlund	En gång i Stockholm
1964	Germany	Nora Nova	Man gewöhnt sich so schnell an das Schöne
1964	Portugal	António Calvário	Oração
1964	Yugoslavia	Sabahudin Kurt	Život je sklopio krug
1964	Switzerland	Anita Traversi	I miei pensieri
1965	Spain	Conchita Bautista	¡Qué bueno, qué bueno!
1965	Germany	Ulla Wiesner	Paradies, wo bist du?
1965	Belgium	Lize Marke	Als het weer lente is
1965	Finland	Viktor Klimenko	Aurinko laskee länteen
1966	Monaco	Tereza Kesovija	Bien plus fort
1966	Italy	Domenico Modugno	Dio, come ti amo
1967	Switzerland	Géraldine	Quel cœur vas-tu briser?
1970	Luxembourg	David Alexandre Winter	Je suis tombé du ciel
1978	Norway	Jahn Teigen	Mil etter mil
1981	Norway	Finn Kalvik	Aldri i livet
1982	Finland	Kojo	Nuku pommiin
1983	Turkey	Çetin Alp and The Short Waves	Opera
1983	Spain	Remedios Amaya	Quién maneja mi barca?
1987	Turkey	Seyyal Taner and Grup Locomotif	Şarkım Sevgi Üstüne
1988	Austria	Wilfried	Lisa Mona Lisa
1989	Iceland	Daniel Ágúst	Það sem enginn sér
1991	Austria	Thomas Forstner	Venedig im Regen
1994	Lithuania	Ovidijus Vyšniauskas	Lopšinė mylimai
1997	Norway	Tor Endresen	San Francisco
1997	Portugal	Célia Lawson	Antes do adeus
1998	Switzerland	Gunvor	Lass' ihn
2003	United Kingdom	Jemini	Cry Baby
2004 Semi	Switzerland	Piero & The MusicStars	Celebrate
2009 Semi	Czech Republic	Gypsy.cz	Aven Romale
2015	Germany	Ann Sophie	Black Smoke
2015	Austria	The Makemakes	I Am Yours

2. Under the current scoring system from 2016 onwards

Year	Country	Performer	Song
2016 Final (Public)	Czech Republic	Gabriela Gunčíková	I Stand
2017 Final (Jury)	Spain	Manel Navarro	Do It For Your Lover
2017 Final (Public)	Austria	Nathan Trent	Running On Air
2018 Semi (Public)	Iceland	Ari Ólafsson	Our Choice
2019 Semi (Public)	Austria	PÆNDA	Limits
2019 Final (Jury)	Israel	Kobi Marimi	Home
2019 Final (Public)	Germany	S!sters	Sister
2021 Semi (Public)	Czech Republic	Benny Cristo	Omaga
2021 Final (Jury)	United Kingdom	James Newman	Embers
2021 Final (Public)	United Kingdom	James Newman	Embers
2021 Final (Public)	Germany	Jendrik	I Don't Feel Hate
2021 Final (Public)	Spain	Blas Cantó	Voy a quedarme
2021 Final (Public)	Netherlands	Jeangu Macrooy	Birth of a New Age

Highest Scores in Finals

Including the points awarded by juries and public televoting from 2016 onwards as separate totals:

Year	Country	Performer	Song	Points	Position
2009	Norway	Alexander Rybak	Fairytale	387	1
2017 Juries	Portugal	Salvador Sobral	Amar Pelos Dois	382	1
2017 Public	Portugal	Salvador Sobral	Amar Pelos Dois	376	1
2012	Sweden	Loreen	Euphoria	372	1
2015	Sweden	Måns Zelmerlöw	Heroes	365	1
2016 Public	Russia	Sergey Lazarev	You Are The Only One	361	1
2017 Public	Bulgaria	Kristian Kostov	Beautiful Mess	337	2
2016 Public	Ukraine	Jamala	1944	323	2
2016 Juries	Australia	Dami Im	Sound of Silence	320	1
2021 Public	Italy	Måneskin	Zitti e buoni	318	1
2018 Public	Israel	Netta	Toy	317	1
2015	Russia	Polina Gagarina	A Million Voices	303	2
2006	Finland	Lordi	Hard Rock Hallelujah	292	1
2015	Italy	Il Volo	Grande Amore	292	3
2014	Austria	Conchita Wurst	Rise Like a Phoenix	290	1
2013	Denmark	Emmelie de Forest	Only Teardrops	281	1
2004	Ukraine	Ruslana	Wild Dances	280	1
2017 Juries	Bulgaria	Kristian Kostov	Beautiful Mess	278	2
2008	Russia	Dima Bilan	Believe	272	1
2018 Juries	Austria	Cesár Sampson	Nobody But You	271	3
2007	Serbia	Marija Šerifovic	Molitva	268	1
2017 Public	Moldova	Sunstroke Project	Hey, Mamma!	264	3
2019 Public	Netherlands	Duncan Laurence	Arcade	261	1

With combined final points totals from 2016 onwards:

Year	Country	Performer	Song	Points	Position
2017	Portugal	Salvador Sobral	Amar Pelos Dois	758	1
2017	Bulgaria	Kristian Kostov	Beautiful Mess	615	2
2016	Ukraine	Jamala	1944	534	1
2018	Israel	Netta	Toy	529	1
2021	Italy	Måneskin	Zitti e buoni	524	1
2021	France	Barbara Pravi	Voilà	499	2
2019	Netherlands	Duncan Laurence	Arcade	498	1

Eurovision Winners - Winning Margins

(since the introduction of the modern points system in 1975)

Year	Winner	Points	Runner-up	Points	Winning Margin	Margin as Percentage
2009	Norway	387	Iceland	218	169	78%
1982	Germany	161	Israel	100	61	61%
2010	Germany	246	Turkey	170	76	45%
1997	United Kingdom	227	Ireland	157	70	45%
2012	Sweden	372	Russia	259	113	44%
1996	Ireland	162	Norway	114	48	42%
1994	Ireland	226	Poland	166	60	36%
2000	Denmark	195	Russia	155	40	26%
1986	Belgium	176	Switzerland	140	36	26%
1978	Israel	157	Belgium	125	32	26%
1995	Norway	148	Spain	119	29	24%
2017	Portugal	758	Bulgaria	615	143	23%
1987	Ireland	172	Germany	141	31	22%
2014	Austria	290	Netherlands	238	52	22%
2018	Israel	529	Cyprus	436	93	21%
2015	Sweden	365	Russia	303	62	20%
2013	Denmark	281	Azerbaijan	234	47	20%
2005	Greece	230	Malta	192	38	20%
2008	Russia	272	Ukraine	230	42	18%
2006	Finland	292	Russia	248	44	18%
1985	Norway	123	Germany	105	18	17%
2011	Azerbaijan	221	Italy	189	32	17%
2007	Serbia	268	Ukraine	235	33	14%
1993	Ireland	187	United Kingdom	164	23	14%
1990	Italy	149	France	132	17	13%
1977	France	136	United Kingdom	121	15	12%
2001	Estonia	198	Denmark	177	21	12%
1980	Ireland	143	Germany	128	15	12%
1999	Sweden	163	Iceland	146	17	12%
1976	United Kingdom	164	France	147	17	12%
1992	Ireland	155	United Kingdom	139	16	12%
1975	Netherlands	152	United Kingdom	138	14	10%
1979	Israel	125	Spain	116	9	8%
2002	Latvia	176	Malta	164	12	7%
2019	Netherlands	498	Italy	472	26	6%
2004	Ukraine	280	Serbia & Mont	263	17	6%
1998	Israel	176	United Kingdom	166	10	6%
1984	Sweden	145	Ireland	137	8	6%
1989	Yugoslavia	137	United Kingdom	130	7	5%
2021	Italy	524	France	499	25	5%
2016	Ukraine	534	Australia	511	23	5%
1983	Luxembourg	142	Israel	136	6	4%
1981	United Kingdom	136	Germany	132	4	3%
2003	Turkey	167	Belgium	165	2	1%
1988	Switzerland	137	United Kingdom	136	1	1%
1991	Sweden	146	France	146	0	0%

Performance on Debut

Country	Debut Year	First Artist	Finish
Serbia	2007	Marija Šerifović	Winner
Serbia & Montenegro	2004	Željko Joksimović & Ad-Hoc Orchestra	2nd in final
Belgium	1956	Fud Leclerc	2nd
France	1956	Mathé Altéry	2nd
Germany	1956	Walter Andreas Schwarz	2nd
Italy	1956	Franca Raimondi	2nd
Luxembourg	1956	Michèle Arnaud	2nd
Netherlands	1956	Corry Brokken	2nd
Poland	1994	Edyta Górniak	2nd
Switzerland	1956	Lys Assia	2nd (with first song)
Denmark	1957	Birthe Wilke & Gustav Winckler	3rd
Latvia	2000	Brainstorm	3rd
Hungary	1994	Friderika Bayer	4th
Israel	1973	Ilanit	4th
Norway	1960	Nora Brockstedt	4th
Sweden	1958	Alice Babs	4th
San Marino	2008	Sirusho	4th in final
Australia	2015	Guy Sebastian	5th in final
Cyprus	1981	Island	6th
Ireland	1965	Butch Moore	6th
Moldova	2005	Zdob și Zdub	6th in final
United Kingdom	1957	Patricia Bredin	7th
Albania	2004	Anjeza Shahini	7th in final
Yugoslavia	1961	Ljiljana Petrović	8th
Armenia	2006	André	8th in final
Azerbaijan	2008	Elnur & Samir	8th in final
Russia	1994	Youddiph	9th
Spain	1961	Conchita Bautista	9th
Finland	1961	Laila Kinnunen	10th
Austria	1957	Bob Martin	10th (last)
Greece	1974	Marinella	11th
Monaco	1959	Jacques Pills	11th (last)
Georgia	2007	Sopho	12th in final
Portugal	1964	António Calvário	13th
Ukraine	2003	Olexandr	14th
Croatia	1993	Put	15th
Bosnia & Herzegovina	1993	Fazla	16th
Iceland	1986	ICY	16th
Morocco	1980	Samira Bensaïd	18th
Malta	1971	Joe Grech	18th (last)
Andorra	2004	Marta Roure	18th in semi-final
North Macedonia	1998	Vlado Janevski	19th
Slovakia	1994	Tublatanka	19th
Turkey	1975	Semiha Yankı	19th (last)
Belarus	2004	Aleksandra and Konstantin	19th in semi-final
Bulgaria	2005	Kaffe	19th in semi-final
Romania	1994	Dan Bittman	21st
Slovenia	1993	1X Band	22nd
Montenegro	2007	Stevan Faddy	22nd in semi-final
Estonia	1994	Silvi Vrait	24th
Lithuania	1994	Ovidijus Vyšniauskas	25th (last)
Czech Republic	2007	Kabát	28th in semi-final (last)

League Table of Appearances

Country	Years entered
Germany	64
France	63
United Kingdom	63
Belgium	62
Netherlands	61
Switzerland	61
Sweden	60
Spain	60
Norway	59
Ireland	54
Finland	54
Austria	53
Portugal	52
Denmark	49
Italy	46
Israel	43
Greece	41
Luxembourg	37
Cyprus	37
Turkey	34
Iceland	33
Malta	33
Yugoslavia	27
Croatia	26
Slovenia	26
Estonia	26
Monaco	24
Poland	23
Russia	23
Romania	21
Lithuania	21
Latvia	20
North Macedonia	20
Bosnia & Herzegovina	19
Hungary	17
Albania	17
Belarus	16
Moldova	16
Ukraine	16
Armenia	13
Serbia	13
Azerbaijan	13
Georgia	13
Bulgaria	13
Montenegro	11
San Marino	11
Czech Republic	9
Slovakia	7
Andorra	6
Australia	6
Serbia & Montenegro	2
Morocco	1

Top 5 closest voting relationships

Since the introduction of the modern points scoring system in 1975, including semi-finals.
"% of max" is the percentage of the maximum one country could give to the other in all contests.

1) Most Points Awarded Between Two Countries

									Average	
Pos	Country	Gave to	Total	% of max	Country	Gave to	Total	% of max	Total	% of max
1	Cyprus	Greece	491	93%	Greece	Cyprus	482	89%	487	91%
2	Norway	Sweden	454	65%	Sweden	Norway	316	48%	385	57%
3	Denmark	Sweden	449	72%	Sweden	Denmark	289	50%	369	61%
4	Denmark	Norway	280	47%	Norway	Denmark	291	49%	286	48%
5	United Kingdom	Ireland	302	52%	Ireland	United Kingdom	219	37%	261	45%

2) Highest Percentage of Possible Points Awarded Between Two Countries

									Average	
Pos	Country	Gave to	Total	% of max	Country	Gave to	Total	% of max	Total	% of max
1	Turkey	Azerbaijan	72	100%	Azerbaijan	Turkey	84	100%	78	100%
2	Romania	Moldova	263	91%	Moldova	Romania	257	97%	260	94%
3	Cyprus	Greece	491	93%	Greece	Cyprus	482	89%	487	91%
4	Montenegro	Serbia	179	93%	Serbia	Montenegro	69	82%	124	88%
5	Andorra	Spain	60	83%	Spain	Andorra	54	90%	57	87%

3) Most Number of Times Any Points Awarded Between Two Countries

									Average	
Pos	Country	Voted for	Times	% of max	Country	Voted for	Times	% of max	Times	% of max
1	Sweden	Denmark	38	88%	Denmark	Sweden	41	91%	40	90%
2	Norway	Sweden	44	88%	Sweden	Norway	37	77%	41	83%
3	Ireland	United Kingdom	37	82%	United Kingdom	Ireland	37	84%	37	83%
4	Greece	Cyprus	35	97%	Cyprus	Greece	37	100%	36	99%
5	Denmark	Norway	31	74%	Norway	Denmark	35	83%	33	79%

4) Highest Percentage of Possible Times Two Countries Have Awarded Points to each Other

									Average	
Pos	Country	Voted for	Times	% of max	Country	Voted for	Times	% of max	Times	% of max
1	Albania	Greece	25	100%	Greece	Albania	22	100%	24	100%
2	Russia	Ukraine	21	100%	Ukraine	Russia	19	100%	20	100%
3	Moldova	Romania	19	100%	Romania	Moldova	19	100%	19	100%
4	Croatia	N Macedonia	19	100%	N Macedonia	Croatia	19	100%	19	100%
5	Albania	N Macedonia	17	100%	N Macedonia	Albania	20	100%	19	100%

.. And the Bottom 5 (or the Countries who receive points but don't reciprocate)

Since the introduction of the modern points scoring system in 1975, including semi-finals.
"% of max" is the percentage of the maximum one country could give to the other in all contests.

1) The Most One-Sided Points Totals

Pos		Gave to	Total	% of max		Gave to	Total	% of max	Difference Total	Difference % of max
1	Russia	Latvia	30	12%	Latvia	Russia	240	67%	-210	-55%
2	Russia	Estonia	64	21%	Estonia	Russia	251	65%	-187	-44%
3	Lithuania	United Kingdom	22	7%	United Kingdom	Lithuania	193	49%	-171	-42%
4	Sweden	Denmark	289	50%	Denmark	Sweden	449	72%	-160	-22%
5	Turkey	France	38	10%	France	Turkey	190	44%	-152	-34%

2) The Most One-Sided Points as a percentage of the total points possible

Pos		Gave to	Total	% of max		Gave to	Total	% of max	Difference Total	Difference % of max
1	Andorra	Portugal	10	17%	Portugal	Andorra	64	76%	-54	-59%
2	Armenia	Turkey	16	13%	Turkey	Armenia	75	69%	-59	-56%
3	Russia	Latvia	30	12%	Latvia	Russia	240	67%	-210	-55%
4	Ukraine	Andorra	0	0%	Andorra	Ukraine	49	51%	-49	-51%
5	Russia	Montenegro	8	6%	Montenegro	Russia	123	54%	-115	-48%

3) The biggest difference between the number of times countries vote for each other

Pos		Voted for	Times	% of max		Voted for	Times	% of max	Difference Times	Difference % of max
1	Sweden	Spain	8	18%	Spain	Sweden	30	65%	-22	-47%
2	Sweden	United Kingdom	21	48%	United Kingdom	Sweden	40	78%	-19	-30%
3	Sweden	Slovenia	6	23%	Slovenia	Sweden	24	77%	-18	-54%
4	Ireland	Portugal	6	17%	Portugal	Ireland	24	65%	-18	-48%
5	Israel	Germany	11	28%	Germany	Israel	29	64%	-18	-36%

4) Countries who keep voting for others but get nothing in return - based on percentage of maximum possible

The change to the voting system in 2016 and the inclusion of jury and public sets of points separately in the voting stats has meant that there are no instances remaining where a currently participating country has always voted for another but received nothing from either the jury or public from that country at every opportunity.

5) Countries who keep voting for others but are never voted for in return

Pos		Voted for	Times	% of max		Voted for	Times	% of max	Difference Times	Difference % of max
1	Sweden	San Marino	0	0%	San Marino	Sweden	10	77%	-10	-77%
2	Norway	San Marino	0	0%	San Marino	Norway	10	71%	-10	-71%
3	Belgium	North Macedonia	0	0%	North Macedonia	Belgium	8	44%	-8	-44%
4	United Kingdom	San Marino	0	0%	San Marino	United Kingdom	7	70%	-7	-70%
5	Denmark	San Marino	0	0%	San Marino	Denmark	7	64%	-7	-64%

(Excludes statistics for Yugoslavia and Serbia & Montenegro - as those entities no longer exist, their figures will be permanent, and also excludes those for Morocco whose appearance in 1980 looks to be one-off.)

Each Country's Closest Voting Partners

The highest total points received from the same country since the start of the 1975 voting system, including semi-finals, and how many points those countries awarded in Finals over the last ten years. "% of max" is the percentage of the total points it has been possible for the awarding country to give.

Based on total points received

Country	Received most points from:	Points	% of max
Albania	North Macedonia	263	84%
Andorra	Spain	54	90%
Armenia	Russia	187	82%
Australia	Poland	115	56%
Austria	**Switzerland**	132	24%
Azerbaijan	Russia	213	74%
Belarus	Ukraine	155	72%
Belgium	Netherlands	233	45%
Bosnia & H	Croatia	194	70%
Bulgaria	North Macedonia	160	58%
Croatia	Slovenia	203	63%
Cyprus	Greece	482	89%
Czech Republic	Iceland	76	32%
Denmark	Norway	291	49%
Estonia	Finland	211	61%
Finland	**Estonia**	204	57%
France	**Switzerland**	174	32%
Georgia	Lithuania	147	77%
Germany	Spain	203	34%
Greece	Cyprus	491	93%
Hungary	Serbia	156	59%
Iceland	**Finland**	209	42%
Ireland	United Kingdom	302	52%
Israel	France	257	48%
Italy	Spain	221	58%
Latvia	Lithuania	189	83%
Lithuania	Ireland	227	54%
Luxembourg	Portugal	76	33%
Malta	United Kingdom	152	34%
Moldova	Romania	245	93%
Monaco	Italy	33	55%
Montenegro	Serbia	69	82%
Netherlands	Belgium	249	48%
North Macedonia	Albania	183	73%
Norway	Sweden	286	47%
Poland	Germany	140	45%
Portugal	France	242	48%
Romania	Moldova	257	97%
Russia	Estonia	251	65%
San Marino	**Albania**	59	45%
Serbia	**North Macedonia**	208	79%
Slovakia	Malta	27	45%
Slovenia	Croatia	140	47%
Spain	Portugal	184	33%
Sweden	**Norway**	454	65%
Switzerland	Austria	159	34%
Turkey	Germany	208	48%
Ukraine	Belarus	215	72%
United Kingdom	Ireland	219	38%

Based on % of maximum possible points

Country	Received most points from:	Points	% of max
Albania	North Macedonia	263	84%
Andorra	Spain	54	90%
Armenia	Russia	187	82%
Australia	Iceland	94	60%
Austria	Bulgaria	75	45%
Azerbaijan	Turkey	84	100%
Belarus	Ukraine	155	72%
Belgium	**Netherlands**	233	45%
Bosnia & H	Serbia	78	81%
Bulgaria	Cyprus	132	65%
Croatia	Bosnia & H	176	67%
Cyprus	Greece	482	89%
Czech Republic	Croatia	64	44%
Denmark	**Iceland**	261	51%
Estonia	Latvia	203	74%
Finland	Estonia	204	57%
France	Monaco	53	55%
Georgia	Armenia	141	78%
Germany	**Slovakia**	27	38%
Greece	Cyprus	491	93%
Hungary	Serbia	156	59%
Iceland	Australia	62	57%
Ireland	United Kingdom	302	52%
Israel	France	257	48%
Italy	Albania	146	81%
Latvia	Lithuania	189	83%
Lithuania	Latvia	201	67%
Luxembourg	Malta	25	52%
Malta	Luxembourg	27	56%
Moldova	Romania	245	93%
Monaco	Italy	33	55%
Montenegro	Serbia	69	82%
Netherlands	Belgium	249	48%
North Macedonia	Serbia	135	87%
Norway	Slovakia	47	49%
Poland	Germany	140	45%
Portugal	Andorra	64	76%
Romania	Moldova	257	97%
Russia	Belarus	212	88%
San Marino	Albania	59	45%
Serbia	Montenegro	179	93%
Slovakia	Malta	27	45%
Slovenia	Bosnia & H	110	54%
Spain	Andorra	60	83%
Sweden	Denmark	449	72%
Switzerland	**Austria**	194	38%
Turkey	Azerbaijan	72	100%
Ukraine	Belarus	215	72%
United Kingdom	Luxembourg	123	54%

Bold denotes change from the previous year.

Which Countries Have Never Awarded Points To Another?

(In semi-finals and finals, where voting for the recipient would have been possible, due to being drawn in the same semi-final). Includes either Jury or Public votes since 2016.)

	Countries never voted for:	Change on 2019	The Unfortunates:	First time awarded points in 2021 to:
Albania	0	-	none	
Andorra	8	-	Belarus, Bulgaria, Croatia, Czech Republic, Estonia, FYR Macedonia, Georgia, Serbia	
Armenia	2	-	Andorra, Monaco	
Australia	1	0	Albania	
Austria	3	0	Andorra, Montenegro, Morocco	
Azerbaijan	3	-	Andorra, Armenia, Slovakia	
Belarus	1	-	Monaco	
Belgium	4	0	Andorra, North Macedonia, Montenegro, Morocco	
Bosnia-H	3	-	Andorra, Luxembourg, San Marino	
Bulgaria	5	-1	Andorra, Monaco, Montenegro, Slovakia	San Marino
Croatia	2	0	Luxembourg, Monaco	
Cyprus	2	0	Andorra, Slovakia	
Czech Republic	1	0	Spain	
Denmark	4	-1	Andorra, Morocco, Slovakia	San Marino
Estonia	1	0	Montenegro	
Finland	1	0	Morocco	
France	2	0	Andorra, Morocco	
Georgia	4	0	Andorra, Ireland, Montenegro, Slovakia	
Germany	3	0	Andorra, Morocco, Slovakia	
Greece	1	0	Morocco	
Hungary	3	0	Andorra, Monaco, Slovakia	
Iceland	2	0	Monaco, Morocco	
Ireland	3	0	Montenegro, Morocco, San Marino	
Israel	1	0	Slovakia	
Italy	1	0	Slovakia	
Latvia	3	0	Andorra, Monaco, Slovakia	
Lithuania	4	0	Monaco, Montenegro, San Marino, Slovakia	
Luxembourg	4	-	Bosnia, Croatia, Morocco, Slovenia	
Malta	0	-	none	
Moldova	0	-	none	
Monaco	8	-	Andorra, Armenia, Bulgaria, Hungary, Moldova, Poland, Russia, Yugoslavia	
Montenegro	2	-	Andorra, Germany	
Morocco	8	-	Belgium, Finland, Greece, Ireland, Italy, Luxembourg, Netherlands, Portugal	
Netherlands	2	0	Morocco, Slovakia	
North Macedonia	1	0	Monaco	
Norway	3	0	Morocco, San Marino, Slovakia	
Poland	1	1	Montenegro	San Marino
Portugal	1	0	Morocco	
Romania	2	0	Andorra, Monaco	
Russia	1	0	Monaco	
San Marino	1	0	Andorra	
Serbia	1	0	Andorra	
Serbia & Mont	15	-	Andorra, Armenia, Austria, Belarus, Belgium, Denmark, France, Germany, Latvia, Malta, Monaco, Poland, Portugal, Spain, United Kingdom	
Slovakia	4	-	Bulgaria, France, Georgia, Latvia	
Slovenia	1	0	Monaco	
Spain	2	0	North Macedonia, Morocco	
Sweden	2	0	Morocco, San Marino	
Switzerland	3	-1	Andorra, Morocco, Slovakia	San Marino
Turkey	3	-	Morocco, Serbia, Slovakia	
Ukraine	2	0	Andorra, Monaco	
United Kingdom	4	-1	Andorra, Montenegro, Morocco, Slovakia	San Marino
Yugoslavia	0	-	-	

(Net change takes into account the first time one country could vote for another, so the number of countries never voted for can increase depending on the semi-final draw).

The Least Friendly Pairs - Public Voting (2016 onwards)

Using the new points allocation system from 2016, which countries' voting public have shunned each other? (Includes semi-finals)

Country	Voting public have never awarded points to or received points from:	Total
Albania	Serbia, Latvia, Malta, Georgia, Belarus	5
Armenia	Azerbaijan, Lithuania, United Kingdom, Ireland, Slovenia	5
Australia	-	0
Austria	United Kingdom, Montenegro	2
Azerbaijan	Serbia, Armenia, Finland	3
Belarus	Germany, Spain, Malta, United Kingdom, North Macedonia, Albania	6
Belgium	Bosnia & H	1
Bosnia & H	Belgium, Italy, Israel, Germany, Poland, Lithuania, Spain, Latvia, Georgia, United Kingdom, Finland, Greece, Moldova, Estonia, Iceland	15
Bulgaria	-	0
Croatia	Georgia	1
Cyprus	-	0
Czech Republic	-	0
Denmark	Serbia, Spain	2
Estonia	Bosnia & H	1
Finland	Azerbaijan, Germany, Malta, Georgia, Greece, Bosnia & H	6
France	Germany, Latvia, United Kingdom, San Marino	4
Georgia	Croatia, Spain, Malta, Switzerland, Ireland, Albania, Bosnia & H, Montenegro	8
Germany	France, Belarus, Bosnia & H, Finland, Montenegro	5
Greece	Lithuania, Latvia, Bosnia & H	3
Hungary	-	0
Iceland	Ukraine, Bosnia & H	2
Ireland	Serbia, Georgia, Armenia, Slovenia	4
Israel	Bosnia & H	1
Italy	Bosnia & H	1
Latvia	Serbia, Albania, Bosnia & H, France, Greece, Montenegro	6
Lithuania	Serbia, Armenia, Slovenia, Bosnia & H, Greece	5
Malta	Serbia, Georgia, Albania, Belarus, Finland, Slovenia	6
Moldova	United Kingdom, Bosnia & H	2
Montenegro	Germany, Poland, Latvia, Georgia, Austria, United Kingdom	7
Netherlands	-	0
North Macedonia	Spain, United Kingdom, Belarus	3
Norway	Spain, Armenia	2
Poland	Bosnia & H, Montenegro	2
Portugal	United Kingdom, Albania	2
Romania	Spain, Lithuania, United Kingdom, Albania, Finland, Slovenia	6
Russia	-	0
San Marino	France	1
Serbia	Azerbaijan, Lithuania, Latvia, Malta, United Kingdom, Albania, Ireland	7
Slovenia	Lithuania, Malta, United Kingdom, Armenia, Ireland	5
Spain	Georgia, Bosnia & H, Belarus, Denmark, North Macedonia	5
Sweden	Georgia	1
Switzerland	Georgia	1
Ukraine	-	0
United Kingdom	France, Serbia, Austria, Armenia, Belarus, North Macedonia, Slovenia, Bosnia & H, Montenegro	9

(As 2016 was the first year the public vote was treated separately from the jury vote, this list will include losing semi-finalists to whom some of the finalists will not yet have had an opportunity to award points.)

Jury/Public Vote Points Split in Finals since 2016

Countries with no split shown have not qualified for the final since 2016.

Jury/Public Vote Points Split in Finals since 2016

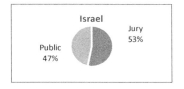

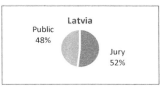
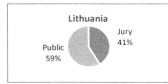
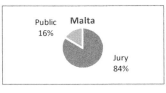
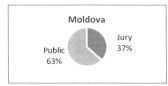

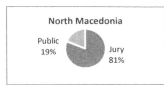

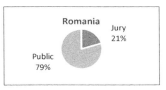

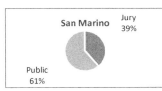

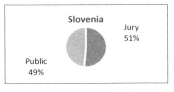
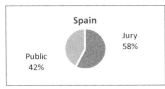

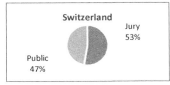
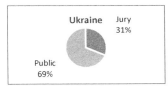
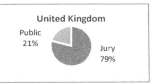

Most Points Received Since 1975

Despite most of Eastern Europe only joining in the 1990's, the results are not quite what you'd think....
(includes combined jury/public voting points since 2016)

Semi-finals

Country	Total Points Received	Contests	Average Points
Albania	1289	10	129
Andorra	157	6	26
Armenia	1308	12	109
Australia	991	5	198
Austria	942	11	86
Azerbaijan	1551	12	129
Belarus	1025	16	64
Belgium	1334	16	83
Bosnia & H	945	8	118
Bulgaria	1501	13	115
Croatia	1105	14	79
Cyprus	1520	15	101
Czech Republic	784	9	87
Denmark	1490	15	99
Estonia	1230	17	72
Finland	1389	16	87
France	-	-	-
Georgia	946	13	73
Germany	-	-	-
Greece	1771	14	127
Hungary	1042	11	95
Iceland	1513	16	95
Ireland	904	15	60
Israel	1592	15	106
Italy	-	-	-
Latvia	946	12	79
Lithuania	1369	13	105
Luxembourg	-	-	-
Malta	1453	15	97
Moldova	1618	15	108
Monaco	46	3	15
Montenegro	483	11	44
Morocco	-	-	-
Netherlands	1483	16	93
North Macedonia	1108	17	65
Norway	1757	14	126
Poland	1006	14	72
Portugal	1261	14	90
Romania	1465	13	113
Russia	1892	12	158
San Marino	533	11	48
Serbia	1372	12	114
Serbia & Mont	263	1	263
Slovakia	102	4	26
Slovenia	1050	17	62
Spain	-	-	-
Sweden	1980	12	165
Switzerland	1189	16	74
Turkey	790	7	113
Ukraine	1847	12	154
United Kingdom	-	-	-
Yugoslavia	-	-	-

Finals

Country	Total Points Received	Contests	Average Points
Albania	835	16	52
Andorra	-	-	-
Armenia	1276	10	128
Australia	1821	5	364
Austria	1980	33	60
Azerbaijan	1775	12	148
Belarus	366	6	61
Belgium	2303	33	70
Bosnia & H	1242	18	69
Bulgaria	1415	5	283
Croatia	1216	18	68
Cyprus	2100	31	68
Czech Republic	479	3	160
Denmark	2743	34	81
Estonia	1464	16	92
Finland	1532	33	46
France	3766	45	84
Georgia	631	7	90
Germany	3062	45	68
Greece	3054	38	80
Hungary	1112	14	79
Iceland	1924	26	74
Ireland	3079	35	88
Israel	3058	35	87
Italy	3795	27	141
Latvia	835	13	64
Lithuania	1054	12	88
Luxembourg	935	19	49
Malta	2105	24	88
Moldova	1322	11	120
Monaco	330	5	66
Montenegro	81	2	41
Morocco	7	1	7
Netherlands	2710	33	82
North Macedonia	674	9	75
Norway	3244	42	77
Poland	809	14	58
Portugal	1931	33	59
Romania	1471	18	82
Russia	3531	22	161
San Marino	141	3	47
Serbia	1271	10	127
Serbia & Mont	400	2	200
Slovakia	42	3	14
Slovenia	723	15	48
Spain	2380	46	52
Sweden	5096	45	113
Switzerland	2590	31	84
Turkey	1996	33	60
Ukraine	2749	16	172
United Kingdom	3453	46	75
Yugoslavia	730	13	56

Eurovision 2021 East v West

(With 22 countries from the "west" and 17 from the "east" taking part this year, how strong was geographical voting?)

Semi-Final 1 (8 "eastern" voting countries, 11 "western" voting countries)

Points received from Juries

East	Total	East	% of max	West	% of max
Lithuania	66	17	20%	49	37%
Slovenia	36	18	21%	18	14%
Russia	117	42	50%	75	57%
North Macedonia	12	10	12%	2	2%
Croatia	57	33	39%	24	18%
Romania	58	22	26%	36	27%
Azerbaijan	47	18	21%	29	22%
Ukraine	103	46	55%	57	43%
Average		25.75	31%	36.3	27%

Points received from Public

East	Total	East	% of max	West	% of max
Lithuania	137	35	29%	102	77%
Slovenia	8	8	7%	0	0%
Russia	108	52	43%	56	42%
North Macedonia	11	11	9%	0	0%
Croatia	53	26	22%	27	20%
Romania	27	5	4%	22	17%
Azerbaijan	91	48	40%	43	33%
Ukraine	164	70	58%	94	71%
Average		31.9	27%	43.0	33%

Points received from Juries

West	Total	East	% of max	West	% of max
Sweden	91	25	19%	66	55%
Australia	26	25	19%	1	1%
Ireland	16	3	2%	13	11%
Cyprus	92	43	33%	49	41%
Norway	38	7	5%	31	26%
Belgium	70	37	28%	33	28%
Israel	99	45	34%	54	45%
Malta	174	73	55%	101	84%
Average		32.3	24%	43.5	36%

Points received from Public

West	Total	East	% of max	West	% of max
Sweden	51	13	10%	38	29%
Australia	2	2	2%	0	0%
Ireland	4	1	1%	3	2%
Cyprus	78	34	26%	44	33%
Norway	77	35	27%	42	32%
Belgium	47	25	19%	22	17%
Israel	93	40	30%	53	40%
Malta	151	59	45%	92	70%
Average		26.1	24%	36.8	26%

Semi-Final 2 (10 "eastern" voting countries, 11 "western" voting countries)

Points received from Juries

East	Total	East	% of max	West	% of max
Estonia	29	21	19%	8	6%
Czech Republic	23	12	11%	11	8%
Poland	18	3	3%	15	11%
Moldova	56	30	28%	26	20%
Serbia	56	16	15%	40	30%
Georgia	1	1	1%	0	0%
Albania	74	23	21%	51	39%
Bulgaria	149	60	56%	89	67%
Latvia	4	4	4%	0	0%
Average		18.9	17%	26.7	20%

Points received from Public

East	Total	East	% of max	West	% of max
Estonia	29	15	14%	14	11%
Czech Republic	0	0	0%	0	0%
Poland	17	7	6%	10	8%
Moldova	123	55	51%	68	52%
Serbia	68	22	20%	46	35%
Georgia	15	11	10%	4	3%
Albania	38	9	8%	29	22%
Bulgaria	101	41	38%	60	45%
Latvia	10	6	6%	4	3%
Average		18.4	17%	26.1	20%

Points received from Juries

West	Total	East	% of max	West	% of max
San Marino	76	38	32%	38	32%
Greece	104	56	47%	48	40%
Austria	53	26	22%	27	23%
Iceland	140	62	52%	78	65%
Portugal	128	55	46%	73	61%
Finland	84	38	32%	46	38%
Switzerland	156	74	62%	82	68%
Denmark	9	3	3%	6	5%
Average		44.0	37%	49.8	41%

Points received from Public

West	Total	East	% of max	West	% of max
San Marino	42	28	23%	14	12%
Greece	80	51	43%	29	24%
Austria	13	3	3%	10	8%
Iceland	148	61	51%	87	73%
Portugal	111	38	32%	73	61%
Finland	150	79	66%	71	59%
Switzerland	135	64	53%	71	59%
Denmark	80	32	27%	48	40%
Average		44.5	37%	50.4	42%

Eurovision 2021 - East v West

(With 22 countries from the "west" and 17 from the "east" taking part this year, how strong was geographical voting?)

FINAL (17 "eastern" voting countries, 22 "western" voting countries)

Finalists

		Points received from Juries					Points received from Public			
East	Total	East	% of max	West	% of max	Total	East	% of max	West	% of max
Albania	22	0	0%	22	8%	35	11	5%	24	9%
Russia	104	39	16%	65	25%	100	71	30%	29	11%
Serbia	20	20	8%	0	0%	82	41	17%	41	16%
Moldova	53	38	16%	15	6%	62	37	15%	25	9%
Bulgaria	140	48	20%	92	35%	30	5	2%	25	9%
Lithuania	55	13	5%	42	16%	165	54	23%	111	42%
Ukraine	97	41	17%	56	21%	267	120	50%	147	56%
Azerbaijan	32	24	10%	8	3%	33	28	12%	5	2%
Average		**27.9**	**12%**	**37.5**	**14%**		**45.9**	**19%**	**50.9**	**19%**

West	Total	East	% of max	West	% of max	Total	East	% of max	West	% of max
Cyprus	50	12	6%	38	15%	44	22	9%	22	9%
Israel	73	38	19%	35	14%	20	13	5%	7	3%
Belgium	71	31	15%	40	16%	3	3	1%	0	0%
Malta	208	79	39%	129	51%	47	2	1%	45	18%
Portugal	126	67	33%	59	23%	27	0	0%	27	11%
United Kingdom	0	0	0%	0	0%	0	0	0%	0	0%
Greece	91	45	22%	46	18%	79	48	19%	31	12%
Switzerland	267	107	52%	160	63%	165	80	32%	85	34%
Iceland	198	86	42%	112	44%	180	46	18%	134	53%
Spain	6	4	2%	2	1%	0	0	0%	0	0%
Germany	3	1	0%	2	1%	0	0	0%	0	0%
Finland	83	40	20%	43	17%	218	99	39%	119	47%
France	248	94	46%	154	61%	251	101	40%	150	60%
Norway	15	1	0%	14	6%	60	23	9%	37	15%
Netherlands	11	4	2%	7	3%	0	0	0%	0	0%
Italy	206	125	61%	81	32%	318	161	64%	157	62%
Sweden	46	12	6%	34	13%	63	11	4%	52	21%
San Marino	37	17	8%	20	8%	13	10	4%	3	1%
Average		**42.4**	**21%**	**54.2**	**22%**		**34.4**	**14%**	**48.3**	**19%**

Notes:

"% of max" is the most points a country could have received, so for example there were 22 "western" countries voting in the final, so the most points a "western" country could have received from other "western" countries was 21 x 12 points, but "eastern" countries could have received 22 x 12 points.

Whether a country falls into the category of "western" or "eastern" is of course, fairly arbitrary. The above statistics allocate countries along what is normally considered traditional east and west groupings, with Australia, Israel, Greece and Cyprus being included in the "western" category.

Eurovision 2021 Bloc Voting in Final

Jury voting

Balkan bloc

Country	Average points received from Balkan bloc	Other countries
Albania	0.00	0.65
Serbia	5.00	0.00
Total	**5.00**	**0.65**

Scandinavian bloc

Country	Average points received from Scandinavian bloc	Other countries
Iceland	6.33	5.11
Norway	1.67	0.29
Sweden	4.00	0.97
Total	**12.00**	**6.37**

Former Soviet Union bloc

Country	Average points received from Former Soviet bloc	Other countries
Russia	2.88	2.61
Moldova	2.50	1.06
Lithuania	1.38	1.42
Ukraine	4.50	1.97
Azerbaijan	2.75	0.32
Total	**14.00**	**7.39**

Public voting

Balkan bloc

Country	Average points received from Balkan bloc	Other countries
Albania		
Serbia		
Total	**0.00**	**0.00**

Scandinavian bloc

Country	Average points received from Scandinavian bloc	Other countries
Iceland		
Norway		
Sweden		
Total	**0.00**	**0.00**

Former Soviet Union bloc

Country	Average points received from Former Soviet bloc	Other countries
Russia		
Moldova		
Lithuania		
Ukraine		
Azerbaijan		
Total	**0.00**	**0.00**

Notes on voting countries in each bloc (not all participated this year):

Balkan bloc:

Albania, Croatia, North Macedonia, Montenegro, Serbia, Slovenia, Bosnia

Scandinavian bloc:

Denmark, Iceland, Norway, Sweden

Former Soviet Union bloc:

Armenia, Azerbaijan, Belarus, Estonia, Georgia, Latvia, Lithuania, Moldova, Russia

Eurovision 2021: Who Votes for Who? (And Who Doesn't)

Since the introduction of the modern points scoring system in 1975, including semi-finals. Since 2008, this figure is based on which semi-final each country was drawn to vote/perform in and which countries then made the final. Previous voting arrangements are also taken into account, including the 2004 voting boycott by France, Poland & Russia. "% of max" is the percentage of the maximum one country could have given to the other in the semi-finals and final. From 2016 the analysis of the awarding of 12 points includes the jury and public televoting points separately but the total points and the frequency that any points have been awarded are based on the final combined score.

Albania

	Albania awarded points to:				Frequency	
	Total	% of max	12's	% of max	Times	% of max
Albania	-	-	-	-	-	-
Andorra	6	13%	0	0%	1	25%
Armenia	42	15%	0	0%	8	44%
Australia	56	36%	2	15%	6	86%
Austria	26	11%	0	0%	6	46%
Azerbaijan	104	33%	0	0%	14	74%
Belarus	13	6%	0	0%	3	20%
Belgium	42	15%	0	0%	9	53%
Bosnia & H	70	49%	1	8%	8	67%
Bulgaria	103	43%	0	0%	11	85%
Croatia	38	17%	0	0%	8	53%
Cyprus	96	32%	2	8%	11	61%
Czech Republic	3	2%	0	0%	2	25%
Denmark	20	6%	0	0%	7	32%
Estonia	16	6%	0	0%	5	29%
Finland	39	13%	0	0%	7	35%
France	57	22%	0	0%	10	59%
Georgia	5	2%	0	0%	2	13%
Germany	49	19%	0	0%	9	53%
Greece	264	71%	9	29%	25	100%
Hungary	59	22%	0	0%	10	53%
Iceland	28	9%	0	0%	5	23%
Ireland	20	9%	0	0%	4	27%
Israel	58	19%	0	0%	11	61%
Italy	146	81%	7	47%	10	100%
Latvia	1	0%	0	0%	1	5%
Lithuania	14	5%	0	0%	4	21%
Luxembourg	0	-	0	-	0	-
Malta	59	23%	0	0%	13	76%
Moldova	47	15%	1	4%	9	43%
Monaco	2	6%	0	0%	1	33%
Montenegro	43	51%	2	29%	5	83%
Morocco	0	-	0	-	0	-
Netherlands	40	15%	0	0%	7	44%
North Macedonia	183	73%	8	38%	17	100%
Norway	54	17%	1	4%	9	43%
Poland	23	9%	0	0%	5	31%
Portugal	55	24%	1	5%	7	47%
Romania	42	18%	0	0%	8	44%
Russia	72	23%	1	4%	10	45%
San Marino	59	45%	0	0%	7	88%
Serbia	41	15%	0	0%	13	76%
Serbia & Mont	17	47%	0	0%	3	100%
Slovakia	4	17%	0	0%	1	50%
Slovenia	24	12%	0	0%	4	31%
Spain	55	21%	2	9%	8	47%
Sweden	90	27%	0	0%	17	81%
Switzerland	94	34%	0	0%	9	53%
Turkey	113	78%	3	25%	12	100%
Ukraine	42	13%	0	0%	8	38%
United Kingdom	31	12%	0	0%	6	35%
Yugoslavia	0	-	0	-	0	-

Andorra

	Andorra awarded points to:				Frequency	
	Total	% of max	12's	% of max	Times	% of max
Albania	6	7%	0	0%	1	14%
Andorra	-	-	-	-	-	-
Armenia	3	4%	0	0%	1	14%
Australia	0	-	0	-	0	-
Austria	8	22%	0	0%	2	67%
Azerbaijan	15	42%	0	0%	2	67%
Belarus	0	0%	0	0%	0	0%
Belgium	8	11%	0	0%	2	33%
Bosnia & H	6	5%	0	0%	2	20%
Bulgaria	0	0%	0	0%	0	0%
Croatia	0	0%	0	0%	0	0%
Cyprus	6	10%	0	0%	2	40%
Czech Republic	0	0%	0	0%	0	0%
Denmark	18	21%	0	0%	4	57%
Estonia	0	0%	0	0%	0	0%
Finland	49	45%	1	11%	7	78%
France	26	36%	0	0%	5	83%
Georgia	0	0%	0	0%	0	0%
Germany	5	7%	0	0%	1	17%
Greece	34	35%	0	0%	6	75%
Hungary	17	35%	0	0%	4	100%
Iceland	24	29%	0	0%	3	43%
Ireland	6	8%	0	0%	2	33%
Israel	45	42%	1	11%	6	67%
Italy	0	-	0	-	0	-
Latvia	12	14%	0	0%	2	29%
Lithuania	13	18%	0	0%	3	50%
Luxembourg	0	-	0	-	0	-
Malta	18	21%	0	0%	4	57%
Moldova	5	6%	0	0%	2	29%
Monaco	17	47%	0	0%	3	100%
Montenegro	1	3%	0	0%	1	33%
Morocco	0	-	0	-	0	-
Netherlands	19	26%	0	0%	4	67%
North Macedonia	0	0%	0	0%	0	0%
Norway	26	27%	0	0%	5	63%
Poland	10	14%	0	0%	1	17%
Portugal	64	76%	4	57%	6	86%
Romania	34	31%	0	0%	6	67%
Russia	22	23%	0	0%	5	63%
San Marino	2	17%	0	0%	1	100%
Serbia	0	0%	0	0%	0	0%
Serbia & Mont	3	8%	0	0%	2	67%
Slovakia	0	-	0	-	0	-
Slovenia	8	11%	0	0%	1	17%
Spain	60	83%	5	83%	5	83%
Sweden	32	33%	0	0%	6	75%
Switzerland	9	13%	0	0%	3	50%
Turkey	15	14%	0	0%	3	33%
Ukraine	49	51%	1	13%	6	75%
United Kingdom	6	8%	0	0%	2	33%
Yugoslavia	0	-	0	-	0	-

Armenia

	Armenia awarded points to:				Frequency	
	Total	% of max	12's	% of max	Times	% of max
Albania	6	3%	0	0%	2	13%
Andorra	0	0%	0	0%	0	0%
Armenia	-	-	-	-	-	-
Australia	13	10%	0	0%	5	83%
Austria	30	16%	0	0%	6	60%
Azerbaijan	3	1%	0	0%	2	11%
Belarus	58	35%	1	7%	8	73%
Belgium	36	18%	0	0%	8	62%
Bosnia & H	19	14%	0	0%	5	50%
Bulgaria	31	18%	0	0%	6	60%
Croatia	17	9%	0	0%	5	45%
Cyprus	121	53%	5	26%	9	75%
Czech Republic	43	26%	0	0%	6	75%
Denmark	18	8%	0	0%	6	43%
Estonia	24	12%	0	0%	4	31%
Finland	14	6%	0	0%	2	12%
France	73	36%	1	6%	12	92%
Georgia	141	78%	4	27%	13	100%
Germany	11	5%	0	0%	2	15%
Greece	146	53%	0	0%	17	94%
Hungary	10	5%	0	0%	3	21%
Iceland	26	11%	1	5%	6	38%
Ireland	4	2%	0	0%	2	18%
Israel	68	28%	1	5%	7	47%
Italy	37	26%	0	0%	6	75%
Latvia	5	3%	0	0%	2	20%
Lithuania	6	3%	0	0%	2	15%
Luxembourg	0	-	0	-	0	-
Malta	85	44%	1	6%	8	67%
Moldova	81	34%	0	0%	10	67%
Monaco	0	0%	0	0%	0	0%
Montenegro	44	37%	1	10%	6	75%
Morocco	0	-	0	-	0	-
Netherlands	62	26%	0	0%	8	57%
North Macedonia	39	25%	0	0%	4	40%
Norway	61	27%	0	0%	13	87%
Poland	14	8%	0	0%	5	45%
Portugal	49	34%	1	8%	5	50%
Romania	26	12%	0	0%	9	56%
Russia	217	82%	12	55%	18	100%
San Marino	14	13%	0	0%	4	57%
Serbia	26	15%	0	0%	5	45%
Serbia & Mont	0	-	0	-	0	-
Slovakia	0	-	0	-	0	-
Slovenia	6	4%	0	0%	2	18%
Spain	13	6%	0	0%	4	31%
Sweden	100	35%	3	13%	13	72%
Switzerland	42	25%	0	0%	6	55%
Turkey	16	13%	0	0%	3	30%
Ukraine	102	50%	3	18%	12	86%
United Kingdom	15	7%	0	0%	4	31%
Yugoslavia	0	-	0	-	0	-

Australia

	Australia awarded points to:				Frequency	
	Total	% of max	12's	% of max	Times	% of max
Albania	0	0%	0	0%	0	0%
Andorra	0	-	0	-	0	-
Armenia	11	11%	0	0%	2	40%
Australia	-	-	-	-	-	-
Austria	11	13%	0	0%	3	75%
Azerbaijan	15	9%	0	0%	4	50%
Belarus	8	7%	0	0%	2	40%
Belgium	70	36%	4	25%	6	67%
Bosnia & H	0	-	0	-	0	-
Bulgaria	51	43%	0	0%	4	80%
Croatia	7	10%	0	0%	3	100%
Cyprus	42	19%	0	0%	6	60%
Czech Republic	37	28%	1	9%	4	67%
Denmark	46	35%	1	9%	5	83%
Estonia	23	24%	0	0%	4	80%
Finland	18	17%	0	0%	4	80%
France	37	28%	0	0%	3	50%
Georgia	13	9%	0	0%	3	43%
Germany	15	11%	0	0%	2	33%
Greece	25	17%	0	0%	3	43%
Hungary	16	11%	0	0%	3	43%
Iceland	62	57%	1	11%	4	80%
Ireland	24	29%	0	0%	3	75%
Israel	65	34%	1	6%	6	67%
Italy	28	21%	0	0%	4	67%
Latvia	27	23%	0	0%	4	67%
Lithuania	46	32%	0	0%	6	86%
Luxembourg	0	-	0	-	0	-
Malta	65	49%	0	0%	6	100%
Moldova	71	54%	2	18%	4	67%
Monaco	0	-	0	-	0	-
Montenegro	7	7%	0	0%	1	20%
Morocco	0	-	0	-	0	-
Netherlands	24	15%	0	0%	5	71%
North Macedonia	16	19%	0	0%	3	75%
Norway	49	26%	1	6%	8	89%
Poland	28	17%	1	7%	4	50%
Portugal	34	28%	0	0%	3	50%
Romania	11	11%	0	0%	2	40%
Russia	44	31%	0	0%	6	86%
San Marino	9	8%	0	0%	2	40%
Serbia	28	15%	1	6%	6	67%
Serbia & Mont	0	-	0	-	0	-
Slovakia	0	-	0	-	0	-
Slovenia	19	10%	0	0%	4	44%
Spain	14	11%	0	0%	2	33%
Sweden	110	51%	5	28%	8	80%
Switzerland	23	27%	0	0%	3	75%
Turkey	0	-	0	-	0	-
Ukraine	56	33%	0	0%	5	71%
United Kingdom	29	22%	1	9%	3	50%
Yugoslavia	0	-	0	-	0	-

Austria   Azerbaijan

	Austria awarded points to:				Frequency			Azerbaijan awarded points to:				Frequency	
	Total	% of max	12's	% of max	Times	% of max		Total	% of max	12's	% of max	Times	% of max
Albania	65	27%	1	5%	11	79%	Albania	72	27%	2	9%	10	63%
Andorra	0	0%	0	0%	0	0%	Andorra	0	0%	0	0%	0	0%
Armenia	39	22%	1	7%	6	60%	Armenia	0	0%	0	0%	0	0%
Australia	30	28%	2	22%	3	60%	Australia	20	13%	0	0%	3	43%
Austria	-	-	-	-	-	-	Austria	12	6%	0	0%	3	30%
Azerbaijan	46	20%	1	5%	6	50%	Azerbaijan	-	-	-	-	-	-
Belarus	25	12%	0	0%	3	21%	Belarus	56	52%	3	33%	5	83%
Belgium	77	15%	0	0%	19	50%	Belgium	22	10%	0	0%	6	50%
Bosnia & H	108	50%	4	22%	12	71%	Bosnia & H	24	25%	0	0%	4	57%
Bulgaria	88	41%	1	6%	10	91%	Bulgaria	47	33%	1	8%	6	86%
Croatia	117	35%	1	4%	16	73%	Croatia	19	9%	0	0%	6	55%
Cyprus	32	6%	0	0%	9	25%	Cyprus	43	14%	0	0%	8	50%
Czech Republic	51	33%	1	8%	5	71%	Czech Republic	23	15%	0	0%	4	57%
Denmark	120	22%	2	4%	20	50%	Denmark	17	8%	0	0%	4	29%
Estonia	55	15%	0	0%	13	54%	Estonia	26	14%	0	0%	7	58%
Finland	52	11%	0	0%	10	28%	Finland	11	5%	0	0%	3	21%
France	138	26%	4	9%	18	46%	France	15	7%	0	0%	3	23%
Georgia	2	2%	0	0%	1	11%	Georgia	89	62%	1	8%	10	100%
Germany	131	25%	1	2%	23	59%	Germany	6	3%	0	0%	2	15%
Greece	57	11%	0	0%	15	38%	Greece	107	36%	1	4%	15	79%
Hungary	79	27%	1	4%	12	63%	Hungary	69	32%	0	0%	9	64%
Iceland	93	23%	0	0%	14	50%	Iceland	7	3%	0	0%	2	12%
Ireland	196	39%	4	10%	24	63%	Ireland	20	10%	0	0%	6	46%
Israel	123	23%	3	7%	20	54%	Israel	116	42%	1	4%	13	81%
Italy	120	32%	0	0%	16	62%	Italy	41	23%	0	0%	6	60%
Latvia	24	11%	0	0%	5	33%	Latvia	31	20%	0	0%	6	60%
Lithuania	9	3%	0	0%	4	21%	Lithuania	33	13%	0	0%	9	60%
Luxembourg	47	22%	0	0%	9	50%	Luxembourg	0	-	0	-	0	-
Malta	77	20%	1	3%	14	54%	Malta	112	49%	1	5%	11	85%
Moldova	42	15%	0	0%	9	53%	Moldova	102	40%	0	0%	13	87%
Monaco	14	19%	0	0%	3	50%	Monaco	0	-	0	-	0	-
Montenegro	0	0%	0	0%	0	0%	Montenegro	34	28%	0	0%	5	63%
Morocco	0	0%	0	0%	0	0%	Morocco	0	-	0	-	0	-
Netherlands	171	30%	3	6%	24	60%	Netherlands	28	12%	0	0%	5	38%
North Macedonia	37	15%	1	5%	6	38%	North Macedonia	34	28%	0	0%	3	50%
Norway	82	15%	1	2%	17	41%	Norway	70	24%	1	4%	12	67%
Poland	60	26%	2	11%	10	63%	Poland	21	13%	0	0%	6	55%
Portugal	60	14%	1	3%	7	21%	Portugal	42	32%	1	9%	5	63%
Romania	86	31%	1	4%	13	65%	Romania	85	39%	0	0%	13	87%
Russia	106	32%	1	4%	13	57%	Russia	220	76%	10	42%	17	94%
San Marino	9	6%	0	0%	3	43%	San Marino	44	28%	0	0%	7	70%
Serbia	111	49%	2	11%	13	100%	Serbia	12	7%	0	0%	2	18%
Serbia & Mont	36	100%	3	100%	3	100%	Serbia & Mont	0	-	0	-	0	-
Slovakia	3	8%	0	0%	1	33%	Slovakia	0	0%	0	0%	0	0%
Slovenia	35	13%	0	0%	9	45%	Slovenia	24	13%	1	7%	5	45%
Spain	68	13%	0	0%	12	30%	Spain	4	2%	0	0%	3	23%
Sweden	188	33%	4	9%	24	59%	Sweden	48	15%	0	0%	11	61%
Switzerland	194	38%	3	7%	25	68%	Switzerland	28	16%	0	0%	5	45%
Turkey	70	21%	1	4%	11	39%	Turkey	72	100%	6	100%	6	100%
Ukraine	37	16%	0	0%	8	53%	Ukraine	167	70%	3	15%	15	100%
United Kingdom	168	31%	7	16%	24	60%	United Kingdom	7	3%	0	0%	2	15%
Yugoslavia	24	17%	0	0%	5	42%	Yugoslavia	0	-	0	-	0	-

Belarus

Belgium

	Belarus awarded points to:				Frequency			Belgium awarded points to:				Frequency	
	Total	% of max	12's	% of max	Times	% of max		Total	% of max	12's	% of max	Times	% of max
Albania	24	10%	1	5%	3	18%	Albania	63	20%	0	0%	12	60%
Andorra	4	7%	0	0%	1	20%	Andorra	0	0%	0	0%	0	0%
Armenia	92	45%	1	6%	13	93%	Armenia	126	50%	5	24%	14	82%
Australia	57	37%	0	0%	7	100%	Australia	89	44%	3	18%	7	78%
Austria	32	14%	0	0%	5	36%	Austria	131	26%	4	10%	21	55%
Azerbaijan	71	37%	0	0%	9	75%	Azerbaijan	42	15%	0	0%	9	53%
Belarus	-	-	-	-	-	-	Belarus	4	1%	0	0%	1	6%
Belgium	53	20%	1	5%	8	47%	Belgium	-	-	-	-	-	-
Bosnia & H	21	12%	0	0%	5	33%	Bosnia & H	26	10%	0	0%	7	32%
Bulgaria	78	33%	4	20%	7	50%	Bulgaria	57	26%	0	0%	8	67%
Croatia	36	16%	0	0%	7	47%	Croatia	20	6%	0	0%	9	41%
Cyprus	49	18%	1	4%	7	41%	Cyprus	99	17%	0	0%	19	48%
Czech Republic	39	25%	0	0%	3	38%	Czech Republic	52	31%	0	0%	6	75%
Denmark	36	12%	0	0%	9	43%	Denmark	115	22%	1	2%	20	50%
Estonia	64	22%	1	4%	11	58%	Estonia	50	14%	1	3%	10	38%
Finland	27	11%	0	0%	6	35%	Finland	60	10%	0	0%	12	27%
France	11	5%	0	0%	2	13%	France	168	29%	1	2%	22	51%
Georgia	88	43%	1	6%	12	86%	Georgia	32	17%	0	0%	8	67%
Germany	8	3%	0	0%	1	6%	Germany	141	24%	0	0%	22	51%
Greece	66	23%	1	4%	13	65%	Greece	157	26%	2	4%	27	61%
Hungary	37	15%	0	0%	9	56%	Hungary	52	19%	1	4%	10	53%
Iceland	53	22%	2	10%	9	53%	Iceland	106	23%	1	3%	15	44%
Ireland	11	5%	0	0%	4	25%	Ireland	181	33%	5	11%	30	71%
Israel	83	27%	1	4%	14	74%	Israel	164	26%	1	2%	27	61%
Italy	18	12%	0	0%	4	44%	Italy	103	28%	1	3%	14	54%
Latvia	47	26%	0	0%	10	77%	Latvia	43	17%	1	5%	6	33%
Lithuania	101	35%	0	0%	14	74%	Lithuania	49	16%	0	0%	7	35%
Luxembourg	0	-	0	-	0	-	Luxembourg	53	23%	0	0%	8	42%
Malta	57	24%	1	5%	11	65%	Malta	80	22%	0	0%	10	37%
Moldova	104	48%	1	6%	14	88%	Moldova	38	13%	0	0%	9	43%
Monaco	0	0%	0	0%	0	0%	Monaco	16	17%	0	0%	3	38%
Montenegro	5	6%	0	0%	2	33%	Montenegro	0	0%	0	0%	0	0%
Morocco	0	-	0	-	0	-	Morocco	0	0%	0	0%	0	0%
Netherlands	36	14%	0	0%	5	31%	Netherlands	249	46%	8	18%	30	75%
North Macedonia	22	8%	0	0%	5	25%	North Macedonia	0	0%	0	0%	0	0%
Norway	99	34%	1	4%	13	68%	Norway	147	24%	1	2%	27	60%
Poland	60	29%	0	0%	10	77%	Poland	62	20%	2	8%	9	43%
Portugal	34	16%	0	0%	4	27%	Portugal	112	22%	2	5%	17	44%
Romania	27	11%	0	0%	10	53%	Romania	81	25%	0	0%	14	56%
Russia	212	88%	15	75%	18	100%	Russia	108	28%	1	3%	18	64%
San Marino	11	13%	0	0%	2	50%	San Marino	2	2%	0	0%	1	14%
Serbia	44	16%	0	0%	9	53%	Serbia	26	10%	0	0%	6	38%
Serbia & Mont	20	56%	0	0%	3	100%	Serbia & Mont	10	28%	0	0%	2	67%
Slovakia	3	8%	0	0%	1	33%	Slovakia	4	7%	0	0%	2	40%
Slovenia	31	13%	0	0%	7	44%	Slovenia	22	6%	0	0%	6	25%
Spain	2	1%	0	0%	1	6%	Spain	128	22%	3	6%	25	57%
Sweden	80	28%	0	0%	13	65%	Sweden	220	33%	5	9%	33	69%
Switzerland	33	15%	0	0%	6	43%	Switzerland	135	27%	3	7%	19	51%
Turkey	18	12%	0	0%	5	38%	Turkey	140	34%	6	18%	18	53%
Ukraine	215	72%	8	32%	20	95%	Ukraine	98	28%	0	0%	12	52%
United Kingdom	6	3%	0	0%	3	19%	United Kingdom	149	25%	7	14%	21	48%
Yugoslavia	0	-	0	-	0	-	Yugoslavia	45	29%	1	8%	7	54%

Bosnia & Herzegovina

	Bosnia awarded points to:				Frequency	
	Total	% of max	12's	% of max	Times	% of max
Albania	43	36%	0	0%	9	90%
Andorra	0	0%	0	0%	0	0%
Armenia	25	17%	0	0%	5	50%
Australia	13	54%	0	0%	1	100%
Austria	53	26%	1	6%	8	53%
Azerbaijan	53	44%	0	0%	7	88%
Belarus	8	7%	0	0%	3	30%
Belgium	22	10%	0	0%	3	18%
Bosnia & H	-	-	-	-	-	-
Bulgaria	18	17%	0	0%	5	63%
Croatia	176	67%	6	27%	18	90%
Cyprus	2	1%	0	0%	1	6%
Czech Republic	22	31%	1	17%	2	50%
Denmark	12	6%	0	0%	4	24%
Estonia	19	8%	0	0%	5	26%
Finland	20	10%	0	0%	5	31%
France	59	25%	1	5%	10	53%
Georgia	5	5%	0	0%	2	29%
Germany	33	14%	0	0%	6	33%
Greece	63	24%	0	0%	12	57%
Hungary	14	9%	0	0%	6	55%
Iceland	9	4%	0	0%	3	15%
Ireland	54	25%	1	6%	9	50%
Israel	34	15%	0	0%	7	39%
Italy	12	17%	0	0%	2	40%
Latvia	5	3%	0	0%	1	8%
Lithuania	4	2%	0	0%	2	14%
Luxembourg	0	0%	0	0%	0	0%
Malta	68	25%	2	9%	12	57%
Moldova	10	6%	0	0%	2	15%
Monaco	0	0%	0	0%	0	0%
Montenegro	38	63%	1	20%	4	100%
Morocco	0	-	0	-	0	-
Netherlands	21	9%	0	0%	6	35%
North Macedonia	114	68%	1	8%	13	93%
Norway	44	19%	0	0%	10	53%
Poland	25	13%	0	0%	4	27%
Portugal	12	6%	0	0%	5	28%
Romania	24	13%	0	0%	6	38%
Russia	57	22%	0	0%	10	50%
San Marino	10	28%	0	0%	1	50%
Serbia	110	92%	6	60%	9	100%
Serbia & Mont	34	94%	2	67%	3	100%
Slovakia	11	18%	0	0%	2	40%
Slovenia	110	54%	2	12%	17	100%
Spain	30	13%	0	0%	5	26%
Sweden	74	27%	2	9%	14	64%
Switzerland	8	6%	0	0%	3	25%
Turkey	133	55%	4	20%	16	80%
Ukraine	54	28%	1	6%	9	60%
United Kingdom	33	14%	0	0%	7	37%
Yugoslavia	0	-	0	-	0	-

Bulgaria

	Bulgaria awarded points to:				Frequency	
	Total	% of max	12's	% of max	Times	% of max
Albania	29	13%	0	0%	6	43%
Andorra	0	0%	0	0%	0	0%
Armenia	102	53%	1	6%	12	92%
Australia	32	33%	1	13%	2	50%
Austria	81	42%	3	19%	8	80%
Azerbaijan	74	39%	3	19%	10	83%
Belarus	40	19%	1	6%	9	64%
Belgium	52	25%	1	6%	5	42%
Bosnia & H	31	22%	0	0%	6	50%
Bulgaria	-	-	-	-	-	-
Croatia	36	18%	0	0%	7	54%
Cyprus	76	35%	2	11%	10	77%
Czech Republic	26	20%	0	0%	3	43%
Denmark	32	12%	1	4%	7	39%
Estonia	23	11%	0	0%	6	46%
Finland	38	18%	0	0%	6	43%
France	34	17%	1	6%	3	23%
Georgia	40	21%	0	0%	9	69%
Germany	21	10%	1	6%	3	23%
Greece	140	65%	4	22%	14	100%
Hungary	47	23%	0	0%	8	62%
Iceland	17	8%	0	0%	3	20%
Ireland	13	6%	0	0%	5	36%
Israel	81	27%	0	0%	12	67%
Italy	28	21%	0	0%	2	29%
Latvia	1	1%	0	0%	1	8%
Lithuania	44	16%	0	0%	9	53%
Luxembourg	0	-	0	-	0	-
Malta	31	16%	0	0%	6	46%
Moldova	64	28%	0	0%	10	67%
Monaco	0	0%	0	0%	0	0%
Montenegro	0	0%	0	0%	0	0%
Morocco	0	-	0	-	0	-
Netherlands	28	14%	0	0%	5	42%
North Macedonia	109	50%	2	11%	14	93%
Norway	25	10%	0	0%	9	56%
Poland	22	15%	0	0%	4	50%
Portugal	33	16%	0	0%	5	38%
Romania	53	25%	0	0%	11	69%
Russia	73	43%	2	14%	9	75%
San Marino	2	2%	0	0%	1	25%
Serbia	84	37%	2	11%	11	85%
Serbia & Mont	4	33%	0	0%	1	100%
Slovakia	0	0%	0	0%	0	0%
Slovenia	14	10%	0	0%	3	30%
Spain	13	6%	0	0%	4	31%
Sweden	34	13%	0	0%	8	44%
Switzerland	21	9%	0	0%	5	36%
Turkey	96	62%	2	15%	13	100%
Ukraine	101	35%	2	8%	16	84%
United Kingdom	19	9%	1	6%	2	15%
Yugoslavia	0	-	0	-	0	-

Croatia

	\multicolumn{4}{c}{Croatia awarded points to:}	\multicolumn{2}{c}{Frequency}
	Total	% of max	12's	% of max	Times	% of max
Albania	101	38%	0	0%	17	100%
Andorra	2	4%	0	0%	1	25%
Armenia	13	6%	0	0%	3	21%
Australia	25	21%	1	10%	3	60%
Austria	44	13%	0	0%	9	43%
Azerbaijan	83	28%	0	0%	11	65%
Belarus	17	8%	0	0%	3	21%
Belgium	19	6%	0	0%	6	29%
Bosnia & H	194	70%	6	26%	21	95%
Bulgaria	60	26%	0	0%	8	62%
Croatia	-	-	-	-	-	-
Cyprus	103	23%	2	5%	15	52%
Czech Republic	64	44%	1	8%	6	86%
Denmark	65	17%	2	6%	12	44%
Estonia	30	8%	0	0%	7	28%
Finland	29	10%	0	0%	4	20%
France	61	16%	0	0%	10	38%
Georgia	16	11%	0	0%	3	27%
Germany	35	10%	0	0%	10	40%
Greece	72	19%	0	0%	13	48%
Hungary	112	39%	3	13%	12	63%
Iceland	32	9%	0	0%	7	28%
Ireland	70	18%	1	3%	15	56%
Israel	73	18%	1	3%	9	36%
Italy	86	48%	2	13%	8	80%
Latvia	31	15%	0	0%	7	47%
Lithuania	51	13%	1	3%	10	38%
Luxembourg	0	0%	0	0%	0	0%
Malta	135	31%	3	8%	20	69%
Moldova	29	11%	0	0%	9	53%
Monaco	0	0%	0	0%	0	0%
Montenegro	17	35%	0	0%	3	100%
Morocco	0	-	0	-	0	-
Netherlands	76	18%	1	3%	10	37%
North Macedonia	158	55%	4	15%	19	100%
Norway	75	17%	1	3%	14	47%
Poland	14	6%	0	0%	3	18%
Portugal	42	14%	0	0%	6	27%
Romania	30	10%	0	0%	7	33%
Russia	138	36%	2	6%	18	69%
San Marino	3	3%	0	0%	2	40%
Serbia	175	73%	7	35%	15	100%
Serbia & Mont	36	100%	3	100%	3	100%
Slovakia	8	13%	0	0%	1	20%
Slovenia	140	47%	2	8%	21	95%
Spain	36	10%	0	0%	7	27%
Sweden	60	13%	0	0%	14	45%
Switzerland	69	22%	0	0%	11	52%
Turkey	56	19%	1	4%	11	46%
Ukraine	107	32%	1	4%	15	65%
United Kingdom	71	19%	2	6%	12	46%
Yugoslavia	0	-	0	-	0	-

Cyprus

	\multicolumn{4}{c}{Cyprus awarded points to:}	\multicolumn{2}{c}{Frequency}
	Total	% of max	12's	% of max	Times	% of max
Albania	30	11%	0	0%	6	33%
Andorra	0	0%	0	0%	0	0%
Armenia	111	49%	2	11%	12	86%
Australia	38	21%	0	0%	6	75%
Austria	58	13%	0	0%	13	39%
Azerbaijan	116	37%	0	0%	15	83%
Belarus	45	21%	0	0%	8	57%
Belgium	81	15%	0	0%	15	41%
Bosnia & H	7	3%	0	0%	2	10%
Bulgaria	132	65%	3	18%	12	100%
Croatia	61	16%	0	0%	13	48%
Cyprus	-	-	-	-	-	-
Czech Republic	30	15%	0	0%	5	50%
Denmark	81	17%	0	0%	17	46%
Estonia	47	13%	0	0%	9	36%
Finland	51	11%	0	0%	11	33%
France	117	24%	0	0%	21	58%
Georgia	57	32%	1	7%	8	67%
Germany	55	11%	2	5%	9	25%
Greece	491	93%	34	77%	37	100%
Hungary	46	15%	0	0%	7	35%
Iceland	48	10%	1	3%	10	30%
Ireland	105	22%	1	3%	18	49%
Israel	128	24%	1	2%	22	59%
Italy	137	48%	2	8%	16	84%
Latvia	24	10%	0	0%	7	39%
Lithuania	65	19%	0	0%	13	57%
Luxembourg	32	22%	0	0%	5	42%
Malta	103	27%	0	0%	16	59%
Moldova	58	20%	0	0%	11	58%
Monaco	4	11%	0	0%	1	33%
Montenegro	6	5%	0	0%	2	25%
Morocco	0	-	0	-	0	-
Netherlands	50	11%	0	0%	11	33%
North Macedonia	5	2%	0	0%	2	12%
Norway	93	18%	0	0%	18	47%
Poland	21	8%	0	0%	7	37%
Portugal	60	14%	1	3%	10	31%
Romania	106	37%	1	4%	17	77%
Russia	193	54%	3	10%	22	88%
San Marino	10	8%	0	0%	1	17%
Serbia	43	19%	0	0%	8	57%
Serbia & Mont	30	83%	0	0%	3	100%
Slovakia	0	0%	0	0%	0	0%
Slovenia	32	9%	0	0%	7	28%
Spain	123	24%	1	2%	19	51%
Sweden	173	29%	4	8%	25	58%
Switzerland	76	19%	0	0%	17	55%
Turkey	12	3%	0	0%	2	6%
Ukraine	119	35%	1	4%	18	78%
United Kingdom	80	16%	0	0%	21	57%
Yugoslavia	59	49%	1	10%	9	90%

Czech Republic

	Czech Rep awarded points to:				Frequency	
	Total	% of max	12's	% of max	Times	% of max
Albania	16	8%	0	0%	4	36%
Andorra	7	29%	0	0%	1	50%
Armenia	85	47%	4	27%	10	100%
Australia	41	26%	1	8%	5	71%
Austria	30	18%	0	0%	5	63%
Azerbaijan	109	50%	2	11%	10	91%
Belarus	22	15%	0	0%	5	63%
Belgium	37	21%	0	0%	7	78%
Bosnia & H	22	31%	0	0%	4	80%
Bulgaria	69	36%	1	6%	9	90%
Croatia	19	13%	0	0%	3	38%
Cyprus	40	15%	0	0%	5	38%
Czech Republic	-	-	-	-	-	-
Denmark	31	22%	0	0%	5	63%
Estonia	21	12%	0	0%	5	56%
Finland	34	16%	0	0%	6	55%
France	19	11%	0	0%	3	33%
Georgia	18	12%	0	0%	5	56%
Germany	3	2%	0	0%	1	11%
Greece	28	12%	0	0%	5	42%
Hungary	48	29%	1	7%	6	67%
Iceland	71	30%	0	0%	8	62%
Ireland	31	43%	0	0%	3	75%
Israel	61	28%	3	17%	7	58%
Italy	32	24%	0	0%	5	83%
Latvia	25	17%	0	0%	6	67%
Lithuania	9	6%	0	0%	5	56%
Luxembourg	0	-	0	-	0	-
Malta	42	27%	0	0%	7	78%
Moldova	54	30%	0	0%	5	56%
Monaco	0	-	0	-	0	-
Montenegro	8	7%	0	0%	2	29%
Morocco	0	-	0	-	0	-
Netherlands	38	24%	0	0%	4	57%
North Macedonia	25	26%	0	0%	5	83%
Norway	20	13%	0	0%	3	33%
Poland	38	23%	0	0%	4	44%
Portugal	80	42%	1	6%	8	73%
Romania	6	7%	0	0%	1	17%
Russia	66	46%	1	8%	8	100%
San Marino	14	11%	1	9%	2	33%
Serbia	48	25%	1	6%	6	60%
Serbia & Mont	0	-	0	-	0	-
Slovakia	0	-	0	-	0	-
Slovenia	42	29%	1	8%	6	75%
Spain	0	0%	0	0%	0	0%
Sweden	81	36%	3	16%	8	62%
Switzerland	34	24%	0	0%	4	50%
Turkey	7	10%	0	0%	3	50%
Ukraine	78	54%	4	33%	8	100%
United Kingdom	15	9%	0	0%	3	33%
Yugoslavia	0	-	0	-	0	-

Denmark

	Denmark awarded points to:				Frequency	
	Total	% of max	12's	% of max	Times	% of max
Albania	48	15%	0	0%	8	38%
Andorra	0	0%	0	0%	0	0%
Armenia	8	4%	0	0%	3	20%
Australia	92	59%	2	15%	7	100%
Austria	118	23%	0	0%	21	58%
Azerbaijan	40	16%	0	0%	6	38%
Belarus	5	2%	0	0%	3	19%
Belgium	120	25%	2	5%	14	39%
Bosnia & H	76	35%	1	6%	12	67%
Bulgaria	70	28%	1	5%	8	57%
Croatia	10	3%	0	0%	3	13%
Cyprus	80	16%	0	0%	15	42%
Czech Republic	6	5%	0	0%	1	17%
Denmark	-	-	-	-	-	-
Estonia	92	28%	0	0%	18	78%
Finland	96	22%	1	3%	13	39%
France	73	14%	1	2%	17	45%
Georgia	6	3%	0	0%	2	14%
Germany	191	36%	6	14%	27	69%
Greece	47	10%	0	0%	14	38%
Hungary	50	16%	1	4%	10	48%
Iceland	203	51%	3	9%	25	83%
Ireland	187	37%	4	10%	28	74%
Israel	80	15%	0	0%	19	50%
Italy	31	9%	0	0%	8	33%
Latvia	70	22%	0	0%	13	62%
Lithuania	57	16%	0	0%	11	48%
Luxembourg	32	17%	0	0%	9	56%
Malta	90	24%	2	6%	15	60%
Moldova	40	12%	0	0%	6	27%
Monaco	14	23%	0	0%	2	40%
Montenegro	5	5%	0	0%	1	14%
Morocco	0	0%	0	0%	0	0%
Netherlands	188	33%	1	2%	23	59%
North Macedonia	24	9%	0	0%	4	22%
Norway	280	47%	10	20%	31	74%
Poland	27	10%	0	0%	8	44%
Portugal	43	10%	0	0%	8	24%
Romania	64	20%	0	0%	13	57%
Russia	87	23%	2	6%	14	52%
San Marino	12	8%	0	0%	2	25%
Serbia	22	7%	0	0%	5	28%
Serbia & Mont	17	47%	0	0%	2	67%
Slovakia	0	0%	0	0%	0	0%
Slovenia	22	7%	0	0%	3	14%
Spain	38	7%	1	2%	11	28%
Sweden	449	72%	18	35%	41	91%
Switzerland	154	31%	1	2%	23	66%
Turkey	90	23%	0	0%	14	42%
Ukraine	81	22%	1	3%	15	60%
United Kingdom	141	27%	2	5%	25	64%
Yugoslavia	52	39%	2	18%	6	55%

Estonia
Finland

Estonia awarded points to:

	Total	% of max	12's	% of max	Times	% of max
Albania	5	2%	0	0%	4	21%
Andorra	8	13%	0	0%	2	40%
Armenia	15	6%	0	0%	4	25%
Australia	34	26%	0	0%	5	83%
Austria	91	26%	2	7%	12	55%
Azerbaijan	49	18%	0	0%	8	47%
Belarus	50	18%	0	0%	10	56%
Belgium	93	26%	1	3%	16	64%
Bosnia & H	2	1%	0	0%	2	9%
Bulgaria	74	31%	2	10%	7	54%
Croatia	27	8%	0	0%	8	32%
Cyprus	81	19%	0	0%	11	41%
Czech Republic	47	26%	1	7%	6	75%
Denmark	144	39%	2	6%	21	81%
Estonia	-	-	-	-	-	-
Finland	204	57%	5	17%	21	88%
France	67	18%	1	3%	12	46%
Georgia	45	25%	0	0%	9	75%
Germany	48	13%	1	3%	11	44%
Greece	36	8%	0	0%	10	32%
Hungary	107	33%	1	4%	16	76%
Iceland	117	30%	0	0%	18	69%
Ireland	96	30%	1	4%	15	63%
Israel	25	7%	0	0%	7	29%
Italy	39	20%	0	0%	6	55%
Latvia	137	57%	3	15%	18	100%
Lithuania	113	35%	1	4%	15	68%
Luxembourg	0	-	0	-	0	-
Malta	71	20%	0	0%	16	64%
Moldova	33	10%	0	0%	7	32%
Monaco	2	6%	0	0%	1	33%
Montenegro	0	0%	0	0%	0	0%
Morocco	0	-	0	-	0	-
Netherlands	119	28%	3	8%	15	52%
North Macedonia	2	1%	0	0%	1	5%
Norway	156	39%	2	6%	22	79%
Poland	29	9%	1	4%	5	23%
Portugal	45	14%	0	0%	7	32%
Romania	33	11%	1	4%	7	30%
Russia	251	65%	9	28%	28	100%
San Marino	25	14%	0	0%	4	44%
Serbia	18	6%	0	0%	6	32%
Serbia & Mont	1	3%	0	0%	1	33%
Slovakia	6	7%	0	0%	1	14%
Slovenia	30	10%	0	0%	6	26%
Spain	13	3%	0	0%	4	15%
Sweden	220	54%	8	24%	26	90%
Switzerland	77	28%	2	9%	8	44%
Turkey	14	6%	0	0%	3	16%
Ukraine	122	38%	2	7%	17	74%
United Kingdom	53	14%	0	0%	11	42%
Yugoslavia	0	-	0	-	0	-

Finland awarded points to:

	Total	% of max	12's	% of max	Times	% of max
Albania	38	12%	0	0%	7	33%
Andorra	5	7%	0	0%	1	17%
Armenia	29	10%	0	0%	7	37%
Australia	74	47%	1	8%	6	86%
Austria	102	20%	2	5%	15	41%
Azerbaijan	24	8%	0	0%	7	39%
Belarus	14	6%	0	0%	3	19%
Belgium	126	21%	3	6%	20	47%
Bosnia & H	53	21%	1	5%	8	40%
Bulgaria	70	32%	0	0%	8	67%
Croatia	21	7%	0	0%	7	35%
Cyprus	108	20%	0	0%	16	44%
Czech Republic	42	19%	0	0%	6	60%
Denmark	118	24%	1	2%	19	51%
Estonia	211	61%	8	28%	22	96%
Finland	-	-	-	-	-	-
France	135	24%	3	7%	24	59%
Georgia	20	9%	0	0%	5	33%
Germany	81	15%	2	4%	16	39%
Greece	104	16%	0	0%	23	49%
Hungary	114	37%	3	12%	15	71%
Iceland	209	42%	5	12%	22	65%
Ireland	129	28%	1	3%	25	69%
Israel	203	36%	4	9%	28	68%
Italy	169	45%	4	13%	22	85%
Latvia	39	17%	1	5%	8	50%
Lithuania	36	14%	0	0%	6	33%
Luxembourg	55	24%	1	5%	9	47%
Malta	56	15%	0	0%	14	50%
Moldova	40	13%	0	0%	7	35%
Monaco	17	18%	0	0%	4	50%
Montenegro	3	2%	0	0%	1	11%
Morocco	0	0%	0	0%	0	0%
Netherlands	109	22%	1	2%	16	44%
North Macedonia	9	4%	0	0%	3	16%
Norway	174	30%	6	13%	24	55%
Poland	31	10%	0	0%	4	20%
Portugal	95	18%	2	5%	17	44%
Romania	30	10%	0	0%	7	29%
Russia	133	37%	2	7%	20	77%
San Marino	11	6%	0	0%	4	40%
Serbia	42	16%	1	5%	8	50%
Serbia & Mont	20	56%	0	0%	2	67%
Slovakia	2	4%	0	0%	1	25%
Slovenia	39	14%	0	0%	9	47%
Spain	80	14%	0	0%	14	33%
Sweden	295	50%	8	16%	33	77%
Switzerland	187	35%	2	5%	26	65%
Turkey	55	14%	0	0%	13	39%
Ukraine	53	21%	1	5%	9	53%
United Kingdom	106	19%	0	0%	18	43%
Yugoslavia	35	22%	1	8%	7	54%

France

	France awarded points to:				Frequency	
	Total	% of max	12's	% of max	Times	% of max
Albania	24	9%	0	0%	7	37%
Andorra	0	0%	0	0%	0	0%
Armenia	142	66%	7	39%	15	100%
Australia	62	40%	1	8%	7	100%
Austria	101	19%	2	5%	15	39%
Azerbaijan	38	15%	0	0%	7	44%
Belarus	18	8%	0	0%	3	19%
Belgium	171	32%	6	13%	25	61%
Bosnia & H	71	25%	0	0%	13	57%
Bulgaria	78	33%	0	0%	11	79%
Croatia	34	10%	0	0%	6	24%
Cyprus	59	11%	1	2%	13	35%
Czech Republic	21	13%	0	0%	5	63%
Denmark	128	22%	2	4%	23	55%
Estonia	76	18%	0	0%	13	45%
Finland	60	11%	0	0%	13	33%
France	-	-	-	-	-	-
Georgia	10	4%	0	0%	2	13%
Germany	116	20%	1	2%	18	41%
Greece	139	23%	0	0%	24	53%
Hungary	68	18%	0	0%	15	60%
Iceland	87	18%	1	2%	14	39%
Ireland	102	21%	0	0%	22	56%
Israel	257	48%	6	13%	33	85%
Italy	167	43%	2	6%	22	81%
Latvia	28	10%	0	0%	4	20%
Lithuania	10	3%	0	0%	3	15%
Luxembourg	56	26%	2	11%	9	50%
Malta	68	15%	0	0%	14	44%
Moldova	72	22%	1	4%	12	57%
Monaco	27	32%	0	0%	5	71%
Montenegro	7	6%	0	0%	1	14%
Morocco	0	0%	0	0%	0	0%
Netherlands	161	26%	3	6%	23	53%
North Macedonia	15	6%	0	0%	2	11%
Norway	74	11%	0	0%	15	31%
Poland	78	23%	1	4%	16	70%
Portugal	278	50%	8	17%	30	73%
Romania	94	29%	1	4%	15	63%
Russia	81	20%	0	0%	15	54%
San Marino	17	8%	0	0%	3	30%
Serbia	118	36%	3	11%	15	79%
Serbia & Mont	16	67%	0	0%	2	100%
Slovakia	1	1%	0	0%	1	14%
Slovenia	32	10%	0	0%	9	39%
Spain	150	25%	2	4%	25	56%
Sweden	171	26%	3	5%	33	67%
Switzerland	117	24%	1	3%	17	47%
Turkey	190	44%	8	22%	21	58%
Ukraine	42	13%	0	0%	9	39%
United Kingdom	152	25%	5	10%	23	51%
Yugoslavia	21	15%	0	0%	7	58%

Georgia

	Georgia awarded points to:				Frequency	
	Total	% of max	12's	% of max	Times	% of max
Albania	15	6%	0	0%	4	27%
Andorra	0	0%	0	0%	0	0%
Armenia	146	76%	5	31%	13	100%
Australia	31	15%	0	0%	4	44%
Austria	42	27%	0	0%	6	67%
Azerbaijan	174	73%	6	30%	15	100%
Belarus	87	43%	3	18%	11	85%
Belgium	53	26%	1	6%	7	64%
Bosnia & H	2	3%	0	0%	1	17%
Bulgaria	54	25%	0	0%	8	67%
Croatia	11	9%	0	0%	3	38%
Cyprus	63	26%	1	5%	6	46%
Czech Republic	32	19%	2	14%	4	50%
Denmark	34	13%	0	0%	8	50%
Estonia	49	27%	0	0%	7	64%
Finland	11	5%	0	0%	2	14%
France	23	11%	0	0%	6	46%
Georgia	-	-	-	-	-	-
Germany	15	7%	0	0%	4	33%
Greece	73	25%	0	0%	13	72%
Hungary	28	11%	0	0%	7	44%
Iceland	34	14%	0	0%	6	40%
Ireland	0	0%	0	0%	0	0%
Israel	47	21%	1	5%	9	69%
Italy	54	30%	0	0%	8	80%
Latvia	70	36%	0	0%	9	82%
Lithuania	112	52%	2	11%	13	93%
Luxembourg	0	-	0	-	0	-
Malta	32	16%	0	0%	7	54%
Moldova	55	24%	1	5%	9	69%
Monaco	0	-	0	-	0	-
Montenegro	0	0%	0	0%	0	0%
Morocco	0	-	0	-	0	-
Netherlands	35	16%	0	0%	7	58%
North Macedonia	6	4%	0	0%	4	40%
Norway	46	17%	0	0%	8	47%
Poland	27	11%	0	0%	5	38%
Portugal	69	34%	2	12%	7	58%
Romania	25	13%	0	0%	4	29%
Russia	81	38%	0	0%	13	93%
San Marino	44	28%	1	8%	6	75%
Serbia	38	12%	0	0%	6	33%
Serbia & Mont	0	-	0	-	0	-
Slovakia	0	0%	0	0%	0	0%
Slovenia	25	10%	0	0%	5	36%
Spain	2	1%	0	0%	1	8%
Sweden	91	32%	3	13%	11	65%
Switzerland	38	20%	0	0%	6	50%
Turkey	37	34%	0	0%	8	89%
Ukraine	170	64%	4	18%	16	100%
United Kingdom	7	3%	0	0%	3	23%
Yugoslavia	0	-	0	-	0	-

Germany

Germany awarded points to:

	Total	% of max	12's	% of max	Times	% of max
Albania	31	12%	0	0%	8	47%
Andorra	0	0%	0	0%	0	0%
Armenia	59	27%	0	0%	10	67%
Australia	78	43%	0	0%	8	100%
Austria	112	22%	2	5%	19	50%
Azerbaijan	22	8%	0	0%	5	29%
Belarus	2	1%	0	0%	1	6%
Belgium	117	21%	2	4%	19	45%
Bosnia & H	79	27%	0	0%	13	54%
Bulgaria	64	27%	1	5%	8	57%
Croatia	92	26%	0	0%	18	75%
Cyprus	69	14%	0	0%	15	42%
Czech Republic	12	11%	0	0%	2	33%
Denmark	148	25%	2	4%	23	55%
Estonia	51	16%	0	0%	11	46%
Finland	90	18%	2	5%	19	48%
France	141	24%	3	6%	19	43%
Georgia	24	13%	0	0%	3	25%
Germany	-	-	-	-	-	-
Greece	148	27%	3	7%	22	52%
Hungary	67	23%	1	4%	10	53%
Iceland	84	21%	1	3%	15	47%
Ireland	159	27%	2	4%	27	61%
Israel	191	29%	4	7%	30	64%
Italy	113	29%	3	9%	19	70%
Latvia	62	22%	1	4%	8	40%
Lithuania	48	13%	0	0%	8	33%
Luxembourg	42	18%	1	5%	7	37%
Malta	118	23%	0	0%	22	63%
Moldova	26	9%	0	0%	5	28%
Monaco	23	21%	0	0%	4	44%
Montenegro	2	2%	0	0%	1	14%
Morocco	0	0%	0	0%	0	0%
Netherlands	178	30%	1	2%	25	60%
North Macedonia	30	9%	1	4%	4	17%
Norway	189	25%	5	8%	29	55%
Poland	140	45%	4	15%	19	86%
Portugal	105	20%	2	5%	17	43%
Romania	65	16%	0	0%	13	46%
Russia	127	31%	2	6%	19	68%
San Marino	1	1%	0	0%	1	13%
Serbia	73	26%	0	0%	11	69%
Serbia & Mont	25	69%	1	33%	3	100%
Slovakia	0	0%	0	0%	0	0%
Slovenia	31	8%	0	0%	8	31%
Spain	84	14%	2	4%	13	29%
Sweden	250	35%	9	15%	34	67%
Switzerland	157	29%	3	7%	22	55%
Turkey	208	48%	8	22%	22	61%
Ukraine	72	20%	0	0%	8	35%
United Kingdom	153	26%	2	4%	25	56%
Yugoslavia	16	10%	0	0%	6	46%

Greece

Greece awarded points to:

	Total	% of max	12's	% of max	Times	% of max
Albania	229	68%	2	7%	22	100%
Andorra	4	7%	0	0%	1	20%
Armenia	158	57%	3	13%	16	89%
Australia	40	26%	0	0%	4	57%
Austria	96	19%	3	7%	18	50%
Azerbaijan	116	37%	3	12%	17	89%
Belarus	51	22%	0	0%	10	67%
Belgium	85	16%	1	2%	14	36%
Bosnia & H	20	7%	0	0%	4	18%
Bulgaria	93	46%	1	6%	11	100%
Croatia	40	12%	0	0%	10	43%
Cyprus	482	89%	30	67%	35	97%
Czech Republic	31	15%	0	0%	5	56%
Denmark	46	9%	1	2%	11	30%
Estonia	57	15%	1	3%	10	38%
Finland	101	17%	1	2%	17	39%
France	159	29%	2	4%	25	63%
Georgia	83	36%	0	0%	14	93%
Germany	36	7%	0	0%	10	25%
Greece	-	-	-	-	-	-
Hungary	45	13%	0	0%	8	35%
Iceland	71	14%	0	0%	13	37%
Ireland	108	23%	2	5%	14	38%
Israel	68	13%	0	0%	15	38%
Italy	126	35%	1	3%	17	68%
Latvia	15	6%	0	0%	4	22%
Lithuania	11	4%	0	0%	4	20%
Luxembourg	24	13%	1	6%	5	31%
Malta	95	25%	0	0%	19	68%
Moldova	120	37%	0	0%	16	76%
Monaco	16	19%	1	14%	2	29%
Montenegro	18	14%	0	0%	3	38%
Morocco	0	0%	0	0%	0	0%
Netherlands	73	14%	1	2%	15	42%
North Macedonia	8	4%	0	0%	3	18%
Norway	84	15%	2	4%	16	36%
Poland	46	13%	0	0%	14	58%
Portugal	81	16%	0	0%	17	45%
Romania	113	39%	1	4%	16	70%
Russia	174	45%	3	9%	22	79%
San Marino	43	24%	0	0%	9	90%
Serbia	57	21%	0	0%	10	59%
Serbia & Mont	24	67%	0	0%	3	100%
Slovakia	7	12%	0	0%	2	40%
Slovenia	27	8%	0	0%	6	26%
Spain	140	25%	0	0%	23	56%
Sweden	66	12%	0	0%	13	32%
Switzerland	92	19%	1	3%	19	53%
Turkey	36	10%	0	0%	6	19%
Ukraine	74	27%	0	0%	13	68%
United Kingdom	85	15%	2	4%	15	37%
Yugoslavia	30	25%	1	10%	7	70%

Hungary

	Hungary awarded points to:				Frequency	
	Total	% of max	12's	% of max	Times	% of max
Albania	35	17%	0	0%	6	40%
Andorra	0	0%	0	0%	0	0%
Armenia	28	15%	0	0%	6	46%
Australia	60	38%	1	8%	6	86%
Austria	57	25%	0	0%	8	57%
Azerbaijan	110	48%	5	26%	12	80%
Belarus	31	17%	1	7%	5	45%
Belgium	37	19%	1	6%	5	38%
Bosnia & H	1	1%	0	0%	1	10%
Bulgaria	72	46%	3	23%	7	78%
Croatia	44	18%	0	0%	7	44%
Cyprus	44	16%	1	4%	8	47%
Czech Republic	47	33%	1	8%	5	71%
Denmark	112	37%	4	16%	15	75%
Estonia	55	20%	0	0%	9	50%
Finland	36	16%	1	5%	6	38%
France	15	6%	0	0%	5	29%
Georgia	26	14%	0	0%	9	69%
Germany	24	10%	1	5%	4	24%
Greece	71	23%	1	4%	12	55%
Hungary	-	-	-	-	-	-
Iceland	109	41%	3	14%	14	74%
Ireland	48	27%	0	0%	7	54%
Israel	51	21%	0	0%	7	47%
Italy	35	21%	0	0%	7	70%
Latvia	22	12%	0	0%	6	46%
Lithuania	13	6%	0	0%	3	21%
Luxembourg	0	-	0	-	0	-
Malta	56	20%	1	4%	7	39%
Moldova	46	19%	0	0%	9	56%
Monaco	0	0%	0	0%	0	0%
Montenegro	4	3%	0	0%	1	13%
Morocco	0	-	0	-	0	-
Netherlands	119	41%	3	13%	12	71%
North Macedonia	12	8%	0	0%	2	18%
Norway	106	34%	1	4%	15	71%
Poland	65	27%	0	0%	11	69%
Portugal	32	16%	1	6%	3	21%
Romania	65	26%	2	10%	10	56%
Russia	102	35%	1	4%	13	65%
San Marino	36	20%	1	7%	6	60%
Serbia	62	25%	2	10%	9	60%
Serbia & Mont	2	17%	0	0%	1	100%
Slovakia	0	0%	0	0%	0	0%
Slovenia	41	19%	0	0%	7	50%
Spain	18	7%	0	0%	4	24%
Sweden	86	29%	1	4%	14	70%
Switzerland	38	20%	0	0%	8	57%
Turkey	30	23%	0	0%	7	64%
Ukraine	63	28%	1	5%	10	67%
United Kingdom	38	15%	1	5%	7	41%
Yugoslavia	0	-	0	-	0	-

Iceland

	Iceland awarded points to:				Frequency	
	Total	% of max	12's	% of max	Times	% of max
Albania	56	17%	1	4%	9	41%
Andorra	6	10%	0	0%	1	20%
Armenia	25	9%	0	0%	7	39%
Australia	94	60%	1	8%	6	86%
Austria	98	19%	1	2%	12	32%
Azerbaijan	60	19%	0	0%	12	63%
Belarus	19	8%	0	0%	5	33%
Belgium	82	14%	1	2%	12	29%
Bosnia & H	18	7%	0	0%	5	23%
Bulgaria	37	16%	0	0%	4	31%
Croatia	44	14%	0	0%	10	43%
Cyprus	104	18%	3	6%	16	41%
Czech Republic	76	32%	2	10%	7	58%
Denmark	261	51%	10	23%	29	74%
Estonia	103	29%	1	3%	16	67%
Finland	197	32%	5	10%	25	57%
France	116	20%	1	2%	17	40%
Georgia	15	7%	0	0%	4	29%
Germany	75	13%	1	2%	12	28%
Greece	83	15%	0	0%	17	45%
Hungary	91	28%	1	4%	13	59%
Iceland	-	-	-	-	-	-
Ireland	82	22%	1	3%	15	52%
Israel	81	14%	0	0%	12	29%
Italy	59	15%	0	0%	9	33%
Latvia	55	20%	0	0%	11	55%
Lithuania	36	13%	0	0%	8	40%
Luxembourg	9	4%	0	0%	3	16%
Malta	58	14%	0	0%	12	39%
Moldova	36	12%	0	0%	5	26%
Monaco	0	0%	0	0%	0	0%
Montenegro	2	1%	0	0%	1	10%
Morocco	0	0%	0	0%	0	0%
Netherlands	108	20%	4	9%	13	34%
North Macedonia	9	4%	0	0%	2	13%
Norway	203	34%	7	14%	28	61%
Poland	56	17%	0	0%	13	57%
Portugal	143	25%	4	8%	14	33%
Romania	46	18%	0	0%	9	45%
Russia	96	26%	1	3%	18	67%
San Marino	18	9%	0	0%	5	45%
Serbia	40	16%	0	0%	9	60%
Serbia & Mont	7	19%	0	0%	1	33%
Slovakia	5	14%	0	0%	1	33%
Slovenia	29	10%	0	0%	7	35%
Spain	26	4%	0	0%	9	20%
Sweden	298	46%	7	13%	35	73%
Switzerland	124	23%	1	2%	18	45%
Turkey	31	7%	0	0%	8	22%
Ukraine	71	25%	1	4%	10	50%
United Kingdom	44	7%	1	2%	9	20%
Yugoslavia	48	31%	1	8%	6	46%

Ireland

	Ireland awarded points to:				Frequency	
	Total	% of max	12's	% of max	Times	% of max
Albania	11	4%	0	0%	5	28%
Andorra	5	8%	0	0%	2	40%
Armenia	4	2%	0	0%	2	13%
Australia	39	25%	0	0%	4	57%
Austria	129	23%	3	6%	20	49%
Azerbaijan	52	17%	0	0%	11	58%
Belarus	14	6%	0	0%	5	31%
Belgium	151	26%	5	10%	20	47%
Bosnia & H	24	9%	0	0%	7	32%
Bulgaria	89	37%	1	5%	8	62%
Croatia	54	13%	0	0%	11	39%
Cyprus	115	20%	2	4%	18	44%
Czech Republic	18	15%	0	0%	4	67%
Denmark	195	33%	8	16%	29	66%
Estonia	121	34%	0	0%	20	77%
Finland	103	20%	1	2%	15	38%
France	149	25%	1	2%	22	50%
Georgia	14	9%	0	0%	4	36%
Germany	148	25%	1	2%	27	61%
Greece	61	11%	0	0%	15	36%
Hungary	37	13%	1	4%	7	37%
Iceland	81	19%	1	3%	12	38%
Ireland	-	-	-	-	-	-
Israel	151	22%	1	2%	21	45%
Italy	104	28%	3	10%	16	62%
Latvia	122	46%	5	23%	14	74%
Lithuania	227	54%	11	31%	24	89%
Luxembourg	65	30%	1	6%	10	56%
Malta	143	32%	2	5%	20	65%
Moldova	38	14%	0	0%	10	53%
Monaco	17	18%	0	0%	3	38%
Montenegro	0	0%	0	0%	0	0%
Morocco	0	0%	0	0%	0	0%
Netherlands	178	30%	2	4%	28	65%
North Macedonia	17	5%	0	0%	3	15%
Norway	224	32%	3	5%	33	65%
Poland	93	31%	1	4%	12	55%
Portugal	42	9%	0	0%	7	19%
Romania	113	30%	2	6%	19	70%
Russia	134	34%	0	0%	17	61%
San Marino	0	0%	0	0%	0	0%
Serbia	14	6%	0	0%	3	20%
Serbia & Mont	9	25%	0	0%	2	67%
Slovakia	6	10%	0	0%	2	40%
Slovenia	39	10%	1	3%	7	25%
Spain	48	8%	0	0%	11	24%
Sweden	229	34%	7	13%	31	63%
Switzerland	151	27%	2	4%	23	56%
Turkey	24	6%	0	0%	7	20%
Ukraine	89	25%	0	0%	15	63%
United Kingdom	219	37%	1	2%	37	82%
Yugoslavia	34	24%	1	8%	8	67%

Israel

	Israel awarded points to:				Frequency	
	Total	% of max	12's	% of max	Times	% of max
Albania	13	5%	0	0%	3	18%
Andorra	6	8%	0	0%	2	33%
Armenia	110	48%	2	11%	13	81%
Australia	84	47%	3	20%	6	75%
Austria	106	22%	3	8%	13	37%
Azerbaijan	103	36%	2	8%	15	83%
Belarus	63	23%	2	9%	11	65%
Belgium	106	18%	0	0%	19	46%
Bosnia & H	6	3%	0	0%	3	15%
Bulgaria	73	28%	1	5%	8	53%
Croatia	40	12%	0	0%	12	55%
Cyprus	113	21%	0	0%	21	57%
Czech Republic	48	31%	2	15%	5	63%
Denmark	144	27%	2	5%	24	62%
Estonia	84	26%	0	0%	12	55%
Finland	95	18%	0	0%	19	49%
France	173	32%	3	7%	24	60%
Georgia	48	25%	0	0%	9	69%
Germany	79	14%	2	4%	11	27%
Greece	134	24%	2	4%	21	51%
Hungary	56	20%	1	4%	8	44%
Iceland	67	16%	1	3%	12	38%
Ireland	90	16%	1	2%	20	48%
Israel	-	-	-	-	-	-
Italy	80	23%	1	3%	13	54%
Latvia	54	23%	1	5%	9	50%
Lithuania	57	16%	0	0%	10	43%
Luxembourg	35	17%	1	6%	6	35%
Malta	95	23%	0	0%	15	52%
Moldova	56	25%	0	0%	11	69%
Monaco	19	20%	0	0%	4	50%
Montenegro	8	7%	0	0%	2	25%
Morocco	0	-	0	-	0	-
Netherlands	139	28%	3	7%	24	67%
North Macedonia	21	7%	0	0%	5	24%
Norway	125	20%	2	4%	22	48%
Poland	23	8%	0	0%	5	26%
Portugal	44	9%	2	5%	6	17%
Romania	182	51%	3	10%	23	85%
Russia	205	61%	6	21%	22	92%
San Marino	11	7%	0	0%	2	22%
Serbia	13	5%	0	0%	4	29%
Serbia & Mont	15	42%	0	0%	2	67%
Slovakia	0	0%	0	0%	0	0%
Slovenia	48	13%	0	0%	13	52%
Spain	118	21%	3	7%	22	54%
Sweden	208	34%	5	10%	27	60%
Switzerland	112	22%	1	2%	21	55%
Turkey	42	11%	0	0%	11	33%
Ukraine	172	51%	2	7%	20	91%
United Kingdom	146	26%	4	9%	23	56%
Yugoslavia	52	36%	2	17%	6	50%

Italy   Latvia

	Italy awarded points to:			Frequency			Latvia awarded points to:			Frequency	
	Total	% of max	12's	% of max	Times	% of max		Total	% of max	12's	% of max	Times	% of max
Albania	97	54%	5	33%	8	89%	Albania	16	4%	0	0%	5	22%
Andorra	0	-	0	-	0	-	Andorra	0	0%	0	0%	0	0%
Armenia	11	8%	0	0%	3	43%	Armenia	31	14%	0	0%	7	47%
Australia	47	23%	1	6%	6	67%	Australia	73	41%	1	7%	8	100%
Austria	78	21%	4	13%	13	48%	Austria	34	13%	0	0%	8	50%
Azerbaijan	47	20%	2	10%	5	38%	Azerbaijan	64	22%	0	0%	12	67%
Belarus	8	6%	0	0%	2	25%	Belarus	53	26%	0	0%	8	57%
Belgium	83	21%	0	0%	12	44%	Belgium	78	27%	1	4%	9	47%
Bosnia & H	11	18%	0	0%	3	60%	Bosnia & H	4	2%	0	0%	2	13%
Bulgaria	34	26%	0	0%	4	67%	Bulgaria	43	19%	0	0%	7	54%
Croatia	8	6%	0	0%	2	29%	Croatia	25	10%	0	0%	6	35%
Cyprus	70	19%	0	0%	13	57%	Cyprus	32	10%	0	0%	8	36%
Czech Republic	4	4%	0	0%	1	20%	Czech Republic	15	10%	0	0%	4	50%
Denmark	104	26%	3	9%	13	48%	Denmark	128	32%	2	6%	19	73%
Estonia	34	26%	1	9%	5	56%	Estonia	203	74%	7	30%	19	95%
Finland	46	14%	0	0%	5	21%	Finland	72	26%	0	0%	10	53%
France	126	33%	1	3%	17	63%	France	37	12%	0	0%	8	38%
Georgia	17	12%	0	0%	3	38%	Georgia	58	25%	0	0%	9	64%
Germany	86	22%	1	3%	14	52%	Germany	44	14%	1	4%	8	38%
Greece	61	17%	1	3%	14	54%	Greece	26	7%	0	0%	7	28%
Hungary	15	8%	0	0%	4	36%	Hungary	32	12%	0	0%	9	50%
Iceland	50	21%	0	0%	9	53%	Iceland	104	31%	0	0%	15	63%
Ireland	109	28%	5	16%	16	57%	Ireland	55	21%	0	0%	11	58%
Israel	97	24%	1	3%	15	58%	Israel	22	6%	0	0%	8	35%
Italy	-	-	-	-	-	-	Italy	49	27%	1	7%	6	60%
Latvia	17	10%	0	0%	3	33%	Latvia	-	-	-	-	-	-
Lithuania	56	25%	0	0%	7	54%	Lithuania	201	67%	3	12%	19	95%
Luxembourg	41	21%	2	13%	7	44%	Luxembourg	0	-	0	-	0	-
Malta	95	36%	0	0%	14	88%	Malta	66	20%	0	0%	15	68%
Moldova	105	49%	2	11%	12	100%	Moldova	83	24%	0	0%	10	45%
Monaco	33	55%	1	20%	5	100%	Monaco	0	0%	0	0%	0	0%
Montenegro	9	8%	0	0%	2	29%	Montenegro	2	2%	0	0%	1	13%
Morocco	7	58%	0	0%	1	100%	Morocco	0	-	0	-	0	-
Netherlands	69	17%	0	0%	15	58%	Netherlands	75	23%	3	11%	8	40%
North Macedonia	23	17%	0	0%	5	71%	North Macedonia	13	5%	0	0%	2	11%
Norway	102	22%	2	5%	16	52%	Norway	130	34%	2	6%	19	76%
Poland	62	34%	0	0%	10	100%	Poland	37	12%	0	0%	9	47%
Portugal	56	19%	0	0%	10	48%	Portugal	78	33%	3	15%	7	44%
Romania	95	49%	3	19%	11	92%	Romania	22	7%	0	0%	6	27%
Russia	70	29%	0	0%	10	71%	Russia	240	67%	10	33%	23	92%
San Marino	17	16%	0	0%	4	67%	San Marino	6	4%	0	0%	3	33%
Serbia	40	21%	0	0%	9	90%	Serbia	13	5%	0	0%	4	25%
Serbia & Mont	0	-	0	-	0	-	Serbia & Mont	10	28%	0	0%	3	100%
Slovakia	0	0%	0	0%	0	0%	Slovakia	0	0%	0	0%	0	0%
Slovenia	27	11%	0	0%	5	33%	Slovenia	37	13%	0	0%	10	53%
Spain	95	25%	2	6%	14	52%	Spain	13	4%	0	0%	3	14%
Sweden	97	20%	1	2%	16	50%	Sweden	182	42%	5	14%	21	75%
Switzerland	90	25%	1	3%	17	65%	Switzerland	69	25%	1	4%	10	56%
Turkey	23	13%	0	0%	3	20%	Turkey	2	1%	0	0%	1	7%
Ukraine	135	56%	3	15%	13	100%	Ukraine	177	49%	4	13%	19	79%
United Kingdom	100	26%	1	3%	16	59%	United Kingdom	30	10%	0	0%	10	48%
Yugoslavia	17	14%	0	0%	3	30%	Yugoslavia	0	-	0	-	0	-

Lithuania

Luxembourg

	Lithuania awarded points to:				Frequency			Luxembourg awarded points to:				Frequency	
	Total	% of max	12's	% of max	Times	% of max		Total	% of max	12's	% of max	Times	% of max
Albania	1	0%	0	0%	1	5%	Albania	0	-	0	-	0	-
Andorra	2	4%	0	0%	1	25%	Andorra	0	-	0	-	0	-
Armenia	10	4%	0	0%	4	27%	Armenia	0	-	0	-	0	-
Australia	49	31%	2	15%	6	86%	Australia	0	-	0	-	0	-
Austria	71	26%	1	4%	8	47%	Austria	14	6%	0	0%	3	17%
Azerbaijan	107	34%	2	8%	13	68%	Azerbaijan	0	-	0	-	0	-
Belarus	83	31%	1	5%	14	82%	Belarus	0	-	0	-	0	-
Belgium	93	34%	0	0%	11	65%	Belgium	48	21%	1	5%	8	42%
Bosnia & H	7	4%	0	0%	2	13%	Bosnia & H	0	0%	0	0%	0	0%
Bulgaria	49	19%	0	0%	7	50%	Bulgaria	0	-	0	-	0	-
Croatia	28	8%	0	0%	8	33%	Croatia	0	0%	0	0%	0	0%
Cyprus	42	12%	0	0%	10	43%	Cyprus	8	6%	0	0%	2	17%
Czech Republic	27	20%	0	0%	3	43%	Czech Republic	0	-	0	-	0	-
Denmark	71	19%	0	0%	16	64%	Denmark	26	14%	0	0%	6	38%
Estonia	141	49%	4	17%	18	90%	Estonia	0	-	0	-	0	-
Finland	50	21%	0	0%	8	47%	Finland	21	9%	0	0%	6	32%
France	71	23%	0	0%	10	48%	France	89	41%	3	17%	12	67%
Georgia	147	77%	6	38%	14	100%	Georgia	0	-	0	-	0	-
Germany	32	10%	0	0%	7	33%	Germany	67	29%	2	11%	11	58%
Greece	35	11%	0	0%	7	30%	Greece	29	16%	0	0%	6	40%
Hungary	29	12%	0	0%	7	41%	Hungary	0	-	0	-	0	-
Iceland	61	22%	0	0%	10	50%	Iceland	13	14%	0	0%	2	25%
Ireland	87	25%	2	7%	13	57%	Ireland	96	44%	0	0%	14	78%
Israel	56	14%	0	0%	12	50%	Israel	76	37%	1	6%	11	65%
Italy	68	38%	0	0%	7	70%	Italy	64	33%	1	6%	9	56%
Latvia	189	83%	10	53%	16	100%	Latvia	0	-	0	-	0	-
Lithuania	-	-	-	-	-	-	Lithuania	0	-	0	-	0	-
Luxembourg	0	-	0	-	0	-	Luxembourg	-	-	-	-	-	-
Malta	61	17%	0	0%	15	63%	Malta	27	56%	1	25%	3	75%
Moldova	37	15%	0	0%	6	38%	Moldova	0	-	0	-	0	-
Monaco	0	0%	0	0%	0	0%	Monaco	17	28%	1	20%	3	60%
Montenegro	0	0%	0	0%	0	0%	Montenegro	0	-	0	-	0	-
Morocco	0	-	0	-	0	-	Morocco	0	0%	0	0%	0	0%
Netherlands	83	25%	3	11%	12	57%	Netherlands	61	30%	2	12%	11	65%
North Macedonia	4	1%	0	0%	1	5%	North Macedonia	0	-	0	-	0	-
Norway	150	35%	3	8%	19	68%	Norway	33	14%	0	0%	9	47%
Poland	71	30%	1	5%	12	71%	Poland	0	-	0	-	0	-
Portugal	42	18%	2	10%	5	29%	Portugal	51	22%	0	0%	10	53%
Romania	28	9%	0	0%	8	38%	Romania	0	-	0	-	0	-
Russia	178	53%	4	14%	22	96%	Russia	0	-	0	-	0	-
San Marino	0	0%	0	0%	0	0%	San Marino	0	-	0	-	0	-
Serbia	16	6%	0	0%	5	29%	Serbia	0	-	0	-	0	-
Serbia & Mont	3	8%	0	0%	2	67%	Serbia & Mont	0	-	0	-	0	-
Slovakia	0	0%	0	0%	0	0%	Slovakia	0	-	0	-	0	-
Slovenia	34	11%	0	0%	8	38%	Slovenia	0	0%	0	0%	0	0%
Spain	12	4%	0	0%	2	10%	Spain	67	29%	0	0%	12	63%
Sweden	153	38%	0	0%	22	81%	Sweden	59	27%	0	0%	11	61%
Switzerland	70	22%	0	0%	10	50%	Switzerland	80	35%	3	16%	15	79%
Turkey	16	8%	0	0%	4	24%	Turkey	19	10%	0	0%	4	25%
Ukraine	198	55%	3	10%	20	83%	Ukraine	0	-	0	-	0	-
United Kingdom	22	7%	0	0%	5	24%	United Kingdom	123	54%	4	21%	18	95%
Yugoslavia	0	-	0	-	0	-	Yugoslavia	24	15%	0	0%	5	38%

Malta   Moldova

	Malta awarded points to:				Frequency			Moldova awarded points to:				Frequency	
	Total	% of max	12's	% of max	Times	% of max		Total	% of max	12's	% of max	Times	% of max
Albania	39	15%	0	0%	6	33%	Albania	31	10%	0	0%	6	32%
Andorra	3	5%	0	0%	1	20%	Andorra	4	8%	0	0%	1	25%
Armenia	52	22%	1	5%	8	50%	Armenia	88	33%	0	0%	14	82%
Australia	50	32%	1	8%	5	71%	Australia	61	39%	0	0%	7	100%
Austria	44	12%	1	3%	9	38%	Austria	26	11%	0	0%	6	43%
Azerbaijan	138	46%	5	20%	14	78%	Azerbaijan	179	60%	3	12%	18	100%
Belarus	51	22%	0	0%	10	63%	Belarus	77	43%	1	7%	11	85%
Belgium	37	11%	1	3%	5	20%	Belgium	39	15%	0	0%	8	47%
Bosnia & H	30	10%	0	0%	8	33%	Bosnia & H	21	13%	0	0%	5	38%
Bulgaria	83	38%	2	11%	8	62%	Bulgaria	80	44%	0	0%	9	90%
Croatia	95	23%	2	6%	12	43%	Croatia	19	10%	0	0%	5	42%
Cyprus	145	34%	4	11%	20	69%	Cyprus	39	14%	0	0%	7	41%
Czech Republic	15	10%	0	0%	4	50%	Czech Republic	28	18%	0	0%	4	57%
Denmark	93	23%	0	0%	19	68%	Denmark	30	9%	0	0%	7	32%
Estonia	46	14%	1	4%	8	33%	Estonia	57	21%	1	4%	12	63%
Finland	44	12%	0	0%	9	33%	Finland	35	13%	0	0%	6	33%
France	39	9%	0	0%	8	26%	France	23	9%	0	0%	4	25%
Georgia	29	15%	0	0%	5	36%	Georgia	52	27%	0	0%	9	75%
Germany	32	8%	0	0%	10	33%	Germany	10	4%	0	0%	2	13%
Greece	136	31%	2	6%	22	69%	Greece	101	30%	0	0%	16	73%
Hungary	34	10%	0	0%	9	41%	Hungary	27	10%	0	0%	8	44%
Iceland	82	20%	3	9%	11	35%	Iceland	45	16%	0	0%	8	44%
Ireland	97	25%	2	6%	16	57%	Ireland	9	4%	0	0%	4	27%
Israel	124	27%	1	3%	16	52%	Israel	47	19%	1	5%	6	38%
Italy	163	68%	7	35%	13	87%	Italy	37	21%	0	0%	6	60%
Latvia	69	26%	2	9%	9	47%	Latvia	34	13%	1	5%	9	53%
Lithuania	51	14%	0	0%	10	40%	Lithuania	30	13%	0	0%	7	47%
Luxembourg	25	52%	0	0%	3	75%	Luxembourg	0	-	0	-	0	-
Malta	-	-	-	-	-	-	Malta	34	14%	0	0%	6	43%
Moldova	27	10%	0	0%	6	35%	Moldova	-	-	-	-	-	-
Monaco	1	2%	0	0%	1	25%	Monaco	2	8%	0	0%	1	50%
Montenegro	18	17%	0	0%	3	43%	Montenegro	19	12%	0	0%	3	30%
Morocco	0	-	0	-	0	-	Morocco	0	-	0	-	0	-
Netherlands	128	29%	2	5%	17	61%	Netherlands	31	10%	0	0%	6	32%
North Macedonia	40	13%	0	0%	9	41%	North Macedonia	24	14%	1	7%	5	42%
Norway	130	24%	1	2%	24	63%	Norway	77	26%	0	0%	13	68%
Poland	21	7%	0	0%	6	27%	Poland	20	8%	0	0%	6	40%
Portugal	36	10%	0	0%	7	25%	Portugal	54	28%	1	6%	7	58%
Romania	123	33%	1	3%	16	62%	Romania	257	97%	20	91%	19	100%
Russia	113	26%	2	6%	17	59%	Russia	245	68%	6	20%	23	96%
San Marino	40	24%	1	7%	6	67%	San Marino	31	18%	0	0%	6	67%
Serbia	30	11%	0	0%	9	56%	Serbia	29	11%	0	0%	7	41%
Serbia & Mont	10	28%	0	0%	2	67%	Serbia & Mont	1	8%	0	0%	1	100%
Slovakia	27	45%	1	20%	3	60%	Slovakia	7	19%	0	0%	1	33%
Slovenia	34	10%	0	0%	9	38%	Slovenia	15	7%	0	0%	4	27%
Spain	48	11%	1	3%	9	29%	Spain	13	5%	0	0%	3	19%
Sweden	242	44%	4	9%	28	74%	Sweden	89	26%	0	0%	16	76%
Switzerland	100	27%	3	10%	15	56%	Switzerland	42	23%	0	0%	5	45%
Turkey	87	27%	1	4%	12	44%	Turkey	11	10%	0	0%	2	22%
Ukraine	102	30%	0	0%	16	73%	Ukraine	188	63%	3	12%	19	95%
United Kingdom	128	30%	2	6%	21	68%	United Kingdom	5	2%	0	0%	2	13%
Yugoslavia	4	11%	0	0%	2	67%	Yugoslavia	0	-	0	-	0	-

Monaco

	Monaco awarded points to:				Frequency	
	Total	% of max	12's	% of max	Times	% of max
Albania	3	6%	0	0%	1	25%
Andorra	0	0%	0	0%	0	0%
Armenia	0	0%	0	0%	0	0%
Australia	0	-	0	-	0	-
Austria	10	14%	0	0%	2	33%
Azerbaijan	0	-	0	-	0	-
Belarus	1	3%	0	0%	1	33%
Belgium	26	27%	1	13%	3	38%
Bosnia & H	28	47%	2	40%	3	60%
Bulgaria	0	0%	0	0%	0	0%
Croatia	16	27%	0	0%	3	60%
Cyprus	24	50%	1	25%	3	75%
Czech Republic	0	-	0	-	0	-
Denmark	33	46%	0	0%	4	67%
Estonia	5	14%	0	0%	1	33%
Finland	27	25%	0	0%	4	44%
France	53	55%	2	25%	7	88%
Georgia	0	-	0	-	0	-
Germany	32	33%	1	13%	5	63%
Greece	31	32%	0	0%	4	50%
Hungary	0	0%	0	0%	0	0%
Iceland	6	17%	0	0%	2	67%
Ireland	31	29%	0	0%	4	44%
Israel	43	40%	2	22%	6	67%
Italy	15	25%	0	0%	3	60%
Latvia	10	21%	0	0%	2	50%
Lithuania	11	23%	0	0%	2	50%
Luxembourg	10	17%	0	0%	2	40%
Malta	5	8%	0	0%	1	20%
Moldova	0	0%	0	0%	0	0%
Monaco	-	-	-	-	-	-
Montenegro	0	-	0	-	0	-
Morocco	0	-	0	-	0	-
Netherlands	32	30%	0	0%	6	67%
North Macedonia	4	6%	0	0%	2	33%
Norway	9	8%	0	0%	3	33%
Poland	0	0%	0	0%	0	0%
Portugal	8	8%	0	0%	3	38%
Romania	11	23%	0	0%	2	50%
Russia	0	0%	0	0%	0	0%
San Marino	0	-	0	-	0	-
Serbia	0	-	0	-	0	-
Serbia & Mont	14	39%	0	0%	3	100%
Slovakia	0	-	0	-	0	-
Slovenia	7	19%	0	0%	2	67%
Spain	14	15%	0	0%	4	50%
Sweden	22	23%	0	0%	4	50%
Switzerland	29	27%	0	0%	7	78%
Turkey	11	15%	0	0%	2	33%
Ukraine	15	25%	0	0%	4	80%
United Kingdom	42	44%	2	25%	5	63%
Yugoslavia	0	0%	0	0%	0	0%

Montenegro

	Montenegro awarded points to:				Frequency	
	Total	% of max	12's	% of max	Times	% of max
Albania	121	78%	3	23%	10	100%
Andorra	0	0%	0	0%	0	0%
Armenia	68	33%	1	6%	9	69%
Australia	27	15%	0	0%	5	63%
Austria	3	2%	0	0%	2	22%
Azerbaijan	81	36%	1	5%	11	79%
Belarus	24	17%	0	0%	7	78%
Belgium	18	9%	0	0%	5	42%
Bosnia & H	77	80%	4	50%	7	100%
Bulgaria	29	27%	0	0%	5	83%
Croatia	60	50%	1	10%	7	100%
Cyprus	40	17%	0	0%	7	54%
Czech Republic	15	8%	0	0%	5	56%
Denmark	31	16%	0	0%	5	42%
Estonia	8	4%	0	0%	3	25%
Finland	5	3%	0	0%	2	17%
France	12	7%	0	0%	3	27%
Georgia	4	3%	0	0%	2	22%
Germany	0	0%	0	0%	0	0%
Greece	77	34%	3	16%	9	64%
Hungary	46	19%	1	5%	7	50%
Iceland	29	13%	0	0%	5	36%
Ireland	4	4%	0	0%	3	38%
Israel	26	14%	0	0%	7	58%
Italy	61	42%	0	0%	8	100%
Latvia	5	3%	0	0%	2	20%
Lithuania	3	2%	0	0%	2	22%
Luxembourg	0	-	0	-	0	-
Malta	50	28%	1	7%	6	55%
Moldova	56	25%	0	0%	9	64%
Monaco	0	-	0	-	0	-
Montenegro	-	-	-	-	-	-
Morocco	0	-	0	-	0	-
Netherlands	15	7%	0	0%	6	50%
North Macedonia	51	71%	0	0%	5	100%
Norway	44	22%	0	0%	7	54%
Poland	6	3%	0	0%	3	25%
Portugal	26	20%	0	0%	4	50%
Romania	32	19%	0	0%	5	42%
Russia	123	54%	0	0%	13	87%
San Marino	39	25%	0	0%	5	56%
Serbia	179	93%	13	81%	11	100%
Serbia & Mont	0	-	0	-	0	-
Slovakia	0	-	0	-	0	-
Slovenia	91	45%	1	6%	12	100%
Spain	6	3%	0	0%	2	18%
Sweden	54	20%	0	0%	9	56%
Switzerland	5	6%	0	0%	1	17%
Turkey	15	21%	0	0%	4	67%
Ukraine	65	34%	1	6%	8	67%
United Kingdom	2	1%	0	0%	1	9%
Yugoslavia	0	-	0	-	0	-

Morocco

	Morocco awarded points to:				Frequency	
	Total	% of max	12's	% of max	Times	% of max
Albania	0	-	0	-	0	-
Andorra	0	-	0	-	0	-
Armenia	0	-	0	-	0	-
Australia	0	-	0	-	0	-
Austria	3	25%	0	0%	1	100%
Azerbaijan	0	-	0	-	0	-
Belarus	0	-	0	-	0	-
Belgium	0	0%	0	0%	0	0%
Bosnia & H	0	-	0	-	0	-
Bulgaria	0	-	0	-	0	-
Croatia	0	-	0	-	0	-
Cyprus	0	-	0	-	0	-
Czech Republic	0	-	0	-	0	-
Denmark	2	17%	0	0%	1	100%
Estonia	0	-	0	-	0	-
Finland	0	0%	0	0%	0	0%
France	1	8%	0	0%	1	100%
Georgia	0	-	0	-	0	-
Germany	10	83%	0	0%	1	100%
Greece	0	0%	0	0%	0	0%
Hungary	0	-	0	-	0	-
Iceland	0	-	0	-	0	-
Ireland	0	0%	0	0%	0	0%
Israel	0	-	0	-	0	-
Italy	0	0%	0	0%	0	0%
Latvia	0	-	0	-	0	-
Lithuania	0	-	0	-	0	-
Luxembourg	0	0%	0	0%	0	0%
Malta	0	-	0	-	0	-
Moldova	0	-	0	-	0	-
Monaco	0	-	0	-	0	-
Montenegro	0	-	0	-	0	-
Morocco	-	-	-	-	-	-
Netherlands	0	0%	0	0%	0	0%
North Macedonia	0	-	0	-	0	-
Norway	4	33%	0	0%	1	100%
Poland	0	-	0	-	0	-
Portugal	0	0%	0	0%	0	0%
Romania	0	-	0	-	0	-
Russia	0	-	0	-	0	-
San Marino	0	-	0	-	0	-
Serbia	0	-	0	-	0	-
Serbia & Mont	0	-	0	-	0	-
Slovakia	0	-	0	-	0	-
Slovenia	0	-	0	-	0	-
Spain	5	42%	0	0%	1	100%
Sweden	6	50%	0	0%	1	100%
Switzerland	7	58%	0	0%	1	100%
Turkey	12	100%	1	100%	1	100%
Ukraine	0	-	0	-	0	-
United Kingdom	8	67%	0	0%	1	100%
Yugoslavia	0	-	0	-	0	-

Netherlands

	Netherlands awarded points to:				Frequency	
	Total	% of max	12's	% of max	Times	% of max
Albania	9	4%	0	0%	5	29%
Andorra	7	12%	0	0%	1	20%
Armenia	141	56%	6	29%	14	82%
Australia	41	26%	1	8%	5	71%
Austria	104	21%	1	2%	15	42%
Azerbaijan	65	21%	0	0%	14	74%
Belarus	6	3%	0	0%	3	20%
Belgium	233	45%	5	12%	29	74%
Bosnia & H	90	33%	0	0%	14	64%
Bulgaria	45	22%	2	12%	4	33%
Croatia	54	14%	1	3%	11	41%
Cyprus	84	16%	1	2%	11	31%
Czech Republic	16	15%	0	0%	3	60%
Denmark	205	36%	6	13%	28	68%
Estonia	69	18%	1	3%	12	43%
Finland	52	11%	0	0%	13	36%
France	152	28%	4	9%	21	51%
Georgia	13	8%	0	0%	4	33%
Germany	149	27%	5	11%	24	59%
Greece	129	25%	0	0%	23	59%
Hungary	82	25%	0	0%	12	57%
Iceland	76	20%	0	0%	11	38%
Ireland	150	27%	3	7%	25	60%
Israel	195	35%	3	7%	29	74%
Italy	70	19%	1	3%	11	44%
Latvia	23	10%	0	0%	5	29%
Lithuania	44	13%	0	0%	9	39%
Luxembourg	45	22%	1	6%	8	47%
Malta	98	22%	0	0%	17	59%
Moldova	31	9%	0	0%	5	23%
Monaco	18	19%	0	0%	2	25%
Montenegro	6	5%	0	0%	1	13%
Morocco	0	0%	0	0%	0	0%
Netherlands	-	-	-	-	-	-
North Macedonia	18	7%	0	0%	4	22%
Norway	207	31%	4	7%	33	69%
Poland	43	16%	0	0%	9	45%
Portugal	96	21%	3	8%	16	44%
Romania	53	14%	0	0%	13	50%
Russia	103	24%	0	0%	18	62%
San Marino	4	3%	0	0%	1	13%
Serbia	72	26%	0	0%	13	76%
Serbia & Mont	26	72%	1	33%	3	100%
Slovakia	0	0%	0	0%	0	0%
Slovenia	38	11%	0	0%	7	28%
Spain	60	11%	0	0%	13	31%
Sweden	247	37%	6	11%	28	58%
Switzerland	150	33%	1	3%	18	53%
Turkey	168	42%	7	21%	23	70%
Ukraine	85	22%	0	0%	13	50%
United Kingdom	112	20%	2	4%	20	48%
Yugoslavia	25	17%	0	0%	4	33%

North Macedonia

	\multicolumn{4}{c}{N Macedonia awarded points to:}	\multicolumn{2}{c}{Frequency}
	Total	% of max	12's	% of max	Times	% of max
Albania	263	84%	16	62%	20	100%
Andorra	1	2%	0	0%	1	20%
Armenia	41	17%	0	0%	9	56%
Australia	37	24%	0	0%	4	57%
Austria	14	5%	0	0%	4	25%
Azerbaijan	71	26%	0	0%	11	69%
Belarus	44	15%	0	0%	9	45%
Belgium	41	13%	0	0%	9	45%
Bosnia & H	116	60%	3	19%	16	100%
Bulgaria	160	58%	4	17%	15	94%
Croatia	172	57%	2	8%	19	100%
Cyprus	51	16%	0	0%	6	30%
Czech Republic	28	21%	0	0%	3	43%
Denmark	31	9%	1	3%	5	22%
Estonia	32	11%	1	4%	6	30%
Finland	36	13%	0	0%	9	43%
France	27	9%	0	0%	5	25%
Georgia	15	8%	0	0%	5	36%
Germany	11	4%	0	0%	2	10%
Greece	58	18%	0	0%	12	52%
Hungary	29	12%	0	0%	5	29%
Iceland	15	6%	0	0%	6	32%
Ireland	16	5%	0	0%	4	21%
Israel	75	18%	0	0%	14	56%
Italy	73	41%	1	7%	10	100%
Latvia	31	13%	0	0%	7	41%
Lithuania	20	6%	0	0%	5	23%
Luxembourg	0	-	0	-	0	-
Malta	116	32%	2	7%	15	63%
Moldova	49	19%	0	0%	9	53%
Monaco	0	0%	0	0%	0	0%
Montenegro	27	56%	1	25%	4	100%
Morocco	0	-	0	-	0	-
Netherlands	54	17%	0	0%	9	47%
North Macedonia	-	-	-	-	-	-
Norway	43	11%	0	0%	10	40%
Poland	13	7%	0	0%	5	38%
Portugal	23	10%	0	0%	3	19%
Romania	79	23%	2	7%	13	52%
Russia	109	34%	0	0%	15	68%
San Marino	13	14%	0	0%	2	40%
Serbia	208	79%	7	32%	16	100%
Serbia & Mont	30	83%	0	0%	3	100%
Slovakia	3	6%	0	0%	1	25%
Slovenia	75	30%	0	0%	14	82%
Spain	5	2%	0	0%	2	10%
Sweden	68	17%	0	0%	16	62%
Switzerland	39	13%	0	0%	8	40%
Turkey	125	65%	2	13%	16	100%
Ukraine	106	32%	1	4%	16	73%
United Kingdom	28	9%	0	0%	5	25%
Yugoslavia	0	-	0	-	0	-

Norway

	\multicolumn{4}{c}{Norway awarded points to:}	\multicolumn{2}{c}{Frequency}
	Total	% of max	12's	% of max	Times	% of max
Albania	21	8%	0	0%	5	28%
Andorra	2	3%	0	0%	1	20%
Armenia	7	3%	0	0%	2	13%
Australia	79	44%	1	7%	7	88%
Austria	67	13%	0	0%	11	30%
Azerbaijan	63	20%	0	0%	9	45%
Belarus	4	2%	0	0%	2	14%
Belgium	96	18%	0	0%	18	46%
Bosnia & H	92	37%	3	14%	11	52%
Bulgaria	86	38%	3	16%	7	54%
Croatia	34	9%	0	0%	12	44%
Cyprus	76	15%	1	2%	15	41%
Czech Republic	16	17%	1	13%	2	40%
Denmark	291	49%	8	16%	35	83%
Estonia	63	20%	0	0%	12	52%
Finland	153	31%	4	10%	23	59%
France	151	26%	3	6%	28	64%
Georgia	2	1%	0	0%	2	13%
Germany	102	17%	2	4%	18	41%
Greece	88	16%	0	0%	21	49%
Hungary	57	18%	0	0%	11	52%
Iceland	179	44%	3	9%	26	81%
Ireland	180	29%	5	10%	33	72%
Israel	177	28%	1	2%	29	64%
Italy	98	26%	2	6%	15	56%
Latvia	64	24%	1	5%	11	61%
Lithuania	162	41%	4	12%	18	69%
Luxembourg	38	17%	1	5%	6	32%
Malta	122	25%	2	5%	16	47%
Moldova	30	11%	0	0%	7	41%
Monaco	10	10%	0	0%	3	38%
Montenegro	3	4%	0	0%	1	17%
Morocco	0	0%	0	0%	0	0%
Netherlands	162	26%	2	4%	22	50%
North Macedonia	21	7%	0	0%	3	16%
Norway	-	-	-	-	-	-
Poland	82	24%	0	0%	16	67%
Portugal	65	13%	2	5%	9	23%
Romania	91	24%	0	0%	15	58%
Russia	88	22%	0	0%	18	67%
San Marino	0	0%	0	0%	0	0%
Serbia	66	23%	0	0%	10	59%
Serbia & Mont	16	44%	0	0%	2	67%
Slovakia	0	0%	0	0%	0	0%
Slovenia	32	8%	0	0%	7	26%
Spain	59	10%	0	0%	14	31%
Sweden	454	65%	15	26%	44	88%
Switzerland	141	26%	1	2%	23	56%
Turkey	59	13%	0	0%	16	43%
Ukraine	76	20%	0	0%	13	54%
United Kingdom	122	20%	2	4%	23	51%
Yugoslavia	31	20%	1	8%	5	38%

Poland

	Poland awarded points to:				Frequency	
	Total	% of max	12's	% of max	Times	% of max
Albania	25	9%	0	0%	5	29%
Andorra	7	15%	0	0%	2	50%
Armenia	68	35%	2	13%	12	92%
Australia	115	56%	2	12%	9	100%
Austria	40	16%	1	5%	7	41%
Azerbaijan	67	28%	1	5%	10	67%
Belarus	40	21%	0	0%	8	67%
Belgium	109	35%	4	15%	12	60%
Bosnia & H	20	9%	0	0%	4	22%
Bulgaria	40	21%	0	0%	5	50%
Croatia	24	10%	0	0%	7	37%
Cyprus	34	10%	0	0%	8	36%
Czech Republic	32	19%	0	0%	6	75%
Denmark	80	26%	1	4%	14	70%
Estonia	63	22%	1	4%	10	50%
Finland	86	29%	2	8%	13	65%
France	54	16%	1	4%	10	43%
Georgia	59	25%	0	0%	9	64%
Germany	64	20%	1	4%	9	41%
Greece	68	17%	0	0%	15	54%
Hungary	95	34%	2	9%	11	61%
Iceland	93	27%	2	7%	13	54%
Ireland	53	19%	1	4%	12	57%
Israel	78	23%	0	0%	11	50%
Italy	52	31%	0	0%	6	67%
Latvia	67	25%	1	5%	8	47%
Lithuania	61	23%	2	9%	10	56%
Luxembourg	0	-	0	-	0	-
Malta	33	11%	0	0%	8	36%
Moldova	57	21%	0	0%	9	53%
Monaco	1	4%	0	0%	1	50%
Montenegro	0	0%	0	0%	0	0%
Morocco	0	-	0	-	0	-
Netherlands	61	20%	1	4%	7	35%
North Macedonia	8	5%	0	0%	1	8%
Norway	129	31%	2	6%	20	69%
Poland	-	-	-	-	-	-
Portugal	75	23%	3	11%	8	36%
Romania	45	19%	0	0%	8	44%
Russia	80	25%	0	0%	13	57%
San Marino	30	18%	0	0%	3	33%
Serbia	52	17%	0	0%	9	53%
Serbia & Mont	5	21%	0	0%	1	50%
Slovakia	5	8%	0	0%	1	20%
Slovenia	83	23%	0	0%	13	54%
Spain	21	6%	0	0%	6	26%
Sweden	133	34%	3	9%	17	65%
Switzerland	72	29%	1	5%	9	53%
Turkey	11	5%	0	0%	3	18%
Ukraine	183	64%	9	38%	18	100%
United Kingdom	37	11%	0	0%	8	35%
Yugoslavia	0	-	0	-	0	-

Portugal

	Portugal awarded points to:				Frequency	
	Total	% of max	12's	% of max	Times	% of max
Albania	32	11%	0	0%	6	32%
Andorra	10	17%	0	0%	2	40%
Armenia	20	10%	0	0%	5	38%
Australia	34	26%	0	0%	4	67%
Austria	80	18%	1	3%	14	41%
Azerbaijan	56	25%	1	5%	8	57%
Belarus	15	7%	0	0%	4	27%
Belgium	165	31%	3	7%	21	54%
Bosnia & H	20	8%	0	0%	4	18%
Bulgaria	70	34%	0	0%	10	83%
Croatia	41	15%	0	0%	14	67%
Cyprus	64	12%	0	0%	16	44%
Czech Republic	50	26%	2	13%	6	60%
Denmark	81	17%	0	0%	22	61%
Estonia	94	28%	4	14%	11	48%
Finland	69	13%	0	0%	12	31%
France	148	27%	3	7%	25	61%
Georgia	21	13%	0	0%	5	45%
Germany	165	31%	3	7%	23	56%
Greece	126	21%	1	2%	19	45%
Hungary	47	20%	0	0%	9	53%
Iceland	134	27%	2	5%	19	53%
Ireland	128	27%	1	3%	24	65%
Israel	149	29%	2	5%	21	55%
Italy	207	59%	6	21%	23	92%
Latvia	48	22%	0	0%	8	50%
Lithuania	46	18%	1	5%	6	33%
Luxembourg	76	33%	2	11%	12	63%
Malta	54	16%	1	3%	13	48%
Moldova	146	58%	4	19%	15	94%
Monaco	18	19%	0	0%	5	63%
Montenegro	12	10%	0	0%	3	38%
Morocco	0	0%	0	0%	0	0%
Netherlands	109	23%	2	5%	17	47%
North Macedonia	5	2%	0	0%	1	6%
Norway	102	18%	1	2%	23	52%
Poland	16	6%	0	0%	6	32%
Portugal	-	-	-	-	-	-
Romania	85	39%	1	6%	13	76%
Russia	82	30%	0	0%	15	71%
San Marino	9	7%	0	0%	1	14%
Serbia	38	17%	0	0%	8	57%
Serbia & Mont	17	47%	0	0%	2	67%
Slovakia	9	15%	0	0%	2	40%
Slovenia	49	16%	0	0%	10	45%
Spain	184	33%	8	17%	23	55%
Sweden	194	31%	2	4%	28	60%
Switzerland	131	27%	1	2%	23	62%
Turkey	21	5%	0	0%	4	11%
Ukraine	129	49%	5	23%	16	84%
United Kingdom	156	28%	4	9%	25	60%
Yugoslavia	11	7%	0	0%	3	23%

Romania

Romania awarded points to:

	Total	% of max	12's	% of max	Times	% of max
Albania	20	8%	0	0%	7	41%
Andorra	0	0%	0	0%	0	0%
Armenia	56	26%	0	0%	11	69%
Australia	31	23%	1	9%	6	100%
Austria	44	17%	2	10%	7	41%
Azerbaijan	100	40%	1	5%	12	75%
Belarus	14	6%	0	0%	5	33%
Belgium	41	15%	0	0%	8	40%
Bosnia & H	24	12%	1	6%	3	18%
Bulgaria	48	25%	0	0%	7	58%
Croatia	39	15%	0	0%	7	39%
Cyprus	56	18%	0	0%	11	52%
Czech Republic	11	15%	0	0%	2	50%
Denmark	84	23%	2	7%	16	67%
Estonia	17	6%	0	0%	6	30%
Finland	36	13%	0	0%	7	32%
France	27	9%	0	0%	5	24%
Georgia	6	4%	0	0%	2	17%
Germany	38	13%	1	4%	9	43%
Greece	166	49%	5	18%	20	80%
Hungary	136	52%	1	5%	17	94%
Iceland	25	10%	0	0%	3	16%
Ireland	47	15%	0	0%	10	45%
Israel	98	26%	0	0%	20	77%
Italy	52	33%	1	8%	7	78%
Latvia	13	6%	0	0%	4	25%
Lithuania	27	9%	0	0%	5	26%
Luxembourg	0	-	0	-	0	-
Malta	95	27%	0	0%	13	57%
Moldova	263	91%	16	67%	19	100%
Monaco	0	0%	0	0%	0	0%
Montenegro	7	7%	0	0%	1	14%
Morocco	0	-	0	-	0	-
Netherlands	89	26%	3	10%	12	55%
North Macedonia	67	22%	1	4%	11	52%
Norway	79	19%	0	0%	16	59%
Poland	23	14%	0	0%	4	31%
Portugal	38	19%	0	0%	4	29%
Romania	-	-	-	-	-	-
Russia	138	38%	2	7%	17	68%
San Marino	9	6%	0	0%	2	25%
Serbia	37	17%	0	0%	6	46%
Serbia & Mont	24	67%	0	0%	3	100%
Slovakia	3	8%	0	0%	1	33%
Slovenia	42	15%	0	0%	9	47%
Spain	48	16%	0	0%	9	43%
Sweden	96	24%	2	6%	16	59%
Switzerland	75	26%	0	0%	9	45%
Turkey	107	56%	1	6%	15	94%
Ukraine	88	28%	0	0%	14	67%
United Kingdom	20	7%	1	4%	4	19%
Yugoslavia	0	-	0	-	0	-

Russia

Russia awarded points to:

	Total	% of max	12's	% of max	Times	% of max
Albania	19	7%	0	0%	6	32%
Andorra	4	8%	0	0%	1	25%
Armenia	187	82%	11	58%	16	100%
Australia	25	19%	0	0%	6	100%
Austria	27	10%	0	0%	5	28%
Azerbaijan	213	74%	6	25%	18	100%
Belarus	89	62%	4	33%	10	91%
Belgium	75	26%	0	0%	11	52%
Bosnia & H	15	6%	0	0%	3	16%
Bulgaria	10	8%	0	0%	2	29%
Croatia	36	12%	0	0%	10	48%
Cyprus	93	28%	0	0%	13	59%
Czech Republic	8	7%	0	0%	2	40%
Denmark	61	18%	1	4%	10	42%
Estonia	64	21%	0	0%	11	48%
Finland	43	16%	1	4%	6	30%
France	66	20%	1	4%	10	43%
Georgia	70	45%	0	0%	11	100%
Germany	38	12%	0	0%	7	30%
Greece	119	33%	0	0%	21	78%
Hungary	54	18%	0	0%	11	52%
Iceland	32	10%	0	0%	10	42%
Ireland	39	13%	1	4%	6	27%
Israel	87	29%	0	0%	11	55%
Italy	47	28%	1	7%	5	50%
Latvia	30	12%	0	0%	9	50%
Lithuania	58	19%	0	0%	13	65%
Luxembourg	0	-	0	-	0	-
Malta	88	24%	1	3%	10	42%
Moldova	185	57%	7	26%	20	91%
Monaco	0	0%	0	0%	0	0%
Montenegro	8	6%	0	0%	2	22%
Morocco	0	-	0	-	0	-
Netherlands	32	9%	0	0%	7	30%
North Macedonia	28	13%	0	0%	4	27%
Norway	119	30%	2	6%	14	52%
Poland	32	13%	0	0%	7	37%
Portugal	4	2%	0	0%	1	6%
Romania	68	22%	3	12%	13	57%
Russia	-	-	-	-	-	-
San Marino	9	6%	0	0%	3	33%
Serbia	49	19%	0	0%	9	53%
Serbia & Mont	16	67%	0	0%	2	100%
Slovakia	1	3%	0	0%	1	33%
Slovenia	50	18%	0	0%	10	53%
Spain	22	7%	0	0%	6	26%
Sweden	82	20%	1	3%	15	56%
Switzerland	28	13%	0	0%	6	40%
Turkey	25	12%	0	0%	6	35%
Ukraine	172	55%	1	4%	21	100%
United Kingdom	38	12%	1	4%	8	35%
Yugoslavia	0	-	0	-	0	-

San Marino

	San Marino awarded points to:				Frequency	
	Total	% of max	12's	% of max	Times	% of max
Albania	62	34%	1	7%	9	82%
Andorra	0	0%	0	0%	0	0%
Armenia	54	32%	0	0%	9	82%
Australia	31	20%	0	0%	5	71%
Austria	12	6%	0	0%	3	30%
Azerbaijan	72	29%	1	5%	10	63%
Belarus	1	1%	0	0%	1	17%
Belgium	26	17%	0	0%	5	56%
Bosnia & H	6	8%	0	0%	1	20%
Bulgaria	59	38%	2	15%	6	86%
Croatia	18	15%	0	0%	4	67%
Cyprus	65	30%	0	0%	7	64%
Czech Republic	27	17%	0	0%	4	57%
Denmark	35	16%	1	6%	8	67%
Estonia	13	6%	0	0%	2	17%
Finland	35	16%	0	0%	6	46%
France	34	18%	0	0%	4	36%
Georgia	17	10%	0	0%	5	50%
Germany	14	7%	0	0%	1	9%
Greece	141	53%	6	27%	11	69%
Hungary	64	23%	0	0%	10	63%
Iceland	57	24%	0	0%	7	47%
Ireland	23	19%	1	10%	4	50%
Israel	52	24%	2	11%	7	58%
Italy	110	61%	2	13%	9	90%
Latvia	35	24%	1	8%	5	56%
Lithuania	23	14%	0	0%	4	40%
Luxembourg	0	-	0	-	0	-
Malta	69	32%	1	6%	11	92%
Moldova	82	38%	0	0%	8	67%
Monaco	0	-	0	-	0	-
Montenegro	29	20%	0	0%	4	44%
Morocco	0	-	0	-	0	-
Netherlands	79	33%	3	15%	10	83%
North Macedonia	7	10%	0	0%	3	75%
Norway	77	31%	0	0%	10	67%
Poland	37	18%	0	0%	6	50%
Portugal	29	19%	1	8%	3	38%
Romania	27	15%	0	0%	5	42%
Russia	69	29%	2	10%	8	53%
San Marino	-	-	-	-	-	-
Serbia	43	17%	0	0%	8	62%
Serbia & Mont	0	-	0	-	0	-
Slovakia	0	-	0	-	0	-
Slovenia	21	13%	0	0%	5	56%
Spain	1	1%	0	0%	1	9%
Sweden	72	30%	2	10%	10	71%
Switzerland	32	19%	0	0%	5	50%
Turkey	19	53%	0	0%	3	100%
Ukraine	49	26%	2	13%	5	45%
United Kingdom	31	16%	0	0%	7	64%
Yugoslavia	0	-	0	-	0	-

Serbia

	Serbia awarded points to:				Frequency	
	Total	% of max	12's	% of max	Times	% of max
Albania	13	5%	0	0%	5	31%
Andorra	0	0%	0	0%	0	0%
Armenia	16	11%	0	0%	4	40%
Australia	57	32%	0	0%	7	88%
Austria	20	12%	0	0%	5	56%
Azerbaijan	25	12%	0	0%	6	46%
Belarus	25	11%	0	0%	6	43%
Belgium	44	22%	0	0%	8	67%
Bosnia & H	78	81%	5	63%	8	100%
Bulgaria	98	45%	0	0%	11	100%
Croatia	89	53%	3	21%	11	100%
Cyprus	37	16%	0	0%	8	62%
Czech Republic	20	14%	0	0%	3	43%
Denmark	45	15%	1	4%	9	50%
Estonia	22	9%	0	0%	7	44%
Finland	40	21%	0	0%	4	33%
France	32	15%	0	0%	5	38%
Georgia	17	7%	0	0%	4	25%
Germany	18	8%	0	0%	2	15%
Greece	94	36%	0	0%	13	76%
Hungary	156	59%	8	36%	14	88%
Iceland	53	25%	0	0%	6	43%
Ireland	3	2%	0	0%	1	10%
Israel	51	22%	0	0%	8	67%
Italy	78	46%	0	0%	7	78%
Latvia	6	3%	0	0%	3	27%
Lithuania	27	11%	0	0%	5	31%
Luxembourg	0	-	0	-	0	-
Malta	37	17%	0	0%	7	54%
Moldova	68	27%	0	0%	10	63%
Monaco	0	-	0	-	0	-
Montenegro	69	82%	3	43%	5	100%
Morocco	0	-	0	-	0	-
Netherlands	34	14%	0	0%	6	46%
North Macedonia	135	87%	7	54%	10	100%
Norway	63	22%	0	0%	9	53%
Poland	7	3%	0	0%	3	25%
Portugal	51	22%	1	5%	8	57%
Romania	22	12%	0	0%	6	50%
Russia	106	44%	1	5%	14	88%
San Marino	11	7%	0	0%	3	43%
Serbia	-	-	-	-	-	-
Serbia & Mont	0	-	0	-	0	-
Slovakia	7	19%	0	0%	2	67%
Slovenia	97	48%	0	0%	11	92%
Spain	2	1%	0	0%	1	8%
Sweden	73	29%	2	10%	13	87%
Switzerland	34	20%	0	0%	6	67%
Turkey	3	3%	0	0%	1	11%
Ukraine	95	34%	1	4%	13	76%
United Kingdom	10	5%	0	0%	2	15%
Yugoslavia	0	-	0	-	0	-

Serbia & Montenegro

	Serbia & Mont awarded points to:				Frequency	
	Total	% of max	12's	% of max	Times	% of max
Albania	22	46%	0	0%	3	75%
Andorra	0	0%	0	0%	0	0%
Armenia	0	0%	0	0%	0	0%
Australia	0	-	0	-	0	-
Austria	0	0%	0	0%	0	0%
Azerbaijan	0	-	0	-	0	-
Belarus	0	0%	0	0%	0	0%
Belgium	0	0%	0	0%	0	0%
Bosnia & H	41	68%	2	40%	5	100%
Bulgaria	1	4%	0	0%	1	50%
Croatia	42	70%	1	20%	5	100%
Cyprus	6	13%	0	0%	3	75%
Czech Republic	0	-	0	-	0	-
Denmark	0	0%	0	0%	0	0%
Estonia	4	11%	0	0%	1	33%
Finland	15	31%	0	0%	2	50%
France	0	0%	0	0%	0	0%
Georgia	0	-	0	-	0	-
Germany	0	0%	0	0%	0	0%
Greece	35	73%	1	25%	4	100%
Hungary	14	58%	0	0%	2	100%
Iceland	2	6%	0	0%	1	33%
Ireland	1	2%	0	0%	1	25%
Israel	6	13%	0	0%	2	50%
Italy	0	-	0	-	0	-
Latvia	0	0%	0	0%	0	0%
Lithuania	6	13%	0	0%	2	50%
Luxembourg	0	-	0	-	0	-
Malta	0	0%	0	0%	0	0%
Moldova	11	31%	0	0%	2	67%
Monaco	0	0%	0	0%	0	0%
Montenegro	0	-	0	-	0	-
Morocco	0	-	0	-	0	-
Netherlands	1	2%	0	0%	1	25%
North Macedonia	59	82%	2	33%	6	100%
Norway	6	13%	0	0%	2	50%
Poland	0	0%	0	0%	0	0%
Portugal	0	0%	0	0%	0	0%
Romania	12	25%	0	0%	3	75%
Russia	12	25%	0	0%	3	75%
San Marino	0	-	0	-	0	-
Serbia	0	-	0	-	0	-
Serbia & Mont	-	-	-	-	-	-
Slovakia	0	-	0	-	0	-
Slovenia	14	39%	0	0%	2	67%
Spain	0	0%	0	0%	0	0%
Sweden	9	19%	0	0%	3	75%
Switzerland	2	4%	0	0%	1	25%
Turkey	2	4%	0	0%	1	25%
Ukraine	25	42%	0	0%	4	80%
United Kingdom	0	0%	0	0%	0	0%
Yugoslavia	0	-	0	-	0	-

Slovakia

	Slovakia awarded points to:				Frequency	
	Total	% of max	12's	% of max	Times	% of max
Albania	4	7%	0	0%	1	20%
Andorra	0	-	0	-	0	-
Armenia	7	29%	0	0%	2	100%
Australia	0	-	0	-	0	-
Austria	9	19%	0	0%	3	75%
Azerbaijan	29	48%	1	20%	4	80%
Belarus	4	8%	0	0%	2	50%
Belgium	26	36%	0	0%	3	50%
Bosnia & H	41	38%	1	11%	6	67%
Bulgaria	0	0%	0	0%	0	0%
Croatia	32	44%	1	17%	4	67%
Cyprus	3	4%	0	0%	3	43%
Czech Republic	0	-	0	-	0	-
Denmark	16	22%	0	0%	3	50%
Estonia	50	42%	1	10%	6	60%
Finland	2	3%	0	0%	1	17%
France	0	0%	0	0%	0	0%
Georgia	0	0%	0	0%	0	0%
Germany	27	38%	1	17%	3	50%
Greece	23	21%	0	0%	4	44%
Hungary	10	17%	0	0%	2	40%
Iceland	24	29%	0	0%	5	71%
Ireland	29	30%	0	0%	5	63%
Israel	20	42%	0	0%	3	75%
Italy	5	21%	0	0%	1	50%
Latvia	0	0%	0	0%	0	0%
Lithuania	7	10%	0	0%	1	17%
Luxembourg	0	-	0	-	0	-
Malta	31	37%	3	43%	5	71%
Moldova	16	19%	0	0%	3	43%
Monaco	0	-	0	-	0	-
Montenegro	0	-	0	-	0	-
Morocco	0	-	0	-	0	-
Netherlands	5	7%	0	0%	1	17%
North Macedonia	6	10%	0	0%	3	60%
Norway	47	49%	0	0%	6	75%
Poland	7	12%	0	0%	2	40%
Portugal	11	13%	0	0%	3	43%
Romania	7	8%	0	0%	2	29%
Russia	9	13%	0	0%	2	33%
San Marino	0	-	0	-	0	-
Serbia	21	29%	0	0%	3	50%
Serbia & Mont	0	-	0	-	0	-
Slovakia	-	-	-	-	-	-
Slovenia	9	13%	0	0%	2	33%
Spain	4	5%	0	0%	2	29%
Sweden	48	50%	2	25%	5	63%
Switzerland	6	13%	0	0%	2	50%
Turkey	3	4%	0	0%	1	17%
Ukraine	30	36%	1	14%	5	71%
United Kingdom	15	18%	0	0%	3	43%
Yugoslavia	0	-	0	-	0	-

Slovenia

	Slovenia awarded points to:				Frequency	
	Total	% of max	12's	% of max	Times	% of max
Albania	35	14%	0	0%	10	63%
Andorra	5	8%	0	0%	2	40%
Armenia	18	9%	0	0%	5	36%
Australia	56	25%	1	5%	8	80%
Austria	77	29%	1	5%	11	58%
Azerbaijan	54	19%	0	0%	9	50%
Belarus	22	9%	0	0%	4	25%
Belgium	97	26%	1	3%	14	58%
Bosnia & H	151	57%	5	23%	17	77%
Bulgaria	52	25%	0	0%	6	50%
Croatia	203	63%	8	30%	22	92%
Cyprus	77	17%	0	0%	13	45%
Czech Republic	53	37%	2	17%	5	71%
Denmark	122	32%	2	6%	15	56%
Estonia	56	17%	1	4%	11	46%
Finland	39	14%	0	0%	6	30%
France	46	12%	0	0%	10	38%
Georgia	16	7%	0	0%	5	33%
Germany	34	9%	0	0%	7	28%
Greece	76	19%	0	0%	13	45%
Hungary	42	15%	0	0%	8	44%
Iceland	59	18%	0	0%	10	43%
Ireland	42	12%	2	7%	13	48%
Israel	44	10%	0	0%	12	43%
Italy	95	47%	0	0%	10	83%
Latvia	63	24%	0	0%	9	50%
Lithuania	19	5%	0	0%	5	21%
Luxembourg	1	8%	0	0%	1	100%
Malta	65	17%	0	0%	10	38%
Moldova	52	18%	0	0%	10	53%
Monaco	0	0%	0	0%	0	0%
Montenegro	63	44%	0	0%	8	89%
Morocco	0	-	0	-	0	-
Netherlands	81	21%	0	0%	15	58%
North Macedonia	131	55%	2	9%	16	94%
Norway	109	23%	1	3%	19	59%
Poland	43	12%	0	0%	11	46%
Portugal	50	17%	2	8%	6	29%
Romania	38	12%	0	0%	8	35%
Russia	118	33%	2	7%	14	56%
San Marino	3	2%	0	0%	1	14%
Serbia	197	68%	11	46%	17	100%
Serbia & Mont	34	94%	2	67%	3	100%
Slovakia	3	5%	0	0%	1	20%
Slovenia	-	-	-	-	-	-
Spain	20	5%	0	0%	7	27%
Sweden	179	36%	4	10%	25	76%
Switzerland	61	24%	0	0%	10	56%
Turkey	18	7%	0	0%	4	19%
Ukraine	107	27%	2	6%	15	58%
United Kingdom	50	13%	0	0%	10	38%
Yugoslavia	0	-	0	-	0	-

Spain

	Spain awarded points to:				Frequency	
	Total	% of max	12's	% of max	Times	% of max
Albania	27	8%	0	0%	6	26%
Andorra	54	90%	3	60%	5	100%
Armenia	121	42%	3	13%	14	74%
Australia	69	44%	1	8%	6	86%
Austria	103	19%	2	4%	16	41%
Azerbaijan	44	14%	0	0%	9	45%
Belarus	7	3%	0	0%	1	7%
Belgium	138	23%	2	4%	21	47%
Bosnia & H	12	4%	0	0%	4	17%
Bulgaria	108	53%	1	6%	11	100%
Croatia	35	10%	2	7%	7	28%
Cyprus	118	20%	1	2%	16	40%
Czech Republic	67	33%	0	0%	6	67%
Denmark	98	18%	0	0%	19	46%
Estonia	63	15%	1	3%	14	48%
Finland	93	14%	0	0%	20	43%
France	151	25%	0	0%	21	47%
Georgia	13	6%	0	0%	4	29%
Germany	203	34%	8	16%	28	62%
Greece	201	28%	3	5%	31	61%
Hungary	66	19%	0	0%	11	46%
Iceland	148	27%	1	2%	23	59%
Ireland	151	29%	3	7%	23	56%
Israel	159	28%	3	6%	24	57%
Italy	221	58%	9	28%	24	89%
Latvia	27	10%	1	4%	5	25%
Lithuania	20	7%	0	0%	6	30%
Luxembourg	51	22%	1	5%	9	47%
Malta	97	24%	1	3%	16	53%
Moldova	89	26%	0	0%	14	64%
Monaco	17	18%	0	0%	3	38%
Montenegro	5	3%	0	0%	2	22%
Morocco	0	0%	0	0%	0	0%
Netherlands	133	23%	1	2%	23	55%
North Macedonia	0	0%	0	0%	0	0%
Norway	92	15%	3	6%	18	38%
Poland	33	9%	0	0%	9	36%
Portugal	252	45%	8	17%	29	69%
Romania	169	59%	6	25%	19	83%
Russia	102	25%	0	0%	14	47%
San Marino	26	14%	0	0%	4	36%
Serbia	32	12%	0	0%	8	47%
Serbia & Mont	14	39%	0	0%	2	67%
Slovakia	2	3%	0	0%	1	20%
Slovenia	34	10%	0	0%	9	39%
Spain	-	-	-	-	-	-
Sweden	169	27%	3	6%	30	64%
Switzerland	97	19%	0	0%	16	41%
Turkey	55	13%	1	3%	14	39%
Ukraine	91	32%	0	0%	15	75%
United Kingdom	133	22%	1	2%	25	54%
Yugoslavia	22	14%	0	0%	4	31%

Sweden

	Sweden awarded points to:				Frequency	
	Total	% of max	12's	% of max	Times	% of max
Albania	27	10%	0	0%	7	41%
Andorra	2	3%	0	0%	1	20%
Armenia	47	18%	0	0%	11	65%
Australia	96	53%	4	27%	7	88%
Austria	101	20%	1	2%	20	53%
Azerbaijan	57	18%	0	0%	9	47%
Belarus	4	2%	0	0%	2	13%
Belgium	102	18%	1	2%	18	43%
Bosnia & H	127	42%	1	4%	17	71%
Bulgaria	25	12%	0	0%	4	31%
Croatia	29	7%	0	0%	10	36%
Cyprus	107	18%	2	4%	18	43%
Czech Republic	19	11%	0	0%	6	67%
Denmark	289	50%	10	21%	38	88%
Estonia	119	35%	3	11%	17	68%
Finland	191	38%	3	7%	24	63%
France	132	22%	0	0%	25	57%
Georgia	15	8%	0	0%	4	31%
Germany	124	21%	2	4%	19	43%
Greece	68	13%	2	4%	15	38%
Hungary	65	22%	1	4%	11	55%
Iceland	207	44%	3	8%	28	80%
Ireland	224	41%	6	13%	31	74%
Israel	141	24%	1	2%	23	55%
Italy	75	20%	0	0%	11	42%
Latvia	53	18%	0	0%	11	55%
Lithuania	60	17%	0	0%	10	42%
Luxembourg	52	24%	0	0%	8	44%
Malta	129	26%	2	5%	20	59%
Moldova	51	16%	0	0%	6	30%
Monaco	22	26%	1	14%	2	29%
Montenegro	15	10%	0	0%	5	50%
Morocco	0	0%	0	0%	0	0%
Netherlands	171	27%	3	6%	24	55%
North Macedonia	18	7%	0	0%	6	32%
Norway	316	48%	10	18%	37	77%
Poland	45	15%	0	0%	10	48%
Portugal	90	17%	2	5%	14	35%
Romania	48	14%	0	0%	10	40%
Russia	115	27%	1	3%	16	55%
San Marino	0	0%	0	0%	0	0%
Serbia	60	26%	0	0%	9	64%
Serbia & Mont	28	78%	2	67%	3	100%
Slovakia	3	5%	0	0%	1	20%
Slovenia	30	8%	0	0%	6	22%
Spain	43	7%	0	0%	8	18%
Sweden	-	-	-	-	-	-
Switzerland	93	19%	3	7%	15	39%
Turkey	91	19%	0	0%	15	38%
Ukraine	79	21%	0	0%	14	54%
United Kingdom	133	22%	3	6%	21	47%
Yugoslavia	35	24%	1	8%	6	50%

Switzerland

	Switzerland awarded points to:				Frequency	
	Total	% of max	12's	% of max	Times	% of max
Albania	180	54%	3	11%	20	95%
Andorra	0	0%	0	0%	0	0%
Armenia	7	3%	0	0%	3	18%
Australia	47	36%	2	18%	5	83%
Austria	132	24%	3	7%	17	45%
Azerbaijan	25	9%	0	0%	8	44%
Belarus	2	1%	0	0%	2	13%
Belgium	83	16%	0	0%	11	29%
Bosnia & H	84	41%	3	18%	12	71%
Bulgaria	70	24%	1	4%	8	50%
Croatia	101	30%	0	0%	20	87%
Cyprus	68	13%	0	0%	17	47%
Czech Republic	11	7%	0	0%	1	11%
Denmark	76	13%	0	0%	21	51%
Estonia	28	9%	1	4%	4	20%
Finland	104	18%	1	2%	18	42%
France	174	32%	4	9%	25	61%
Georgia	2	1%	0	0%	2	13%
Germany	160	29%	5	11%	25	61%
Greece	108	19%	1	2%	22	52%
Hungary	62	22%	1	4%	10	50%
Iceland	96	22%	0	0%	15	45%
Ireland	197	36%	7	15%	29	71%
Israel	186	30%	1	2%	30	70%
Italy	174	45%	2	6%	24	89%
Latvia	46	17%	0	0%	9	50%
Lithuania	45	12%	0	0%	8	33%
Luxembourg	26	11%	1	5%	5	26%
Malta	68	16%	0	0%	13	43%
Moldova	14	6%	0	0%	3	19%
Monaco	16	17%	0	0%	3	38%
Montenegro	3	4%	0	0%	2	33%
Morocco	0	0%	0	0%	0	0%
Netherlands	149	28%	2	5%	23	62%
North Macedonia	102	33%	1	4%	16	76%
Norway	145	22%	0	0%	23	49%
Poland	27	10%	0	0%	5	28%
Portugal	204	40%	4	10%	24	63%
Romania	33	10%	0	0%	8	32%
Russia	33	10%	0	0%	7	30%
San Marino	2	1%	0	0%	1	11%
Serbia	171	65%	8	36%	15	100%
Serbia & Mont	36	100%	3	100%	3	100%
Slovakia	0	0%	0	0%	0	0%
Slovenia	12	5%	0	0%	3	16%
Spain	158	28%	3	6%	29	69%
Sweden	193	31%	3	6%	27	59%
Switzerland	-	-	-	-	-	-
Turkey	154	37%	3	9%	21	60%
Ukraine	27	9%	0	0%	6	30%
United Kingdom	143	25%	2	4%	23	55%
Yugoslavia	18	12%	0	0%	4	31%

Turkey   Ukraine

	Turkey awarded points to:				Frequency			Ukraine awarded points to:				Frequency	
	Total	% of max	12's	% of max	Times	% of max		Total	% of max	12's	% of max	Times	% of max
Albania	60	45%	0	0%	11	100%	Albania	7	3%	0	0%	3	20%
Andorra	3	5%	0	0%	2	40%	Andorra	0	0%	0	0%	0	0%
Armenia	75	69%	1	11%	9	100%	Armenia	78	46%	1	7%	11	92%
Australia	0	-	0	-	0	-	Australia	51	35%	1	8%	6	100%
Austria	71	23%	1	4%	13	50%	Austria	16	8%	0	0%	3	25%
Azerbaijan	84	100%	7	100%	7	100%	Azerbaijan	133	62%	4	22%	14	100%
Belarus	8	7%	0	0%	2	22%	Belarus	155	72%	8	44%	14	93%
Belgium	63	18%	1	3%	10	34%	Belgium	63	26%	0	0%	7	47%
Bosnia & H	175	69%	6	29%	19	90%	Bosnia & H	22	13%	0	0%	3	21%
Bulgaria	49	51%	1	13%	8	100%	Bulgaria	40	17%	0	0%	8	57%
Croatia	55	21%	0	0%	9	41%	Croatia	69	26%	0	0%	12	67%
Cyprus	10	3%	0	0%	3	10%	Cyprus	34	12%	0	0%	7	39%
Czech Republic	1	3%	0	0%	1	33%	Czech Republic	14	19%	0	0%	1	25%
Denmark	32	8%	0	0%	12	36%	Denmark	51	16%	0	0%	8	36%
Estonia	22	11%	1	6%	3	19%	Estonia	41	19%	0	0%	10	63%
Finland	40	11%	0	0%	9	30%	Finland	21	13%	0	0%	3	25%
France	38	10%	0	0%	12	36%	France	53	22%	1	5%	5	31%
Georgia	65	60%	0	0%	9	100%	Georgia	115	64%	2	13%	12	100%
Germany	86	22%	3	9%	13	39%	Germany	10	4%	0	0%	2	13%
Greece	81	23%	2	7%	14	47%	Greece	35	16%	0	0%	6	38%
Hungary	25	19%	0	0%	6	55%	Hungary	61	24%	0	0%	11	69%
Iceland	34	10%	0	0%	7	26%	Iceland	18	9%	0	0%	4	27%
Ireland	124	32%	2	6%	22	69%	Ireland	12	5%	0	0%	6	33%
Israel	63	17%	2	6%	11	35%	Israel	92	31%	1	4%	12	67%
Italy	76	40%	0	0%	12	75%	Italy	33	23%	0	0%	3	38%
Latvia	6	4%	0	0%	1	8%	Latvia	45	21%	0	0%	8	53%
Lithuania	4	2%	0	0%	2	13%	Lithuania	82	26%	1	4%	13	65%
Luxembourg	26	14%	0	0%	7	44%	Luxembourg	0	-	0	-	0	-
Malta	93	32%	1	4%	15	63%	Malta	46	17%	0	0%	8	47%
Moldova	42	39%	1	11%	6	67%	Moldova	121	46%	4	18%	14	78%
Monaco	5	8%	0	0%	1	20%	Monaco	0	0%	0	0%	0	0%
Montenegro	5	21%	0	0%	1	50%	Montenegro	12	17%	0	0%	3	60%
Morocco	0	0%	0	0%	0	0%	Morocco	0	-	0	-	0	-
Netherlands	95	28%	1	4%	19	68%	Netherlands	40	13%	1	4%	6	30%
North Macedonia	72	40%	0	0%	12	80%	North Macedonia	27	13%	0	0%	6	40%
Norway	57	14%	1	3%	11	31%	Norway	81	24%	1	4%	14	67%
Poland	8	5%	0	0%	2	15%	Poland	77	38%	1	6%	10	77%
Portugal	48	12%	1	3%	10	29%	Portugal	36	19%	0	0%	5	38%
Romania	55	29%	0	0%	12	75%	Romania	36	13%	0	0%	10	53%
Russia	50	25%	0	0%	9	53%	Russia	154	56%	5	22%	19	100%
San Marino	5	42%	0	0%	1	100%	San Marino	4	4%	0	0%	1	20%
Serbia	0	0%	0	0%	0	0%	Serbia	29	12%	0	0%	6	40%
Serbia & Mont	15	42%	0	0%	2	67%	Serbia & Mont	27	75%	2	67%	3	100%
Slovakia	0	0%	0	0%	0	0%	Slovakia	14	39%	1	33%	2	67%
Slovenia	18	9%	0	0%	4	24%	Slovenia	36	14%	0	0%	7	41%
Spain	118	29%	2	6%	19	56%	Spain	6	3%	0	0%	2	13%
Sweden	97	21%	1	3%	20	53%	Sweden	95	27%	1	3%	16	70%
Switzerland	60	16%	0	0%	11	35%	Switzerland	22	12%	0	0%	3	25%
Turkey	-	-	-	-	-	-	Turkey	39	23%	0	0%	9	64%
Ukraine	69	38%	2	13%	10	67%	Ukraine	-	-	-	-	-	-
United Kingdom	126	31%	2	6%	21	62%	United Kingdom	9	4%	0	0%	2	13%
Yugoslavia	80	56%	4	33%	10	83%	Yugoslavia	0	-	0	-	0	-

United Kingdom

	UK awarded points to:				Frequency	
	Total	% of max	12's	% of max	Times	% of max
Albania	30	9%	0	0%	9	45%
Andorra	0	0%	0	0%	0	0%
Armenia	15	6%	0	0%	4	24%
Australia	76	49%	0	0%	7	100%
Austria	131	24%	3	7%	21	53%
Azerbaijan	33	11%	0	0%	5	28%
Belarus	4	2%	0	0%	2	12%
Belgium	121	21%	1	2%	22	52%
Bosnia & H	16	6%	0	0%	5	23%
Bulgaria	129	49%	2	9%	11	73%
Croatia	34	9%	0	0%	15	54%
Cyprus	158	28%	2	4%	25	63%
Czech Republic	16	8%	0	0%	4	40%
Denmark	168	29%	4	8%	27	63%
Estonia	83	25%	1	4%	14	58%
Finland	109	19%	2	4%	15	36%
France	108	18%	0	0%	21	47%
Georgia	27	11%	2	10%	4	25%
Germany	147	25%	1	2%	27	60%
Greece	150	25%	5	10%	22	50%
Hungary	28	11%	0	0%	7	39%
Iceland	153	31%	2	5%	20	56%
Ireland	302	52%	8	17%	37	84%
Israel	179	29%	3	6%	29	66%
Italy	38	10%	0	0%	9	33%
Latvia	86	30%	0	0%	14	74%
Lithuania	193	49%	6	18%	22	81%
Luxembourg	57	25%	0	0%	10	53%
Malta	152	34%	3	8%	24	73%
Moldova	58	21%	1	4%	8	47%
Monaco	24	25%	0	0%	4	50%
Montenegro	0	0%	0	0%	0	0%
Morocco	0	0%	0	0%	0	0%
Netherlands	115	20%	1	2%	24	59%
North Macedonia	24	8%	2	8%	2	10%
Norway	133	20%	3	5%	22	44%
Poland	92	27%	2	7%	14	61%
Portugal	101	18%	1	2%	14	33%
Romania	59	20%	1	4%	9	39%
Russia	65	18%	0	0%	11	42%
San Marino	9	8%	0	0%	2	33%
Serbia	16	6%	0	0%	5	31%
Serbia & Mont	11	31%	0	0%	2	67%
Slovakia	0	0%	0	0%	0	0%
Slovenia	18	5%	0	0%	3	12%
Spain	67	11%	0	0%	21	46%
Sweden	261	37%	4	7%	40	77%
Switzerland	170	28%	3	6%	24	55%
Turkey	143	30%	4	10%	24	60%
Ukraine	71	21%	0	0%	13	57%
United Kingdom	-	-	-	-	-	-
Yugoslavia	47	30%	2	15%	6	46%

Yugoslavia

	Yugoslavia awarded points to:				Frequency	
	Total	% of max	12's	% of max	Times	% of max
Albania	0	-	0	-	0	-
Andorra	0	-	0	-	0	-
Armenia	0	-	0	-	0	-
Australia	0	-	0	-	0	-
Austria	23	16%	0	0%	5	42%
Azerbaijan	0	-	0	-	0	-
Belarus	0	-	0	-	0	-
Belgium	32	21%	0	0%	5	38%
Bosnia & H	0	-	0	-	0	-
Bulgaria	0	-	0	-	0	-
Croatia	0	-	0	-	0	-
Cyprus	52	43%	1	10%	8	80%
Czech Republic	0	-	0	-	0	-
Denmark	7	5%	0	0%	2	18%
Estonia	0	-	0	-	0	-
Finland	22	14%	0	0%	5	38%
France	56	39%	3	25%	7	58%
Georgia	0	-	0	-	0	-
Germany	33	21%	1	8%	6	46%
Greece	17	16%	0	0%	4	44%
Hungary	0	-	0	-	0	-
Iceland	4	5%	0	0%	1	14%
Ireland	38	26%	0	0%	10	83%
Israel	54	38%	2	17%	8	67%
Italy	62	52%	1	10%	8	80%
Latvia	0	-	0	-	0	-
Lithuania	0	-	0	-	0	-
Luxembourg	37	24%	1	8%	6	46%
Malta	13	36%	0	0%	3	100%
Moldova	0	-	0	-	0	-
Monaco	4	17%	0	0%	1	50%
Montenegro	0	-	0	-	0	-
Morocco	0	-	0	-	0	-
Netherlands	40	28%	0	0%	7	58%
North Macedonia	0	-	0	-	0	-
Norway	11	7%	0	0%	2	15%
Poland	0	-	0	-	0	-
Portugal	14	9%	0	0%	3	23%
Romania	0	-	0	-	0	-
Russia	0	-	0	-	0	-
San Marino	0	-	0	-	0	-
Serbia	0	-	0	-	0	-
Serbia & Mont	0	-	0	-	0	-
Slovakia	0	-	0	-	0	-
Slovenia	0	-	0	-	0	-
Spain	26	17%	0	0%	7	54%
Sweden	49	34%	1	8%	9	75%
Switzerland	61	39%	1	8%	9	69%
Turkey	42	29%	1	8%	6	50%
Ukraine	0	-	0	-	0	-
United Kingdom	57	37%	1	8%	8	62%
Yugoslavia	-	-	-	-	-	-

Printed in Great Britain
by Amazon